GLOBAL
Social Problems

GLOBAL
Social Problems

JAMES A. GLYNN
Bakersfield College

CHARLES F. HOHM
San Diego State University

ELBERT W. STEWART
Bakersfield College

HarperCollins*CollegePublishers*

Acquisitions Editor: *Alan McClare*
Developmental Editors: *Nancy Crochiere, Ann Marie Kirby*
Project Coordination and Text Design: *Thompson Steele Production Services*
Cover Design: *Kay Petronio*
Cover Photograph: *Digital Stock Corp., Photodisk Inc.*
Photo Researcher: *Corrine Johns*
Electronic Production Manager: *Eric Jorgensen*
Manufacturing Manager: *Hilda Koparanian*
Electronic Page Makeup: *Interactive Composition Corporation*
Printer and Binder: *RR Donnelley & Sons Company*
Cover Printer: *New England Book Components, Inc.*

For permission to use copyrighted material, grateful acknowledgment is made to the copyright holders on p. 460, which are hereby made part of this copyright page.

Global Social Problems

Library of Congress Cataloging-in-Publication Data

Glynn, James A.
     Global social problems / James A. Glynn, Charles F. Hohm, Elbert W. Stewart
          p.   cm.
     Includes bibliographical references and index.
     ISBN   0-673-99158-X
     1. Social problems. 2. Social history—1970-   I. Hohm, Charles F.
     II. Stewart, Elbert W. III. Title.
HN17.5G593   1995   95-33356
361.1—dc20   CIP

95 96 97 98 9 8 7 6 5 4 3 2 1

Dedication

To the memory of my father, James A. Sciortino Glynn—J.A.G.

*To my late father-in-law and mother-in-law, Bob and Van Carlson;
to my parents, Jim and Ida Hohm; to my children, Anna-Marie, Jonathan,
and Alexandra Hohm; and to my wife, Linda Carlson Hohm—C.F.H.*

To Rachel, Renée, Tara, Travis, and Ian—E.W.S.

Brief Contents

Detailed Contents

chapter 3

HUMAN SEXUALITY: POWER AND POLITICS   55

chapter 4

THE HUMAN CONDITION: HEALTH AND AFFLICTION   87

xii DETAILED CONTENTS

chapter 7

FROM VILLAGE TO MEGACITY: URBANIZATION   201

chapter 8

GLOBAL COMPETITION   233

chapter

chapter

chapter

Preface

As the nations of the world have drawn closer through telecommunications, international trade, and ease of travel, it has become increasingly clear that social problems are global. Workers everywhere compete in a global economy. Pollution spreads from country to country and from sea to sea. Urbanization proceeds most rapidly in countries that were recently rural, and irretrievably changes customs, mores, and family structures. In many places, ethnic conflicts cause enormous increases in international migration. War and threats of war move many countries to greater attempts at international cooperation.

Global Social Problems approaches the study of social problems by focusing on the whole planet, not just one country or region. Each chapter treats a social problem common to all countries, and uses examples from around the world.

Consider the shrinking of the middle class in developed countries. Without understanding how countries compete on the international scene, one cannot explain the dramatic changes in social class structure that are characterizing developed countries. In Chapter 8, we deal with this complex issue by exploring pre- and post-industrial nations, trade policies, economic growth, and governmental influences in both Eastern and Western nations.

Consider the grinding poverty in less developed countries. It is virtually impossible to explain the intractability of this problem and the difficulties these nations face in becoming developed without a grasp of the social, political, and economic relationships between more developed and less developed nations. We give this problem international consideration in Chapter 9, which discusses many factors that contribute to and maintain both poverty and plenty.

Consider drug abuse. Most social problems textbooks focus on illegal drugs in one country, namely the United States. Too little is said about the international implications: a Cold-War policy of supporting anti-Communists who engage in the drug trade; the peasants who can find no marketable crop other than cocaine; or the exploitation of desperate refugees by those who profit from the drug trade. Without considering these worldwide aspects, one's understanding of the "drug problem" in any one country is incomplete. In Chapter 12, we present such a global view of the criminal, organizational, and political aspects of growing and selling illegal drugs.

FEATURES OF THE BOOK

Global Social Problems includes several pedagogical features that should prove interesting and useful to students.

Opening Vignettes

Each chapter opens with a compelling anecdote or quotation that will engage students in the subject matter. In Chapter 8, we see a tiny African village whose only modern possession is a television set on which people watch "Home Improvement." In Chapter 6, we meet Hamed

Celik, a Moslem, used as a human minesweeper by his Serbian captors; in Chapter 4 we read the story of Toda, a small girl who, like thousands of others, died in 1994 of a curable disease like measles.

Contemporary Global Examples

Examples of the most current social problems are drawn from all parts of the world, including Chinese political prisons, genocide in Rwanda, neo-Nazis in Germany, refugees from Bosnia, forced prostitution in Brazil and Thailand, health care and insurance in the United States and Canada, population and deforestation in South America.

"Toward A Solution" Box

After reading about the many serious social problems that exist in the world, it is possible to feel overwhelmed with their enormity. To show that the study of social problems includes consideration of how to address these problems, chapters feature a "box" that demonstrates progress toward a solution in a particular nation or by a particular group. Encouraging examples are often found where least expected: a sudden drop in fertility rates in sub-Saharan Africa; medical advances from the shamans of the rainforest of Suriname; increasing prosperity for the White Mountain Apache Nation. In the chapter on war, an insert called "Avoiding Armageddon" points out the steps countries have taken to reduce the possibility of a nuclear war. There is hope, and the most promising hope of all—we still have time to work on our social problems.

Study Questions

At the end of each chapter, study questions focus on the important themes and issues of the chapter. These questions will help students review this material and reflect on what they have read.

Key Terms

Important concepts and terms are boldfaced upon introduction in the text, defined in a list at the end of each chapter, and appear in a general glossary at the end of the book. This reinforces understanding of the sociological concepts embodied by the terms.

ACKNOWLEDGMENTS

Writing a textbook is a major undertaking that can test the nerve and patience of all involved. We are fortunate to have HarperCollins as our publisher, and have enjoyed the encouragement, creativity, and assistance from the HarperCollins team. Hal Levinson, regional representative, encouraged us to submit our proposal to HarperCollins. Alan McClare, sponsoring editor, provided invaluable assistance in getting the project off the ground. Anyone who has written a textbook can attest to the critical importance of the developmental editor, and we had the good fortune to work with two. Ann Kirby's early editorial work, suggestions, and insights improved the book dramatically. When Nancy Crochiere took over, she did a marvelous job with the task of coordinating three authors spread throughout California and guiding us through the later drafts. Other members of the HarperCollins team who deserve our thanks are Art Pomponio, Margaret Loftus, and Corrine Johns.

Our colleagues have also offered their assistance in reviewing the manuscript. Larry Herzog, Kenji Ima, and Rolf Schulze at San Diego State University read various chapters and gave valued criticism and ideas. Linda Carlson Hohm also read and edited some chapters and we are indebted to her for her input. We would also like to thank Mary Sannwald, Administrative Coordinator of the Sociology Department at San Diego State University, for inputting text on a number of chapters.

We were very fortunate to have talented and committed reviewers whose insights, criticisms, and suggestions improved the manuscript immeasurably. We thank:

Patricia Atchison
Colorado State University
Karen Baum
Mira Costa College
Valerie Brown
Cuyahoga Community College
Gerald Bill
Fresno City College
Lee K. Frank
Community College of Allegheny County
Mark A. Foster
Johnson County Community College
Larry H. Frye
St. Petersburg Junior College
Neda Saburi Hicks
Randolf-Macon College
Gary F. Jensen
Vanderbilt University
Maralee Mayberry
University of Nevada, Las Vegas
Anne R. Peterson
Columbus State Community College
Leslie F. Ulgee
Maryville University
Robert A. Weyer
County College of Morris
Paul C. Whitehead
University of Western Ontario

We would like especially to thank Joni Lee Heleotis of Rutgers University. She went "beyond the call of duty," providing an incredible list of ideas and constructive suggestions that had a major impact on the manuscript.

James A. Glynn
Bakersfield College

Charles F. Hohm
San Diego State University

Elbert W. Stewart
Bakersfield College

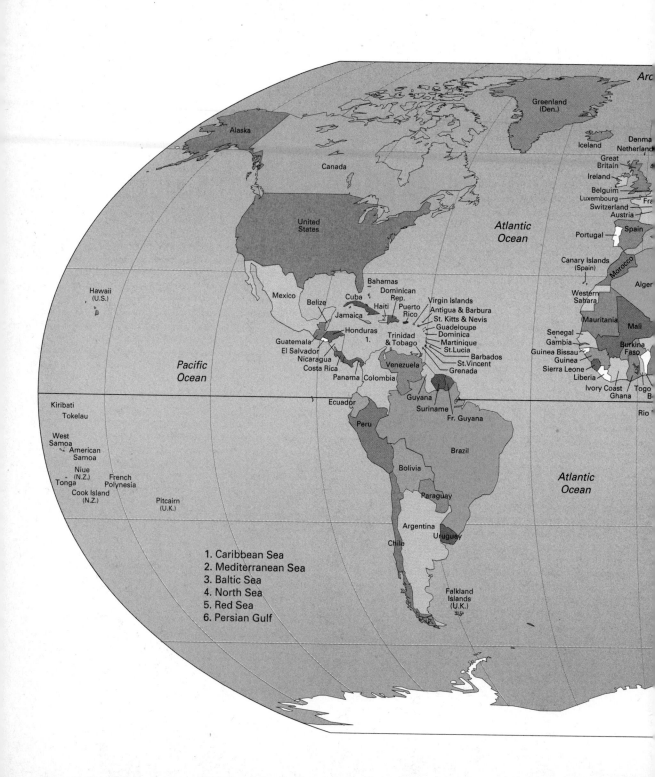

Arc

Greenland
(Den.)

Iceland

Denma

Netherland

Great
Britain

Ireland

Belguim
Luxemburg
Switzerland
Austria

Portugal   Spain

Canary Islands
(Spain)   Morocco

Western
Sahara   Alger

Mauritania   Mali

Senegal
Gambia   Burkina
Guinea Bissau   Faso
Guinea
Sierra Leone
Liberia   Togo
Ivory Coast   B
Ghana

Rio

Atlantic
Ocean

Alaska

Canada

United
States

Hawaii
(U.S.)

Mexico   Bahamas
Dominican
Belize   Rep.
Cuba   Virgin Islands
Jamaica   Haiti   Antigua & Barbura
Puerto   St. Kitts & Nevis
Rico   Guadeloupe
Honduras   Dominica
Guatemala   1.   Martinique
El Salvador   Trinidad   St.Lucia
Nicaragua   & Tobago   Barbados
Costa Rica   St.Vincent
Panama   Colombia   Venezuela   Grenada

Ecuador   Guyana
Suriname
Peru   Fr. Guyana

Brazil

Bolivia   Atlantic
Ocean

Paraguay

Argentina
Uruguay
Chile

Falkland
Islands
(U.K.)

Pacific
Ocean

Kiribati
Tokelau

West
Samoa
American
Samoa
Niue
(N.Z.)
Tonga
Cook Island   French
(N.Z.)   Polynesia
Pitcairn
(U.K.)

1. Caribbean Sea
2. Mediterranean Sea
3. Baltic Sea
4. North Sea
5. Red Sea
6. Persian Gulf

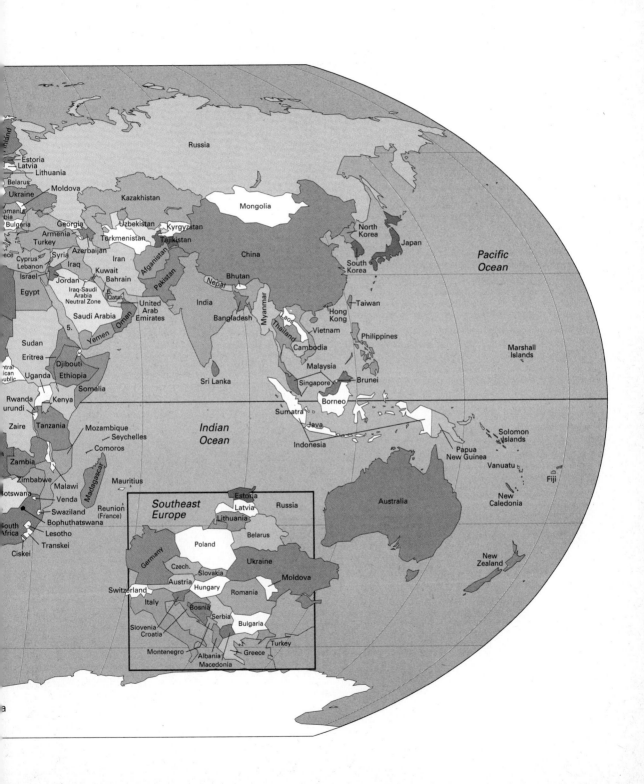

Russia

Estoria
Latvia
Lithuania
Belarus
Ukraine Moldova
Kazakhistan
Mongolia
omania
bia
Bulgaria
Georgia
Armenia Uzbekistan Kyrgyzstan
Turkey
Turkmenistan Tajikistan
eece
Syria Azerbaijan Iran Afganistan
Cyprus Lebanon
Israel
Iraq Kuwait
Bahrain
Jordan
Iraq-Saudi
Arabia
Neutral Zone
Qatar
Pakistan
United
Arab
Emirates
Oman
Egypt
Saudi Arabia
5.
Yemen

North
Korea
Japan
South
Korea

China

Bhutan
Nepal
India
Myanmar
Bangladesh
Laos
Thailand
Vietnam
Cambodia
Hong
Kong
Taiwan
Philippines

Pacific
Ocean

Marshall
Islands

Sudan
Eritrea
Djibouti
Ethiopia
Somalia
ntral
ican
ublic
Uganda
Rwanda
urundi
Kenya
Zaire
Tanzania
Mozambique
Seychelles
Comoros
Sri Lanka
Malaysia
Singapore Brunei
Borneo
Sumatra
Java
Indonesia

Solomon
Islands

Zambia
Zimbabwe
Malawi
Madagascar
Mauritius
Reunion
(France)
otswana Venda
Swaziland
Bophuthatswana
outh Lesotho
Africa Transkei
Ciskei

Indian
Ocean

Papua
New Guinea
Vanuatu

Fiji

New
Caledonia

Australia

New
Zealand

a

Southeast
Europe
Estoria
Latvia
Lithuania
Russia
Belarus
Germany
Poland
Czech.
Slovakia
Ukraine
Switzerland
Austria
Hungary
Moldova
Romania
Italy
Bosnia
Serbia
Slovenia
Croatia
Bulgaria
Montenegro
Albania
Macedonia
Greece
Turkey

c h a p t e r

SOCIAL PROBLEMS AND SOCIOLOGICAL ANALYSIS

It was the best of times, it was the worst of times, it was the age of wisdom, it was the age of foolishness, it was the season of Light, it was the season of Darkness, it was the spring of hope, it was the winter of despair . . .

So opens *A Tale of Two Cities* by Charles Dickens (1859), describing a small part of the world of 1789. As we move through the 1990s, we can think of no better description of social reality than Dickens's, but now it applies to the entire earth, not just revolutionary France.

Never have the arts and sciences advanced more brilliantly, and never has commerce flowed more freely or in such enormous tonnage and priceless value. Never have such endless acreages of land been under irrigation, and never has the harvest of the earth been more abundant. The inventiveness that once brought us smoke-stifled factories now brings us the gleaming halls and laboratories of high technology. The old epidemics that once wiped out multitudes of people, especially children, have largely succumbed to medicines and immunologies. Even the mysteries of life are being fathomed, and the first steps have been taken to eliminate the genetic ills of humankind. Satellites circle the earth, conveying information on a scale never before deemed possible. The hidden resources of the earth are harvested from their hiding places, whether in the frozen polar regions, the tropics, or under the seas. Along with this type of development goes the amassing of great fortunes and, in the more advanced countries, even people of modest incomes live in an abundance that once belonged only to the chosen few.

hidden from ordinary citizens, as are many of the secret machinations of governments. Despite a century of struggle, women and minorities are far from their goal of equality. The earth is being stripped of irreplaceable natural resources at an alarming rate. And the fortunes amassed in the modern world stand in mocking contradistinction to the poverty, hunger, and untimely death that await so many millions of people in the poorer parts of the world. Never have so many people been so overfed, and never have so many people been so hungry.

If we are to describe ours as the best of times, we must also describe it as the worst of times. Perhaps that has been true to some degree of all stages of human history. The story of the human species is a story of social problems, some minor, some virtually apocalyptic; occasionally solved, sometimes partly solved; frequently ignored or accepted as inevitable. Before we go further with such observations, however, it is time to turn to a discussion of social problems, how they are defined by sociologists, and different viewpoints from which they can be analyzed.

THE DOWNSIDE OF THE STORY

But, there is a downside to the story, just as there is a downside to the above quotation. For much of the world, it is the worst of times, a season of darkness, a winter of despair. The very brilliance of the science by which we live has left us hostage to nuclear weapons, deadly chemical poisons, and the possible destruction of the protective layer of the earth's upper atmosphere. The old-smoke-and-smog industries are by no means gone, and their fallout poisons the rain, killing the lakes and forests into which it falls. The keys to genetic manipulation, which are both promising and terrifying, are in the hands of corporations unregulated by the people who could become victims of their mistakes. The information beamed by the satellites is often

EXPLAINING SOCIAL PROBLEMS

The "downside of the story" above is really a list of social problems, some of which have received more publicity than others, and some of which are matters of concern to larger numbers of people than others. Most problems on the list are relatively new dilemmas that have arisen because of advances in industrial technologies, such as nuclear and chemical developments, the emergence of genetic engineering, and the increasing complexity of "high technology." Others are the grievances of antiquity: unequal treatment of women and minorities, governmental duplicity, mismanagement of resources, and chronic poverty.

Modern societies have often reinterpreted some of these old problems. In fact, some of them were not even regarded as problems until fairly recent times. Poverty, female inequality, child maltreatment, and the subordination of some people to others were once looked upon as the will of God or as dire necessities rather than as conditions amenable to improvement. Circumstances that are accepted universally as part of the natural and inevitable order of the world are not regarded as social problems. They fall into a class with earthquakes, volcanoes, and bad climate—matters completely beyond human control.

Social Problems Defined

Social problems can be defined as situations, policies, or trends that are (1) distressing or (b) threatening to large numbers of people, (2) contrary to the **mores** (essential practices) or moral beliefs of the society, and (3) partly or wholly correctable through the actions of social groups. This definition probably assumes more unity of public opinion than usually exists, but it makes a good starting point for this discussion and is consistent with the sociological treatment of social problems. We must be mindful, however, that even the mores of society may be called into question by certain factions. For example, is it a **mos** (the singular of mores) that we must protect any human life? Even if that life is yet unborn? Even if, after that life is born, it will be abandoned because its mother does not want it? Even if that life came into being through incest or rape? Religious groups may vary considerably in their answers to these questions; so might political groups, like pro-choice and pro-life groups. **Values**—the feelings and beliefs one develops that define his or her notions of right or wrong—play an important role in one's definition of social problems. Even when there is agreement that a social problem exists, values come into play in determining how to handle the problem.

Certainly, nuclear bombs are terrifying to all of us and pose a threat to our species. Their existence is contrary to our beliefs in peace and survival. It is generally believed that, with top-level statesmanship, societies should be able to save themselves from nuclear extinction. Yet over the years our political officials have had a difficult time trying to limit certain categories of missiles. Furthermore, with the disintegration of the Soviet Union, the whereabouts and control of a large portion of the world's missiles are questionable.

Similarly, no one is happy to see air, lakes, seas, and rivers contaminated by poisons and sewage. No one wants to witness our land erode or our great forests disappear. We see such developments as threatening to everyone (present and future generations), contrary to moral values (no one has a right to pollute), and correctable to a considerable degree through collective social action (laws and regulations). But, each year global pollution worsens and more species (animal and plant) are destroyed.

There is no question that women and minorities fall far short of equal treatment in most societies. In the United States, women, Hispanics, and African Americans are subject to great economic inequity. Parallels are found in other societies such as among the Tamil people in Sri Lanka and Ainu people on the northernmost island of Japan. Their inequality is contrary to what we believe to be right. Although improvements, through the passage of laws and enactments of regulations, are possible, changes may not occur or may occur too slowly to be satisfactory.

Last on our "downside" list is extreme poverty. We find examples not only in the poorer countries of the world, but even in the wealthy ones. In the United States, poverty exists among thousands, maybe millions, of "street people." Indeed, the proportion of the U.S. population that has been called the "poverty-burdened underclass" has been increasing during the last decade (Sivard, 1993:37). As we shall see, conditions elsewhere in the world are much worse.

Extreme poverty, then, meets all criteria of our definition of a social problem. It affects large numbers of people in undesirable ways, is contrary to what we regard as "right," and is

Grinding poverty among the urban underclass in U.S. cities continues to be a severe problem, especially among Afican Americans. Single-parent households face inumerable barriers.

solvable, especially in a wealthy nation like the United States. Yet, the number of people living below the poverty level increased from 29 million in 1980 to more than 35 million in 1991 (U.S. Bureau of the Census, 1993:469). Why does a rich nation like the United States still have economic discrimination, homeless people, and extreme poverty? Cannot a wealthy nation like the United States provide adequate shelter and nutrition to its people? It can, but the solutions involve both social and economic costs.

Social Problems and Social Priorities

Whether we respond to social problems with a ho-hum sigh or a burst of moral outrage is a reflection of our values. One value is that of hard work; another is that of charity. We can imagine a very charitable couple spending time, money, and considerable effort to help the homeless street people of their city. Their neighbors, in the name of the hard-work ethic, refuse to cooperate. "After all," they say, "most of those people don't work as hard as we do, and that's why they're in trouble." Even the less charitable neighbors might see homelessness as a problem, but they don't see it as a high societal priority. Similarly, if women's pay is seen as secondary income for the family,

not as a vital necessity, giving equal pay for comparable work will not be a priority.

For purposes of this discussion, we define **priorities** as what we are willing to do, either passively or actively, about our feelings and beliefs of right and wrong. A young woman from the United States who feels it is wrong for millions of people to starve to death in Ethiopia and Somalia and, consequently, who does not object to the government spending some of her tax money on famine relief is *passively* setting a higher priority on help to the needy than on keeping a higher proportion of her earnings. On the other hand, if she joins the Peace Corps because she feels she has skills and knowledge that she can use personally to improve conditions in less developed countries (LDCs), then she is *actively* placing a higher priority on feeding people than on personal comfort and, possibly, safety. Suffragettes of the early twentieth century who agitated for the right to vote for women, Freedom Riders who went into the U.S. south in the 1950s to register African Americans to vote, and civil-rights workers who risked—and sometimes gave—their lives to secure civil rights legislation in the 1960s all held equality as a very high priority.

Extreme poverty exists in both LDCs and MDCs but is more widespread in the less developed countries. Here a mother in Baidon, Somalia, is attempting to clean her malnourished children.

From another perspective, one might say the same of the leaders of the Bolshevik Revolution in Russia in 1917, the followers of Mao Ze-dong in China in the late 1940s, and the guerrillas who fought beside Fidel Castro in Cuba in the late 1950s. Similar movements are currently taking place in a number of less developed countries. Does this mean we can equate civil-rights workers and Bolsheviks? Certainly, some Americans who fought for equality were called "pinkos" or "commies." However, their views were very different from those of the communists. The point is that all of these groups obviously put a high value on equality; however, equality is only one value. We need to understand that people have **constellations**, or sets, of values and, while all of the above groups shared equality as a priority, they may have differed on priorities among other values. For example, based on the studies of Milton Rokeach (1960), we know that, while Stalinists and Maoists place a high value on equality, they have a negative value for freedom. Humanists, on the other hand, place high values on both equality and freedom.

Values are deeply involved in many other social issues, not only in the United States, but throughout the world. Ruth Leger Sivard (1993:6) calls into question the values and priorities of the world community as reflected in our military spending compared with our spending on basic human needs. She points out that in 1991 the world spent an average of $1,070 per school-aged child and nearly $27,000 per soldier. The outcome of this differential is predictable. About 1.5 billion people, or more than one-quarter of the earth's inhabitants, still lack basic health care (Sivard, 1993:26) and 2.5 million children die every year because they were not vaccinated for measles, tetanus, and whooping cough (Sivard, 1993:27). One-fifth of the planet's population goes hungry every day and 192 million children suffer stunted growth, lack of resistance to infection, and premature death due to malnutrition (Sivard, 1993:28). These are annual figures for a year when world military spending surpassed $600 billion (U.S.) (Sivard, 1993:5).

The end of the Cold War has resulted in declining worldwide expenditures on military matters. The amount spent on the military, worldwide, has declined for five successive years (Sivard, 1993). Russia, the primary republic in the former Soviet empire, has slashed military funding in an attempt to rebuild itself. The United States has decreased spending on the military from a high of $303.6 billion in 1991 to

$272.8 billion in 1993 (U.S. Bureau of the Census, 1993:350), a 10 percent decrease in military spending by the United States in two years. Still, we are all aware of situations where military spending is not decreasing such as those in Bosnia, North Korea, and the Middle East.

It is apparent that this appalling situation fits our definition of a social problem. Certainly we have been discussing large numbers of people who are mortally threatened by a correctable condition, which offends our sensibilities. Would the world tolerate another Hiroshima every three days? The first atomic bomb dropped on Hiroshima in 1945 left 120,000 people dead. That many children die unnecessarily every three days.

Besides such well-understood problems as poverty, the denial of equal rights, nuclear weapons, and pollution, other causes of distress and worry have attracted less attention. They could be called **latent** problems, or problems in the making.

Latent Problems

You may have noticed that several of the grievances mentioned as part of the "downside of the story" do not seem to fit the given definition of social problems. For instance, up until now, no large numbers of people are known to have suffered as a result of a decline in the protective ozone layer of the earth's upper atmosphere. Although experts expect a large increase in skin cancers because of the change (Marwick, 1992:3041), there is not as yet any strong public outcry. The same is true of complaints about biotechnology or genetic engineering. The results of interference with genetic structure that have been made known as of this writing are clearly beneficial; no one has suffered injury, and we can at least hope no one will. Still, many knowledgeable people worry about possibilities and argue that new technologies, like medicines, always seem to produce unwanted side effects. No expert in the field thinks we are suddenly going to create monsters, but it is quite possible

that new life forms might endanger older forms, not just the microorganisms that we would like to destroy (Weir, 1987:147–157).

Another latent problem involves secret government operations, such as the United States' sale of weapons to Iran in 1987. It cannot be proven to have cost many American lives and the economic cost was not major. The real worry is about the future of open, honest, constitutional government and the eclipse of democracy if such developments were to continue or recur.

These **latent problems** are not yet clearly perceived and have not yet become issues of widespread public debate. Sociologist Robert K. Merton (1957) argues that our customs, institutions, and policies have both **manifest functions**, which are intended, obvious, and clearly seen, and **latent functions**, which are unintended and little noticed. When applied to social problems, the theory suggests that some new developments, generally welcomed by the society, might very well result in social problems later. Such is the case with chlorofluorocarbons, which for years served well for refrigerants, making foamy plastics, and spray cans, but which now are ruining the earth's protective ozone layer. Such might be the case with genetic manipulations that will bring freedom from certain genetic diseases but that might create new environmental hazards.

Another example of a technical breakthrough that could result in a social problem is amniocentesis, a procedure that allows a physician and parents to ascertain the gender of the fetus. A possible latent side effect of this medical advance is the aborting of fetuses that do not meet the "gender specifications" of the parents. This is more likely to adversely affect female than male fetuses, given the worldwide preference for male infants over female infants. Whether one defines the aborting of fetuses based on their gender as a problem might depend on one's views on abortion and rights of females. An additional latent social problem associated with this is an unbalanced sex ratio. In Chapter 3 we discuss the tremendous imbalance of males over females in one province in China that was caused by selective infanticide, how there are ten times as many marriageable men as women, and how many men then, cannot find spouses. How much of a worldwide problem this becomes remains to be seen. The point is, abortion based on gender was not possible before the advent of amniocentesis.

One example of a latent problem that has developed into a manifest one is pollution. In the early days of the Industrial Revolution there was a tremendous demand for a source of energy, and the burning of coal was welcomed as a blessing on the burgeoning new factories of England. Although plumes of smoke were visible rising from these huge manufacturing edifices, the effect of the smoke on air quality was not initially perceived as a social problem. But by the 1950s Birmingham, England, was a blackened and unwholesome city, and London was experiencing choking fog intensified by coal smoke; hundreds died. A latent social problem had become a manifest one. A future problem associated with coal-burning factories—acid rain—was not even suspected!

As these examples suggest, social problems are dynamic and fluid. What is a social problem in one time period may not be a social problem in another and what is not a social problem today might well constitute one in the future.

Let's go back to our discussion of the coal-burning factories of nineteenth-century London. Had they known that deaths would result from the factory smoke, would the barons of industry of the nineteenth century have discontinued the use of coal? Today, is everyone in favor of tightened environmental controls? As we shall see, there is a divergence of opinion about the priorities that society adopts.

Various Theoretical Perspectives

Sociology, like other academic disciplines, utilizes various **theories** or perspectives to explain and analyze phenomena. A social theory

Technological advances often result in latent problems, such as chlorofluorocarbons diminishing the earth's protective ozone layer. Here a mother applies sunscreen to her child to minimize the effects of increased solar radiation resulting from a diminished ozone layer.

or perspective represents a particular way of making sense out of the world in which we live. Two of these perspectives are macro in nature, attempting to explain the workings and conditions of large groups of people, even whole societies.

One macro view is that societies contain oppositional forces, some favoring solutions to perceived problems and others failing to perceive the existence of a problem. This view, called the **conflict perspective,** has been most successfully argued by Karl Marx (1867) and, more recently, by C. Wright Mills (1951; 1956; 1959). Marx, who wrote in the 1800s, was of the opinion that two main opposing groups were to be found in capitalist societies—the **bourgeoisie** and the

Amniocentesis is a medical diagnostic test that identifies birth defects and the sex of a fetus. In societies where boys are valued more than girls, this information can lead to selective abortion, a problem that did not exist prior to the advent of amniocentesis.

proletariat. The bourgeoisie is the class of people that owns the means of production, that is, the owners of factories, landlords, and the like. The proletariat is the class that has only its labor to provide, that is the laborers and workers. Marx thought the bourgeoisie exploited the proletariat and that, in time, the proletariat would rise up and violently overthrow the bourgeoisie. Then capitalism would cease to exist and a socialistic society would take its place, ensuring a fair distri-

bution of opportunities and material goods. Though the fall of communism has definitely put a damper on Marxism, the conflict perspective, which has its roots in Marxism, is still used extensively by sociologists explaining social problems.

There must be a minimum of societal loyalty and observance of laws and customs or a society would cease to exist. The conflict perspective centers on the clash of interests that lies behind all of the practical agreements that hold society together. In this perspective, society is an arena of conflicts, some of which are mere matters of opinion. In the case of nuclear weapons, some would argue for keeping an overwhelming force as the only way to be safe in a hostile world. Others would reply that the power to blow up the world many times over is not particularly reassuring. Such arguments will go on indefinitely and are necessary in societies that value freedom of speech and democratic decisions.

A type of conflict theory that is global in scope and uses countries as the unit of analysis is **world systems theory**, which was developed during the 1970s by Immanuel Wallerstein (1979). World systems theory states that a country's progress toward modernity cannot be analyzed only in terms of that country's economic characteristics and achievements. Each country is tied into a world economic system that largely depends on the activities of **core societies** that were early entrants to the Industrial Revolution—the United States and Western European countries. Countries with close ties to these countries were likely to advance economically. These core societies are viewed as wielding tremendous influence over the world economy, composed mainly of **peripheral societies**. The peripheral societies are the mainly agricultural countries of Latin America, Africa, and Asia. They depend on the core societies, which may choose to export or to withhold technology from the poorer countries. Whether a country will modernize depends on its position in the world economy, especially relative to the core societies. This perspective is quite useful when the approach is global, as it is in this book.

The opposite macro view is the **functionalist perspective**. This school of thought sees the agreements of society as the glue that holds the whole together. Emile Durkheim (see Simpson, 1963), one of the founders of sociology, theorized that societies would move away from **mechanical solidarity**—a system held together because of the likeness of its members and their desires — to **organic solidarity**—a system that emerges because, as the parts of society become more diverse, they must be more interdependent for the good of the whole. Two twentieth-century sociologists, Talcott Parsons and Robert Merton, have been particularly important in refining this theory. According to this perspective, social problems arise when imbalances occur within a social system. Imbalances may occur for numerous reasons: the failure to socialize individuals adequately; the failure of a society to control aggression; and rapid social change. This last factor—rapid social change—can lead to social disorganization by producing **cultural lag**, which refers to the inability of social structure and culture to keep up with rapid technological change. For example, the advances of medical science in the first half of the twentieth century resulted in major decreases in the death rates of infants and children. Human fertility patterns failed to adjust to these declines in mortality however, and the population of our species has exploded as a result (see Chapter 5). In this section of the chapter we will contrast the conflict and functionalist views of society relative to social problems.

The conflict perspective goes beyond mere differences of opinion; it emphasizes vested interest. A **vested interest** is a special economic or political interest one has in a social practice, policy, or institution. Vested interest can be determined by answering the question, "What have I to gain or lose by keeping things as they are?" For example, the current income-tax code

in the United States favors very wealthy families. A change in the tax code that would generate more income for the federal government by taxing the very wealthy families more would obviously not be viewed in a positive light by these families, even though it would lessen the burden on the less wealthy. Another example is the vested interest that social workers have in the welfare system as it is currently constituted in the United States. Though social workers may say that they look forward to the day poverty is eliminated, such a turn of events would mean their services were no longer needed.

Vested interest often plays a role in the formation of a social problem. Military policy is one such issue. From a functionalist view, we could say that everyone favors adequate defenses, but adequacy is a matter of opinion. Such opinions are usually based on one's vested interest. If you were the head of a firm making lucrative profits by manufacturing missiles, it would be hard to convince you that we already have enough missiles. If you were a worker in a missile plant, had a good job, and had no chance of another equally good one, it would be hard for you to believe that we already have enough missiles. If you were a congressperson representing a district whose biggest industry was a missile plant, you would be sure to vote for more missiles. And, if you worked in the science department of a university whose research grants came almost entirely from the U.S. Department of Defense, you would find it hard to take a strong stand against keeping up military expenditures.

This point was documented when, in late 1987, the U.S. Congress agreed to cuts in defense spending. Among the strongest opponents to the cuts were several prominent universities that receive much of their research funding from the Department of Defense. Although the research might not be strictly military, such funding is provided because "some of the basic research could lead to advances in technology for Star Wars weapons, high-performance aircraft, missile warheads, and antisubmarine warfare" (Perlman, 1987). Note that vested interest works both ways: universities have a vested interest in a big defense budget for research funding, so they fight for increased spending; the Department of Defense has a vested interest in the products of their research, so it gives universities grants. The research might be entirely reasonable and worthwhile, but vested interest in its defense applications is clear and persuasive. We can extend this line of thinking to nearly any social problem that comes to mind.

On the subject of environment, for example, a reform-minded person might well assume that everyone agrees (functionalist view) that the environment must be saved and a big part of its salvation is to discontinue the use of pesticides.

"You're nuts!" says a worker from a chemical plant that produces the ingredients for a very effective pesticide used widely in agriculture. "You get pesticides or you get bugs, and that's all there is to it. If the government regulations drive us out of business, the bugs will take over the earth. And they'll get you, too, my bug-loving friend."

The man with the pesticide job has greatly overstated his case (although he is correct to the extent that we couldn't suddenly outlaw all pesticides), and his opinion is undoubtedly justified by his need for a job (vested interest) and what others in the industry have said to him (stating their vested interests).

Similarly, a functionalist view of equality for women and/or minority groups might well be stated as, "We all believe in full equality. It's the American way." But in conflict perspective, a white male in a high position might add under his breath, "But that doesn't mean I'm giving up my hard-earned vice presidency in the company!"

This type of thinking is **zero opinion analysis,** which theorizes that one person's gain must be another person's loss. For example, we might jump to the conclusion that poverty can only be

alleviated if we're willing to give up something of value. The dynamics of this type of analysis are visible in some of the poorest countries of the world where the ruling classes see clear advantage in keeping the lower classes poor and ignorant. In fact, many countries, both rich and poor, develop a vested interest in poverty.

While the functionalist and conflict perspectives are macro in nature, the **interactionist perspective** is micro in nature, in that it focuses mainly on the behavior of individuals and small groups of individuals. The interactionist perspective views **socialization**—the process by which an individual learns to think and act in a particular culture—as a very important component explaining social life. This approach relies heavily on the work of the American social scientist-philosopher George Herbert Mead. Mead (1934) stated that our species' ability to communicate in symbols, like words and gestures, is what separates us from other species. As children grow up and become socialized they learn to use symbols, to think, and to "take the role of the other" in pretending to be another person, such as "mother" or "doctor." A person's **self-concept**, central to the interactionist perspective, evolves out of the socialization process. Self-concept refers to the mental image one has of herself or himself. In time, children learn to take the role of a **generalized other**, developing the ability to respond to the values and norms of people in general. As socialization continues, a person develops **reference groups,** which are groups with which the person wishes to identify.

The interactionist perspective has been used very much by social-problems scholars and has helped us understand the origin and persistence of various problems such as gang behavior, drug dependence, and mental illness. Also, the interactionist perspective has played the major role in the study of *how* problems come to be defined. For example, wife-beating is a phenomenon that has existed since time began. However, it wasn't until the 1970s that it began

These assembly line workers have a vested interest in the missile industry because they help produce "Hellfire Warheads" in a plant in Middletown, Iowa.

to be defined as a social problem (Tierney, 1982). Kathleen Tierney shows how the battered women's movement developed in the United States and how feminist organizations (such as the National Organization for Women) and professionals in the fields of law, mental health, and social work voiced their concerns to the media and government officials. Eventually, what had been an individual problem and a private affair became a social problem as concerned organizations and professionals argued that the U.S. society itself was paying a high price for wife-beating. As a result, laws against wife-beating have been passed and new organizations have been created to help battered women, batterers, and their children.

Analysis of Social Problems

Sociologists study social problems by the **scientific method,** which relies on both logic and observation. As Earl Babbie (1992:27) states, "A scientific understanding of the world must make sense and correspond with what we observe." Babbie (1992:27) also notes that "both of these

elements are essential to science and relate to three major aspects of the overall scientific enterprise: **theory, research methods,** and **statistics**." Theory refers to the logical aspect of science that seeks to explain how and why a phenomenon exists. (We briefly discussed some sociological theories, or perspectives, in the preceding section of this chapter.) Research methods refer to the techniques, ranging from qualitative to quantitative, that social scientists use in their research. Statistics allow us to compare what was expected from the theory and what was actually observed.

Sociologists use **independent variables** to explain variation on **dependent variables.** The dependent variable is what the researcher is interested in explaining. The independent variables are the factors that affect or perhaps cause the dependent variable in question. For example, a researcher might want to study teenage pregnancy. Teenage pregnancy would be the dependent variable. Factors that might explain why some teenagers become pregnant while others do not would be the independent variables. Whether a teenager comes from a broken home, performance in school, social class, religious orientation, and race are examples of independent variables that could affect teenage pregnancy.

The research methods used by sociologists to gather information on social problems are quite varied. Sociologists find **public records** very useful. The United States government has many agencies that gather social and economic data. The U.S. Bureau of the Census conducts a census each decade and information from this enumeration is very valuable to researchers. The Bureau of Justice, the Labor Department, and the Centers for Disease Control and Prevention are also U.S. agencies that provide information to sociologists. The United Nations, the International Labor Organization, and the World Bank are international agencies that gather and distribute data that sociologists use to analyze global social problems. Private, nongovernmental organizations like the Population Reference Bureau and the Worldwatch Institute are also good sources of data.

The **social survey** is another source of information for researchers of social problems. Typically, social surveys rely on questionnaires designed to elicit information on a particular topic. For example, a family sociologist studying teenage pregnancy could produce a questionnaire specifically designed to provide information on this topic. Most of the time such a questionnaire is distributed to a **sample** instead of a **population**. A population refers to the whole group in which the researcher is interested. In this example it would be all teenagers in the United States. Because it would be extremely expensive and time consuming to interview all the teenagers in the United States, a sample, or subset, of the population is selected. In this example, a sample of 1,500 teenagers could be selected for investigation.

Yet another source of information for researchers of social problems is the **experiment**, with a **control group** and an **experimental group**. Both groups are identical in all aspects except for the **stimulus**. The experimental group is given the stimulus, while the control group is not. Any difference in the outcome can then be attributed to the stimulus. For example, a researcher may want to see if a new program designed to enhance self-esteem will reduce teenage pregnancy. Two similar groups of teenagers (from the same race, social class, etc.) could be involved in such an experiment. One group would be exposed to a program to enhance self-esteem and the other group would not. Difference in the pregnancy rates of the two groups of teenagers could then be attributed to the effect of the self-esteem program.

Finally, sociologists also use the **case study** method to shed light on social problems. This technique typically involves a small number of respondents who are studied in detail. **Personal interviews** and **participant observation** are the two most frequently used techniques in the case study. Personal interviews are often very lengthy (five or more hours) and probe into a particular topic. For example, Arlie Hochschild (1989) interviewed a limited number of couples in depth, in order to see how working husbands and wives shared household and child-rearing tasks. Participant observation is by a researcher who joins the group being studied. A researcher could, for example, act like a homeless person and interact with the homeless in an attempt to understand the reasons for homelessness.

Poverty and Vested Interest

A prominent sociologist, Herbert J. Gans (1971), once wrote an essay in which he listed the uses of poverty and showed that the poor can be a source of profit. They are exploited, he explained, by loan sharks, unscrupulous merchants, pawn brokers, slum landlords, narcotics peddlers, and many more; but above all, they are a source of cheap labor. One reason so many people come to the United States from Mexico, often on a seasonal basis, is to take farm jobs that pay too little to interest most United States citizens. In other words, citizens of the United States are not poor enough to serve the purpose. Similarly, many U.S. (and now Japanese) manufacturers have found it profitable to set up assembly plants in Mexico so that they can bene-fit from cheap labor (see Chapter 7). Industries from many **more developed countries** (postin-dustrial societies such as the United States, Japan, and European countries where people live with some level of abundance and hereafter referred to as **MDCs**) move to many **less developed coun-tries** (societies not yet developed economically that have large proportions of extremely poor people and hereafter referred to as **LDCs**), not just Mexico, for the same purpose.

Before we continue and discuss vested inter-ests and poverty, it should be made very clear that there is a very important connection to the status of a country being "less" or "more" devel-oped. The status of "less" developed is often a consequence of the economic and resource exploitation by "more" developed countries. Because we are interested in a worldview of social problems, let us take a look at vested interests in poverty in a land much more distant from the United States than Mexico—India.

In the carpet factories of Mirzapur, India, chil-dren of 10 years of age or younger work 12 to 16 hours a day. They must be brought into the trade while young because "only tiny fingers can tie the four hundred knots per square inch of a top-quality Mirzapur carpet" (Ganguly, 1987). Many of the 120,000 children who work at Mirzapur are bonded laborers, sold into servitude by impoverished parents to pay off debts. The chil-dren are beaten to keep them at work; they are provided only wretched sleeping mats and barely enough food to keep them alive, according to a suit brought before the Indian Supreme Court. "They are nonbeings, exiles of civilization, living a life worse than that of animals," says Chief Justice P. N. Bhagwati (Ganguly, 1987).

Indian organizations are now taking up the cause of the children. Swami Agnivesh has spent three years in jail for his opposition to the child-labor system. However, none of the exploiters of child labor has been sent to jail, and none has paid a fine of more than $40 (U.S.). Profiting from poverty is more extreme and heartless in

some parts of the world than in others, but prof-its from poverty are widespread.

The merchants of Mirzapur would not agree with the functionalist view that children need to be protected from unscrupulous people who exploit their innocence, and they are not alone in their beliefs. There are many other cases in which social norms appear to line up on one side of an issue and vested interest on the other (see Figure 1.1). Readers can undoubtedly think of many conflicts between what "everyone" believes and actual facts of internal conflicts about social prob-lems. Such conflicts of interest within societies are common the world over.

THE NEED FOR A GLOBAL PERSPECTIVE

Throughout this book, we use illustrations from around the world to show that other countries face the same social problems as the United States. Historically, it was possible for countries to be isolated from one another and hence, to have their special social problems and possible solu-tions. In today's world, societies are intricately connected. When the stock market plummets in New York, the stock markets in Tokyo, London, Buenos Aires, and Berlin are affected as well. Analyzing social problems in one society in isola-tion from the rest of the world does not make much sense in this "shrinking global village." The need to address social problems on a worldwide scale is increasing with every passing decade.

Kenneth E. Boulding (1985) suggests that one reason countries experience similar problems is that the world is a *total system*. According to him, a system is "anything that is not in chaos . . . and exhibits order and pattern" (Boulding, 1985:9). Boulding points out that all societies develop family systems, the concept of the city, a method for production and distribution of goods and services, a belief system that transcends the indi-vidual psyche, some means of medical care, methods for settling disputes, and so forth. It was

Focus on the United Kingdom

Social Research Is Becoming Less Expensive

In the United Kingdom, as in other countries, conducting research on social problems has been facilitated by the development of personal computers and other information technologies. In the not too distant past, one had to be associated with major universities like Cambridge, Oxford, and the London School of Economics in order to have access to powerful computers and data banks. The average academician, and certainly the average citizen, simply did not have access to the tools necessary to do research on serious social problems. That situation has changed dramatically in the last 10 years, and especially in the last few years.

Powerful personal computers that are costing less and less to purchase are now within the reach of almost anyone who wishes to conduct research. Sociologist Earl Babbie (1995:366) puts the issue of availability and power of computers into focus when he points out that he recently purchased a battery-operated laptop microcomputer that is the size of a metropolitan telephone directory and has a memory of 8 megabytes, which is more than 333 times the memory of a mainframe IBM 1620 computer owned by the survey research center at the university where he did graduate work 30 years ago. The IBM 1620 was as large as six or seven refrigerators. In those days, one had to have an account at a university computing center and one had to rely on computer center personnel to handle the computer instructions and processing.

Today, one can purchase an IBM 486 personal computer with a quality printer for around $1,500 that, together with modern statistical software, can handle fairly large data sets with ease. As Earl Babbie (1995:363) has stated, "What the microscope was to biology, what the telescope was to astronomy—that's what the computer has been to modern social research."

The revolution in social research starts with how the "literature search" is conducted. The literature search refers to locating all published work on a particular topic. Suppose one were interested in finding out what other researchers had found out about juvenile gangs in England. In the "old days" one would have to journey to major libraries of universities like Cambridge, Oxford, and the London School of Economics. There one would go through the card catalog to see what books and monographs had been written on the topic and one would consult the various indexes to see what articles were published on the topic in professional journals. Then one would physically find the pertinent sources in the "stacks" of the library and read the literature.

Today one can conduct most of these tasks from one's home, with the help of a modern personal computer. And it doesn't make any difference how remote one is from a major urban center. With the use of a modem, a computer, and a telephone, an interested citizen living in a remote village can access various data bases to search for articles and books on various topics. By entering the code words "juvenile gang" and "England," one would be instructing the computer to go through a particular data base and find all the literature on that topic. Many data bases also contain extracts of articles and books so that a researcher can determine whether a particular piece is worth pursuing. It is also possible to have an entire article printed out on the researcher's printer (for a fee). The *Internet*, a worldwide information system allowing individuals to communicate with each other, offers boundless sources of information and data, further facilitating the research process.

After the literature has been reviewed, the researcher may use secondary data, information already assembled by another institution or individual. Modern computing technology has made it possible for a researcher to analyze data on a personal computer. The data might be made available on a 5.25-inch "floppy disk", a 3.5-inch diskette, or a CD-ROM disk. In the very recent past, this was not possible, and one had to use a computer center at a university or think tank to research social problems.

The revolution in computer technology is recent and is accelerating. What will be available in just a few years will make present technology obsolete. What is a certainty, however, is that with the declining cost of powerful personal computers and the development of new information technologies, it is becoming easier for concerned individuals to conduct research on serious social problems.

SOURCE: E. Babbie, *The Practice of Social Research*, 7th ed. (Belmont, CA: Wadsworth, 1995.)

These children were sold into servitude by their impoverished parents and work as virtual slaves in a carpet factory in Baranasi, India, providing enormous profits to the owner of the factory.

not until recently, however, that these systems reached a vital level of interdependence. This interdependence—reminiscent of Durkheim's notion of organic solidarity, but on a global scale—is mainly a consequence of modern industrial needs, modes of transportation, and communications.

Boulding (1985:75) points out that the "Mayan Empire could collapse in the ninth and tenth centuries without this affecting either Charlemagne in Europe or the Emperor of China, for neither of them ever heard about it." But, today, events in one part of the world have effects elsewhere. The powerful technologies that we have now were not imaginable only a few decades ago. Our poisons are so toxic that chemical spills in upstream countries have disastrous effects on downstream countries. The explosion at Chernobyl (outside Kiev in the former Soviet Union) spread nuclear fallout over parts of Northern, Central, and Southern Europe. According to Robert P. Gale (1987), who coordinated treatment of the Chernobyl victims, about 60 percent of the estimated 60,000 future deaths from the accident will occur outside the former Soviet Union. Smog from fossil-burning factories in the United States causes acid rain in Canada. Modern transportation systems allow drugs to spread all over the world.

This "world superculture," as Boulding calls it, is difficult to understand because it comprises a broad spectrum of local cultures that have languages, customs, religions, occupations, stratification patterns, and other practices that are independent of the whole. Still, what happens in one country is so likely to affect other countries that it is becoming increasingly difficult to study social problems without taking the whole world into consideration. When our friends in tropical countries deforest their land, they may be influencing the climate of the entire world in an unfavorable way. Above all, the world has become a much smaller place than it was in the days of Columbus and Magellan. Sometimes we glow with enthusiasm over what human ingenuity has accomplished. Other times we wonder if we haven't somehow overextended ourselves, rushing too fast for our limited world. In one of his *Fables for Our Times*, humorist James Thurber (1956:169) expresses that idea.

The Thurber fable is "Oliver and the Other Ostriches." In it, an elderly ostrich is lecturing his fellow ostriches about the superiority of their species. However, one of the younger ostriches, Oliver, does not agree. He feels a certain sense of inferiority because Man [*sic*] can fly so fast and even fly sitting down, whereas ostriches can't fly at all.

The old ostrich is greatly annoyed at Oliver and lets him know, in no uncertain terms, that Man has no future. The old ostrich glares at him severely, first with one eye and then the other. "Man is flying too fast for a world that is small

and round," he says. "Soon he will catch up with himself in a great rear-end collision, and Man will never know that what hit Man from behind was Man."

If we are to avoid the great rear-end collision, we must know more about the world and the people that dwell therein. We must study social problems and realize that they are, for the most part, world problems. Human ingenuity occurs

Functionalist Versus Conflict Perspectives

Functionalist view	Conflict view
We wish to see the end of the illegal drug traffic.	Billions of dollars are made on drugs by dealers, corrupted officials and even by small-scale marijuana growers who might otherwise be on welfare. They will fight to keep drugs.
Our friends and allies also believe in doing away with drugs.	But Colombia, Peru, and Ecuador gain much of their incomes from drugs. So do remote parts of Burma, Thailand, Laos, and Pakistan.
We believe in honest, open government; no secrecy.	Presidents and government officials, especially in the CIA, have a strong vested interest in keeping some of their activities hidden.
We believe in good management of resources, especially soil conservation.	But not if we can strip mine a large land area at enormous profit. After all, it's our land.
Tropical countries also believe in soil conservation.	But many of their business interests and politicians see immediate gain in cutting their forests and shipping lumber abroad, while soil washes away.
Communist China believes in peace and opposes the profit motive.	But it must have made a tidy profit on Silkworm missiles that went to Iran.
Everyone believes in fighting AIDS.	But not if TV networks might offend audiences (and lose money) by advertising condoms.
Everyone believes our young people should have a first-rate education.	But hundreds of taxpayers' committees oppose school bonds because schools are expensive.
We and our good allies all oppose selling munitions and secret high "tech" to potential enemies.	But firms in Western countries have been profiting by doing this for years.

Figure 1.1
This chart illustrates how someone adopting a functionalist perspective will view a particular issue differently from someone applying a conflict perspective.

in all lands, and is another important reason for a global perspective.

SOCIAL PROBLEMS IN GLOBAL PERSPECTIVE

In writing a social-problems textbook, the authors face the problem of what to include and what to exclude. When taking a global perspective, this is a particularly difficult decision because, while the world is getting smaller and smaller, it is still a huge supersystem of very complex relationships. We have tried to select for inclusion those problems that affect virtually all nations, yet will be familiar to our students in North America and most English-speaking parts of the world.

Family: Changing Structure and Social Roles

We begin our investigation by addressing the issue of how various social roles change as the world continues to change. Imagine the outrage of the patriarch of an upper-Egyptian family who sees his granddaughter not only refuse to marry the man that her parents selected for her, but also run off to Cairo where women are beginning to think that they may be as good as men! On the other side of the world, a congresswoman from Colorado considered running for president of the United States. Other women complained because, although doing work comparable to men's, they were getting only 70 percent as much income.

In the meantime, we can witness some reverses in the trend toward modernization. Iran had been making progress toward Western ways when the Shah was deposed and replaced by a reactionary government led by the Ayatollah Khomeini in 1979. Khomeini had his country return to Islamic tradition; for example, women who had been wearing European designer jeans had to wear the *chaddor* (the long veil that covers them from head to toe) at all times in public. As we shall see, although social change is constant, it is not unidirectional and is not even.

Photographs of Planet Earth have done much to raise our consciousness about the interdependence of societies on earth. The social problems of one area of the planet are relevant to the concerns of the other areas.

Human Sexuality: Power and Politics

Chapter 3 addresses problems associated with human sexuality. The unequal status of women and men varies from one society to the next. Inequality based on sex is definitely causally related to problems such as rape, prostitution, child molestation (girls are ten times more likely to be molested), sexual harassment, and infanticide (girl babies are much more likely to be killed than boy babies). This chapter shows that equality between the sexes must be achieved before any of the aforementioned problems can be solved.

The Human Condition: Health and Affliction

Chapter 4 points out that health problems are similar in all MDCs, as is also true in all LDCs. We will learn how historically, diseases have spread over great land masses and how in modern times AIDS (Acquired Immune Deficiency Syndrome) has become a *pandemic* disease (affecting nearly all parts of the world). In ages past, separation of land masses imposed barriers to the spread of diseases. Tuberculosis was unknown in the Americas before the coming of Europeans, and it is generally believed that syphilis was unknown in Europe in pre-Columbian times. The black death (the great plague that ravaged European populations) was confined to the Old World. Now epidemics are worldwide. No country appears to be completely escaping AIDS, and each blames the others for its introduction and spread.

There is a tremendous disparity in health care between the developed world and the underdeveloped world. The number of physicians per one thousand people is one means of measuring health care. The developed countries average one doctor for every 680 people; the less developed countries average one doctor per 3,490 people. But, the availability of doctors does not tell the whole story. It may cost more money to ease the death of a single elderly patient in an intensive care unit in the United States than it costs for the health care (poor, though it is) of all of the children of Yemen.

Population: Explosion and Decline

Chapter 5 addresses the issue of population. In the eighteenth century, European populations began to gain control of infectious disease, largely through prevention. As the death rate declined, population literally exploded at a pace never before realized for a sustained period anywhere on earth. By the middle of the twentieth century, though, nearly all people of European origin had controlled this explosion. They had gained the confidence that they could have very few children and live to see those children enter adulthood. As a result, not only did the population explosion cease but a decline began. Now, few of these countries are having children at a replacement level.

South of the equator, the story is very different. Though fertility rates are starting to drop, couples continue to have many children. The reasons for this are numerous: children provide social security in old age; high infant mortality necessitates more births as parents must deal with the realities of replacing children who die prematurely; the economic benefits of children who earn more money than is spent on them; the low status of women dictating that women have little input on their own reproductive options; and the age-old religious and cultural beliefs that dictate numerous offspring.

As we will see, tackling the modern population explosion in the developing world will require knowledge of the reasons people have many children. Peoples of various cultures have many reasons for the number of children they have. But, by and large, so long as people lack the wealth to develop interests outside the family, their joy and prestige in life will be their abundance of children.

Rising populations in the LDCs affect the entire world. It provides cheap labor to compete with Western nations; it increases the need for famine relief and other foreign aid; and it accelerates destruction of soil and forests as people overtax the land in an effort to survive.

Race, Ethnicity, and Ethnocentrism

Chapter 6 addresses a problem common to nearly all people: **ethnocentrism,** (a feeling or belief that our way is right and that our people are somehow superior to other people). Migration helps to intensify this situation, as foreign people enter a culture with their different languages and social patterns, and their own ethnocentrism. Modern transportation has exacerbated the problem by making it relatively easy for large numbers of people to transverse broad geographical regions.

Often ethnocentrism leads to **prejudice** (an unfounded negative attitude about a people) and **discrimination** (the treatment, usually unfavorable and limiting, of a group). In the United States, discrimination has been experienced by every ethnic group. Even where the major ethnic groups live in relative equality (Switzerland, for example), smaller ethnic groups of more recent migration who do most of the menial work (Pakistanis, Saudis, and Egyptians) suffer from discriminatory patterns. Discrimination can be subtle, even unintended, or it can be violently obvious.

From Village to Megacity: Urbanization

In Chapter 7, we'll see that people involved in subsistence farming are being driven from their ancestral lands by the imposition of industry and large-scale, mechanized farming. This happens in poor countries and rich ones alike. In MDCs, like the United States, the small and mid-range farmers can no longer compete with agribusiness. Neither can the farmers of Mexico or the herdsmen of Kenya. The U.S. farmer sells his land at a rock-bottom price and moves to Kansas City. The Mexican farmer leaves his land and moves to Mexico City. The city draws people who are looking for a future that doesn't exist in the countryside anymore. In LDCs, the rapid urbanization of the population causes horrendous problems to the infrastructure (sewers, water system, transportation, etc.) of a city.

Global Competition

This chapter begins by examining the transition the MDCs have made from the nonmechanized existence of preindustrial society to the complex, almost incomprehensible technologies of postindustrial society. These changes were initiated by the Industrial Revolution of the late eighteenth and nineteenth centuries when Europe and countries of European origin mechanized many processes. Business transactions were accelerated by the invention of the cash register, word processing by the typewriter, mechanical power by the steam engine. Intense competitiveness, a product of the Protestant Reformation of earlier times, drove people to improve the machines for greater productivity and profit.

Toward the end of the nineteenth century, the notion that common people could obtain education stimulated the process of modernization. As a greater percentage of the population obtained some level of education, overall expectations about the future increased. The new demands could only be satisfied by developing better systems of mass production. As economies expanded, they became interconnected. Any doubts of this phenomenon should have been dashed in 1987 when a U.S. stock market crash on a Monday in November was followed the very next day by crashes in Europe, Japan, Hong Kong, and virtually every other industrialized part of the world.

Of course, not every part of the world was affected because not all nations have made this transition to postindustrial society. A country that still relies mostly on subsistence farming for its economic base will hardly worry about the price of IBM's stock or the current level of the Dow-Jones Industrial Averages. As we will see, countries are often classified according to where they are in the transition from preindustrial through industrial to postindustrial society.

Abundance and Poverty

In Chapter 9 we will address the issues of abundance and poverty. By and large, people in the postindustrial societies or MDCs live with some level of abundance while those in LCDs live at some level of poverty. We will point out that the nature of modern industry and finance tends to widen the gap between rich and poor (between MDCs and LDCs) and, within MDCs, between the upper classes and the lower classes. This occurs because the exploitation of cheap labor in LDCs tends to cheapen labor in the industrially advanced countries. This is obviously seen as unfair competition by American, Canadian, European, and Japanese workers, but it is an opportunity for jobs and industrial development by the LDCs—another good example of conflict of interest.

The real contrasts between abundance and poverty can best be understood by examining the tremendous differences in the quality of life between MDCs and LDCs. Life expectancy is higher than it has ever been in modern countries and low in preindustrial countries. If we were to take the gross national product (the sum of all goods and services produced and sold) and divide it evenly among all people in each country, every person in the MDCs would be relatively wealthy and every person in the LDCs would be absolutely, not relatively, poor. But, because wealth is never evenly distributed, poverty is a worldwide problem, whether relative or absolute. Poverty tends to destabilize governments, cause frustrations at nearly all levels of society, and make fertile ground for the emergence of

radical or reactionary dictatorships, which can have an adverse effect on the United States and its allies.

Environmental Pollution and Global Destruction

Chapter 10 deals with the pollution of the environment and Chapter 11 deals with how our species is destroying the environment. These two chapters examine the world as one great ecosystem (a community of plant life and animal life existing with a physical and chemical environment). In these chapters, we look at the extent and effects of water and air pollution, the problems associated with the construction of the great dams erected in LDCs, and the effects of deforestation, desertification, and soil erosion.

More developed countries are increasingly exporting their pollution to poorer countries in many ways. One example is the location of chemical-producing plants in LDCs whose priorities for income are greater than their concerns about protecting their populations from contamination. But, if the world is a single ecosystem, then it would follow that destruction of one part of the world will have repercussions on every part of the earth.

Global Corruption, Crime, and the Drug Trade

Chapter 12 examines international crime and violence, and notes some differences in violent crime in MDCs and LDCs. The deadliness of **white-collar crime** (crimes committed by people who seem to be respectable and by multinational corporations) is discussed.

Before leaving the subject of crime, we'll look at the scope of the international drug trade. In glaring contradistinction to most other issues raised in this book, LDCs seem to be exploiting MDCs in this one area. The drug trade is so well organized that it must be attacked on a global basis; only international cooperation can possibly provide a remedy.

Deadly Combat

Deadly combat is the theme of the next chapter. Often this derives from age-old patterns of ethnocentrism. Compared to the eighteenth and nineteenth centuries, the twentieth century has witnessed far more deaths in war, perhaps a consequence of advanced technology, perhaps a result of a failure of diplomacy.

A global arms trade, fueled by the greed of defense contractors and multinational corporations, makes modern weapons available to even the most primitive of nations. Where organized armies do not exist, war prevails in the form of terrorism, the only alternative available to severely oppressed people with no resources, embassies, or world sympathy.

Even though the former Soviet Union has disintegrated and the direct conflict between that former country and the United States is diminishing, the world is still stocked with thousands of nuclear weapons with unbelievable destructive power. All of the explosive power used during World War II seems insignificant compared to the destructive power of just a few modern missiles. Nuclear weapons in the hands of terrorists, dictators, or warlords is of more concern now than before the demise of the Soviet Union.

Human Rights and World Cooperation

Chapter 14 deals with the issues of freedom and oppression. The Western world, with few exceptions, has experienced generations of freedom, to a greater or lesser extent. It is a value that we take for granted, sometimes, because we have become used to it. Often we forget how hard our ancestors fought for these freedoms and how hard we must fight to keep them.

Elsewhere in the world such freedoms are unknown. Torture is a widespread problem, bitterly opposed by Western nations, accepted by its victims. Often oppression is accompanied by fanaticism, as is the case in Iraq. In the People's Republic of China, personal freedom is sometimes a matter of degree. Even in the United States, the degree of surveillance practiced by organizations like the Federal Bureau of Investigation and certain congressional committees is seldom, if ever, completely known. Certain nongovernmental agencies, such as fundamentalist groups, would like to suppress scientific theories and investigations. To what extent freedom is possible is an important topic of debate. On a world scale, probably nothing would promote progress more rapidly than freedom of information.

Also in Chapter 14, we discuss global attempts at cooperation to bring solutions to our many shared social problems. There exist certain agreements among nations concerning fishing territories, protection of endangered species, sovereignty of airspace, and so forth. However, we still need to create consensus regarding trade, outstanding national debts, and scientific collaboration. Above all else, we must seek agreement regarding dismantling of nuclear warheads and the safe storage or disposal of the radioactive material from the warheads. President Clinton and the leaders of Russian, the Ukraine, and other former republics of the USSR, are making progress in this area.

Very briefly, then, these are the topics considered in this text, undoubtedly expanded upon and supplemented by both instructors and students. It will become increasingly clear why we have repeated the old statement, "It was the best of times, it was the worst of times." For many, it will continue to be the worst of times until greater understanding of the world and its peoples comes about. In some respects, a social-problems course appears to emphasize the negative; after all, it *is* about problems yet to be solved. Recall, however, from our earlier definition that social problems are conditions considered amenable to improvement through social action. We should not forget that some very serious social problems are, in fact, being solved. For example, just a few years ago, the Soviet Union and the United States had thousands of nuclear missiles aimed at each other and the entire planet was living under this terrible threat. However, with the disintegration of the Soviet Union, this problem is being solved. Both the United States and the Russians are dismantling many of their missiles. Other republics of the former Soviet empire are agreeing to scrap their nuclear arms. The Ukraine has agreed to eliminate its nuclear warheads in exchange for Western aid and Russian assistance in disposing of the arsenal (Condon, 1994). One should not conclude, however, that the problem of nuclear warheads is completely solved. The United States still has an abundance of nuclear weapons and the problem of nuclear weapons in the hands of terrorists and dictators is still with us, as is the problem of disposing of the radioactive materials in nuclear warheads being dismantled. However, the threat of the world being destroyed by a nuclear holocaust has been dramatically decreased in the last few years.

In short, there is not a single problem, or combination of problems, in the following pages that will inevitably seal our doom. With knowledge, interest, and concern, we can make progress against them all, and a growing segment of humanity and its descendants can eventually change the worst of times into the best of times.

A Note of Caution

Before we start to discuss various social problems from a global perspective, you should be aware that the ethnocentrism discussed previously (the tendency to view one's values, norms, and behavior patterns as "correct" while viewing those of other cultures as "incorrect") will continually hamper your ability to appreciate and understand various social problems, espe-

cially problems of other countries. We make every attempt in this book to go beyond simple description of a problem to help you understand how the values, norms, and history of a particular culture are associated with and explain a particular problematic condition. We ask that you attempt to "remove yourself" as much as possible from your own particular society and then to "put yourself" in the foreign cultures that we will be discussing.

SUMMARY

In this chapter we introduced the area of sociology called social problems. Social problems are situations that are distressing to large numbers of people, are contrary to the moral beliefs of people, and are partly or wholly correctable through the actions of social groups. The degree to which a particular social problem gets attention depends on what priority society, as a whole, places on solving that problem. This priority is, in turn, affected by the values of members of society.

Latent social problems are unintended and are the result of some other action or invention. Initially, these problems are not clearly perceived and do not generate public support until later.

There are three major perspectives on social problems: the functionalist perspective, the conflict perspective, and the interactionist perspective. The functionalist perspective tends to see the agreements of society as the glue that holds the whole together, and sees the joint efforts of groups as the way to solve problems. The conflict perspective is a way of viewing society that emphasizes the conflicts within. This view tends to focus on vested interests of certain groups as a way of explaining why various social problems exist. The interactionist perspective focuses on the socialization process and small groups in an effort to understand social problems, and also is the best perspective to use when explaining how a particular phenomenon gets defined as problematic.

Along with one or more of the above perspectives, sociologists study social problems by using the scientific method. Researchers use public records, social surveys, experiments, and case studies to generate data to test hypotheses regarding social phenomena which are deemed to be problematic.

It was argued that there is a need to study social problems from a global perspective rather than a national perspective. Because of the revolution in telecommunications, the planet is quickly becoming "smaller." What occurs in one part of the world has a definite impact on other parts of the world. One cannot truly understand a problem without having the "big" picture—the global view.

KEY TERMS

Bourgeoisie The class of people that owns the means of production.

Case study method The research approach in the social sciences that involves a small number of respondents who are studied in detail.

Conflict perspective Emphasis on the conflicts and clash of interests between and among various social classes and groups.

Constellation of values A set, or certain mix, of numerous values.

Cultural lag The inability of social structure and culture to keep up with rapid technological change.

Control group The group in an experiment that is not given the stimulus.

Core societies The dominant, economically well-developed societies in world systems theory.

Dependent variable The factor that the researcher is interested in explaining.

Discrimination The treatment, usually unfavorable and limiting, of a group that has minority status.

Ethnocentrism A condition in which a group or society feels that its way is right and that its people are somehow superior to other groups or societies.

Experiment A test to see if a particular stimulus has an impact on another variable.

Experimental group The group, in an experiment, that is given the stimulus.

Functionalist perspective The point of view that the agreements of society are the glue that holds the whole together.

Generalized other, taking the role of A person's ability to respond to the values and norms of people in general.

Independent variable The factor that explains variation in another, dependent variable.

Interactionist perspective The perspective that is micro in nature, and that focuses mainly on the behavior of individuals and small groups of individuals.

Latent function The unintended and little noticed function for which an institution or policy is designed.

Latent problem A problem that is in the making and not yet readily apparent.

Less developed countries (LDCs) Societies that are not yet developed economically and that have large proportions of extremely poor people.

Manifest function The intended function for which an institution or policy is designed.

Mechanical solidarity The concept that a system is held together because of the likeness of its members and their desires.

More developed countries (MDCs) Post-industrial societies like the United States, Japan, and European countries where people live with some level of abundance.

Mores Moral beliefs and practices of a society.

Mos Singular of *mores.*

Organic solidarity The idea that, as parts of society become more diverse, they must come to be more interdependent for the good of the whole.

Participant observation The research technique that involves the researcher joining the group under investigation.

Peripheral societies The dependent, less economically developed societies in world systems theory.

Personal interview In-depth, lengthy interviews of respondents in a case study.

Population The total group in which the researcher is interested.

Prejudice An unfounded negative attitude about a subgroup of people based on preconceived notions.

Priorities What we are willing to do, either passively or actively, about our feelings of right and wrong.

Proletariat The class of people that has only its labor to provide.

Public records Social and economic data gathered by public agencies and used by researchers.

Reference groups Groups with which a particular person wishes to identify.

Research methods The techniques, ranging from qualitative to quantitative, that social scientists use in their research.

Sample A subset of a population that a researcher selects for investigation.

Scientific method An approach to investigating a topic that relies on both logic and observation.

Social problems Situations, policies, or trends that are (a) distressing or threatening to large numbers of people, (b) contrary to the moral beliefs of the society, and (c) partly or wholly correctable through the actions of social groups.

Social survey A survey of a population or sample that relies on a questionnaire to elicit information on a particular topic.

Socialization The process by which an individual learns to think and act in a particular culture.

Self-concept The mental image one has of herself or himself.

Statistics Analytical techniques that allow us to compare what was expected from a theory to what was actually observed.

Stimulus That which is administrated to the experimental group but not the control group, in an effort to test cause and effect.

Theoretical perspective A particular way of explaining or making sense out of the social world.

Theory The logical aspect of science that explains how and why a certain phenomenon exists.

Values The feelings and beliefs that define notions of right or wrong.

Vested interest A special economic or political interest that one has in a social practice, policy, or institution.

White-collar crime Crimes committed by people who seem to be otherwise respectable or by multinational corporations.

World systems theory A conflict perspective developed by Immanuel Wallerstein that explains the status and well-being of a society based on where that society is located in the global economic stratification system

Zero opinion analysis Theory that resources are finite so that one person's gain requires another person's loss.

1. What three factors define a social problem?

2. How do values affect the definition of social problems?

3. How does the passive setting of priorities differ from the active setting of priorities?

4. What is a latent social problem? Give an example.

5. What is the difference between a manifest function and latent function?

6. Define the conflict and functionalist perspectives and discuss how they might be used to explain poverty.

7. How would world systems theory explain the poverty of a less developed country like Nigeria?

8. How could one's vested interest affect one's opinion about the manufacturing of missiles?

9. What is the difference between a population and a sample?

10. What kind of research problem might lend itself to the technique of participant observation?

chapter 2

FAMILY: CHANGING STRUCTURE AND SOCIAL ROLES

ex. It was intended for the enjoyment of men and to provide childbearing ability for women. As absurd as this view may seem to the college student in any Western country, it is still held is some parts of the world. For example, in Ethiopia, baby girls must routinely undergo genital mutilation, having the clitoris surgically removed. When they marry—often by age 14 or 15 to a man who may be anywhere from 30 to 45—they are not allowed to speak to their husbands. When they are menstruating, they are considered unclean and must hide themselves from view. If they bear daughters instead of sons, they may be divorced by their husbands. In some places, there is no notion of equality between men and women. But in other places, social roles are changing.

Equality is coming to the women of Eritrea, once the northern province of Ethiopia. It was an Italian colony before World War II. It was administered by the British from the end of the war until 1952, when it was annexed to Ethiopia under the government of Haile Selassie, the hereditary ruler who traced his ancestry back to the Queen of Sheba and King Solomon. However, Eritrea never accepted the rule of Ethiopia and has waged war for its independence for more than a quarter of a century. The soldiers of the Dergue, the socialist government of Ethiopia, are all men, but a high percentage of the army of the Eritrean People's Liberation Front is *women. By proving themselves in battle, the women of Eritrea improved their social status and no longer have to fight to be considered equal. Yet, the 40 percent of the army that is female is composed of volunteers (Robertson, 1987).*

In the United States, Canada, and most other more developed countries (MDCs), we are not often reminded how the roles of men, women, and children have changed. However, drastic changes have occurred, perhaps with less drama than has been reported about the women of Eritrea. We'll begin our examination of this topic by looking at the traditional and changing family structures of societies.

THE FAMILY IN ANTIQUITY

The **family** may be defined as "an intimate kin-based group consisting of at least a parent–child nucleus, [and] the minimal social unit that cooperates economically and assumes responsibility for the rearing of children" (Howard and Dunaif-Hattis, 1992:623). It is probably the oldest social institution, even preceding the evolution of our species. Lenski and Lenski (1987:13–15) suggest that our strong reliance on learning (through the process of socialization) is responsible for the development of human beings—and our primate ancestors—as social animals.

Originally, the family and society were virtually synonymous. When hunting and gathering societies first formed, about 40,000 years ago, a "society" probably consisted of 6 to 30 people dwelling in caves or following herds. These tiny societies, however, developed rather ingenious ways of allocating jobs, distributing property, defining rights and obligations, and determining potential marriage partners for each individual. In addition, the family was also the basic economic, political, religious, and educational institution. Most problems were problems of basic survival; social problems were probably limited to selection of

mates and distribution of food and other basic resources.

As societies have evolved and become increasingly complex, family form and structure has likewise become more varied from one culture to the next.

FORMS OF MARRIAGE ACROSS CULTURES

William Kephart and Davor Jedlicka (1991:17) identify four family functions that are found so frequently around the world that they can be called **cultural universals**. These functions are (1) reproduction, (2) socialization of children, (3) transferral of inheritance, and (4) regulation of sexual behavior. Families can be formed in numerous ways, however, to meet the above functions.

Polygamy

Polygamy refers to either one woman being married to several men or one man being married to several women (Kephart and Jedlicka, 1991:18–22). The former is **polyandry** and the latter is **polygyny**. Although polyandry is far less common than polygyny, there are societies (the Todas of India, the Sherpa of Nepal, the peasants of Tibet and others) in which one woman is married to two or more men. Polygyny is not only more common than polyandry, it is the preferred form of marriage—70 percent of societies prefer marriage arrangements where one husband has two or more wives (Friedl and Whiteford, 1988:246). Though most societies prefer polygyny, this form of marriage is generally not attainable for most males in polygynous societies due to the lack of available women and the cost of supporting multiple wives.

Monogamy

Monogamy refers to marriages of one husband and one wife. There are two forms of monogamy. **Serial monogamy** refers to situations in which, at any one time, one man is married to one woman but, at different periods of their lifetimes, husbands and wives are married to two or more spouses. Though the death of a spouse can lead to remarriage, serial monogamy is usually associated with relatively high rates of divorce. **Strict monogamy** is the "till death does us part" version in which a spouse will only remarry in the event of the other spouse's death. Monogamy is the only type of marriage accepted in all societies (Kephart and Jedlicka, 1991:23). Even though the vast majority of societies prefer nonmonogamous marriages, the overwhelming majority of our planet's inhabitants follow the monogamous model.

THE FAMILY AND SEX ROLES IN LDCs

The most recent evidence from the less developed world suggests that current family structures and the relationships between men and women is increasing hardship and exploitation of women. Centuries-old religious, cultural, social, and legal traditions have institutionalized and legitimized discriminatory actions against females. Nations like the People's Republic of China, that had made great progress toward sexual equality, are now moving in the opposite direction. Opportunities for women in China are decreasing and female status is reverting to one of subjugation and servitude. In most developing countries, the belief that women are inferior is ingrained in cultural and social life, and discrimination often begins at birth (Anderson and Moore, 1993:6). In this section, we will discuss

Although polygyny is the preferred form of marriage in many cultures, it is not generally possible. This family from Bangladesh consists of one husband and his many wives and children.

Women in New Delhi, India, carry loads of dried cow dung, which will be used for cooking fires. In India and other LDCs, women have lower status than men and do the majority of hard labor.

the plight of women in five developing countries: India, Brazil, China, Egypt, and Saudi Arabia.

India

In the Indian village of Gandhi Nagar a weathered 31-year-old mother fed her newborn daughter a poisonous mixture of oil and crushed oleander seeds. After the infant died, the mother buried her in a shallow grave in a nearby field. This type of murder is called **infanticide**, and is much more likely to involve infant girls than boys. How prevalent is infanticide? Due to its clandestine nature, official statistics are unreliable. However, in a recent survey by the Community Services Guild of the city of Madras, India, more than half of the 1,250 women questioned stated that they had killed infant daughters (Anderson and Moore, 1993:6). Even more sobering is the fact that female infanticide is known to be much more prevalent in rural areas.

Although such a statistic might shock us, infanticide is common practice in many parts of the world. After all, the value of girls and women in India, as in other developing countries, is very low.

Why are girls valued so little in rural India? There are many reasons. First, girls are given away in marriage, along with a hefty dowry, which is a monetary or material gift to the bridegroom's family. Many times a dowry will drain the bride's family of all its economic reserves. A girl is regarded as a temporary family member that dissipates the family's wealth. R. Venkatachalam, director of the Community Services Guild of Madras, notes, "They say bringing up a girl is like watering a neighbor's plant" (quoted in Anderson and Moore, 1993:6). Second, males are regarded as the "chief breadwinners" and boys, the future breadwinners, are thusly provided more of scarce resources. Finally, sons (and their wives) are usually responsible for taking care of their parents in their old age. Women do not provide support for their old parents in India: as part of their husband's family they must take care of his parents.

In India, as in other developing countries, girls are given less than boys, in all aspects of life. Girls are fed less than boys; in fact, infant boys are breastfed longer than infant girls. Girls are withdrawn from school earlier, given less medical care, and are forced into hard labor younger than boys. This pattern of gender discrimination continues through adolescence and adulthood. Though life is hard for all in the less developed countries, it is harder for females than for males.

Brazil

Rosa María Santos is a 33-year-old mother of six who lives with her husband, Carlos, in a traditional farming community in the impoverished northeastern part of Brazil. Rosa has been pregnant 13 times; 3 of these pregnancies ended in miscarriage and 4 babies died before they reached the age of two. The high incidence of miscarriage and infant and child mortality in this part of Brazil is due, in part, to the grinding poverty. Rosa and her husband try to scratch a living from their small rented farm but most of the time the family goes hungry. Insufficient food and protein make mothers more prone to miscarry and infants and children more susceptible to fatal diseases.

Another problem is the lack of birth control. Many of Rosa's neighbors are ignorant of birth control and the closest family planning clinic is 20 miles away. However, Rosa has learned about family planning from a friend and wanted to have a tubal ligation after her last birth. Carlos would not hear of it. In his eyes it would make Rosa "less of a woman." He also refuses to use condoms because "such things are not used by real men." Rosa has just found out that she is pregnant again, but continues to work in the fields alongside her husband, to prepare meals for him and the children, and to keep their modest house as clean as possible. It seems to Rosa that she and her female friends are carrying a disproportionate part of the load, that they put in many more hours than their husbands. Her mother once told her that God intended men to be the rulers of their homes and women to be subservient to them. This God surely is a man.

China

"Women hold up half the sky." This was one of the slogans put forth by Mao Zedong's Communist Party as it took over power in the People's Republic of China in 1949 (Sun, 1993:9). Mao sought a total restructuring of Chinese society—including replacing the Confucian view of the family, which placed the husband in charge and the wife in submission. The Communist Party's stated goal was an egalitarian society in which men and women had equal status and opportunity. The state took over many functions of the family such as child care, and women were brought into the work force. As late as 1977, the percentage of women in China who were employed outside of the home exceeded that of most Western countries (Sun, 1993:9). Then, in 1978, numerous economic reforms were instituted in an attempt to modernize the country. For example, the decentralization of planning gave individual factories more power to fire and hire and more responsibility for their own profits and losses.

There is evidence that these economic reforms have resulted in a return to Confucianist norms of male dominance in the family and outside of the home (Sun, 1993:9). According to Chinese and Western researchers alike, the gender gap in China is increasing and there is increasing discrimination against females in employment outside the home, in inheritance of property, and in educational opportunities (Sun, 1993:9). If women work outside of the home, they are likely to be involved in "traditional" women's occupations which are low paying and considered "dead end": street sweepers, nursery school teachers, and nurses. At the same time, women are expected to perform the tedious housework without the conveniences and appliances that Westerners take for granted, and they are also expected to tend elderly parents.

Another interesting change, or return to tradition, in China is the reviving importance of physical beauty of females. Increasingly, beautiful young mistresses or wives, referred to as "modern flower vases," confer status upon men (Sun, 1993:9). Women are also finding that physical beauty is, in many situations, a qualification for employment. It appears that the Confucianist values of unequal status between men and women were much more ingrained than some thought. Long gone are the days of "Mao" suits that conferred equal status on men and women.

Egypt and Saudi Arabia

Most women in Western countries would find the status of women in contemporary Arab countries very confining and frustrating. Caryle Murphy (1993) interviewed a number of educated women in Egypt and Saudi Arabia and found that age-old cultural values place women in untenable positions, both at work and at home. For example, when a woman wants to get or renew a passport, she must have written permission from her husband or some other male relative. Also, Islamic law states that a man can divorce his wife by simply saying so, for any purpose whatsoever. A wife, however, cannot divorce her husband for any reason, including his taking a second wife. In fact, Egyptian national identity cards for males have space for the names of four wives.

Arabic culture generally doesn't value the presence of females in the external work force. Women are seen as too fragile and emotional to do jobs for which only men are qualified. What makes things especially hard for aspiring women in Arabic countries is the cultural expectation that they be in total charge of the home, even if they work outside of the home. Husbands are not expected to help in any way, shape, or form. Given the general lack of labor-saving appliances in third-world countries, this means that women who work outside of the home endure very long hours.

Saudi Arabia is an even more difficult place than Egypt for women with ambition. In Saudi Arabia, women can't drive, walk alone in public,

or socialize with men who are not relatives. If a woman desires to open a business, all the paperwork must be filed in the name of her husband or another male relative. Some women go through extraordinary measures to run a business (Murphy, 1993:10–11). For example, a Saudi woman running a shop would have her husband open the shop in his name. She would have to deal with the bank and government by proxy, sending papers via male drivers or employees, and have a letter of permission (from her husband) to travel even to a nearby town. As bad as things are presently for Arabic women, many worry that the future may be even more dismal, given the contemporary revival of Islamic fundamentalism.

How do sociologists view these gender roles in less developed countries? It depends on their perspectives. Conflict sociologists, and especially feminists—scholars who call for equal economic, social, and political rights for women and men— view the dire situation of third-world women as a direct result of the inferior social position women occupy in their societies. Functionalists would see the position of women in the third world as a function of the different but complementary roles that males and females play in those societies. As these societies become developed, functionalists would predict that the roles of men and women would change and become more equal. Interactionists would focus on socialization and discuss the manner in which attitudes about men and women are learned and handed down from father to son and from mother to daughter.

THE FAMILY AND SEX ROLES IN MDCs

Family structure and the roles that men and women play are undergoing profound change in all the more developed countries. Although these changes may be more pronounced in some MDCs like the United States, they are occurring in all MDCs. Some of these changes are viewed as problematic by some observers, but not so by others.

Changing Family Composition

Family composition has changed dramatically in most MDCs in the last 20 years and change is expected to continue, albeit at a much slower pace. Table 2.1 presents data on family composition for the United States, from 1970 to the year 2000. The changes for the United States mirror, to a large extent, trends in other MDCs. The table shows that the proportion of families made up of a married couple with children has decreased from 49.6% of all families in 1970 to less than 37% in 1990. This type of family is expected to represent 34.5% of all families by the year 2000. Married couples without children have increased their representation from 37.1% in 1970 to 41.7% in 1990.

Single-Head Households

As Table 2.1 shows, single-head households have increased substantially over the last quarter of a century. Part of the explanation for this trend is the increase in divorce, which is discussed later in this chapter. However, much of this increase

in single-head households is a result of men and women *choosing* to remain single, and in many cases, with children. The family type that has increased the most, proportionally, is the female-headed family with children, going from 5.7% of families in 1970 to 10.2% in 1990. Single-parent families are most prevalent in minority populations. According to Ahlburg and De Vita (1992:7), single parent families with children represent 20% of white families with children, one-third of Hispanic families with children, and 60% of African American families with children. Recent research (Morgan et al., 1993) using 1910 U.S. Census manuscripts shows that the sharp differences that exist today between African American and white families in the United States existed at the turn of the century. Then, as now, African American households were more likely to be headed by women and less likely to be **nuclear**—a family consisting of two parents and their natural or adopted children—than white households. Also, African American women were much more likely than white women to have children who were living not with them, but with relatives. Morgan and his colleagues suggest that part of the difference between African American and white household configurations at the turn of the century is due

Family Composition in the United States, 1970–2000				TABLE 2.1
Type of family	1970	1990	1995	2000
All families (in millions)	51.2	64.5	68.0	71.7
Total	100.0%	100.0%	100.0%	100.0%
Married couple with children	49.6	36.9	36.2	34.5
Married couple without children	37.1	41.7	41.8	42.8
Female head with children	5.7	10.2	10.0	9.7
Male head with children	0.7	1.8	2.2	2.7
Other families	6.9	9.4	9.8	10.3

SOURCE: Projections prepared by Decision Demographics. Data for 1970 from U.S. Bureau of the Census, *Current Population* Reports p.20, no. 218; as cited in Ahlburg and De Vita, 1992:7.

The proportion of households consisting of single parents and their children has risen in many countries, due partly to the increase in divorce and partly to the fact that some parents choose not to marry.

better environment for the child; greater access to health care and education; and to provide companionship and assistance to childless relatives (Morgan et al., 1993:222–237).

The persistence of differences in African American and white family structures can be at least partially explained by societal structural factors such as segregation. The U.S. Census Bureau projections suggest that the increase in female-headed families has leveled off and may even decline slightly by the year 2000.

Gay and Lesbian Families

In most MCDs, homosexuals are the victims of prejudice and discrimination. The institution of marriage is solely for heterosexual couples and the legal and societal benefits (such as tax laws, health plans, etc.) that married hetereosexuals enjoy do not accrue to homosexual couples. Still, about three-fourths of lesbian couples and more than one-half of gay male couples cohabitate (Harry, 1983:225) and deal with the same problems that heterosexual couples do—who will do the laundry, who will mow the lawn, and who will put dinner together.

In times past, social-problems textbooks presented homosexuality as the "problem." In fact, the manner in which societies deal with homosexuality is the real problem. For example, gay and lesbian couples who desire to raise children are blocked from doing so. The courts generally view homosexual couples as potentially harmful to the development of children, though no evidence is available to support this contention. The child in question could be the offspring of one of the homosexual partners or a child the couple wants to adopt. In any event, most societies make it very difficult, if not impossible, for homosexual couples to raise children.

The Return to the Nest

Due to the economic recession in the United States, a growing number of people in their

to the influence of cultural predispositions traced back to West Africa, the ancestral home of most African Americans. For example, in sub-Saharan Africa, people tend to have very strong ties and obligations to kin outside of the immediate family. In fact, ties to extended kin can rival those in the immediate family. A normal feature of West African families is the institution of *fosterage*, where children are raised not by the parents but by other relatives. In Africa there are many reasons to send one's children to live with relatives: economic hardship; the desire for a twenties are moving back in with their parents (Boo, 1992). More than 18 million single adults aged 18 to 34 years live with their parents. In a society that values independence, moving back home with mom and dad can be embarrassing and shameful for the young adult. Also, the parents may resent giving up their privacy and freedom and the additional expense of having their children move back in with them.

It has been suggested (Boo, 1992) that this trend of adult children moving back in with their parents may not be problematic, but healthy. Other developed countries such as France, Spain, Italy, Greece, Russia, and Japan have always had higher proportions of their populations living in intergenerational households, and they seem to thrive on it. Most Europeans live at home much longer than their American counterparts. While the higher cost of living in Europe partially explains this, research suggests that Europeans have a greater appreciation for the economic and emotional benefits of family life. Katherine Boo argues that Europeans are more likely to want to continue to be involved in their children's and grandchildren's lives than are Americans.

> When French grandparents were polled a few years ago about what they wished to devote their retirement to, the answer most frequently given was, 'to help the children.' They mean it. One-third of infants were looked after by their grandparents while their parents work; one-half of children spend their annual holidays with their grandparents. Perhaps most astoundingly, a full 50 percent of French people live within 20 miles of their parents. (Boo, 1992:35)

Boo (1992:35) concludes by suggesting that the difference between the cultures of many other developed countries and the United States is that the former "tend to view the parent–child commitment as a lifelong one: a continuum of sacrifice and repayment," while the latter does not.

Separation of Reproduction and Sex

Historically, human sexual behavior and the reproduction of the species went hand in hand. Increasingly, these two factors are being seen as separate. At one time, one became sexually active, married, and entered the work force at roughly the same time. A number of factors have changed. First, the age of sexual maturity has been declining, due mainly to improved nutrition. Second, the need for formal education has increased the average age for entry into the work force. Peter Laslett (1992:10) points out that the period of childhood has been shortened by four years while adolescence has been lengthened by eight years. Also, the general malaise in the economies of most MDCs and the huge restructuring of the marketplace occurring in all MDCs has resulted in a paucity of jobs for younger people entering the work force.

Two-Paycheck Families

All MDCs have experienced an increase in the proportion of families where both husband and wife work. Table 2.2 presents data on the percentage of mothers in the labor force in eight MDCs. Sizeable percentages of mothers with children under the age of 18, and even under the age of 3, are working outside of the home. This is especially true in the Scandinavian countries of Denmark and Sweden, where the percentage of mothers working is approaching 90 percent.

Family structure is changing in the United States as well, as shown in Figure 2.1. The most dramatic trend in family structure is the marked decline in the proportion of families that fit the "father-breadwinner/mother-homemaker" model. This family type has decreased from nearly 70 percent of families in 1940 to about 20 percent in 1990. Conversely, the proportion of other family types has increased since 1940, especially the dual-worker family, which has risen from less than 10 percent of families in 1940 to more than 40 percent in 1990.

Mothers in the Labor Force in Selected Countries, 1988	TABLE 2.2	

Percentage of mothers in the labor force with children

Country	Under age 18	Under age 3
United States	65	53
Canada	67*	58
Denmark	86	84
Germany (Western)	48	40
France	66	60
Italy	44	45
Sweden	89*	86**
United Kingdom	59	37

*Children under 16 years
**Children under 7 years

NOTE: Data for United States, Canada, and Sweden are for 1988; data for other countries are for 1986.

SOURCE: C. Sorrentino, *Monthly Labor Review* (March 1990); as cited in Ahlburg and DeVita, 1992:26.

Figure 2.1
The proportion of families in the United States that conform to the breadwinner/homemaker model has declined markedly in the last 50 years. Other family models, such as the dual-worker family, are becoming more prevalent.

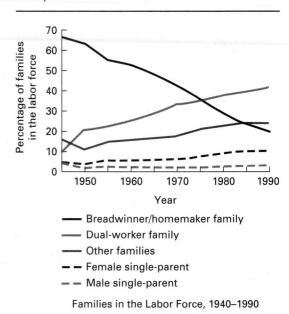

——— Breadwinner/homemaker family
——— Dual-worker family
——— Other families
– – Female single-parent
– – Male single-parent

Families in the Labor Force, 1940–1990

The increase in the number of mothers working outside the home is partly due to the impact of the Women's Liberation Movement on the roles of men and women. In the late 1960s and 1970s, women called for more equality in education and the workplace. As a result, social barriers have been coming down and women are starting to find themselves in occupations that had been reserved for men. Although women continue to make less money than men, the disparities of income are diminishing, albeit slowly. In 1975, fully employed females earned about 59.5 percent as much as fully employed males. By 1991, women were earning 72 percent of what men were making (U.S. Bureau of the Census, 1991b). This represents a move in the right direction but is still less than .8 of 1 percent improvement per year.

Another factor contributing to the increase in two-paycheck families is the economic necessity of two incomes to make ends meet. The

U.S. Census Bureau (1991) data show that the earnings of women are playing an ever more important role in family finances. The median annual family income of families with wives working outside the home was $47,000 in 1990 compared to $30,000 in families in which the wife did not work outside the home. The size and purchasing power of the average husband's paycheck has been slipping over the last two or three decades, and without the wife's employment, most families would have experienced a decline in their standard of living. Richard Easterlin (1987) has shown that if the rate at which wives had participated in the labor force had remained the same from 1968 to 1982, real family income would have gone down by 8 percent. The loss of the good-paying blue-collar

This physician exemplifies the trend of women becoming involved in occupations that had been practiced only by men.

jobs that uneducated men used to find in abundance and the rising cost of housing have contributed to these trends.

Changing Roles of Family Members

The increased participation of women in the work force has led to a redefinition of the roles that men and women are expected to play. Men are now expected to contribute more to housework. Men are also expected to show a more nurturing side and to spend more time parenting. The mass media in the United States are spending more time and space on the changing role of men in the home. Although segments of each generation of American men are becoming increasingly involved in parenting, society continues to question the extent to which fathers should be responsible for the emotional development of their children. For example, teachers and pediatricians routinely assume that the mother is in charge of the children. Employers, even those that provide paternity leave, continue to penalize dads who show as much or more commitment to their children as they do to their work. Men are expected to be committed 110 percent to their work and employers tend to give raises and promotions to the "workaholics" instead of the less committed male employees. While "flex-time" and part-time employment may be options for mothers, they are less likely to be available for fathers. Also, some wives are reluctant to give equal parental responsibility to their husbands, either because they are reluctant to give up the power that accompanies such a change or because they don't feel their husbands are competent enough or responsible enough to care for the children adequately. The sad fact is that men are often less prepared for parenthood than women because girls are taught to be caregivers from an early age and boys are not.

Recent research (Pleck, 1992) shows that indeed, U.S. men are increasing their involvement with their children. Though everyone does not view the increased participation of women in the work force and the increased participation of men in domestic affairs in a positive light, most view these developments as long overdue and healthy.

Although women still do the vast majority of housework and child care, men are starting to participate more in these activities.

While men are becoming more involved at home, they are still not "equal" to their wives. Research continues to demonstrate that working women still do most of the household chores and child-care duties after they get home from work. Frances Goldscheider and Linda Waite (1991) studied the distribution of household work among husbands, wives, and children in the United States and found that for all tasks except yard work, wives did the lion's share of the work and children and husbands tended to alternate as the chief assistants to the wife. Figure 2.2 shows that for laundry, shopping, cooking, cleaning, dishwashing, paperwork, and childcare, wives do 60 percent to 81 percent of the work. Yard work is the only task on which the wife is not disproportionately represented. In fact, this is the only task in which husbands come close to doing their fair share.

The amount of household work by husbands does, however, vary with the occupations of wives. L. Suzanne Dancer and Lucia Albino Gilbert (1993) divided a group of U.S. couples into three family types: single-wage traditional, dual-earner types in which wives or husbands held jobs or careers and, dual-earner types in which both

husbands and wives held careers. They found more sharing of housework in the dual-earner types, particularly for the dual-career families. Also, disparity between amount of time put in on household and childcare is more likely in lower socioeconomic households. As social class and income increase and as the prestige of the wife's occupation increases, so does the amount of effort expended by the husband at home.

Another major change is the increase in **blended families**, which are formed when divorced individuals remarry and where one or more children from previous marriages are involved. Various new roles accompany this family form—stepfathers, stepmothers, stepsiblings, and half-siblings—and there seems to be quite a bit of ambiguity regarding these roles. Exactly how much discipline should a stepfather or stepmother exert on a stepchild? How much respect and love does a stepchild owe a stepparent? How should a relationship between full siblings be compared to that between half-siblings or stepsiblings? These and other important questions about roles in new family forms are currently being asked. Andrew Cherlin (1978) argues that American society is much more supportive—both legally and institu-

Figure 2.2
Although husbands and children share some responsibility for household tasks like cleaning, dishwashing, child care, and yard work, wives continue to bear the brunt of household labor.

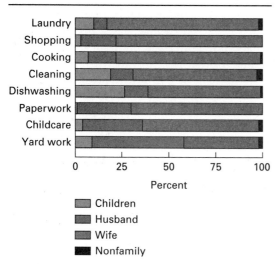

Distribution of Household Tasks by Family Members, mid-1980s

Source: Goldscheider and Waite, *New Families, No Families?*, 1991, using National Longitudinal Surveys of Young Women and Mature Women; as cited in Ahlburg and DeVita, 1992: 27.

tionally—of first marriages and marriages involving one or more widows, than it is of blended marriages. He suggests that the higher divorce rate for remarriages after divorce is a result of the uncertainly of family members' roles and the lack of societal guidelines for handling problems inherent in blended families. In addition to the ambiguity about disciplining stepchildren, legal relationships between members of blended families are also often blurred. Finally, based on the complexity generated by the linkages between several households, blended families experience more strain than other families. Cherlin (1978) argues for more research so that we can properly understand the extent and configuration of blended families. He also calls for new societal guidelines on how to define and conduct relationships in these families.

Change in the role of family members is also evident in Japan. Many observers continue to see the Japanese wife as submissive and dependent on her husband with no role other than raising children and caring for her family. Sumiko Iwao (1993) challenges many of these stereotypes. Her study of women in Japanese society starts in the early 1930s and documents many unheralded changes in gender roles in that country. Before World War II, a woman's place in Japanese society was one of absolute inferiority to men; today her place is much more powerful, albeit in subtle ways. Iwao points out that Japanese women are becoming better educated and are starting to become noticed as novelists, artists, and in other professional capacities. Her research suggests that many Japanese women consider their "liberation" more advanced than that of American women. Unlike American women, Japanese women do not necessarily want to mimic the occupational and life profiles of their men. Instead of long hours of the pressure-packed jobs of their husbands, Japanese women are charting career and life courses that combine much of the positive from both their traditional and modern roles. Iwao points out that Japanese women have been able to rewrite their scripts because (1) Japanese women have traditionally controlled the family's finances, and (2) Japanese society is oriented to "singles" rather than to "couples." An absentee father who spends most of his time with his co-workers is the norm; the husband and wife are not expected to do things as a couple, and women form extensive lifelong networks with each other.

The Increase in Age of Marriage, the Decrease in the Marriage Rate, and the Increase in Divorce

All MDCs have witnessed an increase in the age of marriage, a decrease in the marriage rate, and an increase in the divorce rate during the last 30 to 40 years, though the change in these rates appears to have stabilized. Individuals in the United States, as

---

in other MDCs, are postponing marriage longer and are more likely to forego marriage altogether than in the past (Ahlburg and De Vita, 1992:11). In 1955 the median age at first marriage was 22.6 years for men and 20.3 years for women; in 1991 it was 26.3 years for men and 24.1 years for women (Ahlburg and De Vita, 1992:12). Figure 2.3 presents data on marriage rates in the United States from 1940 to 1990. While the overall marriage rate per 1,000 people has remained fairly stable since the 1950s, the rate per 1,000 unmarried women aged 15 to 44 has plummeted since the late 1940s. This demonstrates that men and women of the baby boom generation, that huge cohort born between 1946 and 1964, have been delaying marriage. This is one of the main reasons that the fertility rate is below replacement in the United States; it is even lower in other MDCs (Haub and Yanagishita, 1994).

An increase in the divorce rate has accompanied delayed marriage in most MDCs. Again, while some observers decry this trend, others welcome it, saying that it frees unhappy people from unsuccessful relationships. Various factors account for this increase. Many MDCs are characterized by ideologies of individualism, individual growth, and self-actualization which, when extended to both women and men, result in a greater propensity to end unfulfilling marriages. Also, violence against women (discussed later in this chapter), which is less and less acceptable in MDCs, is related to the increase in the divorce rate. Finally, the increased financial and personal independence of women has given them more options and power and has resulted in increased divorce (Riche, 1991). In the past, women were more likely to be full-time homemakers without personal income and did not have the option of leaving their husbands and striking out on their own. Table 2.3 presents divorce rate data for a number of MDCs. All of the countries in the table witnessed sizeable increases in their divorce rates from 1960 to 1988. Although the divorce rate in the United States remained the highest, all of the countries, with the exception of Japan, witnessed appreciable increases in their divorce rates from 1960 to 1988.

Economic Effects of Divorce

Research on the economic effects of divorce shows that females are more negatively affected by divorce than are males. A study using longitudinal data (Duncan and Hoffman, 1985) showed

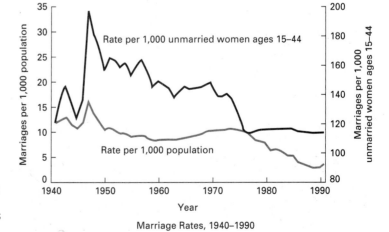

Figure 2.3
While the overall U.S. marriage rate has remained fairly stable for the last four decades, the marriage rate for unmarried women aged 15 to 44 has plummeted during this same time period.

Source: National Center for Health Statistics, *Advance Report of Final Marriage Statistics, 1988,* and provisional data; as cited in Ahlburg and DeVita, 1992: 12.

Divorce Rates of Selected Countries, 1960–1988				TABLE 2.3

Divorces per 1,000 married women

Country	1960	1970	1980	1988
United States	9.2	14.9	22.6	20.7
Canada	1.8	6.3	10.8	12.6
France	2.9	3.3	6.3	8.4
Germany (Western)	3.6	5.1	6.1	8.8
Japan	3.6	3.9	4.8	4.9
Sweden	5.0	6.8	11.4	11.4
United Kingdom	2.0	4.7	12.0	12.3

SOURCE: *U.S. Statistical Abstract*, 1991; as cited in Ahlburg and DeVita, 1992: 15.

that while women (who, 90 percent of the time, are the custodians of the children, after divorce) suffer significant declines in their incomes following divorce, men actually improve their economic positions. This is because men usually leave a marriage with much greater earning power than women and because men typically do not shoulder a fair share of child support when the mother retains custody of the children (Furstenberg, 1990:385). Data from the U.S. Bureau of the Census (1989) shows that fewer than 25 percent of mothers with custody of their children were receiving full and regular child support from their former husbands.

Lenore Weitzman's (1985) seminal research on the effects of no-fault divorce, which first appeared in California in the early 1970s, showed that it carries unexpected negative social and economic consequences for children and women. Initial proponents of no-fault divorce saw the new legislation as progressive because it allowed "irreconcilable differences" as cause for divorce and did not require that one party be judged guilty of some fault such as cruelty or adultery. Unfortunately, this gender-neutral approach to divorce had some unintended consequences. As Weitzman (1985:xi) says,

gender-neutral rules—rules designed to treat men and women "equally"—have in practice served to deprive divorced women (especially older homemakers and mothers of young children) of the legal and financial protections that the old law provided. Instead of recognition for their contributions as homemakers and mothers, and instead of compensation for the years of lost opportunities and impaired earning capacities, these women now face a divorce law that treats them "equally" and expects them to be equally capable of supporting themselves after divorce.

Weitzman's research demonstrated that the no-fault rules for dividing marital property generally benefited the husband much more than the wife because *future* earnings are, for the most part, not included. The most valuable assets that most couples accumulate in their marriages involved the major earner's education, license, salary, pension, goodwill (if self-employed) and future earning power. The exclusion of some or all of these items from divorce settlements explains why divorced women and their children have become the new poor in the United States.

Terry Arendell's (1986) in-depth study of 60 middle-class divorced mothers in the San Francisco Bay area lends support to Weitzman's conclusions. Arendell found that the most difficult part of divorce for these middle-class women was having to cope with decreases in economic status and financial insecurities. Her research also showed that *none* of the husbands of these women experienced the same decline in economic status that they did. By and large, the husbands did not adequately support their children. Only 38 percent of these divorced mothers received child support on a regular basis; 40 percent received no financial assistance at all from the fathers of their children. Arendell (1986:157) concludes that divorce in the United States is a socially structured phenomenon that "reflects the gender-based organization of our society, with all its related inequities."

Toward A Solution

Focus on France

A Social Contract That Targets Children

In the early 1930s, Americans elected Franklin D. Roosevelt as President. Roosevelt's "New Deal" policies promised economic security for people who were blind and had other disabilities, and for families with dependent children. At the time, these programs were hailed as a new social contract that could exist between a government and its people in a free-market economy.

However, 60 years later, 17 percent of this nation's white children are living in poverty, and an almost unbelievable 46 percent of African American children live in this unacceptable condition (Bennett, 1995). Despite these appalling statistics, the U.S. Congress seems intent on severely limiting federal entitlements to the nation's children, including school lunch programs for the poor. The United States stands virtually alone among industrial nations in having no family leave for new mothers and no government-subsidized day care for the children of working parents.

In France—and in fact, in most western European societies—such conditions are no longer tolerated. The French citizen can take comfort in cradle-to-grave care that is the inalienable right of all people within that society. Actually, coverage starts some time before the cradle—pregnant women are entitled to prenatal care paid for by the government. In the third month of pregnancy, a woman begins to accrue monthly benefits that will eventually total hundreds of dollars (in French currency, of course) per month.

When the baby is born, the French mother will be paid her full salary for 16 weeks while she stays home to care for her new infant. If she decides not to return to work, she is eligible for the equivalent of nearly $600 a month in "parental education benefits" (Smolowe, 1992:58). If she returns to work, then the government will subsidize day care for her baby. In addition, the family gets more than $1,000 of annual tax deductions.

These entitlements don't come free, as if by magic. French parents pay an income tax of about 44 percent to fund family benefits, including social security (Smolowe, 1992:58–59). In France, children are considered a public responsibility, a concept very different from America's high value on rugged individualism. In the United States, raising children is a private issue, one not to be meddled with by politics or government policy. But American children suffer because of the ideology. They are more likely than their French counterparts to die before their first birthday, less likely (by almost 50 percent) to have all of their immunizations, and less likely to be covered by medical insurance (Smolowe, 1992:59).

French policies regarding the family can be traced back to the horror of World War II. France was conquered by Germany and lost many of its young men to the casualties of battle. After the war, population declined because of the small cohort of men to father the next generation. The government created a package of special benefits to encourage young adults to marry and procreate. Gradually, French society came to see its children as "conservators of their family and traditions" (Smolowe, 1992:59). The children of a family are seen as the future of the collective whole, part of a solidarity between generations.

In the United States, with a more heterogeneous population than France has, it may be more difficult to conceive of any family's children as the collective future of the nation. Also, the United States has one of the fastest growing populations among industrial nations, partly as a result of high immigration (see Chapter 5). France, on the other hand, is not replacing its population, has a small immigration factor, and can expect a decline in its population early in the next century. Under such conditions, it is easy to understand why a country like France would cherish each of its children.

Sources: C. E. Bennett. 1995. The Black Population in the United States: March 1994 and 1993. Washington, D.C.: U.S. Bureau of the Census; J. Smolowe. 1992. "Where Children Come First," *Time*. Nov. 9: 58–59.

The Increase in Out-of-Wedlock Births

One of the most important changes in the family is the increase in births occurring out of wedlock. Peter Laslett (1992) asserts that nearly one-third of British babies are now born outside of wedlock and that the same pattern exists in other European countries. This increase is most prevalent in minority groups but has also occurred in the white populations of MDCs. Furthermore, this trend has occurred in all socioeconomic groups. The increased participation of women in the work force that has resulted in more divorce has also given many women the option of having children without the father present. Data on this trend in the United States from 1960 to 1989 is shown in Figure 2.4. In less than three decades, the number of births to unmarried women rose almost 500 percent, from 224,000 in 1960 to one million in 1989. It is interesting to note that this trend is largely driven by women who are 20 years old and older. In 1970, about half of all births to single mothers were to women over 20 years old. By 1989, the percentage of births to unmarried women in this age group had increased to more than two-thirds.

Though the United States has seen a dramatic increase in the percentage of births to unmarried women, other MDCs have witnessed even larger increases. Table 2.4 shows that the percentage of births to unmarried women went from 11.3% of births in Sweden in 1960 to more than of 50% of births in 1989. For France, the proportion went from 6.1% in 1960 to 28.2% in 1989. Only Japan did not witness a dramatic increase in such births. The proportion of births to unmarried women in Japan has remained low and constant at about 1%.

Out-of-Wedlock Births to Teens

Out-of-wedlock births to teens has been increasing in all MDCs, markedly in some. Many

Figure 2.4
The number of births to unmarried women in the United States increased fivefold from 1960 to 1989, and the vast majority of these births were to women 20 years old and older.

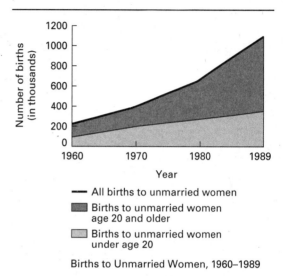

Births to Unmarried Women, 1960–1989

Source: National Center for Health Statistics, *Advance Report of Final Natality Statistics, 1989;* as cited in Ahlburg and DeVita, 1992: 22.

observers see this trend as very problematic. Teenage women who have children out of wedlock are often uneducated, poor minorities and their children are thus likely to be poor and disadvantaged. Teenage pregnancy among white middle-class teens is also on the increase, although abortion is more often an option for this group. The higher rate of teenage pregnancy in the lower classes can be explained partly by limited opportunities and lack of power, which result in low self-esteem.

Though increased premarital sex is correlated with increases in out-of-wedlock births to teens, there are great differences in this trend among MDCs. For example, the rate of teen out-of-wedlock births in the United States is five times that of most MDCs. Table 2.5 shows that while the birthrate to teens aged 15 to 19 years was 58.1 per 1,000 for the United States in 1989, it

Percentage of Births to Unmarried Women in Selected Countries, 1960–1989				TABLE 2.4
Percentage of all births				
Country	1960	1970	1980	1989
United States	5.3	10.7	18.4	27.1
Canada	4.3	9.6	12.8	23.0
France	6.1	6.8	11.4	28.2
Germany (Western)	6.3	5.5	7.6	10.2
Japan	1.2	0.9	0.8	1.0
Sweden	11.3	18.4	39.7	51.8
United Kingdom	5.2	8.0	11.5	26.6

SOURCE: *U.S. Statistical Abstract,* 1991, and country vital statistics reports; as cited in Ahlburg and DeVita, 1992:23.

Birthrates to Girls Aged 15–19 in Selected Countries, 1970–1989 (Per 1,000)				TABLE 2.5
Country	1970	1980	1985	1989
United States	68.3	53.0	51.3	58.1
Denmark	32.4	16.8	9.1	9.2
France	27.0	17.8	11.6	9.2
Germany (Western)	35.8	15.2	8.6	11.1
Japan	5.0	7.6	9.0	9.8
Netherlands	17.0	6.8	5.0	5.9
United Kingdom	49.1	30.5	29.6	31.7

SOURCE: Eurostat, *Demographic Statistics, 1991;* Japan Ministry of Health and Welfare; and U.S. National Center for Health Statistics, *Final Natality Statistics, 1989;* as cited in Ahlburg and DeVita, 1992:20.

was less than 10 for Denmark, France, Japan, and the Netherlands. Furthermore, this table demonstrates than while many European countries experienced major declines in the teenage birthrates from 1970 to mid and late 1980s, the United States did not. In Europe, teens are provided more comprehensive sex education, and birth control and abortion are much more available than in the United States.

Deadbeat Dads?

As divorce rates and out-of-wedlock births have risen in MDCs, the responsibility of fathers for the children they have produced has become the focus of much discussion. How can fathers ignore their children, financially and/or emotionally, after a divorce? Frank Furstenberg and Andrew Cherlin's research (1991) suggests that fathers view marriage and childcare as an inseparable role-set and that as a result, fathers often cut the ties with their children after divorce. Furstenberg and Cherlin also found that remarriage by either the mother or father tends to speed up this disengagement process between children and their noncustodial fathers.

Hard-pressed taxpayers are tiring of footing the welfare bills for fatherless homes and have demanded that fathers be responsible for their children. In 1988 the U.S. Congress passed the Family Support Act, which requires states to standardize child-support levels computed on a fixed percentage of a father's wages. Procedures to collect support monies are also becoming quite routine by the garnishing of wages, just like income taxes are deducted from paychecks. While the Family Support Act of 1988 represents some progress in this area, much more needs to be done to ensure that fathers contribute financially, socially, and psychologically to their children's development and livelihood.

The Losers: The Children

Though perspectives on the trends mentioned in this section vary, one conclusion is inescapable—children have been the losers. Men and women in all MDCs have more options and more freedom to end unsatisfactory relationships, and as a result are more likely to get divorced and remarried. Blended families and stepfamilies are therefore more common. This hasn't been easy for the

Teenage pregnancy is a growing problem in all MDCs. Teenage mothers and their children are at a severe disadvantage when it comes to education, employment, and income.

children. Although being a child in an unhappy or volatile marriage may not be easy, moving from a situation with both natural parents to a situation with stepparents and stepsiblings has also been shown to be stressful for children. It is interesting to note that research has shown (Popenoe, 1993) that children from broken families are the strongest advocates of strong families comprised of mother, father, and their natural children. They are determined to achieve strong and permanent marital relationships.

Most longitudinal studies that have followed children as they grew up have shown that being raised in single-parent households (due to the mother's choice, divorce, or desertion) is related to behavioral problems in children. M. E. J. Wadsworth (1979) followed a cohort of 5,000 children born in 1946 in the United Kingdom for 30 years and found that children raised in intact families were less likely to become delinquent than children raised in families experiencing divorce or desertion. Sheppard Kellam and his associates (1982; 1977) followed a cohort of several hundred poor African American first-grade boys in Chicago. They found that, after ten years, independent of the level of family income, boys raised in mother-only families were more likely to be delinquent than boys raised in families with multiple adults, and that the lowest delinquency rates were reported for boys who were raised by both their mothers and fathers.

Another important study by the U.S. Department of Health and Human Services (Dawson, 1991) in 1988 looked at the family situations of 60,000 children in the United States. After controlling for sex of the child, income, and race, it was found that, children living in two-parent families were substantially better off than children living with a never-married or divorced mother. Children living with both natural parents were only half as likely as children in single-parent families to have been expelled or suspended from school, or to have shown emotional or behavioral problems. These differences persisted when controlling for family income.

It should also be pointed out that a 60-year longitudinal study (Clausen, 1993) that followed the lives of 300 people found no indications that divorce, by itself, created problem children. The study did find, however, that parental conflict (with or without separation) did lead to various problems for children.

These trends have resulted in ever increasing poverty rates for children in MDCs. Though poverty rates for the elderly have declined in recent decades in most MDCs, the same cannot be said of poverty rates for children. David J. Eggebeen and Daniel T. Lichter's research (1991), which used data from 1960 to 1988, demonstrates that the increased poverty of American children can be linked to changes in family structure, specifically the increase in female-headed, single-parent families. The authors found that if family structure had remained the same since 1960, child poverty rates would have been one-third less in 1988 and that the changing structure of the American family accounted for almost one-half of the increase in child poverty rates since 1980. Also, their research suggests that since 1960, the growing difference between the proportion of African American families headed by single women compared to white families, has made the persistent difference between the poverty of black and white children even more severe.

FAMILY VIOLENCE: BEHIND CLOSED DOORS

Much attention has been focused recently on family violence, including spousal abuse, maltreatment of children, and abuse of elders. Many people are under the impression that there has been a massive increase in family violence. It is more likely we are just more aware of family violence because of an increase in the *reporting* of family violence and coverage of this topic in the media. There is no evidence that family violence has increased dramatically since previous generations. In all likelihood, the increase in the visibility of family violence is due to the change in what developed countries perceive as permissible family behavior. What used to be considered the private business of the family, especially of the husband, is now open to public scrutiny. Linda Gordon's (1988) research on the history of family violence in the United States demonstrates that family violence has definitely been a severe social problem, historically. Even though family violence may not be increasing, it is still very prevalent in most societies.

Spousal Abuse

Although women have been known to abuse their husbands emotionally and physically, it is husband-to-wife abuse that is most common and problematic. The primary reason is that men are usually stronger physically than their wives. Also, historically, men have had complete legal control over their wives and children, which were viewed as property. Roman law, for example, gave the husband permission to kill his wife for drinking wine, committing adultery, or other "inappropriate" behavior (Steinmetz, Clavan, and Stein, 1990:460). In discussing the situation in the United States, Murray Straus (1990:26) asserts that efforts to reduce wife abuse by battered women's shelters and treatment programs are starting to yield results and that the incidence of spousal abuse has decreased somewhat in the last decade. However, spousal abuse is still a serious problem and the *National Crime Surveys* indicate that at least 2.1 million American women experience domestic violence at least once a year (Davidson and Moore, 1992:232).

Why do some husbands beat their wives? Research suggests numerous reasons. The first theory is the **cycle of abuse**, which means that abusive behavior is learned and passed from one generation of husbands to the next. In the same manner, the acceptance of abuse is passed from one generation of wives to the next. Human beings learn how to behave; our behavior patterns are not innate. If one's father routinely beat one's mother, this behavior is often viewed as normal by the child. Second, alcohol abuse has been shown to be related to spousal abuse. One research investigation (Roscoe and Benaske, 1985) implicated alcohol in 56 percent of cases of physical abuse of wives. Also, abusive husbands are more likely to suffer from low self-esteem (Goldstein and Rosenbaum, 1985) and are more likely to have low levels of education (Szinovacz, 1983). Financial stress and job problems have been shown to be causal factors in wife abuse, as is **social isolation** of the family, that is, the family is not integrated socially into the community. Finally, the less the wife depends financially on her husband, the less likely she is to be abused (Aguirre, 1985).

Maltreatment of Children

In the United States, more than two million cases of suspected child abuse are reported to the authorities each year (Jamieson and Flanagan, 1989:324). As previously discussed, the large number of reported cases reflects not just the incidence of child maltreatment but the recent recognition of child abuse as a social problem. Indeed, children in the more developed countries today are accorded much more respect and have many more rights than in the past. Also, there is some evidence that actual child maltreatment may be decreasing. Richard Gelles and Murray Straus (1987) conducted national family violence surveys both in 1975 and 1985 and noted a significant decrease in child maltreatment in this ten-year period. This is a good example of an area in which the sociologist's use of survey methods may be detecting patterns quite different from those being detected by a governmental agency. It should be stated, however, that even though child maltreatment rates may be declining, as long as one child suffers from abuse, we must attempt to understand it and eliminate it.

What kinds of child maltreatment exist and why do parents mistreat their children? First of all, child maltreatment is generally broken down into three types: physical abuse, sexual abuse, and neglect. The cycle of abuse that was discussed relative to spousal abuse is operative here as well. Parents learn how to raise their offspring and mostly from their own parents (Jamieson and Flanagan, 1988:324). For example, parents who were physically abused as children tend to use the same aggressive techniques on their own children. People who were sexually abused as children are more likely to sexually abuse their own children than are parents who were not sexually molested. Finally, child neglect also appears to be transmitted from one generation to the next. In addition to abusive behaviors being handed down, the following factors have been be associated with child maltreatment: social isolation, lower income, mental health problems, and the father being unemployed (Rosenthal, 1988:263).

Although physical abuse and neglect have been found to be associated with lower socioeconomic status, child sexual abuse appears to be an "equal opportunity" type of maltreatment—it is a problem in *all* socioeconomic groups. Diane Russell's classic survey (1986) of adult women in San Francisco found that an astounding 16 percent had been victims of incest and that all income levels were represented.

Abuse of Elders

The most recently studied form of family violence is elder abuse, the mistreatment of seniors by their own children, spouses, or personnel in institutions such as nursing homes. In a survey conducted in Boston by Karl Pillemer and David Finkelhor (1988:53), it was found that the rate of prevalence per 1,000 people over 65 years of age was 32. This included physical violence, chronic verbal aggression, and neglect. The authors did not find any differences in elder abuse by race, religion, educational level, or income level. Also, more than three-fourths of the perpetrators of elder abuse are not the children, but spouses of the elderly (Pillemer and Finkelhor, 1988:53). Though it is difficult to document, stealing is another way that elders are abused. Dipping into a parent's bank accounts or taking control of the Social Security check is abusive and needs to be studied as a form of elder abuse.

FAMILY VALUES: PAST AND PRESENT

The fact that more mothers are raising children without husbands, has generated a tremendous amount of public debate. In 1992 then Vice President Dan Quayle commented on the out-of-wedlock birth of a child to the popular television character Murphy Brown, a well-to-do single television commentator. Quayle indicated that this trend illustrated a decline in "family values" and that society should not condone such behavior. Others responded to Quayle by stating that women who could afford to raise children by themselves had every right to do so.

Dan Quayle's criticism of "Murphy Brown" and unwed mothers touched off a "family values" debate in 1992 that is still raging. Changes in family composition, processes, and functions have resulted in many diatribes against the diverse family structures of the 1990s. Various commentators have blamed the breakdown of the traditional family for society's ills and have suggested that a return to the "nuclear" family, with Dad at work and Mom at home with the kids, would solve many, if not most of our problems.

The Way We Never Were

A historical study (Coontz, 1992) suggests that the "Leave It to Beaver" model of the 1950s American family was more fiction than fact and that the American family of that time was very heterogeneous. Though the American family is beset with problems today, it was not without its problems in the past. Stephanie Coontz (1992:4) provides data showing that the poverty rate of American children today is no greater than it was

at the turn of the century. She also asserts that although many fathers are not adequately held accountable for their children today, in the 1920s a divorced father was under absolutely no legal duty to support his children. Further evidence (Coontz, 1992:5) suggests that even a smaller percentage of high school students graduated in the 1940s than do today and that the per capita consumption of alcohol in the 1820s was three times higher than it is today. In short, the historical record suggests that no one family form has successfully protected its members from poverty or social disruption, and it is highly unlikely that any single form of family will be able to address the many vagaries of the modern world. Rather than being the culprit responsible for much of society's contemporary problems, the contemporary American family has been adversely affected by societal changes, from the way we produce and reproduce to the way we distribute power and economic rewards.

Myths About the American Family

There are additional myths about the American family that need to be analyzed. The work of Maxine Baca Zinn and D. Stanley Eitzen (1990:9–20) offers support for Coontz's ideas. They discuss five myths about the American family that have been perpetuated over the years. The first myth is that, in the past, the American family has been stable and harmonious and much better than the family of today. Like Coontz, they argue that this assertion is not based on fact and that families of old were beset with problems as well. The divorce rate was not so high as it is today, but many marriages were ended, nevertheless, by legally unrecognized desertion.

The second is the "myth of separate worlds," which is the belief that work and family roles operate in different spheres and that the family is a haven from a competitive and cruel world. This myth assumes that the family unit is somehow independent from the rest of society and is not

The 1950s television show "Leave It to Beaver" depicted a family with a father who worked and a mother who stayed at home with the children, nurturing and caring for the family. Research shows that only a minute proportion of families fit this model.

affected by outside societal forces and events. Yet historical and contemporary analyses suggest that the family has been, and continues to be, very much linked and affected by other societal institutions, such as schools, work organizations, and welfare systems.

The third is the "myth of the monolithic family form," which is a nuclear family comprised of a father who is the breadwinner and mother who is at home taking care of the children, all living in a single-family dwelling. As Stephanie Coontz did, Zinn and Eitzen show that this "Leave it to Beaver" model was more fact than fiction and that the American family has always been a varied and heterogeneous institution.

The fourth is the "myth of undifferentiated family experience," the notion that all family members have similar needs, interests, and experiences. However, members of American families have experienced, and continue to experience, family life quite differently, depending on gender and age. For example, a husband who comes home from work may find his house as a haven

from the outside world, a place to relax and forget about the troubles at work. His wife, however, is more likely to come home from her job and find many household chores need to be done.

The final myth discussed by Zinn and Eitzen is the "myth of family consensus," the idea that the family operates on the principles of harmony and love. This myth fails to address the many contradictions associated with the family, contradictions based on differential power relationships within families and the intense emotional component of family life. Families can be nurturing but they can also be emotionally destructive. They can be loving but they can also be characterized by violence and brutality. No other institution in our society is characterized by as many extremes as the family.

Are U.S. Family Values Congruent with U.S. Family Behavior?

Since Americans have expended so much energy in discussing "family values," it might be interesting to see how closely aligned American family values are with American family behavior. Norval Glenn (1992) found that Americans' high regard for traditional family values was not reflected in actual family life. Although Americans say that family is their number one priority, surveys demonstrate that the majority of Americans place their careers, financial pursuits, and personal freedom above their family responsibilities. This lack of congruity between values and behavior is due, according to Glenn, to a change in peoples' perceptions of the family: an increased doubt about the permanence of marriage; a growing negative picture of parenting; and an increased value placed on personal achievement and materialism.

Again, what sociologists say about the trends in family structure in the more developed countries depends on their perspectives. Conflict theorists would explain many of these changes by focusing on the increased power that women have assumed in the developed world. For example, the increase in the divorce rate would be seen as a function of the increased ability of women to take care of themselves brought about by increases in their levels of education and occupational mobility. Conflict theorists would also explain the severe problems that divorced women face in the developed world as a function of the inequality that remains between the sexes. Functionalists tend to view the changes in family structure in the developed world as a response to the rapid changes that have taken place in technology and the work and home environments. Cultural lag would explain why some of the trends in family structure are problematic and the dysfunctions of these trends are also analyzed. For example, the negative effects on children and society in general of the increase in out-of-wedlock births is given much attention by functionalists. Finally, interactionists tend to focus on how gender and family roles have changed over time in the developed world, and how changing socialization patterns

will continue to alter family roles in the future. For example, the changing role expectations for a father in the developed world (to be more nurturing with the children and more emotionally available to his wife) and the way these new role expectations will be passed on to the children is of much interest to interactionists.

RESOLVING FAMILY PROBLEMS AND FAMILY POLICY

How can we best solve these family problems? First of all, we must distinguish between the less developed and more developed countries. It appears that the most serious problems of the family in the LDCs stem from the inferior position that females occupy in these societies. High birthrates and accompanying poverty result in a vicious cycle that perpetuates gender inequality. Research has shown that LDCs can progress without immense degrees of economic development and industrialization. However, one of the necessary conditions for advancement is increased educational and occupational opportunities for women. As long as women are viewed as inferior and not afforded equal status, high birth rates and pressing poverty will continue to plague these societies.

The problems of the family in the MDCs are complex. Some wish to turn back the clock and return to the family form of a working dad, a mom who is a full-time homemaker, and two kids. Such a reversal is unlikely. The MDCs are likely to continue to experience diversity in family structure and the roles of men and women will, in all likelihood, continue to change. Rather than blaming the diverse family of today for societal ills, we should be searching for ways to strengthen the family.

The first thing that governments of MDCs and businesses could do to assist families is to make society more "family friendly." Work schedules that are flexible for parents, maternity and paternity leaves that allow parents to bond with their infants, and first-rate child day-care programs are some of the things that should be seriously addressed. Many people assume that the reason women generally make less money than men is because they tend to have occupations that accommodate parenting needs. However, research shows that mothers working more than 30 hours per week are not more likely than mothers working fewer than 30 hours per week to be in jobs that are "parent friendly" (jobs with flexible schedules and easy tasks), nor are jobs dominated by females likely to have characteristics that reduce job–family conflict. In short, even occupations traditionally defined as feminine in the United States are not "family friendly" (Glass and Camarigg, 1992).

Child day care is extremely important in societies where more women are entering the work force. Some MDCs, such as Sweden, have developed effective and efficient day-care programs. Other MDCs, like the United States, are in the infant stage of day-care development. Some U.S. companies are just now starting to realize that day-care programs on site can be cost effective and increase morale and productivity.

Programs designed to make fathers and mothers more accountable are also needed. We should start by sensitizing children to the responsibilities of parenthood. Learning the sacredness, importance, and seriousness of producing a new human being is the first step in developing a sense of responsibility. For those men who continue to be irresponsible about the financial and emotional support of their children, society should come down with all the force necessary to ensure compliance. Societal pressure can take numerous forms, from subtle and not-so-subtle messages in the media to garnishing of paychecks.

Given the complexity of the rapidly changing world in which we live, the family will need the help of a host of institutions —employers, public schools, and governments—in order to survive and prosper.

SUMMARY

The institution of the family goes back as far as our species does—and so do the problems associated with this institution and the changing roles of family members. The major functions of the family are reproduction, socialization of children, transferral of inheritance, and regulation of sexual behavior. The major family forms are polygamy and monogamy.

The most recent evidence from the less developed countries suggests that current family structures and the relationships between men and women result in increasing exploitation of women. The central problem is that in LDCs, there is a social and cultural attitude that women are inferior—and discrimination starts at birth. Infanticide is a serious problem in less developed countries and is more likely to involve girl babies than boy babies. Women from LDCs are more likely to be overworked than their male counterparts, and to experience discrimination in the work force.

Family structure and the roles of family members have been changing dramatically in the more developed countries of the world. In all MDCs, the traditional family comprised of father, mother, and the children, is becoming less prevalent. One-parent families, blended families, and nontraditional families (such as homosexual couples) are becoming more prevalent.

A number of factors such as the separation of reproduction and sex, the women's liberation movement, and the need for dual incomes, have revolutionized families in the MDCs. Families with both parents working are characterized by positive factors such as egalitarian relationships between spouses and the personal satisfaction that comes when both spouses have meaningful careers. The downside is the great amount of stress that modern families experience in trying to "do it all." Though men are starting to contribute more to domestic life, equality in this sphere has not yet been reached. Women tend to put in much longer hours than men: they do the 9-to-5 routine and then come home and do the housework and tend to the children.

MDCs are also experiencing increases in the age of marriage, decreases in the marriage rate, and increases in divorce. The increase in divorce is viewed as problematic by some and healthy by others. Though divorce may liberate both the husband and wife from an unhappy marriage, research shows that the negative economic effects of divorce are much worse for women than men. The children, because they usually stay with the mother, also suffer financial setbacks as a result of divorce.

An alarming trend in MCDs is the increase in out-of-wedlock births, especially to teenagers. Children born out of wedlock are at a very real disadvantage emotionally and financially. Fathers of these children tend not to take emotional and financial responsibility for their children. The cost to society is immense and greater efforts must be made to engage these fathers in the lives of their children.

Family violence is a problem that has recently received much attention. Spousal abuse, child maltreatment, and elder abuse have been with us as long as we have had families; they were just "behind closed doors." Family violence was not considered a "social problem" because it was considered a private matter. In all likelihood, most of the recent "increase" in reported family violence is due to the recent legislation mandating the reporting of family violence, and a heightened sensitivity toward the subject. That does not mean that family violence is not a serious social problem. We must continue to be vigilant and deal with the factors leading to family violence.

There is evidence to show that the problems modern families are encountering are neither new nor necessarily more serious than the problems faced by families of yesteryear. The changes in family structures and roles is not so much the cause of current societal problems, but rather a reflection of major changes in the structure of modern societies.

The resolution of family problems calls for specific changes. In less developed countries, there is a desperate need for equality between the sexes. Increased educational and occupational opportunities for women would go a long way in the betterment of their lives. In the more developed countries, governments and businesses must do more to make society more "family friendly." Work schedules that are more flexible for parents, maternity and paternity leaves that allow parents to bond with their infants, and first-rate child-care programs are just some of the things that should be seriously addressed. Finally, programs designed to make parents more accountable for their children are also needed.

KEY TERMS

Blended families Families formed when divorced individuals remarry and one or more children from previous marriages are involved.

Cultural universals The family functions that are found frequently around the world: reproduction, socialization of children, transferral of inheritance, and regulation of sexual behavior.

Cycle of abuse Abusive behavior that is experienced and learned and passed from one generation to the next.

Family An intimate kin-based group consisting of at least a parent-nucleus, the minimal social unit that cooperates economically and assumes responsibility for the rearing of children.

Infanticide The murder of infants.

Monogamy A marriage of one husband and one wife.

Nuclear family A family consisting of two parents and their natural or adopted children.

Polyandry The status of one woman being married to several men.

Polygamy The status of one women being married to several men or one man being married to several women.

Polygyny The status of one man being married to several women.

Serial Monogamy Situations in which, at any one time, one man is married to one woman but, at different periods of their lifetimes, husbands and wives are married to two or more spouses.

Social isolation The situation in which the family is not integrated socially into the community.

Strict monogamy The "till death does us part" version of monogamy in which a spouse will only remarry in the event of the other spouse's death.

STUDY QUESTIONS

1. What are the four family functions found in nearly all societies?

2. What are the reasons for the devaluation of girls in less developed countries?

3. What are the trends in family composition in the more developed countries?

4. What social and economic forces are responsible for the increase in the divorce rate in the more developed countries?

5. Discuss the changing roles of family members in the more developed countries.

6. What problems are blended marriages more likely to experience than first marriages or marriages involving widows? Why?

7. Discuss the trends in the age of marriage, the marriage rate, and the divorce rate in the more developed countries.

8. Discuss the relationship between teenage sexuality and teenage pregnancy. Why is there a stronger correlation between these two factors in some countries (like the United States) than in others (like Sweden)?

9. What factors are related to family violence?

10. Discuss the five myths regarding the American family that have been perpetuated over the years.

HUMAN SEXUALITY:
POWER AND
POLITICS

As the world approached the midpoint of the twentieth century, the late anthropologist Margaret Mead wrote her observations of human sexuality in her book, Male and Female. Instead of beginning the book with a statement, she asked this fundamental question: "How are men and women to think about their maleness and their femaleness in this twentieth century, in which so many of our old ideas must be made new?" (Mead, 1949: 36). That question is perhaps even more important now as we approach a new century than it was 50 years ago.

SEX AS A SOURCE OF NORMATIVE PROBLEMS

In every society, there exist **norms,** socially accepted rules that govern which behaviors are to be approved and which are to be forbidden. Many of the social problems associated with sex are really normative problems, which violate the norms of a particular society. Even in very tolerant societies, certain sexual practices are nearly always forbidden: sex between adult and child, for example, and incest (sex between close relatives). But even these are not universal; for example, Alorese mothers in Indonesia believe that masturbating their children calms them and brings them a feeling of well-being. In Africa, the highest chiefs among the Azande people are expected to marry their daughters (Robertson, 1989).

Some societies have gone much further in attempting to regulate sex than the two prohibitions just mentioned. Often, the ideal norms permit sex only between married adults. Adultery, especially on the part of women, is severely condemned. Premarital sex is also forbidden, but neither universally nor so severely. Several decades ago, Ford and Beach (1951) studied nearly 200 societies and found that only ten of them shared prohibitions against both extramarital and premarital sex.

How one thinks of his maleness or her femaleness is a function of internalizing societal norms. Each generation tries to pass its social norms to the next, but this doesn't always happen successfully or completely. In times of rapid social change, society may experience a condition that French sociologist Émile Durkheim (1951) called **anomie.** Anomie refers to a sense of instability, a time in society when the norms are rapidly changing or a time when people don't understand exactly what the norms are. If we accept the premise that the world is changing faster now than at any point in history (Lenski, Lenski, and Nolan, 1991), then it is easy to understand why

there may be confusion about gender identification (maleness and femaleness), sexual practices, and other approved or disapproved behavior.

Silence Regarding Sex

In some societies, the problem of gender identification may be exacerbated simply because adults neglect to discuss sex and sexual practices with their children. In the People's Republic of China, both the ancient teaching of Confucius and the more recent Communist ideology have tended to preclude talk about sex. Confucius emphasized modesty, but Mao Ze-dong ruled that Communist theory called for a concentration on service to society, not a preoccupation with personal pleasures such as sex. Consequently, sex education was virtually nonexistent. Often brides were told about sexual practices only on their wedding days, if at all. Interestingly, it was taken for granted that grooms were either sexually experienced or "somehow knew about sex." This implies that women have to learn about sex, while men instinctively or hormonally are prepared for the marital bed.

In reality, we suspect that the virgin groom is as confused and embarrassed as the virgin bride, especially when their marriage is arranged by their parents. In traditional China, it was not uncommon for bride and groom to meet for the first time at the wedding ceremony. Although arranged marriages may seem strange to students in the Western world, Ching-kun Yang (1959) says that these marriages were at least as happy as those in Europe or North America.

Similarly, in much of Latin America, norms forbid open discussion of sexuality; consequently sex education about healthy and safe sexual behavior has been neglected. Both social norms and religious beliefs call for virginity at marriage. But, there is a double standard of morality and a clear difference between ideal culture and real culture. While young women are held to the strict societal ideal, at least among families of higher socioeconomic status, young

In much of the Middle East, sexual restraints for women include wearing clothes that hide the body, face, and hair. The oppression of women is so complete that a wife's infidelity can be punished by death.

men are expected to be sexually experienced. In fact, this double standard extends to life after marriage. In the villages of many Latin American countries, a man may gain **machismo** (a strong sense of manliness) by fathering children by both his wife and his mistress (Schaefer, 1993). For poor people, sexual relations are likely to come at an early age, with little knowledge of contraceptives or of safer sexual practices to reduce risks of sexually transmitted diseases (STDs).

Restrictive Societies

In some countries, there are strong beliefs urging restraint in sexual matters. However, the restraints are usually imposed upon women by men. Where men's behavior is restrained, the restraints are nearly always self-imposed, and therefore, optional. Allowing or disallowing practices depends on the construction of reality and who does the constructing. The men of several New Guinea tribes stay away from women for a good part of the year for fear of weakening themselves. Among the Cheyenne people of the North American West, standards were quite puritanical. Premarital and extramar-

ital sex were forbidden and seldom took place. Sexual energy was considered to be limited and had to be used sparingly. Restraint from sexual activity was greatly admired. If a man avoided sexual relations for a number of years after his son was born, it was believed to bestow good character and power to the son (Hoebel, 1960). Notice in both examples how the construction of reality totally disregards the welfare or the wishes of the wife and the character and other qualities of the daughter.

Other examples of the oppressive control of females and their sexuality can be found in the Middle East where women who are not virgins at the time of marriage may be killed by their own families, and prostitutes may be stoned (Kusha, 1992). Some Iranian cities were becoming Westernized until the Islamic Revolution of 1979. Today, in many parts of Iran, women hardly dare be seen in public without their *chaddors* (the long garments that cover all but their faces).

Some of the most conservative sections of the Middle East are Saudi Arabia and Oman, where there are arranged marriages, heavily veiled women, killing of prostitutes, and a claim of absolute Koranic law. Nevertheless, the sexual restraints imposed on the women and common people apparently do not apply to wealthy Arab men, some of whom go on "sex vacations" to Thailand. Many of them bring sexually transmitted diseases, including AIDS (Acquired Immune Deficiency Syndrome), back to their own countries, where any discussion of sex or AIDS is strictly forbidden. The power and politics of sex is clearly part of an exclusively male agenda.

Highly Permissive Societies

By contrast, many of the peoples of the South Pacific not only freely discuss sex, but encourage young people to participate in sexual behavior. Before the arrival of Christian missionaries, Tahitians instructed children of both sexes in masturbation and premarital intercourse (Davenport, 1962). In Samoa it was not unusual for a man to prefer to marry a young woman who has already had a baby. Once again, we have to be careful to observe the construction of reality. The man has the power to make the decision. The young woman, who is less powerful, may be seen by the man as an easily controllable child. So, the major question that arises is, permissive to whom?

Margaret Mead (1966) described the Samoans as imposing virtually no restraints on sexuality. She found them to be a happy people with a carefree nature. But, their happiness might be attributed to living within a large, extended family that loved and cared for all babies regardless of the marital status of their parents, and not just their society's permissiveness regarding sex.

Additionally, not all would agree about the nature of happiness and sexual satisfaction. Kissing, for example, is simply unknown in many societies. In Bolivia, the Siriono people consider it a repulsive act. During sexual intercourse, they gain great pleasure in poking each other in the eyes. In the Brazilian jungle, women of the Apinaye tribe bite off portions of their mates' eyebrows during intercourse. And Choroti women

of a neighboring tribe are expected to spit in their partners' faces (Robertson, 1989).

As one can see, there is a myriad of thinking about what is right and what is wrong in terms of sexual practice. Many of the societies we have discussed are going through a transition because of increased contact with the rest of the world and exposure to different customs and cultures, such as Western movies and television. In a few cases, the changes have been drastic enough to be labeled a sexual revolution, but, in general, change occurs slowly, over time. The term *sexual revolution* usually refers to changes in the United States and similarly industrialized nations of the West at particular times. Let us turn our attention to the United States. Is it highly restrictive or permissive? How drastically has it changed?

THE SEXUAL REVOLUTION

The term *sexual revolution* refers to the liberalizing changes in sexual practices and social tolerance over the last few decades, but the term *revolution* may be too extreme. Many observers have an exaggerated view of a sexual revolution that assumes that people in the nineteenth century and before lived up to idealized norms; for example, that no one had sexual relations outside of marriage. But, in 1871, French traditionalist Frédéric Le Play wrote a social history of Europe in which he chastised Europeans of his time for their rampant adultery and for "substituting . . . sexual gratification for self-sacrifice . . ." (Gies and Gies, 1987:5). Le Play's major point was that when people act in self-interest rather than in the interest of the traditional extended family, they contribute to social disorganization.

In this respect, Le Play agreed with the "Father of Sociology," Auguste Comte. Writing during the nineteenth century, Comte insisted that "the family, not the individual, should be thought of as

Nineteenth-century clothing for American women kept body, arms, and legs well hidden, emphasizing chastity, which was expected of women, but not of men.

the social unit for study in the developing science of society" (Stewart and Glynn, 1984:351). Translated into a sexual context, the writing of both authors indicates that for the good of the extended family, sexual relations should be a part of marriage and take place only within the context of a large traditional family.

Undoubtedly, many people met the expectation, especially women, but some men and women did not. Studies of U.S. birth records indicate that, in Colonial times (1607–1775) and even in Puritan colonies, large numbers of brides were pregnant at the time of marriage. During the Revolutionary War (1775–1783), sexual activity appears to have been a usual part of courtship, again leading to large numbers of premarital pregnancies. The number of pregnant brides declined in the more settled period after that war. So, there appear to have been cycles of strict and less strict standards (Larkin, 1988).

Historian Page Smith (1989) thinks that one major difference between historic America and twentieth-century America has been in men's perception of women. Nineteenth-century women were not expected to enjoy sexual relations, and far more men than now went to prostitutes. This raised a serious problem to a society that had not yet discovered penicillin and other "wonder drugs." Venereal diseases spread from prostitutes to their patrons and often to the patrons' spouses. Elizabeth Blackwell (1821–1910), the first woman to receive a medical degree in the United States, campaigned against prostitution and warned of the damages of venereal diseases to wives and children; but efforts at reform foundered.

One factor that contributed to the high incidence of prostitution in the nineteenth and early twentieth centuries was the inequality between men and women. The belief was almost universal that men should have considerable sexual license,

Focus on the United States

More Accurate Surveys Can Be Done: The Case of Sexual Behavior in the United States

Individuals in Western developed countries are bombarded with news about the decline of social institutions, especially the family. One factor put forth as a cause of family problems is the sexual revolution that started in the 1960s and supposedly continues to this day. In the United States, popular magazines such as *Playboy* and *Redbook* have often published the results of membership surveys on sexual attitudes and behavior. Sometimes, as in the survey by *Playboy*, the respondents report very active sex lives, with sizeable proportions of respondents claiming multiple sex partners.

How accurate are these surveys? Unfortunately, they are notoriously inaccurate. One might think that, given the interest in the topic, there would be many scientifically designed studies on this subject. This is not the case. If one looks at sexual behavior in the United States, almost all of the studies are, from a scientific viewpoint, seriously flawed. Alfred Kinsey (1948, 1953) conducted studies on sexual behavior in the United States in the late 1940s and early 1950s. Although his studies became famous and were widely read and cited, they were fraught with serious design problems. Kinsey was a biologist and was not trained in the areas of survey design and implementation, sampling procedures, and statistical analysis. Kinsey himself did not think it possible to get a random sample to discuss the personal, sensitive subject of sexuality. He therefore used what social scientists call "convenience samples." These samples are not randomly drawn, that is, every individual in the population does not have an equal chance of being selected. Kinsey got his human subjects wherever he could find them—in boardinghouses, prisons, mental wards, and college fraternities. Though Kinsey's report on Americans' sexual habits was based on more than 11,000 subjects, the conclusions he reached (such as that more than half of Americans were having extramarital sex) were based on interviews with people who were self-selected.

The *Playboy* and *Redbook* sex surveys of magazine subscribers mentioned earlier are also based on nonscientific methods. Subscribers to these magazines are hardly representative of the American population. Shere Hite's *Hite Report* is yet another example of a sex survey that received significant press but was not based on a scientifically selected sample. All of these nonscientific surveys suffer from the same serious problem—their respondents are not representative of the entire population. Individuals who elect to fill out a questionnaire included in *Playboy* or *Redbook* are not typical of the general population for two reasons. First, people who read the above magazines probably fall into narrow ranges with regard to age, marital status, income, and other important variables. Second, the individuals who decide to take the time to fill out the questionnaire and send it back to the magazine probably differ in significant ways from the readers who don't. They may be more sexually active or they may have sexual problems that they want to "vent." In any event, the "results" of such "surveys" are unlikely to reflect accurately the sexual behavior of the total population.

A comprehensive survey of sexual behavior in the United States that was scientifically designed and implemented was recently completed. The results are published as *The Social Organization of Sexuality* by the University of Chicago Press (1994). The authors of the report are sociologists with extensive training and experience in survey design, sampling, and statistical analysis. Edward Laumann, Robert Michael, and Stuart Michaels are from the University of Chicago and John Gagnon is from the State University of New York at Stony Brook. The authors worked with the internationally acclaimed National Opinion Research Center (NORC) located at the University of Chicago to design the sampling strategy. They then used computers to select addresses in the United States at random. Next, they randomly chose which member of a household to interview. Two-hundred and twenty interviewers underwent rigorous training on how to discuss the delicate subject of sex. Respondents were interviewed in person and if they declined to be interviewed, they were revisited as many as 15 times. Of 4,369 initial subjects, and astounding 79 percent were eventually interviewed.

What did Laumann and his colleagues find out about sexual behavior in the United States? The most important finding is that Americans' sexual behavior is quite conservative and does not resemble the portrayal of sex in American popular culture. One-third of the sample had sexual relations twice a week or more, one-third a few times a month, and the remaining third a few times a year or not at all. The study also found that Americans are, for the most part, monogamous. Of married people, 94 percent were faithful to their spouses in the past year. No matter how sexually active individuals are before and between marriages, they appear to be faithful to their partners during marriage. Other findings were that married couples have the most sex and are more likely to have orgasms than the unmarried, and that vaginal sex is the most preferred kind of sex. Homosexuality was also found to be less prevalent than the often cited figure of 10 percent. One of the surprises in the study was that people who masturbate the most are the ones who have the most sex. This is the opposite of the "conventional wisdom" on this, which holds that people who masturbate the most do not have sex very often.

In summary, this scientifically conducted survey of sexual behavior in the United States, the first major survey on this subject to use sophisticated sampling, interviewing, and statistical analysis, found that U.S. citizens are fairly conservative and straightlaced when it comes to sex. They do not fit the image that comes through so loudly and clearly in the media and popular culture.

SOURCES: E. Lauman, R. Michael, S. Michaels, and J. Gagnon, *The Social Organization of Sexuality* (Chicago: University of Chicago Press, 1994).

A.C. Kinsey, W. Pomeroy, and C.E. Martin, *Sexual Behavior in the Human Male* (Philadelphia: W.B. Saunders, 1948); A.C. Kinsey, W. Pomeroy, C.E. Martin, and P. Gebhard, *Sexual Behavior in the Human Female* (Philadelphia: W.B. Saunders, 1953)

but that a women's virtue was a condition of her chastity. Only "bad" women were believed to enjoy sexual activity. This attitude held more strongly for the middle and upper classes than for the poor, but it was held to a considerable degree throughout society. During the twentieth century, marriage manuals gradually began to change the perception of women from passive creatures with little interest in sex to people who are entitled to some sexual pleasure. The number of prostitutes declined as a percentage of society as mutual sexual enjoyment by husband and wife became more acceptable. A significant change in sexual mores was coming about, characterized by less egregiously unequal standards for men and women, as well as by less restrictive sexual standards in general.

EARLY SEXUAL RELATIONS: POSSIBLE CONSEQUENCES

Teachers estimate that, by the tenth grade, about 25 percent of students are sexually active (United Press, 1989). A 1986 study of the sexual relations of 1,400 junior high school students in Florida , along with a follow-up study two years later (Billy, Lansdale, Grady, and Zimmerle, 1988), places the figure somewhat higher. It showed that, by ages 13 and 14, boys were more likely than girls to have had sexual relations. Forty-seven percent of white boys and 29 percent of white girls had sexual relations. For African Americans, the figures were dramatically higher. Ninety-one percent of black boys and 60 percent of black girls had sexual experiences.

An interesting aspect of this study is that a number of questions were investigated regarding psychological adjustment, attitudes toward sex, and attitudes about school and the future. Over the two years, no problems were found in regard to psychological adjustment, and attitudes toward sex became more positive. The bad news concerned school and the future. For males, experiencing sex during this time of maturation had a strong negative effect on grades. For females, there was an equally negative effect on their interest in going to college. The only explanation offered by the authors of the study is a direct and obvious one: sex became enough of a preoccupation to downgrade other interests.

The authors conclude that, because school grades and academic plans for the future definitely correlate with success in life, early sexual activity may bode ill for the future. The study would have to cover many more years of the students' lives to produce results that could be stated with a high degree of confidence. There is no question, however, that one possible consequence of early coitus is early pregnancy.

Unwanted Pregnancies

At first glance, it would seem that the problem of unwanted pregnancies could be solved quite easily. There are pills, condoms, and other devices to prevent pregnancy, but unwanted pregnancies persist. Why is unwanted pregnancy, especially among teenagers, so persistent? In 1993 there were 1,528,930 abortions performed in the United States, or a rate of nearly 24 per 1,000 females between the ages of 15 and 45 (*World Almanac*, 1995). About 25 percent, or more than 380,000, were performed on young women between 15 and 19 years of age, a figure higher than in any other country (Wright, 1993). It should also be noted that a large majority of pregnancies among teenage females (as well as sexually transmitted diseases, including AIDS) is caused by *adult* males. The most recent National Center for Health Statistics data show that *only one-third* of births among teenage mothers involved teenage fathers. The remainder, the vast majority, were caused by adult men over the age of 20 (Males, 1993).

Part of the problem lies in the way sex education is taught (or not taught) in the United States, and the conflicting messages teenagers receive about sexuality. On one hand, they are encouraged to say no, but at the same time, they are bombarded with sexually explicit movies, advertisements, videos, and music. Ambivalence in our society about sexual openness as opposed to

stricter social controls is reflected in the struggle over sex education. Consequently, young people have great difficulty with the question of how they should think about their sexuality

Dilemmas of Sex Education

It is difficult for many people to understand why sex education for children has presented so many problems. However, if we think a bit about the founding of the United States, we might come close to solving the puzzle. Most of the earliest European settlers were Puritans, fundamentalist Protestants who were fleeing the repression of the Church of England. Later, they were joined by other religious groups, for example Quakers and Huguenots. But it was the Puritans who had gained political sophistication in Europe and knew how to use the power of the courts.

For a long time, church officials supervised education, cared for the poor, and performed other functions that the modern American would associate with government, rather than with religion. The rules imposed by the church were very strict, even requiring people to desist from work during the Sabbath, a period of time beginning on Saturday afternoon and extending until Sunday night. Everyone was expected to spend this time in prayer, and, if one were caught breaking the Sabbath, he or she received sentence from the local court. Courts regularly put people in the pillory (wooden structures to bind one's head and hands that are similar to modern handcuffs, but the pillory required the penitent to stand in the middle of the village where he or she suffered public humiliation, as well as the physical suffering that occurs when one is restrained) or the ducking stool (a chair fastened to the end of a long pole, used for "ducking" people under water several times while the villagers jeered). The local justice would order use of these devices also on people who were accused of swearing, disturbing the peace, or drinking to excess.

A major weakness of sex education in the United States may be that it is provided too late. By the ninth and tenth grades, many students are already sexually active.

The Puritans also brought with them Old World superstitions about women. Men of the church believed that women had evil powers and could cast spells on people, a notion dubiously traceable to the Old Testament account of Eve tempting Adam in the Garden of Eden. If a woman used this power once too often—in some cases, once was too often—she was accused of practicing witchcraft. If the court agreed with the accusation, the court could order the "witch" to be publicly whipped or imprisoned. Some were even executed.

However, Puritanical values began to change in the latter part of the nineteenth century, and the Kinsey studies of the late 1940s and early 1950s made people begin to question old aphorisms (Kinsey, Pomeroy, and Martin, 1948; Kinsey, Pomeroy, Martin, and Gebhard, 1953). In the 1990s, a majority of people favor sex education, but many others feel that it tends to promote early sexual activities, often with a variety of partners.

To try to please those who favor sex education as well as those who oppose it, many school districts water down their sex-education courses.

Norman Lear of People for the American Way, an anticensorship group, reported 157 cases of censorship or attempted censorship in the nation's schools during the 1987–1988 school year, many of the cases having to do with sex education (Associated Press, 1987). In Bartow, Florida, the school board caved in to pressure to eliminate any discussion of contraceptive methods in sex-education courses, allowing only abstinence to be mentioned. Clearly, the idea of sex only within the confines of marriage has not died with the passing of years. In fact, Laumann, Michael, Michaels, and Gagnon (1994) found that 94 percent of people in intact marriages report being faithful to each other, regardless of how sexually active they were before or between marriages.

With respect to AIDS education, the 14.6 million-member Southern Baptist Convention has taken a position similar to that of the Bartow School Board: The federal government's pamphlet on AIDS is not to be used in instruction because it fails to condemn all sex outside of marriage ("Abortion," 1988). On the other hand, the World Bank (1993:101), which commissions studies on teenage pregnancy and other topics, says that young people, "both in and out of school, need comprehensive education on reproduction and reproductive health issues". It is the World Bank's opinion that such education must begin before children become sexually active, 12 to 14 years old in many countries. "Reaching boys," according to the report, "is particularly important because men so often dominate the sexual relationship" (World Bank, 1993:101). But, both boys and girls need to know about all potential behavioral choices (World Bank, 1993:102).

Timing of Sex Education

The Alan Guttmacher Institute points out that a major weakness of sex education in the United States is that it is usually given in the ninth and tenth grades, by which time many students are already sexually active. When Institute researchers spoke to teachers about this situation, they found that 93 percent of public-school teachers in the sample wanted a solid course in sex education at an early age, which would emphasize the prevention of pregnancy and **sexually transmitted diseases** (STDs). The researchers also discovered that 85 percent of adults in the United States agree with the teachers, up from 76 percent in 1975 (Alder, 1993).

Although good sex education may be *necessary* to explain to young women why they should abstain from sex, it may not be sufficient. Studies over the past decade (Freedman and Thorne, 1984; Bem, 1993) have suggested that teenage females who are familiar with and have access to contraception are nonetheless reluctant to initiate use of it for fear of being perceived as "having planned to have sex" or "having premeditated the possibility of sexual intercourse." Young women reported they felt it was a lesser jeopardy to their "reputations" to be perceived as having "impulsively succumbed" to male-initiated advances than to be seen as "having been ready and waiting for it." Obviously, the double standard of morality is at work, just a bit more subtly than in the circumstances we've previously discussed.

Figure 3.1
The median age for first intercourse is 16.6 years for boys and 17.4 for girls, according to the latest available data. But nearly 20 percent (of both sexes) remain virgins throughout their teenage years.

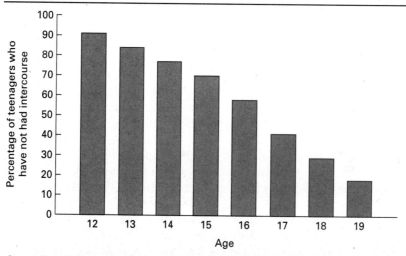

Source: From M. Ingrassia, "Virgin Cool," *Newsweek,* Oct. 17, 1994: 61.

Another criticism of sex-education courses is that they do not make condoms readily available, although some large, urban schools do freely distribute condoms and other types of birth control to students. A comparison with European countries suggests that the lack of availability of contraceptives has been a crucial problem. The countries with the lowest teenage pregnancy rates are those with a thorough sex-education policy and readily available contraceptives. Whereas the pregnancy rate for U.S. females between 15 and 20 years of age is 96 per 1,000, the rate in neighboring Canada is less than half that (44 per 1,000). The rate for European countries varies from 43 in France to 4 in the Netherlands, despite the fact that the Netherlands is one of the world's most permissive countries for both males and females (Gregerson, 1986). Some people have tried to attribute this higher U.S. rate to racial factors, but this accounts for very little in the total. White teenagers have a pregnancy rate that is more than twice that of France or Canada and more than 20 times that of the Netherlands (Shearer, 1985).

Some Good News in the United States

Despite the inadequacy of school sex-ed courses, the notion of remaining a virgin has become "cool" (Ingrassia, 1994). Although this may be a short-term fad for both males and females, the new value being placed on virginity may provide an alternative to peer pressure on teenagers to engage in sexual intercourse. Figure 3.1 shows that almost one of five young people are currently getting through their teenage years with their virginity intact. Nevertheless, nearly one of ten 12-year-olds has already experienced sexual intercourse. While Figure 3.2 shows that more than one-third of teenagers have experienced sexual intercourse, two-thirds have opted for other sexual activity. Of those two-thirds, 90

Figure 3.2
Sexual experimenting soars in high school, especially between sophomore and junior years.

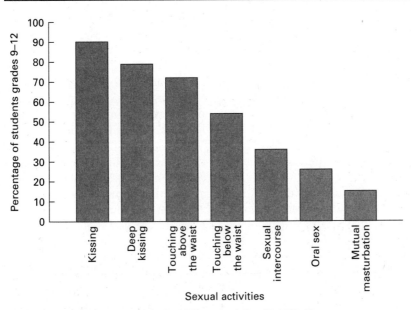

Source: From M. Ingrassia, "Virgin Cool," *Newsweek*, Oct. 17, 1994: 64.

percent have engaged in kissing, about 25 percent have had oral sex, and 15 percent have tried mutual masturbation. The reason the figures add up to more than 100 percent is that students could respond to more than one category. For example, a teenager who has not engaged in sexual intercourse might have engaged in kissing, deep kissing, touching above and below the waist, and mutual masturbation. For young women who *have* engaged in sexual intercourse, one possible consequence is pregnancy and one possible alternative to bearing a child is abortion.

The Abortion Issue

Large numbers of unwanted pregnancies lead to economic problems and moral dilemmas. Babies born into very poor families may need welfare support and other human services. This is especially true of babies born to young, unmarried mothers who have not yet completed high school. Dropping out of school could lead to a deprived life, and that life-style could become relatively permanent. The alternative, used in more than 1.5 million cases annually for the past several years in the United States (*World Almanac*, 1995), is abortion—a subject of intense debate in the United States and many other countries. Opinion polls on the subject vary, but generally find the public supporting abortion in some cases, but not in others. If a pregnant woman seeks an abortion during her *first trimester* (first three months), 45 percent of the public favor the woman's right to obtain the abortion, and 45 percent do not (Henslin, 1995).

Current abortion law in the United States is based on the 1973 *Roe v. Wade* Supreme Court decision, which stated that state governments cannot prohibit abortion during the first trimester. Many people felt a responsibility to choose sides regarding the ruling. Those who supported the ruling became known as **Pro-choice** advocates; those who opposed the

law were **Pro-life** advocates. For a decade and a half, pro-choice definitely had the upper hand. Then in 1989, a far more conservative Supreme Court with Justice Antonin Scalia holding high the pro-life banner, decided that states could place certain restrictions on abortion in *Webster v. Reproductive Services*. Later that same year, in *Casey v. Planned Parenthood*, the court upheld a somewhat restrictive law in the state of Pennsylvania. The ruling involved several issues: Once an adult woman has confirmation that she is pregnant, she must wait at least 24 hours before obtaining an abortion; if the woman is younger than 18 years old, she must obtain the consent of at least one parent; abortion clinics must inform potential clients of other options, and this instruction may include materials that describe the fetus; and a married woman does not have to inform her husband that she is getting or has had an abortion (Henslin, 1995:607–608).

From a sociological point of view, abortion in and of itself is not a social problem. The problems are that this issue divides society and becomes a question of fetal rights versus women's rights. Some antiabortionists attempt to close clinics and hospitals where abortions are performed; some have resorted to violent attacks on physicians who perform abortions. In 1993 David Gunn, a physician who performed abortions, was shot to death in Pensacola, Florida. In response, the U.S. Congress passed the Freedom of Access to Clinic Entrances Act in 1994. This law makes it a federal crime to use force, threats, or physical obstruction to block entrances to clinics where abortions take place. Under the provisions of the act, there must be a free zone, an area that cannot be occupied by protesters, of 300 feet surrounding clinics and hospitals. Nevertheless, on August 4, 1994, John Britton, another abortionist, was killed by antiabortionist Paul Hill outside another clinic in Pensacola. In that attack, clinic defense volunteer James Barrett was also shot to death and Janet Barrett was injured (*World Almanac*, 1995).

At the time of this writing, Paul Hill has been convicted and sentenced to death. But the violence continues. Police allege that, in early January 1995, John Salvi entered an abortion clinic in Brookline, Massachusetts, took a rifle out of a black bag, killed the receptionist, and then sprayed the rest of the room with bullets. Ten minutes later, he repeated this scene at a nearby clinic, fatally shooting its receptionist and then spraying the rest of the room. The following day, at a clinic in Norfolk, Virginia, he allegedly played out the same scene. Fortunately no one was killed in Virginia, but in two days two human beings had been killed and five injured (Lemonick, 1995:34).

Pro-life advocates see the act of abortion as a moral issue rather than a political and economic one: To them, abortion is taking a life. Ironically, conservative policies usually oppose increased welfare costs, which could result from outlawing abortion.

Pro-choice advocates argue that a woman has a right to decide what goes on in her body and that equality between the sexes is impossible if pregnancies cannot be terminated. They further remind us that when abortions were illegal, they were nevertheless performed, often by poorly trained medical personnel and at very serious risk to the woman's life.

According to the Gallup organization (Reinisch and Beasley, 1990), the majority of people in the United States have no absolute position on the abortion issue. Even among those who said that abortion should be illegal, about half agreed that an abortion should be performed if necessary to save the mother's life, and nearly half believed abortion was warranted in cases of rape. Similarly, if a woman's life is endangered by the process of parturition (the birth of a baby), she is granted an exception to the "no abortion rule." The supposition is that "it's not her fault"; she would otherwise be willing to bear the child or want to assume the role of motherhood but finds her plans thwarted by forces outside her control. Abortion, as with other matters concerning human sexuality, becomes really a question of who has the power and controls the politics regarding the issue.

International Comparisons

Most East Asian countries permit abortion as one means of preventing rapid population increase. In Europe, the majority of countries permit abortion, but with restrictions. Ireland is the only European country in which abortion is completely forbidden, mainly because of the power of the Roman Catholic Church in this predominantly Catholic country. Many Irish women who want an abortion go to England for medical assistance. In 1992, however, an Irish woman was arrested for attempting this. However, her case was eventually dismissed. Irish opinion appears to be changing to some degree; a majority of the Irish public approved the dismissal of the charge.

Spain, also a predominantly Catholic country, allows abortion only in cases of rape or serious threat to the mother's life, or if there is strong evidence that the baby will be deformed. Many sociologists also wonder if this latter exception might be an attempt at **eugenics,** the science of the improvement of hereditary qualities of human beings by selective breeding. Most of the world condemned Hitler for such attempts before and during World War II (1939–1945).

Prior to the reunification of Germany, abortions were legal in East Germany, but were severely restricted in West Germany. Now, united Germany has legalized abortion with a few restrictions, but there is political protest, especially in the Western sector. In Belgium, abortions are outlawed, but the law is only enforced in rural areas. By contrast, in Sweden, abortion is legal, but the abortion rate is low because of the widespread use of contraceptives, which are available to teenagers as well as adults.

France is of particular interest. Abortions have been legal since 1975, yet female sexuality is the center of controversy. The new contraceptive pill,

RU 486, was developed in France and is now in use there. RU 486 is a pill that causes the embryo to be aborted. Although widely used in some Western European countries, it is not being marketed in the less developed countries, where it could be a great force for slowing rapid population growth. Neither is it marketed at present in the United States, but there is increasing pressure to make the pill available to American women. It is currently being tested at about 20 facilities in the country, including one of the abortion clinics in Massachusetts where two people were killed (Lemonick, 1995).

The USSR had by far the highest abortion rate in the world, with about 11,000,000 abortions per year, and the policy in Russia has not changed. Abortion is the primary means of contraception because very little information about preventive methods is available. Because the large number of abortions places strain on an overworked medical system, one would expect that Russia would change to a policy promoting contraceptives. But Russia, like Western Europe, has a low birthrate and will probably try to keep it low by either one means or another (Anderson and Moore, 1993).

Japan and the People's Republic of China have low birthrates also, partly because of contraception and partly because of abortions. In fact, there have been times when the government of China has insisted on abortions to control population growth. In both countries, more female than male fetuses are aborted, which can result in a serious imbalance of the national sex ratios. The New China News Agency reports that there have been so many female abortions and female infanticides (the killing of infants soon after birth or simply allowing them to die) in one Chinese province that about half a million bachelors cannot find wives. Men of marriageable age outnumber women by about ten to one (Anderson and Moore, 1993)

India, like China, has a sex ratio imbalance, and for the same reasons. Both societies promote and reinforce **misogynist attitudes**, the hatred for and distrust of women. Notice that the social problem, as stated by the New China News Agency, is the inconvenience the imbalance causes for men. It does not address the impact of practices like female abortion and female infanticide on the psychological and social lives of girls and women. In these countries, the birth of a girl is a great tragedy, but the birth of a boy is a time for great celebration. Imagine what a young Chinese or Indian girl must think when she asks herself the question posed by Margaret Mead, What am I to think about my femaleness?

THE HOMOSEXUAL MINORITY

No one really knows why some people are homosexual and some are not, but one area of investigation is the field of genetics. Homosexuality is not a disease, mental illness, or social problem. The social problem is society's attitudes and reactions to homosexuality. Ideally all people, including gays (homosexual males) and lesbians (homosexual females), should be accepted in society. However, many societies, including the United States, have shown little tolerance for homosexuals, who have suffered much violence and discrimination. Even families often show bitter disappointment in offspring who are gay or lesbian. Let's see how these problems came about.

Homosexuality in Western Tradition

During certain periods in ancient Greece and Rome, homosexuality was fairly well tolerated. After the Roman Empire collapsed in A.D. 473, Western Europe entered the Dark Ages, a time during which advances in science came to a screeching halt. However, even during the Dark Ages, gay men were allowed to marry, even within the Church. And homosexuality was widespread, at least among the upper classes. Often male servants were required to service their masters' sexual needs. The master's wife, however, did not enjoy the same privilege; she faced a death

Medical doctors Dean Hamer and Victoria Magnuson look at DNA markers to see whether there is a gene connected with homosexuality.

penalty if she were caught in a homosexual act (Gies and Gies, 1987:29).

During the Middle Ages (about A.D. 1000 to A.D. 1500), the Church began to formalize its position on various sexual practices in a series of writings called Penitentials. According to the Penitential of Columban, homosexuality was severely punished, and it was assumed that only men could be homosexual. Later, the Penitential of Theodore recognized that women could have homosexual relations and prescribed the penalty for this offense against God: "If a woman practices vice with a woman, she shall do penance for three years"(Gies and Gies, 1987:64–65). If the woman had a husband, the penance was more severe.

The first big change came with the Napoleonic Code of 1804, which did away with punishments for private homosexual relations between consenting adults. The tolerance that was gradually spreading in Europe was struck a serious blow with the rise of the Nazi state in Germany. Between 1933 and 1944, more than 50,000 homosexuals were sent to Nazi concentration camps; between 5,000 and 15,000 were executed. Heinrich Himmler was the leader of actions against gays, expressing the opinion that they spread a "homosexual infection."

Both homosexuality and abortion were hated by the Nazis because Germany was trying to increase its birthrate (Plant, 1987.)

During the long reign of the Communist Party in the Soviet Union, homosexuals were treated very harshly. Although no homosexuals were executed for engaging in homosexual behavior, five-year sentences were imposed. As of this writing, Latvia and the Ukraine have decriminalized both male and female homosexuality. Russia has done likewise, but many convicted gays and lesbians have not been released from prison (Tuller, 1993).

Despite incidents to the contrary, the trend in modern, industrial societies is in the direction of greater tolerance of homosexuality. The 1960s and 1970s witnessed the rise of a Gay Liberation Movement that has helped to change attitudes about gays and lesbians and to give them a measure of political clout, especially in big cities. Today the American Psychological Association no longer considers homosexuality a psychopathology (mental illness) and, in 1973, eliminated it as a diagnostic category.

It must be understood, however, that the practice of dividing people into categories based on their sexual activity has not existed for more than a century or so. Of course, homosexual behavior existed in earlier times, but the identification of individuals as a function of their sexual activity is fairly new. Before modern times, some people had sex with a same-sex partner, but this was not perceived as an indicator of what type of people (homosexual or heterosexual) they were. In 1868, Karl Kertbeny of Germany coined the terms *homosexual* and *heterosexual,* although homosexual *behavior* had existed probably for thousands of years (Bullough, 1976). The categories of homosexual and heterosexual are social constructs, and, although his methodology was quite faulty, we have Kinsey to thank for letting us know that these are not mutually exclusive polar extremes. Now, the outbreak of AIDS, which has been especially prevalent among homosexuals, has been a setback to their progress toward acceptability.

AIDS and Homosexuals

The condemnation of homosexuals has been so strong in the past that some people have wrongly concluded that AIDS is an exclusively "gay disease." Even in San Francisco, generally noted for its tolerance, hardly a day goes by without a case of **gay bashing**, violent crimes against homosexuals that sometimes cause serious injuries or death (Caldwell, 1989). Many gay bashers blame homosexuals for spreading AIDS. When AIDS was first identified in the early 1980s, it appeared to spread rapidly among gay men. However, the gay community responded to the disease by promoting safe-sex education and other measures, leading to an eventual decline in the rate of new cases. In a real sense, gays have been made scapegoats, responsible for this morbid disease. A **scapegoat** is a person or group falsely blamed for some condition. It is then presumed that if the person or group could somehow be destroyed, then the unpleasantness would magically disappear. In Germany during the 1930s, Hitler blamed the economic depression on the Jews; in the United States today,

Despite incidents to the contrary, the trend in industrial societies is toward greater tolerance of gays and lesbians.

many Americans blame the existence and spread of AIDS on homosexuals.

Occupational Problems

A study of occupational choice among gay men in the United States and Brazil (Whitman and Dixon, 1980) found only minor differences between homosexual and heterosexual men; but in both countries there was discrimination against homosexuals in nearly all fields, except for the arts and entertainment. Consequently, gay men who have jobs in business and industry have to keep their sexual orientations secret. Again, paraphrasing Margaret Mead, what problem of identity is caused when the gay man asks, "What am I to think of my maleness?"

Lesbians face the same kind of occupational discrimination. In addition, they are burdened by general discrimination against women; namely, women are paid less than men for comparable work, and employers are less likely to hire women when there are male applicants for the same job. This is an extension of the double standard that we previously discussed. In this case, many employers assume that the woman's income is a secondary income. Her husband has the real job and earns the majority of the family income. Of course, a lesbian does not have the luxury of this male paycheck to enhance her income.

Homosexuals often suffer from a form of subtle discrimination. For example, a college professor who has tenure has a relatively safe job and can likely reveal her or his sexual preference. However, the professor may be less likely to be chosen as department chair or get one of the higher-paying jobs in administration. Health-care professionals in private practice are relatively immune from occupational discrimination because they are their own employers. Health care professionals who may have private practices include physicians, nurses, occupational therapists, dentists, speech therapists, physical therapists, optometrists, and so on. Other business categories that have many self-employed people include bookkeeping, law, and accounting. But any of these professionals can be victimized by gay bashing or more subtle forms of discrimination, like lack of referrals. Lawyers often refer clients to accountants and vice versa. An occupational therapist relies on referrals from physicians. And many physicians get referrals from other physicians. So, no job is ever completely free from potential discrimination for a homosexual who makes her or his sexual preference known. In many of the examples given, if the referrals stop coming, the business won't survive.

Military Service

During the 1992 presidential campaign, the question about homosexuals in the military became a political issue, with Bill Clinton promising to end discrimination against homosexuals in the armed services. The issue led to an examination of the policies of other countries regarding homosexuals. In October 1992, Canada agreed to end discrimination based on sexual orientation in the military service; the director-general for personnel policy found it impossible to prove that homosexuality "had that deleterious effect on cohesion and morale that everyone talked about" (Lancaster, 1992:14). Australia adopted the same policy one month later. However, the majority of NATO (North American Treaty Organization) member nations (Germany, Italy, France, Norway, Denmark, Sweden, and the Netherlands) had long had policies permitting homosexual service personnel. Israel has had such a policy for many years, and its army, almost ceaselessly in battle, has had no morale problems (Lancaster, 1992).

The military establishment in the United States was strongly opposed to a change in its policy not to accept homosexuals in the armed services. After Clinton was elected president, a compromise was established as a quasi-policy: "Don't ask; don't tell; don't pursue." In theory, this should end the policy of shadowing men and women suspected of being gay in order to force them out of the service; but it still means that anyone who admits to being a homosexual can be discharged. At present, there are cases before the courts to decide whether expelling gays or exempting them from military service violates their constitutional rights.

PROSTITUTION

Prostitution, the rental of one's body to someone for use in sexual activities, is often referred to as the "oldest profession," perhaps because it has existed in virtually all societies and for all of recorded time. In the Biblical story of the destruction of the city of Jericho, it was the harlot Rahab who successfully hid Joshua's spies. In return, when Jericho fell, she and her kin were spared, while all other inhabitants were put to the sword. In the late 1600s, English poet John Milton wrote a poem, "Samson Agonistes," modeled after an Israeli mythical hero in the Book of Judges, who is caught and blinded by the Philistines because he was betrayed by Dalila (Delilah, in the original myth), a prostitute who had been his mistress. By contrast, in the last quarter of the nineteenth century, French author Guy de Maupassant wrote "Boule-de-Suif" ("Ball of Fat"), in which the chubby little prostitute is the only decent person. The kind-hearted prostitute has been a standard character in American film from "Gone with the Wind" (1936) to "Pretty Woman" (1990).

There are several reasons for sympathizing with or even glamorizing the prostitute in fiction. One is that prostitutes are usually exploited people, victims of a cruel world. Another is that, in a sexist society in which women are still seen by many men as property, prostitution supports the assumption that women can be bought and sold. It was this assumption that was attacked by early **conflict theory.** Conflict theory was originated by Karl Marx who with Friedrich Engels, wrote *The Communist Manifesto* in 1848 which united the various Communist parties of Europe. It was their observation that all societies are divided into the "haves" and "have-nots." In their time, they could witness the tremendous power wielded by the **bourgeoisie** (those who owned the means of production) over the **proletariat** (those who had to sell their labor for very low wages because the size of the wage was determined by the bourgeois class). In more recent times, German sociologist Ralf Dahrendorf refined conflict theory by substituting **authority** (power that derives from control). As we'll see, either theory applies when we attempt to analyze prostitution.

Prostitution from a Conflict Perspective

Although early conflict theory is attributed to Karl Marx, his friend and sometimes collaborator Friedrich Engels focused much of his work on family issues. In 1884 Engels published *The Origin of the Family, Private Property and the State*, in which he addressed certain issues that we can apply to the analysis of prostitution. His assertion is that as societies evolved from **matrilineal descent,** in which the family line is traced only along the woman's side of the family, to **patrilineal descent,** in which the family history follows only the man's branch, another important transformation was taking place. Men's and women's roles changed form **egalitarian** (equal authority between males and females) to **patriarchal** (authority and ownership of the family assets in the exclusive domain of the male). Charlotte O'Kelley, a sociologist at Providence College, provides the following interpretation, based on the work of Engels:

> Chastity and monogamy were enforced on wives to ensure the paternity of the male's heirs. But sexual freedom was allowed to males wealthy enough to buy or support several wives or to buy the sexual favors of unattached women—thus the development of prostitution. Engels held that the economic dependence of women forced them to sell themselves either as wives or as whores. Truly affectionate, loving marriages were no longer possible under capitalism because women had to depend on their relationships with men for economic support. Women had become just another form of private property (O'Kelley, 1980:8).

The conflict perspective emphasizes the struggle over scarce commodities: prestige, wealth, and power. Conflict analysis argues that "industrialization—and capitalism in particular—sharply lowered the social standing of women" (Johnson, 1992:348). The reason for this, maintain some conflict theorists, is that capitalism is an economic **zero-sum game,** meaning that if one group obtains a precious commodity, like power, then another group must lose an equal portion of the commodity, because commodities are in limited supply. Consequently, as societies moved from being matrilineal to being patrilineal, men gained greater prestige because they controlled the family's descent and women lost status because their side of a family's ancestry was either lost or ignored. As societies changed from being egalitarian to being patriarchal, men gained power and women lost it, becoming little more than domestic slaves.

Prostitution reflects the power relationships within a society. Most societies attach criminal sanctions to those who commit prostitution, while the client, or "john," enjoys relative impunity. According to Allan Johnson (1992: 243), prostitution is the only crime primarily (but not exclusively) committed by women. If Engels was correct in saying that many women had no value other than their bodies to satisfy men's sexual needs and desires, then Ian Robertson (1989:163–164) asks this penetrating question, If prostitution exists to cater to sexual needs, why are there not hordes of males prostituting themselves to women? Viewing it as a zero-sum game, his answer is that prostitution benefits the men—clients and pimps (as well as madams of brothels)—at the expense of women, whose prestige and power decline because they are forced to have sexual relations when the customer wants. They must do what they are told, when they are told, and however the client wants it done.

Also, within the prostitution organization, the profits seldom benefit the female prostitute. If she works for a pimp, he will likely demand all of the money she earns in return for protection. If she works in a brothel, the madam will probably take half of her earnings. Conflict theorists claim that the majority of prostitutes come from poor, lower-class backgrounds and have few, if any, alternatives to the prostitute's life-style. Their

sexuality may be their only economic commodity. And, this commodity is devalued over time; that is, as prostitutes age, they become less desirable, and customers will likely seek younger women.

It should be instructive to see if the adoption of a conflict perspective by the policy makers of society would increase the status of women, treating them as human beings rather than property. In this regard, the former Soviet Union, from its earliest position papers, dedicated itself to the emancipation of women.

Prostitution in the Former Soviet Union and Modern Russia

Initially, the Bolsheviks (majority party) were true to their word, at least in theory. Laws were passed that assured women of equality with men and equal pay for equal work. Women were given the right to vote and the right to receive pay for household work. A women's freedom movement started, and the state set up programs to guarantee the safety and welfare of mothers and children. However, most of the "new rights" were cosmetic, merely symbols of Marxist doctrine. For most women, life did not change appreciably.

In 1917 Vladimir Ilyich Lenin became the leader of the Bolsheviks, hence, the leader of Soviet Union. By this time, there was virtually no political opposition from the Mensheviks (minority party). Toward the end of the year, he negotiated an end to hostilities with Germany, and turned his attention to healing the wounds of his country. Lenin led as a tyrant, but he suffered a stroke in 1922 and never really accomplished many of his national policies. By the time he died in 1924, Joseph Stalin had worked his way to the top of the power structure. By 1929 he was recognized as a dictator. Because of the devastating loss of adult males during World War I (1914–1918), Soviet leaders became worried about its declining birthrate. Stalin reaffirmed that the family was the core of society. Abortions, which had been legalized under Lenin, were banned. The government declared various activities to be illegal, including homosexuality and prostitution.

Millions more of the Soviet Union's young males died in World War II (1939–1945), and Stalin was concerned that there was a serious imbalance in the country's sex ratio, with too few young men to father children that the surplus of women could provide. Stalin issued a Family Edict in 1944, which was intended to strengthen the family by placing strong restrictions on divorce, premarital pregnancy, and "casual marriages," those not recognized by the state. O'Kelly (1980:300) also points out that the new "law absolved men of all responsibility toward their lovers and children and encouraged a frivolous attitude toward women." Under Stalin's policies, women were to become child-bearing machines. Conditions for women were no better than they had been before the revolution under control of a czar.

In 1991, after 74 years of ruling nearly the entire western part of Asia, the Communist Party (previously known as the Bolsheviks) failed, and the Soviet Union came to an end. Under the leadership of Boris Yeltsin, the new republics began a process of democratization and free-market capitalism. Now, perhaps, women would see change. But at this writing, men still hold power, and women remain powerless, often having to turn to prostitution. The new capitalist system got off to a shaky start, and lay-offs became commonplace over the next few years. However, 70 percent of workers who were laid off were women (MacFarquhar, 1994). If these now unemployed women were young and pretty, they might get jobs as "secretaries," in many cases a lightly veiled euphemism for prostitutes.

Victoria Pope (1994:56) reports the following want ads published in respectable newspapers throughout modern Russia:

> I invite applications for secretary . . . Not older than 25; bright appearance, long legs compulsory.

An ad for secretary-housekeeper specifies a women 'without complexes, very communicative and full of sex appeal. She should cook delicious food and keep a good house. Her age: No older than 25.'

Pope goes on to explain that many of the young women who answer the advertisements know they are simply selling their bodies as expensively as possible. The guise of being a secretary protects their reputations, while the job requirements call for sex at the behest of the employer. Pope says that they "sell themselves not as street prostitutes, but get indirectly involved in this business" (Pope, 1994:56).

"Many first-wave democrats," she concludes, "consider a traditional hearth and home a human right that was long denied to the unisex Soviet citizen" (Pope, 1994:56). She claims that few, if any, of these new entrepreneurs ever bought the party line about sexual equality. In the division of "haves" and "have-nots," women are the losers. For example, of those people in Russia who are currently unemployed and actively seeking work, 71 percent are women (Pope, 1994:56). In modern Russia, the answer to the problem that women face is pretty simple: One must be young and pretty to get a job. Imagine how a short-legged, plain-looking woman in Moscow would answer the question, How am I to think about my femaleness in this new utopian society?

Prostitution in Less Developed Countries

In most LDCs, prostitution is increasing dramatically. Local beliefs and customs encourage prostitution, and many boys cannot become "men" without the service of a prostitute. Jodi L. Jacobson (1992:13) tells us that in Guatemala and Ecuador "the transition to 'manhood' supposedly requires a young male to have his first intercourse with a prostitute" (13). This "forced use" of a prostitute is another example of the double standard of morality: Men are to be sexually experienced from an early age; women are to remain chaste until marriage.

In parts of sub-Saharan Africa, social and religious taboos prevent husbands and wives from having sexual intercourse during certain times of the year, when the wife is menstruating, or during the period (sometimes two years) when the wife is breastfeeding an infant. These periods of abstinence may encourage men to seek prostitutes as partners. Once again, let's look at the construction of reality. Who decided that boys in Central and South America are to be sexually experienced? Who decided that in sub-Saharan Africa women could not have sex with their husbands during certain times? We suggest the answer is "those who hold power," and that these powerful people are exclusively male because, in either case, the male gets sexual gratification; the female must wait until marriage or until she has met some qualification not of her choosing.

Another societal factor that determines who is and who is not sexually deviant is the ongoing process of **urbanization.** Urbanization refers to three interconnected trends: (1) the growth of cities, both in number and in size, (2) the movement of rural people into urban areas so that the cities grow faster than the surrounding non-metropolitan area, and (3) the casting off of a rural life-style for new migrants and the adoption of the more cosmopolitan life of the urban dweller. Again, Jacobson (1992) provides useful insight:

> Deepening poverty among women is contributing to a documented rise in prostitution in cities from Russia to Zimbabwe. Rapid urbanization, too, has driven up the number of men seeking prostitutes. . . . This complicated scenario begins with economic development policies that enrich urban areas at the expense of rural ones, which leads to migration by farm workers in search

of jobs in the city. Especially in Africa, and to a large extent in Asia, the vast majority of migrants to cities have been male. Whether married or single, these men tend to return home infrequently. To meet their sexual needs, they are apt either to take a second wife or girlfriend, or to seek the services of a prostitute (p. 13).

Notice, once more, the zero-sum game: If the urban areas prosper, the rural areas must sink deeper into poverty. Again, the sexual needs of the male are an excuse for prostitution. Frequently women become prostitutes because they have no alternative. For example, in Niger, Uganda, and the Central Republic of Africa, barren women (women who cannot bear children) and abandoned women who are no longer virgins are shunned by the village and may be forced to move to one of the few large cities. Having no marketable skills and being no longer eligible for marriage, their only choice for keeping themselves alive is prostitution. Unfortunately, in these countries, it is only a matter of time before they contract STDs and often AIDS.

As mentioned, prostitution is not exclusively practiced by women. In the Middle East and Southeast Asia, young boys are often requested by wealthy men. But prostitution, overall, is still the woman's burden. Prostitution is common in India and much of Southeast Asia. In recent years it has been especially prevalent in Thailand, attracting many foreign visitors. Very young girls from poor families are often recruited to "work in town." They come to the city with their recruiters and find themselves locked up in a brothel. In some cases, they are even sold by their families. It is commonly said in Bangkok's red-light district: At 10, you are a woman. At 20, you are an old woman. At 30, you are dead (Sachs, 1994:25).

Prostitution has long been prominent in Thailand for certain cultural reasons. For example, it is strictly forbidden for a young man to have sexual relations with his fiancée;

but having sex is an important part of the rite of manhood, just as it is in the Central and South America. In a survey of recruits into the Thai army, 73 percent said that they had lost their virginity in a brothel. Among the upper classes, hosts are expected to provide girls (preferably between the ages of 10 and 14) for their guests.

In recent years, Thailand has had yet another reason for prostitution: the tourist trade and the money it brings. Even though foreign tourists are aware of the AIDS threat, there are still tours, mainly for sex, from such diverse countries as Japan, South Korea, Australia, and the United States. The Thai government fears that there may be as many as 400,000 cases of HIV (human immunodeficiency virus) in the country and is campaigning to get people to use condoms. Within the government, there is pressure to curb sex tours from abroad, but the countervailing pressure to keep the matter hushed up so the profitable trade will continue is almost irresistible (Moreau, 1992). Unfortunately, the government is not effective in stopping the practice of forcing young girls and boys into prostitu-

tion against their wills—a situation in which prostitution becomes rape.

PORNOGRAPHY, RAPE, AND CHILD MOLESTATION

Often, the general public links pornography to both rape and child molestation, both of which are persistent social problems. **Pornography** is the depiction of erotic behavior in pictures, films, videocassettes, and writing that is intended to cause sexual excitement. On this basis, it would be easy to call much of the advertising, television, and cinema in North America and Western Europe pornographic.

Usually, though, when a storm is raised against pornography, it is not about advertisements, plays, or movies that are erotic, but about very explicit sexual material found in adult bookstores, movie houses, and peek shows. Movies, home videos, magazines, and books are sold that feature sexually explicit materials. In some countries in Western Culture, city and state laws attempt to limit access to such establish-

Thailand has become a sex mecca, drawing men from many parts of the world to its houses of prostitution. Women are often forced into the job at a very early age. As might be expected, AIDS cases are increasing rapidly.

ments and materials to adults. However, the presence of such stores and materials is disconcerting to self-proclaimed moral purists who call for censorship. Those who oppose censorship nearly always cite freedom of speech as their rationale for permitting these materials to circulate among adults. A question arises, though, as to what harm pornography actually does, and whether it does more harm than would enforced censorship.

Commission Reports on Pornography

In 1970, the National Advisory Commission of Obscenity and Pornography (NACOP) completed a report and submitted it to the President of the United States (NACOP, 1970). The commission had been at work for two years trying to determine whether there was a relationship between pornography and antisocial behavior. Among the commission's members were sociologists, psychologists, and legal experts. The commission was thorough, conducting interviews with more than 3,000 people regarding their experiences with pornography and their sexual attitudes and practices. Responses from convicted rapists and child molesters were compared to a control group of randomly selected adults and teenagers who had no history of sex-related crimes. To its surprise, the committee found that rapists and child molesters had seen *less* pornography than the general population (as represented by the control group). The NACOP concluded that much of our problem with both pornography and sex crimes results from our inability to talk frankly about sexual behavior (Nathan and Harris, 1975). Rapists and child molesters were more likely to be the products of homes that were highly repressive about sex than of homes in which sex could be discussed with a degree of freedom.

The result of NACOP's findings were three recommendations: (1) repeal federal, state, and local laws prohibiting the sale or showing of pornographic materials to adults, (2) prohibit the sale of such materials to minors, and (3)

institute a good sex-education program for minors. Fifteen of the eighteen members of the commission agreed with the recommendations (NACOP, 1970).

European and Canadian Reports

A number of European countries and Canada have also raised questions about the potential harm of pornography. Denmark investigated the matter, concluded it did no major damage to society, and legalized pornography in 1967. Surprisingly, child molestation fell 50 percent over the next six years. The Federal Republic of Germany (before East and West Germany were united) also adopted very permissive rules on pornography, and sex crimes declined by 11 percent in the years between 1972 and 1982 (Nobile and Nadler, 1986).

In 1979 the William Committee of England and Wales reported on pornography along similar lines, concluding that pornography was not a major cause of sex crimes. In 1984 Canada's Fraiser Committee, after a similar investigation, reported that pornography was not found to be a significant factor in violent crime or in the abuse of children (Nobile and Nalder, 1986:257). So, European and Canadian studies seemed to be consistent with the NACOP.

Rape as Power and Control

Rape usually refers to forced sexual intercourse with, oral copulation by, or anal penetration of, mature women. However, children of either sex are often raped, usually by members of their own families. Rape is an expression of power and control rather than an act of sex. It is usually true that the rapist is likely expressing contempt for the victim or for whom or what she represents. Enloe (1988) suggests rape represents a symbolic violation or contamination of a piece of property, the man's ownership of the woman.

This last premise seems to be confirmed by accounts of rape during wartime, when women

People celebrate at an antirape rally, demanding that women be able to "Take back the night." Growing protests about rape are having their effect; court cases are still an ordeal for victims, but rapists are prosecuted and convicted more now than in the past.

have often been forced into sexual relations with members of conquering armies. There were many charges of the rape of Belgian women by German troops in World War I. During World War II, as they advanced to the east, German soldiers raped Polish and Russian women. Later, as the Russians counterattacked, Russian soldiers raped Polish and German women. In the 1990s, similar events occurred in Bosnia (Eastern Europe) and Rwanda (Sub-Saharan Africa). There is an old axiom: To the victors go the spoils. In these cases, women were seen as property of the vanquished, and were therefore part of the "spoils of war."

In the United States, 154,500 cases of rape were reported annually to police between 1973 and 1987 (Wright, 1993). Between 1988 and 1992, another 505,200 rapes were reported (*World Almanac*, 1995:214) So many women refused to report rapes and attempted rapes that the statistics are practically worthless. Twenty-five percent of women who did not report rape or attempted rape said they did not report the rape because they considered it a personal problem, and they wanted to solve it themselves; 23 percent

feared reprisals by the rapist; and another 23 percent thought that the police would be ineffectual and insensitive (Wright, 1993:239). The Bureau of Justice Statistics, which conducted the survey, acknowledges that some victims do not even inform the National Crime Survey interviewer of crimes against them. Therefore, all data probably represent an undercount.

Coser, Nock, Steffan, and Spain (1991) claim that about one-third of rapists are known to the victim as members of the family, family friends, acquaintances, and dates. Awareness and reporting of "date rape" has been increasing in recent years partly because one of the myths about rape is that victims "ask for it" by provocative clothing or promiscuous behavior. This double standard is likely to make rape a continuing social problem so long as society lacks respect for women and accepts the notion of male dominance and female passivity.

Child Molestation

Child molestation refers to acts that range from improper fondling of children by an adult to rape or sodomy. Most experts believe that bizarre sexual behaviors are not ordinarily learned from viewing pornography, but are the result of abuse and sexual molestation during the molester's own childhood (Galtney, 1992). The sexual abuse of children has occurred for generations, but the available statistics make it appear much more common now than in the past. One report (Wright, 1993) says that substantiated cases of child rape in the United States had risen from 6,000 in 1973 to 55,400 in 1987. Table 3.1 shows that the average number of rapes per year of 12- to 15-year-olds during that time period was 16,800; in addition, there were 37,600 average annual rapes of 16- to 19-year olds. However, notice from the table that an estimated 70 percent of rapes of young children,

and fewer than half of rapes of older teenagers are actually reported. Overall, the report contends that 53 percent of attempted or completed rapes are ever disclosed to police or other officials (Wright, 1993). The data for the latter years probably reflect increased willingness to report such cases, including more vigilance by doctors and school authorities; hence it is possible that there has not been a significant increase in the number of incidents. But there is no question that child molestation is a widespread problem.

Imagine the young person who has been molested in childhood trying to answer the question "What am I to think about my femaleness or my maleness?" as she or he enters the tough decision-making years of young adulthood.

Reporting of Rape by Women, by Characteristics of the Crime and the Victim, 1973–1987			TABLE 3.1		
Characteristics of crime or victim	Average annual number of rapes	Percentage of incidents reported to police	Characteristics of crime or victim	Average annual number of rapes	Percentage of incidents reported to police
All rapes	154,500	53%	Age of Victim:		
Attempted	101,600	50	12–15	16,800	70%
Completed	52,900	59	16–19	37,600	48
Victim-offender relationship:			20–24	41,000	48
Nonstranger	58,800	47%	25–34	41,600	51
Stranger	89,900	57	35–49	11,800	56
Presence of weapon:			50–64	3,800	74
No weapon	101,600	47%	65 or older	1,800	55
Weapon	36,500	71	Marital status of victim:		
Presence of injury:			Married	27,100	54%
No injury	93,00	48%	Widowed	3,900	62
Injury	60,700	61	Separated/divorced	36,500	51
Minor injury[a]	41,200	55	Never married	86,500	53
Serious injury[b]	19,300	74			
Race of victim:					
White	121,400	52%			
Black	29,900	56			
Other	3,200	50			

[a] Includes bruises, black eyes, cuts, scratches, swelling, and undetermined injuries requiring less than two days of hospitalization.
[b] Includes gunshot wounds, broken bones, loss of teeth, internal injuries, lacerations, loss of consciousness, and undetermined injuries requiring two or more days of hospitalization. SOURCE: U.S. Bureau of Justice Statistics, *Female Victims of Violent Crime* (1991)

SOURCE: J.W. Wright, Ed., *The Universal Almanac* (Kansas City: Andrews and McMeel, 1993), p. 239.

HARASSMENT: POWER AND POLITICS

The majority of sex-related complaints, especially on the job, are about sexual harassment. **Sexual harassment** refers to verbal or physical conduct that is clearly sexual in nature and unwanted by the person toward whom it is directed. The fact that nearly all such complaints come from women against men, who are usually in dominant positions, is a good indication that sexual harassment is a "power" phenomenon. There are cases in which an employer, supervisor, or professor demands sexual favors for employment, promotion, or grades. These are clearly cases of the exploitation of a dominant position. Sometimes the harassment is a matter of unwanted or embarrassing comments on a person's clothing, references to a woman's figure, or suggestive remarks. One study estimates that 50 to 88 percent of women experience some form of sexual harassment at some time in school or in their workplaces. About 90 percent of them remain silent, not wanting to jeopardize their jobs or provoke a scene (Eskenazi and Gallen, 1992).

There are other situations in which power is abused. A psychiatrist is in a strong authoritative position and a patient may trust and rely on the psychiatrist and may feel that the only path to a cure is to do as the psychiatrist insists. Sexual relations between psychiatrist and client, therefore, are forbidden by the American Psychiatric Association. Nevertheless, in the most thorough study available at this writing, 7 percent of male psychiatrists and 3 percent of female psychiatrists admitted to having had sexual relations with their clients. It's interesting to note that when women are in the power position, they too will use their dominance (though not as frequently) to gain sexual control (Beck, Springen, and Foote, 1992).

Unfortunately the psychiatric profession is not alone in this regard. A number of other medical doctors have been accused of having had sexual relations with their patients. Priests and ministers have been accused of child abuse and harassment of women. Male prison guards have been accused repeatedly of having sex with female prisoners—the guards wielding extreme power and the women not daring to say no.

Famous Cases of Harassment

Two famous cases of sexual harassment in the United States have called national attention to the issue. Clarence Thomas, a federal judge named to the U.S. Supreme Court by President George Bush, faced questioning in the Senate for job confirmation. During the hearings, Anita Hill, a former clerk to Judge Thomas, charged him with sexual harassment. According to the charges, he was very fond of pornographic literature and pictures. Hill refused to go on dates with him, but according to her testimony, he took an interest in her and recounted to her much of the pornography he had read. The case became that of one person's word against another's. Many people seemed to think that Hill was at fault for having remained silent on the matter until the time of Judge Thomas's confirmation hearings. Like many women who are the victims of rape, Hill may have feared being put on trial herself. Nevertheless, she willingly took and passed a lie-detector test. In the end, the Senate confirmed Clarence Thomas, by an extremely narrow vote.

What proved much more important about the case than the truth or falsehood of the charges was the reaction of millions of American women to the whole procedure. They felt that a woman had been battered and brutalized by an all-male Senate committee. Stories of sexual harassment began to surface by the thousands. More women than ever before entered races for the Senate and House of Representatives, and the largest number in history won. The publicity about Anita Hill had had its influence.

Another event that added to a feeling of outrage on the part of American women was the Tailhook Scandal of September 1991. The

Tailhook Association (named for the hook on a naval airplane that grabs landing cables on aircraft carriers) is an organization of active and retired naval pilots. As in previous years, the get-together was a rowdy one with lots of liquor. There were formal meetings of Navy "brass" (high-ranking officers) on the first floor of the hotel. On the third floor, Navy squadrons had rented hospitality suites, featuring such gags as a mannequin of a green knight with a penis that dispensed drinks. Many of the women went to the party knowingly (previous years had been similar), but some did not. One pilot had visited local high schools, inviting teenage girls to drop in. Women were sexually assaulted (patted, groped, pinched, bitten, and stripped) as they "ran the gauntlet" along the hall of the third floor. Thirty or more complained of sexual harassment, including one female lieutenant, a Navy pilot herself who, when forced to "run the gauntlet," reportedly feared that she was going to be gang raped (Waller, King, and Salholz, 1992).

The aftermath of the event was a long investigation by the Navy, which at first seemed to be a cover-up. A year later, however, two admirals were forced into retirement for failure to pursue the investigation. The military services have grown sensitive to charges of harassment. Well before the Tailhook scandal, the government had moved to stop sexual harassment in the workplace and elsewhere by creating the Equal Employment Opportunity Commission (EEOC), which developed statutes that prohibit unwelcome sexual advances, requests for sexual favors, and other verbal or physical conduct of a sexual nature as a condition of employment or promotion.

Law and Politics

The creation of the EEOC to do away with sexual harassment does not mean that such harassment has come to an end. Often a woman finds it easiest to remain silent. Charges are hard to prove and lawsuits involve a great amount of effort and expense. A good illustration is the case of 23 women who had leveled sexual harassment charges against Senator Bob Packwood of Oregon. Packwood was re-elected to the Senate in 1992, having succeeded fairly well in keeping the charges silenced until after the election. By early 1993, however, so many charges were made by so many

Anita Hill brought charges of sexual harassment against Clarence Thomas, candidate for the U.S. Supreme Court. Although Thomas was confirmed, many people were incensed by the way Hill was treated by the press and especially by the all-male Senate committee that investigated the case.

women that Packwood became a laughingstock for television comedians. Packwood turned on his accusers, questioning their characters and sexual histories. The tactic backfired because his accusers were so numerous and of good reputations and all told similar stories of unwanted kissing, hugging, patting, and requests to "meet later" (King and Cohn, 1993). Packwood resigned from the Senate in September 1995. Nevertheless, even cases like this, which seem unequivocal, are hard to prove. And, politicians tend to protect each other.

An extreme case of women being in a position from which they dared not voice complaints occurred at the Georgia Women's Correctional Institution. Because prison employees had full control over women prisoners, including the possibility of parole and of keeping custody of their children, the women were in no position to refuse their requests. The result was years of forced sexual relations, including oral sex and sadomasochistic relations (Carlson, 1992). The situation is comparable to rape of women in warfare. Obviously, in many circumstances, women suffer from the politics of power expressed in sexual ways.

An international study of harassment (Wilkes, 1993) notes that men also complain of harassment: fourteen percent of British men had such complaints. In other countries, the statistics were not very precise. The report claimed that sexual harassment of males occurred least in Sweden, France, and the United States. At the bottom of the list for male sexual harassment was Bangladesh, a Moslem country in which women work hard in the fields, bear many children, and suffer the most sexual harassment of any country.

In other Moslem countries, although they have far from equal status, women may be somewhat protected from harassment through rigid conformity to societal customs. They must have a designated male guardian who protects them from other males. As a result of a conservative religious trend, women are finding protection in old customs. More of them are donning the *hijab* scarf that hides ears, hair, and forehead, which gives them a measure of protection and dignity in a patriarchal society. Women so dressed can move about Cairo unharassed, not gawked at or in any way molested. Full subordination to religious fundamentalism, then, becomes the price of freedom from harassment (Miller, 1992).

But, whether women wear *chador* and *hijab* in the developing part of the world or miniskirts in a modern office building in an industrial society, all women should be free of harassment and free to define their sexuality—their femaleness—in their own way.

SUMMARY

Throughout the chapter, we have asked some variation of Mead's question, What are we to think about our maleness or our femaleness in this era of dramatic change? Problems concerning human sexuality are normative problems. Anomie occurs when the norms are changing, and this leaves the people of a society with a sense of instability. Sometimes, the norms are inconsistent, resulting in a double standard of morality which tends to put control and power in the hands of men at the price of the subordination of women.

Certain societies are rather restrictive in regard to sexual practices, and others are highly permissive. In either case, however, we must ask who sets the standards and who creates the image of reality. By looking at a variety of cultures, we see that there are no universal standards.

In the United States, the cultural *ideal* regarding sexual behavior has probably never been followed by all people. The Kinsey Reports of the late 1940s and early 1950s shed some light on the differences between real and ideal culture.

Recent studies have pointed out that it is likely that more very young people are sexually active than was true in the past. Preoccupation with sex may negatively affect young males' performance in school and young females' expectations for the future. While much attention has been focused on births to teenage mothers, little mention has been made of the fact that two-thirds of the fathers are adult men.

Attempts at adequate sex education have been hampered by a lack of consensus among today's citizens. Canada and European countries have programs that have kept teenage pregnancy rates low. However, even in the United States, nearly one of every five teenagers remains a virgin.

Although the *Roe v. Wade* Supreme Court decision assured women that they could get a legal abortion during their first trimester of pregnancy, recent U.S. Supreme Court decisions have placed some restrictions on them. Controversy between pro-choice groups (who favor a woman's right to decide about abortion) and pro-life groups (who oppose abortion) are likely to continue for some time in the United States. In Europe, public policy varies from abortions being forbidden in Ireland to very few restrictions in most nations. Some less developed countries rely on abortion as a means of birth control.

When a society responds to homosexuality with intolerance and violence, it creates social problems. Western civilization has been inconsistent in its attitudes toward homosexuality, sometimes exhibiting acceptance, other times, rejection. Dividing people into categories based on sexual behavior is a recent phenomenon. The occurrence of AIDS has increased incidents of gay-bashing and discrimination in employment.

Prostitution may have originated because a change of family patterns made women property. Even in the former Soviet Union, sexual relations between men and women were trivialized, giving unofficial sanction to prostitution. In less developed countries, prostitution is encouraged by customs and trends like urbanization. Thailand has become the sex capital of the world.

In the United States, many people see a clear connection between pornography and rape and child molestation. However, various commissions and Canadian and European experience tend to discount this idea. Both rape and child molestation can best be understood as the exercise of control and power, which can be glorified, enhanced, and encouraged by pornography.

Sexual harassment has been brought to public consciousness by recent cases like Anita Hill's allegations regarding Judge Clarence Thomas and the Navy's Tailhook scandal. These myriad problems connected to our sexuality certainly may lead us to question what we are to think of our maleness and femaleness in these changing times.

KEY TERMS

Anomie A sense of being without rules; confusion that occurs when norms are changing rapidly.

Bourgeoisie Literally, the middle class in France, generally used to refer to people who own the means of production.

Child molestation Adult sexual acts with children.

Cognitive dissonance Attempt to simultaneously hold two or more perceptions that are inconsistent.

Conflict theory The type of sociological theory that perceives social strife at almost every level of society.

Deferred gratification Putting off immediate pleasures for later gratification.

Double standard of morality Different standards of sexual behavior for men and women; men are expected to be sexually experienced, while women are suppose to remain virgins until marriage.

Egalitarian authority   Power is shared by all parties, in a marriage by husband and wife.

Eugenics   The science of improving human beings through selective breeding.

Female infanticide   The killing of female babies.

Freedom of Access to Clinic Entrances Act   Congressional act passed in 1994 that makes it a federal crime to block the entrance to an abortion clinic; established a "free zone" of 300 feet around clinics and hospitals.

Gay bashing   Speaking ill of, and in the extreme, committing violence toward people simply because they are homosexuals.

Machismo   A sense of power and manliness.

Matrilineal descent   Family heritage traced through the woman's family; generally children take the mother's family name.

Misogynist attitudes   Antifemale attitudes.

Norms   The behaviors accepted and expected within a society.

Patriarchal authority   Power is held by males; females are subordinate.

Patrilineal descent   Family heritage traced through the man's family; generally children take the father's family name.

Pornography   Pictures, videos, printed material, or other matter that exceeds the community standards of decency and stirs sexual interest.

Pro-choice   The attitude that a woman has a right to a legal abortion.

Proletariat   Those who must sell their labor for whatever price the bourgeois class is willing to pay.

Pro-life   The attitude that abortion is wrong; abortion is the taking of a life.

Prostitution   The exchange of sexual activities for money or other considerations.

Scapegoat   A person or group who is blamed for problems of which he, she, or they are not guilty.

Sexual harassment   Unwanted sexual advances; usually made repeatedly by someone in a position of power over the victim.

Sexually transmitted disease (STD)   Diseases, like syphilis, gonorrhea, and AIDS, that are passed from person to person through sexual acts.

Urbanization   The growth of cities by comparison to rural growth.

Zero-sum game   The situation played out with the belief that someone's gain equals another person's loss.

STUDY QUESTIONS

1. Why are some societies essentially silent about sexual behavior? What are some consequences of such secrecy?

2. Discuss the "creation of reality" with regard to "restrictive" and "permissive" societies.

3. Do you believe that the United States has experienced a "sexual revolution?"

4. What reasons might some people in the world have for practicing female infanticide?

5. What are some consequences of early sexual experiences?

6. What arguments can be made for and against including homosexuals in the military service?

7. What do you think can be done to decrease the rate of teenage pregnancies?

8. What do you suppose accounts for the wide range of attitudes toward abortion in Europe?

9. Why does it seem that all problems, including those with regard to human sexuality, are so much worse in the less developed than more developed countries.

10. Do you think there are correlations among: pornography, prostitution, child molestation, and sexual harassment?

4 chapter

THE HUMAN
CONDITION: HEALTH
AND AFFLICTION

Last Monday, a little girl—let's call her Toda—didn't feel very hungry. Even though she was slightly malnourished, she skipped her meal and complained of feeling warm. On Tuesday, again she didn't eat very much and was running a fever. Her appetite was completely gone by Wednesday, her temperature was much higher, and she began coughing. Thursday, a florid rash appeared on her body and the fever raged on. Days passed and the rash spread to all parts of her body. Her skin got dry and she began to experience bouts of diarrhea. This Monday, we can see that her eyes are infected and inflamed; she hasn't eaten for a week. The rash has begun to peel away and her skin is now marked by open sores. The diarrhea and the coughing persist. She is too weak to eat and, although her thirst is unbearable, she doesn't seem able to swallow water. This Tuesday, she is severely dehydrated; her body is almost devoid of nutrients. The coughing is not so violent anymore. She is now too weak to clear her lungs, and even the weak coughing puts excessive strain on her feeble heart. By the end of the week, her family will bury what is left of her ravaged body.

Toda is one of the 880,000 children under the age of five who died in this fashion in 1994. Her disease is not some exotic tropical illness. No researcher will write up her symptoms for a medical journal; they're simply too common to deserve special attention. Toda died of measles. Next year, one million or more "Todas" will die because they have not been immunized against the disease that causes this agonizing death. Another million will die of tetanus, in a series of racking spasms, and half a million will succumb to whooping cough, choking to death on their own bodily fluids. All of these debilitating diseases could be eradicated at the cost of about $5.00 per child, an almost insignificant sum in the more developed countries (MDCs) of the world, but a luxury beyond reach for many in the less developed countries (LDCs). In fact, according to the United Nations Children's Fund, four million young lives each year could be saved for an investment of $25 billion, less than half the money that U.S. citizens spend annually on beer (Roark, 1992).

In health and health care, we find a wide gap between the rich and poor nations of the world. In MDCs, significant numbers of people are overweight; in the poorer countries significant numbers of people are underfed, and must struggle to get enough food to prevent weight loss. Families in MDCs are likely to experience the death of an elderly member, perhaps a grandparent or even great-grandparent. In the poorest countries, however, the death of an infant or young child is common. The major health threats in wealthy countries are heart disease, cancer, and other conditions usually associated with old age. In the poorest countries, the biggest health threats are childhood diseases, as well as diarrhea, dysentery, schistosomiasis, malaria, typhoid, and many other diseases that had been almost eradicated in the more developed countries decades ago. In the wealthiest one-fifth of the world's countries, governments spent $1,860 per capita in 1990 on the health of their people; in the poorest one-fifth of the world, they spent $24 per capita that year (World Bank, 1993). In the LDCs, the children suffer most. Approximately one-fifth of the world loses one-half of its population before they live ten years.

Consistent with such observations are great differences in life expectancy. In the period between 1990 and 1995, a child born in the central region of Africa could expect to live 52 years; in Europe or North America, life expectancy is about 76 years. Taking the most extreme examples available, a baby born today in Japan can expect to live 79 years. Another baby born in Sierra Leone (Western Africa) or Afghanistan (Southern Asia) will, with average luck, live 43 years (Wright, 1993).

In the more developed countries, medical acclaim goes to achievements in organ transplants, prevention of genetic defects, saving of premature babies, and keeping terminal patients from dying for weeks, months, or maybe even years. In the poorest countries, the celebrated medical event is a decline in infant mortality, childhood diseases, or conditions linked to poor nutrition. In these respects, the MDCs and LDCs are extremely uneven. One medical concern, however, is shared by the entire world. We are now in the shadow of one of the world's pandemics (an epidemic occurring over a wide geographical area and affecting an exceptionally high proportion of the population) for which no cure is known: AIDS. The implications of this disease must be given considerable space; but first we will look at the more common problems of health and affliction in the advanced capitalist countries, Communist and formerly Communist countries, and in the less economically developed countries.

HEALTH PROBLEMS IN THE MDCs

In some respects, the United States, Western Europe, Canada, Australia, New Zealand, Japan, and similarly advanced countries can be quite self-congratulatory. All have very low infant mortality rates (IMRs), the number of babies per 1,000 live births who die in the first year of life. The rate in the United States in the early 1990s has ranged from 8.3 to 10, and 29 other countries do even better. In 1991, Japan had the world's lowest IMR, a mere 4 per thousand (Wright, 1993). Infant mortality rate is one of the best possible measures of the overall health of a country (see Table 4.1). Life expectancy is

another good indicator of health, and the countries named above have life expectancies for males in the low seventies and for females in the high seventies. In Japan, a girl born in the nineties can expect to live 82 years! (*The World Almanac and Book of Facts,* 1994). The United States, although its record is quite good in both IMR and life expectancy, is not at the top of the list in either. Although the world's leader in medical research and many kinds of intensive

Nations with Highest and Lowest Infant Mortality Rates, 1991		TABLE 4.1	
Nation	Infant mortality rate	Nation	Infant mortality rate
Highest Infant mortality		**Lowest Infant mortality**	
Western Sahara	177	Japan	4
Afghanistan	164	Austria	5
Angola	151	Liechtenstein	5
Sierra Leone	151	Switzerland	5
Guinea	144	Belgium	6
Central African Rep.	138	Denmark	6
Gambia	138	Finland	6
Malawi	136	France	6
Bhutan	135	Ireland	6
Chad	134	Italy	6
Mozambique	134	Spain	6
Niger	129	Sweden	6
Cambodia	125	Taiwan	6
Guinea-Bissau	125	Andorra	7
Laos	124	Canada	7
Liberia	124	Germany	7
Yemem	121	Iceland	7
Benin	119	Luxembourg	7
Burkina Faso	119	Netherlands	7
Bangladesh	118	Norway	7
Cameroon	118	United Kingdom	7
Nigeria	118	Australia	8
Djibouti	117	Monaco	8
Equatorial Guinea	116	San Marino	8
Somalia	116	Singapore	8
Ethiopia	114	Israel	9
Mali	114	Cyprus	10
Rwanda	110	Greece	10
Togo	110	United States	10

SOURCE: J. W. Wright, Ed., *The Universal Almanac* (Kansas City: Andrews and McMeel, 1993), p. 352.

care, the United States does not distribute medical care as evenly as Canada or most Western European countries. This fact has been a major concern of the Clinton administration, with Hillary Rodham Clinton recommending significant changes to existing policy.

Medical Costs

The cost of medical care has risen more rapidly than other costs in all medically advanced countries. In the United States, especially, health costs have risen faster than the general cost of living and increased as a percentage of the gross national product. According to Harvard University economist Joseph Newhouse, per capita spending on health care increased 1.4 percent per year between 1929 and 1940 and accounted for only 4 percent of the gross domestic product (GDP). But it grew by 4 percent per year after World War II and now accounts for 13.4 percent of the GDP (Collins, 1993). Figure 4.1 shows how the United States compares to four other economically advanced countries in terms of health-care expenditure as a percentage of the GDP. In some cases—Sweden is a prime example—the cost of a visit to the doctor is nominal. A

Swedish doctor will charge not more than $8.00 "whether for a hangnail or brain surgery" (Rosenbloom, 1988). Although the difference in what doctors charge patients and what they actually receive from the government is paid through very high taxes, the Swedish people continue to support the system, which they feel provides a fair return on their tax investment. In the late 1980s, the government did contract with private hospitals in two of its largest cities—Stockholm and Goteborg—to perform cataract, heart bypass, and hip replacement surgery, but nearly all other services are provided by the nationalized health system (Nelson, 1988a). Other European systems are similar, although not always so generous as the Swedish system. Table 4.2 shows that Europeans are significantly more satisfied with their health-care systems than are U.S. health-care consumers.

Most Western European governments require some kind of medical care for everyone (Nelson, 1988b). England, known for years for its free medical care, has had to impose charges for medicine to prevent exploitation of the system. The administrations of Margaret Thatcher in the 1980s and of John Major in the 1990s, were dedicated to cutting expenses and failed to support the health system very generously. Consequently, there are long waits for medical services of a nonemergency type, accompanied by considerable grumbling. Harry Nelson (1988b:A10) reported that 700,000 patients had

Figure 4.1
Costs of medical technology have contributed to the world's rising health-care expenditures.

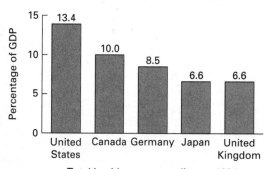

Total health-care expenditures, 1991

Source: S. Collins, "Saving Lives Isn't Cheap," *U.S. News & World Report,* June 7, 1993: 58.

Percentage of Populations Satisfied by Health-care System	TABLE 4.2
Netherlands	47%
Germany	41%
France	41%
Sweden	32%
Britain	27%
United States	10%

SOURCE: J. Havemann, "Diagnosis: Healthier in Europe," *Los Angeles Times,* Dec. 30, 1992: A1, A9.

to wait long periods for elective surgery at the end of the 1980s.

Whether medical care is funded by governments, insurance companies, or private individuals, the cost is a problem to all countries. It is considerably more of a problem when funded by private insurance companies whose sole reason for existence is to make a profit. In the 1990s, the United States (government, corporations, insurance plans, and individuals) spent $2,867 per capita on health care; Germany spent $1,659; France, $1,650; and Canada, $1,915 (Easterbrook, 1993).

Joseph A. Califano (1986), who was the U.S. Secretary of Health and Welfare during the Carter administration and later worked for the Chrysler Corporation on its health insurance programs, has written extensively about coping with health costs. His work with Chrysler revealed that the corporation was paying an unreasonable amount for employee health care, enough to add $530 to the price of every auto produced. Califano reasoned that the first problem was the noncompetitive market in which doctors and hospitals set their own rates and insurance companies paid unquestioningly. He negotiated for a hospital plan that would promise to hold down costs. Because the Chrysler medical bill was a huge one, the insurance corporation was willing to negotiate. A second problem that added to the company's health-care cost was workers' abuse of the system. Califano addressed the problem by instituting a small, employee-paid fee for each illness. Under the new system, far fewer employees got sick.

Chrysler also conducted an investigation revealing various sources of fraud. Workers' absences had been fraudulently reported by doctors. One chiropractor supplied fake injury reports to 1,895 automotive workers, who collected $1.4 million in disability from the "Big Three" auto manufacturers (Chrysler, Ford, General Motors). One worker obtained from doctors enough Valium (a tranquilizer) prescriptions for about 25 tablets per day—tablets that

bring a good price on the black market. Hospital stays for maternity cases doubled in length as soon as insurance payments were certain. Investigators found that back troubles had increased greatly for no apparent reason, and that 85 percent of hospital admissions for such problems should never have taken place. The cost to Chrysler was more than $1 million (Califano, 1986:19–21). Studies such as Califano's led to health-care and insurance reforms, saving millions of dollars for Chrysler and other companies that followed. It should be noted however, that a sizeable proportion of this so-called abuse may have been by employees taking advantage of medical services that previously had been unaffordable.

Califano also adopted the philosophy, and the services, of Health Maintenance Organizations (HMOs). Because HMOs receive a fixed amount for each person under their care, it is no longer to their economic disadvantage to keep their clients healthy. Some people fear that HMOs will be more hesitant to call in a specialist or order expensive tests. Califano found no cases of that kind, however.

Attempts are made in all countries to do something about medical costs. The United States government pays about 42 percent of the nation's health-care expense. The Swedish government, on the other hand, picks up 90 percent of its country's tab (Havemann, 1992). Table 4.3 shows that European governments cover a much higher percentage of health-care expense than does the U.S. The ratio of doctors to population is about the same in Europe as in the United States, but Europe has many more general practitioners than the United States. For example, more than two-thirds of Great Britain's physicians and half of Canada's are in general practice, as compared to only 10 percent of U.S. physicians (Gorman, 1992). The United States has the largest percentage of specialists of any country—90 percent. Depending on specialists, of course, drives up the cost of medical bills. Although a large proportion of specialists might

Share of Health-care Spending by Governments, and Private Individuals and Insurers	TABLE 4.3	
	Governments	Private
France	75%	25%
Germany	72	28
Britain	87	13
Italy	79	21
Netherlands	73	27
Sweden	90	10
United States	42	58

SOURCE: J. Havemann, "Diagnosis: Healthier in Europe," *Los Angeles Times*, Dec. 30, 1992: A1, A9.

be reassuring to people with unusual and threatening conditions, it should be noted that this "reassurance" is fostered by an overall occupational ideology that equates degrees of specialization (and high tech) with levels of competence—an ideology that is suspect. Such a skewed distribution in favor of specialists is not only unnecessary but, for many patients actually counterproductive. Finally, all geographical areas, especially rural areas, need more generalists than specialtists.

There is great economic motivation for U.S. medical students to enter specialties. According to Milton Terris (1990), the average annual income for family physicians and general practitioners is $87,120 and $79,910 respectively. However, a urologist earns $145,000; a plastic surgeon makes $179,170; an orthopedic surgeon, $193,300; a neurosurgeon, $236,460; and a cardiovascular surgeon, a whopping $271,550. It should be noted however, that even though there are income differentials by medical specialty (or nonspecialty), all physicians' incomes are considerably higher than the median U.S. income, which is about $34,000 per year.

Old Age and Medical Expense

For countries in which life expectancy extends well into the seventies or even the eighties,

medical costs are sure to rise. As we have noted, people in the MDCs live much longer than in years past and even in a few LDCs life expectancy is increasing sharply. The World Bank (1993:289) estimates that more than 19 percent of the U.S. population will be over age 65 by the year 2025, up from slightly less than 13 percent in 1991. In Japan, which is "graying" faster than other MDCs, more than one-fourth of the population will be over 65 years of age in 2025, compared to slightly more than 12 percent in 1991. In all of the more affluent societies, the aged are rapidly increasing as a percentage of the total population.

In the United States, the great majority of people over 65 live at home and are in reasonably good health. Between 50 and 80 percent of these senior citizens claim that they feel good, very good, or excellent (Pol, May, and Hartranft, 1992). Social gerontologist Kenneth J. Doka (1992) says that they are most interested in travel and educational activities. But, they are more prone to illnesses than they were in their prime years. A large number of them, especially those in their eighties and older, must be cared for in the kinds of facilities that, in the United States, are euphemistically called convalescent homes. In very many cases, patients who enter such nursing-care homes spend the remainder of their lives there. The cost of nursing homes, regardless of the quality of care, is often beyond the reach of any but the well-to-do. It is important to ask why the costs of nursing home care are so great, especially since the overwhelming majority of patient-care tasks are carried out by low-wage nurse's aides. The conflict perspective would point out that the goal of an owner of a nursing home is to maximize profit at the expense of clients. In the majority of cases, families run out of funds for nursing-home care and must resort to state assistance. Often state policies virtually force poverty upon the patient's family.

In the United States, neither Social Security nor private pension plans provide long-time

In the economically wealthy countries of Western Europe and North America, life expectancy is now about 76 years. These senior citizens participating in an Elderhostel mini-course show that many older people enjoy good health and remain physically active.

nursing care. Consequently, if need continues long enough, Medicaid must be depended upon. Medicaid is medical assistance to individuals who are poor (as opposed to Medicare which provides medical assistance to the elderly). A healthy spouse left at home can keep only a very small amount, ranging from $162 per month in Delaware to $640 in Alaska. Some believe that on net balance, Hillary Rodham Clinton's recommendation to the president could result in more losses than gains for some elders. Figure 4.2 shows an analysis of the Clinton plan by the staff of the *Los Angeles Times,* which says that retirees relying on Medicare may experience new restrictions on payments to doctors and hospitals which could limit access to care for Medicare beneficiaries.

Health Habits and Medical Costs

One strategy for reducing medical costs is to induce people to take care of themselves. Even before the Clinton administration proposed drastic changes to the health-care system, C. Everett Koop, U.S. Surgeon General in both the Reagan and Bush administrations, was an outspoken critic of industries that supported poor health habits.

One of Koop's favorite targets was the tobacco industry. Although the use of cigarettes has been decreasing in the United States, it has become a global health problem. People in the United States have cut per capita consumption in half since 1963. But, along with Germany and Japan, the United States still has one of the world's highest smoking rates (2,140 cigarettes per person annually). Japanese people consume 2,533 cigarettes per person each year, and Germans smoke 2,004 "cancer sticks" per person annually (Kane, 1993). Roughly half of all adult men and 10 percent of the women, worldwide, smoke cigarettes, and the rate is increasing at 2 percent per year (Mosley and Cowley, 1991). If that rate holds, the number of smokers will double in 35 years!

The health consequences of cigarette consumption are almost unbelievable. Each year, tobacco use causes more than 400,000 U.S. deaths; more than the number of deaths due to alcohol, cocaine, heroin, homicide, suicide, automobiles, and AIDS, combined (Mosley and Cowley, 1991:16).

As Americans became aware of cigarette-related health hazards, many people curtailed their smoking or quit altogether. Figure 4.3 shows that, while cigarette consumption was

Figure 4.2
The advantages and disadvantages of the Clinton health plan are applied to five typical health-care consumers.

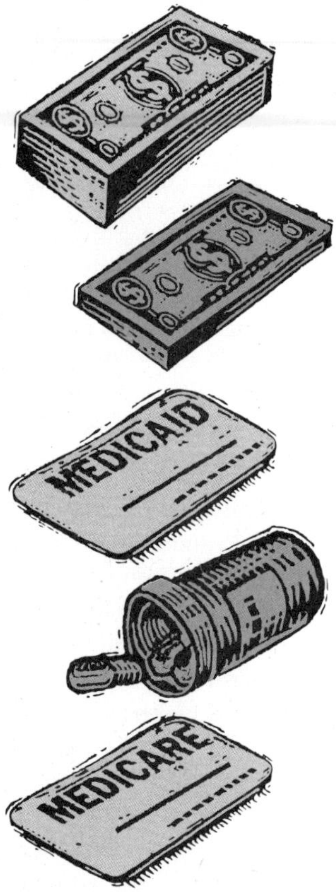

Family description	Gains	Losses
Family making $50,000 a year with good employer-provided insurance	Assured coverage, even if job is lost	Premium deductions may be greater than family now pays as its share of employer's medical plan
Family making $20,000 without insurance	Assured coverage	Some payroll deductions, with partial subsidies likely
Welfare family currently relying on Medicaid	Access to more doctors and broader coverage	None
Single person without insurance now and who can't get coverage because of current illness	Assured coverage despite existing illness	Some payroll deductions
Retiree relying on Medicare	Additional benefits, including some coverage for prescriptions and in-home care	New restrictions on payments to doctors and hospitals could limit access to care for Medicare beneficiaries

Source: R. Rosenblatt, E. Chen, C. Erskine, and K. Oelerich, "Health Care and You," *Los Angeles Times*, Sept. 23, 1993: A6.

declining in the United States after the 1960s, cigarette production worldwide continued to increase. One reason is the creation of new markets in developing countries. For example, South Korea now has a rate of 1,940 cigarettes per person per year. The figures for China and Brazil are 1,408 and 1,088, respectively. Poor countries have lower rates: Indonesia, 764; Kenya, 230; and Zimbabwe, 219. Russia does not have facilities to supply Russian demands, so R. J. Reynolds International is building factories there to produce an additional 22 billion cigarettes a

year (Kane, 1993:98). Once again, it is instructive to listen to the words of former U.S. Surgeon General Koop:

> It is reprehensible for industrial nations to export disease, death, and disability in the way of cigarette smoke to developing countries, putting on their backs a health burden that they will never be able to pay for 20 to 30 years from now. (Mosley and Cowley, 1991:17)

Cigarette companies have also increased their sales by targeting the female market. In the United

States, among females who smoke, the largest growing segment is adolescent girls. The connection with the U.S. culture's obsession with thinness and increased smoking among adolescent girls should not go unnoticed. Smoking depresses the appetite in many people, and U.S. girls who want to fit society's image of beauty may view smoking as a means to that end. In Spain, only 3 percent of women over 63 years of age ever smoked, but half of 20-year-old women now have the habit. Hal Kane (1993:98) points out that if "the share of Chinese women who smoke begins to approach that of men—70 percent—hundreds of millions more people will be at risk."

Alcoholism and drug abuse are additional means by which people undermine their health. Alcoholism and drug abuse overtax both public-health facilities and jails and are very difficult to control or stop. There is a great deal of public resentment of paying the costs of medical bills and disastrous accidents related to alcohol or drugs. Millions of people require medical care for problems related to cigarettes, alcohol, or other drugs. Often, the real problem is never treated; emphysema patients continue to smoke, cirrhosis patients continue to drink. Some suggest certain types of medical services be

limited for people whose life-styles contribute to illnesses. Specifically, some propose denying heart surgery to people who continue to smoke.

In the anticigarette fight, however, vested interest shows its hand. While the United States leads the propaganda barrage against cigarettes, it still subsidizes the tobacco industry. The U.S. tobacco industry has taken advantage of major increases in tobacco use in LDCs during the last 15 years. For example, India witnessed a 33 percent increase and Egypt a 138 percent increase. Other "new" markets include Japan, Taiwan, South Korea, and China (Chandler, 1986; Mosley and Cowley, 1991).

The use of drugs can also result in expensive health care. For example, a pregnant woman who uses "crack" cocaine will pass that addiction on to her child. The daily cost of U.S. hospital care for a crack baby is $2,000.

Other factors contribute to increasing health costs. For example, numerous malpractice lawsuits have resulted in expensive premiums for medical practitioners, and the higher costs are passed on to consumers. In the United States, the increased cost of medical insurance has resulted in a staggering 25 percent of Americans being uninsured.

Figure 4.3
While cigarette consumption is decreasing in the Unites States, world cigarette production continues to increase.

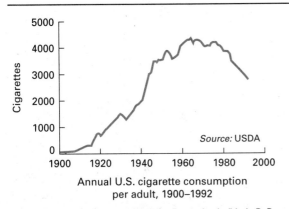

Annual U.S. cigarette consumption per adult, 1900–1992

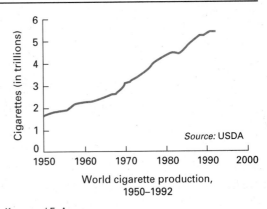

World cigarette production, 1950–1992

Source: H. Kane, "Cigarette Smoking Drops Again." In L. R. Brown, H. Kane, and E. Ayres, Eds. *Vital Signs* (New York: W.W. Norton, 1993), pp. 98–99.

Medical Inequality

Access to quality medical care varies widely from one MDC to another. In this section we will look at medical insurance and discuss the situations in the United States, Canada, and Western Europe.

Medical Insurance

The United States. The United States is the only major industrialized country that does not have universal health coverage. With regard to health insurance, there are three categories of individuals in the United States: those who are privately insured, those who are insured by Medicaid and Medicare, and those who are not insured. The first group is made up of individuals wealthy enough to buy their own medical insurance or who work for companies that offer medical insurance as a benefit. The second group is made up of citizens covered by federal programs that were established to assist the poor (Medicaid) and the elderly (Medicare). The last group, the uninsured, represents those without any medical insurance. Thirty-six million U.S. citizens, or 13 percent of the population, fall into this category, and their numbers are growing, both absolutely and proportionately to the population of the United States (Weissman and Epstein, 1994:133). People in this category tend to be in the working class or middle class and are uninsured because they make too much money to be eligible for Medicaid, but not enough to afford private insurance. Also, the research of Himmelstein and Woolhander (1992:5) shows that one out of four U.S. citizens, or 63 million people, lose their health insurance for some period of time during any two-year period. These facts and trends explain why so many U.S. citizens see medical insurance, or lack of it, as a serious social problem.

Another fact that does not escape the U.S. public is the rapidly expanding cost of medical care in the United States. Currently, health-care expenditures constitute more than 14 percent of the U.S. gross domestic product (GDP) (Weissman and Epstein, 1994:133). If nothing changes, health care will gobble up 18.9 percent of the U.S. GDP by the year 2000. And, it should be noted that the proportion of GDP going to health care is much higher in the United States than in MDCs with universal medical coverage. For example, the current proportion of GDP going into health care in the United States is 50 percent higher than in Canada, 75 percent higher than in Germany or France, and 300 times higher than in England (Schieber, Poullier, and Greenwald, 1993). Table 4.4 shows that although the United States ranks number 1 out of 24 MDCs on health expenditures, it ranks very low on how well health care is used and on health outcomes, such as infant mortality and life expectancy.

Uninsured individuals in the United States tend to be employed or the spouses and children of uninsured employed people. Table 4.5 shows that nearly 42 percent of the uninsured are fully employed people and their families. Another 40 percent of the uninsured are part-time workers and their families. Only 12.2 percent of the medically uninsured in the United States are unemployed individuals and their families. Another important fact presented in Table 4.5 is the predominance of children in the uninsured category of U.S. citizens. Nine and a half million children in the United States are not covered by health insurance.

What are the consequences of this system? Weissman and Epstein (1994:134–135) assert that the medical evidence shows that the uninsured are negatively affected in numerous ways: They are less likely to have a regular primary physician; they are more likely to receive care from emergency departments or hospital outpatient clinics; the waiting time to see a doctor is greater; they receive fewer preventive health services; they delay seeking care and hence, come to hospitals more severely ill; their lengths of stay

Rank of the U.S.A. among 24 OECD countries on Selected Indicators of Health Expenditure, Utilization, and Outcome	TABLE 4.4
Measure	**Rank**
EXPENDITURE	
Total health expenditures as a percentage of GDP, 1991	1
Per-capita health spending in U.S. dollars, 1985–1991	1
Excess health-care inflation (ranking out of 5 selected countries), 1985–1991	1
UTILIZATION	
Beds per 1,000 population, 1990	21
Admission rate (% population), 1989	18
Average length of stay (days), 1990	20
Physicians per 1,000, 1990	14
Physician contacts per capita, 1990	15
OUTCOME	
Infant mortality (deaths per 1,000 live births), 1990	4[a]
Life expectancy at birth, males (years), 1990	18
Life expectancy at birth, females (years), 1990	15

SOURCE: Data from Schieber, Poullier, and Greenwald, 1993, cited on page 2 of Weissman and Epstein, 1994.

OECD = Organization for Economic Cooperation and Development; GDP = Gross domestic product.

[a]The low number indicates poor health status outcome.

in hospitals are short; they use fewer discretionary high-cost procedures; and the quality of their care is often compromised.

Lack of adequate insurance is probably the primary reason for the disparity of low birth weight between white babies and African American infants. Low birth weight is the major cause of infant mortality, and African Americans experience the phenomenon more than twice the rate for whites (18.6 for U.S. blacks, 8.1 for U.S. whites). Low birth weight and, consequently, infant mortality is attributed to four pregnancy problems: infection or rupture of the amniotic membrane, premature labor, high blood pressure, and uterine bleeding. All of these conditions, accounting for 81 percent of underweight births, are treatable ("A Question of Color," 1992). However, African Americans, who are disproportionately poor, lack insurance or sufficient income to seek treatment.

If the U.S. health system is so costly, yet inefficient, and certainly inequitable with regard to who receives quality health care, why does the system persist? It may come as a surprise that there were many times in U.S. history when universal health coverage was almost made the law of the land. National health insurance was on the platform of the Bull Moose ticket of Teddy Roosevelt when he ran for president in 1912 (Ginzberg, 1994:1,51). Support for national health insurance reemerged periodically (in the mid thirties, the late forties and the mid seventies), but it never materialized (Ginzberg, 1994:51–52). The conflict perspective would ask, Who benefits from the present arrangement and would not like to see a national health insurance plan instituted? According to Victor R. Fuchs (1983:142), physicians, drug companies, and the insurance companies have the most to lose if a national plan is instituted, and they can be

Uninsured Population by Employment Status of Family Head and by Dependent Status, 1991		TABLE 4.5
Family head	**Number without health insurance (millions)**	**Percentage of total uninsured**
Worker, full-time, full-year	9.7	26.6
Adult dependents	2.1	5.9
Children	5.5	15.0
Other worker	10.8	29.8
Adult dependents	1.0	2.6
Children	2.8	7.8
Nonworker	2.0	5.6
Adult dependents	1.2	3.2
Children	1.2	3.4
Total	36.3	100.0

Note: Nonelderly population. The definition of full-year worker in this table is slightly different from previous usage. In this table, EBRI analysts consider workers full-year only if they were never unemployed and looking for work. In previous usage, workers could be full-year even if they had short periods of unemployment.

Source: Adapted from Foley, 1993, Table 7; data from March 1992 CPS, cited on page 35 of Weissman and Epstein, 1994.

expected to fight any change with a tenacious effort. For example, insurance companies, which take a 25 percent cut of health-care expenditures, can now drop someone with a serious disease and can refuse coverage for a prospective customer who may have a debilitating disease or has a family member with such a disease. Hence, these "expensive" clients are culled from the insurance companies' medical rolls and the profits are much higher. Uninsured people with serious medical problems are left "out in the cold." One major reason that medical costs are higher in the United States than in other MDCs is because its health-care system is funding a multi-billion-dollar insurance industry—an expense that is avoided in other MDCs, like Canada.

Canada. Unlike the United States, Canada does have universal health coverage. Figure 4.4 compares the United States and Canada on how one gains and loses medical coverage. In Canada, one achieves medical coverage by becoming a citizen and one loses coverage by losing citizenship. It isn't that simple in the United States.

Canada's national health insurance is funded from general federal and provincial revenues and the vast majority of health care in Canada is conducted in private medical offices by private physicians on a fee-for-service basis. The fees are set and closely monitored by the federal government and physicians bill the national health insurance system for their services (Roemer, 1991:167). A major component in the 1984 Canada Health Act is a provision to deal with physicians who "extra bill." According to Milton Roemer (1991:167), "To discourage or eliminate extra billing, it [the 1984 Canada Health Act] provided that federal allotments to the provinces would be reduced by the estimated amounts that physicians collected for extra billings of 'user charges.' Very soon, all provinces had passed legislation prohibiting such noninsured payments by patients." The various administrative strategies employed by the Canadian government and the provincial governments have been quite successful in controlling health-care expenditures. In 1985 the total health system in Canada absorbed 8.6 percent of the country's

GNP, compared to 11 percent in the United States (Roemer, 1991:167).

Opponents of national health insurance in the United States list a number of things that might occur if such a plan were instituted:

Physicians will leave the country in droves; medical school applications will drop; physicians' incomes will decline; physicians will be swamped with work; the quality of medical care will deteriorate; and the free choice of physician

How people get coverage		How people lose coverage	
United States	**Canada**	**United States**	**Canada**
Get a job that offers insurance	Become a citizen	Lose job	Lose citizenship
Get married (to spouse with insurance)		Change jobs (with a pre-existing condition)	
Have parents with insurance		Get sick, lose job	
Qualify for Medicaid • Become pregnant • Become disabled • Lose job • Become poor		Become self-employed	
		Lose income (cannot afford premium)	
		Get divorced	
Qualify for Medicare • Turn 65 • Become permanently disabled • Have end-stage renal failure		Grow up and leave home	
		Get a job (lose Medicaid)	
		Children grow up or leave (lose Medicaid)	
Qualify for Veteran's Assistance		Leave prison	
Enter prison		Leave the Army	
Enter the Army (or be a dependent)		Leave a Native American reservation (leave tribe)	
Buy your own policy		Insurance company denies coverage to group	
Reside in a Native American reservation (as a member of a tribe)		Insurance company folds	
		Insurance carrier cancels contract	
Purchase individual or group policy			

Figure 4.4
How citizens of the United States and Canada obtain and lose health-care coverage.

Source: Cited in J. Weissman and M. Epstein, *Falling Through the Safety Net: Insurance and Access to HealthCare* (Baltimore: Johns Hopkins University Press, 1994), p. 27.

will disappear. The Canadian experience has proved all of the above false (Roemer, 1991:169). Instead of leaving in droves, doctors have been coming to Canada from other countries and medical school applications have risen. Doctors' incomes, which were already high in Canada, have been increasing while their work weeks have been shortened. The quality of medical care has improved and the free choice of physician has not disappeared, but has been enhanced, since every citizen, independent of income, can select his or her doctors (Roemer, 1991:169). It should be noted that, unlike the United States, Canada has an extremely low incidence of malpractice actions against physicians. It is possible that the strict controls on quality of medical care in Canada, which is part of the national health insurance system, is responsible for the low rate of malpractice actions.

Western Europe.   With regard to health insurance, countries in Western Europe fall into two major categories. Countries included in the "welfare-oriented health systems" have a very high proportion, but not 100 percent, of their populations covered with health insurance. The rest of the Western European countries fall into the "comprehensive health system" category (Roemer, 1991:129), in which every individual is covered. We will look at Germany as an example of a country in the first category and Sweden as a country in the second category.

The universal health system of Germany has its roots in the various "sickness societies" that were organized in the 1800s (Roemer, 1991:131; Anderson, 1989:79–88). There "societies" were local cooperatives organized by various occupations. They required workers to pay into the system and later, through bargaining, required employers to contribute. These societies were the origin of Social Security, an idea that eventually spread throughout the world (Roemer, 1991:131). As time went on, the number of sickness funds grew to number more than 1,500.

The German government has made it mandatory to contribute to a fund, if not an occupationally based fund, then a substitute one. Only a fraction of one percent of the German population is not covered by a sickness fund. A typical benefit package includes physicians' fees, hospitalization, dental care, eye care, rehabilitative care, and cash compensation for loss of wages due to sickness (Roemer, 1991:132).

Sweden's national health insurance program covers every citizen. Employers and the federal government fund the general health insurance system, but hospital services (including physicians' salaries) are largely funded by general revenues from the 22 counties in Sweden (Roemer, 1991:209). A number of federal legislative acts have led to a proliferation of community health centers in Sweden. Typically, these centers are staffed by two to four general practitioners, nurses, and ancillary staff, and are financed by the health insurance program (Roemer, 1991:209). Private medical practice has become a rarity in Sweden; only 5 percent of doctors now devote their entire time to private practice (Roemer, 1991:209–210). Even though Sweden's universal health insurance is costly—consuming 9.1 percent of the GDP—it is less expensive than that of the United States (Roemer, 1991:210).

Medical Inequality and Socioeconomic Status

Studies show that death rates differ with socioeconomic status. Researcher Gregory Pappas analyzed the findings of two 1986 nationwide studies of more than 44,000 Americans aged 25 to 64, and compared them with similar studies conducted in 1960. He found a death rate for white, male high school dropouts of 9 per 1,000 in 1960, and 7.6 per 1,000 in 1986. By comparison, the death rates for white male college graduates were 5.7 and 2.8, respectively. Disparities grew with differences in income and race (see Figure 4.5). Pappas concluded that socioeconomic status probably affects many factors that

Figure 4.5
Death rate per 1,000 people aged 24 to 64 years in the United States for 1986, by income, race, and gender.

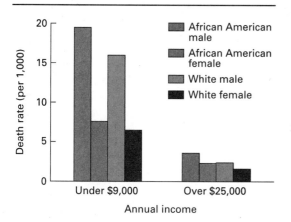

contribute to death, such as diet, exercise, control of disorders like high blood pressure, and smoking (Haney, 1993).

Earlier we stated that health worries in the MDCs tend to center around heart problems, cancer, and problems such as Alzheimer's disease. Diseases such as tuberculosis (TB) are generally thought to be under control. Yet TB is making a comeback in New York City, and it is closely associated with poverty and lack of proper care. The Centers for Disease Control and Prevention, in a severely damning report, says that "New York City has been fiddling while the infection burned through its shelters and poorest neighborhoods (Monmaney and McKillop, 1988:69)." Harlem, a mostly African American section of New York, had a rate of 130 cases per 100,000 people, 13 times as high as the national average and second only to Haiti as the Tuberculosis Center of the Western Hemisphere. Approximately one-fourth of the cases involve people with AIDS, who are very susceptible, but it also takes a very high toll on malnourished children (Monmaney and Mckillop, 1988:70). Although no country has better medical facilities than the United States, it remains a moral dilemma that conditions exist that most people

think of as occurring only in lands of poverty and underdevelopment.

Ironically, the United States had the lowest rate of tuberculosis in modern history in 1984. Despite the evidence from Harlem, little was done to arrest this once easily treated disease. By 1992 the U.S. rate had increased by 16 percent. At that time, young African American men in New York experienced 345 cases per 100,000 people. In migrant-labor camps in North Carolina, the rate among U.S.-born African Americans was 3,600 cases per 100,000 people. Although tuberculosis was once under control, changing social conditions have led to a spectacular comeback for the illness. Facilities for the homeless with so many people crowded into such little space offer the tuberculosis bacterium a place to spread easily. Ordinarily, the body's defense system holds the germ in check, and nine out of ten carriers suffer no symptoms. But if the immune system is weakened by poor diet, poor sanitation, or HIV infection, the disease ravages the lungs and can spread to other organs, including the liver, kidneys, and brain. About half of the TB victims with weakened systems die (Cowley, Leonard, and Hager, 1992).

To make matters worse, drug-resistant forms of the disease are developing. A study conducted in the early 1990s showed that 19 percent of the tuberculosis cases in New York City were resistant to the most commonly used tuberculosis-fighting drugs ("U.S. Announces Plan to Fight Drug-Resistant Tuberculosis," 1992). Strains of tuberculosis become drug-resistant when a victim does not complete the drug therapy, allowing the germ to build an immunity to the medicine. In New York City, the disease jumped from 1,300 cases in 1988 to 3,700 cases in 1991. Worldwide, 1.7 billion people are infected with the disease and about 3 million victims die annually (Wright, 1993:210). Because of this resurgence of TB, the National Multidrug-Resistant Tuberculosis Task Force, part of the Centers for Disease Control and Prevention, has suggested a nationwide surveillance of drug resistance

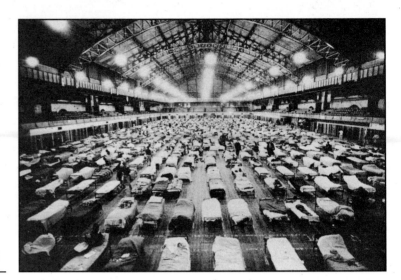

Illness spreads more easily when people live in crowded conditions. This shelter for homeless people in New York City is a natural breeding ground for diseases like tuberculosis.

among TB patients, quarantining uncooperative patients who may otherwise spread the disease, and helping to establish TB programs in countries whose citizens frequently emigrate to the United States, like the Philippines, Korea, and Mexico. However, even with occasional outbreaks of disease, as the United States is now experiencing with TB, the MDCs do significantly better at controlling them than do the LDCs.

Moral Dilemmas in Medicine

Moral dilemmas arise in many areas related to health care. Should society take on the task of watching us all to make sure we do not smoke or drink or even live mainly on greasy potato chips or "junk food"? Another, more subtle but no less real, moral dilemma exists when such unhealthy practices are promoted and glamorized by industries that choose to continue to sell these products. Medical science also is confronted with a large number of dilemmas.

Rationing of Life

Serious moral dilemmas accompany medicine. The first dilemma has to do with the "rationing of life," and economics is generally involved. In Great Britain only limited funds are provided to each district for health care, and health care must be rationed. Wealthy people can pay for private care, but poor people cannot. In a sense, life is rationed. In the United States, a similar rationing of life occurs. Between 1981 and 1985, an estimated 700,000 children and 567,000 senior citizens lost their Medicaid benefits because of changes in government policy (Califano, 1986:183). An inhuman manner of health-care rationing in the United States is that done by insurance companies. Most of the health care in the U.S. is handled by the private sector, so that is where many critical-care decisions are made. Many insurance companies cancel people's coverage when they contract a costly disease, or refuse to pay for certain kinds of treatments for some of their insured (liver transplants, for example).

New Diagnostic Tools and Tests

Another dilemma involves new and better diagnostic tools and tests. Magnetic Resonance Imaging (MRI) is capable of producing "pictures" of internal soft-tissue abnormalities that earlier technology could not detect. This means that tumors can be detected when they are very small and still operable. Years ago, such abnormalities might not have been noticeable until the patient was in critical condition. Computerized Tomography (CT), a highly advanced form of X ray that allows a technician to see an internal organ from various angles and "slice" into its internal structure, was utilized 300,000 times in 1980, but doctors prescribed 1,500,000 CT scans in 1991 (Samuelson, 1993). These new medical tests are very expensive. They are often overprescribed for the rich and insured and not used for the poor and uninsured. As mentioned earlier, there is a rationing of health care and different classes of people do not benefit equally from these innovations. How much money is wasted on overprescribed medical tests and how many people die from disorders that could have been detected earlier had medical tests (like an MRI) been used?

New medical tests also present dilemmas. Amniocentesis, a test of the fluid surrounding the fetus, is given to pregnant women to determine the health of the fetus. It has been widely used to detect abnormalities such as Down's syndrome, a condition that causes mild to severe retardation. In the case of an abnormality, some parents choose to have an abortion.

Amniocentesis can also detect the sex of the unborn child. Although not a problem in the United States, in countries where boys are greatly preferred it may have serious consequences. The percentage of male births has increased in both Korea and Japan, indicating that more females are aborted. The result could be a disproportionate number of males and a shortage of females in years to come. Such an outcome could change the status of women, for better or worse. It might also leave a large population of unmarried males, which could be a disruptive force in the society, as the unmarried males would not be able to have families and children.

There are other conditions in which knowledge of the future is at best a mixed blessing. Huntington's disease, for example, is very destructive, both physically and mentally,

although the symptoms do not develop until the victim is about 40. Those who have at least one parent afflicted with it can take a test to find out if they have a 50 percent chance of eventually developing Huntington's disease as well. However, few people actually take the test; most prefer to wait and cling to hope.

Knowledge of predisposition to ailments like Huntington's disease could lead to discrimination. For instance, if a person has a 50 percent chance of developing the disease, why hire him or her for a permanent position? This is obviously one way that newfound medical abilities can cause social problems. What damage might we do if we find predictive factors in alcoholism or in drug addiction? We can easily imagine such a prediction becoming a self-fulfilling prophecy. As a matter of fact, studies have been conducted in criminology in an attempt to isolate physical factors in proneness to criminal violence (Stolberg, 1993a; 1993b). A consequence could easily be strong prejudice against people showing such traits, which might then drive them to crime. Fortunately, few people from the medical world have turned their attention to such types of prediction.

Improvements in Medical Skills

Dramatic improvements in medical skills will continue. For example, in 1970, 14,000 heart bypass surgeries were performed in the United States. In 1991 this procedure, which requires a highly skilled team of medical personnel, was performed 407,000 times, an increase of more than 2,800 percent (Samuelson, 1993:32). But as Figure 4.6 shows, the increased use of new technologies and complex medical treatment have sent the cost of health care soaring. In the early 1990s, it cost about $20,000 for an annual dose of growth hormones to a child with a severe deficiency, $49,000 for coronary bypass surgery, and $3.75 for a single aspirin administered in a psychiatric hospital (Castro, 1991). The main reason that the prices of inexpensive treatments

Figure 4.6
The soaring costs of health care in the United States.

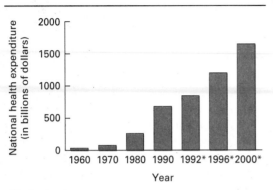

*Projection

Source: R.J. Samuelson, "Health Care: How We Got into This Mess," *Newsweek*, Oct. 4, 1993: 32.

like aspirin are so high is that they are driven up to subsidize more expensive treatments.

Increased Life Expectancy and Bioethics

Additional moral dilemmas in the field of medicine have accompanied increases in life expectancy. These dilemmas have led to increasing interest in **bioethics,** a discipline dealing with the ethical implications of medical advancements. For centuries, the cornerstone of medical ethics has been the Hippocratic oath, through which medical doctors vow that they will preserve life whenever possible and never knowingly do harm to a patient. One moral dilemma for doctors is the question of how long life should be preserved, if prolonged life amounts only to prolonged misery. Are there cases in which mercy killing, **euthanasia,** should be permitted? Between 1990 and 1994, Dr. Jack Kevorkian, often referred to as "Dr. Death," assisted in the suicides of 20 terminally ill people (Shapiro and Bowermaster, 1994). To allow a person to die without every possible type of medical intervention is considered contrary to medical tradition. Religions have usually ruled against euthanasia, even in cases of incurable and painful illness. Yet even conservative religious opinion is not completely united on the issue. The conservative Pope Pius XII in 1957 ruled that in cases in which no hope exits, it is the primary duty of the physician to relieve pain, even if the means for doing so are inconsistent with prolonging life. State laws have been varied on the matter of euthanasia. Consequently, in many hospitals doctors are careful not to put in writing any instruction to terminate life-preserving measures, even if those measures are directed mainly at prolonged suffering. However, it is possible for people to make living-will declarations asking that resuscitory measures be ended if there is no possibility of recovery. Every U.S. state has either a living-will or a durable-power-of-attorney statute (Choices in Dying, 1993). Such documents pertain to a phenomenon called **negative euthanasia,** that is, allowing people to die, but not aiding the process.

The Netherlands has become the most permissive country in what is called **positive euthanasia,** which amounts to actually terminating the life of a hopeless and suffering patient. To do so requires that a document calling for such treatment was made by the patient at a time when he or she was mentally capable of such a decision. Several doctors must be consulted, and in cases of extreme pain, a lethal shot can be administered to produce what the Dutch call *milde dood,* or mild death. Pieter Admiraal, a physician influential in making such a law in the Netherlands, says euthanasia is more widely practiced than is commonly acknowledged. "They administer the good death nearly everywhere in Europe," he says. "The difference is that we (Dutch) are less hypocritical about it. Everywhere they do it but do not talk about it; here the debate is always open. Here we can speak of euthanasia" (Clark, Gosnell, and Shapiro, 1991:53). Admiraal claims that negative euthanasia via withdrawal of life support results in a long period of suffering before death finally occurs. The only kindly death, he says, is one administered by the doctor or by patients themselves.

In the Netherlands, a majority of people (64 percent) approve of the law permitting euthanasia, and it now accounts for about 7.5 percent of deaths there. In the opinion of some moralists, only God can decide the time of death. In Admiraal's view, the right to choose helps protect the free will in which most moralists believe.

HEALTH CARE IN FORMERLY COMMUNIST AND COMMUNIST COUNTRIES

State-supported health care had been a promise of the Communist countries that comprised the Soviet Union. In a few cases, East Germany and Czechoslovakia, health care was reasonably good before Communist government took control. In the majority of cases, though, health care had been good only for the elite, and average life expectancy was far below present-day standards.

Eastern Europe and the Former Soviet Union

Among the egalitarian dreams of communism were the provision of free and good medical care. In some respects, the results were impressive. Michael Kaser (1976) wrote quite favorably of the system in his study of medicine in Eastern Europe. Medical standards were not quite uniform for every country, but basically all the people were covered by free, cradle-to-grave medical care. During the 30 years from the end of World War II until publication of the study, infant mortality declined from 80 to 20 per 1,000 live births. A later study by Henry P. David (1982) showed that rates in Bulgaria and Czechoslovakia had dropped below 20 infant deaths per 1,000 live births, and East Germany's rate fell to 12, comparable to the rate in the United States at the time.

Life expectancy in the USSR rose from 44.5 years for males at the end of World War II to 66.1 years in 1966; for females, from 47 to 69.5 years. By the early 1990s, however, it decreased to 63.8 years for men and 67.2 years for women. Today, one-third of Russian men do not live until their sixtieth birthday (Goldberg, 1992). Czechoslovakia (now the Czech Republic and the Slovak Republic, also known as Slovakia) and Hungary, by contrast, have done quite well, each having an average life expectancy of 72 years (Wright, 1993:328).

Food shortages throughout Eastern Europe took priority over health care in the 1950s and 1960s, but by the 1970s the Soviet Union had made serious progress in matters of public health. However, the 1990s have created new health problems for Russia and several other members of the Commonwealth of Independent States (CIS).

The Soviet Union/Russia

In terms of numbers of medical personnel, the former Soviet Union had an extensive system. In the early 1990s, there were 1.3 million doctors in the Soviet Union, approximately twice as many as in the United States; there were 13 hospital beds per 1,000 people, slightly more than in the United States. In 1991 the Russian Federation maintained its lead with 4.69 doctors and 13.8 hospital beds per 1,000 people. The figures for the United States were 2.38 and 5.3, respectively (World Bank, 1993:208–209). However, given the miserable health of so many of its people, writes Yale historian Paul Kennedy, "the large numbers of doctors claimed by Soviet statistics became meaningless" (Kennedy, 1993:235).

Some of Russia's medical facilities are among the world's best, such as Dr. Fyodorov's eye clinic, which attracts patients from all over the world. Nevertheless, the health of the Soviet people lags behind that of people in the United States and Western Europe. For example, in 1990 the United States, the United Kingdom, Australia, New Zealand, the Netherlands, Germany, Finland,

Norway, and Canada all had 10 or fewer cases of tuberculosis per 100,000 people; 56 out of every 100,000 Russians had the disease. The extreme case among the present member nations of the CIS is Tajikistan, which has an annual incidence rate of tuberculosis of 133 per 100,000 people (World Bank, 1993:206–207).

In the late 1980s, many people were treated by *feldshers,* health workers trained in the prevention of disease and who can treat minor medical emergencies. A *feldsher* is also trained to know when a patient needs a physician (Nelson, 1988d). Ordinarily, people received health care from a *polyclinic,* the basic unit of the Soviet health system. About 80 percent of treatment took place in these multipurpose clinics located near large apartment complexes. Children had special pediatric polyclinics in each neighborhood.

Ambulance service was among the best in the world. In Moscow, for instance, a central ambulance control dispatched 7,000 ambulances each day. Any Soviet citizen could obtain an ambulance simply by dialing a central telephone number. If the person who summoned the ambulance was suffering from any symptom associated with a heart problem, the ambulance would bear a cardiologist, a *feldsher* or nurse, as well as the driver.

Although the system was well organized, it was not without major problems. As is the case with almost every commodity, there were shortages of antibiotics, oxygen, monitoring equipment, disposable needles, and nearly all other types of medical necessities. According to diagnoses, about 150,000 patients annually needed cardiac bypass surgery, but Soviet physicians could only perform about 15,000 operations. The country had only about half of the cardiac clinics that it needed. And although Russian medical schools graduate 35,000 doctors a year (in the United States, the number is 16,000), many of them are poorly trained.

After the collapse of the Soviet system, the health-care system deteriorated quickly. Tuberculosis, a good index of public health, is increasing dramatically. All kinds of disease are increasing as food prices outstrip wage increases, and levels of nutrition drop. In hospitals, syringes are used over and over, despite widespread publicity about an incident in the city of Elista in 1989. In one of Elista's clinics, 41 infants contracted AIDS because they were injected with infected needles (Efron, 1993:A8).

One of the problems of resuscitating the Russian health system involves switching from a centrally planned system of entrenched bureaucracies to a free-market system. The medical system in post–Cold War Russia is disintegrating and the public health is suffering as a result. Diphtheria, once almost eradicated, is back in dramatic proportion (Efron, 1993). In addition, Murry Feshbach (cited in Goldberg, 1992:A13) says that about 70 million Russians live in cities with air that is unfit to breathe. In the city of Perm, children are 3.4 times more likely to get a blood disease than their counterparts in less polluted cities. Food allergies have also increased because pollutants taint produce and packaged goods. Conditions are so bad that many women are deciding not to have children. Mikhail Nezhirenk (cited in Goldberg, 1992), chief doctor at Children's Hospital No. 2 in Rostov-on-Don, says, "We have very bad pregnancies among our women; that's problem No. 1. The children are born and they're already sick, and the ecology works on the immune system and weakens the child further."

STDs in Russia.   In 1971, the Soviet Union's leaders passed a law that established both civil and criminal sanctions against anyone who contracted a sexually transmitted disease (STD) and refused to submit to treatment and reveal the names of sexual partners. Upon disclosure, the "patient" was then sent to one of the nation's 42 high secu-

In Russia, special hospitals that treat people with sexually transmitted diseases, like the psychiatric hospital pictured here, resemble prisons more than health treatment centers.

rity hospitals, which more closely resembled jails than treatment centers. Despite the fact that most cases of syphilis and gonorrhea could be cured with a single injection of antibiotics, patients were kept in these medical prisons a month or more. Standard care included being treated like a criminal and receiving daily injections of weak Soviet-made antibiotics. Finally, when patients were released, their official release forms indicated that they had been treated for a noncontagious skin disease, but only if the patient had been docile. Uncooperative patients were threatened with prolonged hospital time and a true accounting of the reason for their incarceration.

In post–Soviet Russia, the ministry is gradually closing such hospitals. But the public is still skeptical, and many people who contact STDs purchase penicillin through the underground market. This raises the possibility that disease rates are higher than those officially reported. According to official sources, political liberalization and provocative advertising in Russia's developing free-market system have given birth to a sexual revolution. There has been a veritable explosion of prostitution and pornography. This has been accompanied by an eightfold increase in syphilis in just five years. In 1988 Russia's rate of syphilis was 4.4 per 100,000 people; in 1992, 13.4; in 1993, 32.3! In the city of Cheboksary, by 1993, the syphilis rate increased to 20 times what it had been in 1990 (Efron, 1994).

Other STDs are more common. The gonorrhea rate is 211.4 cases per 100,000 people. Chlamydia is so widespread that it has become the major cause of infertility in women. The first Russian case of AIDS was reported in 1987. By 1994, there were 717 active cases, and 83 people had died of the illness (Efron, 1994:A10).

Public-health officials believe there are three causes for the skyrocketing increase of STDs: (1) unrestricted travel out of and into the country, which had been highly restricted during the Communist era, (2) increasing rates of unemployment among women, causing a marked rise in prostitution, and (3) the large number of refugees settling in Russia from war-torn areas of the former Soviet Union, like the Caucasus and Tajikistan. Although the old controls were overly restrictive, they were effective in controlling the spread of STDs. For example, under the Soviet system, sailors were not allowed to wander around foreign ports unless they were accompanied by a KGB (secret service) guard. Now many Russian sailors visit prostitutes in far-off lands and return home with syphilis.

Additionally, there has been virtually no sex education in Russia, although some AIDS prevention programs exist. The average citizen is strongly biased against the use of condoms; domestically produced condoms are thick and unreliable, the subject of many jokes.

However, the Russian medical community is trying to respond to the needs of the people. For example, as of 1994, four hospitals were allowed to import and sell antibiotics, supplied by UNICEF for $0.39 per dose (Efron, 1994:A10). As word spreads that some STDs (not AIDS, of course) can be cured with a single injection, the public may begin to change its collective mind about the medical community.

Poland

Like health care in Russia, the situation in Poland seems to be worsening. The reason is not a shortage of doctors; there are 2.06 per 1,000 people, as compared to 2.38 per 1,000 in the United States (World Bank, 1993:209). The problem is due to general economic troubles in Poland which cause the government to skimp on foreign purchases, including medical supplies. The shortages are wide-ranging; everything from cotton gauze to antibiotics to surgical supplies are in short supply. Patients often have long waiting periods for the pharmaceuticals they need, even though public drives are made to raise money for the needed supplies.

The price of drugs in Poland is very low, and prescriptions are free to veterans, pensioners, military personnel, and many more. The low prices may be part of the problem; it is suspected that there is a black market through which drugs are smuggled out of the country to be sold at world-market prices. The distribution system within the county is also very bad so that even drugs manufactured within the country are nonexistent in many areas (Kaser, 1976:136).

Despite the lack of general medical equipment, 98 percent of children under 1 year of age have been immunized against diphtheria, pertussis, and tetanus (DPT), compared to only 67 percent in the United States, and 94 percent have received immunization against measles, as compared to 80 percent in the United States (World Bank, 1993:209).

The People's Republic of China

Although health care in the People's Republic of China has a long way to go, no other country has made such rapid strides under adverse circumstances. China has also accomplished what the World Health Organization (WHO) is advocating in all the less developed countries—a system in which the people themselves play an important role, and not just in urban centers, but at the village level. In the early days of the Communist revolution, health care was considered a priority, but China lacked the doctors necessary for its vast population. Even by 1965, China had only one physician for every 3,780 people. By 1992 the numbers had improved to 646 individuals per doctor, and about 95 percent of children under 1 year of age were immunized against DPT and measles (*World Almanac and Book of Facts 1994,* 752).

On the order of the revolutionary leader, Mao Ze-dong (1949–1976), medicine was to meet four criteria: (1) serve the masses, (2) put preventive medicine first in order of importance, (3) launch mass campaigns to popularize cleanliness and health care, and (4) integrate Chinese traditional medical beliefs with modern Western medicine (Rosenthal, 1987).

To provide medical care to a population that even then numbered well over 800 million (it is now about 1.2 billion), was a challenge that could be met only by doctors with much less training than doctors would receive in the Western countries. These Chinese doctors, trained in at least rudimentary care, have long been referred to as the "barefoot doctors," a term that appears not to have been pejorative. They

A "barefoot doctor" in Cambodia practices "cupping," placing warm glass jars on the patient's back, to cure an upper-respiratory infection. Millions of people throughout China and Southeast Asia rely on such traditional treatments from birth to death.

were trained hurriedly, and in tremendous numbers. Often a man or woman from a particular village who was known for a background in medical lore and herbal knowledge, or who had successful experience as a midwife, would become the village doctor. A short term of formal medical training was added to his or her traditional skills. Even in their early service, the barefoot doctors brought improved medical care, cleanliness, and immunizations. Infant mortality rates dropped, which helped the government realize that drastic measures should be taken for birth control (see Chapter 5). By 1991 life expectancy in China had become long enough to take the country out of the category of LDC insofar as health is concerned: 69 years for males and 72 for females, up from 54 and 55, respectively, in 1965 (World Bank, 1993:238; *World Almanac and Book of Facts 1994*:752).

With permission of the government, certain concessions were made to ancient tradition. Acupuncture was, and is, practiced. Acupuncture consists of inserting needles into the body at various points to cure illness and to relieve pain. Although it is controversial, many cures have been attributed to acupuncture, and it has advo-

cates in the Western world. It has been effective as a pain reliever and, as such, has been helpful in surgery when modern anesthesia was not available. Chinese herbalists continue to practice their skills, and they are generally regarded as creditable healers of many conditions.

HEALTH CARE IN THE LDCs

An Overview

While the more developed countries devote the major part of their medical skill and technology to saving the lives of elderly people, the people of the less developed countries struggle to save the lives of their children. Every year in the LDCs, 14 or 15 million children die before the age of 5. Africa, Asia, and Latin America account for 88 percent of the world's births and 98 percent of the world's deaths among children under age 5. According to UNICEF, 95 percent of the 14.5 million deaths of infants and children in LDCs in 1990 were preventable (Mosley and Cowley, 1991:8). So much of the less developed world,

Focus on Suriname

Medical Lessons from the Rain Forest

There are shamans in the Amazon rain forest who know a large number of medicinal plants that relieve pain and even cure a variety of ailments. Just as with the Chinese folk cures, however, the explanation for their curing ability is quite foreign to Western thinking. The work of the shaman is always aided by what modern doctors would compare to a placebo effect, that is, taking medicine makes the patient feel better regardless of whether the medicine has an effect on the sickness. Hence, a good shaman will not only administer medicine, but he will dance frantically, take something hallucinogenic in order to have visions, beat drums, and make as much noise as possible in order to frighten the evil spirits that cause sickness. All this sounds absurd to modern doctors, so they have paid too little attention to one aspect of the treatment: some of the medicines work. Many doctors and botanists have become interested in the plants of the rain forest, which form a medical cornucopia that has been largely overlooked.

Mark J. Plotkin, an ethnobotanist, made repeated trips to the rain forest of Suriname, to the northeast of the great Amazon river. He was able to make contact with the Tirios, a very small tribe living so far inland as to have retained most aspects of their culture, including their shamans. Plotkin had two aims in mind: (1) to take note of all herbal medicines the shaman would show him and report on them to the outside world, and (2) to make sure the forest people profited in some way for helping him with his research. Neither the chief nor the jaguar shaman (the most prestigious medicine man of the tribe) were enthusiastic about the strange foreigner who said he wanted to learn from them. No other foreigner had ever wanted to learn from them; in fact, foreigners had acted as though the Tirios knew nothing about medicine or anything else.

Despite misgivings, the jaguar shaman practiced his healing art in the presence of Mark Plotkin. A young boy was very sick, dangerously sick. The shaman blew smoke on him, took hallucinogens, talked with the spirits, danced frantically, then made a concoction of plant juices, which the boy drank. Next morning his fever was gone and his energy and appetite came back. Most cures were not that dramatic, but there seemed to be a "right" tree, vine, fruit, or herb for every disease that the shamans had known since time immemorial, although not necessarily for diseases introduced since the coming of the whites.

Plotkin kept a plant press and a notebook at all times, entering everything he learned. He also learned from personal experience what to rub on a bee sting and on a burn or what to take for a stomachache or diarrhea. He was surprised, though, to find that he seemed to be the only apprentice the old jaguar shaman had. The people had been taught that the foreign medicine that came in little bottles and boxes was better. Thus the knowledge of centuries was going to waste, and no one was testing the chemical composition of herbs that might become cures for cancer, heart disease, or any of a thousand afflictions.

When back in the United States, Plotkin published his findings in great detail, not only in English, but in Tirio. He took the book of Tirio medicine back to the village, where he now had many good friends who addressed him as "Jaco" (brother). The chief greeted him and accepted the book. The chief called a meeting of all the people and said that the book brought back by their "brother" should be kept in the school and taught to all the people. The knowledge was important, he said, and he appointed two Tirio friends of Plotkin's to be shamans.

By this time (1990), many people were becoming interested in learning all the plants of the rain forest, only about 2 percent of which were known. Mark Plotkin wanted to contact the pharmaceutical companies, but only if a percentage of the profits from cures would go back to the native people. He became acquainted with a woman by the name of Lisa Conte, who agreed with his ideas. She was a very efficient businessperson, and more than willing to help the indigenous people. She and a number of others founded a new pharmaceutical company. Almost immediately the new company became successful with extracts from the rain forest turned to medicines for herpes, flu, and respiratory problems, and a fund was started to go partly to the Tirio people, partly to botanical research in the region, and partly to setting aside forest areas that would never be destroyed.

This whole development has given the Tirio a sense of importance, which white civilization usually robs from indigenous people. Not only that, but studies of native medicine have affected other regions. The Bribri Indians of Costa Rica have started a project for their shamans to get their knowledge into writing. And the Bribri have influenced others to do likewise. Not only are medicines being saved, but there is increased impetus to save the forests, and the whole movement is breathing life into what once appeared to be dying cultures.

Causes of Death of Children Under Age 5 in Developing Countries		TABLE 4.6
Causes of death	Number (thousands)	Percentage of deaths
Diarrheal diseases	4,000	27.4
Immunizeable diseases	3,700	25.3
Measles	2,000	13.7
Whooping cough	600	4.1
Tuberculosis	300	2.1
Neonatal tetanus	775	5.3
Polio	25[a]	0.2
Acute respiratory infections	2,375	16.3
Malaria	750	5.1
Other infectious/parasitic diseases	450	3.1
Perinatal causes	2,425	16.6
Injuries	200	1.4
Other causes	700	4.8
Total	14,600	100.0

[a]Polio causes about 250,000 paralytic cases annually, of which about 10 percent die.

SOURCE: W. H. Mosley and P. Cowley, *The Challenge of World Health*, (Washington, DC: Population Reference Bureau, 1991), p. 11.

especially in rural areas, lives in unsanitary conditions and drinks bacterially infested water that "the single biggest killer remains diarrheal dehydration, accompanied by malnutrition, which killed between 3 and 4 million children per year in the mid 1980s" ("UNICEF Says Seven Million Lives Could Be Saved", 1987). By 1990 the use of oral rehydration therapy (ORT) saved at least 1 million lives, but still 2.5 million infants and children died due to diarrhea (Mosley and Cowley, 1991:13). Table 4.6 shows the annual death toll in LDCs due to common childhood illnesses, most of which can be easily prevented or treated.

The LDCs have 77 percent of the world's population, but they account for only 4 percent of the world's health expenditures. High-income countries of the world spent an average of $1,500 per year per person for health care; the poorest countries spent $41 per year per person (World Bank, 1993:4). In 1991, at the extremes, Mexico used only 1.9% of its total expenditures for health care, India 1.6%, Guinea-Bissau, 1.4%, and Pakistan, 1.0%, while the corresponding

Child Mortality Rates (1993)	TABLE 4.7

COUNTRIES WHERE MORE THAN 25 PERCENT OF CHILDREN DIE BETWEEN BIRTH AND 5 YEARS OF AGE:

Country	Childhood Mortality Rate[a]
Madagascar	360
Niger	320
Afghanistan	307
Mozambique	280
Guinea	268

COUNTRIES WHERE AT LEAST 20 PERCENT OF CHILDREN DIE BETWEEN BIRTH AND 5 YEARS OF AGE:

Country	Childhood Mortality Rate[a]
Malawa	222
Somalia	214
Angola	214
Chad	212
Rwanda	200

[a]Childhood Mortality Rate is the number of children who die between birth and 5 years of age per 1,000 live births.

SOURCE: World Bank, *World Development Report 1993: Investing in Health* (Oxford: Oxford University Press, 1993), pp. 200–201.

percentages in developed countries were 13.8 % for the United States, 15.3 % for France, and 18.3 % for Germany. Two notable exceptions to the pattern were in Latin America, where Panama spent 20.5% and Costa Rica dipped into its budget for 32.0% that was used for health care (World Bank, 1993:258–259). At present, only one country (Zimbabwe) in sub-Saharan Africa has an infant mortality rate of less than 50 per year. All the arid regions extending from Senegal and Mauritania eastward as far as Chad have infant mortality rates of 130 to 160 per 1,000 live births, and the same is true of Ethiopia (World Bank, 1993:292). In four countries of Africa, as well as in Afghanistan, more than 25% of children die before the age of 5 years. Other African countries, as shown in Table 4.7, were not far behind (World Bank, 1993:200–201).

Almost as shocking as high mortality rates of infants and children are high rates of blindness. In this respect, too, the contrast between LDCs and MDCs is very great, differing by a margin of about four to one. Less than one-quarter of 1 percent of the people in MDCs are blind; in the LDCs the figure averages about 1 percent. That 1 percent, however, includes some extreme cases. In Oman, Yemen, and Liberia, more than 3 percent of the people are blind, and in Chad, nearly 4 percent. In Mali, whole villages are infected with parasites, transported by black flies, that cause *onchocerciasis*—better known as *river blindness*. Currently, the World Health Organization (WHO) is administering an American-made drug that interrupts the reproductive cycle of the parasitic worms. WHO is also involved with a program to eradicate the flies that deposit the parasites (Kraft, 1987). Despite heroic efforts to distribute the drug, there are now two million more people who are blind because of the ailment than there were in 1987 when the drug, Mectizan, was approved for use (Moody, 1993). Figure 4.7 shows the distribution of river blindness, the total number of people at risk of contracting it, and the number of people already affected. The World Health Organization estimates it will cost about $200 million and take as long as 15 years to provide the medication to all who need it (Moody, 1993:H6).

In life expectancy, the contrast of MDCs and LDCs is also very great. The MDCs have attained an average life expectancy of 71 years; the LDCs average only 52 years. Within the LDC category, life expectancy varies widely. As noted previously, China, although an LDC on the basis of per-capita income, has a life expectancy comparable to that of MDCs. At the most unfavorable extreme of the LDC category are Sierra Leone and Niger, with a life expectancy of only 38 years (World Bank, 1993:200). Maternal mortality rates, the number of women who die while giving birth per 1,000 live births, are also very

Figure 4.7
"River blindness" is a serious medical problem in various less developed regions of the world.

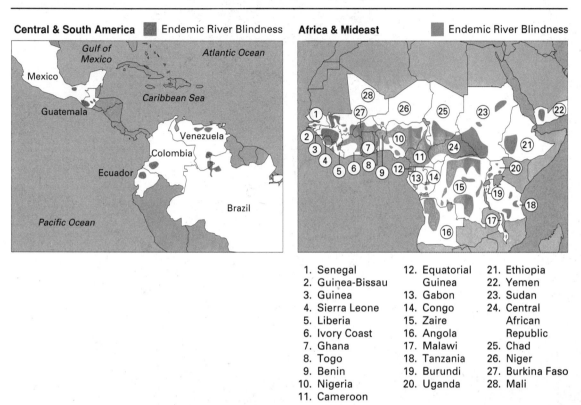

| **Central & South America** ■ Endemic River Blindness | **Africa & Mideast** ■ Endemic River Blindness |

1. Senegal	12. Equatorial	21. Ethiopia
2. Guinea-Bissau	Guinea	22. Yemen
3. Guinea	13. Gabon	23. Sudan
4. Sierra Leone	14. Congo	24. Central
5. Liberia	15. Zaire	African
6. Ivory Coast	16. Angola	Republic
7. Ghana	17. Malawi	25. Chad
8. Togo	18. Tanzania	26. Niger
9. Benin	19. Burundi	27. Burkina Faso
10. Nigeria	20. Uganda	28. Mali
11. Cameroon		

Source: M. Moody, "Speaking of River Blindness," *Los Angeles Times*, Nov. 23, 1993: H6.

high: two to six per 1,000 births. This ranges from 100 to 500 times the rates in MDCs (Goliber, 1989). Better diet, prenatal care, and sanitary practices could significantly reduce these numbers.

Unsafe drinking water and insufficient food contribute to the high death rate, as well as shortages of doctors, clinics, medicine, immunizations against childhood diseases, and a lack of medical knowledge at the village level.

Life-Styles and Disease

Sometimes peoples' traditional practices and ways of life pose a variety of health risks. Life-styles can relate directly to health conditions, such as unsanitary use of animal products and close living with domestic animals. For example, the rural Barabaig people of East Africa use cattle products in ways that Western medicine would regard as very unsafe. The Barabaig occupy a territory just south of Eastern Kenya. As described by anthropologist George Klima, their way of life is typical of many herding tribes of East Africa:

Among the Barabaig, the infant's first food will be cow's milk, for they believe that the first few days' supply of mother's milk will be contaminated. Throughout life, the Barabaig

This little girl in Mexico is dressed up for her First Holy Communion. Her natural beauty is in stark contrast to the filth around her, where danger lies in the bacteria that breed in open trenches such as the one running beside her.

will think of milk as the best food, and, next to milk, cattle blood, which is drunk straight or mixed with butter or milk. Cattle have other uses as well. Cow dung is mixed with mud to plaster the walls of huts, and cow urine is used for cleaning bowls and for a disinfectant for wounds (Klima, 1970:4–6).

The cattle complex takes its toll of human population. Many of the cattle are carriers of tuberculosis, which is spread to the people. Cattle hides sometimes contain the spores of anthrax, a nearly always fatal disease. At night, ticks spread from cattle to people, often giving them relapsing fever, which can be fatal to children or to any individual in a weakened condition.

Dietary Deficiencies

The drinking of cattle blood is common among some of the pastoral peoples of East Africa. One can say that their diet is rich in protein, and if not contaminated, is probably more wholesome than the diets of many of the world's poorest people. In many of the poorest countries, foreign interests have acquired much of the land so that peasants who once had corn and chickens to live on must

buy all their food at prices they can ill afford. In some cases, mothers adopt from Western advertising the idea of using formula for babies rather than depending mainly on breast-feeding. In so doing, they sometimes try to save on food expenses by diluting the formula with too much water (Clinton, 1985). A frequent result is less protein than necessary for normal growth and brain development. In extreme cases, undernutrition can lead to a condition called *kwashiorkor,* severe protein deficiency resulting in abdominal swelling, mental dullness, lackluster eyes, and faded brittle hair. This condition frequently is seen in televised pictures of famines—the latest in Ethiopia, Somalia, and Madagascar.

It is encouraging to know that when famine becomes sufficiently widespread to attract world attention, relief agencies spring into action, and many lives are saved. It is also encouraging to know that some governments take measures to keep down food prices. India has long followed such policies, and its people are better fed than in the past. The same is true of China, and to an even greater degree. While 33 other LDCs showed a net loss in food production per capita for the period from 1979 to 1991, India increased

Men from a "squatter city," erected on a municipal dump outside Mexico City, scavenge for saleable junk. Many third-world cities are growing so rapidly that many thousands of people are forced to live among disease-carrying rats and insects, without a source of safe water.

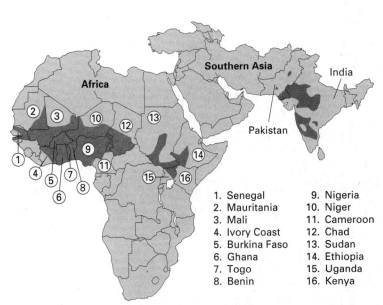

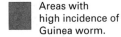 Areas with high incidence of Guinea worm.

1. Senegal
2. Mauritania
3. Mali
4. Ivory Coast
5. Burkina Faso
6. Ghana
7. Togo
8. Benin
9. Nigeria
10. Niger
11. Cameroon
12. Chad
13. Sudan
14. Ethiopia
15. Uganda
16. Kenya

Source: M. A. Hiltzkiz, "Guinea Worm: How and Where This Crippling Disease Strikes," *Los Angeles Times*, Nov. 6, 1989: B3.

Figure 4.8
"Guinea worm" is a crippling disease in parts of Africa and Southern Asia.

production by 1.6 percent per year and China increased its food supply by 3 percent annually (World Bank, 1993:244).

Water-borne Diseases

The World Health Organization considers lack of safe water to be a primary cause of diseases—especially gastrointestinal diseases such as cholera, typhoid, bacillary dysentery, and in some cases, hepatitis. During the past two decades, the migration of village people to urban centers in search of jobs has created abominable living conditions, in which tens of thousands of people live in city dumps or squatter "cities" without a source of safe water.

In the adult population as well as in the child population, diseases of many kinds are more common in LDCs than in the industrialized societies. *Dracunculiasis*, otherwise known as Guinea Worm, infected about 10 million people a year in India, Pakistan, and 16 countries in Africa in the late 1980s, as Figure 4.8 shows (Hiltzik, 1989). Although the disease is seldom fatal, it causes debilitating pain and makes it virtually impossible for its victims to work. People are infected repeatedly throughout their lives. The disease is communicated to humans through drinking water containing microscopic crustaceans, which carry the worm's larvae. The larvae metamorphose into worms that are eight to ten inches long. Over a period of about six months, they travel through the body, until they become visible as large blisters (usually on the legs). Eventually the worms break through the skin. The victim can then, painfully, pull them out.

Figure 4.9
Although the developed world is largely free of malaria, it remains well entrenched across the tropical regions of the planet. In Africa, there are 97 million cases per year; in Latin America, 1 million cases per year; in Asia, 9 million cases per year.

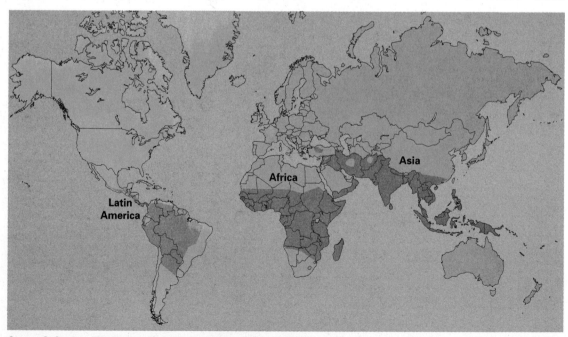

Source: G. Cowley, "The Endless Plague," *Newsweek,* Jan. 11, 1993: 58.

The infected victim often tries to allay the burning and itching by standing in ponds or streams that provide water to the village. When the worm breaks through the skin, it deposits thousands of eggs in the water, and the cycle of infection begins anew. However, with help from the World Health Organization, many of these areas improved their water delivery systems and learned to strain their drinking water through a cloth. Consequently, Pakistan hoped to have eradicated the disease by 1992 and Cameroon, Senegal, and India hoped to have accomplished this by 1993. Between 1987 and 1993, the number of annual cases fell from 653,000 to 201,000 in Nigeria, from 180,000 to 33,000 in Ghana, and from 17,000 to 900 in India. Currently, there are fewer than one million cases worldwide (World Bank, 1993:92).

The Return of Malaria

Malaria is a disease that much of the Western world thinks of as a thing of the past. Malaria had been almost brought under control in the mid 1950s, due to two developments: DDT, a pesticide that curbs the number of mosquitoes that carried the parasites, and new drugs to treat the disease. In the years since, however, both the mosquitoes and the parasites developed resistances to these chemicals. Resistant strains were first reported in Colombia and Thailand in the early 1960s, but they are now common in many parts of the world. All they need is year-round warm climate, an abundance of standing water, and another factor we might not think of: poverty. Figure 4.9 shows that the poorest countries of the world suffer many millions of cases of malaria annually.

José Najera-Morrondo, director of the malaria program for WHO, reminds us that, in the United States, the South used to have about one million cases of malaria per year; yet by the 1950s, the disease disappeared from the country (see Sitwell, 1986:72). Just as important as medicine, he says, is economic development and consequent good nutrition, health, and health services. When economic resources are sufficient, cases are detected sooner, mosquito sources sought and eradicated, and therefore, the disease is less likely to continue to be transmitted.

The control of malaria will require a number of strategies: draining swamps to eliminate breeding grounds of the anopheles mosquito, training health-care workers in proper treatment

People are crowded in unsanitary conditions in this Manila slum in the Philippines. Diseases like cholera are endemic to areas like this.

techniques, and selective use of pesticides. One encouraging report is discussed by Mosley and Cowley (1991:12). In the Gambia, insecticide-impregnated netting placed over infants' beds may reduce infant and child mortality by about 40 percent in malaria-endemic communities. But, that still means the world will continue to witness hundreds of millions of cases until an improved drug or vaccine is invented.

The Return of Cholera

Cholera has been endemic (restricted to a particular area) to parts of Asia and Africa, but it had not been a major problem in South America for the past 70 or 80 years, until 1991. At that time, a cholera epidemic swept across Peru, sickening about 100,000 people and killing more than 600 of them (Thomassie, 1991). Cholera is an acute diarrheal disease that develops in the small intestine after contaminated water or food is ingested. After an incubation period of one to five days, the victim experiences watery diarrhea, followed by vomiting. The deaths that occur are usually due to dehydration. Antibiotics can shorten the

period of time that the germs are active and oral hydration therapy can quickly relieve the effects of dehydration. However, treatment is rare where people are poor and sanitary conditions cannot be maintained.

By 1992 the epidemic had spread to 11 other Latin American countries, and 400,000 cases had been reported. About one of every hundred people who had been affected died. Peru was hardest hit with 320,000 cases and 29,000 deaths due to cholera. Ecuador experienced 46,000 cases and nearly 700 deaths; Colombia had 12,000 cases and 200 deaths, and Mexico reported 2,700 cases and 34 deaths. The disease even made its way into the United States, to the north, and Argentina, to the south (Long, 1992).

In 1993 a new strain of cholera, resistant to all known vaccines, began sweeping across Southeast Asia. The first cases were detected in Madras, India, and Bangladesh, and claimed thousands of lives. The World Health Organization immediately started to distribute doses of a vaccine made from killed cholera bacteria, but the vaccine is short-lived and not very effective. Consequently, health-care experts had little hope

Nearly every inch of space on this sidewalk in Calcutta, India, is claimed by a homeless person. Under these conditions, it is virtually impossible to halt the spread of disease.

of containing the epidemic, predicting that it would affect nearly all countries in the southern part of Asia and eventually make its way into Africa. They were right. In a single month, and in a single hospital in Calcutta, there were 22,000 cases reported (McGirk, 1993). The bacteria are drawn to areas marked by poverty, crowding, and unsanitary conditions.

In early 1994, a cholera outbreak in the northern part of Somalia spread to the capital city of Mogadishu ("Officials Fear Cholera Outbreak in Somalia May Turn Epidemic," 1994). The Somalis, recovering from both famine and war, were especially susceptible to the disease. By the end of March, more than 3,600 people were suffering from the disease, overwhelming the feeble health-care system ("Cholera Spreads Through Somalia," 1994). In some areas, cases were increasing ninefold in a single week. Under such conditions, cholera could ultimately claim more lives than the famine and war combined. Finally, the bloodletting in Rwanda in 1994 also resulted in a devastating outbreak of cholera, killing thousands of people.

Coping with Sickness in the LDCs

Infant mortality correlates with hunger; in general, in countries where people have enough to eat, the infant mortality rate falls below 50 per 1,000 live births. As so measured, and despite all the brutal statistics given above, there has been worldwide improvement, especially in countries with high or moderate incomes. Previous to 1900, no country in the world had an infant mortality rate of less than 50 per 1,000 live births; now all MDCs and a growing number of LDCs (mainly in Asia and Latin America, not Africa) have rates below that figure. By the mid 1980s, writers for The Hunger Project (1985) pointed to Thailand, Indonesia, the Dominican Republic, and South Korea as good examples of rapid improvement in health. These countries have all received foreign aid, and are pointed to with pride by Hunger Project advocates of

foreign aid. Figure 4.10 shows the countries where most of United States–supplied foreign aid was going in early 1990s. Those who think foreign aid is often wasted and/or is used mainly to gain control over LDCs point to China as a country that has done better all by itself.

Other countries have not fared so well. In the 1990s about 2 billion of the world's 5.5 billion people suffer from some degree of malnutrition. A recent survey by the United Nations Food and Agriculture Organization (FAO) points out that malnutrition and hunger exist in almost every country. There are three categories of hunger: acute hunger, chronic hunger, and hidden hunger. **Acute hunger** exists in poverty-stricken, resource-poor, and overpopulated countries like Mozambique, Zimbabwe, Malawi, and Somalia. In such countries, as many as 35 million people live on the verge of starvation. **Chronic hunger** exists in similar countries, like Bangladesh, Pakistan, India, and Sri Lanka, where most people are not in immediate danger of dying, but food is so scarce that it is inadequate for health, growth, and energy needs. **Hidden hunger** is a worldwide phenomenon, where peoples' stomachs may be reasonably full, but their diets lack adequate protein, minerals, and vitamins. In the United States, people suffering from hidden hunger increased from 20 million in 1985 to 30 million in 1992 (Wright, 1992).

The MDCs and Health Problems in the LDCs

The horrendous health conditions in the less developed countries that we have delineated result at least partly from the economic and resource exploitation by the more developed countries. Recall the example of U.S. cigarette companies establishing larger and larger markets in LDCs, even as the market for cigarettes in the United States is declining. World system theory would suggest that this and other examples of poor health conditions in the LDCs can be explained by the dominance of core countries

Figure 4.10
This map shows where U.S. foreign aid monies are spent. Four to ten U.S. agencies have programs in each of these countries to relieve sickness and hunger and to provide emergency assistance.

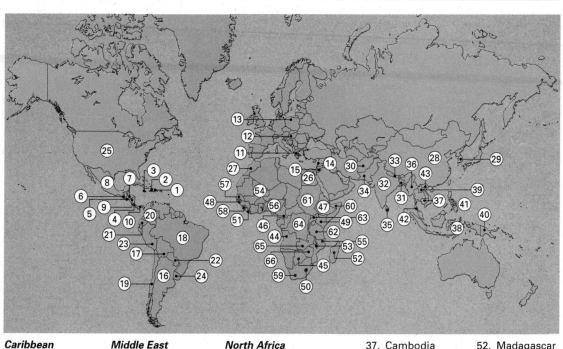

Caribbean
1. Dominican Republic
2. Haiti
3. Jamaica

Central America
4. Costa Rica
5. El Salvador
6. Guatemala
7. Honduras
8. Mexico
9. Nicaragua
10. Panama

Europe
11. Greece
12. Hungary
13. Poland

Middle East
14. Israel
15. Jordan

South America
16. Argentina
17. Bolivia
18. Brazil
19. Chile
20. Colombia
21. Ecuador
22. Paraguay
23. Peru
24. Uruguay

North America
25. United States

North Africa
26. Egypt
27. Morocco

East Asia
28. China
29. South Korea

South Asia
30. Afghanistan
31. Bangladesh
32. India
33. Nepal
34. Pakistan
35. Sri Lanka

Southeast Asia
36. Myanmar (Burma)
37. Cambodia
38. Indonesia
39. Laos
40. Papua New Guinea
41. Philippines
42. Thailand
43. Vietnam

Sub-Saharan Africa
44. Angola
45. Botswana
46. Cameroon
47. Ethiopia
48. Gambia
49. Kenya
50. Lesotho
51. Liberia
52. Madagascar
53. Malawi
54. Mali
55. Mozambique
56. Nigeria
57. Senegal
58. Sierra Leone
59. South Africa
60. Somalia
61. Sudan
62. Tanzania
63. Uganda
64. Zaire
65. Zambia
66. Zimbabwe

Source: P. Gonzales and V. Kotowitz, "Speaking of: International Relief," *Los Angeles Times*, Apr. 20, 1993: H6.

over the peripheral and semiperipheral countries. Another example would be the introduction of hazardous chemicals into the environment along the U.S.-Mexican border. While U.S. manufacturers are barred from dumping hazardous chemicals in the United States, they often do so on the other side of the border with their assembly plants that hire Mexican workers.

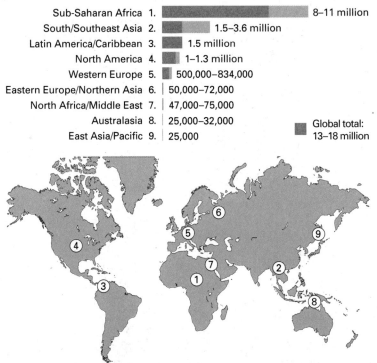

Sub-Saharan Africa 1. ▮▮▮▮▮▮ 8–11 million
South/Southeast Asia 2. ▮▮▮ 1.5–3.6 million
Latin America/Caribbean 3. ▮▮ 1.5 million
North America 4. ▮ 1–1.3 million
Western Europe 5. ▮ 500,000–834,000
Eastern Europe/Northern Asia 6. │ 50,000–72,000
North Africa/Middle East 7. │ 47,000–75,000
Australasia 8. │ 25,000–32,000
East Asia/Pacific 9. │ 25,000

▮ Global total:
13–18 million

Figure 4.11
Cases of AIDS have been found all over the world. As of mid 1993, estimates of various health organizations, based on cases reported to them, range from 13 to 18 million people suffering with AIDS. This global distribution shows that sub-Saharan Africa, with 8 to 11 million cases, has been the hardest hit region.

Source: D. Perlman, "Top Scientists Gather for Ninth AIDS Conference," *San Francisco Chronicle*, June 5, 1993: A10.

AIDS: A NEW PLAGUE

A relatively new health problem now affecting the entire planet is Acquired Immune Deficiency Syndrome (AIDS). Many parallels have been drawn between AIDS and bubonic plague, popularly called the black death, which wiped out approximately one-third of the world's population in the seventeenth century. There are, of course, some reassuring differences. Bubonic plague was spread by fleas, which bit infected rats and spread the disease to people. The Human Immunodeficiency Virus (HIV), which leads to AIDS, is not spread quite so easily; no insect acts as an intermediary. This virus is spread mainly through sexual contact, but also by addicts who share needles, and sometimes through blood transfusions, unless great care is taken by blood banks. Babies can be born with the AIDS virus if their mothers are carrying the infection.

Although there is no cure for AIDS, there is room for hope: AIDS is a preventable disease. People can choose to abstain from sexual relations or engage in responsible sexual behavior—drastically reducing promiscuity, using condoms, or better yet, having sexual intercourse with only one partner. In MDCs, blood donations are now screened for HIV and other viruses. In some metropolitan areas, free needles are made available to heroin addicts. Even though the idea sounds unfair (why should we pay for their needles?), it might prove much less expensive (in money, not in lives) than having to hospitalize many thousands more patients. It should be remembered, too, that many drug addicts acquire their drug money by prostitution, spreading the disease among the non-addicted population.

The Coming of AIDS

AIDS was first diagnosed in 1980 and has spread very rapidly. It is uncertain when the disease originated. It is probable that a number of AIDS-infected people died of pneumonia or were treated for tuberculoses prior to the identification of the virus. Michael Gottlieb first noted a case of pneumonia with no immune defenses at UCLA in 1980 and discussed with his colleagues the mystery of a patient without immune reaction (Shilts, 1987). Then other reports came in from New York. Something new and terrible was occurring. Soon the medical world became worried about a condition that might develop into a disastrous plague.

At the same time, large numbers of people were dying in Africa, particularly in Uganda and Zaire. They were dying of what they called the "thin disease," which was wasting bodies and eventually leading to death.

Despite the rapid spread of AIDS, the first reactions from many governments was to ignore the disease. In the United States, AIDS was considered mainly a disease of homosexual men. The federal government showed little interest; in fact, it was several years before then President Reagan even uttered the word AIDS. By then, 25,000 Americans had died, the majority of them gay men, who appeared to draw less official sympathy than would other segments of the population. Eventually, then Surgeon General C. Everett Koop addressed the issue, warning that AIDS is not just a gay disease; everyone is susceptible.

AIDS in Africa

In Africa, little or no action was taken except to try to hide the disease. Reporters were thrown out of Zaire for telling the story. Early reactions

in Uganda were similar. Reports to the World Health Organization were not dependable. One problem was that many people were pointing to Africa as the place of origin of AIDS, and African countries felt themselves to be victims of false accusations and of racism. Eventually African countries, like the Unites States, had to face the problem squarely, count the casualties, and ask for help. By 1987, when President Mobutu of Zaire realized the need for action, around 20 percent of the sexually-active people of Kinsasha were infected with the virus (Mann, 1988). Other capital cities of central Africa were equally devastated, including Kampala (Uganda, 15 percent), Lusaka (Zambia, 15 percent), and Kigali (Rwanda, 18 percent) (Kraft, 1987). By the early 1990s, four out of five hospital beds in these cities were occupied by patients with AIDS (Hiltzik, 1991).

In the case of Africa, the afflicted people were overwhelmingly heterosexuals, not homosexuals. Only about 1 percent of AIDS cases in Africa are caused by homosexual relations or intravenous drug use. Eighty percent of the time, the virus is passed through heterosexual activity. The remainder of the cases are passed from mother to child during pregnancy or birth (Kraft, 1992). In Africa, even if a woman sees open sores on her husband's penis, it is almost impossible for her to refuse his demand for sexual relations. This means that when AIDS is present in a family, both mother and father will likely die. Traditionally children would be taken in by relatives or, if the husband dies first, arrangements would be made for the surviving wife to remarry. Now, family members of AIDS victims are shunned. It is likely that major social structures will change as traditional patterns are abandoned. Children may have to stay home from school in order to take care of sick parents, setting back any strides forward that may have been made in recent years.

It is very difficult to organize the large-scale programs needed to prevent the spread of AIDS

Prostitutes ply their trade in Rio de Janeiro's Copacabana. By 1992 700,000 Brazilians had been infected with HIV. Experts expect the number of AIDS cases could approach three million by the late 1990s.

in Africa because of the other massive health problems that plague the continent, the lack of economic resources, poor educational levels among the various populations, and a paucity of clinics and trained medical personnel. Even blood banks, which already had shortages, are affected. In Zimbabwe, for example, blood banks will not accept blood from any of Zimbabwe's soldiers because, when they started screening blood in the mid 1980s, doctors found that more than half of the military men tested HIV positive (Kraft, 1992:16). At this point, it seems that AIDS is truly out of control in Africa.

AIDS in Latin America

Carnival is the pre-Lenten period of celebration in Rio de Janeiro, a time of freedom from the constraint of norms that usually govern sexual behavior. In recent years, Carnival has been feared as a time that AIDS could spread so quickly it might become uncontrollable. Brazilians, and the tourists who flock in for the celebration, were urged to use protection against the disease. But the public-service announcements on radio and television, articles in news-

papers, and pamphlets distributed by the Health Ministry advocating the use of condoms were strongly objected to by the Catholic Church for being too sexually explicit and condoning casual sexual activity.

Brazil, with more reported AIDS cases than any other South American country, had 700,000 people infected with HIV by 1992, and that number was expected to quadruple by 1995 (Black, Collins, and Boroughs, 1992). In the early 1990s, unemployment had hit 17 percent and inflation was an almost unbelievable 2,000 percent. In such an economic environment, Brazil needs $600 million to care for AIDS patients, but its $16-billion foreign debt hampers its efforts to help AIDS victims (Black, Collins, and Boroughs, 1992:55–56).

A major problem confronting workers who want to prevent the spread of AIDS in South America is that victims who suspect the presence of the illness are unwilling to report it. Because of the strong religious values, victims who seek help feel ashamed and ask their physicians to diagnose their symptoms as something else. Many of the men apparently get the disease from the more than 3,000 young women from all over the country who come to Rio de Janeiro's red-light district every night to earn a living from Rio's sex trade ("Globe and Mail," 1992).

Other Latin American countries have similar problems, but to a lesser extent than Brazil. By 1993, Honduras had 2,700 cases of full-blown AIDS, and about 50,000 people who had tested HIV positive. With a small population (about five million in 1993), Honduras has a rate of AIDS cases that is almost twice as high as Brazil's rate (Wilkinson, 1993). In such countries, sex information and health education are very poor, but some governments are attempting to convince people to use condoms, despite the position taken by the Church, which advocates celibacy outside of marriage and monogamous fidelity within marriage.

AIDS Around the World

Elsewhere around the world, AIDS has shown up in nearly every country that reports such statistics. The tiny country of Haiti, which shares the island of Hispaniola with the Dominican Republic, reports that about one of every 11 sugar cane cutters is infected with the disease. But, the State Sugar Council claims that this is not a problem because there are plenty of people to replace those who die (Black, Collins, and Boroughs, 1992:57). Interestingly, the Dominican health department is getting the AIDS message to the Dominican people, but not to the Haitians. However, Dominican prostitutes are used by the Haitian cane cutters, and it is only a matter of time before the disease spreads to a large portion of the Dominican population.

In Southeast Asia, Thailand has a booming tourist sex industry, and 15 to 20 percent of the nation's prostitutes were HIV positive by 1992. Government statistics show that between 200,000 and 400,000 Thais are carrying the AIDS virus, and the World Health Organization estimates that, by the turn of the century, between two million and four million people will be

infected with the deadly virus in this tiny country. Seventy-three percent of the new recruits to the Thai Army had their first experience of sexual intercourse with a prostitute because a trip to the brothel is considered a rite of passage for most men. People in the upper classes are expected to supply a prostitute for their guests (Moreau, 1992). So, the spread of AIDS is, indeed, predictable. In fact, the chief of the World Health Organization's global AIDS program claims:

> While Africa suffers the explosion of AIDS cases as a result of infections 10 years ago, it is in South and Southeast Asia that we are seeing an explosion of infection today. We can soon expect more new infections in Asia than in Africa, and as the epidemic of AIDS takes hold in Asia as it has in Africa, we can anticipate that individuals, families, and communities will be affected in the same tragic way we are already seeing in parts of Africa (Perlman, 1994:A10).

In most of Asia, sex is big business, and men from the top politicians to the local police share in the profits. Much of Asia's population follows a double standard of sexual behavior, making it acceptable for husbands to visit brothels. Men also disdain using condoms. Consequently, by the turn of the century, 1.5 million women in Thailand alone will be HIV positive and so will one-third of their children (Moreau, 1992:1).

AIDS has become a particular concern for women, who are ten times more likely to contract the illness from men than men do from women. Taking a worldview, WHO claims that more than 13 million women will have contracted the disease by the year 2000. In the Unites States alone the number of women infected with AIDS increased 10 percent in the one year between 1991 and 1992 (World Health Organization, 1994). In sub-Saharan Africa, for every five men infected by HIV/AIDS, there are six women infected. In Malawi, for example,

3 percent of women visiting prenatal clinics in 1985 tested positive; by 1993 this figure increased tenfold to 30 percent (World Health Organization, 1994:63). The World Health Organization gives three reasons that women are more susceptible than men. First, during sexual intercourse, women have a larger portion of mucosal surfaces exposed. Sexual behavior is androcentrically (domination by males) defined everywhere and both intercourse (vaginal and anal) and fellatio (oral stimulation of the penis) are much more commonly practiced worldwide than is cunninglingus (oral stimulation of the female genitalia). Through these practices, women have larger portions of their mucosl surfaces (vaginal, anal, and oral) exposed to an ejaculate of semen. Second, women tend to have intercourse with men who are older than they, and these men are more likely to have had numerous sexual partners, increasing their risk of exposure. And finally, in many cultures, men are the controlling figures, so even if a woman desires protection, the man may make the decision not to use a condom (World Health Organization, 1994:63). Obviously, a change of attitudes about women would greatly restrict the spread of this modern plague.

SUMMARY

Health problems, like other kinds of social problems, are not experienced equally by people. Individuals from the less developed countries are much more likely to be afflicted with serious health problems than are individuals from the more developed countries. Likewise, lower income people in the MDCs are more likely to lack adequate health care than are higher income people.

With regard to the MDCs, one of the most serious problems is the increased relative cost of health care. This is especially true for the United States. In the United States, medical care is largely funded by private insurance companies whose sole reason for existence is to make a profit. This is reflected in the per capita amount of money spent on health care in the MDCs, where the United States leads the list both in the absolute amount spent and in the proportionate amount of the gross national product being consumed by health care. Even though the United States spends the most for health-care, it is the only major MDC where significant proportions of people do not have medical insurance and thereby cannot afford quality health care, even if they are middle class.

Increased life expectancy in the MDCs and the aging of their populations are increasing the demand for health care because elderly people are more prone to illness. Unhealthy habits such as tobacco consumption, drug use, excessive use of alcohol, and diets including too much fat and not enough fiber contribute to health problems in the MDCs. Although cigarette consumption per capita has decreased in some MDCs, it is still very high and causes more deaths than any other single factor. Vested interest shows its hand in the anticigarette fight. While the United States leads the propaganda barrage against cigarettes, it still subsidizes the tobacco industry. And, the U.S. tobacco industry has taken advantage of major increases in tobacco use in LDCs.

Though the overall level of health is high in the MDCs, there are marked differences in the health levels that people enjoy. The well-to-do have access to the best that modern medicine has to offer, which is considerable. The poor and the minorities do not have the same access to modern medicine as do the rich, and morbidity and mortality statistics reflect this.

The rationing of life, which occurs under the structures of some universal health-care coverages and private insurance companies, has a detrimental effect on the poor and middle class. Other moral dilemmas that call for attention are the effects of new diagnostic tools and tests, the

vast improvements in medical skills (such as
organ transplants), increased life expectancy, and
bioethics (including topics like euthanasia).

The health problems of the MDCs pale in
comparison with those of formerly Communist
countries and LDCs. The former Soviet Union
has experienced a marked rise in mortality rates
and a huge decrease in life expectancy due to the
collapse of communism and the vacuum left in
the wake of that collapse. Other East European,
formerly Communist countries such as Poland,
are also experiencing major difficulties with their
health systems. The major health problems of the
LDCs center around the grinding poverty that is
endemic to these nations. People are much more
likely to die of diseases such as malaria, cholera,
and tuberculosis than they are from heart disease
and cancer. Inadequate nourishment, unsanitary
conditions, and unsafe water supplies allow the
above killers to ravage the populations of LDCs.
Part of the blame for the insufferable health
conditions in the LDCs must go to the MDCs.
The dominance and exploitation of LDCs by
core countries like the United States and Japan
keep the LDCs from developing and, hence, the
grinding poverty continues to exist, resulting in
serious health problems.

The world community must contend with
some major diseases that threaten the human
population, AIDS being the most serious. The
African continent is being ravaged by this killer
and Southeast Asia is now experiencing rapid
increases in HIV infection. Also, drug-resistant
strains of certain diseases, like tuberculosis, are
gaining ground and are of major concern to
humankind.

KEY TERMS

Acute hunger Hunger in poverty-stricken,
resource-poor, and overpopulated countries,
where very high proportions of the populations
are on the verge of starvation.

Bioethics An academic and research discipline
that deals with the ethical implications of
medical advancements.

Chronic hunger Hunger in very poor countries,
where most people are not in immediate danger
of dying, but where food is so scarce that it is
inadequate for health, growth, and energy needs.

Euthanasia The act of killing an individual who
is hopelessly sick, hence, often referred to as
"mercy killing."

Hidden hunger Hunger where peoples' stomachs
may be reasonably full, but their diets lack
adequate protein, minerals, and vitamins.

Negative euthansia Allowing a person to die, but
not aiding the process.

Positive euthanasia The actual termination of
the life of a hopeless and suffering patient.

STUDY QUESTIONS

1. How do the major health threats in the less
developed countries compare to the major health
threats in the more developed countries? Why is
this the case?

2. How has the U.S. cigarette industry
responded to the decrease in cigarette smoking
in the United States?

3. What are the major differences in medical
insurance among the United States, Canada, and
Western Europe?

4. What groups have the most to lose if a
national health plan is instituted in the United
States? Why?

5. What negative things do opponents of a U.S.
national health insurance plan say will occur?
Which of these things have occurred in Canada,
which has national health insurance?

6. How does rationing of life occur in Great Britain and the United States?

7. How do the new diagnostic tools and tests, such as Magnetic Resonance Imaging (MRI), Computerized Tomography, and amniocentesis, present moral dilemmas?

8. What has happened to life expectancy rates in the former Soviet Union since it collapsed? What are the reasons for this?

9. How are life-styles associated with health problems in less developed countries?

10. What social forces explain why the United States federal government is so slow in reacting to the spread of AIDS in the United States?

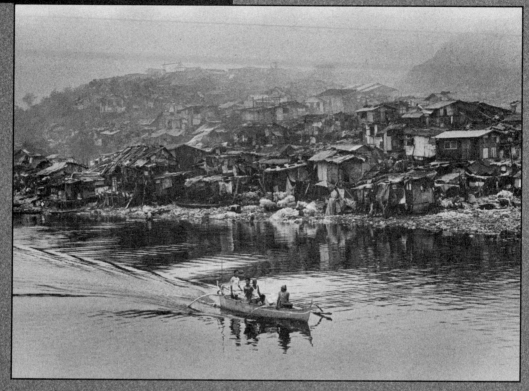

POPULATION

EXPLOSION AND

DECLINE

*U*ganda, located in central Africa, is one of the poorest countries in the world. If we evenly distributed its gross national product (GNP), the total money output for goods and services, each person would have an annual income of $170 (U.S.). Yet, in this impoverished environment, on average, each woman has at least seven children.

Germany, located in central Europe, is one of the wealthiest countries in the world, having a per capita GNP of $23,030 (U.S.). But, in this land of plenty, each woman has only 1.3 children, on average. While Germany's present population of 81.2 million will decline to 73.2 million by the year 2025, Uganda's present population of 19.8 million will nearly triple to 46 million in the same time frame (Haub and Yanagishita, 1994).

The cause of the disparity between these two countries is the subject of this chapter. The *population bomb,* a term coined by Paul Ehrlich (1968), refers to rapidly growing populations due to reduced death rates and continued high birthrates. In the MDCs, the population bomb has been defused, but in the LDCs it is exploding. To some extent, this accounts for the global contrast of abundance and poverty (to be discussed in Chapter 9). We can gain some understanding of this phenomenon by looking at the history of the world's growth in population.

WORLD POPULATION GROWTH TRENDS

Imagine the world as it existed ten thousand years ago. Humankind is just emerging from the Old Stone Age. We live in small tribes and spend some of our waking hours hunting or gathering food. Our life may seem to be a leisurely one, but we may travel hundreds of miles before encountering people from another tribe. Its members probably exist as we do. Life is hard, and it is short.

Most of our babies die during their first year of life. Those who survive are old by age 30 and we'll probably bury them before they see 35 years. World population probably does not exceed 8 million, and this condition will not change for a very long time.

Now, let's move forward a couple of thousand years to the height of the New Stone Age. A couple of million people have settled into small villages and developed a crude system of agricul-ture. Our population increases, but at an almost imperceptibly slow pace.

Gradually, more people settle into villages and villages merge into cities. Still, by the year A.D. 1, world population is only about 250 million. Century follows century and the number of people increases so slowly that it takes until 1830 before world population reaches 1 billion. We're now at the beginning of the Industrial Revolution in Europe and life is about to be dramatically transformed. But in most of the rest of the world, including Africa, Latin America, and Southeast Asia, nothing much has changed.

So, it took all of time, from the emergence of the human species until 1830, for us to develop a living population of one billion. In the next 100 years, we doubled our numbers. Then in just 30 years (around 1960), we added a third billion; 15 years later we reached 4 billion; and 10 years after that, 5 billion. The United Nations estimates slightly more than 6 billion people at the beginning of the twenty-first century (Table 5.1).

As population specialist Kingsley Davis (1949:595) observed, the world's population growth "has been like a long, thin powder fuse

World Population Growth: Time Needed to Add Next Billion	TABLE 5.1
Year	Number Living
1830	1,000,000
(100 years)	
1930	2,000,000
(30 years)	
1960	3,000,000
(15 years)	
1975	4,000,000
(12 years)	
1985	5,000,000
(11 years)	
1998	6,000,000
(projected)	

SOURCES: Murphy, *World Population: Toward the Next Century,* Population Reference Bureau; Haub and Yanagishita, *1992 World Population Data Sheet.*

that burns slowly and haltingly until it reaches the charge and then it explodes." Clearly, the charge was the Industrial Revolution. The initial blast took place in Europe, later in countries of European origin, and now in the LDCs. Figure 5.1 graphically depicts the phenomenon described by Davis.

Elements of Demography

Demography is the statistical description and analysis of human population. Although many disciplines (fields of study) are interested in demographic data, the formal study of demography falls within the area of sociology because the main causes of demographic trends are social. To gain an understanding of this principle, we begin by considering the basic demographic processes.

There are three basic demographic processes: fertility, mortality, and migration. **Fertility** refers to the actual number of births within a population each year. It is always given as a whole number, not as a percentage or rate. For example, the United Kingdom's fertility for 1991 was 805,000, meaning that 805,000 people were born that year. Fertility may be affected by such factors as socioeconomic status. For instance, there is a

tendency for higher-status farmers in India, Bangladesh, Iran, Nepal, the Philippines, and Thailand to have more children than lower-status farmers. In such countries, the more land one owns, the more children he wants to work the farm and provide security for him in his old age (see Kammeyer and Ginn, 1986:197; Hohm, 1975; and Hohm, et al., 1985). On the other hand, in the MDCs of Western Europe, and Australia, Canada, and the United States, early in this century, upper-middle class people started using artificial means of contraception—thereby having fewer children—much earlier than did the lower classes (see Kammeyer and Ginn, 1986:197). As economic development occurs, children become economic liabilities rather than assets, and fertility levels drop accordingly.

Often, especially for the purpose of comparing or projecting populations, it is desirable to convert whole numbers into rates. With regard to fertility, the crude birthrate is commonly used. The **crude birthrate** (CBR) is obtained by dividing the fertility (the actual number of births) by the total population and multiplying the quotient by 1,000. With data from Haub et al. (1992), we can figure the CBRs for the Phillipines and the United Kingdom.

$$\text{Crude birthrate} = \frac{\text{Total number of births/year}}{\text{Total population}} \times 1,000$$

$$\frac{2,055,900}{63,700,000} \times 1000 = 32.$$

$$\frac{805,000}{57,800,000} \times 1000 = 14.$$

Sometimes governments attempt to control the fertility of their populations. Some nations have used **pronatalist policies** designed to increase fertility. German demographers Thomas Buttner and Wolfgang Lutz (1990) argue that such policies in the former East Germany resulted in a 20 percent increase in the East German fertility rate. The pronatalist policies were (1) paid maternity

Figure 5.1
World population A.D. 1 to A.D. 2050: Most of the growth has occurred in the last few decades.

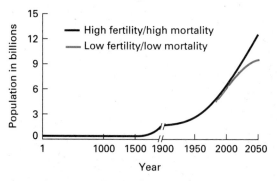

Source: Appeared in W. Lutz, "The Future of World Population," *Population Bulletin,* 49(1), 1994: 4.

leaves from 18 to 26 weeks and (2) paid maternity leaves of one year for mothers with two or more children. The policies resulted in increased fertility for women with larger families and had no effect on the percentage of women remaining childless.

The second demographic process is **mortality**, which refers to the actual number of deaths within a population during a year. Like fertility, it is affected by social factors. For example, people who have better living conditions have longer life expectancies than people who have poor living conditions. As in the case of fertility, it is often desirable to express a population's mortality as a rate, called the **crude death rate (CDR)**, which is determined in the same way as the CBR.

The values of a society exert tremendous influence over its mortality. For example, in India, members of one **caste**, or social level, may not touch members of a different caste. If such a system were strictly followed, surgical transplants would be absolutely forbidden. In South Africa, a country where, until 1994, the leadership believed in the strict separation of races, the heart of a brain-dead man was transplanted into a patient whose own heart was beyond repair. While organ transplants are relatively routine now in many MDCs, this was the first transplant of such a nature in South Africa. Ironically, the recipient was white (as was the leadership class) and the donor was black. So, the values of South African society that disallowed blacks and whites from eating in the same restaurant allowed surgical transplants between races, at least in this case of a white recipient.

Populations experience fairly rapid growth once they are able to lower their CDRs while maintaining fairly high CBRs. The MDCs have now controlled their CBRs; the LDCs have not. In essence, this is one of the causes of the tremendous gap between "have" and "have-not" nations.

For the world as a whole we can say that the **rate of natural increase (NI)** is the CBR minus the CDR. There is tremendous variability among the countries of the world in their rates of natural increase.

Migration is the third demographic process. It refers to the physical movement of people into or out of a geographic region. The term **immigration** indicates the movement of people into a country of which they are not natives, and the term **emigration** identifies movement out of a country of which they are natives or long-term residents.

Many social functions affect migration. For instance, laws affect migration. Nearly all countries have policies setting limits on immigration for various reasons. One reason is to protect local labor markets. For example, an unskilled worker from Mexico can move to the United States and make much more money for his labor than he can at home and still demand lower wages than the native American population.

Some countries also restrict emigration. For example, the former USSR's policy for allowing Jews to emigrate was briefly relaxed at the end of the 1970s. In 1979 more than 50,000 Soviet Jews seized the opportunity to leave. But by the mid 1980s, restrictions again curbed Jewish emigra-

Figure 5.2
Major political events, such as the end of the Cold War between the USSR and the United States, have major effects on emigration—in this case a dramatic increase in Jewish emigration from the USSR.

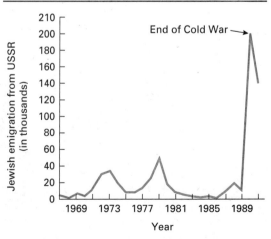

Source: Los Angeles Times, "140,000 Soviet Jews Emigrate to Israel, a Decrease of 23%," Dec. 25, 1990: A21; *Los Angeles Times*, Dec. 27, 1991: A8.

tion. However, there was a dramatic increase in Jewish emigration (primarily to Israel) at the end of the Cold War (Figure 5.2).

Clearly migration affects the population growth of a country. We can determine a country's **rate of growth** as follows. For individual populations, the rate of growth is equal to the rate of natural increase *NI* plus the rate of net migration *NM* (the rate of immigration, *I*, minus the rate of emigration, *E*). If we let *r* stand for the rate of growth of a population, then:

$$r = NI + NM$$

As we will see later in this chapter, MDCs and LDCs differ dramatically in terms of rate of growth, with the former having very low rates and the latter having extremely high ones.

The distribution of populations within countries also changes over time. **Internal migration** is movement from one region of a country to another. The terms *in-migration* and *out-migration* are used to indicate internal migration. For example, in France, one who moves from Nice to Paris is an out-migrant from Nice and an in-migrant to Paris.

The United States has experienced a great deal of internal migration within the past two decades from the "Rust Belt," north-central states identified with "old" manufacturing industry, to the "Sun Belt," southern and western states identified with new, high-technology industry and services (Figure 5.3).

Internationally, immigration and emigration may present specific social problems, and within nations in-migration and out-migration may be problematic.

MEDICAL REVOLUTION OR CHANGE IN VALUES?

A strong argument can be made that the tremendous growth of the world's population has been due to our ability to control the infectious spread

Figure 5.3
This map shows the U.S. population growth in every state from 1980 to 1990. The national average is 11.4%. Internal migration in the United States has resulted in the growth of population in the western and southern states and a decrease in the population of north-central states.

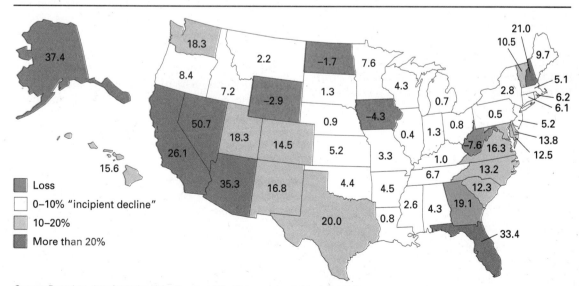

- ■ Loss
- □ 0–10% "incipient decline"
- ▦ 10–20%
- ■ More than 20%

Source: Based on data from the U.S., Bureau of the Census reported in *Information Please Almanac* (Boston: Houghton Mifflin, 1992).

of life-threatening, or morbid, diseases. Some people attribute this progress to developments in medical advancements that have conquered debilitating ailments and increased life expectancy; others claim that education and a consequent change of values are really responsible.

Medicine in Antiquity

Four hundred years before the dawn of the Christian era, Hippocrates, a Greek physician, tried to convince his colleagues that illness was a product of natural causes. The common belief at that time was that disease was of supernatural origin and that its treatment must be of a religious nature. His success ushered in centuries of slow but steady progress in the field of medicine. This progress, however, was seriously impeded by European attitudes during the Middle Ages (about 500–1500 A.D.) when there was a deemphasis on scientific inquiry.

Toward the end of this medieval period, about the middle of the fourteenth century, Europe was devastated by the bubonic plague, or black death. The disease was so contagious that, according to French surgeon Guy de Chauliac, "The father did not visit the son nor the son the father. Charity was dead and hope abandoned" (see Wallis, 1987:54). By the time the epidemic subsided about a decade later, somewhere between one-fourth and one-third of the European population had perished. This incident was one of the more dramatic ways that population was held in check, historically. Over time, many scholars came to believe that populations could not continue to grow without suffering some kind of calamity.

Malthusian Theory

Toward the end of the eighteenth century, Thomas Robert Malthus (1798), an economist and clergyman, warned that the future would not be so bright as some of his colleagues proph-

Thomas Robert Malthus (1766–1834), an English clergyman and economist, examined the relationship between population and food supply. He was the first scholar to point out the dangers of overpopulation.

esied. Although Europe was on the brink of the Industrial Revolution, Malthus foresaw not a "brave, new world," but a world of misery brought on by the rapidly growing population. He reasoned that the human species had the capacity and inclination for rapid reproduction, but the economy and food production could increase only within strict limits.

Based on his study of Egyptian population cycles, Malthus taught that population could double each generation, while food supply would increase much more slowly. As population outgrew food supply, **positive checks** (e.g., famine, pestilence, war, and disease) would increase mortality and bring population back into balance with food supply.

The means of subsistence (including food), according to Malthus, increased arithmetically, while population increased geometrically. In other words, if we start at some point in time when food and population are balanced, we would have one unit of food for each unit of population. A generation later, population would double (increasing geometrically) and food supply would increase by another unit (increasing arithmetically). Now, we have two units of food for two units of population and, although we are still in balance, the important factor is *how* we arrived at the two units, in one case by doubling and in the other case by adding one unit. A generation later, population doubles again to four units, but food supply, adding one more unit, increases only to three. According to what Malthus was writing about two hundred years ago, here is what the food/population ratio would look like today, if food and population were balanced at his time:

Food	1	2	3	4	5	6	7	8	9
Population	1	2	4	8	16	32	64	128	256
		1800	1825	1850	1875	1900	1925	1950	1975	2000

Of course, this relationship does not exist today for a number of factors. First of all, high death rates held population growth in Europe between 1 and 2 percent a year, causing a doubling about every 50 years. Second, many people began using **preventive checks**, as Malthus called them, to population growth. Those advocated by Malthus were celibacy, deferment of marriage, and "moral restraint" within marriage, leading to a lower birthrate. Finally, food production increased faster than had been imagined and food preservation techniques, such as canning, were invented.

While Malthus's predictions did not occur in Europe, we cannot dismiss his theory entirely. Today, the populations of sub-Saharan Africa, tropical Latin America, and Southeast Asia are growing at rates equal to or greater than those imagined by Malthus. But, even Europe's slower growth during the nineteenth century was remarkable compared to all of previous history.

Europe in the Eighteenth and Nineteenth Centuries

One factor propelling Europe's growth was a tremendous increase in individual wealth, attributable to the Industrial Revolution. E. A. Wrigley (1969:177) points out that during the nineteenth century, "improvements in health were a by-product of increases in wealth." In preindustrial Europe, increasing the supply of raw material and food almost always meant putting new lands under cultivation, and land was becoming a scarce commodity. However, industry was based on mineral consumption, especially coal. In a relatively small space, large quantities of material goods could be produced, increasing the total income of the population and, as a by-product, improving its overall health.

Demographer Paul Zopf (1984:190) attributes the decrease in the death rate to four factors. First, during the eighteenth and nineteenth centuries, political order was reestablished, producing a safer environment for people. Second, production and distribution of food and clothing improved to provide most people with adequate nutrition and protection from the elements. Third, sanitation improved, allowing purer water supply and better refuse disposal. Finally, knowledge of disease and methods to prevent and cure it expanded considerably. Antoine van Leeuwenhoek's discovery of bacteria in 1676 and Edward Jenner's discovery of vaccine for smallpox in 1796 are important examples of breakthroughs in medical science that resulted in fewer deaths. But, Zopf (1984:196) points out that improvements in health during the eighteenth century probably resulted more from changes in the human environment than from direct medical intervention.

Kammeyer and Ginn (1986:145) point out that during this same period, the diet of the average western European improved dramatically. Great Britain, particularly, was engaged in brisk trade with the United States and imported great quantities of potatoes and corn (both "New

World" products). The nutritional value of each was an important element in the improvement of health and in increasing people's resistance to disease.

Another very important advance was the decrease of infectious diseases such as cholera, dysentery, typhus, diarrhea, and of microorganisms that contaminated water and food supplies. From the mid 1800s on, countless lives have undoubtedly been saved by the work of Louis Pasteur. Building on van Leeuwenhoek's work, Pasteur showed that, although bacteria live almost everywhere, their spread can be controlled. He made milk, cheese, and beer safe to consume by inventing a controlled heating and cooling process, *pasteurization.*

Finally, a good deal of the decline of mortality in the nineteenth century may be attributable to a change in values. Cleanliness was elevated to a position next to godliness. This was not true before the 1800s. According to an eighteenth-century Englishwoman's diary (see Kammeyer and Ginn, 1986:146), she withstood a bath "better than expected, not having been wet all over for 28 years." It is reasonable to expect that other western Europeans were not much cleaner than the English. But the nineteenth century brought forth a new attitude toward personal hygiene. Soap was less expensive and, in the first 40 years of the nineteenth century, per capita soap consumption increased by 100 percent (see Kammeyer and Ginn, 1986:146). Figure 5.4 shows the effect this combination of occurrences had on mortality in England and Wales.

MDCs in the Twentieth Century

The MDCs entered the twentieth century armed with a hundred years of experience in controlling mortality. By 1900 diseases like smallpox were more readily detected, and noninfected people could be protected from diseased people. Nutrition continued to improve as we came to understand the nature of the human body and its requirements. Starvation gradually began to

Figure 5.4
The decline in death rates in England and Wales in the 1800s and 1900s was due, in part, to improved hygiene.

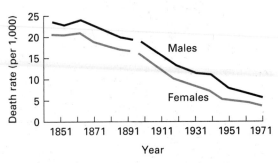

Source: Thomas McKeown, *The Role of Medicine: Dream, Mirage or Nemesis?* (Princeton, N.J.: Princeton University Press, 1979), p. 31. Copyright © 1979 by Princeton University Press; as cited in K. C. W. Kammeyer and H. L. Ginn, *An Introduction to Population* (Chicago: The Dorsey Press, 1986), p. 142.

disappear as a cause of death (although evidence of it may still be found among small, relatively isolated populations). Improvements continued to be made to water supplies and sewage disposal. Cleanliness remained next to godliness and governments began organized programs to ensure the purity of food.

In this century, direct medical intervention has been much more effective in lowering mortality than it was during previous eras. The treatment of disease became more scientific and physicians were able to provide drugs that had positive effects. In the 1940s, working on earlier research by the English bacteriologist Sir Alexander Fleming, a team led by Howard Florey isolated penicillin, the first antibiotic. Initially, it was used to treat scarlet fever, but 98 percent of deaths caused by scarlet fever had been eradicated prior to the introduction of penicillin (see Kammeyer and Ginn, 1986:147). This has caused some researchers to question whether medical intervention has been as effective as we sometimes assume. Still, one must remember that annually hundreds of thousands of cases of pneumonia, streptococcal infections, influenza, and the like (diseases that regularly took the lives of our ancestors) are successfully treated with modern medicines.

The medical profession also became much more interested in the prevention of disease. In 1953 Jonas Salk introduced his vaccine against poliomyelitis, or infantile paralysis. Polio was not only a crippler; it was a killer. In 1952, for example, 58,000 people contracted polio in the United States and about 5,000 of them died. Salk's vaccine was made available to the public in 1955. Now, polio is rare in the MDCs.

Certain organ transplants, like those dealing with the kidney and heart, occur rather commonly, and work continues on development of an artificial heart. But it seems that for every medical triumph, the world is faced with a new challenge. With diseases like polio and smallpox virtually eradicated from the earth, in 1980 a new killer was discovered—AIDS (Acquired Immune Deficiency Syndrome). At this writing, there is no cure for AIDS and 100 percent of its victims eventually die (see Heymann, Chin, and Mann, 1990)

The World Health Organization (WHO) says that 162 countries have reported incidents of AIDS, and it estimates that 100 million people will become infected by 2005. If this occurs and no cure is found, the great plagues that struck down about 25 million people in Europe will seem like a case of a bad cold by comparison. Of course, 100 million people is a smaller percentage of world population than that killed during the plagues, but it is a higher absolute number of deaths. Because AIDS is spread only by intimate contact (i.e., sexual intercourse, sharing of hypodermic needles, exchange of bodily fluids) we, like our European counterparts who had to adopt new values regarding personal hygiene, may have to change our views and behavior regarding sexual practices. Historic precedence exists, and the alternative is disaster.

Medical advances and changes in values and behavior are relatively important in explaining declines in mortality. Some sociologists believe, however, that changes in values and behavior are more important than medical advances in explaining mortality declines, especially in the eighteenth and nineteenth centuries. The evidence suggests that death rates in Europe were starting to drop *before* the major medical advances occurred. Also, in the 1990s, we are witnessing the reverse of the above—old Malthusian foes, such as the bubonic plague that

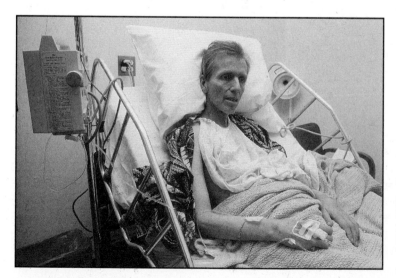

The World Health Organization estimates that 100 million people will become infected with AIDS, like this man waiting for death at Cooke Health Care Facility in New York. There is no cure for the disease.

ravaged Europe in the Middle Ages, are revisiting us. Scores of people died of the plague in India in 1994 while hundreds of thousands of citizens fled their hometowns to escape the disease. The reason for the reappearance of the plague is the deteriorating physical environment that people find themselves living in. The lack of safe water supplies and sewage systems facilitate the spread of diseases.

DEMOGRAPHIC TRANSITION: THREE MODELS

The changes in medical knowledge, personal habits, and social values we've discussed greatly increased the size and nature of the European population, but other parts of the world were largely unaffected by the process of modernization until fairly recently. One theory explaining the transformation of the European population, the **demographic transition theory**, holds that populations originally had very high CBRs that were matched by equally high CDRs. Gradually the CDR decreases, allowing for an increase in the population. As the CDR continues to decline, the people become confident that they can have few children with a reasonable expectation that those children will live into adulthood and be there to care for the parents when the parents reach old age. When that degree of confidence is attained, the CBR begins to decrease until it matches the existing CDR, which, by now, is quite low (see Figure 5.5a).

The transformation of the European population was the model on which the theory was built, and the theory is quite accurate according to the information we have. For example, in 1790 Finland had a high CBR (38 births per 1,000 people) that was nearly offset by a CDR of 32 deaths per 1,000 people. In 1830, although the CBR stayed at 38 per 1,000, the CDR decreased to 24, allowing a rate of natural increase of 14 per 1,000, or 1.4 percent per year. By 1915 the CDR continued to decrease to 17, but the CBR also

Figure 5.5
The demographic transitions in Europe, Asia, and Africa and Latin America follow three models.

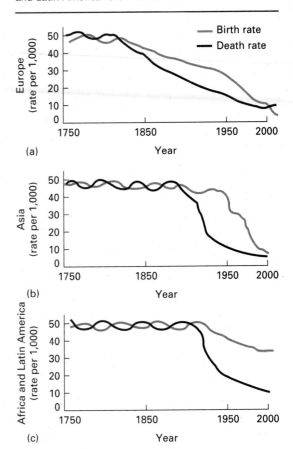

Source: Models are based on data from Population Reference Bureau, Bureau of the Census, and United Nations by James A. Glynn.

decreased to a moderate 29. By this time, population was growing at 16 per 1,000, or 1.6 percent per year. By the mid 1970s, Finland had completed the cycle with a low CBR of 13, nearly matching its CDR of 10, and a population growth approaching zero (actually, 3 per 1,000 or 0.3 percent per year) (Merrick, 1986:9). While most European populations were undergoing this transformation, however, the countries of Africa, Latin America, and Asia were not.

If we were to try to fit the development of population of these three geographic regions into our theory of the demographic transition, we would be frustrated because they simply don't follow the pattern. Birth and death rates began to decline in Asia much later than they did in Europe (see Figure 5.5b) and, although death rates dropped rather dramatically in recent years in Africa and Latin America, birthrates have remained quite high (see Figure 5.5c). The imbalance of these two rates is causing tremendous problems for the LDCs of Asia and Latin America. In general, countries that completed the transition in the European fashion have populations who enjoy good health, have adequate food, and are economically well off. Countries that have not completed the transition usually suffer from opposite conditions.

Latin America

Before the twentieth century, most of the population of Latin America resembled the populations of antiquity, with high birthrates offset by high death rates. Population, however, did expand through immigration from Europe and, later, the slave trade. Also, as Europe exported its medical technology and methods of sanitation, population in Latin America grew, albeit rather slowly when compared to modern rates. Although death rates began to decline in a few Latin American countries in the opening decades of this century, real progress was not made until after World War II. As late as 1965, a number of countries still had relatively high mortality rates (Table 5.2). Over the next three decades or so, however, the death rates of some countries (Colombia, Ecuador, and Guatemala, for instance) were cut in half and other countries, like Bolivia, experienced a lesser reduction.

While death rates fell, birthrates did not decline enough to significantly slow the rate of growth. High birthrates combined with low death rates create a situation in which population grows rapidly. One measure of how fast a population is growing is **doubling time**, the number of years that it will take a country's present population to double in size. A population with an annual rate of growth of 1 percent will take 70 years to double; 2 percent doubles in 35 years; 3 percent, 23 years. Many Latin American countries have had annual growth rates close to, at, or above 3 percent for more than two decades. Table 5.3 shows the 1965 and 1994 figures for the four Latin American countries featured in Table 5.2. Notice that while Colombia and Ecuador are growing slightly slower now and Guatemala is growing at the same rate, Bolivia is growing faster.

The high birthrates in Latin America also affect the age structure of those societies. As Thomas W. Merrick (1986:9) points out, **age structure** "is one of the principal ties between demographic processes and socioeconomic changes." If a society has a high proportion of its population below age 15 and above age 65, it is said to have a high **age-dependency ratio**. That means that the relatively smaller proportion of people between 15 and 65 years old must support not only themselves, but also the young and old who are their dependents. An age-dependency ratio of 100 means that there are as many dependent people (under 15 or over 65) as there are working people. Table 5.4 shows the percentage of Latin American populations under age 15 and the age-dependency ratio. Notice that in 1960 four countries had age-dependency ratios greater than 100 and many places were very close to 100. By 1994 all countries, with the exception of Honduras, had ratios below 100, but all are also quite a bit higher than the United States' age-dependency ratio of 54.

Because some Latin American countries have been growing at rates predicted for Europe by Malthus two hundred years ago, it is not surprising that a neo-Malthusian view of the situation south of the Rio Grande was to emerge. The neo-Malthusians are fearful that the rapid growth of population will place greater demands on monetary and other resources to provide a simple maintenance level. This would, in turn, work

Crude Death Rates (1965 and 1994), Infant Mortality Rates, Life Expectancy (1994), and Per Capita Gross National Products (1992) for Selected Countries				**TABLE 5.2**
	1965 Crude death rate	1994 Crude death rate	1994 Infant mortality rate	1994 Life expectancy	1992 Per Capita GNP
LATIN AMERICA					
Bolivia	21	10	75	61	$680
Colombia	15	5	33	71	$1,290
Ecuador	15	6	53	69	$1,070
Guatemala	16	7	57	65	$980
ASIA					
Bangladesh	22	13	116	53	$220
India	21	10	79	57	$310
Indonesia	20	9	68	60	$670
Nepal	24	15	90	51	$170
Pakistan	21	12	109	60	$410
AFRICA					
Guinea	30	21	147	43	$510
Malawi	27	20	134	44	$210
Mozambique	27	18	147	47	$60
Niger	29	19	123	47	$300
Sierra Leone	33	22	143	43	$170

SOURCE: 1965 data is from The World Bank, *World Development Report 1986*. All other data is from Haub and Yanagishita, *World Population Data Sheet 1994*.

against the possibility of increasing the standard of living of the populations, a step seen as essential to lowering the fertility rate. Neo-Malthusians point out that it was only after Europeans' standard of living improved that their fertility rates began to decline. Stated simply, Latin America may have fallen into a "Malthusian trap" (Merrick, 1986:37) from which it cannot be extricated.

Other views challenge the causal assumption of neo-Malthusians. Structuralists challenge the neo-Malthusian idea that rapid population growth is the root cause of the area's underdevelopment. They argue that present problems of poverty and inequality are tied to Latin America's colonial past. The unequal distribution of land, resources, and political power is to blame. So, the neo-Malthusians push for family planning to lower fertility, and the structuralists press for economic development. However, a third view holds that both socioeconomic development and family planning are necessary to lower fertility and improve the standard of living. This was the central theme of the International Population Conference held in Mexico City in 1984, and it was strongly supported by Latin American governments (Merrick, 1986). The importance of improving the status and well-being of women was added by the Programme of Action of the International

Crude Birthrates (1965 and 1994), Rates of Growth (1965 and 1994) and Current Doubling Time for Selected Latin American Countries					TABLE 5.3
	1965 Crude birthrate	1994 Crude birthrate	1965 Rate of growth	1994 Rate of growth	Current doubling time
Bolivia	46	37	2.5%	2.7%	26 years
Colombia	45	25	3.0%	2.0%	35 years
Ecuador	45	31	3.0%	2.5%	28 years
Guatemala	46	39	3.0%	3.1%	22 years

SOURCES: 1965 data is from the World Bank, *World Development Report 1986* and 1994 data is from Haub and Yanagishita, *World Population Data Sheet 1994.*

Conference on Population and Development, which met in Cairo in September of 1994. Principle number 4 in the Programme of Action asserts that

> Advancing gender equality and equity and the empowerment of women, and the elimination of all kinds of violence against women, and ensuring women's ability to control their own fertility, are cornerstones of population and development-related programmes. The human rights of women and the girl-child are an inalienable, integral, and indivisible part of universal human rights. The full and equal participation of women in civil, cultural, economic, political, and social life, at the national, regional, and international levels, and the eradication of all forms of discrimination on grounds of sex, are priority objectives of the international community (United Nations, 1994:13).

Even if Latin America manages to lower its fertility rate, the number of Latin Americans will continue to soar well into the next century because of a dynamic called population momentum. **Population momentum** is a function of the age structure of a population. If a large percentage of a population is young, as is the case in nearly all Latin American countries,

then, even if fewer children are born to that generation than to the previous generation, the absolute number of children will increase. In turn, even if that future generation has fewer children than their parents had, the absolute number may be as high or higher. Consequently, it is entirely possible that although birthrates may drop significantly in the next several decades, the number of Latin Americans will more than double.

Asia

Asia's populations and its problems are more diverse than those of Latin America. First, there is the industrialized area that has completed the demographic transition in the European tradition and is economically fairly healthy. Countries in this category are Japan, South Korea, and Taiwan. In fact, Abdel Omran (1971) claims that Japan is a good example of an accelerated transition model of demographic change. Before the late 1880s, Japan maintained an isolationist position, not communicating or dealing with the outside world. However a change of political regimes, referred to as the *Meiji Restoration*, cleared the way for trade with western nations, which lead to the diffusion of modern ideas to the Japanese islands.

Population Under Age 15 and Age-Dependency Ratio for Latin American Countries: 1960 and 1994.				TABLE 5.4

Subregion and country	Percentage of population under age 15		Age-dependency ratio (Number per 100 between 15 and 65)	
	1960	1994	1960	1994
SOUTH AMERICA				
Argentina	31	30	57.1	63.9
Bolivia	43	42	85.4	85.2
Brazil	43	35	86.7	66.7
Chile	39	31	77.6	58.7
Colombia	46	34	97.5	61.3
Ecuador	45	39	95.3	75.4
Guyana	48	33	107.5	58.7
Paraguay	46	40	97.3	78.6
Peru	43	38	87.8	72.4
Suriname	48	41	104.9	81.8
Uruguay	28	26	56.2	61.3
Venezuela	46	38	94.4	72.4
MEXICO AND CENTRAL AMERICA				
Costa Rica	48	36	101.9	69.5
El Salvador	45	44	92.2	92.3
Guatemala	46	45	94.9	92.3
Honduras	46	46	91.4	104.1
Mexico	46	38	96.0	72.4
Nicaragua	48	46	101.2	96.1
Panama	44	35	90.5	66.7
CARIBBEAN				
Cuba	34	23	64.4	47.1
Dominican Republic	47	38	98.8	69.5
Haiti	41	40	81.3	78.6
Jamaica	42	33	85.2	69.5
Puerto Rico	43	27	91.9	58.7
Trinidad & Tobago	43	24	88.7	61.3

SOURCES: Merrick, 1986, *Population Pressures in Latin America;* and Haub and Yanagishita, *1994 World Population Data Sheet.*

ween 1870 and 1945, the year World War II ended. In 1955 abortion was approved, and in the next ten years Japan cut its birthrate in half, an unprecedented achievement. For most of that decade, abortions outnumbered live births. In more recent years, however, Japan has continued to lower its birthrate through contraception rather than abortion.

Statistically, Japan resembles the modern countries of Europe and European influence (North America, Australia, and New Zealand). By adopting European technology and knowledge, Japan was able to bring its death rate down swiftly; this was followed by a precipitous decline in the birthrate. Currently, the crude birthrate is a low 10 per 1,000 living population, the crude death rate is 7, and the rate of growth is just 3 percent annually. If the population were to double, and it probably won't, it would take 267 years (see Table 5.5).

Most of the Asian continent is dominated by the People's Republic of China, the world's first demographic billionaire. Because its population is so large, many people think that China must be growing very fast. However, China's growth rate is relatively low, although it did experience rapid growth from the early 1950s through the late 1970s. Before 1650, China's population probably fluctuated between 60 million and 100 million, growing during good times and declining when times were bad. Beginning around 1685, China began steadily growing until it reached 413 million in the late 1840s. This growth spurt was probably due to the diffusion of foodplants like corn, potatoes, and peanuts. This renaissance of agriculture encouraged peasants to have larger families, thereby providing more workers for the fields. But from 1850 until 1950, China's overall population did not change very much, increasing to only 540 million over that century.

After the People's Republic of China was established (1949) and land reform was accomplished, the death rate in China declined drastically, which allowed for annual growth increases ranging from 1 percent to 3 percent (see Table 5.6). The

Japanese success at modernizing over the next hundred years equaled that of Northern and Western Europe. But Japan's birthrate remained relatively high and stable until after World War II. Consequently, Japan's population doubled bet-

Demographic Data: Japan, China, and India (1994)	Japan	China	India
Crude birthrate	10	18	29
Crude death rate	7	7	10
Natural increase	0.3	1.1	1.9
Doubling time	267 yr	61 yr	36 yr
Life expectancy	79	70	57
Infant mortality rate	4.4	31	79
Per capita GNP	$28,220	$380	$310

TABLE 5.5

SOURCE: Haub and Yanagishita, *1994 World Population Data Sheet.*

biggest increases occurred during the 1960s, China's baby boom. Since the early 1970s, China's annual rate of natural increase has declined to very low levels. The famous (or infamous) *one-child policy*, which China adopted in the late 1970s, calls for "only child glory certificates" to be issued to couples who pledge to have only one child. The certificate entitles the couple to free medical care and school tuition for their offspring. In addition, the parents can receive either direct cash or work points, depending on their place of residence and type of work. The family gets preferential housing and the parents will qualify for extended pension benefits when the time comes. There is no doubt that the one-child policy was largely responsible for the impressive declines in fertility from the 1970s through the mid 1980s.

The one-child policy has been relaxed since the second half of the 1980s. The annual rate of natural increase reversed around 1984, inched upward to 1.4 percent in 1992, and then reversed itself again, registering 1.2 percent in 1993 and 1.1 percent in 1994. Whether the relaxation of the one-child policy is the primary cause of the temporary reversal in the rate of increase is debatable. Norman Luther and his colleagues (1990) argue that the relaxation of the one-child family policy has been very instrumental in increasing

China's birthrate. However, Zeng Yi and her associates (1991) broke down the increase in the crude birthrate in China and came to the conclusion that the increase in the birthrate was primarily due to the rising population of women of peak productive age (the baby boom generation creating the "echo effect") and the declining age at marriage. Their analysis (Yi et al. 1991:435) did not show much of an actual increase in marital fertility (the number of children that a couple will eventually have) and they concluded that China's population growth is not "out of control again." Because the birthrate and the rate of natural increase for China appear to have vacillated in the 1980s, the conclusion of Yi and her associates would seem to be the more accurate.

The "echo effect" refers to the increase in births due to a large cohort produced in the 1960s, which is now entering its childbearing time of life. But even with the echo from the baby boom, China's population, now well over one billion people, grows slowly by comparison to its Southeast Asian neighbors (see Table 5.6). For example, Southeast Asian countries growing by 2.3 percent annually or higher include Brunei, Cambodia, Malaysia, the Philippines, and Vietnam. Nearly all of the other Southeast Asian and Southern Asian countries are growing by 2 percent or higher. Singapore and Thailand are exceptions with rates of growth of 1.4 percent and 1.2 percent, respectively, as is Sri Lanka (1.5 percent) and Kazakhstan (1.2 percent). And, most western Asian countries have fairly large rates of natural increase (see Haub et al. 1994).

Special note must be taken of India, a country that pioneered federally operated family planning programs but now has the second largest population in the world. Although some scholars voiced concern about the size of India's population as far back as 1890, the crisis it faces today is a product of the last four decades. Before 1911 India's annual growth rate was far below 1 percent because death rates were nearly as high as birthrates. Between 1911 and 1921 India was devastated by outbreaks of malaria, severe famine, epidemics of plague,

In China, wall posters and huge billboards communicate the message that small families are happy and prosperous. Although the government in Beijing has relaxed its one-child policy, China's overall rate of growth is rather low for an economically underdeveloped country.

cholera, and influenza. After those conditions were controlled, population increase jumped to more than 1 percent per year, and it has never returned to the lower level.

Between 1941 and 1951 there was a slight shift in the otherwise accelerating pace of India's growth. The shift was due to the Bengal famine of 1942–1943 and the division of the Asian subcontinent into India, Pakistan, and East Pakistan (now Bangladesh) after independence from Great Britain was achieved in 1947. From that time on, epidemics have been largely controlled and the mortality rate has steadily declined. At the present time, India has a population of 911.6 million people and is still growing by 1.9 percent annually (see Tables 5.5 and 5.7).

In 1951 the leaders who drew up India's constitution and formulated its first Five-Year Plan hoped to double the per capita income in 27 years. By 1978, while the net national product increased by 162 percent, the rapid growth of population only increased the per capita income by about 47 percent. Sixteen years later, per capita income was still only about $310 annually (see Table 5.5). Furthermore, nearly half of India's population (51 percent of rural Indians and 38 percent of urban ones) live in conditions of absolute poverty. The

Visarias (1981) define *absolute poverty* as consumption of fewer than 2,400 calories per person per day in rural areas and 2,100 calories per person per day in urban areas.

By 1975 things looked so desperate that Prime Minister Indira Gandhi's son, Sanjay, made family planning a key element in the Indian Youth Congress. He declared that family planning must be given "the utmost attention and importance because all our industrial, economic, and agricultural progress would be of no use if the population continued to rise at the present rate" (Visaria and Visaria, 1981:38). The following year, the government's Minimum Needs Program, to hasten development and reduce poverty, included 16 population-related measures. Among other things, it included sharply increasing the monetary rewards given to people who chose sterilization, requiring central government employees to have small families, permitting state legislation to compel sterilization for couples with more than three children, and raising the minimum legal age for marriage.

This last measure is especially important to India because of its age structure. India and China are two of the very few countries in the world where adult men outnumber adult

China's Birth, Death, and Natural Increase Rates 1952–1994			TABLE 5.6
Year	Crude birthrate	Crude death rate	Natural increase rate
1952	37.0	17.0	2.0%
1957	34.0	10.8	2.3%
1962	37.3	10.1	2.7%
1967	34.1	8.1	2.6%
1972	29.9	7.7	2.2%
1977	19.0	6.9	1.2%
1982	20.9	6.4	1.6%
1987	21.0	8.0	1.3%
1992	20.0	7.0	1.4%
1993	18.0	7.0	1.2%
1994	18.0	7.0	1.1%

SOURCES: All data except 1987, 1992, 1993, and 1994 are from Tien, *China: Demographic Billionaire.* Data for 1987 is from Haub et al., *1987 World Population Data Sheet.* Data for 1992 is from Haub and Yanagishita, *1992 World Population Data Sheet.* Data for 1993 is from Haub and Yanagishita, *1993 World Population Data Sheet.* Data for 1994 is from Haub and Yanagishita, *1994 World Population Data Sheet.*

Population Statistics for India: 1901–1994		TABLE 5.7
Census year[a]	Total population (millions)	Average annual growth rate (%)
1901	283.3	0.30
1911	252.3	0.56
1921	251.2	−0.03
1931	278.9	1.06
1941	318.5	1.34
1951	361.0	1.26
1961	439.1	1.98
1971	548.2	2.20
1981	683.8	2.23
1994	911.6	1.90

[a]1901–1981 are actual census years: 1994 is an estimate.

SOURCES: Visaria and Visaria, *India's Population: Second and Growing,* and Haub and Yanagishita, *1994 World Population Data Sheet.*

women. This is due to male preference and subsequent female infanticide (as discussed in Chapter 3), and to a high rate of maternal deaths during childbirth. When the age structure gets out of balance in this fashion, the pool of women of a given age range available for marriage to men of a slightly higher age range is quickly used up. Consequently, the families of the less fortunate men must look to increasingly younger females as potential mates for their sons. Marrying females off early, for example before they can finish their schooling, exacerbates all other problems. Children come early to teenage mothers, the span of fertility (number of years a woman will reproduce) increases, and chances of maternal mortality are higher.

An official target of 4.3 million sterilizations, mostly vasectomies (an operation that prevents sperm from being in semen), was set for 1976–1977 in India. But government administrators went far beyond official policy. "State sterilization targets were divided among different government departments and orders (were) passed down the line that everybody—from teachers and police to government contractors and railway inspectors—must meet monthly quotas or jobs, salaries, or contracts would suffer" (Visaria and Visaria, 1981:39). Through the year, there were incidents of denial of public rations for families with more than three children, the ordering of employees to be sterilized or lose pay, and other negative incentives. Rumors of such coercion caused a backlash against the government.

For the first time in India's independence, the Congress Party (the party of Nehru and Indira Gandhi) was voted out of office. It was replaced by the Janata (People's) Party, which softpedalled the idea of sterilization and contraception. Whereas 8.3 million sterilizations had been performed from 1976 to 1977 (almost double the target), only 948,000 (or 11 percent of the previous year's accomplishment) were performed from 1977 to 1978 under the Janata leadership. In 1980 Indira Gandhi returned to office but "chose to keep a low profile on family planning during her first year back in office" (Visaria and Visaria, 1981:42). Although efforts at family planning have increased in recent years, India is still adding more than 17 million persons per year to its heavily burdened population.

Africa

Declines in mortality came very late to the African continent. As late as 1965, nearly every sub-Saharan country had a crude death rate of more than 20 per 1,000 living persons, and some had 30 or more (see Table 5.2). By contrast, that same year the crude death rate of the United States was nine, of Canada was eight, and the CDRs of Japan and the USSR were seven. For most of its existence, Africa represented the beginnings of our model for the demographic transition; it had very high birthrates that were offset by very high death rates, causing a rate of growth over time of zero. For at least 250 years, from 1650 to 1900, its population totaled about 100 million, a very small number of people for such a large, fertile land mass. The death rate was high because of very high **infant mortality rates**, the number of deaths of infants between birth and 1 year old per 1,000 live births, as well as erratic food supplies from subsistence farming, the slave trade, and tribal warfare (Goliber, 1985:32).

As Europeans began to colonize Africa more intensely after 1900, European diseases were added to African diseases and, by 1930, some leaders began to worry about depopulation. After World War II, more modern medicine and technology was introduced to Africa, lowering the death rate, but not affecting the birthrate. This caused the overall rate of growth to soar. By 1965, 20 years later, Kenya was growing by 3.5 percent annually; Tanzania, 2.9 percent; and Ghana, 2.8 percent (Goliber, 1985:36). In recent decades, death rates have continued to decline slowly in this part of the world, while birthrates have remained high or have gone up even further. This has raised the rate of natural increase. The average rate of increase in Africa in the 1960s was 2.6, and it rose to 2.9 in the

1970s and 3.0 in the 1980s (Goliber, 1989:6). Even with this unprecedented growth, Africa managed to raise incomes and standards of living until the 1970s. Thomas J. Goliber (1985:36) points out that the countries were able to sustain the growing population. But as per capita share of the gross national product declined in the 1980s, this progress appears to have come to a halt. Goliber (1989:12) asserts that "most of the sub-Saharan region has witnessed a decade and a half of economic stagnation and declining living standards." Additionally, Table 5.2 shows that most sub-Saharan countries (42 of Africa's 47 countries that lie below the Sahara Desert) have high infant mortality rates and low life expectancy.

The International Institute of Tropical Africa (IITA) says,

> In Africa, almost every problem is more acute than elsewhere. Topsoils are more fragile, and more subject to erosion and degradation. Irrigation covers a smaller fraction of the cultivated area ... leaving agriculture exposed to the vicissitudes of an irregular rainfall pattern. The infrastructure, both physical and institutional, is weaker. The shortage of trained people is more serious. The flight from the land is more precipitate. ... In one respect, namely the failure to develop farming systems capable of high and sustained rates of production growth, the problems of Africa have reached the stage of crisis. (Brown and Wolf, 1986:188)

Almost every problem mentioned in the IITA report will probably become worse because of the very small doubling time of these countries, ranging from a mere 22 years in Western Africa to 23 years in Eastern and Middle Africa to a high of 26 years in Southern Africa (see Table 5.8).

Lester R. Brown (1987:21) reports, "Once populations expand to the point where their demands begin to exceed the sustainable yield of local forests, grasslands, croplands, or aquifers, they begin directly or indirectly to consume the resource base itself. Forests and grasslands disap-

As populations mushroom in sub-Saharan African cities, traffic jams like this one in Lagos, Nigeria, become common. In poor countries, it is not possible to build roadways, housing, and other necessities for city dwellers whose numbers may double every seven to ten years.

pear, soils erode, land productivity declines, water tables fall, or wells go dry. This in turn reduces food production and incomes, triggering a downward spiral." This has happened already in many parts of Africa. There are food shortages (highlighted by famines such as those experienced by Ethiopia in the mid 1980s and Somalia in the early 1990s), firewood shortages, extremely high rates of unemployment, and a general unavailability of safe water. Although arguments can be made against a neo-Malthusian

viewpoint of Africa's situation, few scholars would not agree that before any other consideration would improve African conditions, the countries must begin to control their growth. Figure 5.5c shows that Africa (and to a slightly lesser extent Latin America and Southeast Asia) is at a new point in the demographic transition. Might this point be the Malthusian trap we discussed earlier, from which escape, if possible, will be extremely difficult?

Lack of Movement Through the Demographic Transition

Why are so many of the world's LDCs having difficulty moving through the demographic transition? Why do so many of them have difficulty bringing down their fertility rates? Some light was shed on this in the three models of Latin America, Asia, and Africa just discussed. Certainly the point in history at which countries start the transition is important. When the present MDCs went through the transition, they were the most powerful countries in the world and could colonialize and exploit other parts of the planet, virtually at will. Obviously, this helped these countries to develop and grow. And, as was mentioned previously, the LDCs of today were able to borrow the medical and scientific advances of the MDCs and immediately slash their mortality rates. However, these mortality declines were achieved with artificial changes, not the substantive improvements in living conditions that was the case of the MDCs. High fertility has continued in the LDCs because substantial increments in the standard of living have not been realized.

In addition, world system theory argues that the immediate interest of the core countries has been the status quo, that is, the lack of development in the LDCs. Core countries can realize more profit by locating assembly plants in the LDCs where very cheap labor can be found. If the LDCs become developed, this cheap labor disappears. As long as peripheral

In many poor countries, mortality rates declined with artificial changes, usually involving technology borrowed from the industrialized countries. Here a mother in poverty-stricken Mali feeds her baby with a bottle, clearly not a traditionally African product. However, unless baby formula is mixed with safe water, babies will die rather than thrive.

Doubling Time in Sub-Saharan Africa, 1994	TABLE 5.8
Sub-Saharan Africa	**Doubling time**
WESTERN AFRICA	**22**
Benin	22
Burkina Faso	22
Cape Verde	24
Côte d'Ivoire	20
Gambia	26
Ghana	23
Guinea	28
Guinea-Bissau	32
Liberia	21
Mali	23
Mauritania	24
Niger	20
Nigeria	23
Senegal	26
Sierra Leone	26
Togo	19
EASTERN AFRICA	**23**
Burundi	24
Comoros	20
Djibouti	23
Ethiopia	22
Kenya	21
Madagascar	21
Malawi	25
Mauritius	47
Reunion	40
Rwanda	30
Seychelles	46
Somalia	22
Tanzania	21
Uganda	23
Zambia	24
Zimbabwe	23
MIDDLE AFRICA	**23**
Angola	26
Cameroon	24
Central African Republic	29
Chad	27
Congo	27
Equatorial Guinea	27
Gabon	26
Sao Tome and Principe	28
Zaire	21
	(continued)

LDCs are undeveloped, it is easy for core MDCs to extract raw resources, often with the blessing of elites in the LDCs, and to sell finished products to the citizens of LDCs. As long as LDCs remain undeveloped, the conditions needed for substantial fertility reduction are absent, and rapid population growth results. In short, the MDCs have been, and continue to be, a large part of the problem of rapid world population growth.

TABLE 5.8	
(continued)	
SOUTHERN AFRICA	26
Botswana	26
Lesotho	36
Namibia	21
South Africa	26
Swaziland	22

SOURCE: Haub and Yanagishita, *1994 World Population Data Sheet.*

THE ELDERLY

In addition to the world's population getting larger, it is also becoming older. The present average age of the planet's population is 28 years. By the year 2030, the average age will be between 31 and 35 years (Lutz, 1994:29). The proportion of the world's population that is 60 and older will also increase from its current level of 9 percent to 13 to 17 percent by the year 2030 (Lutz, 1994:29–30). Though the average age in LDCs is, and will continue to be, considerably lower than in the MDCs, and though the LDCs have a considerably smaller percentage of their populations in the elderly categories, the issue of aging is still very relevant to the LDCs. That is because the absolute number of old people in the LDCs is growing rapidly. By the year 2000, the LDCs will contain 60 percent of the planet's population over 65 years of age (Sokolovshy, 1982:4).

Are the Elderly a Burden?

When families were organized into *consanguine*, or extended family units, as during the pioneer days of the United States or Canada, the elderly were a vital part of the social and economic unit. They provided experience, child care, and a sense of continuity. Where the elderly are venerated, like in ancient China, people are admired for their longevity. As the populations of modern societies get older, some argue that the aged become a burden. Concern about the aging of populations is most prevalent in the MDCs. The reason is that in the MDCs the crude birthrate has been low for a number of decades. A low birthrate "ages" a population; so does the increase in life expectancy (compare Tables 5.9 and Table 5.2). One important demographic indicator is the **total fertility rate (TFR)**, the total number of children that each woman (on average) would have, if her fertility pattern followed the age-specific birthrates (rates for age categories of women) in existence at that time (Weller and Bouvier, 1981:56–60). A TFR of 2.1 is necessary to replace existing population. If the TFR falls below 2.1 and remains low for a period of years, a population will begin to shrink and larger and larger proportions of the society will enter into the elderly category. Table 5.10 shows the actual and middle-range projections of the United States' population aged 65 and older. In 1990, this "retirement cohort" made up 12 percent of the population; they numbered 31 million. With increases in medical technology, improvement in nutrition, and a better overall understanding of health, it is expected that this segment of society will continue to increase absolutely and proportionately as the crude birthrate and TFR remain low.

While the United States may well be concerned about who or what social programs will support the nearly 18 percent of its population that will be 65 years of age or older by the year 2040, France is very worried about the 30 percent of its population that will be at least 65 that same year. Some observers claim that the French are "obsessed" with the problem. Former President François Mitterrand is quoted as calling it "a question of national survival." According to French sociologists, the consequences will be "a general decline in the quality of French life, an unmanageable burden on social services, a disappearance of creativity, more immigration, and an increasing inability to assimilate the newcomers, leading to a loss of specific French identity" (Associated Press, 1984:cc7).

Total Fertility Rates and Life Expectancy for Selected MDCs: 1994	TABLE 5.9	
	Total fertility rate	Life expectancy
NORTH AMERICA		
Canada	1.8	77
United States	2.1	76
OCEANIA		
Australia	1.9	77
New Zealand	2.1	75
EUROPE		
Denmark	1.8	75
Iceland	2.2	78
Austria	1.5	76
France	1.7	77
Germany	1.3	76
Switzerland	1.5	78
Bulgaria	1.5	72
Hungary	1.7	69
Poland	1.8	71
Greece	1.4	77
Portugal	1.5	74
Spain	1.2	77

SOURCE: Haub and Yanagishita, *1994 World Population Data Sheet.*

Population 65 and Older and Median Age of U.S. Population, 1900–1990, and Projections for 2000–2040		TABLE 5.10
Year	Percentage of population aged 65 and older	Median age of total population
ESTIMATES		
1900	4.1	22.9
1910	4.3	24.1
1920	4.7	25.3
1930	5.5	26.5
1940	6.9	29.0
1950	8.2	30.2
1960	9.3	29.5
1970	9.9	28.1
1980	11.2	30.2
1990	12.0	32.6
PROJECTIONS		
2000	12.2	35.5
2010	12.7	36.6
2020	15.5	37.0
2030	18.3	38.0
2040	17.8	37.8

SOURCES: U.S. Bureau of the Census, *Historical Statistics of the United States, Colonial Times to 1970,* and Current Population Reports, Series P-25, No. 704, *Projections of the United States: 1977–2050,* and U.S. Bureau of the Census, *Statistical Abstracts of the United States,* 1991.

France is not alone with these concerns. By 2025, 22.2 percent of the Netherlands' population will be 65 years of age or older, nearly double the 1985 percentage. Most other Western and Northern European countries are not far behind. Meanwhile, the population under age 15 will decrease to less than 17 percent. There is great concern that there will be no base of support for the future elderly. Writing for France's *Le Monde,* Michel Debre warned, "the policy setters, ministers, elected officials, journalists, teachers, priests have a responsibility: to make it understood that in France everything is at stake with this catastrophe of the decline in births—pension plans, social legislation, economic prosperity, freedom" (van de Kaa, 1987:46).

In the United States, it is estimated that it will take more than $85 billion in federal benefits to care for the nation's oldest citizens (those over 80 years) by the turn of the century. At the present time, this is the fastest growing segment of U.S. society, probably increasing by 67 percent between 1985 and 2000 (Associated Press, 1984:A3). This will put more stress on the family because the family, not government or agency programs, provides care for 80 to 90 percent of the elderly. Aside from the emotional burden, there is economic burden. Families already sustain many hidden costs in caring for their elderly members—home modifications, rented equipment, and higher energy expense to heat or cool the premises. Women, who are often the primary caregivers, may also have to sacrifice employment outside the home. Finally, there have been increases in health-care costs and cutbacks in federal programs like Medicare and Medicaid (Day, 1985).

The population of Japan is also aging quite rapidly. According to Linda Martin (1989), the Japan Institute of Population Problems estimates that the population over 65 will be 16.6 percent by the year 2000, 20 percent by the year 2010, and 23.4 percent by the year 2025. This can be compared to only 10.3% of the population being over age 65 in 1985. Japanese policy makers see two major problems connected with this aging of the population: increasing cost of public pensions and increased cost of health care. Japanese politicians and policy makers appear more concerned with the aging of their population than officials and politicians in other aging MDCs. Martin (1989) notes that all recent prime ministers of Japan have publicly recognized the challenge of their aging population.

Recently, major pension, tax, and medical reforms have tried to shift payment to the families of the elderly and away from the government. The burden will increasingly fall on the shoulders of the children of the elderly, which in Japan means the shoulders of middle-aged women. This is happening at the same time that the country's labor force is relying more and more on women, especially in part-time roles.

According to Martin (1989), Japan currently has a low retirement age and high unemployment among older workers. Japan is currently rethinking retirement policy. It may be necessary to make some adjustments to the age at which people retire, how and when their pensions start, and incentives to encourage people to work longer.

Some researchers assert that the "burden of the elderly" is blown out of proportion, and that the elderly are a resource rather than a detriment. Mary K. McMahon and Charles F. Hohm (1994) argue that archaic social measurements such as the age-dependency ratio perpetuate myths about the elderly as burdens to society. Their research shows that categorizing all people over 65 years of age as "dependent" is very problematic. The 65 to 74 age category, for example, was found to be very independent, taking little in the way of societal resources. In fact McMahon and Hohm (1994) found that this and other elderly cohorts provide much of the capital that younger generations need for purchasing homes and businesses. They also found a fairly strong *positive* relationship between the percentage of a nation's population over 65 and its per-capita gross national product—as the percentage of the population over 65 increases, so does the per capita GNP of the country.

Ageism

Robert W. Butler coined the term **ageism** back in 1968. According to Butler (1969:243–46), "Ageism can be seen as a systematic stereotyping of and discrimination against people because they are old, just as racism and sexism accomplish this with skin color and gender. Old people are categorized as senile, rigid in thought and manner, old-fashioned in morality and skills. . . . Ageism allows the younger generation to see older people as different from themselves; thus they subtly cease to identify with their elders as human beings." In a more recent article, Butler (1989:139) talks about the "New Ageism" which portrays the elderly as undeserving of increases in their pensions or Social Security benefits. Butler is of the opinion that concern about the elderly is universal and can be found in diverse societies, cultures, and political systems. He asserts that "Societies are afraid this increasing older population will become unaffordable, lead to stagnation of the society's productive and economic growth, and generate intergenerational conflict" (Butler, 1989:141–142).

Butler (1989:142–145) discusses a number of myths about the elderly that need to be dismissed. The first is that the life span of *Homo sapiens* has been greatly extended. He argues that the reason for the increase in the overall life expectancy rate is that *more* people are living longer, resulting in an increase in survivorship. The second myth is that the elderly are senile and debilitated. Senility, according to Butler, is not inevitable with age but is associated with illnesses like Alzheimer's disease, and only a minority of older people have these diseases. The third myth is that the elderly are affluent. Butler (1989:142) points out that there is a very skewed distribution of wealth among the elderly. For example, in the United States only 5.6 percent of the elderly have annual incomes exceeding $50,000, and 2.6 million elderly fall below the government's poverty line. In addition, 4.5 million U.S. elderly are near-poor. The probability of elderly women being poor is quite high, due to their longevity and also to lower pensions and Social Security payments caused by shorter working periods (because of child rearing) and lower pay. Fully 41 percent of U.S. elderly women are near-poor. The fourth myth about the elderly is that because of their growing older populations, nations will become bankrupt. Butler cites Sweden as an example of a country with a high percentage of its population over 65 (17 percent) that is doing very well economically. The fifth myth about the elderly is specific to the United States—that the U.S. Social Security system is bankrupt so that when young people reach retirement age, there will be no Social Security benefits for them. Butler (1989:143) asserts that this is simply not so and that "Rather, trust funds are becoming enormous; they will be in the trillion-dollar range at the turn of the century and will have $12 trillion when all of the baby boomers are 65 years of age and over."

Equity

Gordon F. Streib and Robert H. Binstock (1990:11) assert that in the late 1970s, as industrialized nations became aware of some of the possible economic and social ramifications of aging populations, the portrayal of the elderly changed from deserving to greedy. They discuss the new stereotype of older people in the United States, that the elderly are now thought to be prosperous, hedonistic, and selfish. "The aged emerged as a scapegoat for an impressive list of American problems" (Streib and Binstock, 1990:11).

Some demographers and child advocates blamed the voting power of the elderly for the problems that children were facing such as inadequate nutrition, education, and health care (for example, see Preston, 1984). Streib and Binstock (1990) argue, however, that the evidence (Rosenbaum and Button, 1989; Binstock, 1988; and Chomitz, 1987) shows that older people were not voting for programs that hurt children and young people.

MIGRATION

A major problem facing the planet today centers around the movement of huge numbers of people across national boundaries. The United Nations Population Fund (1993) reports that unchecked migration is threatening to overwhelm the receiving countries such as Canada, Germany, and the United States. In 1989, 50 million people were living in a country other than their native one. Just three years later, that number had doubled to 100 million (UNFPA/United Nations Population Fund, 1993). Figure 5.6 shows the number of immigrants who moved to 12 MDCs from 1980 to 1990. Germany has been by far the most affected by immigration, taking in 5 million people in the 1980s. Other European countries like France have taken in sizeable numbers of newcomers. Australia, Canada, and the United States have also added huge numbers of immigrants, especially in the late 1980s.

Immigrants can be classified as **refugees** or **permanent settlers**. Refugees are people who have been uprooted, left homeless, or forced to flee one geographic region to settle in another. (The three kinds of refugees—religious, economic, and political—are discussed in the section on Refugees in this chapter.) The term "permanent settlers" refers to immigrants who are not facing the severe and dire forces faced by refugees, but who desire to move to another

Figure 5.6
These graphs show the gross flows of immigrants and asylum seekers in selected MDCs from 1980 to 1990.

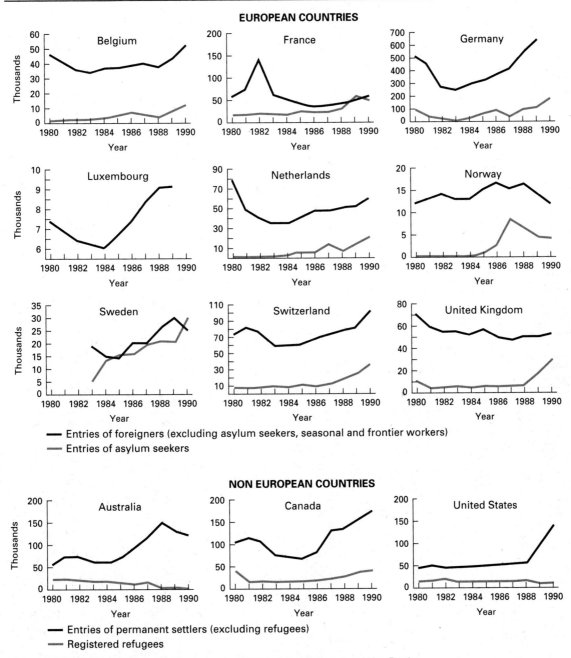

EUROPEAN COUNTRIES

— Entries of foreigners (excluding asylum seekers, seasonal and frontier workers)
— Entries of asylum seekers

NON EUROPEAN COUNTRIES

— Entries of permanent settlers (excluding refugees)
— Registered refugees

Source: OECD, SOPEMI, 1992, pp. 21–22; appeared in UNFPA/United Nations Population Fund.
The State of the World Population, 1993. New York: United Nations Population Fund: p. 18.

country to improve their lives. Figure 5.7 shows that refugees constitute a relatively small part of the immigration scene. Worldwide, refugees make up less than 20 percent of international migrants (Newland, 1994:20).

Permanent Settlers

Present immigration patterns differ considerably from past patterns and generate a distinctive set of challenges. In the past immigrants moved to areas with small populations and low densities. Opportunities for employment and advancement were considerable. Modern-day migrants are likely to encounter a quite different environment. The North American and European cities they are likely to enter are already occupied by others and are under considerable stress (UNFPA, 1993). The probability of finding decent employment and the chances of advancement are not so good as they were for former cohorts of migrants. Immigrants are also made scapegoats in MDCs and suffer from harassment and, in some cases, are killed by native citizens.

Numerous factors account for the growing number of immigrants, worldwide. First, as noted, the planet has been experiencing tremendous population growth, mostly in the less developed regions which do not have a sufficient number of jobs for the working-age population. One option for unemployed or underemployed citizens in the LDCs is to migrate to an MDC in the hope of finding work. For example, World Bank labor force figures suggest that 10 percent of Mexico's domestic labor force resides in the United States (Stanton-Russell and Teitelbaum, 1992:7). A second reason for increased migration from LDCs to MDCs is the loss of jobs in LDCs caused by modern electronic machines that displace human beings (Simmons, 1992). Increased mechanization characterizes the labor forces of LDCs just as it does the MDCs. A third reason for the increase in worldwide migration is environmental degradation. (We deal with the causes of environmental pollution and destruc-

Figure 5.7
The global number of refugees has increased dramatically since the mid 1970s.

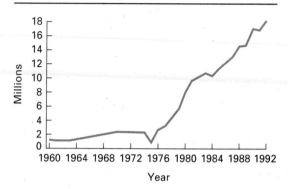

Source: UNHCR, *State of the World's Refugees*, 1993; appeared in K. Newland. *Refugees: The Rising Flood*, Worldwatch Paper 1994. Washington, DC: Worldwatch Institute: p. 18.

tion in later chapters.) Environmental problems such as deforestation, desertificaton, and polluted water supplies often result in people moving to other countries to escape these problems.

Refugees

Even though refugees constitute less than 20 percent of immigrants, the absolute number of refugees has been growing very rapidly. Figure 5.7 shows that from 1960 to 1976, the number of refugees in the world stayed about the same, fluctuating between 1 and 3 million. Since 1976 the number of refugees worldwide has kept increasing, to reach more than 18 million by 1992.

As noted, refugee status can be broken down into religious, political, and economic components. Religious refugees are forced to relocate because their religious beliefs clash with the beliefs of the majority. In 1947 the Asian subcontinent was divided into India and Pakistan in an effort to avoid further bloody revolutions. In turn, this forced the migration of millions of Hindus eastward to India and millions of Moslems westward to Pakistan. Historically, Jews were driven from Germany and, after 1492, from Spain, as well. The Quakers, Mennonites, and

Hutterites are groups with religious beliefs outside the mainstream of a dominant belief system that have escaped persecution only by leaving their native lands.

In some cases, populations may be "fleeing to," rather than fleeing from, a geographical area. When the smoke settled in the Middle East in 1948, the state of Israel had been "carved out of Palestine in fulfillment of the Zionest dream of a national homeland" (Friedlander and Gold-schieder, 1984:3). At that time, the new state had a population of about 650,000 Jews and 156,000 Arabs. Immediately the new government adopted a mass immigration policy to open Israel's doors to any Jew from any part of the world. Within three years, its Jewish population doubled as immigrants streamed in from Europe, Asia, and the United States. Immigration slowed after 1951, but still another million people entered Israel. However, the low crude birthrate among Jews of European origin and the high crude birthrate among Arabs (coupled with Israel's possible intention to annex more land) will bring the Israeli-Arab population into a 50–50 balance by 2015 (Friedlander and Goldschieder, 1984:24). Demographics aside, the migration to Israel is an excellent example of people "fleeing to" a geographical area. Similar migratory patterns are seen among economic refugees.

Economic refugees usually come from a country or region that can no longer support their needs for goods and services. In the 1960s, Ghana was experiencing cycles of economic boom and bust. During boom periods, tens of thousands of Nigerians moved to Ghana to look for employment because unemployment in Nigeria was quite high during the entire decade. During bust periods, the Nigerians were forcibly expelled on at least two occasions. Ironically, in the early 1980s when oil prices were at all-time highs, more than two million illegal alien workers flooded Nigeria's market place. More than half of them were Ghanaians. When oil prices began to decline toward the middle of the 1980s, Nigeria turned the tables and expelled the Ghanaians (Goliber, 1985:10–11).

Political refugees are people whose lives would be endangered if they remained in their homelands. These people usually have chosen the losing side in a war between states, a *coup d'état*, or a revolution. In 1959 the revolutionary forces of Fidel Castro were victorious over the totalitarian rule of Fulgencio Batista. In the four decades since the change of government, conditions for the average Cuban have improved (especially in education and social services), yet nearly every year emigration from Cuba has exceeded immigration. The situation has been characterized as "an exodus of over 800,000 Cubans who left for the Unites States and other countries in an unabated flow that continued into the 1980s with the dramatic Mariel sealift" (Diaz-Briquets and Perez, 1981:25). "Boat people" from war-torn countries like Vietnam and Cambodia (Kampuchea) are also political refugees.

The United States continually adds large numbers of immigrants who could be classified as both economic and political refugees. Figure 5.8 shows the massive increase in legal migration to the United States. For most of the 1980s, approximately 600,000 people per year came. In 1989, that figure rose to more than 1,000,000. By 1990 the number of immigrants to the United States ballooned to more than 1.5 million.

Sometimes it is difficult to determine if people are economic or political refugees, or both. Between 1850 and 1890, one-half the entire population of Ireland emigrated, mostly to the United States. Because of the potato famine and its aftermath, they could be considered economic refugees, but the ongoing (since before the famine) conflict between Ireland and England could lead one to think the move was as much political as economic. Furthermore, a political migration can pave the way for an economic one. For example, there was a civil war in Paraguay in 1947, and thousands of political refugees crossed the border to Argentina when the war ended. In the 1960s, Paraguay experienced a population explosion that was not matched by increased economic development. This left many thousands of people without jobs and without hope.

Figure 5.8
The number of legal immigrants and refugees to the United States had risen sharply since 1988.

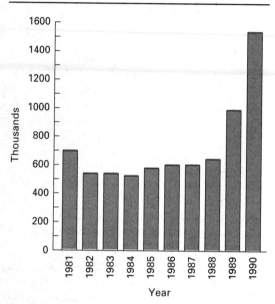

Source: Data from the U.S. Immigration and Naturalization Service, In *Information Please Almanac* (Boston: Houghton Mifflin, 1992).

But, there was a base for these economic refugees in Argentina, which had been established by the political refugees (see Newland, 1979:7). A recent similar example involves the movement of Tamils from Sri Lanka to the former West Germany. Ostensibly, the move was politically motivated because of the Tamils' conflict with the majority Sinhalese peoples. After a brief period of resettlement, however, the Tamils moved on to Newfoundland, obviously not because of political conditions in West Germany (Bouvier and Gardiner, 1986:6–7).

Finally, not all people who leave one country in search of a better life are economic refugees. Many people who could live well in their home countries choose to live better yet in wealthy Arab countries or in industrialized Europe, North America, Australia, or New Zealand. Often, these people are highly skilled or members of profes-

sions like medicine or law. The movement of such people from LDCs to MDCs has been referred to as the *brain drain* to the source countries and the *brain gain* to the host countries. More than any other area of the world, Africa has been losing many of its educated citizens to MDCs. In recent decades, Africa lost about one-third of its highly educated population (United Nations Development Programme, 1992:7). The brain drain had been problematic to India in the 1970s when more than half of its émigrés to the United States were professional and technical workers. But, with changes in global economics in the 1980s, the problem seems to have abated (Visaria and Visaria, 1981:18). Overall, of the 570,000 immigrants legally admitted to the United States in 1985, only 29 percent listed an occupation; the rest were spouses and children. Of those with an occupation, about two-thirds were in a professional or technical field. At the other end of the scale, 22 percent listed themselves as "operators, fabricators, and laborers" (Bouvier and Gardiner, 1986:24–25).

Despite these statistics, it is still usually true that the receiving nation benefits economically, because it can pick and choose which migrants to admit. As Kathleen Newland (1979:17) points out, "All societies invest a substantial portion of their resources in the upbringing, education, and training of the young. If one country bears these costs and another reaps the benefits, there is a clear gain for the latter." She estimates that between 1953 and 1973, the former West Germany saved more than $33 billion through brain gain. Among those admitted to former West Germany, a country with a small Asian population, were 3,000 Korean nurses. Further, she points out that "more senior staff nurses from Bangladesh work in the Middle East than in their own country" (Newland, 1979:17).

Increases in Global Migration

We have discussed numerous factors that increase immigration—rapid population growth; displacement of workers by mechanization; environmental

Not all immigrants from poor countries are economic refugees. A well-educated man like this one may choose to leave his own country in search of a better life-style or to live in a community of scholars. This phenomenon is called the "brain drain" because the wealthy countries benefit from the immigrant's talents while the poor country that educated him must do without his services.

degradation; and political, racial, and religious conflict. Further light is shed on global immigration patterns and trends by world system theory. Alan B. Simmons (1992) argues that current immigration patterns are advantageous to the core MDCs and are not likely to change much in the foreseeable future. Simmons is of the opinion that an attempt to tighten the borders of developed countries or an attempt to hasten the development of less developed countries will not stem the tides of migrants from the poor "Southern," peripheral

countries to the wealthy "Northern," core countries. This is because the developed countries benefit from the current international division of labor that keeps the underdeveloped countries at an economic disadvantage. Simmons (1992:31) discusses four major global trends encouraged by the core MDCs. These include "globalization of production (final assembly based on parts manufactured in various parts of the world); globalization of consumer markets (goods assembled in one nation are sold in many others); the spread of 'structural adjustment' programmes (to favour export-oriented development); the rise of international trading blocs (European Union, the North American Free Trade Agreement, the Southern Cone trading bloc in Latin America, etc.)" (Simmons, 1992:31). Simmons (1992:31) asserts that "globalization is not an accident. It is the result of deliberate policies promoted by the developed nations, by major international institutions, and by many less developed countries that have taken their lead from one of the major players." An important effect of globalization is increased stratification of resources both within and among countries; that is, the rich are getting richer and the poor are becoming poorer. The rich, core countries become richer while the poor, peripheral countries become poorer. The same inequitable distribution of resources between core and peripheral countries that is favored by the core countries also keeps the peripheral countries from meaningful economic development. This, in turn, reinforces high fertility rates, which result in continued high rates of growth, which lead to high rates of underemployment and unemployment. As a result, more and more people from LDCs are migrating, legally and illegally, to MDCs.

POPULATION AND THE FUTURE

The world seems to be drifting toward a demographic dichotomy: some countries (MDCs) where life has been getting better are growing slowly or not at all and other countries (LDCs) where standards of living are declining are growing fast. A major concern about the LDCs is that death rates may begin to rise because of the declining living standards (Brown, 1987). Some of the fast growing countries, like India and Zaire, are currently increasing per capita income, but the possibility of reversal is very real. Another factor that could reverse progress is the spread of disease. In its early days, the United Nations dreamed of eradicating malaria. In fact, considerable progress was made. For example, by 1961 the incidence of malaria in India was down to just 50,000 cases. Unfortunately, by 1970 there had been a tenfold increase to 500,000 cases. About the same time, there were more than 1.5 million malaria victims in Sri Lanka. The reason for the increase was that 51 species of anopheles mosquitoes, the culprits that spread the illness, had developed an immunity to DDT and similar toxins (Goldsmith and Hildyard, 1984:77). In the mid 1990s, 160 million people in the world have malaria and one million die of it annually (Goldsmith and Hildyard, 1984:72). In addition, there has been a marked increase in schistosomiasis, a parasitic disease that spreads where there is no proper disposal of urine and feces. In 1947 there were 114 million cases; three decades later there were 200 million (Goldsmith and Hildyard, 1984:80). Large-scale irrigation has produced conditions conducive to the spread of filariasis, one form of which is elephantiasis. More than a quarter of a million people suffer from this disease (Goldsmith and Hildyard, 1984:84–85).

AIDS in Africa

AIDS (Acquired Immune Deficiency Syndrome) is a disease which no one has yet survived. In 1994 an estimated 6 million Africans were infected with the virus and by the late 1990s, 15 million people in Africa will likely be infected. Although Africa is home to only 10 percent of the world's population, it has 64 percent of the planet's AIDS cases (Kraft, 1992:4). The rate of infection in Uganda is doubling every four to six months. According to the head of Uganda's AIDS prevention program, one-half of the country's population will be infected by the year 2000 (Serrill, 1987:58). The prospects for this African nation are frightening. It is entirely possible that, unless the disease is checked, whole areas of population could be eliminated. And the problem is not confined to Uganda. The total African continent is impacted by AIDS. Kraft (1992:14) reports that the World Bank estimates the average life span in Africa, once expected to reach 60 years, will fall to 47 by the late 1990s.

In Africa, AIDS is spread mostly through heterosexual activity and the typical heterosexual AIDS victim reports having had an average of 32 sexual partners (Serril, 1987:58–59). The mathematics are not complicated. When one has a sexual relationship with a person, he or she is taking a risk equal to having had sexual intercourse with each of that person's previous partners and all of *their* previous partners. Although the disease was only identified in the early 1980s, AIDS antibodies have been found in a blood sample frozen in 1959 (Stone, 1987:36).

Kraft (1992:14) states that one major explanation of the march of AIDS in Africa is secrecy. People do not admit having it, and individuals dying of AIDS in the prime of their lives are said to have died of other causes. Kraft (1992:14) goes on to say, "Also to blame are poor health care, untreated sexually transmitted diseases and the migrant work force—a by-product of industrialization that brought tens of millions of men to the overcrowded cities and left wives behind on the farms." Another serious problem is that many infected persons do not feel sick and do not know they carry HIV. This is an important explanation for the spread of the disease everywhere. Additional factors are people's reluctance to be tested and the fact that in Africa and other less developed regions of the world, there are fewer facilities to test for HIV and other viruses.

Perhaps the biggest reason for the rapid spread of AIDS in Zimbabwe and elsewhere in Africa is culture. Women are the safety net for society, caring for the young and the sick, but the same tradition that leans on them so heavily also keeps them subordinate to men. Even if women want to use precautions against AIDS, they are often unable to do so because men "call the shots." Refusing sexual activity or using condoms is not viewed by men as desirable or necessary. The low status of women is killing them.

To complicate the problem, AIDS can be transmitted through blood transfusion. Present technology cannot guarantee a totally safe blood supply because not all infected blood tests positive. In the United States, however, the chance of an AIDS-infected blood sample slipping through the testing process is 1 in 100,000. Africa, with less money to perform the expensive tests and fewer laboratories and technicians, is not so fortunate. In Rwanda, Uganda, or Zaire, a person who receives a blood transfusion runs an 8 to 18 percent chance of exposure to the disease (Klingholz, 1987:57). The hazard, of course, is not confined to these three countries. AIDS has spread to at least 30 African countries and the testing has been admittedly spotty. The epicenter of the epidemic seems to be the central African countries of Zaire, Uganda, Rwanda, Burundi, Tanzania, and Zambia, referred to as the *AIDS belt* (Goliber, 1989:19–20). A Belgian microbiologist working in that region estimates that between 15 and 25 percent of the entire adult population may already be infected. In Rwanda, a country of 6.8 million people of which nearly half (48 percent) are under 15 years of age, 22 percent of AIDS victims are children (Serrill, 1987:58–59).

The prospects are not good. While Americans are apparently taking to the ideas of "safer sex" (celibacy, monogamy, condoms), Africans are not. Condoms, for example, are not used. A 1986 survey in Kampala, Uganda, showed that one of every ten people had gonorrhea. The number was almost that high in Nairobi, Kenya. The first line of defense in most countries is government-run health-care systems, which are often poorly funded. Doctors have to choose which patients to help; there are not enough resources to treat everyone. A physician may choose to treat many cases of pneumonia for $5.00 to $6.00 worth of medicine per case instead of treating the one case of cryptococcal meningitis (a manifestation of AIDS) for $1,000 worth of medicine. Meanwhile, government leaders choose to hide the problem. Zambia has banned all press statements on AIDS, and Kenya attacks Western news releases on the disease (Serrill, 1987:58–59). In such an environment, the future does not look hopeful. But, given the growth rate of these countries, if AIDS is completely controlled and the birthrate is not, the future may look even worse.

Rapid Growth: Africa and Latin America

Assuming that AIDS or some other affliction does not become pandemic (affecting all countries) and reach proportions of the bubonic plagues that devastated Europe, a long period of continued rapid growth can be expected in Africa and Latin America. In fact, concentrating specifically on Africa, Robinson and McLees (1982:6–7) and Goliber (1989:6) find evidence for an acceleration in its rate of growth. Robinson and McLees point to vast improvements in health care, including delivery systems and better accessibility. Even with the AIDS situation health conditions are better in general now than they have ever been. Second, sanitation and the availability of safe water are improving, although still poor compared to MDCs. It is absolutely true that life expectancy is increasing, which means that more people will live through more years of potential reproduction. There has also been a steady decline in infant and child mortality. Finally, the researchers point out that Africa's strong traditions and customs favor large families.

Goliber (1985:29–30; 1989:23) points out that Africa suffers from four other conditions that tend to keep the birthrate high: low level of education, rural residential patterns, low income, and low status of women. The low status of women in Africa may be the most problematic of factors resulting in high fertility. Goliber (1989:23) points out that as in other poor, agricultural societies, women are not allowed assets or property, and must produce large families to ensure their economic security in old age. These conditions translate into exceptionally high total fertility rates (TFR). Whereas most of Europe's TFRs are well below the replacement level of 2.1, the TFRs in most of Africa are significantly higher (see Figure 5.9). Africans tend to have the number of children they think is desirable (Table 5.11). In examining results from the African countries that participated in the World Fertility Survey in the early 1980s, Goliber finds that only Ghana and Kenya expressed preference for a "desired family size" that was smaller than their actual TFRs (6.1 versus 6.3 for Ghana and 7.2 versus 8.0 for Kenya). In short, the problem of high fertility levels in Africa is not simply one of the need for contraceptive services. Africans desire large families and are having them. If the attitude favoring such large families continues into the next generation, the

growth potential stretches the imagination. The reason is that the current age structure of a country like Kenya shows not only a large percentage of the population below the reproductive age, but also that this is the segment of the population that has been growing fastest in the past. All of this translates into a population momentum that will not be arrested for a long time.

Though things may look bleak for Africa's future, some promising changes are occurring. Goliber (1989:37–38) notes a major change in the attitude of African government officials on population matters. Due to an increasing number of censuses and population surveys (some sponsored by the United Nations), national leaders are becoming informed about the incredible growth rates in Africa and are starting to launch family-planning programs to curtail high fertility levels.

Although Latin America is growing almost as fast as Africa, its situation looks a bit more hopeful.

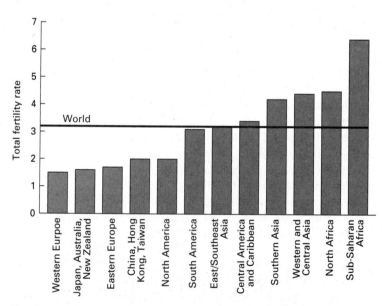

Figure 5.9
Total fertility rates for world regions in 1994 show that rates in Africa are much higher than elsewhere.

Note: The total fertility rate estimates the number of children a woman will have, given current birthrates.

Source: PRB *1994 World Population Data Sheet*, special tabulations; appeared in W. Lutz, "The Future of World Population." *Population Bulletin*, 49(1), 1994: 7.

Fertility Rates and Desired Family Size: World Fertility Survey Findings in 10 Sub-Saharan African Countries	TABLE 5.11	
	Total fertility rate	Average desired family size
Benin	7.1	7.5
Cameroon	6.4	8.0
Ghana	6.3	6.1
Ivory Coast	7.4	8.5
Kenya	8.0	7.2
Lesotho	5.9	5.9
Mauritania	7.7	9.2
Nigeria	6.3	8.4
Senegal	7.1	8.8
Sudan	5.7	6.3

SOURCE: T. J. Goliber, *Sub-Saharan Africa: Population Pressures on Development* (Washington, DC: Population Reference Bureau, 1985).

To begin with, attainment of education for both males and females has dramatically increased since the end of World War II. Second, per capita income, although low compared to standards in the MDCs, is much higher than in Africa. Third, there has been a significant increase in women's use of modern contraceptive methods in the 1980s (Merrick, 1986). For example, in Brazil, the average number of children per woman declined from 4.4 in 1980 to 3.3 by 1990 (Brown, 1991:17). According to Lester Brown (1991:17), "an expansion of government family-planning services and growing access to modern contraceptives in commercial markets" were primarily responsible for this sizeable reduction in the Brazilian birthrate. Finally, almost all Latin American countries experienced declines in their total fertility rates from the mid 1950s to the mid 1970s and literally all of them experienced declines in fertility from the 1970–1975 period to the 1985–1990 period (Table 5.12). If this trend continues, the future of Latin America will be a more hopeful one.

We need to keep in mind that even if Latin America does slow its rate of growth, its population momentum will still cause it to increase from its present 451 million people to 546 million in 2000 and 779 million in 2025. Part of the explanation of population momentum lies in the **youth wave,** the large number of currently young children who will be entering their reproductive years in the future. A glance at the age structure of Mexico for the years 1980, 1990, and 2000 (Figure 5.10) shows that, although the crude birthrate will decline (no expansion at the base of future pyramids), the absolute number of young people (15 to 24 years old) increases, creating a great potential for fertility.

Asia and Europe

As we have seen, future scenarios for Asia differ according to region. It is safe to say that Southeast Asia will continue to grow rapidly or fairly rapidly for some time, perhaps displaying about the same pattern as Latin America. To date, however, educational levels have not increased as they have in Latin America and far fewer women use modern contraceptive methods.

India is again vigorously attacking its high crude birthrate. It is using all methods of mass communication to get its family-planning message across to the people: posters, radio, films, and so on. The legal age for entry into marriage has been increased from 15 to 18 for women and from 18 to 21 for men. But, illiteracy is still so widespread that many people are unaware of what the law requires. The country, consequently, is trying to increase education for both males and females. Nevertheless, India's population will eclipse China's during the next century.

China has experienced some resistance to the one-child policy and has backed off somewhat. However, the policy has already had an effect and it is projected to alter the age structure of Chinese society in the future (Figure 5.11).

The one-child policy has been linked to a significant increase in the preponderance of boy infants over girl infants. Because of male preference, if a couple can have only one child, the couple will want it to be a male. Considerable

Total Fertility Rates for Latin American Countries in Selected Five-Year Intervals: 1955–1990			TABLE 5.12	
(Average number of lifetime births per woman at current age-specific rates)				
Subregion and country	1955–1960	1970–1975	1985–1990	Percent change 1955–1960 to 1970–1975	Percent change 1970–1975 to 1985–1990
SOUTH AMERICA					
Argentina	3.126	3.145	2.958	.6	−5.9
Bolivia	6.690	6.500	6.060	−2.8	−6.8
Brazil	6.150	4.699	3.459	−23.6	−26.4
Chile	5.301	3.630	2.728	−31.5	−24.8
Colombia	6.720	4.780	3.580	−28.9	−25.1
Ecuador	6.900	6.050	4.650	−12.3	−23.1
Paraguay	6.800	5.650	4.578	−16.9	−19.0
Peru	6.853	5.999	4.490	−12.5	−25.0
Uruguay	2.831	3.000	2.610	6.0	−13.0
Venezuela	6.460	4.965	3.469	−23.1	−30.1
MEXICO AND CENTRAL AMERICA					
Costa Rica	7.113	4.335	3.501	−39.1	−19.2
El Salvador	6.806	6.099	4.859	−10.4	−20.3
Guatemala	6.930	6.450	5.770	−6.9	−10.5
Honduras	7.175	7.380	5.550	2.9	−24.8
Mexico	6.750	6.366	3.578	−5.7	−43.8
Nicaragua	7.330	6.710	5.500	−8.5	−18.0
Panama	5.883	4.940	3.139	−16.0	−36.5
CARIBBEAN					
Cuba	3.759	3.470	1.707	−7.7	−50.8
Dominican Rep.	7.400	5.627	3.750	−24.0	−33.4
Guyana	6.765	4.551	2.747	−32.7	−47.0
Haiti	6.150	5.760	4.739	−6.3	−17.7
Jamaica	5.018	5.406	2.856	7.7	−47.2
Puerto Rico	4.817	2.993	2.438	−37.9	−18.5
Suriname	6.560	5.289	2.972	−19.4	−43.8
Trinidad and Tobago	5.304	3.468	2.679	−34.6	−22.8

Source: For data about Total Fertility Rates: Keyfitz and Flieger, 1990 *World Population and Aging: Demographic Trends in the Late 20th Century.*

controversy has surrounded the reporting of fairly large sex ratios at birth for China in the late 1980s (see Figure 5.12). Sten Johansson and Ola Nygren (1991) discussed the "missing girls" in their analysis of the data. H. Yuan Tien and his associates (1992) attribute the increase in the preponderance of boys at birth to four possible factors: (1) female infanticide, (2) aborted female fetuses, (3) a gross underreporting of female births, especially of girls given away in adoptions, and (4) a higher infant mortality for girls due to traditional gender discrimination.

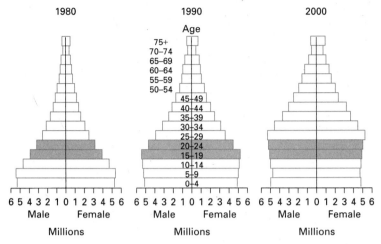

1980   1990   2000

Age
75+
70–74
65–69
60–64
55–59
50–54
45–49
40–44
35–39
30–34
25–29
20–24
15–19
10–14
5–9
0–4

6 5 4 3 2 1 0 1 2 3 4 5 6   6 5 4 3 2 1 0 1 2 3 4 5 6   6 5 4 3 2 1 0 1 2 3 4 5 6
Male   Female   Male   Female   Male   Female

Millions   Millions   Millions

Source: T. W. Merrick, *Population Pressures in Latin America,* Washington, DC: Vol. 41, No. 3, July 1986, p.47. Population Reference Bureau.

Figure 5.10
These three pyramids show Mexico's distribution of people in age ranges for 1980 and 1990, and projected to 2000. Although the CBR (base of pyramids) declines (narrows), the number of people aged 15 to 24 years (shaded bars of pyramids) increases (broadens).

The exact importance of each factor is difficult to determine.

Aside from an imbalance in the age structure of a society, leading to women marrying earlier (one of India's historic problems), this also presents an intergenerational family problem. If an only son marries an only daughter, the couple can only live with one set of parents. Yet, by tradition, the couple will be expected to support both sets of parents when the parents reach old age. For these, and other reasons, China's steady decline in fertility slightly reversed itself in 1986. Art Haupt (1987a:3–4) says four dynamics may be causing the phenomenon: (1) there may be an "echo" from the early 1960s baby boom; (2) the legal age for marriage was lowered in 1980; (3) China seems to have "cycles of implementation" for many of its programs; and (4) a great deal of internal migration may be allowing people to "slip through administrative cracks" of fertility surveillance. The authors of this text, however, believe that the 1986 reversal will not be sustained and China's population can be expected to level off at about 1.4 billion, at which point it will be second only to India's 1.6 billion.

Japan is expected to continue to decrease its rate of growth, already the lowest in Asia. The inhabitable areas of the Japanese islands are over-crowded and MDCs like Japan have the technology to control their growth. Also, the Japanese people are highly educated and have a relatively high per capita income. These characteristics have made it possible to complete the demographic transition. It is expected that Japan's total population will actually shrink in the future. This may be problematic in that Japan would prefer not to import guest workers. *Guest workers* are foreign workers who are allowed to enter a country to do work that the native population either cannot do or prefers not to do. Continued automation and cybernation (the linking of computers to automated processes) may solve that problem. But it will not solve the problems associated with an aging population previously discussed.

Europe will face the same issue of an aging population as a result of what one demographer has called its *second demographic transition.* Dirk J. van de Kaa (1987:5) places the beginning of this transition at about 1965 (a period of time that coincides with the "baby bust" in the United States). The main feature of this transition is a decline in the total fertility rate to below replacement level (see Tables 5.9 and 5.10). This will cause countries to enter an era of absolute population decline. He points out that four countries (Austria, Denmark, West Germany, and Hungary)

Figure 5.11
This population pyramid of China's population by age and sex shows that the one-child policy significantly decreased the population in the mid 1970s.

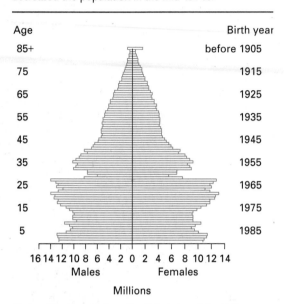

Source: Ten-Percent Sampling Tabulation of the 1990 Population Census of China (Beijing: China Statistical Publishing House, 1991); Table 4-1, cited in H. Yuan Tien, et al., 1992. "China's Demographic Dilemmas," *Population Bulletin*, 47(1).

Figure 5.12
From 1970 to 1987, the number of males per 100 females born in China increased dramatically, especially in the mid to late eighties.

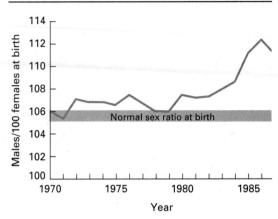

Source: S. Johansson and O. Nygren, "The Missing Girls of China: A New Demographic Account," *Population and Development Review 17*, (1), (March 1991): 39; cited in H. Yuan Tien, et al., "China's Demographic Dilemmas," *Population Bulletin*, 47 (1). (1992).

are already in that position. Van de Kaa argues that the second transition was caused by a shift in personal philosophy from altruism (doing well for others) to individualism (doing well for oneself). He says that the "first transition was dominated by concerns for family and offspring, but the second emphasizes the rights and self-fulfillment of individuals" (van de Kaa, 1987:5). In the second case, having children may involve losses of opportunity, and many young Europeans are choosing not to have babies.

We have discussed France's concern about this new phase of demographic development. Other countries have similar worries. For example, before dictator Nicolae Ceaușescu was executed in December 1989, Romania had a complete ban on abortion and contraceptives. Contraceptives could

neither be manufactured in that country nor imported. Unmarried persons over age 25 and married couples who were childless underwent medical examinations for infertility. If they were found to be capable of bearing children but had not done so, their incomes were subjected to a special 30 percent tax (Haupt, 1987b:3–4). Other European countries tend to use positive incentives, such as tax breaks and paid maternity/paternity leaves, to increase birthrates.

Availability of Contraception

Though parents seem to want more children than the planet needs, there is evidence that many people would have fewer children if contraception were readily available. In an interesting study, John Bongaarts (1991) looked at data from sub-Saharan Africa, North Africa, Asia, and Latin America, and concluded that the average unmet desire or demand for contraceptives was 17 percent of currently married women. Bongaarts

(1991:312) concludes that "since the total number of married women in the developing countries (excluding China) in 1990 was approximately 514 million, a simple calculation (514 × .17) yields the estimate of 87 million married women (or their husbands) who would be current contraception users if their needs for spacing and limiting had been fully satisfied." Clearly, the world community must make effective contraception available to individuals who desire it. Unfortunately, from 1980 to 1992 there was a lack of leadership on contraception. After two decades of leadership in international family planning, the United States, during the presidencies of Ronald Reagan and George Bush, withdrew U.S. funding from both the International Planned Parenthood Federation and the United Nations Population Fund (Brown, 1991:17). Under the Clinton administration, the support of the United States on contraception has been restored.

Fertility, Development, and Industrialization

The Demographic Transition Theory asserts that substantial increases in development and industrialization must occur before fertility will decrease. However, according to Thomas Goliber (1989:39–40), "Now it has been shown that fertility can decline markedly in countries where the economy is not yet highly industrialized, per capita income is low, and the population is still largely rural: China, India, Indonesia, Thailand, and Sri Lanka. Recent fertility declines have been associated less with per-capita income levels than with improvement in life expectancy, female education, and a relatively equitable distribution of income and access to services (including family planning)."

A Two-Tiered System?

Figure 5.13 shows the tremendous shift in demographics that separates MDCs from LDCs. The graph presents projected population sizes by region. We can observe ultimate declines of population in the developed countries and the potential explosion in the less developed regions, especially Africa. The question for the future is, Will the world eventually be a two-tiered system with perhaps 10 (or even 5) percent of its population having a high standard of living in the MDCs and the vast majority living in poverty and subservience in the LDCs?

Women in Lamu, Kenya, receive instruction in family planning. Simply spacing their children further apart in years has a double benefit: fewer children and, because mother's body has had a chance to recuperate from the last birth, healthier children.

Toward A Solution

Focus on Africa

Fertility Levels Drop Dramatically

Many observers of population trends are surprised by changes occurring in many developing nations. Although countries like those in sub-Saharan Africa have not experienced the classic demographic transition of the United States and the countries of Western Europe, taking over a hundred years to go from high birth and death rates to low birth and death rates, the fact is that birthrates are declining in many LDCs.

Europe's transition occurred only after economic conditions improved. In a number of LDCs, however, birthrates are beginning to decline, despite the fact that there has been no substantial change in living conditions. And, this decline is happening faster than experts would have guessed a decade or so ago. "Developing countries appear to have benefited from the growing influence and scope of family-planning programs, and from the educational power of the media," according to Bryant Robey, Shea O. Rutstein, and Leo Morris (1993:60).

One of the differences in the demographic transition of Europe and that of today's LDCs is the availability of effective contraception. Europeans had to rely on abstinence or take their chances with such ineffective means as withdrawal. Frequently, they had to turn to abortion. In the early nineteenth century, many factory workers sold their older children to the factories when a new birth presented them another mouth to feed. Some European countries, mostly those that were part of the former Soviet Union, still rely on primitive methods because of the scarcity of modern devices.

People in today's LDCs can prevent pregnancy by pills (hormones), intrauterine devices, condoms, injectables, and even surgical sterilization through family-planning programs offered by government agencies and donor organizations. "These services have sought clients and have removed or lowered many of the economic barriers to health care and to the availability of contraception" (Robey, Rutstein, and Morris, 1993:64). In Europe, it was probably the control of disease that gave people the confidence to have fewer children.

In places like sub-Saharan Africa, the mass media has a great influence, accelerating the diffusion of information about contraception to rural as well as urban populations. As Robey, Rutstein, and Morris have concluded, "Unlike past generations, millions of people now have direct and instant access to the rest of the world through radio and television" (1993:65).

The authors use the African nations of Kenya, Ghana, and Nigeria as examples of countries that have witnessed significant declines in fertility rates, and they argue that the presence of effective family planning and modern communications are responsible. In Kenya, for example, contraceptive use increased nearly 60 percent between 1984 and 1989, and the desired number of children declined by 24 percent. During this time span, the Kenyan fertility rate declined by 16 percent. Charles Westoff and German Rodriguez of Princeton University analyzed Kenyan fertility survey data and found that women's family-planning decisions were shaped by mass-media campaigns for smaller family size. Westoff and Rodriguez found that "Kenyan women who listened to or watched family-planning messages on radio or television were more likely than others to want smaller families" (Robey, Rutstein, and Morris, 1993:65) and to use contraception. Some of the most popular radio and television programs carry strong family-planning messages.

The phrase "development is the best contraceptive" originated at the 1974 World Population Conference in Bucharest and has been used to suggest that a country's fertility would fail to drop until its economy improved. The review of the literature by Robey, Rutstein, and Morris (1993:65) suggests that although economic development and social changes result in conditions that encourage parents to have smaller families, "contraceptives are the best contraceptive." This is especially true where family planners use modern communication systems.

SOURCE: B. Robey, S. D. Rutstein, and L. Morris. 1993. "The Fertility Decline in Developing Countries," *Scientific American.* Dec.: 60–65.

Figure 5.13
Experts project that populations in less developed regions of the world will grow disproportionately, leaving most of the world's people living in dire poverty.

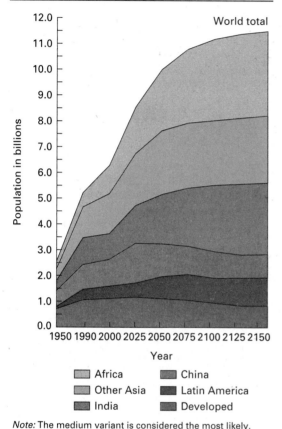

Note: The medium variant is considered the most likely.

Source: United Nations Population Division. Long Range World Population Projections, New York, 1992; appeared in UNFPA/United Nations Population Fund. The State of the World Population, 1993. New York: United Nations Population Fund: p. 6.

S U M M A R Y

The human population on planet Earth was relatively small for most of our species' history. Mortality levels were high and *Homo sapiens* learned to reward high fertility levels to keep the species from dying out. Only in the last 200 years has the population of humankind begun to increase dramatically. The initial increase in human numbers was due to a decline in mortality levels in countries undergoing industrialization, largely as a result of prosperity and better hygiene. With fertility levels remaining high, these countries, which are now the MDCs of the world, experienced significant growth. Over time, however, fertility levels in the MDCs declined, resulting in little or no growth.

The situation in the LDCs is quite different. First, their mortality levels decreased dramatically after medical and scientific developments were borrowed from the MDCs (after World War II). Their mortality rates were reduced not because standards of living improved but by artificial means (spraying for mosquitoes that carry malaria; inoculating babies, etc.). As a result, the fertility levels of LDCs have remained high and their populations have been expanding very rapidly. However, there is substantial variation among LDCs in how they are moving through the demographic transition. Until recently, most Latin American countries were characterized by relatively low mortality and relatively high fertility— they were in the second stage of the transition and were experiencing substantial growth. The fertility rates of Latin American countries have been declining quite rapidly and even though they are above replacement levels, there are reasons to hope that Latin American countries will stabilize their populations. They will grow substantially, however, before they stabilize, because of the population momentum caused by their young populations, which have many potential parents who have yet to bear children.

The continent of Asia is much more varied than Latin America when it comes to the position of countries on the demographic transition continuum. Japan, like other MDCs, has very low fertility and mortality rates and very little growth. India has had difficulty in bringing its fertility rate down, even though it was the first country to organize substantial family-planning drives. India continues to grow rapidly. China is a very interesting country demographically, because it was able to drastically reduce its birthrate, even without substantial economic development. The one-child policy, though controversial, has been effective in curbing China's growth. Though China has more than 1 billion people and will continue to add to its numbers before population stabilization is achieved, it is on the road to stabilization.

African countries, on the whole, appear stuck in the second stage of the demographic transition, and their populations are expanding very rapidly. The high mortality rates of African countries have declined rapidly since 1960, but fertility rates remain very high, accounting for the fastest growing populations in the world. Fertility rates are starting to drop in Africa, however, as women learn of reproductive options.

Future mortality levels of the planet, once thought to be reduced to low levels for all time, are in question. AIDS is ravaging the continent of Africa and may result in major increases in mortality levels in other parts of the world, especially Asia. Other "Malthusian ghosts" such as drug-resistant versions of tuberculosis and malaria represent additional concerns.

The population of the planet is aging, with greater proportions of the people living longer. This is much more the case in MDCs than LDCs. The problems associated with this process, such as greater expenditures for health care or a shortage of workers, are more severe for MDCs. And, the aging of MDC populations will accelerate as we move into the twenty-first century. Numerous scholars argue, however, that various myths about the elderly are perpetuated and that little evidence supports many of the dire claims about aging populations.

Migration flows continue to increase, worldwide. The most significant is from the LDCs to the MDCs. The expanding populations along with the lack of sufficient employment in the LDCs explains the vast majority of these moves. Though refugees constitute a minority of overall migrants, their numbers are increasing very rapidly. This is due to heightened political, religious, and racial conflict as well as deteriorating economic conditions in LDCs.

KEY TERMS

Age structure The manner in which a population is distributed with regard to age.

Age-dependency ratio The ratio of people under the age of 15 and over the age of 65 relative to the rest of the population.

Ageism A systematic stereotyping of, and discrimination against, people because they are old.

Caste A distinct social class designated at birth.

Crude birthrate (CBR) The number of births, per 1,000 people, for a population during a year.

Crude death rate (CDR) The number of deaths, per 1,000 people, for a population during a year.

Demographic transition theory The theory that describes how countries move from a stage with high fertility and high mortality (with little if any growth), to a stage with high fertility and low mortality (with considerable growth), to a stage with low fertility and low mortality (with little if any growth).

Demography The statistical description and analysis of human population.

Doubling time The number of years it will take a country to double its population.

Emigration The movement of people out of a country of which they are natives or long-term residents.

Fertility The actual number of births within a population in a given year.

Immigration The movement of people into a country of which they are not natives.

Infant mortality rate The number of deaths of infants between birth and 1 year old per 1,000 live births.

Internal migration The movement of people from one region of a country to another.

Migration The physical movement of people into or out of a geographic region.

Mortality The actual number of deaths within a population during a year.

Permanent settlers Immigrants who are not facing the severe and dire forces faced by refugees, but who desire to move to another country to improve their lives.

Population momentum The population dynamic that sees the current age of a population as an important force in the future size of that population. A young population is assured of growing, even if couples have replacement-level fertility.

Positive checks Those factors (famine, pestilence, war, and disease) discussed by Thomas Malthus, that increase mortality and bring population back into balance with the food supply.

Preventive checks Those factors (celibacy, deferment of marriage, and "moral restraint" within marriage), discussed by Thomas Malthus, that decrease fertility.

Pronatalist policies Policies designed to increase fertility.

Rate of growth The rate of natural increase plus the rate of net migration.

Rate of natural increase (NI) The crude birthrate minus the crude death rate.

Refugees People who have been uprooted, left homeless, or forced to flee one geographic region to settle in another.

Total fertility rate (TFR) The total number of children that each woman (on average) would have during her reproductive years, if she patterned her fertility after the age-specific birthrates (rates for age categories of women) in existence at that time.

Youth wave The large number of currently young children who will be entering their reproductive years in the future.

STUDY QUESTIONS

1. What are the three basic demographic processes and which two are central in explaining the rapid growth of the world's population? Why?

2. How do the "positive checks" and "preventive checks" of Thomas Malthus's theory of population operate to curtail growth?

3. What factors account for the decline in European mortality in the eighteenth and nineteenth centuries?

4. How are the factors responsible for mortality declines in the current LDCs different from factors responsible for mortality declines in the history of current MDCs? Why is this important in explaining the rapid population growth of LDCs?

5. What factors are responsible for the very rapid population growth in Africa?

6. What are the five myths regarding the elderly that Butler discussed?

7. How do present patterns of immigration differ from past patterns?

8. What factors are responsible for the increasing number of immigrants worldwide?

9. What is the difference between economic refugee status and political refugee status?

10. What is the likely future of population growth in Latin America?

6

RACE,
ETHNICITY, AND
ETHNOCENTRISM

amed Celik, an ambulance driver from the town of Foca in Bosnia, was seized by Serbian soldiers and thrown into a prison camp. There he was starved for long periods of time. At night he was terrified by the screams of fellow prisoners being beaten to death. This abuse went on for more than four months. Then Hamed was taken to the town of Kalenovik and forced to be a human minesweeper, going ahead of the Serbian troops, expecting to be blown up by a land mine to warn those who followed him.

"I saw one colleague from the Foca hospital blown up as he walked ahead of me," the former ambulance driver recalled, his gaunt face flush with emotion. "I was lucky. I said to myself each time, 'Only God can save me!' And he did, because I was never wounded" (Williams, 1993).

What crime had Hamed Celik committed that he should have been thrown in prison and later used as a human minesweeper? The answer is simple: He belonged to the wrong group. He was a Bosnian, not a Serb, and he was a Moslem, not an Orthodox Christian. The Serbs promised to cleanse the land of such people.

The world is faced with a multitude of cases in which the value of people's lives is determined by their religion, ethnicity, or race. We have just given an example of Bosnia in former Yugoslavia. In Northern Ireland, despite occasional truces,

Catholics have been killing Protestants and Protestants have been killing Catholics for decades. In Rwanda, Hutus and Tutsis have killed each other by the hundreds of thousands. In Northern India, episodes of Hindus killing Moslems and of Moslems killing Hindus have gone on since the British withdrew from the area in 1947. In all cases, violent episodes of the past help to reawaken hatreds and lead to further interethnic violence.

Explaining Group Differences

Differences in race, ethnicity, and religion provide lines by which people distinguish themselves from one another. **Race** is a term applied to divisions of the human species based on inherited differences in appearance such as skin color, hair type, average stature, eye shape, and the like. In most respects, these traits have little meaning; they have no bearing on intelligence, morality, or behavior. However, peoples' attitudes toward and beliefs about race can be very important, and in the past, have decided whether people were free or slaves. Even now, in many parts of the world, attitudes can expand or limit opportunities in life. **Racism** is the belief that race is a very important determinant of behavior and that some races are superior to others. This false doctrine has brought about slavery, misery, and war.

Ethnic groups are groups of people who have a common culture or way of life. *Ethnic*, in its broadest sense, can be applied to whole nations of people, like the French, the Italians, or the Canadians. But there are always differences within countries. Most people of the province of Quebec in Canada speak French and think of themselves as culturally French, at least to some degree. In the United States, many Native Americans keep much of their old cultures, so they are different culturally from the majority. In a more serious case of ethnic differences, the Bosnian Moslems and the Bosnian Serbs are at war with each other, although they were long considered part of one nation.

An important derivative from the word *ethnic* is **ethnocentrism,** or the belief that one's own culture is best and that all others should be judged by its standards. An ethnocentric American of Anglo-Saxon descent is sure that his or her cultural traditions are best and worries that they will be distorted by too many immigrants of different backgrounds—Latin Americans, Asians, Mid-Eastern people, or even southern and eastern Europeans. Ethnocentrism is characteristic of people in all countries. In great moderation, it may function for social cohesion and loyalty. When carried to a fanatical extreme, however, it becomes dangerous, leading to contempt for all people who are different. Such ethnocentrism is part of the reason for prejudice and discrimination.

Prejudice is an attitude formed about people that is based on little or no actual knowledge of them. It refers nearly always to other ethnic groups or races, and the attitudes are generally negative. A practice that goes along with a prejudiced attitude is **discrimination,** which is unequal treatment of others. For example, in South Africa, the United States, and other countries dominated by whites but with large black populations, there has been prejudice against black people and discrimination against them in education and hiring. This has meant condemning them to poverty and ignorance, which has reinforced prejudice.

In speaking of ethnic and racial minorities, we must define one more important term, **scapegoating.** This practice is described in Leviticus 16, in which part of a rite of atonement consisted of vesting a goat (called the *scapegoat*) with the sins of the people. The modern use of the term bears quite a similarity: The misfortunes of society are attributed to a minority group. In the United States, animosity toward foreigners and African Americans has always been worse when times were bad, as if they were the cause of economic downturns. High crime rates are often blamed on foreigners, even if their crime rates are not so high as that of the native population. In the fourteenth century, outbreaks of the bubonic plague were blamed on the Jews.

Racial and Ethnic Animosity

It is clear that much of the animosity that develops between groups is based on ethnocentrism, prejudice, and even the need for scapegoating. There are other causes of interracial or interethnic animosity, often based on historical events. For example, in World War II, U.S. animosity against Japan became so great that it spread to Americans of Japanese descent. Large numbers of American citizens of Japanese descent were forced out of their homes and had to spend the war years in concentration camps. Ironically, many young Japanese-American men, often the sons of people in the concentration camps, were fighting for the United States against Germany. Japanese-American units received an unusual number of citings for bravery.

Rivalry for land, trade, waterways, and natural resources can lead to strong ethnic animosities, as can rivalry for jobs and economic opportunities. The hatred of Serbs for Bosnian Moslems, mentioned at the beginning of this chapter has historical roots. Moslems and Christians in Yugoslavia had clashed for centuries. The animosity seemed to have died down, but was rekindled by Serbian desires for more land and a "Greater Serbia."

Prejudice against impoverished groups takes the form of contempt; prejudice against minorities who are too successful takes the form of jealousy, often dangerous jealousy.

Religions, if they are intolerant of all other beliefs, can lead to conflict. The Jews have suffered untold misery, exile, torture, and death for being of an ethnic and religious minority, not just in Germany but in various countries of Europe and the Middle East.

The Jewish Minority

Since their Babylonian captivity, around 500 B.C., the Jewish people have moved to many parts of the world. They were in all the major cities of the Roman Empire, mainly as artisans. The Roman Empire tolerated many religions; however, with the decline and fall of the Empire, the Christian Church became dominant in Europe. In North Africa and the Middle East, Islam became dominant by the early eighth century. Both Christians and Moslems believed they and they alone knew divine truth and that the Jews were a barrier to religious progress.

In parts of the Arab world, the Jews were treated fairly well at times. In many places, no attempt was made to convert them to Islam, because as nonbelievers they had to pay much heavier taxes than Moslems. There were cases, though, in which they were treated savagely.

In Christian Europe, similarly, there were marked differences in treatment, and Jews often had to flee from Eastern Europe to Western Europe. The Medieval Christian doctrine accused the Jews of Satanism. Joshua Trachenberg (1966) sums up Christian thinking in Medieval Europe thus: Since the Jews are intelligent people, it is impossible that they cannot see the truth of Christianity. This being the case, it is obvious that they have sold their souls to the Devil. Therefore, they should receive no sympathy.

The Jews were scapegoated in all disasters. In 1096, at the beginning of the First Crusade, the idea was spread that the Jews had something to do with the fall of Jerusalem to the Moslems. Therefore, especially in Germany, the crusaders robbed, tortured, and killed the Jews before starting for the Holy Land (Garraty and Gay, 1981). Centuries later, they were accused of causing the black death, which wiped out nearly one-third of Europe's population in the fourteenth century.

Actually, for a century or so before the Crusades, the Jews had prospered in much of Europe. Some had become officials and administrators for the Austrian emperor. In many places, the Jews were the nucleus of a middle class of business and trade, with a beneficial effect on the countries in which they lived. In the 1200s and 1300s, they were well treated in Spain, where they established leading schools and helped to begin the intellectual renaissance (reawakening) that occurred in Europe after the Middle Ages.

However, King Ferdinand and Queen Isabella in 1492, decreed that all Jews and Moors must convert to Christianity or leave Spain. Those suspected of being "secret Jews," pretending to be Christians, were tried before the courts of the Inquisition. Many were burned at the stake. The expulsion of the Jews and the Moors from Spain robbed the country of its middle class and probably slowed its progress relative to England and the Netherlands. Many of the Spanish Jews fled to the Netherlands where they helped make Amsterdam the most prosperous city of Europe and Europe's leading intellectual center.

In much of Europe, the Jews were compelled to live in their own part of the city, called the **ghetto.** The ghetto requirement started in Rome in 1550 and remained in force there until 1885. In most other Western European cities, ghettos were no longer required after the French Revolution, but in Russia they were in force until World War I. In Germany they were reinstated by Hitler, preparatory to sending the Jews to death camps.

In Russia the Jews became the victims of **pogroms,** government-sponsored attacks in which they were driven out or killed. A forged document was circulated in Russia claiming the Jews were plotting to take over the world. Although a fraud, the document (called "Protocols of the Elders of Zion") was believed by anti-Jewish fanatics, including Hitler. Hitler believed that the Jews were contaminating the purity of the German "race," and attempted to exterminate the entire

population in gas chambers. Altogether 6 million Jews were killed in the death camps, along with Gypsies, homosexuals, physically handicapped people, and others who were considered a polluting element. In many cases, doctors were put in charge of selecting the people to die, with the explanation that they were curing Germany of the disease of impurity (Lifton, 1986). People who are acquainted with this period of history shudder at the use of the term *ethnic cleansing,* in vogue among the Serbs in the 1990s.

THE WORLDWIDE NATURE OF ETHNIC AND RACIAL PROBLEMS

Since the earliest days of the human species, people have moved from place to place. Often they were looking for greener pastures. If these

The ultimate ethnic atrocity occurred when Hitler and his Nazi followers exterminated 6 million Jews in Auschwitz and other death camps. More recent attempts at genocide have occurred in Rwanda and Bosnia.

pastures were already occupied, a clash may have taken place. In such a case, one group may well have become dominant and the other subordinate, or even enslaved or forced to flee. As populations increased and urbanization took place, conquests occurred and multiethnic empires arose. The best known of the great empires was the Roman Empire. Under the best of its emperors, there was considerable harmony, trade flourished, and Europe enjoyed a period known as *Pax Romana*, or the Roman Peace. Ethnic differences were not eliminated, but they were not allowed to disturb the peace.

In more recent times other multiethnic empires have enforced peace, but not necessarily equality, on their subjects. The world is now learning more about some of the people once held in line by those empires. The Ottoman Empire (Turkey) once ruled North Africa and most of the Balkan Peninsula, including what was known as Yugoslavia. Elsewhere, the Ottoman Empire ruled many of the restive Armenians, Azerbaijanis, and Kurds. To the north, Austria-Hungary ruled the Czechs and Slovaks, the Slovenes, a few of the Serbs, and many of the Romanians. More recently, the Soviet Union ruled vast areas occupied by Islamic peoples: Kazakhstan, Turkmenistan, Uzbekistan, Tajikistan, and Kyrgyzstan. The Soviet Union also ruled the Baltic States, Ukraine, Belorus, Moldavia, and more. Interethnic peace was enforced. Especially in the days of Joseph Stalin, groups were often oppressed, sometimes uprooted and moved to other parts of the USSR. Although they were not allowed to fight one another, many old animosities remained. Indeed, with the demise of the USSR, ethnic clashes have reemerged in many formerly Soviet states.

Other parts of the world have also had to cope with ethnic diversity. The vast country of China contains Mongols, Manchus, Tibetans, and Islamic people more similar to the Afghans than to the Chinese. India speaks a confusion of languages and is divided religiously among Hindus, Moslems, and Sikhs. Southeast Asia contains many nationalities, and most countries of that region have Chinese minorities. Nearly all of Africa was conquered by Europeans and divided into countries that usually contain different tribes and ethnic groups with different languages. The Americas were similarly conquered by different European nations with different languages and cultures. These conquests have had lasting effects on interracial and interethnic problems.

Conquest and Control

The conquest of one people by another was sometimes accomplished quite rapidly and completely, as in the case of the Spanish conquest of the Aztecs and Incas in the early sixteenth century. In both cases the result was a long-time subordination of the native people. Not much later, the Dutch acquired Indonesia, and held control until World War II. Unlike Spain, however, they did not permanently implant their language and religion. Many other European conquests were impermanent, but had a strong effect on ethnic relations. France acquired much of North Africa, with the interesting result that France is now coping with a problem of Algerian and Tunisian immigration. Great Britain became the overlord of India, Pakistan, Bangladesh, Burma, Malaysia, and much of East Africa. Part of the result was the arousal of national ethnocentric feelings in all those countries, and the eventual shaking off of colonial control. Even when foreign rule is benevolent, people hate to be ruled by outsiders.

Conquest by Extermination

Patterns of conquest varied, sometimes using the old technique of dividing subject peoples against each other. Occasionally conquest became a matter of **genocide,** the extermination of an entire people. In the United States, for example, although Native Americans remain, many tribes were exterminated; for those who survived, their way of life was destroyed. The Great Plains Indians were starved into submission, and the majority of them died. The buffalo were exterminated as part of the project because it was known that without the buffalo, the Great Plains Indians would starve. Sociologist Russell Thornton has thoroughly documented the extermination of Native Americans and states that the population of what is now the United States declined from an estimated 8 million people at the time Europeans first made contact with them to a low of fewer than 250,000 in 1920 (Thornton, 1988). Military action, starvation, disease, poverty, and despair had done their work.

Dutch and British people occupied South Africa in much the same manner as the conquerors of the United States first occupied their present territory. The European whites of South Africa imposed a system of racial separation and oppression on the native blacks. However, in some ways they were not so terrible as the United States was to its native peoples. Mistreatment was long and severe, but there was no attempt to exterminate the native African population. In the words of one South African,

> If your American pioneers had not massacred your Red Indians, you would find yourself in the same position (of having to cope with a native majority). You gave them blankets infected with smallpox. We defeated the Blacks in fair battle. (North 1985)

One can understand why a South African, even in the days of racial oppression, could point out that a number of other conquerors had exterminated the native populations, an even worse policy than that of South Africa. The Tasmanians, just south of Australia, were run down and killed by British settlers. The last Tasmanian died in 1870. When Germany tried to conquer Southwest Africa (now Namibia) in the late 1890s, it met strong opposition from the Herero tribe. The German general in charge, Von Trotha, decided on extermination. "[The Herero] nation must vanish from the face of the earth," he said (Thornton, 1988). The Hereroes were driven into the desert where the great majority of them died of thirst.

Colonialism and "Simple Natives"

Extermination, however, has not been the prevailing means of dealing with conquered people. In older times, they were sometimes enslaved. In more recent history, they have worked at types of labor that would enrich the country doing the colonizing. Sometimes European nations found an entrenched class system and were able to ally themselves with the upper classes and subsequently exploit the lower classes. Most frequently, though, they were inclined to consider countries without modern weapons and battleships as lands of "simple natives" in need of European guidance. A few intellectuals were interested in the wisdom of such ancient civilizations as China and India, but the majority saw them only as markets for goods and as sources of raw materials and cheap labor. It was really not until the period after the end of World War II that a real change in thinking about ethnic differences came about, a change very well stated by Jean-Paul Sartre:

> Not so long ago, the earth numbered two thousand million inhabitants—five hundred million men and women, and one thousand, five hundred million "natives." (Sartre, 1963)

One of the great changes of the late twentieth century, Sartre went on to say, is that the "natives" have become "people." Sartre may have been overly optimistic; much arrogance is still shown by people of the more developed countries (MDCs) relative to those in the less developed countries (LDCs). That arrogance declines, however, in direct proportion to the industrial development and fire power of former colonies.

One reason that Europe and the United States had a negative view of the less developed countries was the ethnocentrism discussed previously. Many of the less developed countries had very different cultures and customs. Although their customs regarding marriage, child rearing, food, health, initiations, and religion all make sense to modern anthropologists who study them, people of a century or more ago found different customs "heathenish," "outrageous," or "ungodly."

Technological superiority has also been a criterion for determining a group's superiority. Centuries ago, people with guns considered themselves superior to those who used bows and arrows. Today, a nation's military technology is often accepted as a measure of its worth.

Caste Systems and Ethnic Suppression

Caste systems have functioned to keep ethnic groups separated and to give superior status to conquerors. During the period of Spanish rule in Latin America, especially in the sixteenth and seventeenth centuries, there were four levels of people sufficiently stratified to be called **castes,** although the caste system was not so rigid as that of India. People from Spain were in the top caste; those of Spanish nationality but born in America were a step below them; those of mixed Spanish-Indian blood, called *mestizos,* were a step below pure Spanish. At the bottom of the system were the Native Americans, incorrectly called "Indians," Although the word *caste* is no longer used, the social situation remains similar. The most prosperous people appear to be of European descent. Those of mixed race are inter-mediate. Overrepresented among the very poor are those who appear to be mainly Indian and of Indian descent. However, there are no laws preventing one's status from changing. Indians can hold high office. The Mexican hero, Benito Juarez, was an Indian who overthrew Emperor Maximilian and became president of Mexico.

Caste in India

The classic case of caste was in India where movement from lower caste to a high position was impossible until the middle of the twentieth century. The priestly caste (*Brahmans*) were considered highest. Just below them, and still very high, were the *Kshatriya,* the warrior caste, which included many great landowners and princes. Below them was the ordinary trade-and-craft class (*Vaisya*), and even lower, the servant caste (*Sudra*). Finally, there were "untouchables" or **harijans,** people without caste, at the very bottom of society. The word *untouchable* is very descriptive of older beliefs about them, because high-caste people could be polluted by the very touch, or even the shadow of an untouchable that fell upon them.

It is believed that the untouchables descend from people living in India who were conquered by people from the north. Since the invaders spoke an Aryan language, the episode is called the "Aryan Invasion," and is believed to have occurred between 1500 and 1200 B.C. (Garraty, 1981). It is believed that the Aryans imposed the caste system in India, making themselves the *Brahmans* and *Kshatriya.* Those in their good graces became *Vaisya* and *Sudra,* and those who violated their laws and caste regulations became outcasts or slaves. Also, people who seemed most foreign culturally and dark in skin color were more likely than others to be outcast or enslaved. In fact, the Aryan word for *slave* was the same as their word for *dark* (Garraty, 1981).

In times past, the caste system was upheld both by law and religion. Although Hindus are aware of caste even now, caste distinctions have not had legal validity since 1955. Even untouchables are allowed to vote, hold political office, and enter any occupation they choose. Because they are generally the poorest of the poor, however, they find it hard to get the required education for upper-status jobs. Socially and economically, most of them remain at the bottom, following their traditional jobs of sweeping floors, cleaning bathrooms, skinning and tanning hides, and burying the dead. Ethnically, they seem quite distinct from people of high caste (Caughlin, 1969).

The caste system was probably made rigid by the Aryan invaders. It is likely, too, that even before the Aryan invasion the numerous ethnic groups that made up India had tried to keep their separate identities by banding together and following particular lines of work. Such customs were agreeable to the invaders, who made themselves the highest caste of warriors, or *Kshatriya*. Little by little, however, the priestly caste (the *Brahmans*), with its monopoly on religious learning, writing, and magic, gained the ascendancy (Olcott, 1944). A religious explanation solidified the caste idea: Low caste was the result of sins of a previous life. The road to improvement in the next life lay through humbly accepting one's lot.

It is hard to imagine a more perfect system for keeping people "in their place" and under control. Great Britain was able to fit into the system, and the British were looked upon as high caste, but not quite part of the system. The British were foreigners, with the wrong language, culture, and religion. Consequently, their rule was neither eternal nor totally accepted. Mahatma Gandhi preached passive resistance, and he also reignited in Hindus an intense respect for their own culture and traditions. Following World War II, Great Britain recognized the independence of India and arrangements were made to divide it into India, Pakistan, and East Pakistan (now Bangladesh) so as to separate Hindus from Moslems. A total separation was impossible, however, so there remains a Moslem minority in India and a Hindu minority in Pakistan. Ethnic differences and ethnocentrism on each side continue there, often making relations between India and Pakistan very tense.

The caste system is not unique to India. As Gunnar Myrdal (1964) pointed out, the United States had a caste system without admitting it. Particularly in the southern states, blacks (African Americans) did not interact with whites (Caucasians) as equals. As in all caste systems, intermarriage was outlawed and considered polluting to the white race. Only the lowest occupations were open to blacks. All public places were segregated, including parks, restaurants, rest rooms, schools, and buses. And, like outcasts in India, blacks were expected to accept their lot humbly. The system was, in part, the result of the United States' history of slavery, a caste position. We examine the aftermath of slavery later, but first describe another type of caste that has resulted in war and mass killings.

Caste in Central Africa

Caste and intercaste animosity also exist in Africa, as evidenced by the massacre in Rwanda in July 1994. There are several cases in which pastoral people have made themselves the overlords of gardening people. The classical case is that of the Ankole of Uganda, who are divided into pastoralists known as *Bahima,* and gardeners called the *Bairu.* As described in 1940, the *Bahima* ruled, and only they were allowed to own cattle, carry weapons, or hold high political office. *Bahima* men could take *Bairu* women for concubines, but *Bairu* men could not mate with *Bahima* women (Oberg, 1940). The social system is clearly one of castes.

The relationship between the Tutsis and the Hutus may have once been almost as rigid, but there has been far more intermarriage. The Tutsis are a cattle people, but so are some of the Hutus, although the Hutus were originally gardeners. For centuries, the Tutsis dominated the Hutus in both Rwanda and Burundi, and their upper position was accepted by the Belgians, who had a Trusteeship over the territories until 1961. Since then, the Tutsis have dominated Burundi most of the time, but the Hutus had a period of rule in Rwanda. An attempt of the Hutus to exterminate the Tutsis in a sudden massacre (Winter, 1994) led eventually to their own downfall and the flight of more than 1 million Hutus to Zaire. Although not specifically two castes, they do illustrate interethnic hatred, having waged frequent bloodbaths in Rwanda and Burundi.

SLAVERY AND ITS AFTERMATH

Slavery as an institution has had a number of variations. Among some tribal peoples, a slave was often a captive of war who might eventually be released. Usually slavery consisted of servitude for a limited period of time to pay off debts or to pay for legal offenses. In most cases, the children of slaves were born free (Cohen, 1967). In the United States and many of the Caribbean Islands, a particularly harsh type of slavery prevailed, one that could be called absolute slavery. Slave status lasted for life and was passed on to children and grandchildren. In the United States, marriage between slaves and free people was not permitted, and religious rationalizations were found for slavery as well as for separation of the races.

Any racial slave system defines people of a different race and culture as inferior to another race, that is, inferior to the race in power. In the United States, the people in power were Caucasians. Although the term "Caucasian" includes people from West Asia and North Africa, immigrants to the United States were mainly European. They were "white." The U.S. slaves were Africans. They and their ancestors came mainly from Africa; their skin was "black." Because people were judged by skin color and categorized as either "black" or "white", we use those terms here in our discussion of discrimination and slavery. The definition of "black" was such that any percentage whatever of "black blood" made a person "black."

In the United States, slavery continued until the end of the Civil War in 1865. Even after that, inferior status continued in the form of the "Jim Crow Laws" passed by Southern legislatures. Blacks were kept out of public parks, off sidewalks, allowed only in the back seats of busses, and could not use public drinking fountains or restrooms unless they were specifically marked for blacks. Separate schools for blacks were grossly underfunded. Such laws lasted to some degree until the Civil Rights Act of 1964.

In Spanish possessions in the Americas, slavery was not permitted, but discriminatory treatment of the conquered "Indians" was similar to slavery. Columbus incorrectly thought his first landings were on the East Indies, and therefore called the inhabitants "Indians," a term they seem happy to have replaced by *Native Americans.*

Although we think of both caste and slavery as things of the past, very similar conditions continue. This Haitian boy will, in all likelihood, spend his life cutting sugar cane in the Dominican Republic, kept so far in debt that he will not be allowed to leave.

In Brazil, the first slaves arrived from Africa in the early 1500s, and within a century their "black" descendants accounted for more than half the country's population. By the time slavery was abolished in Brazil in 1888, more than 3.5 million slaves had been brought in—more than six times the number to have arrived in the United States (Long, 1988). Immediately, a policy was undertaken to "whiten" the population by encouraging the immigration of Europeans. Over the years, because of numerous intermarriages, a wide variety of skin color became observable in Brazilian society.

No legal barriers now hold down people of African descent in Brazil, but this does not mean there is no discrimination. A distinction must be made between *de jure* (according to law) and *de facto* (in actual fact). For example, nearly every apartment house for upper-income people has two sets of doors and two elevators, one marked "social" and the other marked "service." Although there is no sign posted regarding who may and who may not use each door or elevator, it is well understood that "social" means "white" and "service" means "black."

Discrimination in Brazil goes much further than names on doors. People of African descent are almost totally absent from high positions. Of the 559 members of Congress, only seven are African Brazilians. In common field and factory jobs, African Brazilians are paid only 60 percent as much as European Brazilians, or whites (Long, 1988). "Blacks" who have made it into top-paying fields earn only 24 percent of the pay of comparably placed "whites."

Unlike the United States, Brazil sees blackness of skin color as a matter of degree. The darkest people suffer more discrimination than the lighter people of mixed ancestry. In Brazil it is said, too, that "money whitens." Economic success or attainment of professional status can almost turn black to white.

PERSISTENCE OF INFERIOR STATUS

Inferior status of non-whites has persisted long after the ending of slavery. There are a number of explanations for such persistence, the first one related to conflict perspective.

Conflict Perspective

Some people think of society as a smoothly functioning system, with each member contributing to the whole; others see it as a field of conflict. In conflict theory, various segments of society are seen as struggling against each other for their fair share of goods, power, and respect. This is most easily seen in a labor strike in which workers and managers struggle to increase their share of the profits. It is also clear in all the systems of conquest and control discussed previously, and in systems of slavery and caste. In all such cases, those in top positions struggle to maintain them.

Even after slavery ended, people of color were kept in inferior positions as sharecroppers, bootblacks, roadworkers, and domestic servants. From a conflict perspective, the reason was that working-class "whites" saw "blacks" as rivals for jobs, and therefore resented them. Laws were passed to segregate them and hold them down. More affluent Caucasians also supported segregation laws to prevent working-class alliances between African Americans and Caucasians, or mixing blacks and whites.

Interactionist Perspective

Another way to explain the persistence of inferior status is in interactionist terms. What happens when interactions are strictly between upper-positioned whites and lower-positioned blacks? Because they were generally given only the menial jobs, people of color were stereotyped in those jobs and looked upon as capable of nothing else. This kind of reasoning, it must be emphasized, was found especially among Caucasians and before the Civil Rights Movement of the 1960s. Before that time, very few African Americans were seen in good jobs. Their low social and economic status appeared simply part of the natural order of things.

Consistent with this reasoning, there developed an educational system that reinforced white superiority feelings about blacks. Black schools received about half the funding of white schools, resulting in poor educational achievement on the part of blacks. This led to a self-serving rationale on the part of whites: "They don't learn much anyway, so why invest too much in their schooling?" Thus, inferior status became a rationale for perpetuating inferior status.

To be treated as inferior obviously has psychological effects. One possibility is smoldering hatred, and another, self-rejection, either of which could well be an explanation for more hypertension and ulcers among blacks than among whites (U.S. Department of Health and Human Services, 1986). Many believe the most positive reaction would be a reinforced effort to prove self-worth, which is helpful unless the struggle becomes a long series of frustrations. For ghetto dwellers, of course, there are many frustrations and defeats. This is undoubtedly a reason that drug dealing is so common among minority youth in American cities.

Institutional Racism

Another sociological explanation for the problems of depressed minorities is not necessarily a result of individual prejudice. It is, instead, that of entrenched habit that pervades all our institutions—**institutional racism.** Institutional racism is the form of discrimination that results from the habitual, hard-to-change ways of a society. For example, most churches remain segregated along racial lines, mainly as a result of age-old

habit rather than belief. As we shall see, legal penalties for cocaine use tend to be stiffer for blacks than whites. Blacks who kill whites are much more likely to get death penalties than whites who kill blacks. Black children are given intelligence tests that have been standardized on white children with quite different experiences. Although housing discrimination is illegal, realtors steer blacks, whites, and Hispanics to "their own" areas. In many institutions of higher learning, preference for entry is given to candidates whose parents are alumni and entered before there were racial-equality rules. Those fired from jobs when times are bad are more likely to be blacks than whites, who are more apt to have seniority, dating to a period before equality rules were enforced. Institutional racism is clearly rooted in the past when all of society was segregated. It changes very slowly.

Successes and Failures

Nevertheless, in the United States, considerable change in race relations has come about. An exciting social movement led by the Reverend Martin Luther King, Jr., successfully attacked both legislated and institutionalized racism. A strong Civil Rights Act was passed in 1964, attempting (with considerable success) to stop race discrimination in employment, organization membership, housing, and education. Over a period of years, much progress was made by black Americans both in employment and politics. More were elected to office, not just as mayors and city council members, but to Congress. In 1992 the first black woman, Carol Mosely-Braun, was elected to the Senate; two years previously, the first black governor, Douglas L. Wilder, had been elected in Virginia. When Martin Luther King, Jr., made his famous "I have a dream" speech in 1963, there were only 300 black public officeholders in the United States. By 1992 there were 7,000. A Black Caucus in Congress was well organized and influential. Blacks were also organized to fight for promotions in medicine, law, and business (Duke, 1993). The athletic and entertainment worlds were open to blacks as never before, although they are still underrepresented in upper positions. In athletics, coaches, owners, and managers are nearly all white. In entertainment, directors and producers are mainly white.

During the 1970s and 1980s many blacks made their way up the social-class scale, despite little government encouragement, especially in the 1980s. By the 1990s, 50 percent were middle class or upwardly mobile working class (Morganthau, 1992). Many had moved from the inner city to the suburbs, where they enjoyed better homes and neighborhoods.

Persistent Problems

Despite these improvements, however, there were many ways in which life for blacks seemed to be falling apart. As the more successful moved to the suburbs, those left behind were worse off than ever. There were virtually no jobs, and transportation to better areas, or rent in better areas, was too expensive (Vobejda, 1993). One-parent (mostly female-headed) homes were becoming the rule, and 65 percent of those homes were very poor. There was only one chance in five that a

black child would grow up in a two-parent home (Ingrassa, 1993).

Twenty-five years ago, Eliot Liebow studied black street-corner men in New York City (Liebow, 1967). Nearly all of them married, an important rite of passage. They left their wives and children fairly soon, though, because they could find no jobs that paid enough to support a wife and children. Now, the pattern is the same, except that marriage is omitted. Women must get by on their own, or on welfare, and children grow up without male role models.

Just as jobs were disappearing and the centers of many big cities were becoming "rust belts," illegal drugs entered the picture on a large scale. The only people making money were the drug peddlers. It was a risky business, but many felt they had nothing to lose. Life was exciting; there were a few big winners; and it was a way of showing contempt for society.

Laws against illegal drugs became increasingly severe, and, deliberately or not, so did discrimination against blacks. Possession of 100 grams of powdered cocaine could draw a one-year prison sentence, but possession of only one gram of crack cocaine could have the same sentence. Powdered cocaine was preferred by the whites who were more likely to have enough money to buy it, and crack cocaine usually went to the blacks who were too poor to buy powdered cocaine. Typically, a black person drew a sentence for 1/100th as much cocaine as would bring a white person the same sentence—a good exam-

In 1992, Carol Moseley Braun from Illinois became the first black woman elected to the U.S. Senate.

Poverty of Americans by Race and Ethnicity					**TABLE 6.1**
Population	Percentage in poverty				
	1975	1980	1986	1988	1990
White	9.7	10.1	11.0	10.0	10.7
Hispanic	26.9	25.7	27.3	26.2	28.1
Black	31.3	32.5	31.1	30.7	31.9

SOURCE: Data (from U.S. Bureau of the Census)

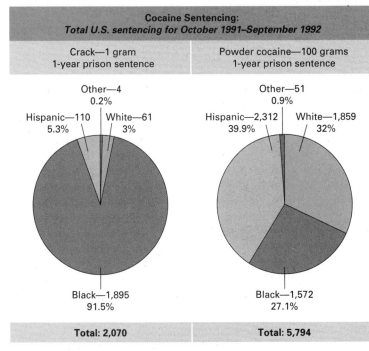

Cocaine Sentencing: Total U.S. sentencing for October 1991–September 1992	
Crack—1 gram 1-year prison sentence	**Powder cocaine—100 grams** 1-year prison sentence

Crack—1 gram, 1-year prison sentence:
- Other—4, 0.2%
- Hispanic—110, 5.3%
- White—61, 3%
- Black—1,895, 91.5%
- **Total: 2,070**

Powder cocaine—100 grams, 1-year prison sentence:
- Other—51, 0.9%
- Hispanic—2,312, 39.9%
- White—1,859, 32%
- Black—1,572, 27.1%
- **Total: 5,794**

Source: San Francisco Chronicle. Aug. 26, 1993.

Figure 6.1
These charts illustrate how cocaine laws discriminate against blacks. A single gram of crack cocaine, used mainly by blacks, draws a one-year prison sentence. It takes 100 times as much powdered cocaine, used mainly by whites and Hispanics, to draw the same sentence.

ple of institutional racism. Moreover, the person with powdered cocaine was fairly apt to get parole; possession of crack cocaine draws a sentence without parole (Associated Press, 1993).

Blacks have always been overrepresented in the prison statistics, part of the reason being discrimination, another part being poverty and place of residence. Whatever the reasons, the United States can hardly scoff at racism in South Africa. *Harper's Index* for June 1993 gives the following statistics on imprisonment:

Number of black men per 100,000 incarcerated in South Africa:	681
Number of black men per 100,000 incarcerated in the United States:	3,370

Finally, although blacks have made considerable progress in terms of equal rights, there is a dangerous racist minority that embitters life for black people and other minorities. As has so often happened at times of rising unemployment and poverty, racist violence is increasing.

Violent white supremacists (of whom there are an estimated 25,000 in various organizations) turn their hatred against blacks, Jews, Asians, and anyone else who is different. Police have found many hate groups stockpiling weapons (Espinoza and Pimentel, 1993).

In the month of July 1993, a headquarters of the National Association for the Advancement of Colored People (NAACP) was bombed, as was a Jewish temple in Sacramento, California; a series of suspicious fires occurred, usually victimizing blacks, Asians, or Hispanics. In Florida, a black man was doused with gasoline and set afire. Nationally, the Federal Bureau of Investigation reported 4,558 hate crimes in 1991 (the last year for which statistics are available), 60 percent of which were racially motivated. Twenty-two deaths were reported from skinhead violence from 1990 to 1993, almost four times as many as in the previous three years (Espinoza, 1993). The word *skinhead* is used synonymously with neo-Nazi because so many neo-Nazis shave their heads or cut their hair very short. In the United States, racial and ethnic differences are strongly associated with violence. The same is true of another country that had a long record of slavery, South Africa.

SOUTH AFRICA AND APARTHEID

In the part of South Africa controlled by the British, slavery was outlawed in the 1830s, but in other parts it lasted for many more years. South Africa is an extreme case of a multiethnic state, and also one strongly influenced by its tradition of slavery. The political background of South Africa lies in conquest by rival white groups, the British and the Boers. The Boers (a Dutch word for *farmer*) were mainly Dutch, but also included French Huguenots, Germans, and a few others. The 1991 population of South Africa was 40.6 million. Of this population, just over 30 million (75 percent) are blacks and an additional 3.3 million are colored, a term in South Africa meaning "of mixed race." The mixture is of blacks and either Europeans or people from India or Malaysia. Asians number a little more than 1 million (3 percent), and are of either Indian or Malaysian origin. This leaves fewer than 6 million whites, less than 14 percent of the population. The whites, in turn, are divided between the Boers, who speak a Dutch-derived language called Afrikaans, and those of British descent. The Dutch are more numerous than the British,

although the British hold more wealth in mines and industry. The Dutch (Boers) have dominated the country politically since World War II.

Race and ethnicity have been of overwhelming importance in South Africa. Until June 1991, everyone was classified into one of nine categories: black, white, colored, Indian, Malay, Griqua, Chinese, and other colored, or other Asians. Rights and freedoms depended on that classification (Schaefer, 1988).

The original inhabitants of South Africa were the Bushmen and the Hottentots, both peoples of small stature and not numerous. Before the seventeenth century, larger black people were entering the Transvaal, the part of South Africa north of the Vaal River. Four tribes were the Swazi, Xhosa, Sotho, and the very powerful Zulus, who became dominant over the others in the early nineteenth century. The first white settlers were the Dutch, who came looking for farmland as early as the seventeenth century, when the region was very thinly populated. During the Napoleonic Wars, Great Britain seized the Dutch colony of Capetown and took permanent control soon after. The Dutch resented British rule, especially when the British outlawed slavery in 1834. The Dutch Boers moved north in an episode known as the Great Trek. They formed two independent republics: Transvaal and the Orange Free State. The Boers were free, but they continued to hold slaves.

The discovery of diamonds in 1867 and gold in the 1880s caused a vast increase in British immigration and control over the territory. The

Racial Groups in the Republic of South Africa (percentages of population)					TABLE 6.2
	Whites	All non-Whites	Black Africans	Coloreds	Asians
1904	22	78	67	9	2
1936	21	79	69	8	2
1951	21	79	68	9	3
1986	18	82	70	9	3
2000 (est.)	10–13	87–90	75–77	9–10	3

SOURCE: R. T. Schaefer, *Racial and Ethnic Groups* (Glenview, IL: Scott, Foresman, 1988), p. 495, Table 17.1.

Dutch fought back in the Boer War at the end of the nineteenth century. The British won, but granted a generous peace. The two white groups seemed to be on good terms when they formed the Union of South Africa in 1910. By a very narrow vote, the Union of South Africa joined the British in World War II. Immediately afterward, however, the political party backed mainly by the Boers gained control and started the policies known as **apartheid** (separateness) to divide white from black. In 1960, South Africa separated from Great Britain and became the Republic of South Africa (see Figure 6.2).

Over the years, the government passed a great many laws to ensure the separate development of blacks and whites: The Native Land Act prohibited blacks from owning land except in a few reservations; the Natives Act required blacks to carry pass books, specifying which parts of a city they could enter for work. There was also a Suppression of Communism Act, aimed at silencing the opposition. All opponents of the government were "Communists."

A unique part of the apartheid policies was the setting up of certain black homelands, or *Bantustans*, so-called self-governing states for blacks. Note that many of the "homelands" are made of noncontiguous areas. Swaziland and Lesotho are the only separate states, made protectorates by the British in 1860. No foreign

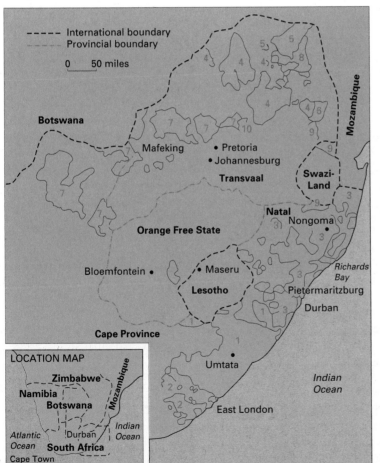

Homeland	People
1. Transkei[a]	Xhosa
2. Ciskei[a]	Xhosa
3. Kwazulu	Zulu
4. Lebowa	Pedi/ N. Ndebele
5. Venda[a]	Venda
6. Gazankulu	Shangaaan/ Tsonga
7. Bophuthatswana[a]	Tswaba
8. Basotho Qwa Qwa	S. Sotho
9. Swazi	Swazi
10. S. Ndebele (Kwandebele)[a]	S. Ndebele

[a] Indicates homelands declared to be independent by South Africa.

Source: From R. J. Southall, *South Africa's Transkei.* Copyright © 1983; cited in R. T. Schaefer, *Racial and Ethnic Groups* (Glenview, IL: Scott, Foresman and Company, 1988), p. 498, Table 17.3.

Figure 6.2
Under South Africa's apartheid policy, an attempt was made to keep each black tribe in a homeland of its own. Besides creating the ethnic confusion shown here, the policy was extremely impractical because blacks had to work in white cities, factories, and mines to make a living.

government recognizes any of the others, and none of them is economically viable, because blacks have to go into white towns for jobs. The country could not run without black labor.

Because their labor is needed, arrangements are made for blacks to live in certain sections of the cities, but housing is crowded, lacks electricity, and in many cases lacks running water and toilets. Houses are tiny huts crammed with an average of 14 people.

Schools are under government control. Until recently, white children went free; blacks paid. Nevertheless, some of the blacks get an education and are needed in technical and professional jobs, another reason that strict apartheid has been impossible.

The South African press became strongly critical of its own government, which led to censoring the press by President Pieter Willem Botha. Foreign opposition to the repressive policies of South Africa grew. For a while South Africa was excluded from the Olympics. Many business firms pulled out. Trade sanctions were imposed by many foreign governments, and proved very effective. In 1989 President Botha resigned and was replaced by Frederik Willem de Klerk. At first de Klerk seemed similar to his predecessor, but in early 1991 he announced plans to end apartheid. Even after that, there were reasons for looking on him with suspicion. He admitted the government had been working to divide the black opposition.

However, the 1990s have brought hope and the first triumphs to the nonwhites of South Africa. Little by little, the strict laws of apartheid were ended. President de Klerk released from prison the leader of the African National Congress (ANC), Nelson Mandela, who had been a political prisoner for 27 years. In the spring of 1994, an election was held in which Nelson Mandela won the presidency. For the first time, a member of the majority black race was the head of the nation. To date, he seems a leader of ability and moderation.

South Africa is far from reaching peace and harmony, however. It is still a land of grueling poverty and violence. Elements among both blacks and whites had at one time opposed a general election. White opponents feared black rule and were determined to keep some type of apartheid, even if it meant dividing South Africa into two countries.

Black opposition to an election came from Mangosuthu Buthelezi, leader of the Zulu-dominated Inkatha Freedom Party. Buthelezi also wished to see the country divided, with considerable territory for his own Zulu people. The Zulus have been famous since the early nineteenth century, when their chief, Shaka, united the Zulus and conquered territories around them (Otterbein, 1967). The Zulus hold considerable territory near the east coast of South Africa (see Figure 6.2). Eventually though, the Zulu leaders withdrew their opposition to the election.

Thousands of South African blacks have died in political violence, especially in the 1970s and 1980s. Until the last few years, nearly all their deaths have been at the hands of white racists. More recently, the death toll is at least partially blamed on the conflict between the African National Congress and the smaller, Zulu-dominated Inkatha Freedom Party. The Inkatha Freedom Party represented the type of separatism that could weaken the black majority and slow the progress toward democracy. As of the mid 1990s, however, it appeared that the Zulus were cooperating with the government.

South Africa has long been a center of world attention because of its mistreatment of people on the basis of race and ethnicity. That dubious distinction, however, is now focused on what used to be Yugoslavia, where Serbs and Croats attempt to weed out a Moslem minority, and in some cases to weed out each other.

ETHNIC CLEANSING

Developments in former Yugoslavia have brought a new term to our vocabulary: **ethnic cleansing**.

The words were first used by Serbians living in Bosnia, attempting to expand their territory and eliminate Moslems. The Moslems, before the present fighting began, made up 43 percent of the population of Bosnia (31 percent are Serbs and 17 percent are Croats). The fighting has involved more than merely the "cleaning out" of Moslems, nearly 200,000 of whom have fled Bosnia. Croatians have also been driven out of Bosnian areas claimed by Serbs, and Serbs have been driven out of Croat-claimed areas. Occasionally Serbs and Croats have cooperated against Moslems, or Croats and Moslems have joined forces against Serbs. An exile from Bosnia, now homeless and penniless, and without hope, says, "I'm a foreigner now wherever I go" (Ottaway, 1993). He joins hundreds of thousands of exiles who will always be foreigners wherever they go. The war has been particularly vicious in the killing of civilians, torture of prisoners, and as noted in Chapter 3, the rape of Moslem women.

The refugees face problems besides exile and loss of homes. Exploiters try to rob them of what little they have, promising to get them into Western Europe. Sometimes they are induced to smuggle drugs to get false visas for France or Germany.

Reasons for Ethnic Cleansing

The reasons for extreme ethnic animosity in former Yugoslavia are hard to understand. Many of the people have lived as friendly neighbors in the past, and there have been intermarriages between Moslems and both Serbs and Croats. But an element among Serbians has long dreamed of a "Greater Serbia," wanting to unite Serbia with Montenegro and add parts of Bosnia. These Serbs have tried to add territory by moving out Moslems and sometimes Croats.

To get public support for such policies, leaders have stirred up historical animosities dating back to the days when the Ottoman Empire (Turkish and Moslem) had seized most of the Balkan Peninsula—six or seven centuries ago. The southern and eastern parts of the Balkan Peninsula had been converted to Orthodox Christianity, and most of the north and west, which includes Slovenia and Croatia, had been converted to Roman Catholicism. Most of Albania, Kosovo, and Bosnia converted to Islam during the long centuries of Turkish rule. This meant that a three-way religious conflict became part of Balkan history. The religious conflict

These Moslems being held prisoner by Bosnian Serbs are victims of ethnic cleansing. The Serbs aim to force them out of their homeland or kill them.

Figure 6.3
Refugees from the former Yugoslavia have been accepted into these countries, but are often homeless and penniless in a foreign land.

COUNTRY	REFUGEES
Germany	300,000
Switzerland	80,000
Austria	73,000
Sweden	62,202
Hungary	40,000
Turkey	18,060*
Italy	16,000
Czech Rep./Slovakia	10,000
Denmark	7,323
Netherlands	7,000
Spain	4,654
Britain	4,424
France	4,200
Norway	3,674
Belgium	3,371
Albania	3,000*
Poland	2,100**
Finland	2,050
Luxembourg	1,618
Ireland	187
Bulgaria	185*
Portugal	150
Greece	7
Others	30,000
Total	643,205

*Not confirmed
**May be as high as 3,000

Source: Data from the U.N. High Commission for Refugees as cited in *The Washington Post Weekly Edition,* August 23–29, 1993: 11.

seemed to have died, but has been resurrected along with dividing nationalism.

In addition to Serbian ambitions, memories of old quarrels, and religious divisions, other factors often bring out ethnic animosities. One is a lack of a cohesive government or ideology to hold people together. Yugoslavia had never achieved statehood in the sense that France, Italy, and Germany had done. Regional loyalties were more important to Yugoslavs than any national state. Marshal Tito, the strongman who had held the country together after World War II, died in 1980. There was no leader of his stature to replace him.

Ethnic animosities are also increased when times are bad and jobs are scarce. Not just in Yugoslavia, but in practically all countries, bad times are blamed on the outsider who becomes the scapegoat. In the case of Yugoslavia, there were Moslems in Serbian territories, Serbs in Croatia, and Croatians in Serbia. Outsiders everywhere provoked rage!

Finally, outside countries had an effect. Germany was quick to recognize Slovenia and Croatia when they declared independence. Other countries followed. A philosophy dating from World War I held that nationalities had a right to self-determination; but there had not been sufficient thought about how far fragmentation should go. Serbia was in a strong position because the former Yugoslavian military establishment was mainly Serbian. There was also hope on Serbia's part that its former ally, Russia, would support it. To date, Russia has not done so.

Effect on the Moslem World

In Saudi Arabia and other parts of the Moslem world there was great anger against the West (especially Western Europe) for standing by complacently while Bosnian Moslems were killed or exiled. The situation could play into the hands of radical fundamentalists (Epstein, 1993). Heavy bombing of Serb positions in the fall of 1995 probably assuaged Arabic feelings and restored faith in NATO.

Other Cases of Ethnic Cleansing

Although the term ethnic cleansing has not been used, there are many other attempts to force people off their lands or to kill them. (In the following chapter we shall mention Sudan in this respect.) In Tibet, Lamaist Buddhism has been suppressed. The Dalai Lama (the high priest of the country) and approximately 100,000 of his followers are in exile. China is accused of trying to wipe out the entire culture of Tibet. In Iran, an attempt is made to suppress non–Iranian tribes of Baluchis and Naroui (Amnesty International, 1992).

Better known as a people under threat are the Kurds. Thousands of them were killed, some with poisoned gas, during Iraq's war with Iran. Then, during the Persian Gulf War against Iraq, it was found that the Iraqi government was trying to wipe out the Kurds on its northern border. Nearly 100,000 Kurds fled to Iran, and many have made their way to Western Europe.

The Kurds illustrate a problem of historical development that has made life difficult for various ethnic groups. The Kurds occupy a territory that lies partly in Turkey, partly in Iraq, and partly in Iran. Although they are rivals, all three countries vehemently oppose the creation of an independent Kurdistan. Small wonder that many Kurds join the 16 million or more people in the world attempting to migrate and find homes elsewhere. One family's situation illustrates the difficulties of emigrating.

The Difficult Road to Exile

Becir Mohammed, a geologist, and his wife, Rasai, and their infant daughter, fled Iraqi Kurdistan in May 1993. By Kurdish standards they were wealthy, with a 1986 Toyota to sell for funds for the trip. They took a taxi to the Iran border, paid bribes to border guards, and walked into Iran. From there they traveled by bus to the Turkish border, where they bought fake Latin American passports. They went north in Turkey to the Black Sea coast, where they took a ferry north to Russian territory. Rasai and the baby were sick all the way because of a heavy storm on the Black Sea. In the Russian town of Sochi, they bought fake Bulgarian passports. From there they made their way to the Polish town of Zgorzelec, and waited to cross the border into Germany, their destination.

In Zgorzelec, Becir, Rasai, and the baby entered a border camp, crowded with refugees of many nationalities: Bulgarians, Belarusians, Ukrainians, Somalis, Armenians, Azerbaijanis, Egyptians, Iraqis, Sri Lankans, Pakistanis, Chinese, and many Romanians. All are waiting for a chance to sneak into Germany. About $60 will get you across the Neisse River, but you must watch to evade border guards. Then about $200 will get you into Dresden, safe from border guards. What will happen in Germany? Will Becir and Rasai be wanted or unwanted immigrants? (Pomfret, 1993).

UNWANTED IMMIGRANTS: EUROPE

While the numbers of people in the world seeking refuge steadily increases, refugees are received with greater and greater reluctance by the countries to which they emigrate. As of 1992, there were an estimated 16.5 million refugees in the world (United Nations, 1993). They include victims of ethnic cleansing, Kurds and others escaping Iraq, and millions fleeing from devastating wars and revolutions or from dire poverty. A very large number of those fleeing Eastern Europe looked for homes in Western Europe, especially Germany.

Germany and the Refugees

Historically, Paris has welcomed refugees, especially intellectuals, artists, musicians, and deposed monarchs and aristocrats. The Netherlands and Scandinavia have also been generous in welcoming refugees, and so has Great Britain.

It was only after World War II that Germany welcomed large numbers of foreigners, including refugees. There were two reasons for German generosity: (1) Germany was prosperous and needed foreign workers, and (2) Germany wanted to demonstrate a deep remorse over the atrocities of the Nazi period. The German policy became one of allowing all refugees to enter and remain, although rules for actually gaining citizenship were extremely restrictive. The feeling was that only Germans could be German citizens (Kramer, 1993).

By the early 1990s, Germany's generous policy had come under attack. For many years, large

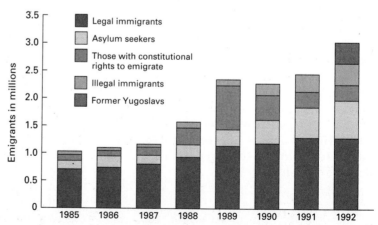

Figure 6.4
By the early 1990s, an increasing flood of immigrants was coming from Eastern Europe, North Africa, and Asia to seek new homes in the prosperous countries of Western Europe; but barriers against immigration were going up, and there were even episodes of attacks on foreigners.

Sources: Organization for Economic Cooperation and Development, "Trends in International Migration," 1992; Jonas Widgren, coordinator for inter-governmental consultations on asylum, refugee and migration policies in Europe, North America and Australia; embassies; U.N. agencies and organizations; as cited in *Washington Post National Weekly Edition*, Aug. 2–8, 1993: 8.

numbers of Turks moved to Germany for jobs. Now, with a job shortage, far fewer are needed. Worse yet, many refugees from former Yugoslavia and elsewhere are trying to get into Germany, where they believe jobs are still plentiful.

Within Germany, gangs of violent young imitators of the Nazis make frequent headlines. They have attacked hundreds of foreigners, and kill about 20 per year. In Ludwigshafen (a small city of Western Germany) the gangs boast of "cracking" people, which means knocking down victims and stomping their heads with heavy boots until they hear the skulls crack. Ender Basaran, a young man of Turkish parentage, was "cracked" by a gang of skinheads. Basaran lived, although his eyesight and coordination are damaged. He had long identified with Germany and almost thought of himself as German, although there was no way for him to become a citizen (Kramer, 1993).

There is some concern about the future of Germany. Will moderation prevail, or will neo-Nazism take over? On the positive side, Germany has shown great generosity about foreigners. It has not only accepted them (about 5.5 million non-Germans live in Germany) but has provided food and shelter for refugees. Skinheads are condemned by the press and by most politicians, yet even when they kill, they get off with light sentences—echoing the case in Germany before the Nazi takeover in 1933. Finally, in Kramer's analysis (Kramer, 1993), far too many Germans appear indifferent to the skinheads or too sure that a right-wing dictatorship can't happen again. In contrast, two-thirds of the 1.8 million Turks living in Germany consider racism a serious problem, and one that is worsening rapidly (Reuters, 1993).

Fortress Europe?

On July 1, 1993, Germany revoked its constitutional guarantee allowing entry to all political refugees. Germany is not alone in tightening immigration policies. France is making it difficult to acquire French citizenship, and its conservative government has declared zero immigration as its goal. Like Germany, France once had need of imported workers, largely from Algeria. Now, French workers see Algerian workers only as competitors for jobs. An extremist party has roused working-class anger against all Moslem immigrants, of whom there are about 3 million in France.

Across the channel in England, ethnic antagonism also occurs, where it is largely turned against "blacks," a word that in England is applied to Pakistanis and Indians as well as African-decended immigrants from Jamaica and other Caribbean Islands. As in continental Europe, racism is strongest among the chronically unemployed, who see the blacks as the cause of their unemployment. Actually, the black unemployment rate (20 percent) is twice as high as that of whites. Because there are no equal employment laws, most firms refuse to hire blacks for even the most menial jobs. There are four black members of parliament (of 650 members), but they are totally ignored by the government. As one black leader says of life for his people, "It is grim and getting grimmer" (Monroe, 1988). The Commission for Racial Equality published a report in 1986 titled "Living in Terror." It pointed out that Asians as well as blacks are routinely harassed and scapegoated as the cause of all the ills of society.

Part of the reason that so much of Europe is shutting its gates is a matter of ethnic and racial prejudice. There are, however, legitimate problems with the great influx of refugees. Often the number seems too great, so that even as generous a country as Sweden is considering restrictions (Robinson, 1993). Denmark contributes to the support of, but is too small a country to accept, a flood of refugees. The economic costs of accepting refugees are high, another reason for a tendency toward a "fortress Europe," with closed gates. Many people fleeing Bosnia and elsewhere have spent, or maybe been fleeced of, all their money and possessions on their way to safety.

Consequently, they must be cared for, at least temporarily. During times of economic stress, it is easy to awaken animosity toward people who cost money and are seen as threats to employment. Are other parts of the world more generous than Europe?

UNWANTED IMMIGRANTS: ASIA AND AFRICA

Europe is not alone in ethnic problems and unequal treatment of different peoples. We mentioned China briefly in connection with Tibet, where China is the aggressor. There are cases, however, in which the Chinese have been the recipients of ethnic animosity and atrocities.

The Overseas Chinese

Approximately 30 million Chinese live outside of China, a few in nearly all countries, but the majority in other parts of Asia. In general, they work hard, are very frugal, and gradually improve their lot economically. For the most part, though, they have not been welcomed by the people with whom they live. Their economic success has often led to persecution. Sociologist Thomas Sowell comments at length on how both economic success and economic failure can lead to ethnic animosity (Sowell, 1983). People who live in poverty are often looked down upon as incapable of anything else. People who succeed are often resented; the majority sees the minority's success as coming at the majority's expense. The actual fact may be just the opposite. When a capable minority is expelled, the whole economy suffers, as was the case when the Chinese were massacred in the Philippines in 1603 and exiled in 1639. In both cases, they were allowed back because they were the only traders who could get the goods that the Philippines wanted (Sowell, 1983).

The most recent anti-Chinese atrocities took place in Indonesia. In 1965–1966, as the present dictator, Suharto, took control, he ordered a general slaughter of Communists, who were his contestants for power. Among the 500,000 people slaughtered, many were not Communists, but were Chinese who had committed the crime of succeeding economically (Bonner, 1988).

In Vietnam, when the troops from the North won the war, the Chinese in the South were deprived of their property, and often driven out. Chinese were the majority of the refugees referred to as the "boat people." Often their boats were attacked as they tried to escape, resulting in rape, pillage, and murder (Sowell, 1983).

Japan and Foreigners

More than other industrialized nations, Japan has had less immigration and a strong sense of racial and ethnic solidarity; but now that it is a leading industrial power, its ethnic isolation is being undermined. The largest number of foreigners are Koreans, who complain of discrimination in hiring and housing. One park in Tokyo has become a meetingplace for the approximately 4,000 Iranians working in Tokyo. Their presence has raised a storm of protest. A member of an antiforeigners group in Japan says, "We believe that nature did not intend different nationalities to live side by side" (Kageyama, 1993).

The reaction to foreigners does not indicate that the Japanese are by nature less tolerant than other nationalities. They have had little acquaintance with foreigners, look upon them with a mixture of curiosity and fear, and, like many Americans and Europeans, do not approve citizenship for people who are so different from themselves.

Asiatic Russia

Many of the former parts of the Soviet Union located in Central Asia, such as Kazakhstan,

Uzbekistan, Kyrgyzstan, and Tajikistan, are inhabited by Moslem people, but contain large Russian minorities. In many cases, Russians in top political positions have been replaced by people native to the republics of Central Asia. For many years there was a forced harmony between Russians and Central Asian people. At present most of the areas are calm and not characterized by anti–Russian policies or oppression; but many Russians have moved back to Russia. (We will see in Chapter 13 the concerns about the future policies of the newly independent Moslem states.) Elsewhere Russia has, like so many countries, crowded native populations such as the reindeer-herding Samoyed and Tungus into inadequate areas.

Africa

Unlike Europe, Africa has no problem of unwanted immigrants, nor a problem of people having to return home. The African problem is more typically one of emigration, as in the case of many north Africans trying to emigrate to France. In other cases, attempts are made to escape devastating wars. Angola has been fighting a civil war for many years; 2 million of Angola's 11,000,000 people are now homeless, but only a handful are ever able to flee (Taylor, 1993).

In Africa, ethnic and racial tensions are not limited to South Africa. In Sudan, constant fighting goes on between the Moslem north and the Christian South. In populous Nigeria, fights have developed between the northern (largely Moslem) tribes and some of the southern (largely Christian) tribes. We must be aware that tribal differences in Africa are important, but they are far too complex to be covered in a short treatment of race and ethnicity. In general, it can be said that the problems of Africa center as much in poverty and power struggles among military leaders as in ethnic differences, although ethnic differences are very important (Richberg,

1944). Such differences led to the mass murders in Rwanda discussed previously.

UNWANTED IMMIGRANTS: THE UNITED STATES

In the United States, especially in the 1960s and 1970s, the main focus of attention regarding racial and ethnic conflict was on the problems of black Americans—people who could hardly be classified as immigrants since their ancestors had been brought to the United States against their wills. In Colonial times, and in the early days of the republic, voluntary immigrants were largely from the British Isles and from the Netherlands and Germany. During the presidency of John Adams, the Alien and Sedition Acts were passed (1798) to allow the president to expel foreigners suspected of "treasonable or secret" inclinations. The real aim was to quiet criticism of the Adams administration and to keep out French agents. The Alien and Sedition Acts were repealed in Jefferson's time, but xenophobia was to appear many more times in American history.

Late in the nineteenth century, a great hue and cry was raised against immigration for two reasons. One problem was that the immigrants were coming in such large numbers. The other problem, seen as even more important, was that the new people bore less similarity to the standard American "type" than had earlier immigrants. Tolerance extended as far as countries of northwestern Europe, but not so far as Italy, Greece, Poland, and Romania. The people looked different, had strange customs, and were apt to be Catholic, Orthodox, or Jewish, whereas the older Americans were mainly Protestant. Language and appearance seemed strange, definitely not "American." Antiforeign sentiment focused even more on Orientals than on southern and eastern Europeans. In California, which received the largest Chinese immigration, laws were passed to keep Chinese children out of public schools, and special taxes were imposed on Chinese businesses, mainly laundries (Hill, 1973). A Chinese exclusion law was passed to keep out Chinese, saying, in effect, that Chinese could not become good American citizens. Early in the twentieth century, the Japanese were also excluded.

Obviously, one reason for exclusionary laws was pure ethnocentrism—too wide a cultural difference was intolerable. The second reason was understandable in conflict terms: The new arrivals were willing to work for incredibly low wages, which pitted them against American workers who were trying to unionize and improve their lot. Immigrants were hungry and desperate for any job that would sustain life; they could hardly understand what offense they had committed, since American industrialists had encouraged them to come. The viewpoint of American laborers, it should be noted, was not too different from that of German and French workers now.

The Antiforeign Panic

The 1920s, following World War I, saw a resurgence of antiforeign sentiment, but in this case the fear was of Communists and subversives, as well as a renewed fear of Catholics. The Ku Klux Klan was revived, its new form being anti–Catholic and antiforeign as well as antiblack. Laws were passed to give preference to immigrants from northwestern Europe, to cut down on Italian, Slavic, and Greek immigration, and to exclude people from the Orient. A quota system, the **National Origins Act,** was passed, giving each country a number of immigrants proportional to how many people it had already contributed to the United States population. The act accomplished its purpose of letting in more northwestern Europeans and cutting back on all others.

In the aftermath of World War II, policies shifted in the direction of racial and ethnic equality, partly in revulsion against the horrors of Nazism. The United States again admitted East Asians. Regarding Jewish immigration, U.S. policies in the late 1930s had been cruel. Boatloads of Jewish refugees from Hitler's Germany were turned back to Germany, where their deaths were almost certain. Narrow interpretations of our quota laws, combined with anti-Semitism, caused their deaths. In 1948 the **Displaced Persons Act,** along with previous directives from President Truman, reversed such policies, but after millions of Jews had already died in gas chambers (Neier, 1987).

In the years since, our policy has been quite generous to refugees from Communist countries, but less so to refugees from other dictatorships, such as the one that usually exists in Haiti. Black leaders have contended that part of the reason for rejecting Haitian refugees is simply that they're black. Another reason is that much of the flight is from grave poverty, and we do not recognize a category of economic refugees (Neier, 1987).

Illegal Immigrants

Immigration laws have always been violated. Sailors jump ship, relatives are smuggled in, stays under visas are violated, and false documents are printed. But in recent years, the major concern with illegal immigration has been with hundreds of thousands of people crossing the U.S. border from the south, mainly Mexican nationals and other Latin Americans. Typically, they have arrived in poverty and are willing to work long hours for low wages. They are accused therefore of having a depressing effect on wages and taking jobs away from United States citizens. They dare not complain about wages for fear of being deported.

There are also concerns about how immigration laws are flouted. The Immigration and

Like much of the Western world, the United States tries to slow immigration, especially from Latin America. Motorists on California's Interstate 5 are cautioned to look for illegal immigrants crossing the highway.

In 1988 a new law was passed to curb illegal immigration. People already here were allowed to apply for legal status, but after that, illegal immigration would be dealt with by fining people who hired illegal immigrants. The law has been a total failure. Fines are too small to frighten most employers, the law is difficult to enforce, and no major effort has been made to enforce it (Turque et al., 1993).

An important reason for not enforcing the law is that too many Americans profit from immigration. Mexican nationals enter in large numbers to take ill-paid farm labor jobs. Conditions of employment are usually bad. Although they work harder than most people do, anti-immigration sentiment has fostered a stereotype of "lazy Mexicans." Mexican Ambassador Jorge Montana complains of how anti-foreign sentiment has been exploited by politicians. Montana says, "There is an equation now that goes: illegal immigrants equal Mexicans, equal criminals, equal someone looking for social services. I think that is absolutely lies" (Sandalow, 1994).

Public Attitudes

Because present-day immigration to the United States is mainly from the poor countries of Latin America, Asia, and the Caribbean, it entails a monetary cost, at least for the short term. Many have no marketable skills and cannot find jobs. Consequently many immigrants require public assistance, although only slightly more than native citizens. In California, which receives by far the most immigrants of any state, 10.4 percent of the new immigrants received public assistance in 1990, compared to 7.7 percent of native Californians (Thomas and Murr, 1993). In complaints about large numbers of immigrants, culturally different immigrants, and immigrants in need of public assistance, the United States and Western Europe have much in common.

A recent opinion survey (Thomas and Murr, 1993) found that 59 percent of the American

Naturalization Service (INS) estimates that 3 million illegal immigrants entered the United States in the decade of the 1980s. The total number of entrants causes concern, whether legal or illegal. During the decade of the 1980s almost 9 million immigrants entered the United States legally, making a total population addition of about 12 million (Mydans, 1993). It is questionable whether the United States will profit from large additions to its population.

public believes past immigration was good; but 60 percent believes present immigration is a bad thing for the United States.

What is more troubling than the numbers of immigrants coming to the United States (more than to all the rest of the industrialized world combined), is the rise in ethnic animosity. Latin Americans and Asians are frequently harassed; and no distinction is made between legal and illegal immigrants by groups who hate foreigners. In Pomona, a city east of Los Angeles, Eddie Cortez, a man assumed to be from Mexico, was pulled over and stopped by immigration agents. He was treated rudely, harassed, and threatened. He was about to be thrown into a police van for deportation to Mexico. Then he identified himself as the Mayor of Pomona. His only offense was looking like a Mexican American (Espinoza, 1993).

In a similar episode, Tom Hsieh and his wife were accosted when going out for dinner. When they stopped for a traffic light, a gang of white men threatened them, spat on their car, and yelled, "You Japs go home!" Mr. Hsieh is a Chinese American whose family has been in the United States for generations and is a well-known member of the San Francisco Board of Supervisors (Espinoza, 1993).

These are the experiences of prominent and politically popular people. Elsewhere, the Washington-based National Immigration Forum has seen a tripling of phone calls by frightened immigrants. The American Friends Service Committee reports a sharp rise in violent beatings of undocumented people near the Mexican border. "We have many cases here in the hospital and in the jail where people have had their jaws broken or their heads split open," said Roberto Martinez of the Service Committee (Espinoza, 1993). This statement is reminiscent of earlier accounts of the neo-Nazi skinheads of Germany.

Whatever the reasons for wanting to reduce immigration to the United States, the long-established norms of America call for rational discussion of policies, not irrational attacks. Unfortunately, there is a small but vocal minority in the United States, England, France, Germany, and elsewhere whose solution to the immigration problems is to bash all foreigners, especially those who look different. In an unpleasant way, their actions show a similarity among people the world over: All are ethnocentric, and reversals of fortune can turn many of them to violence.

Illegal immigrants are often accused of taking jobs away from U.S. citizens, inspiring anti-illegal alien graffiti such as this.

Focus on Canada

Multiethnic Equality

Canada is a prime example of a country that has faced dual nationalism, in its case British and French, and given full equality to each. Switzerland has done the same for her three populations: German, French, and Italian. Both in Canada and in Switzerland, full equality is given to the major languages. We turn to Canada for our example of multiethnic equality, rather than Switzerland, however, because the British–French rivalry seems never to be totally resolved.

The first settlements in Canada were French, Quebec City (1642) and Montreal (1642), and the country was called New France. But Britain acquired Nova Scotia in 1717, and settlers from the British Isles eventually became more numerous than the French. In 1763, New France was acquired by Britain as a result of her victory in the French and Indian War. However, in the Quebec Act of 1774, the French were granted the right to their own language, religion, and civil law.

Many British loyalists fled to Canada at the end of the American Revolutionary War, increasing the British population, mainly in Ontario. The British Parliament, realizing the conflict between the British and French, made Ontario and Quebec separate colonies. But as a result of prodemocracy rebellions in 1837 and 1838, political reforms were granted, and the two provinces were united again. The aim was to lessen the isolation of the French-Canadians and promote feelings of loyalty to Canada.

The attempt to unify the French and British was only a partial success. Further democratization and attempts at unity were contained in the British North America Act of 1867, which provided for a federal parliament that would represent all the provinces of Canada. However, some of the French continued to press for independence.

In 1980 a vote was held on Quebec independence, but the people of Quebec turned it down by a vote of 60 percent to 40 percent. Despite the 1980 vote, agitation for separation from Canada has continued. An election was held in Quebec on September 13, 1994. The Independence Party, led by Jacques Parizeau, won control of the Quebec Parliament, but Parizeau's margin of victory was less than 1 percent—much less than he had expected. Canadian leaders favoring unity are encouraged by the close vote. Jean Chrétien, the Canadian Prime Minister said, "When both parties get almost the same share of the vote, it's a good indication Canada is here to stay" (Swardson, 1994). Most of the Canadian press expressed the same optimism about continued unity.

Not surprisingly, Canadian stock rose and so did the Canadian dollar. Had the Independence Party won an overwhelming victory, the opposite would probably have happened. The Canadian economy is strengthened by unity. Apparently, a large percentage of French-speaking Canadians can see it is to their advantage to remain part of Canada.

Although strong ethnic feelings have caused separatist campaigns, two factors have worked against the separatists. In the first place, there has been no ethnic oppression. The French-speaking population has continued to keep its own language, religion, and civil laws, and has also been able to make Canada bilingual. All road signs and labels are in English and French. A second factor is the belief that Quebec is healthier economically as part of Canada.

One cannot be sure of the future, but it is encouraging to see that equality of treatment and helpful economic policies have, at least until now, helped hold together one of the world's largest countries.

Source: Swardson, A. 1994. "Canadian Leaders Play Down Separatists' Win in Quebec," *San Francisco Chronicle*. Sept. 14: A 12–13.

SUMMARY

Race, ethnicity, and ethnocentrism are explained, with an illustration of how bitter the animosity can become between and among groups. The Jews are among the best known of people to have experienced centuries of oppression because of cultural differences. They have been forced from homelands, restricted to ghettos, suffered massacres, and finally sent to the death camps of Hitler's time.

People of one race or ethnic group have lorded it over others by seizing their lands, driving them out, exterminating them, or incorporating them into multiethnic empires. Caste and slavery are two other extreme measures for controlling people of the "wrong" race or ethnicity. In South Africa, an attempt was made to keep black and white races completely separate by the policy of apartheid, which was abandoned in the 1990s.

People who have long been enslaved are usually discriminated against even after achieving freedom. This is explained in conflict terms as a struggle on the part of people in upper positions to keep those positions by downgrading ex-slaves. Another explanation is that the ex-slaves have always been seen only in inferior positions and are stereotyped as capable of nothing else. Finally, interethnic conduct is ruled greatly by long-established habit, or institutionalization, causing people to discriminate even if they are not prejudiced.

The term *ethnic cleansing* has been used in recent years, first by the Serbians. It refers to an attempt by the majority group to kill off or to drive into exile the people of minority groups. Similar policies have been used by other peoples against the Kurds, the Tibetans, the Baluchis, and many others.

Cruel treatment of minorities in the former Yugoslavia, Iraq, Iran, North Africa, and in war-torn Angola and Mozambique have created a tide of refugees, with few countries willing to accept many of them. The former generous immigration policies of France and Germany have been reversed because of xenophobia. The people of the United States, whose attitude has fluctuated historically on welcoming foreigners, are now in an antiforeign mood, especially relative to illegal immigrants from Latin America. One result has been a number of attacks on people believed to be foreigners, including some who are United States citizens.

KEY TERMS

Apartheid A South African policy, ended in 1992, to divide blacks and whites into separate societies; extreme segregation.

Aryan invasion Invasion of India around 1500–1200 B.C. by an Aryan-speaking people, who are believed to have imposed, or at least strengthened, the caste system.

Caste A rigid system of social classification in which movement from one class to another is impossible and intermarriage between castes is forbidden.

Discrimination The practice of treating people of different ethnic groups unequally, usually because of prejudice against them.

Displaced Persons' Act of 1948 An immigration act making it possible for the United States to admit many people, largely Jewish, fleeing Europe after World War II.

Ethnic cleansing A term used by the Serbs of former Yugoslavia, meaning to rid what they consider their territory of all non-Serbs by driving them out or killing them.

Ethnic group A group of people sharing a common culture or way of life.

Ethnocentrism The belief that one's own culture is best and that all others should be judged by its standards.

Genocide The killing of an entire racial or ethnic group, as in Hitler's attempt to exterminate the Jews.

Ghetto Originally, the Jewish quarter of European cities. Now applied to sections of cities where minority ethnic groups live, usually due to social or economic pressures.

Harijans The very lowest people in the caste system of India, the "untouchables."

Institutional racism Racial discrimination that results from long-established, habitual ways of a society, such as housing discrimination that continues even when outlawed.

National Origins Act of 1921 A federal act to limit immigration from each country on the basis of how many that country had contributed already to the United States population.

Pogroms Organized attacks on the Jews in Russia in the nineteenth and very early twentieth centuries, often encouraged by the government.

Prejudice An unfavorable attitude formed about people (usually a racial or ethnic group) based on little or no actual knowledge of them.

Race A term applied to divisions of the human species based on inherited differences in appearance such as skin color, eye shape, hair type, and bone structure.

Racism The discredited belief that race is a very important determinant of behavior and that some races are superior to others.

Scapegoating The practice of blaming the ills of society on an unpopular person or group.

STUDY QUESTIONS

1. What causes ethnocentrism, and what are its possible consequences?

2. South Africa has made great strides toward racial equality, but what problems, rooted in apartheid, will persist?

3. How were colonial powers able to rule populations much larger than their own?

4. What were the traits of the Hindu caste system that made it an almost perfect system for keeping people "in their place?"

5. What problems generally persist for people who were long held in slavery?

6. What is genocide? Where has it occurred? Is it going on at present?

7. Explain the reasons for the great flood of refugees now seeking a place to live.

8. What do you expect to be the future of ethnic minorities in Germany and France? The United States? Canada?

9. Why have both the overseas Chinese and the Jews often been the victims of attacks, unfair treatment, and even genocide?

10. Many countries are facing the problem of unwanted immigrants, but millions of refugees need somewhere to go. What possible solution is there to the problem? Purely a national problem? A problem calling for international agreement?

7 chapter

PEDESTRIANS PROHIBITED

FROM VILLAGE TO MEGACITY: URBANIZATION

ut of my twenty childhood friends," writes artist and author Prafulla Mohanti (1983), "two died of cholera, one died of typhoid, three were disfigured by smallpox, five girls got married and left the village, six boys went to towns to find work. Only three stayed in the village." Mohanti's village was Nanpur, in the eastern part of India. His story is typical of villages around the world. Villages are groupings of people ranging from 250 to 1,250 (Sirjamaki, 1964:8–9) and in many countries they are dying off, their people moving to the city where, they hope, the quality of their lives will improve. The majority will be disappointed.

More than a hundred years ago, the German sociologist Ferdinand Toennies foresaw the movement away from **Gemeinschaft** (community) to **Gesellschaft** (society). These two types of social organization occupy opposite poles on a continuum of change. *Gemeinschaft* is the close, personal village where everyone knows everyone else. Order is maintained through tradition and custom, rather than through reliance upon formalized law. There is a common language and a homogeneity of thought. The land is the source of wealth and people are bound to each other and to the land. *Gesellschaft*, on the other hand, is the large and associational type of social organization. The people are governed by the rules of business and legislature. The French sociologist Emile Durkheim (1858–1917) also placed great emphasis on the transformations that take place as rural hunting and gathering societies change to urban industrial societies. Like Toennies, Durkheim saw a loss of community as societies change from rural to urban. As the modern sociologist William D. Perdue (1986:81) has put it, "The identity born of community surrenders to the anonymity of mass society."

As is true of many topics, it is possible to understand current trends and problems only by understanding something of their history. For this reason, we begin our discussion by looking at the transformation of the world from one characterized by roving bands of related people to one typified by settled communities, the size of which almost defy the scope of human imagination.

THE HISTORY OF THE CITY

Throughout most of our historical existence, human beings have been hunters and gatherers (Lenski and Lenski, 1987:83). Even today, there are many tribal peoples throughout the world who live this age-old life-style. Consequently, we know a good deal about the lives of ancient peoples by drawing analogies from modern nomads. We must be careful, however, not to confuse analogy with fact because nomads of contemporary times have had contact with other tribal peoples, many of whom possess more sophisticated weapons and tools than existed many thousands of years ago.

For millions of years, life centered around the use of the hand axe, spear, and simply constructed, temporary shelters. People followed herds and depended mainly on hunting for protein and gathering crops for vitamins and other nutrients. Sometime within the last one hundred thousand years, skin clothing probably was developed to provide additional protection from the elements. People traveled in extended families, or kinship groupings, for protection from the rest of the animal kingdom and from other human groups, as well. It is very likely that virtually everyone lived this type of life. Eventually, some tribes turned to fishing and, much later, to maritime activity, consequently becoming traders and transporters.

Eopolis

Sometime during the Neolithic era (a period of time that stretched from about 15,000 years ago to about 7,000 years ago), people settled into tiny villages, called **eopolises**. The word eopolis is from Greek and means "pre-city." Initially, the eopolis was a homogeneous group with virtually no differentiation of labor. All people were engaged full time with the search for food and other basic means of subsistence. All people had about the same knowledge and engaged in about the same sort of labor, so there were probably no social class distinctions. Tools and weapons were probably the only possessions of the people. Even today, there are village people who own virtually nothing. Charles T. Powers (1981:10–12) describes an Ethiopian villager: "His shoes are stitched together with string, the clothes of his children are rags, and the finest possession of his house is a single blue plastic cup, vainly wiped of charcoal and grease, in which coffee is offered to a visitor."

As time passed, a kind of **feudal** society (a society with the social, economic, and political structure of medieval Europe and other preindustrial societies) began to emerge in the fertile river valleys of the world. This probably first occurred in Mesopotamia, the area between the Tigris and Euphrates Rivers in what is now Iraq (see Figure 7.1). In this environment, it was possible to produce a surplus because the selection of grains were high yield and suited to long-term storage. Gideon Sjoberg (1973:19–27) points out that a food surplus is necessary before specialization in labor can occur and before a class structure emerges that facilitates extensive irrigation systems, which in turn lead to even greater increases in the food supply. By this time, of course, both the wheel and a simple plow had been invented and their use led to a multiplication of food production. As more and more people were freed from the land, a greater division of labor became possible. And, gradually, all of the elements needed to operate a city came into being.

Polis

The Greek term **polis** describes the early cities because it carries the connotation of politics. The early cities were, indeed, independent political entities and the source of the only government that existed. Archaeological evidence suggests that the first cities (for example, Eridu, in what is now Iraq) emerged in Mesopotamia between 5,000 and 6,000 years ago. Next, the cities of Thebes and Memphis were founded along the Nile River at about the same time as the great city of Ur emerged in Mesopotamia. Ur was exceptional because of its size. Most cities of that era, between 4,000 and 5,000 years ago, could not have held more than 5,000 or 10,000 people. But the excavator of Ur estimated that, soon after 2,000 B.C., Ur housed about 34,000 people (Sjoberg, 1973:20). Still later, cities like Harappa were founded along the Indus River; Anyang, along the Yellow River; and, by the beginning of the first century A.D., Teotihuacan in Mesoamerica (see Figure 7.1).

The maintenance of a city requires a different type of social organization than does the village. Whole corps of full-time specialists, led by a ruling elite, are needed to supply food and water, operate trading stalls, record events, and build transit systems, sewers, water mains, roads, and buildings. A literate elite was also part of the ancient city. The elite finally replaced the barter economy, typical of the village, with a money standard. In summary, in order to exist, a city

Figure 7.1
The first cities were located in Lower Mesopotamia, followed by urban development along the Nile River, then the Indus and Yellow Rivers, and finally in Mesoamerica.

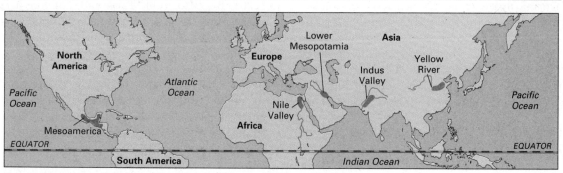

Source: Adapted from G. Sjoberg, "The Origin and Evolution of Cities," *Scientific American, Cities: Their Origin, Growth, and Human Impact* (San Francisco: W. H. Freeman, 1973), pp.19–27.

requires (1) a large population, (2) a division of labor, and (3) a complex economic system. These requirements fit well with Sjoberg's (1973:19–20) definition of a city as "a community of substantial size and population density that shelters a variety of nonagricultural specialists, including a literate elite."

Ancient cities required one additional element: religion. The city was led by a high priest or king who was believed to be of divine origin. Peasants were required to relinquish to the king a substantial portion of the fruits of their labors. The wealth amassed by ancient kings gave them the power to command skilled artisans to build great edifices, nonfarm peasantry to maintain city systems, and soldiers to protect the population. Over time, the king was replaced by a city administrator and the sacred character of the city was replaced by a more secular one. Probably the greatest preindustrial city was Rome of the second century. It had a population that may have surpassed one million and exerted control over an empire of more than 50 million. However, after the decline of the Roman Empire, the city began to shrink in size, reaching a low of 20,000 inhabitants by the ninth century (Thomlinson, 1978:9).

Medieval Cities

The medieval period stretches from about the sixth century to about the fifteenth century. During this era, the remnants of the ancient cities dwindled in size and function. Ficker and Graves (1978:9) point out that "the few remaining cities consisted of mere clusters of dwellings grouped around a monastery or castle and serving mainly as administrative foci for religious, political, or military jurisdiction." Most of the population was composed of peasants who would peddle their agricultural products at weekly markets and annual fairs. With the exception of Paris, Florence, Venice, and Milan, each of which may have amassed populations of 100,000 or more, most cities and towns remained quite small by modern standards. It would have been unusual to find a city of more than 30,000 inhabitants.

The many wars among the various feudal states prevented the establishment of new cities. There was also a slowing of trade between European cities and the cities of the Arab and Byzantine empires—Baghdad, Cairo, Damascus, Antioch, and Constantinople. The era truly deserved its nickname: The Dark Ages. During this period, the black plague wiped out about one-third of the European population, which also contributed to the demise of the city. In 1665, for example, two-thirds of London's 460,000 citizens fled to the safer countryside. In addition, the death toll of city people rose dramatically. Venice lost 46,721 of its population of 160,000, Marseilles was reduced from 90,000 to 50,000, and Messina's population was cut in half (Langer, 1978:106–111). Then, as the various cities of Europe began to recover from the disease and the various wars, the process of urbanization began to accelerate.

Urbanization is the process by which a society sees increasing proportions of its population residing in urban areas and declining proportions living in rural areas. If the rural population grows at the same rate as the city population, then urbanization is not occurring. Urbanization began during the 1600s, but it was really fueled by the Industrial Revolution that started in the mid 1600s. By 1800, both Paris and London had reached populations of a half million people and Vienna and St. Petersburg had surpassed 200,000.

Metropolis

At the opening of the twentieth century, ten cities—London, Paris, Vienna, Moscow, St. Petersburg, Calcutta, Tokyo, Chicago, Philadelphia, and New York—had reached a population of at least one million people (Thomlinson, 1978:10). This can be thought of as the age of the **metropolis**—a large, busy city that often serves as the capital of a country, state, or region. Though there is no agreed-upon definition about how many people a city must have before it can be called a metropolis, certainly cities with one million or more residents can be given this title. If this definition is used, the world was truly becoming metropolized by the 1930s. At that time, there were 27 cities with more than one million inhabitants on the planet (Mumford, 1961:529).

Megalopolis

As cities and their suburbs continue to expand, metropolises are formed, and in some cases these join to form a **megalopolis**. Many countries have one or more megalopolises which can extend for hundreds of miles. For example, in southern California, one can drive from San Diego to Ventura, just north of Los Angeles, and with the exception of Camp Pendleton (a military installation), never leave the urban scene. This megalopolis extends about 200 miles. Similar situations exist in the Great Lakes region and on the East Coast of the United States and also in Europe, where metropolises, cities, and suburbs join each other in a continuous high-density, urban strip.

Problems associated with megalopolises include loss of productive farmland, severe air pollution caused by vehicles and industry, water pollution, traffic congestion, and crime. It seems that the problems of the cities and metropolises are multiplied and exacerbated in the megalopolis. (More time is devoted to the problems of megalopolises in the "Urbanization Patterns" section of this chapter.)

Transfrontier Metropolis

A type of metropolis that is growing in importance worldwide is the **transfrontier metropolis**, an urban area situated on an international border. Lawrence Herzog (1991:519) suggests that "Modern technology has transformed our notions of territory, space, and nation. From labour

migration to banking and corporate practice, social and economic forces operate increasingly at the transnational scale." Herzog (1991:521) argues that borders no longer retain their original military function, since air power and rocketry allow military operations to be staged from nonborder areas of a country. Also, from 1950 to 1980, the changing nature and growing importance of the world economy began to decrease the roles of individual countries in the world economy (Herzog, 1991:521). At the same time, the nature of the production process was changing and major corporations realized that the stages of production could be segmented. Because the assembly stage of production could be separated from other stages (research and development, component production, distribution, etc.), there was every incentive for international business to locate the assembly stage in areas with huge labor pools and low wages (Herzog, 1991:528). This explains the incredible growth of transfrontier metropolises along the United States–Mexico border, of which the San Diego–Tijuana and El Paso–Ciudad Juarez urban areas are the largest. Parts and components are shipped across the border from the United States, are assembled in plants in Mexico, and the finished products are then sent back to the United States. These assembly plants, called **maquiladoras**, began to appear in northern Mexican border cities in the 1960s and their growth has been exponential in the 1980s and early 1990s. It is estimated that of the 1,500 maquiladoras built in Mexico since the mid 1960s, 90 percent can be found in Mexican cities on the United States–Mexico border (Herzog, 1991:528–529). It should be noted that U.S. laborers and labor unions fear that the maquiladoras will take blue-collar jobs away from the United States.

The interconnectedness of Mexican and U.S. cities on the border, and the movement back and forth across the border, is profound. Herzog (1991:525) discusses many types of social and economic activities that result in movement on the United States–Mexico border: legal and ille-

A steel fence constructed of discarded military material stands on the United States–Mexico border. Mexico is in the foreground and the city of San Diego is in the background. Though the fence does not keep people from illegally entering the United States, it has been discussed by U.S. politicians as an example of what can be done to keep out illegal migrants.

This photograph shows the different orientations toward the border between Mexico and the United States. Tijuana is on the right and is densely built, right up to the border. On the left is San Ysidro (a suburb of San Diego) with almost no development on the border. United States citizens do not wish to live near the border; Mexican citizens view the border area more positively.

gal Mexican workers cross the border to work in the United States and then cross back to Mexico after work (it is estimated that, on a daily basis, 160,000 Mexicans do so legally, and many more illegally); Mexican children attend school in the United States; and both U.S. and Mexican citizens cross the border for shopping, entertain-

ment, tourism, and family and social engagements.

Another area of the world with transfrontier metropolises is Western Europe. More than 250,000 workers move across international boundaries in Western Europe each day. By 1980 there were fairly large urban concentrations along the

Swiss, French, German, Belgian, Dutch, and Italian borders (Herzog, 1991:522). The European Community movement toward the unification of European countries will only accentuate this trend, because it will ease the difficulties of moving across national boundaries.

Problems of Transfrontier Metropolises

Transfrontier metropolises are not without problems. Sewage and traffic problems as well as air and water pollution do not respect national boundaries. Binational cooperation is needed to solve these kinds of problems that local officials cannot. A good example is the toxic waste produced by the assembly plants in Tijuana (Sanchez, 1989). There is much concern that the environmental standards employed in Mexico fall far short of U.S. environmental standards and that Mexicans and Americans living near the border may be at considerable risk. A 1990 Council on Scientific Affairs Report stated that the environmental problems in the maquiladora zone are so severe that it is a "virtual cesspool and breeding ground for infectious diseases" (Meinert, 1993:19). The main goal of multinational corporations is profit. Profit can be enhanced by employing low-wage workers, such as poor Mexicans living near the United States–Mexico border, and by taking advantage of lax or nonexistent laws regarding disposal of toxic waste. This is often the case involving maquiladores along the United States–Mexico border.

Although there is much cooperation among citizens of transfrontier metropolises, frequent tensions sometimes erupt. For example, some U.S. citizens are of the opinion that too many illegal migrants are entering the United States from Mexico, and argue that significant sums of money are being spent for education, health, and social services for these illegal migrants, at the expense of American taxpayers. One example that continues to make headlines is that of Mexican mothers who cross the border in time to have their babies born in U.S. hospitals so they can be U.S. citizens.

California Governor Pete Wilson argues that the U.S. Constitution should be changed to eliminate this incentive for illegal entry into the United States. Anti-immigrant groups argue for tighter control of the border and often clash with groups that support both legal and illegal immigration into the United States. Conflicts surrounding the issue of illegal migration seem more intense in times of economic stagnation in the United States. Also, Mexico's relatively young and growing population, combined with serious economic problems in Mexico, assures that more Mexicans will attempt to enter the United States, legally or illegally, in an attempt to find work. Thus, tensions about illegal migration will, in all probability, continue, especially along the United States–Mexico border.

Tensions and conflict regarding migration have also been found in the transfrontier metropolises in Western Europe. Most countries in Western Europe have very low or negative rates of natural increase, and thus need workers from neighboring countries with higher rates of growth in order for their economies to function smoothly. For example, Germany, with a fertility rate well below replacement level, has relied on workers from Turkey to fill various factory positions. Certain segments of the German population, however, do not want these foreign workers and their families living in Germany. This reaction to foreigners appears in many other Western European countries. Residents from transfrontier metropolises on the other side of the border are wanted to fill positions, but are not wanted as full-fledged citizens.

URBAN LIFE AND CHANGE

We have discussed the emergence of the city as a way of organizing economic and social activities. What perspectives have social scientists put forth on the city? In this section we discuss various perspectives.

The "Decline of Community" Thesis

In the first part of this century, most scholars who wrote about the city fit into what William Kornblum (1991:140) refers to as the "decline of community" perspective. These scholars saw cities in a very negative light. Cities were viewed as places where community ties and relationships are replaced with anonymous associations. **Community** refers to a group of people who share a common territory and meet their basic physical and social needs through daily interaction with one another. People living in rural areas or villages experience these community ties and become intimately associated. In urban areas, individuals are seen as involved in anonymous relationships with strangers. The decline of community, according to these writers, results in social disorganization, crime, demise of the family, and anomie (a state of instability, in which individuals no longer feel allegiance to the norms and rules of society). Sociologist Louis Wirth (1938) wrote an article entitled "Urbanism as a Way of Life," which outlined the evils of the city. This anti-urban view permeates much of the social science literature on the city that was written in the first half of the century.

Urban Expansion Models

A number of theories have been developed to explain growth and expansion. One of the earliest and most famous is The **concentric-zone model** by Robert Park and Ernest Burgess (1925). Because Park and Burgess taught at the University of Chicago, the model was based on the city of Chicago. The model saw cities comprised of five circular zones. Figure 7.2

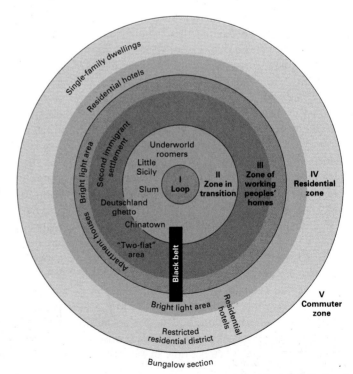

Figure 7.2
The concentric-zone model, as applied to Chicago by Park and Burgess, saw cities comprised of circular zones. The inner zones contained business and manufacturing. As one moves outward one encounters zones of slums, working peoples' homes, and finally, homes of the more affluent residents and commuters.

Sources: W. Kornblum, *Sociology in a Changing World*, 2nd ed. (Fort Worth: Holt, Rinehart, & Winston, 1991), p. 137. *Original Source:* R. Park and E. Burgess, *The City*. (Chicago: The University of Chicago Press, 1925).

shows the various zones, with the "Loop," which contained the downtown businesses and offices, as the center of the circle. Next to the Loop was the "factory zone," followed by the "zone in transition," which was an area being "invaded" by light manufacturing and business. The third circle was the "zone of working peoples' homes," and the fourth zone was the more upscale "residential zone." The outer ring was the "commuter zone." According to Park and Burgess, these zones expand as a city grows. The model asserts that new and poorer immigrant groups tend to "invade" a residential area and the existing residents then move to a better area.

Another model used to explain urban areas is the **sector theory**, developed by Homer Hoyt (1939). Instead of cities comprised of various circular zones, this model sees cities as wedges going from the center of the city to the extremities. According to this model, the various wedges or sectors tend to follow major transportation arteries. The development of the automobile and expressway system was particularly important in the emergence of these pieslice-like pieces of development.

A third urban model is the **multiple-nuclei model** put forth by Chauncey Harris and Edward L. Ullman (1945). This theory was based on the idea that cities do not conform to either the concentric-zone or sector patterns, but tend to be made up of numerous centers or nuclei that are surrounded by different kinds of activities.

Though social scientists have used these models to explain urban growth and change and though they continue to use them to explain various aspects of cities, there are limitations to these models. First, the models tend to apply to a limited number of cities. Many cities, and especially cities not located in North America, simply do not fit the outlines of the models. For example, Latin American cities tend to have their most exclusive housing in the center, not in the outer areas. These models fail to explain the emergence of suburbs and the merging of cities and surrounding suburbs into very large metropolitan areas. Another criticism is that these models fail to address the process of urbanization. Finally, these models fail to deal with the enormity and vastness of contemporary cities throughout the world.

Subculture Theory

More recent perspectives view the city in a more positive light than the "community in decline" view and incorporate aspects of urbanization and urban life that are neglected in the urban expansion models. **Subculture theory** is a recent perspective that sees urban residents involved in numerous groups and communities where meaningful relationships and ties are forged. These communities and groups may not have a specific geographical base as in villages and rural areas, but they are meaningful nevertheless. Such urban communities and groups are based on numerous factors—ethnicity, occupation, kinship, leisure, religion, sexual orientation, and life-style (Fischer, 1987; Street et al., 1978; Suttles, 1967). The point that subculture theorists make repeatedly is that urban residents are not necessarily the lonesome and detached individuals portrayed by many of the early urban scholars. Also, life in non-urban areas is not necessarily as idyllic as one might gather from reading the works of early sociologists. Along with the community ties in these areas comes social control, which can be stifling. In the country, everyone knows everyone else's business and there is pressure to interact with all members of the community. In the city, it is easier to pick and choose your friends and people with whom you interact. There is also the freedom to decide how much interaction one wishes to have with other people and at what level of intimacy.

In a classic treatise on the city, Jane Jacobs (1961) expands on this point and shows how urbanites are able to structure relationships with others in a most efficient manner. For example, the relationship between a customer and the owner of a bakery is cordial, and they may know each other by name, but neither knows, nor cares to know, about intimate and private aspects of each other's lives. Jacobs points out that privacy is cherished and guarded jealously by city dwellers and that rural people and villagers do not experience privacy to the same extent as city dwellers. She also takes city planners to task, asserting that they are guilty of trying to impose rural characteristics, like open space, on urban environments, and that they lack an understanding of what makes great cities function. Jacobs suggests that too often, whole areas of cities are bulldozed and replaced with the planners' version of what the city "ought" to be like— segmented residential and commercial areas with increased open space. She indicates that this desire to have specific areas zoned for residential and commercial use and the desire on the part of planners to bring the "country" into the city is ludicrous. Vibrant, stimulating, and functional cities are characterized by diversity of function, high density of population, and an orientation toward the streets. Diversity of function means that an area of a city would have a healthy mix of shops, businesses, and residences. For example, a diverse urban area might include an apartment complex, a grocery store, a bar, a barber shop, a restaurant, a church, a laundry, and a school. Such a mix means that people are more likely to be able to meet many of their needs in their own neighborhoods and traffic congestion is reduced as a result. Also, mixed use means that pedestrians use the streets on a continual basis and safety is thus enhanced for everyone. A high-density population also tends to increase pedestrian traffic. Pedestrian traffic has a self-policing function. Criminals are less likely to do their deeds when many people are on the street. An orientation toward the street means that shops, businesses, and residences front the street. With "all eyes on the street," people watch out for each other, even though they may be strangers. Street orientation also means that a lot of different things happen there—goods and produce are delivered, adults greet each other and gossip, children play, and

customers walk to shops, bars, and restaurants. In short, Jacobs argues that great cities are vibrant, exciting places and that virtually all the great advances in science, medicine, and art occur there. These advances demand the kind of social and economic organization found in cities, and to blame our social ills and problems on the city is foolish. Social problems may occur in cities, but the solutions to those problems are also found there.

Reissman's Urbanization Theory

Leonard Reissman (1964) has argued that most urban perspectives have three flaws: (1) they are oversimplified—they tend to focus on one factor such as the economic environment, architecture, or political administration; (2) they tend to view the city only within the full gamut of history— they do not see the modern industrial city as distinctly different from previous cities; and (3) they are unable to deal with the great amount of social change associated with industrial cities. Reissman asserts that in order to understand a city, one must understand the nation where that city is found. Also, he argues against the parochialism and provincialism of urban scholars who only study cities in their own cultures. Reissman proposes an urbanization typology, or classifying scheme, that incorporates four variables: urban status, industrial status, prevalence of a middle class, and prevalence of nationalism. Urban status can be measured as the proportion of a country's population living in cities of 100,000 or more people. Industrial status is measured as the percentage of the net domestic product contributed by manufacturing. The prevalence of a middle class is measured by the per capita income (in terms of United States dollars). Finally, the prevalence of nationalism is measured by the proxy index of the percentage of literate persons in the population of 15 years of age and older. Countries are ranked from low to high on these indicators and quartile ranks are assigned on each indicator for each country.

Based on the scores of a particular country on these quartile rankings, it is placed on a continuum with 13 stages, going from the least urbanized (underdeveloped societies) to the most urbanized (metropolitan societies). Reissman is careful to point out that his typology is very crude but that it is an improvement over the urban schemes in existence at that time. Reissman's typology has been changed and modified over the years (by him and others), but his original theory serves as a good illustration of urbanization in a global sense. These ideas and concepts should be kept in mind as we discuss urbanization trends and problems in different countries and different regions of the world.

TRENDS IN URBANIZATION

Urbanization trends vary tremendously both by geographic region and by level of development. This section addresses these major differences.

Urbanization by Geography

Table 7.1 presents data on world urbanization patterns, by region. If we go back to 1965, it is apparent that North America was the most highly urbanized followed by Eastern and Western Europe and Latin America. Only 20.6% of Africa's population and 24.3% of Asia and

Oceania's population was urbanized at that time. By 1990, Africa and Asia-Oceania had increased their proportions of urbanized population to 34.5% and 30.7%, respectively. Latin America also saw its urbanized population increase substantially during this period (from 1965 to 1990), going from 53.4% urban to 72.3% urban.

The projected proportions for 2015 show Latin America as the most urbanized, followed by Eastern and Western Europe and North America. Africa is projected to be 51.4% urbanized by the year 2015, and Asia-Oceania is expected to have slightly less than one-half of its population in urban areas. While Africa and Asia-Oceania are projected to have smaller urbanized proportions of their populations, as compared to the rest of the world, the absolute size of their projected urban populations deserves attention. Asia and Oceania's projected 2,064,000,000 urban residents will make up almost half (49.3%) of the world's urbanized population. If one adds Africa's projected urban population (666,200,000) to that of Asia-Oceania, it becomes clear that more than 65% of the world's urban population in the year 2015 will reside in Africa, Asia, and Oceania.

Urbanization by Development

The most developed regions of the world are also the most urbanized. Figure 7.3 presents data on

	TABLE 7.1					
Proportion and Absolute Numbers (In millions) of Urbanized Population, by Region, 1965, 1990, 2015						
	1965		1990		2015	
Africa	20.6%	65.5	34.5%	223.3	51.4%	666.2
Asia & Oceania	24.3%	437.2	30.7%	949.5	45.9%	2064.0
Eastern & Western Europe	60.5%	405.1	71.1%	558.5	77.5%	657.9
Latin America	53.4%	133.6	72.3%	324.1	82.2%	555.0
North America	72.0%	154.1	74.3%	204.9	76.7%	245.1

SOURCE: Population Crisis Committee, 1990.

urbanization according to the region's level of development. The percentage of the planet's people living in urbanized areas is expected to go from 45% urban in 1990 to 51% in 2000 and 65% by the year 2025. Whereas the urbanization in the more developed regions is expected to increase slightly, from 73% in 1990 to 83% in 2025, urbanization in the less developed regions of the world is predicted to increase dramatically, from 37% in 1990 to 61% by the year 2025.

Also, even though the percentage of the population living in urban areas in the less developed regions will be less than the percentage in the more developed regions, by the year 2025, the *absolute number* of urban residents in the less developed part of the planet will be four times that of the more developed regions (4.4 billion versus. 1.1 billion).

Urbanization Within the Less and More Developed Regions

The information presented in Figure 7.4 suggests much more variation in levels of urbanization in the less developed regions of the world as compared to the more developed regions. In the less developed regions, Africa, Asia (excluding Japan), and Oceania (excluding Australia and New Zealand) had very low levels of urbanization (34%, 33%, and 23% respectively) in 1990, and Latin America was 72% urbanized. Within the more developed regions, the percentage living in urban areas showed much less variation, ranging from a low of 65% in Eastern Europe to 85% in Australia and New Zealand.

The major differences in the percentage of people in urban areas in the less developed regions of the world are expected to continue into the future. Table 7.2 shows that in the less developed regions of the world, the least developed countries will still have a small percentage of people living in urbanized areas by the year 2000 (26%), while in the other less developed countries, the percentage will increase to almost one-half (48%) by the year 2000. The disparity is expected to still exist in the year 2025, when the least developed countries are expected to be 44% urbanized, and the other less developed countries are expected to be 64% urbanized.

URBANIZATION PATTERNS

In an important article, the Population Crisis Committee (1990) presented data on a major

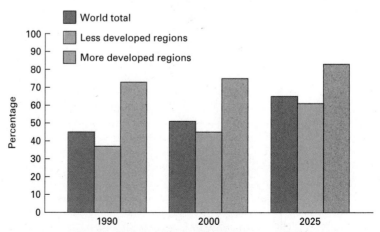

Figure 7.3
The percentage of the world's population living in urban areas is projected to increase, especially in the less developed regions.

Source: United Nations, 1991. *World Urbanization Prospects*. ST/ESA/SER.A/121. Department of International and Social Affairs, New York.

study of the world's 100 largest cities. The authors note that the urbanization patterns of the last 30 years differ in numerous ways from historical urbanization patterns.

First, urban residents are more likely to be found in extremely large urban concentrations. For example, in 1950 only ten metropolitan areas in the world had populations of 5 million or more

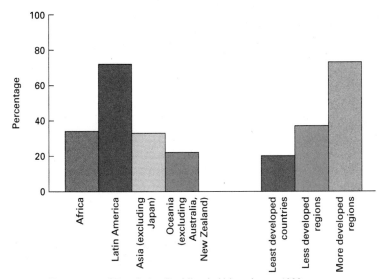

Percentage of Population Residing in Urban Areas, 1990

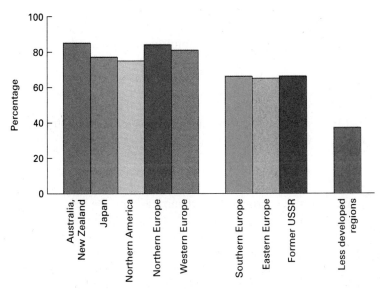

Percentage of Population Residing in Urban Areas, More Developed Regions, 1990

Source: United Nations, 1991. *World Urbanization Prospects.* ST/ESA/SER.A/121. Department of International and Social Affairs, New York, pp. 5, 13.

Figure 7.4
The levels of urbanization in the less developed regions of the world are much more varied than in the more developed regions of the world.

Percentage of Population Living in Urban Areas, 1990, 2000, and 2025			TABLE 7.2
Region	1990	2000	2025
Less developed regions	37%	45%	61%
Least developed regions	20%	26%	44%
Other less developed countries	39%	48%	64%

SOURCE: United Nations, 1991:4

inhabitants. Compare that to the 33 metropolitan areas in 1990 with as many residents. Furthermore, in 1990 there were 15 **hypercities**, cities with 15 million or more people; there had been none in 1950. Many urban experts are of the opinion that these sprawling, congested urban concentrations are taking us into uncharted waters and that humanity may not be able to effectively and efficiently manage cities with so many people. Even Japan, despite its efficiency, cannot make traffic flow smoothly, nor keep its air clean. Police are forced, occasionally, to go to oxygen stations to revive their vigor. Also, the problem of vacating the world's large cities, due to an earthquake or fire emergency, regardless of precautionary measures, is terrible to contemplate.

The second way in which modern urbanization differs from urbanization in the past is that more and more of the world's largest cities can be found in the less developed countries (LDCs) than in the more developed countries (MDCs). Table 7.3 lists urban agglomerations (contiguous cities of 8 million people or more) for developed and less developed regions for the years 1950, 1970, 1990, and projections for the year 2000. In 1950 there were only two cities with populations of 8 million or more (New York and London), and both were in developed countries. By 1970 there were 10 such cities, with half located in developed regions and the other half in less developed regions. In 1990 the less developed part of the planet dominated the developed segment with 14 cities with at least 8 million people, compared with 6 in the MDCs. Projections for the year 2000

show this trend continuing, with the less developed regions having 22 urban agglomerations of 8 million or more people, compared to only 6 such cities in the developed regions.

Table 7.4 lends support to this trend of the world's largest cities being found in the less developed rather than developed regions. In 1950 seven of the 10 largest urban agglomerations were located in the developed world. By 1990 only three of the world's 10 largest urban areas were in the developed world.

This tendency for current and future urbanization to be associated with a lack of development is in contrast to the situation of the past, when urbanization was associated with the degree of economic development and industrialization. Industrialization is no longer the major factor affecting urbanization. Also, large cities in the LDCs are growing at a much greater rate than cities in the MDCs ever did. For example, it took 130 years for London to reach a population of 8 million, but Mexico City went from 1 million to 20 million in just 50 years.

If industrialization and economic development are not responsible for the incredible growth in urbanization in the less developed world, what is? The answer is the unprecedented large rates of natural increase discussed in Chapter 5 (Population: Explosion and Decline). Recall that major decreases in mortality in the LDCs, without commensurate decreases in fertility, have resulted in very high rates of increase. The lack of work in the rural areas acts as a major factor, "pushing" rural peasants to the urban areas, looking for work. It is important to note, however, that only 40 percent of the growth of urban areas in the LDCs can be explained by the migration of rural people to urban areas. The remaining 60 percent of growth is attributed to the rate of natural increase in the urban areas themselves, which is double that of the West during the Industrial Revolution (Kasarda and Crenshaw, 1991:468). Therefore, any attempt to moderate the rapid growth of urban areas in the

LDCs must deal with the high fertility rates in urban areas, as well as rural areas.

URBANIZATION TRENDS ACROSS THE WORLD

Urbanization patterns and problems vary widely from region to region. We will first look at urbanization trends for the developed world and

---

TABLE 7.3

Urban Agglomerations of 8 Million or More Persons

1950	1970	1990	2000
More Developed Regions			
New York	New York	Tokyo	Tokyo
London	London	New York	New York
	Tokyo	Los Angeles	Los Angeles
	Los Angeles	Moscow	Moscow
	Paris	Osaka	Osaka
		Paris	Paris
Less Developed Regions			
None	Shanghai	Mexico City	Mexico City
	Mexico City	São Paulo	São Paulo
	Buenos Aires	Shanghai	Shanghai
	Beijing	Calcutta	Calcutta
	São Paulo	Buenos Aires	Bombay
		Bombay	Beijing
		Seoul	Jakarta
		Beijing	Delhi
		Rio de Janeiro	Buenos Aires
		Tianjin	Lagos
		Jakarta	Tianjin
		Cairo	Seoul
		Delhi	Rio de Janeiro
		Metro Manila	Dhaka
			Cairo
			Metro Manila
			Karachi
			Bangkok
			Istanbul
			Teheran
			Bangalore
			Lima

SOURCE: United Nations, *World Urbanization Prospects*. ST/ESA/SER.A/121. Department of International and Social Affairs, New York. 1991:24.

TABLE 7.4

World's 10 Largest Urban Agglomerations, Ranked by Population Size (in millions), 1950–2000

	1950				1960	
Rank	Agglomeration	Population		Rank	Agglomeration	Population
1	New York	12.3		1	New York	14.2
2	London	8.7		2	Tokyo	10.7
3	Tokyo	6.7		3	London	9.1
4	Paris	5.4		4	Shanghai	8.8
5	Shanghai	5.3		5	Paris	7.2
6	Buenos Aires	5.0		6	Buenos Aires	6.8
7	Chicago	4.9		7	Los Angeles	6.5
8	Moscow	4.8		8	Moscow	6.3
9	Calcutta	4.4		9	Beijing	6.3
10	Los Angeles	4.0		10	Chicago	6.0

	1970				1980	
Rank	Agglomeration	Population		Rank	Agglomeration	Population
1	New York	16.2		1	Tokyo	16.9
2	Tokyo	14.9		2	New York	15.6
3	Shanghai	11.2		3	Mexico City	14.5
4	Mexico City	9.4		4	São Paulo	12.1
5	London	8.6		5	Shanghai	11.7
6	Buenos Aires	8.4		6	Buenos Aires	9.9
7	Los Angeles	8.4		7	Los Angeles	9.5
8	Paris	8.3		8	Calcutta	9.0
9	Beijing	8.1		9	Beijing	9.0
10	São Paulo	8.1		10	Rio de Janeiro	8.8

	1990				2000	
Rank	Agglomeration	Population		Rank	Agglomeration	Population
1	Mexico City	20.2		1	Mexico City	25.6
2	Tokyo	18.1		2	São Paulo	22.1
3	São Paulo	17.4		3	Tokyo	19.0
4	New York	16.2		4	Shanghai	17.0
5	Shanghai	13.4		5	New York	16.8
6	Los Angeles	11.9		6	Calcutta	15.7
7	Calcutta	11.8		7	Bombay	15.4
8	Buenos Aires	11.5		8	Beijing	14.0
9	Bombay	11.2		9	Los Angeles	13.9
10	Seoul	11.0		10	Jakarta	13.7

SOURCE: United Nations, *World Urbanization Prospects*. ST/ESA/SER.A/121. Department of International and Social Affairs, New York. 1991:21.

will then analyze the situation in Asia, Latin America, and Africa.

Australia, Europe, Japan, New Zealand, and North America

As discussed earlier, the levels of urbanization in the more developed areas of the world are already fairly high and not too varied. Figure 7.4 shows that Australia and New Zealand have the highest rate of urbanization (85%), followed by Northern Europe (84%), Western Europe (81%), Japan (77%), Northern America (75%), Southern Europe (66%), the former USSR (66%), and Eastern Europe (65%). Although these developed regions can expect their urban populations to increase from 73% in 1990, to 75% by the end of the century, and to 83% by the year 2025, (Figure 7.2) they will not face the magnitude of urban growth and the resultant problems that the less developed part of the world will face during this time span. The main reason is the very low or negative growth rates characterizing the developed countries. It might also be useful to point out that the relationship between total populations of countries and their urbanization rates is uncertain, to say the least. As just indicated, Australia and New Zealand have the highest urbanization rates in the world but their population sizes are relatively small. On the other hand, both India and China have huge populations, but, as we will see, they are relatively unurbanized.

The problems facing the cities of developed countries include rising levels of crime, congestion, and various types of pollution. Also, because most of the cities in developed countries are relatively old, a good part of their infrastructures need to be replaced. Replacing worn-out mass rapid transit systems, sewers, water mains, roads, and buildings is a huge and expensive task. However, these problems pale in comparison to those that undeveloped countries are experiencing and will continue to face.

Asia (excluding Australia, New Zealand, and Japan)

Relatively speaking, Asia is not very urbanized but is rapidly becoming so, and a large proportion of the world's future urban residents will be from Asia. Though Asian urbanization patterns are similar is some ways to Western urbanization patterns, there are important differences: (1) Asian urban settlements are more densely settled; (2) Asian urban areas are characterized by a greater reliance upon, and development of, basic public transportation; (3) there is a greater mix of land uses in Asian urban areas; and (4) there is greater pressure on Asian cities to accommodate excess population from rural areas. In the cases of London and Paris, for example, over the last three centuries many rural peasants who might have migrated to these cities moved to the Americas and Oceania instead (Costa et al., 1989:3–4). One other major difference between Asian and Western urbanization patterns is the predominance of gigantic cities in Asia. Of the 22 urban agglomerations (8 million or more people) that are expected to exist by the year 2000, at least 15 will be in Asia (see Table 7.3).

India and China are the two most populous countries on the planet. India's 897,400 people and China's 1,178,500 people constitute 38 percent of the world's population (5,506,000) (Haub and Yanagishita, 1993). They have the same low current urbanization rate (26 percent) and both countries are expected to continue to become urbanized. The result is that the earth's urban population will increase appreciably. India is continuing to experience huge waves of poor, displaced rural peasants migrating to its stressed urban centers. Calcutta, Bombay, Delhi, and Bangalore continue to draw these peasants because the country still has a high rate of growth and India's government has not paid much attention to the development of its rural areas (Bose, 1990).

China, like India and most developing countries, is also becoming more urbanized. At the outset, however, it should be noted that China has the "longest continuous urban tradition in the world" (Guldin, 1992:229). Pannell (1992:16) asserts that 17 percent of China's population was urbanized at the time of the Han dynasty (206 B.C. to A.D. 220) and increased to 21 percent during the Sung dynasty (A.D. 960 to A.D. 1280). Urbanization is not new to China. Also, in no other developing country is the boundary between what is "urban" and "rural" so blurred. This is due to the policy of the Communist Party to promote industrialization and the development of the agricultural sector simultaneously. A number of Chinese anti-urban policies since 1949 have been responsible for a relatively low level of urbanization, compared to other developing countries. These policy measures are aimed at moving large numbers of urban dwellers to the countryside; banning migration from rural to urban areas; efforts suppressing urban consumption; and enacting programs of rural industrialization (Chan, 1992:275). Even though the strategies of the regimes since Mao Ze-dong's rule (1949–1976) have been quite varied, they have all attempted to discourage mass migration from the countryside to the large urban centers of China.

More recently, the government of China has been attempting to keep the unemployed peasants from migrating to the large cities by promoting the location of new industries in rural areas and small towns. Thus, a growing proportion of the Chinese population is involved in nonagricultural activities but is still considered rural. The net result is that even though China has been industrializing quite rapidly since the early 1980s, the proportion of individuals classified as urban has remained relatively low (Chan, 1992:275).

Though there is recent evidence that the large Chinese cities like Shanghai, Beijing, and Tianjin are attracting increasing numbers of poor, unemployed, and homeless peasants (Guldin, 1992:226), China has indeed presented an alternative model of development to other less developed countries. The Chinese model emphasizes the industrial development of rural areas and small towns, in an attempt to keep massive numbers of peasants from migrating to megacities where no employment exists.

Latin America

As already pointed out in the discussion of Table 7.1, of all the underdeveloped regions of the world, Latin America has the highest urbanization rate (72.3%). It is expected to have the highest urbanization rate (82.2%) of any region, developed or underdeveloped, by the year 2015. Though the percentage of the population in Latin American that is urban will continue to increase in the next 20 years, a number of trends are of interest: (1) the annual rate of population growth of the biggest urban agglomerations, such as Mexico City, São Paulo, Buenos Aires, Rio de Janeiro, and Lima, has started to decline, (2) the growth of the central district, or core, of each agglomeration is slower than that of the outer rings; (3) the greatest rate of growth is occurring in the mid-sized agglomerations and smaller urban centers; (4) urbanization occurring since the late 1970s has been spreading to regions that were unsettled or very thinly settled before 1980; and (5) during the 1990s, the rural areas will experience an absolute decline in numbers (Hardoy, 1992: xi). What this means is that future growth of urban areas in Latin America will depend primarily on natural increase within the urban areas, not on migration from the rural areas.

Even though the rate of growth is declining in the large urban areas of Latin America, the absolute number of people being added to these areas is still extremely large. One must remember that we are dealing with very large population bases, and even lower rates of growth can mean sizeable additions to existing urban areas. This, combined with the severe economic crisis faced by Latin America in the 1980s and early 1990s, has meant that the urban problems of the 1960s and 1970s have become much more accentuated (Hardoy, 1992: xi–xvii). Jorge E. Hardoy (1992: xvi) has stated that "Even if the worst visible effects of the economic crisis end and the slow-down in the growth rate of urban populations is confirmed, a continuation of current trends spells a bleak future." Hardoy asserts that by the year 2000, Latin America can expect more shantytowns and tenement districts; increased competition among low-income people for cheap or vacant lands to occupy; poorer services and an unsanitary environment, causing an increase in disease; increases in unemployment, illegal workers, and households with unstable incomes; more homeless people, especially children; urban agglomerations spreading endlessly outward, which will result in an increase in the costs for building and maintaining the infrastructure and will make commutes longer and more expensive; and unprecedented environmental pollution in some metropolitan areas, due to industrial and automotive emissions.

Hardoy (1992:xvi) continues by saying that around 40 percent of urban dwellers in Latin America live in degraded environments, and that "Urban planning has proved fruitless when faced with agglomerations adding 100,000, 200,000, 300,000, or even more new inhabitants per year, especially when most social policies are discontinued because of the pressures of economic readjustment programs. Latin American cities are now built—as in the past—by countless individual and community initiatives outside the norms and regulations of local authorities." Hardoy (1992:xvi) concludes by saying that never in the history of Latin American cities has the gap between the needs of city residents and the resources available to them been as great as it is today.

The contrast between the poor shantytowns surrounding São Paulo, Brazil (foreground) and the expensive high-rise housing of São Paulo (background) is profound.

Brasilia: A City Planned from Scratch

Brasilia, the capital of Brazil, is an interesting exception to the unplanned, unzoned cities of Latin America. Brasilia was built from scratch in 1957, in an effort to develop the interior of Brazil. Edward Cornish, the president of the World Future Society, summarizes (1991) an important book by James Holston (1989), *The Modernist City: An Anthropological Critique of*

Visitors to Brasilia notice the lack of people on the city's streets. The expressway system keeps cars and people off the streets; the window shopping and congested intersections that enliven other cities do not exist in Brasilia.

Brasilia, which delineates many serious problems that resulted from the way the city was laid out.

Building this city was an urban planner's dream come true because an existing city with all its problems and constraints did not have to be dealt with. The planners were allowed to guide the total construction of this city.

What did the urban planners plan? They designed a city with buildings that were identical multistory structures. The goal was to eliminate the traditional Latin American cityscape that had a mix of building types. They also planned a city with no streets in order to eliminate a lot of the "street problems" experienced by traditional Latin American cities. Instead, Brasilia was built with highways that did not have stop lights for traffic from cross streets.

What is it like to live in Brasilia? Most Brazilians don't like this city and the Brazilian government is hard pressed to get people to come to this city or stay here. Why? Because there is no street life. Because there are no streets or city squares, there is no window shopping or "people watching." There are no vendors selling food or restaurants that one can find by walking the streets. The urban sounds, smells, and sights

that many folks find enjoyable are absent in Brasilia.

Also, because walking is so difficult and public transportation is minimal, people must rely on their cars more in Brasilia than in other Brazilian cities. This has a negative effect on the environment because more fuel is consumed to move people around the city and more air pollution is produced.

It should be noted that the original intent of Brasilia's planners was to create a city that was egalitarian and not plagued by serious social class divisions. Unfortunately,

> the rigid divisions of the city into work and residential sectors has encouraged a greater geographic segregation of the classes than exists in traditional Brazilian cities. Thus, the planners' efforts to abolish social classes in Brazil have completely backfired. (Cornish, 1991:32)

What can we learn from this example? The main lesson is that we shouldn't completely abandon existing urban conditions and patterns when planning new urban areas. As Holston (1989) asserts, planning needs to incorporate a balance of alternative urban forms and existing conditions.

Africa

As noted, Africa is not highly urbanized. In 1990 34.5% of Africa's people lived in urban areas (Table 7.1), and this is expected to increase to 51.4% of the population by the year 2015. What distinguishes Africa from the rest of the underdeveloped regions of the world is its relatively high rate of natural increase (as discussed in Chapter 5) and its poverty. While Latin America's annual rate of increase is 1.9% a year and Asia's is 1.7% a year, Africa's rate of increase is 2.9% (Haub and Yanagishita, 1993). What this translates into in doubling time is 36 years for Latin America, 40 years for Asia, and a mere 24 years for Africa (Haub and Yanagishita, 1993). While Latin America and Asia have low per capita GNP figures of $2,360 and $1,770 respectively (in 1991 U.S. dollars), Africa is characterized by an even lower per capita income of $600 (Haub and Yanagishita, 1993). The relatively low current urbanization rate of Africa, combined with its very high rate of growth, pressing poverty, and severe droughts since the mid 1970s, means that huge proportions of rural residents are migrating to Africa's cities to seek a better life. The "bottom line" is

an absolute explosion in Africa's urban population. Whereas the average annual rate of growth for Latin American cities in the 1980s was 4.2% and the rate of growth for South Asian cities was 4.0%, the annual rate of growth for sub-Saharan African cities was an astounding 6.2% (World Bank, 1990).

If African cities are having problems now, these problems will only become worse as the twentieth century winds down. The projected problems mentioned in the preceding section on Latin America apply to Africa as well, only more so. Even though Africa had only one of the 20 urban agglomerations of 8 million or more people in 1990 (Cairo) and is projected to have only two of the 28 urban agglomerations by the year 2000 (Cairo and Lagos) (Table 7.3), African cities will be stressed to the breaking point, as rural migrants and newborn urban residents compete for shelter, food, clean water, and employment. It should be noted that AIDS, other diseases, and famine may curb this tremendous growth. As we discussed in Chapter 6, one way for population growth to be controlled is for mortality rates to rise to meet high fertility rates.

Some areas of Africa will be more pressed than others. Table 7.5 shows that Southern Africa is already quite urbanized (54.9% in 1990) and is not projected to experience as much future

TABLE 7.5

Percentage of Population in Urban Areas in Africa, by Region

	1990	2000	2015
Africa, Total	34.5%	40.7%	51.4%
Eastern Africa	21.8%	29.0%	39.6%
Middle Africa	37.8%	45.6%	57.0%
Northern Africa	44.6%	51.2%	60.7%
Southern Africa	54.9%	61.3%	69.3%
Western Africa	32.5%	39.8%	51.0%

SOURCE: United Nations, 1991, Table A.1.

urbanization as Middle and Northern Africa. Also, Eastern Africa is not expected to urbanize as quickly as the rest of Africa. Its 21.8% urbanization rate in 1990 is expected to increase to only 29.0% by the year 2000 and 39.6% by the year 2015.

MAJOR PROBLEMS OF CONTEMPORARY CITIES

We have alluded to a number of serious urban problems. In this section we will discuss more specifically problems affecting cities in both the less developed and more developed regions of the world.

Inadequate Infrastructure

Recall that the infrastructure of cities are the sewer and water systems, gas and electrical hookups, housing, roadways, and communication systems. The most important parts of the infrastructure are the sewer and water systems because sanitation and health are tied directly to the adequacy of these systems. Cities in the LDCs are most likely to experience problems in this regard. Quite simply, the population of most of these cities is quickly outstripping the capacity of the infrastructure. The city of Karachi, Pakistan, serves as an example. The sewer system has not been significantly improved since 1962 (Linden, 1993: 35) and yet the city is growing at the rate of 6 percent a year, meaning that its current estimated population of 8.4 to 11 million could increase to 19 million by the year 2002. The potable (drinkable) water supply is 30 percent less than the citizens of Karachi need. The poor are forced to drink from untreated sources, which are often contaminated with viruses such as hepatitis.

Why is this grossly inadequate infrastructure in cities of LDCs so frightening? The answer is

that the possibility of a major epidemic, resulting in massive loss of life, has never been so great. In the 1300s, the bubonic plague swept Europe and 80 percent of Europe's urban population was annihilated. That was the bad news. The good news was that 95 percent of Europe's population lived in rural areas, where the disease spread much less quickly, due to the low density of population (Linden, 1993: 32).

The situation is very different today, with much larger proportions of people living in urban areas. If there is an outbreak of a serious contagious disease, much more of the world's population is at risk.

Unprecedented Levels of Pollution

Mexico City, with a population of 14 to 20 million, leads the world's cities in pollution. Situated in a high altitude with mountains forming a rim around it, Mexico City is primed for air pollution. Add to this the millions of vehicles without air-pollution control devices, the use of leaded fuel, and the 35,000 industrial sites spewing forth pollutants (Linden, 1993: 36). A recent ozone reading of 0.35 parts per million was four times the level considered safe in California (Linden, 1993:35). Mexico City is attempting to address this severe problem by starting to equip cars with emission controls, eliminating diesel buses, and so forth. However, with the population of the city growing at such a high rate, such attempts may be "too little, too late."

Garbage and Trash Removal

Even cities in the developed world have severe problems with garbage and trash removal. Tokyo, Japan, the world's largest city with 25.8 million (Linden, 1993:36), is running out of places to dump its trash. The city produces 22,000 tons of trash each day, even though recycling and incineration are extensive. Artificial islands are being built in Tokyo Bay to hold this

Tokyo has so much trash and garbage to contend with that the city has built artificial islands in Tokyo Bay to store the garbage. This island has ten years' worth of garbage.

trash, but fishing and shipping will be affected adversely by this. Clearly, such large conglomerations of people are testing humanity's ability to deal with the by-products of its own activities.

Homelessness

Before we can discuss the problem of urban homelessness from a global perspective, we must first deal with the differences in how the term is defined. Irene Glasser's (1994) global analysis of homelessness shows that this concept is defined quite differently in the MDCs and LDCs. For example, in Finland, "the official definition of homelessness includes not only people in shelters, living outside, and doubled-up with other families, but people who are currently living apart from one another because of a lack of housing" (Glasser, 1994:123). As Glasser points out, perhaps Finland can "afford" the above inclusive definition of homelessness, because the country has few truly homeless people, as compared to a country like India which has literally thousands of people living without a roof over their heads.

The United Nations, through its Centre for Human Settlement (1990), compiled a report on homelessness throughout the world. The study concluded that about one billion individuals (about one-fifth of the planet's population) either live in conditions of inadequate shelter or are without any housing whatsoever. Most of these people live in the LDCs and it is estimated that as many as one-half of the residents of some LDC cities reside in slums. The reasons for homelessness in underdeveloped countries are numerous: extremely high rates of population growth; high rates of urbanization fueled by rural-to-urban migration and high natural rates of increase in urban areas; large-scale unemployment and underemployment; and huge amounts of external debt (United Nations Centre for Human Settlements, 1990). The report asserts that, in most cases, these homeless or under-housed individuals are parts of families.

This same United Nations report found that although MDCs do not suffer the same degree of homelessness and inadequate housing as LDCs, they are experiencing increasing problems in this area. Many MDCs have seen a marked decrease

Homelessness has become a severe problem in the United States. This man in New York City has built a squatter home in an attempt to protect himself from the elements.

in government spending on housing. For example during the administration of U.S. President Ronald Reagan, the funding for subsidized housing programs in the United States was decreased by 75 percent (Levitas, 1990). It is not surprising then, that the number of homeless men, women, and children in the United States has increased dramatically. In addition to the decrease in subsidized housing, the release of mentally ill patients from institutions and the lack of sufficient employment are factors related to homelessness in the United States. Much of the blame for the rise in homelessness has been placed on the dein-

stitutionalization of the mentally ill, but some researchers think too much emphasis has been placed on this factor. David Snow and his colleagues (1993; 1986) conducted an in-depth case study of homeless people in Austin, Texas, in the mid-1980s. They concluded that the growth in low-paying, dead-end jobs was a much more important explanation for the growth in homelessness than the release of the mentally ill from institutions. The fact that entire families make up an increasing proportion of the homeless population lends support to this view. Finally, there is evidence that urban renewal has contributed to homelessness. The work of Peter Rossi (1989:181–186) shows that in many U.S. cities, urban renewal led to the removal of much of the older, low-cost, affordable housing that the poor relied upon.

City Entrapment

As indicated earlier in this chapter, the cities of the LDCs are plagued with huge numbers of poor residents who lack adequate housing, food, water, and employment. Cities in the developed countries also have problems with extremely poor residents who do not appear able to break the chains of poverty. For example, most large American cities have significant proportions of their populations residing in ghettos and **barrios.** Historically, the term *ghetto* referred to a section of a city in a European country in which all Jews were required to live. Today, the term refers to an area of an American city inhabited by poor African Americans.

The term *barrio* refers to a section of an American city inhabited by Spanish-speaking people, usually of Latin American descent. The ghettos and barrios typically are plagued with high levels of unemployment, drug use, and crime. Various spokespersons from the African American and Latino communities assert that institutional discrimination is responsible for the high unemployment and subsequent high levels of crime and drug use. Institutional discrimination refers to "the systematic exclusion of people from equal participation in a particular institution because of their group membership" (Kornblum, 1991:684). The system of "tracking," used in many of the educational systems in the United States, is a good example of institutional discrimination. This system results in differential placement of students in tracks with more or less challenging coursework, based on racial and socioeconomic criteria. Minority and low socioeconomic children and youth are less likely to be placed in the more challenging classes, independent of their abilities.

After the civil-rights movement in the 1960s and President Johnson's "War on Poverty," many observers of the American urban scene were hopeful that minorities would be lifted from poverty. However, three decades have passed, and significant numbers of minorities are still mired in poverty. The civil-rights movement has resulted in a significant number of African Americans and Latinos moving into the middle and upper-middle classes. Most of these individuals have sufficient incomes to move out of the ghettos and barrios and into the comfortable suburbs. Various writers have observed that this movement of successful minorities from their original areas results in a lack of role models for poor minority youths. Indeed, important institutions such as churches, schools, and businesses rely on educated, middle-class minorities to lead or run them and suffer mightily when these individuals leave the ghettos and barrios.

Is the Significance of Race Declining?

In 1973 William Julius Wilson, an influential African American sociologist wrote *The Declining Significance of Race*. In that famous book, Wilson presented data to show that class status was becoming more important than race in explaining life chances of African Americans. Wilson asserts that access to education, which is highly associated with social class, is predictive of economic success for African Americans (1973:151).

The differences in social class within the African American community is creating large variations in life-chances. As Wilson (1973:151) states:

On the one hand, poorly trained and educationally limited blacks of the inner city, including that growing number of black teenagers and young adults, see their job prospects increasingly restricted to the low-wage sector, their unemployment rates soaring to record levels (which remain high despite swings in the business cycle), their labor-force participation rates declining, their movement out of poverty slowing, and their welfare roles increasing. On the other hand, talented and educated blacks are experiencing unprecedented job opportunities in the growing government and corporate sectors, opportunities that are at least comparable to those of whites with equivalent qualifications.

Wilson (1973:151–152) continues,

In view of these developments, it would be difficult to argue that the plight of the black underclass is solely a consequence of racial oppression, that is, the explicit and overt efforts of whites to keep blacks subjugated, in the same way that it would be difficult to explain the rapid economic improvement of the more privileged blacks by arguing that the traditional forms of racial segregation and discrimination still characterize the labor market in American industries. The recent mobility patterns of blacks lend strong support to the view that economic class is clearly more important than race in predetermining job placement and occupational mobility. In the economic realm, then, the black experience has moved historically from economic racial oppression experienced by virtually all blacks to economic subordination for the black underclass. And as we begin the last quarter of the twentieth century, a deepening economic schism seems to be developing in the black community, with the black poor falling further and further behind the middle- and upper-income blacks.

Twenty-three years after Wilson wrote these words, and just four years before the twenty-first century begins, the trends he delineated continue, and the huge gap between the African American underclass and the African American population that has fled the ghettos of American cities grows even larger.

In his book *The Truly Disadvantaged*, Wilson (1987) focuses on the African American underclass residing in American inner-cities. Wilson argues that the plight of African Americans in the ghetto can be tied to the broader problems of the American society and economy (1987:148). In the 1950s and 1960s, there were numerous jobs for African Americans in manufacturing, such as automobile production. These jobs did not require advanced education, yet paid quite well. Since the 1970s, these types of jobs have been decreasing as the American economy has become more automated and more service- and information-oriented. Since the latter type of jobs require more education, many African Americans have found themselves without work. Also, many of the jobs that African Americans held in prior decades have been exported to less developed countries. The employment status of African American males has been especially degraded and this has resulted in a much smaller pool of "marriageable" African American males (Wilson, 1987:145). Hence, African American females are more likely not to get married, and have their children out of wedlock.

What can be done to change this situation? Wilson (1987:150) envisions a new comprehensive economic policy aimed at the general population, that would contain educational programs, training and apprenticeship programs, child-care programs, and deficit reduction measures. Wilson suggests that such programs will benefit all poor people in this country, from the African American underclass in the inner-cities to the many poor whites who currently receive two-thirds of the welfare budget. Finally, the United States should investigate the policies of numerous European countries where child support assurance programs and child-care programs provide support to all families with children (Wilson, 1987:152–154).

SOLVING THE PROBLEMS OF THE CITIES

How can we fix these major problems of cities, especially the hypercities of the less developed regions? Although some consider these problems impossible, we might consider the example of Mayor Jaime Lerner and his city of Curitiba, Brazil. "Toward a Solution: Focus on Brazil" suggests that people, even poor people, are a resource and, if adequately tapped, can solve seemingly impossible problems. Leadership with vision, such as that of Mayor Lerner, can certainly facilitate solutions to urban problems.

If Curitiba is an example of how an LDC city can be successful, Kinshasa serves as an example of how an LDC city can fail. Kinshasa is the capital of the African country of Zaire. Zaire is a country blessed with an abundance of minerals, superb agricultural land, water, and inexpensive electrical power (Linden, 1993:30). By all accounts, Kinshasa should be a thriving metropolis. However, the city is overcome with urban problems. The primary reason for Kinshasa's problems is a lack of leadership. Kinshasa is in a country ruled by a ruthless and extremely corrupt dictator, Mobutu Sese Seko. In September of 1991, a group of elite government troops were angry that they had not been paid, and went on a looting spree. They were quickly joined by ordinary citizens. In a three-day period, almost $1 billion worth of goods were stolen. Foreign businessmen and their money departed soon thereafter. The economy fell apart, and since the government had no funds to buy parts and

Focus on Brazil

An LDC City That Works

What can be done to fix the major problems of cities, and especially the hypercities of the less developed part of the world? Although some consider these problems impossible to solve, we might consider the example of Mayor Jaime Lerner and his city of Curitiba, Brazil.

Curitiba with a population of 2.2 million people (Linden, 1993:30) is Brazil's tenth largest city. Curitiba is the capital of Parana, the farm-belt state, and is located about 500 miles south of Rio de Janeiro (Margolis, 1992:44). Like other LDC cities, Curitiba has been saddled with the host of problems accompanying rapid growth. However, this city has shown that many urban problems are, in fact, solvable. One factor is leadership.

Curitiba is fortunate to have such leadership in its mayor, Jaime Lerner. Mayor Lerner, the son of a Polish immigrant, has a degree in architecture and was a city planner before he was elected mayor. He has studied urbanization formats all over the world and has applied his knowledge, in a very pragmatic way, to Curitiba (Margolis, 1992:44). The most important thing about Lerner's approach to solving urban problems is to "think small and cheap." In Lerner's mind, too many LDC cities try to solve their problems with solutions that are too expensive or impossible to implement. The six things Mayor Lerner did to make his city work follow:

1. *Take a bus*. Mayor Lerner thinks there are better things to do with a poor city's finances than invest them in expensive subways. Lerner believes that bus systems can be just as efficient as subways, and cost one-hundredth of what a subway system would cost to build. Curitiba's bus system is organized like no other system in the world. Citizens enter an elevated tubelike transfer station, where they prepay their boarding fee and wait for the bus, protected from the elements. When the bus arrives, an extension shoots out from the bus to the elevated transfer station. The passengers quickly enter the bus, and because the driver doesn't have to collect fares, the time of travel is cut back considerably. The buses of Curitiba travel at an average of 20 miles per hour and can transport 3.2 times as many people as stan- dard buses can during the same time interval.

2. *Integrate transit*. In addition to a quick and effi- cient bus system, Curitiba has a totally integrated transit system. For a single, inexpensive fare, a passenger can ride streetcars and buses from various parts of the city. Because Mayor Lerner realizes the importance of the bicycle, under his leadership, 90 miles of bicycle paths were added, helping commuters and shoppers considerably.

3. *Rescue Children*. Curitiba has started a program that helps get street children off the street. Every shop and institution is encouraged to "adopt" 10 to 15 street children who can help with various chores in exchange for a meal and a basic wage.

4. *Promote linkage*. Mayor Lerner has organized "free fairs" where numerous street vendors sell their wares at regularly scheduled open-air markets. These markets move from neighborhood to neigh- borhood, allowing the poorer segments of the population access to reasonably priced goods.

5. *Maintain balance*. Mayor Lerner is of the opinion that urban leaders must maintain a balance between taking care of immediate problems of the city and thinking and planning for tomorrow. According to Lerner, "The mayor who tends only to current necessities forfeits the city of tomorrow, while the mere visionary stumbles over the potholes of the present" (Margolis, 1993:44).

6. *Foster a city spirit*. This is probably Mayor Lerner's crowning achievement. The city of Curitiba has devised innovative ways of using poor people to solve city problems. For example, litter and garbage used to be scattered around the city. Now a part of the city's recycling program gives bus passes and sacks of vegetables in exchange for sacks of litter and trash. Another recycling example is the use of old trolley cars for day-care centers. The city also gives free trees to citizens who agree to plant and water them. The goal is to plant 1.5 million saplings over the next 20 years.

SOURCES: E. Linden. 1993. "Megacities." *Time*, Jan. 11: 30–38; M. Margolis. 1992. "A Third-World City That Works." *World Monitor*, Mar.: 43–50.

Mayor Jaime Lerner relaxes on the "24-hour street," an enclosed mall he inaugurated in Curitiba's shopping district.

Curitiba residents disembarking a bus through the "tube station" that facilitates bus traffic.

supplies from abroad, the service sector of the city has broken down. Put bluntly, the city of Kinshasa is in a downward spiral, and the people are hurting. Unemployment is at 80 percent, medicines are scarce, and food is both very expensive and in short supply. Diseases like tuberculosis and malaria are spreading quickly. The future of this African city looks very dim indeed.

SUMMARY

In this chapter we discussed the urbanization of our planet and the social problems associated with this process. First, we saw that urbanization is a relatively recent phenomenon. For thousands of years our species was largely nomadic or

The market area of Kinshasa, Zaire, shows how densely populated this city is. However, Kinshasa does not have the infrastructure to accommodate its population.

agrarian. Only in the last one hundred years or so have human beings moved in the direction of urban life. By the end of this century, more than half of the world's population is expected to be living in cities and by the year 2025, 65 percent of the world's inhabitants will be urban residents.

Trends in urbanization vary tremendously, both by geographic region and by level of development. In the mid 1960s, North America and Europe were the most urbanized areas, followed by Latin America, Asia and Oceania, and Africa. Since the mid 1960s, Latin America has been urbanizing rapidly and is projected to be the most urbanized region by the year 2015. Asia and Oceania are also urbanizing with great speed, as is Africa. Africa is experiencing the greatest rate of urbanization, from being one-fifth urbanized in the mid 1960s to one-half urbanized by the year 2015.

Urbanization patterns have changed dramatically, and posed serious problems. First, urban residents are much more likely to be found in extremely large urban concentrations, often in cities of more than 15 million people. Many urban researchers question whether cities with such sheer size can be managed. Second, the vast majority of these new, huge cities are in the less developed regions of the world, rather than the more developed regions. The infrastructures of the huge, exploding cities in the LDCs fall far short of meeting the needs of residents, and prospects look dim.

The tendency for current and future urbanization to be associated with a lack of development is in contrast to the situation of the past, where urbanization was associated with economic development and industrialization. The factor responsible for the incredible growth in urbanization in the less developed world is the unprecedented large rate of natural increase, both in the rural areas and in the urban areas.

In short, though cities in the developed regions of the earth are not without their problems, the problems of cities in the undeveloped parts of the planet are much more severe. Two things must occur in order to solve the problems of cities in the less developed countries: (1) a reduction in the rate of population growth, accomplished by reducing fertility levels, and (2) new and innovative ways of organizing our cities and solving urban problems, as the citizens of Curitiba are now doing.

KEY TERMS

Barrio A section of a U.S. city inhabited by poor Spanish-speaking people, usually of Latin American descent.

Community A group of people who share a common territory and meet their basic physical and social needs through daily interaction with one another.

Concentric-zone model The model developed by R. Park and E. Burgess that sees cities comprised of circular zones, with business zones in the center and residential zones emanating toward the exterior.

Eopolis The Greek term to describe tiny villages or "pre-cities" characterized by homogeneity and no differentiation of labor.

Feudal society A society with the social, economic, and political structure of medieval Europe and other preindustrial societies.

Gemeinschaft The close, personal village where everyone knows everyone else and where order is maintained through tradition and custom, rather than reliance on law.

Gesellschaft The large and associational type of social organization where the people are governed by the rules of business and legislature.

Hypercities Cities with 15 million or more inhabitants.

Maquiladoras Factories located in Mexico, near the United States–Mexico border, that use low-wage Mexican labor and specialize in the assembly of components sent from developed countries.

Megalopolis A very large urban area formed by the merging of metropolises and their suburbs.

Metropolis A large, busy city that often serves as the capital of a country, state, or region.

Multiple-nuclei model The urban model stating that cities tend to be made up of numerous centers of nuclei, which are surrounded by different kinds of activities.

Polis The Greek term to describe the early cities which were independent political entities and the source of the only government that existed.

Sector theory The urban model developed by Hoyt that sees cities made up of wedges going from the center to the extremities, following major transportation arteries.

Subculture theory A perspective that sees urban residents involved in numerous groups and communities where meaningful relationships and ties are forged.

Transfrontier metropolis An urban area situated on an international border.

Urbanization The process by which a society sees increasing proportions of its population residing in urban areas and declining proportions living in rural areas.

STUDY QUESTIONS

1. What is the difference between *Gemeinschaft* and *Gesellschaft*?

2. Briefly outline the history of the city.

3. Define "transfrontier metropolis" and discuss the special problems associated with this type of metropolis.

4. Briefly outline the various perspectives on urban life and change. Which do you find most useful in understanding urban problems? Why?

5. Discuss the different urbanization trends in various geographic regions of the world.

6. How do the less developed and more developed regions of the planet differ in urbanization trends? Why?

7. It was noted that recent urbanization patterns differ in numerous ways from historical urbanization patterns. What are the differences? Why are they important in explaining contemporary urban social problems?

8. Brasilia, the capital of Brazil, was planned from scratch. Are there problems with the design of this city? If so, what are they?

9. Discuss the major problems of contemporary cities.

10. What steps did the city of Curitiba, Brazil, take to solve some of its problems?

8

c h a p t e r

GLOBAL
COMPETITION

*I*t's nine o'clock on a Saturday night in the remote jungle village of Franceville, Gabon. Although there is no electricity in Franceville, villagers are in their wooden shacks watching "Home Improvement" on televisions powered by small generators. Television, used mostly for political manipulation of the population by the leadership of many sub-Saharan African nations, however, is about the only sign of twentieth-century technology that one could observe in this part of the world. The many countries that make up today's interdependent planet differ greatly in level of technological development.

DEVELOPMENTAL STAGES

The stages of development that countries fit into are matters of technological difference and means of livelihood. They do not imply that one type of society is better than another in any moral or philosophical sense. It is important to note that listing a country as being in the preindustrial stage does not mean that its people are incapable of moving rapidly to the industrial, or even postindustrial, stage. All countries change with the passage of time, and some change with dramatic suddenness.

Preindustrial Society

Preindustrial is the term applied to the entire world before a series of inventions that replaced human and animal power with mechanical power and ushered in an age of factories and mass production. Our remote ancestors, from the age of polished stone weapons and tools, had been inventive, but the pace of change was slow, speeding up only gradually. But after the medieval period a rash of inventions for building, warfare, and navigation came into existence. The discovery of mechanical principles led to the development of gears and waterwheels to turn mills and grind grain. Soon the mills provided power for the growing textile industries of England and France. But the steam engine, as improved upon in Scotland by James Watt in 1769, is considered the definitive breakthrough to industrialism. Like the waterwheel, it did not derive its power from human or other animal sources; going beyond the waterwheel, it provided mobile power that could be used anywhere. Soon Watt's engine began to power factories, steamships, and locomotives.

The industrial age developed rapidly in England, the United States, France, the Netherlands, and Germany. Although the people of the less developed world were often very ingenious in crafts, architecture, the fine arts, literature, and philosophy, they soon found themselves outclassed in economic and military power. Many of them, including such an ancient civilization as India, were reduced to the status of colonial possessions.

Industrial Societies

Industrial societies are characterized by heavy industry powered by nonhuman labor. Steam engines, although still around, have been largely replaced by internal combustion engines, electricity, and atomic power. Much energy is generated in petroleum or coal-burning power plants, and human labor is performed in factories on assembly lines. Sociologist Daniel Bell (1973) distinguished between industrial societies and postindustrial societies. Industrial societies can be thought of as depending mainly on "smokestack industries," a work force that need not be well educated, and factories with assembly-line production. The majority of the labor force is divided between manufacturing and agriculture, with only a small service sector. Obviously, there must be stores and salespeople, offices, restaurants, repair shops, doctors, lawyers, and the like, but they make up a much smaller percentage of the employed than they do in a postindustrial society. Figure 8.1 shows that at the turn of the century in the United States, about two-thirds of the work force was employed either in **primary industry** (gathering or extracting raw materials) or **secondary industry** (manufacturing). Employment in primary industry began to decline as the secondary sector grew.

Postindustrial Societies

After the decade of the 1950s, however, secondary industry began to decline as well. In **postindustrial societies** a declining percentage of economic activity centers in heavy industry; it shifts instead to high technology, management, and services. Figure 8.1 shows that since the 1950s the United States has made a complete turnaround, with slightly more than two-thirds of the work force now employed in **tertiary industry** (services). The labor force no longer consists mainly of industrial workers on assembly lines. Education, reeducation, and adaptability are much more important than in the past. Postindustrial society is sometimes described as the "knowledge society." Muscle power loses much of its importance; brain power gains. What matters is highly developed skill and inventiveness.

Figure 8.1
Since the early 1900s, the percentage of workers in the United States involved in primary economic activities has plummeted, while the percentage involved in tertiary economic activities has increased dramatically.

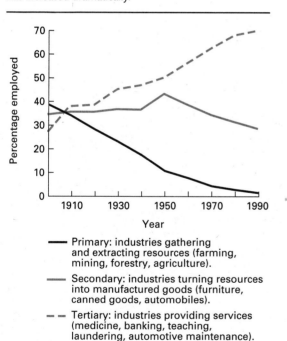

Sources: Adapted from U.S. Department of Labor. Lenski, Gerhard, Jean Lenski, and Patrick Nolan. 1991. *Human Societies: An Introduction to Macrosociology.* New York: McGraw-Hill, p. 274. Data for 1990 estimated from "Employment by Industry, 1970-1992, and by Selected Characteristics, 1992," *Statistical Abstract of the United States 1993.* 1993. Washington, DC: Bureau of the Census, p. 409.

Critiques of Postindustrialism

Although the terms **industrialism** and **preindustrialism** are well established, the word **postindustrialism** is debated. One criticism of the concept is that it has brought out some overly optimistic appraisals, as if suddenly a bright, new world had appeared. Actually, many of the service jobs associated with postindustrialism do not pay as well as the older manufacturing jobs did when unions were strong. Furthermore, jobs are not as permanent as they were in the past because postindustrialism calls for constant change, demanding new skills and making old skills obsolete. People with those skills are also obsolete unless they can adapt quickly to new conditions and requirements—and are given a chance to adjust.

Postindustrialism does not mean that all heavy industry will die out. The idea of postindustrialism is simply that high technology and service industries are gradually taking the lead, both in profits and employment, in many of the most advanced societies. This does not mean that heavy industry has disappeared any more than that the coming of industrialization meant the end of agriculture. The United States, a leader in industrialism (and now postindustrialism) remains the world's most successful agricultural society. Postindustrialism, then, refers to trends and leading developments, not to absolute differences between the present and the past.

In summary, and admittedly in an oversimplified manner, preindustrial society could be pictured by horse-drawn wagons and peasant agriculture, industrial society by smoky factories and assembly lines, and postindustrial society by computerized systems, laboratories, and technical experts. All three systems are a means to a livelihood, and all have their problems.

The Postindustrial Transition

The transition to postindustrialism is of great importance because postindustrialism rearranges the job structure of a society. At the top of the employment structure are many well-paying jobs in management, designing, and technology that enrich a highly prepared, well-educated class of people—an upper-middle class. Such a class grows in size, prestige, and income in all countries that are well on the road to postindustrialism: the United States, Japan, Germany, Sweden, Canada, France, and many more. At the same time, a previously well-paid class of unionized factory and mine workers declines in number, income, and prestige, and their unions lose power. A service sector absorbs a larger and larger percentage of the total work force, in sales, clerical work, restaurants, supermarkets, department stores, and many other jobs that are rather poorly paid. (Law and medicine are also services and pay much better, but the great growth in service jobs is not at the top level of the service sector.) A great need is seen to enter science, business, technology, and the professions to avoid becoming poorly paid service workers.

About four decades ago, a prominent American sociologist, C. Wright Mills (1951), coined the term **status panic** to describe the efforts of members of the middle class to maintain status in a world of rapidly changing requirements. The years have only added to the panic of which Mills spoke. In the United States, the status panic has particularly affected the young, upwardly mobile, well-educated professionals. In Japan, the status panic is much worse, and it starts in early childhood. Mothers send their children to the best preschools they can afford so as to qualify them for the best kindergartens, then the best grade schools, high schools, and colleges, so that they can eventually work for the most prestigious firms. There is even a special term for the hard-pushing mothers—*kyoiku mamas* or "education mothers" (Simons, 1987). The booming Korean economy, suddenly bursting into an age midway between industrialism and postindustrialism, has a similar status panic.

More than the work force is at stake in the change to postindustrialism. Many industries that have been slow to modernize are faced with hostile takeovers or even closings. More mergers take place. New technology, such as powerful computers and FAX machines, makes information available to executives a thousand miles away or completely across the world, spurring phenomenal growth of multinational corporations. Location becomes meaningless, and so does country of origin. For some types of production, it pays to move into a low-wage country; for others, to the country of greatest skill, regardless of cost. Loyalty to "home base" becomes irrelevant. Because multinational corporations are under the control of neither one national government nor a world government (like the United Nations), they can often get away with actions that are harmful both to the natural environment (pollution) and people (lower wages). Because countries, both developed and underdeveloped, feel they must compete to have multinational corporations locate with them, government officials often "look the other way" when the behavior of corporations is questionable.

The level of international competition increases as leading countries attempt to be first and foremost in various lines of technology. Those in the lead see their national treasuries grow, along with their stature in the world. Those that fall too far behind can expect a destabilizing effect on their stock markets and possibly even on their governments.

WORLD SYSTEM THEORY AND GLOBAL COMPETITION

Immanuel Wallerstein's (1974, 1979, 1980, 1991) world system theory was briefly discussed in the Chapter 1. This theory is useful when discussing the problems of present-day underdeveloped countries that are attempting to go through the aforementioned stages of development. Recall that world system theory views peripheral societies (mainly the LDCs) as dependent on the wishes and demands of core societies (mainly the MDCs). Semiperipheral countries are viewed as somewhat less dependent on the core countries, compared to the peripheral ones. This theory emphasizes the economic and power inequities of the international "pecking order" of nations. A division of labor exists in which core nations like Germany, Japan, and the United States exploit the labor of peripheral, poor countries like Nigeria, Bolivia, and Bangladesh. Core countries are characterized by sophisticated, highly educated labor forces while peripheral countries are characterized by unskilled labor forces. Semiperipheral countries like South Korea, Mexico, Brazil, and Taiwan find themselves in the middle, in terms of wealth and occupational structure. While semiperipheral countries are exploited by core countries, they (the semiperipheral countries) also exploit the peripheral nations. Capitalism drives this arrangement. Capitalism necessitates profit, and the need for core countries to control less developed countries to ensure profit results in vast disparities of wealth. World system research shows that the gap between the poor and rich nations is getting larger, and a small segment of humankind is getting wealthy at the expense of the vast majority of the world's people.

Wallerstein argues that this growing international stratification of nations is allowed to take place because of three factors. First, the core nations have superior military power, which mitigates against a violent change in the system by peripheral nations. Second, leaders of core, peripheral, and semiperipheral countries *all* benefit from the present system and do not wish to change it. The leaders of peripheral and semiperipheral nations attempt to convince their populations to work within the present system. Third, the semiperipheral nations function as a middle class does within a nation—symbolizing to the peripheral, poorest countries that progress is actually possible. Thus, the semiperipheral nations function as intermediaries that help keep the system from polarizing into two camps,

which could lead eventually to the demise of the system. In short, world system theory asserts that the present stratification of countries benefits the core countries, and to some extent the semiperipheral countries, and that it is not in the interest of core countries for the peripheral countries to develop economically and socially.

WORLD DIVISIONS

There are very few countries in which no industrialism whatever has taken place, but a very large part of the world has gone only a short step in that direction. Generally speaking, countries that are the least advanced industrially are also the poorest (a subject discussed at length in Chapter 9). They are the less developed countries (LDCs), which tend to be peripheral or semiperipheral in the world system.

Problems of Preindustrial Societies

In times past, countries whose economies were based mainly on agriculture, forestry, hunting, and fishing were sometimes quite well off. In fact, Thomas Jefferson hoped that the United States would forever remain a country of farmers. Now, however, most countries that depend on farming for the employment of the majority of their people are very poor. One problem is that agricultural produce brings a low price relative to the prices of manufactured goods that must be imported. In many cases, too, agriculture and pastoralism are the only ways of life known to the people, but they live in territories that are not productive enough to feed their growing populations. Often, the best land in the country is owned by a small minority of people or by foreign corporations, and its products go to an overseas market, not to the people themselves.

Other problems haunt the preindustrial nations. As was discussed in Chapter 5, high birthrates and low death rates are common in these countries, and they result in populations in which nearly half the people are 16 years of age or younger. Often only a minority can read or write, and poorly educated people are easily controlled by governments that do not represent their interests. Often such governments cooperate well with foreign investors interested in mining or other enterprises, but the investments enrich mainly the foreign investors and the wealthy rulers of the preindustrial society. Warren T. Brooks (1987), a writer based in Washington, D.C., points to many examples of World Bank loans and other forms of aid going mainly to the rich. Although the World Bank started with good intentions in the early days of the United Nations, it now often helps governments to "cripple their economies, maul their environments, and oppress their people." Other forms of foreign aid can be just as fruitless. For years, Chad has received 14 percent of its income in foreign aid, but it has had a 0.7 percent decline in economic growth every year since 1960. Mali, Niger, and Somalia have set similar records (Brooks, 1987).

In fairness, it must be mentioned that foreign aid has sometimes been very helpful to the people of LDCs. Both South Korea and Taiwan were transformed from dire poverty to economic recovery by foreign aid, mainly from the United States, and the same was true for much of Europe in the days following World War II. The Peace Corps, in its person-to-person approach, has accomplished much for the world's poor and has won considerable goodwill. However, too many examples can be found of aid that has helped only the rich and/or only promote the military interests of the country giving the aid.

Examples of Preindustrial Societies

Preindustrial societies are ubiquitous on the continent of Africa, especially in the predominantly desert countries of the north—Niger, Chad, Mauritania, and Sudan, among others. Egypt has a textile industry and petrochemical industry, but half of its people are employed in agriculture. Sudan, to the south of Egypt, is a land of which only 5 percent of the soil is arable, but 78 percent of the people depend on agriculture (including the grazing of animals) for a living. Many African countries hold considerable mineral wealth (oil in Nigeria and Libya, for example), but, with the exception of South Africa, industry employs very small percentages of their people.

Africa is not the only continent in which preindustrial societies are common. In the Middle East, several preindustrial societies have achieved prosperity based on oil production, but others must depend mainly on agriculture or the herding of animals.

One need not concentrate on arid lands for examples of preindustrialism. In some cases, the land is fertile and productive, but is called upon to produce more than is possible. Bangladesh is situated atop the rich soil built up from the Ganges and Brahmaputra rivers and is awash in monsoonal rains. Rice, jute, and many other crops grow abundantly; there is some mineral production and a considerable textile industry, but three-quarters of the people farm for a living. Although the soil is rich and well watered (sometimes subject to flooding), the population density is an incredible 1,824 per square mile. By comparison, that of the United States is 66 per square mile. Too much is expected of the land in Bangladesh. In general, Southeast Asia, with the exception of busy and prosperous Singapore, is either preindustrial or just entering the industrial age. The same is true of many countries of Latin America, although a few of them are definitely in early stages of industrialization. However, industrialism does not develop from dreams; it is brought about by great effort and at least temporary sacrifice.

The Beginnings of Industrialism

In the early days of industrialism in England and the United States, wages and working conditions were incredibly bad. In Chapter 1, we mentioned the child workers of the carpet mills in Mirzapur, India. In Chapter 2 we explored the wretched conditions of working youth during the last century. Such well-known writers as Charles Dickens and Victor Hugo have left indelible pictures of similar conditions among the poverty-stricken working classes of England and France, and Karl Marx documented the abuse of labor in those countries and in Germany, as well. One problem is simply that of people's inhumanity to each other, but there is also the economic problem of finding the money to invest in industry. One way is to underpay the workers to keep production costs low. Then goods can be exported and sold at a profit, and the profit can be reinvested. Regardless of wages, England and Germany had more people than could be supported on the farms, so the poor flocked to factories and accepted any pay and any conditions. In France, the pace of industrialization was slower for a number of reasons, one of which was that the peasants had been given their land in the great French Revolution and were less willing to move to the cities. Working conditions were somewhat less deplorable in the United States than in England because, as a last resort, people could take up land in the West.

If we look for countries that resemble England and Germany in the early days of the Industrial Revolution, we should look for those with a great surplus of people in the countryside, now rushing to the cities, looking for any kind of work at any wage. These conditions exist in many semi-peripheral countries now undergoing industrial development, such as India, Brazil, and Mexico.

It is hard to draw a fine line of distinction between preindustrialism and early industrialism. India, for instance, is a producer of steel and chemicals, machinery, appliances, and even automobiles. Nevertheless, more than 70 percent of its people are still employed in agriculture, but that is down from 80 percent at the end of World War II. Mexico, although burdened with debts and poverty, is moving somewhat faster in the direction of industrialism, with impressive gains in the production of steel, chemicals, electrical appliances, automobiles, petroleum, and a number of other minerals. Less than half of its people are currently employed in agriculture.

Mexico is in a special position because of its proximity to the United States. As unemployed people from Mexico cross the border northward, a number of industries are crossing the border southward, looking for cheap production costs. Hence, we have the anomaly of a country that is barely entering the industrial age, but that has many industrial plants along its border engaged in the production of high-technology equipment. For example, a Pennsylvania electronics company assembles 30,000 printed circuit boards per month for use in medical and computer products, and the work is done in Tijuana, Mexico. Thus, as previously noted, levels of industrial development sometimes merge. What is happening in Mexico is also occurring in other Latin American countries, such as Brazil, Argentina, and Chile, and in some of the newly industrializing countries of East Asia. In nearly all such countries, wages are low, insufficient attention is paid to workers' health and safety, and environmental laws tend to be lax. In large part, this is because multinational corporations operating in these countries have considerable influence on domestic policies, and the domestic policies often condone low wages, lax environmental laws, and nonexistent or weak occupational health and safety regulations.

Juan Forero's (1993) investigative report on the exploitation of Mexican workers who are employed by foreign *maquiladoras* shows that Mexicans who are paid $1.00 per hour can barely survive in the more expensive border cities like Tijuana. Forero discusses the case of María García, a 51-year-old woman who earns $1.00 per hour at a U.S.-owned company that makes plastic coat hangers. Forero's (1993) description of García's home shows how little such a wage in Tijuana provides.

Mexicans working in *maquiladoras* along the United States–Mexico border do not earn enough to afford adequate housing. This woman and child live in a poor "colonia," or neighborhood, without running water, electricity, or sewer hookups.

The dwelling she calls home is more a haphazard collection of scrap wood, corrugated metal and mesh fencing precariously built on a rock-strewn canyon—discarded tires and dirt packed below to provide a foundation. García's home lacks piped water and electricity, save for the gasoline generator the family uses to power the television and two overhanging lightbulbs. Without plumbing, family members are forced to relieve themselves in a metal basin, the waste tossed over a hillside. In colder months,

biting winds whip through the structure's many open spaces.

Forero (1993) reports that although *maquiladoras* along the U.S.–Mexican border pay almost twice the Mexican minimum daily wage, they average only $1.64 an hour, compared to an averaged $2.35 per hour in all Mexican manufacturing. Because many Mexicans feel exploited by the *maquiladoras,* unions are starting to organize workers in an attempt to better their bargaining position with the *maquiladoras.*

A few countries that one might expect to be classified as in the early stages of industrialization have actually reached fairly advanced status in a very short time: South Korea, Taiwan, Hong Kong, and Singapore. They are sometimes referred to as The Four Tigers because of the pace at which they have burst upon the industrial, and even postindustrial, scene.

THE FUTURE OF LDCs

Many postindustrial countries of today once had characteristics commonly found in less developed countries: a rush of rural people to the cities, very low wages and bad working conditions, and governments that showed little concern for the working classes. Such countries have remedied conditions and now give the common people a voice in government. The question that comes to mind when thinking of the success of the United States, Western Europe, Japan, and similarly advanced countries is, Will the present preindustrial and industrializing countries eventually go the same route, improving conditions for their people, raising wages, providing education, health facilities, and a measure of democracy?

The answer is in doubt. One can certainly point to examples of countries that were once underdeveloped but have now joined the MDCs. We have referred especially to South Korea, Taiwan, Hong Kong, and Singapore in this regard. Not all of them are democratic, but they appear to be moving in that direction, and the living conditions of their people are definitely improving. On the other hand, Brazil, Mexico, India, and Indonesia are all countries in which considerable industrial progress is being made, but with little improvement on the depressed economic conditions of their burgeoning populations. Indonesia is a dictatorship, Brazil has had many periods of military rule, Mexico is dominated by one political party, and India (the most nearly democratic of the four) has had frequent complaints made about its election process.

Barriers to Progress

The LDCs have barriers to progress that appear greater than those faced by the United States, England, and other countries that started industrialization in the eighteenth century. One possible barrier may be rapid population growth. The four countries mentioned above—Mexico, Brazil, India, and Indonesia—are all increasing their gross national products, but each year they have many more people to support. As was pointed out in Chapter 5, birthrates are declining in much of the world, especially in the MDCs. It is possible that population stability will eventually be achieved in the LDCs, too, and that overpopulation may no longer loom as a major problem. The Four Tigers are all doing well despite crowded populations. Nevertheless, our fear is that much of the less developed world will suffer greatly from too many mouths to feed and few of them are increasing production fast enough to stay ahead.

A very real problem for the LDCs is that they are part of a much more competitive world than was faced by England during its period of supremacy in the nineteenth century. England, France, the Netherlands, and other colonial powers had found new worlds to conquer. They could sell high-priced manufactured goods to their colonies and buy cheap raw materials. The present LDCs have no such colonial empires to

exploit; they must instead enter the competition with the most technologically sophisticated countries. In many cases, the old colonial powers (now core nations), although they have abandoned political control, are still economically linked to their former colonies. They still sell them manufactured goods and buy raw materials from them, and they see no reason for changing the arrangement by helping them to develop industrially. Although a few former LDCs have made the leap into modernity and become competitors in industrial and postindustrial production, it is questionable whether there is room for them all.

This last point is central to world system theory. Peripheral societies' dependency is largely a function of the huge debts they owe to core societies. The debt itself results from unequal trade, which is controlled by the core societies. Many LDCs have gigantic foreign debts. As a general rule, the largest amounts of money were borrowed prior to the oil crisis of 1973. Brazil, Mexico, and other countries borrowed money to help build industry, intending to pay interest with agricultural proceeds until their new industries began to make profits. These countries were attempting to move toward industrialization and envisioned enough profit from new industry to pay at least the interest on their loans. Then came the rapid boost in oil prices, which drove up their costs of agricultural production and export. Money did not roll in as they had hoped, and they found themselves deeply in debt at high interest rates. Loans must be negotiated annually to prevent any major country from defaulting and more loans are made so the debtors can pay interest and a rescheduling fee. As a way out of this madness, a number of *debt-equity swaps* have been made. Through a debt-equity swap, a country is allowed to issue to the loaning agency an interest (often 51 percent) in some of its industries, rather than paying off its debt. The resultant controlling foreign interest creates yet another form of dependence on the MDCs. Borrowing has not led to industrial freedom.

Latin America: A Turnaround?

Though the problems of the less developed contries are immense, Latin America is making progress in the area of economic and social development. Just ten years ago, Latin America was written off by many as hopeless—underdeveloped countries with loans they could not pay off and unbelievable inflation rates.

John Naisbitt (1994:260–269) reports that South America, Central America, and Mexico are all beating the odds on their demise. Latin American countries such as Argentina and Bolivia, which had astronomical inflation rates (Bolivia's rate was 23,000 percent in 1985) have managed to get inflation rates under control. This turnaround has occurred because democratic governments have been elected and trade barriers among Latin American countries are being eliminated. The trade alliances these countries are forming are proving very beneficial to all.

THE COMMUNIST ROUTE TO INDUSTRIALISM

The Communist Revolution in Russia in 1917 gave birth to a government that was looked upon with great hostility by the rest of the world. The reason for this hostility is that communism did away with private property. Under communism the state owned the basic means of production, such as farmland and factories. Officials and leaders of other countries were concerned that these ideas about property ownership would spread to other countries. Although some industrialization had started, Russia in those days was essentially industrially backward. The Communists were determined to build heavy industry but because they had no foreign friends, they could not borrow funds. The only way to achieve their aim was to work their people hard and with little reward. Industrial workers were given preferential treatment (better and cheaper housing, vacation time, etc.) over the peasants, especially the

better-off peasants called *kulaks*, who were cruelly oppressed. Millions of *kulaks* died during the early years of the Communist Revolution, partly as a result of civil wars and invasions that beset the country, partly because of crop failures, but also because of the actions of Vladimir Lenin and the Communist Party, who viewed the *kulaks* as excessively wealthy farmers. Their farms were expropriated and they were often killed. Joseph Stalin, who took power as a dictator after the death of Lenin, forced collective farmers (farmers who jointly farmed state-owned land) to give most of their produce to the government. *Kulaks* and other peasant farmers opposed being forced to join collective farms and destroyed much of their crops and livestock. Stalin punished these individuals by sending millions of them to prison labor camps in Siberia and Soviet Central Asia.

Though Stalin ruled with an iron hand and eliminated millions of his real and imagined adversaries, he did succeed in building up the economy, in industrializing the nation, and in enhancing the Soviet Union's power, worldwide. The Union of Soviet Socialist Republics (USSR) was formed in December of 1922, two years before Lenin's death, and included a number of republics, Russia being the most important and powerful. Slowly the situation improved for most Soviet citizens. Most people were adequately, if not comfortably, housed; everyone was employed; and the food supply was sufficient. Just as improvement seemed definitely under way, Germany invaded during World War II, bleeding the Soviet Union as few countries in history have ever been bled. Twenty million Soviet servicemen and women were killed and wounded in World War II, with most of the damage coming from Germany. The German invasion resulted in the deaths of millions of Soviet civilians; the destruction of major Soviet cities; and the shattering of the Soviet economy.

Eventually, Germany was beaten by the Allied Forces, which included the United States, France, Britain, and the Soviet Union. Slowly, the Soviet Union recovered from the war and the country's rapid industrialization continued under a number of five-year plans. These five-year plans included renewed restrictions on workers (workers had to get government permission before quitting or changing jobs), the reorganization and enlargement of collective farms, and new waves of political arrests and executions under the Stalinist regime. Nikita Khrushchev eventually assumed power after Stalin's death in 1953, and one of his primary goals was to raise the Soviet standard of living. He shortened the work week to 40 hours, cut down on the terrorist activities of the secret police, and stepped up government efforts at increasing production of food, clothing, household appliances, and other goods. By the mid 1980s, industrialization had been achieved. The labor force, which had once been overwhelmingly agricultural, was devoted mainly to industry and services.

The Experiment Fails

Though the Soviet Union became industrialized via the Communist route, the structural weaknesses of communism were becoming apparent, even to the Soviets, by the end of the 1980s. General Secretary Mikhail Gorbachev, though a Communist, knew that the Soviet Union was not competitive with the rest of the industrialized world, and attempted to change some of the basic structures of Soviet communism. The real problem with the Soviet economy was that is was isolated from the world economy and simply was uncompetitive. The Soviet Union's inability to compete with the industrialized world led to one of the most incredible political phenomena of the century—the breakup of the USSR in 1991. The former Soviet empire is now 15 countries, Russia being the most predominant.

The Future of Russia

The future of Russia is very much in question. Strobe Talbott (1992) pointed out that Russian President Boris Yeltsin has his hands full because this country is actually going through three revo-

lutions at once: (1) from totalitarianism to democracy, (2) from a command economy to a free market, and (3) from a multinational empire to a nation-state. As he states (Talbott, 1992:34), "Any one of these would be arduous enough all by itself. Undertaking three revolutions simultaneously with so little warning and preparation has overloaded the circuits."

The breakup of the Soviet Union has provided opportunities for some Russians. Adi Ignatius (1994) writes about how Russia's chaotic economy has created incredible opportunities for instant wealth. His story about Grigory Nersesyan illustrates the entrepreneurship in Russia. Nersesyan is an intellectual who was on a fixed state salary and who wrote English translations in his spare time for pocket money. When the USSR collapsed, he borrowed $30,000 and opened a Tex-Mex restaurant down the road from the Kremlin. He rented prime space from a beautiful turn-of-the-century theater that used to rely on state subsidies and now is in desperate need of cash. It didn't cost much for Nersesyan to fix up the restaurant. He hired some former Soviet rocket designers, who were desperate for cash, to build a swinging saloon door, and he found someone to paint a Western piano-bar scene on the wall. A few sombreros on the wall and a big blown up Corona beer bottle in the window finished his decorating. Nersesyan recouped his total investment in just six weeks.

For every success story like Nersesyan's, however, there are many more dreadful ones. Carey Goldberg (1994) reports about the shutdown of the "March 8 Weaving Mill" in Ivanovo, Russia, and the severe toll the shutdown has taken on the mill's 1,500 workers. According to Goldberg (1994:4) "The mill's troubles started when the Soviet Union collapsed in 1991, jeopardizing the supply of cotton from Central Asia. . . In 1992, cotton prices shot up, and by the time Ivanovo plants could persuade the government to lend them money to buy it, there was almost none left. So their output dropped radically. And when the factories' loans came due in early 1993, they had to borrow more—this time at 213 percent interest." As a result, the factories are deep in dept and unable to pay their loans, employee salaries, energy bills, or suppliers. These factories are so much in debt that their suppliers won't provide cotton until they are paid for previous orders. The vicious cycle continues.

The serious problems being faced in Russia have taken their toll on the population. Life expectancy is plummeting in Russia. Within the course of one year, life expectancy for Russian men dropped from 62 to 59 years and for women it declined from 73.8 to 73.2 (Cooperman, 1994:25). Murray Feshbach, research professor of demography at Georgetown University asserts that "It's a spectacular decline, the largest one-year decline since the war. It's really unprecedented for any developed country" (quoted in Cooperman, 1994:25). According to Cooperman (1994:25), "The figures quantify what many Russians feel in their bones: poverty, violence, disease, and stress are taking a huge toll on public health."

The Future of Communism Worldwide

Before the Soviet Union fell, Communist East Germany had reunited with capitalist West Germany. When the Soviet Union collapsed, so did the other Communist governments in Eastern Europe. Cuba is still Communist but is suffering mightily since no financial aid is forthcoming from the former Soviet Union (McGeary and Booth, 1993). Though the Cuban population has access to universal education and health care, the lack of adequate food and housing is an increasingly serious problem. Though Cubans are unhappy with the current dire economic situation, there does not appear to be a widespread movement afoot to displace Fidel Castro, who has ruled Cuba since 1959 (McGeary and Booth, 1993). Cubans are proud of their universal education, health care, and social security system and are also proud that their society is much more egalitarian than it was before Castro's revolution. The world will be watching Cuba when Fidel Castro finally passes from the scene.

One other Communist country clinging to the original ideology even after the demise of the Soviet Union is North Korea. This country's per capita income is one-seventh that of its neighbor, South Korea. A large proportion of North Korea's GNP goes to fund its military machine. North Korea is also failing to cooperate with international organizations that wish to verify nuclear weapons.

The lack of adequate housing is a serious problem in Cuba. This scene of dilapidated housing and an old American automobile is common in Havana.

The other two Communist countries, Vietnam and China, are adopting capitalist patterns to develop their economies. Vietnam has been accepting large infusions of foreign capital and allowing foreign companies to build factories. The United States was the only industrialized country not involved in Vietnam, until February 1994 when the U.S. Congress voted to lift the embargo against its former military foe. It will be interesting to see how the United States becomes involved in the development of Vietnam. The American writer, John Naisbitt (1994:249) said, "The Vietnamese seem to have forgiven Americans for the war long before we forgave ourselves; and in any case, more than half the population of Vietnam has no memory of the war, but they have a strong appetite for all things American."

The People's Republic of China is the other Communist country successfully utilizing capitalism to develop. Its transformation is looked at later in this chapter.

INDUSTRIAL AND POSTINDUSTRIAL NATIONS

The postindustrial society is what sociologists refer to as an **ideal type**, meaning a type that is definable and that is approached in the real world, but never completely realized. As indicated previously, the perfect postindustrial society would no longer depend on heavy manufacturing industries, but purely on high technology, finance, scientific development, and all types of "knowledge industry." Its workers would be technical experts, closely aligned with management, and drawing high salaries. Drudgery and monotony on the job would be at an end; the only possible problem would be tensions resulting from extremely great competition. Such a description makes it clear that none of the world's industrial nations is 100 percent postindustrial.

In looking at real cases we find a great decline in agricultural employment, as would be expected in both industrial and postindustrial society. France, the richest agricultural land of Western Europe, has only about 9 percent of its people employed in that field (*World Almanac,* 1994). In the United Kingdom, the agricultural sector employs only a little more than 1 percent of the population (World Almanac, 1994). Other Western European countries fall somewhere between those figures, as do the United States, Canada, Australia, and New Zealand. The rest of the labor force is employed in industry, trade and commerce and, increasingly, services (*World Almanac,* 1994). Typically, the industrial sector declines as a source of employment and services increase. In East Asia, Japan, Korea, and Taiwan are following this example. We must give special consideration to these countries as we emphasize the modern race for economic supremacy.

In all the industrially advanced countries, there are occasional labor problems, but fewer than in the early days of industrialization. Distribution of wealth is by no means even, but average standards of living are moderate to good. Japan and Sweden distribute wealth with greater equity than most, and living standards are comparable. Average annual income (in U.S. dollars) ranges from $15,900 in Great Britain to $21,700 in Switzerland, compared to $380 in India, $130 in Ethiopia, or $1,010 in El Salvador (*World Almanac,* 1994). Generally, lives in postindustrial countries are very comfortable, in contrast to the abject poverty of the nonindustrialized world or parts of the world just entering the industrial age.

There are serious problems for all the postindustrial societies, though. They are engaged in intense competition. There appears to be a question as to how many countries can reach the zenith of postindustrialism. There are also questions regarding which route to follow. The United States, Canada, France, Germany, and many other countries closely approach **free capitalism**, economies with limited government control or government direction. In certain other countries, economies—although run for corporate profit—are more closely linked to the government for direction. Japan and South Korea are the outstandingly successful examples of this model. Both countries are characterized by gigantic corporate enterprise.

The Competitive Struggle of Postindustrialism

There is no question that from the viewpoint of the United States, the world is becoming much more competitive in the post-industrial era. Well within the memory of elderly Americans was a time when Japanese goods were considered cheap and tacky, although so extremely low-priced that they sold well in this country. Then came World War II. Although Japan showed a surprising military ability, it was utterly crushed after two atomic bombs were dropped in 1945. Most of the world believed Japan would never again be more than a third-rate power, either militarily or economically. There were even worries, both in Japan and throughout the rest of the world, as to how the Japanese population could possibly be supported, especially with the collapse of the Japanese overseas empire. Korea and Taiwan were released from Japanese control and were expected to return to LDC status, probably for at least a century into the future. Even in Europe, economic competition had fallen to a low level. Germany was devastated, and even the winning European allies were in serious need, economically. An American century had dawned. The United States dollar was the worldwide measure of value, and it was very strong against all currencies. The United States was the great creditor nation, the almost exclusive producer of automobiles, first in steel and petroleum production, overwhelmingly first in food production, not to mention being the sole possessor of the weapon that, it was believed, would guarantee the nation's safety far into the future—the atomic bomb.

The United States Faces Competition

Forty years after the war ended, the United States had gone from the world's greatest creditor nation to the greatest debtor. In 1981 the national debt was nearly $1 trillion ($998 billion). In just five years, the debt more than doubled ($2.125 trillion in 1986), and by 1992 had doubled once again (to $4.065 trillion) (*World Almanac*, 1994:101). Its basic industries were challenged, its trade balance was grossly unfavorable, and its military position was no longer secure. Other powers, particularly the Soviet Union and China, had developed atomic bombs.

Controversy raged over what had happened to lower the envious position of the United States, and there was also debate as to whether things really looked bad in the long run. As long as Ronald Reagan occupied the presidency, cheerful, upbeat messages emanated from the White House: Prosperity had never lasted so long; the trade balance would soon turn in the United States' favor; the country was making real headway toward balancing the budget; the United States' military and naval power was the greatest it had ever been; there was still a "safety net" for the needy; Americans were better off than ever before.

Contrary to the presidential assurances, many disturbing notes were sounded in addition to those about debts and trade balances. Laboring people complained of a loss of good jobs, as companies moved their operations overseas in search of cheap labor. Barry Bluestone and Bennet Harrison (1982) joined the outcry with pages of statistics about the flight of American industry. It was also pointed out (Reich, 1983) that the United States suffers from many obsolete or poorly managed industries that the government tries to prop up with tax breaks. It was suggested that the United States take a cue from Japan and give special aid to those industries most promising for the future, as well as helping and encouraging all exporting industries. David Halberstam (1987) tells the story about how an inefficient, overconfident automobile industry in America was being bested by Japan. More ominously, it has been argued (Kennedy, 1988) that many changes must come about or the United States will continue a relative decline, which has already started.

Laura D'Andrea Tyson (1992:1) has written that there is general agreement that the United States' economic competitiveness "is in slow but perceptible decline." According to Tyson (1992:1), "The debate in Washington has shifted from whether the nation has a competitiveness problem to what should be done to solve it." Tyson points out that some of the most controversial questions in this new debate center around the nation's trade policies. Tyson analyzed a number of case studies involving trade conflict between nations and concluded that some problems facing the United States are caused by foreign trading polices such as government facilitation in technology development, tariffs, and so forth. She suggests (1992:295–296) that America needs to institute trade policy initiatives that are:

> designed to improve foreign market access for American companies or to counter the effects of foreign targeting programs. Such initiatives are defensible in a world in which trade is manipulated by government intervention, and structural differences impede competition between producers from different nations. The policy task in such a world is to use the nation's trade policies to serve the national interest, but to do so in ways that foster the development of new multilateral rules, reflecting the growing integration of global high-technology industries.

Edward N. Luttwak (1993) agrees with Tyson about the danger of the United States slipping from developed to under-developed status and also lays the blame at the feet of U.S. political and corporate leaders who are naive about the nature of the new world order that has emerged since the end of the Cold War. He (Luttwak, 1993:34–39) argues that while traditional warfare and military threats still are used by backwater countries, a new form of economic warfare, "geo-economics," is currently being used by Japan and the European Community, but not by the United States. Geo-economics involves numerous things. One item is government

support of key technological industries; the support that the Japanese government provides to Japanese automotive and electronic industries exemplifies this. Second, tariffs and hidden trade barriers can protect and benefit a country's domestic producers. The rice industry in Japan serves as an example; without the tariffs placed on American rice, Japanese rice growers would find it very difficult, if not impossible, to compete. Third, various customs-house conspiracies that circumvent the GATT rule (that states that arbitrary tariffs and quotas are illegal) can be employed. For example, a country can state that imports have to be inspected by an official before those imports can be marketed. If the country "conveniently" lacks enough inspection officials, the imports will get bottle-necked at the customs house and will not be salable. Luttwak (1993:27–32) discusses the emergence of Airbus Industrie as a prime example of geo-economics. Airbus Industrie is a European consortium, supposedly a commercial company, that builds jet airliners to compete with U.S. firms like McDonnell-Douglas and Boeing. However, this venture is heavily subsidized and financially guaranteed by the French, British, German, and Spanish governments. The goal of the consortium is to put U.S. airliner firms out of business. Luttwak (1993:28–29) discusses how Airbus Industrie sold drastically underpriced airliners to Eastern Airline, an American company, in an attempt to get a foothold in the United States. Airbus was able to do this only with subsidization by European governments. And, points out Luttwak, all of this happened without much reaction from Boeing, McDonnell-Douglas, or the U.S. Congress. Luttwak argues that U.S. idealogues who champion free trade are very naive about the economic games currently being played in the new world order.

Luttwak (1993) asserts that in order to compete in this new geo-economic climate, the United States must find ways to (1) turn around the educational system so that highly skilled labor is available, (2) increase the rate of savings so that more capital is available for business and technological development, (3) develop national technology programs through which the government works with the business community to meet various technological and market goals, and (4) utilize various methods (tariffs, etc.) to protect U.S. markets.

Not everyone views the United States' situation so grimly. Alfred Balk (1990) argues that the assumptions of U.S. decline have been overstated. He suggests that the declinist view is more American than non-American. And, in his experience with foreigners, the United States in *not* viewed as a "has-been" nation whose best years are past. Balk (1990:3) contends that the United States, indeed the world, is experiencing a "triple revolution." According to Balk (1990:3),

> One revolution is globalization: an internationalization of economics, politics, science/technology, culture, and communications that is fundamentally altering human affairs. A second revolution is reindustrialization: a postindustrial upheaval that futurist Alvin Toffler calls "the third wave," built on high technology and the internationalization of economic activity. A third revolution is the ascent of a scientific, technocratic, megascale culture of incessant, ever-accelerating change and stress for which we are institutionally and temperamentally unprepared. All three revolutions alter the context in which both absolute and comparative power should be measured. Disruptive as they are, in the long term all work in favor of the United States than of any other single nation.

Balk (1990:117) is of the opinion that the "true decline problem" for the United States is not in its economic performance or in its international status, but in its national spirit—its "values, perspectives, resource allocation, . . . and popular culture." Growing proportions of people who are homeless and malnourished in the United States, a growing inner-city underclass that is alienated, the drug culture, random violence, the lack of affordable housing, the growing proportion of

single-parent families, and the lack of investment in public works—these are the problems the United States must address. We should note here that the change in values, perspectives, resource allocation, and popular culture that Balk addresses are, at least in part, a direct result of the deindustrialization in the United States—an economic transformation that had a profound impact on the occupational structure of the country and resulted in a shrinking middle class.

Richard Rosecrance (1990:9–13) predicted that the United States would come back economically but that a number of things would have to happen to ensure this comeback: (1) the U.S. "economic plant" must be remodeled—tax increases and budget cuts will be needed to finance foreign policy and entitlement programs and to reduce the government deficit; (2) Americans—workers, managers, and corporate executives alike—will have to work harder and more efficiently and receive less money for their work, in order for American products to be more competitive globally; (3) the United States must focus on production of high-value, sophisticated products; and (4) the United States must reduce the amount of money spent on the American military presence in Europe and the Far East. Rosecrance (1990:11) thought the odds are good in the United States' favor, due to a large manufacturing base, unmatched creative potential in pure science, and the fact that America's challengers are one-dimensional powers.

Five years later, it is interesting to take note of Rosecrance's predictions and his various points. It seems that, by and large, he was correct; most of the "corrections" he called for have been made or are in the process of being made. The Clinton administration has started to reduce the national deficit, through budget cuts in entitlements and tax increases. Americans are also working harder, and for less money, than their competitors. David Wessel (1994) points out that at current exchange rates, U.S. workers cost $16.70 per hour, compared to $19.30 for Japanese workers and $25.50 for German workers.

Figure 8.2
At current exchange rates, workers from the United States cost considerably less than workers from Germany or Japan.

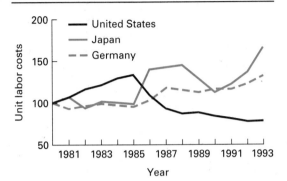

Labor costs in manufacturing for U.S., Japan, and Germany (1980 = 100; based on market exchange rates), 1981–1993

Source: *Wall Street Journal,* January 10, 1994, Part A.

Rosecrance's third point—the need for high-value, sophisticated products—is also appearing to be met, along with the cost-effective work force. Robert Rose (1994) discusses how Cummins Engine Company, (the U.S. diesel engine producer) in Columbus, Indiana, is successfully competing with foreign firms. Refurbished plants are using Japanese-style organization in which workers are part of the decision-making process. The efficiency and productivity of the plant mirrors the recent resurgence of the old "Rust Belt" section of the United States (the Midwest) in manufacturing. A major reason for Cummins's new competitive edge is the reduction of wages. The Cummins plant that reopened in Columbus, Indiana, pays an average $8.60 per hour, which is half the wage at the company's main heavy-duty engine plant (Rose, 1994). The union was forced to agree to lower wages to have the plant reopened.

The U.S. automobile industry has also revamped and is finally turning out high-quality, competitively priced products. The *Wall Street Journal* (1993) reports that for the first time in a decade, U.S. automobile and truck production is exceeding Japanese automotive production. The

December 1993 cover story of *Time* magazine was devoted to the resurgence of the "Big Three" auto makers—Chrysler, Ford, and General Motors.

The job picture has changed drastically in the United States. At first it was the loss of good-paying jobs in manufacturing and then it was the proliferation of low-paying, dead-end jobs in the service sector. More recently, the white-collar professional segment of the American work force has been hit hard with the loss of permanent, well-paying jobs. Temporary and consultant jobs, without benefits, have increased 250 percent since 1982, compared to less than a 20 percent increase in the total employment picture (Morrow, 1993). In 1988 contingent or temporary workers constituted one-fourth of the U.S. work force; they are projected to represent one-half of the work force by the turn of the century (Morrow, 1993:41). Also, well-paying jobs such as being an executive or engineer for IBM—jobs that were once very secure—are vanishing (Hage et al, 1993). Furthermore, there is evidence that the disappearance of such white-collar jobs in the United States is permanent and structural (Church, 1993). In short, U.S. businesses have become more competitive on a global scale because their employees have taken pay cuts. Real wages in the United States have been decreasing since 1978 and the middle class has been shrinking as a result. An observation by Rose (1994) about the Cummins engine plant puts the whole discussion in perspective: The workers who are making the "new" lower wage of $8.60 an hour do not make enough money to buy the Dodge pickup trucks that are outfitted with the Cummins engine.

This loss of jobs is due partly to the dramatic change in the manufacturing process from traditional assembly lines to computer-assisted production, which calls for more highly educated workers able to innovate and change as conditions and markets change. The result of this change, which is taking place increasingly in American industry, is that U.S. productivity has risen rapidly since 1982. Contrary to the expectations of many writers on the subject of postindustrial society, U.S. manufacturing output has actually increased. But there is a downside to the story: The number of jobs in manufacturing has declined while industrial output has risen. The rise in production is small consolation to workers who have had to trade well-paying jobs for poorly paying jobs, or for none at all.

The changes in the occupational and pay structure of the United States are sobering for the American worker, but there is much more to the story on jobs in the United States. There is increasing evidence that sweatshops (companies that do not pay minimum wage and that violate many employment laws) are multiplying in the United States. This is especially evident in the garment industry. Recent reports on garment sweatshops in New York, Dallas, and Los Angeles (Headden, 1993), hearken back to the days of child labor at the turn of the century. For far less than the minimum wage ($4.25 per hour), 10-year-old children sew buttons on skirts in American factories where the temperature can exceed 90°F and where other working conditions are intolerable. Immigrant couples work twelve-hour days, six days a week, in U.S. garment factories for *combined* pay of $111 per week. There is much money to be made in producing clothes. As

Figure 8.3 shows, the lion's share of the profit goes to the company that designs the clothes and subcontracts the work, and to the retailers. Of the selling price of $54 for a "Limited" skirt, only $3 goes to the laborers who make the skirt, less than 6 percent of the selling price. When consumers see labels on manufactured goods that say, "Made in the U.S.A." they often assume the workers who made them are paid decent union wages. Unfortunately, this is not always correct.

Competition for Other Western Countries

If we turn our attention to Europe or to Canada, we see some of the same changes coming about in economic competition. Productivity rises, but unemployment remains high. Quality of product must be constantly upgraded, and inefficient firms must fail. France, Germany, Italy, and other Western European nations in the European Economic Community (EEC) cooperate with each other more closely than ever before, but they still must vie with one another for markets. France, virtually devoid of coal or oil, has become a major producer of electricity through atomic energy. It competes in steel, autos, electronic equipment, and airlines, and has a rapid rail system second only to that of Japan. True to

Figure 8.3
This skirt from "The Limited" retails for $54. The contractor receives $4.25 to sew it, $3 of which is paid to laborers. Less than 6 percent of the selling price of a garment goes to the people who make it.

Labor Costs to Produce a Skirt

Waistband with facing	72¢
Hem, skirt	6¢
Hem, lining	7¢
Serging, skirt	14¢
Serging, lining	4¢
Cutting threads	5¢
Belt loops (4)	10¢
Sewing belt loops on skirt (4)	8¢
Zipper	17¢
Pressing	15¢
Ironing loops	ea. 15¢

Source: S. Headden, 1993. "Made in the USA," *U.S. News & World Report,* Nov. 22: 50.

This 9-year-old boy is working in a garment factory in Brooklyn, New York. Child labor, which is illegal and was believed eliminated in the United States, is a serious contemporary problem.

cultural tradition, France remains an important producer of luxury goods and the arts.

Germany has a much larger population than France in an area only about two-thirds the size. Consequently, it finds a great need to export to support its people. Germany has long been famous for industrial technology, and remains a major industrial producer, ahead of the United States in industrial product per capita. The United Kingdom and Italy are no less crowded than Germany, and Belgium and the Netherlands are even more so. All enjoy a good standard of living, at least compared with the LDCs, but they must keep up their exports to maintain their living standards. The competitive struggle is leading them all to more technology, more computers, and higher quality exports. They invest abroad and in multinational corporations. They compete with each other, but, like the United States, find themselves in greater competition with the countries of East Asia.

At present, Europe finds itself with numerous economic and social problems. The euphoria that followed the fall of the Berlin Wall and the demise of communism has given way to the grim realities of bringing the former East-European Communist countries into the twentieth century economically. High levels of unemployment continue to plague Europe, with rates ranging from 7 to 19 percent. Homelessness, which was almost unheard of in Europe, is becoming a serious problem in some countries, such as Germany (Geiger, 1994). Europeans blame not only their leaders but also foreign residents.

Xenophobia, an unreasonable fear or hatred of foreigners, has become a serious problem in Europe. A good example is the case of members of the U.S. luge team, who were attacked in a German bar in 1993 while training for the Olympics. From 1991 to 1993 scores of immigrants in Europe were killed in physical attacks by native Europeans (Knight, Marks, and Coleman, 1993). David Howell, a respected member of the British Parliament put the European situation in perspective,

A sense pervades that communities are falling apart, values are collapsing, institutions are crumbling, nation-states weakening. High expectations after the end of the Cold War have given way to bitter disappointments. People feel misled" (quoted in Knight, Marks, and Coleman, 1993:54).

Figure 8.4

High unemployment rates, ranging from 7 to 19 percent, present serious problems for European countries.

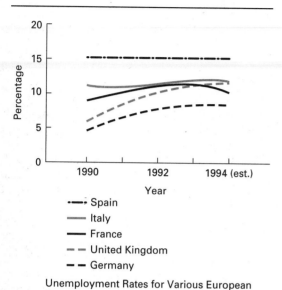

Unemployment Rates for Various European Countries, 1990, 1992, and 1994

Source: U.S. News & World Report, June 14, 1993: 54.

High unemployment in Europe has led to angry reactions to the presence of foreigners, as these neo-Nazis demonstrate in Germany.

Most Europeans cherish their relatively high wages and "cradle-to-grave" welfare systems. It appears that Europe may find it difficult to compete with Asian countries and the United States without compromising somewhat on these items. However, change is never easy. The French government, in an attempt to bring down the country's 12.2 percent unemployment rate, cut the minimum wage for unskilled workers younger than 25 years of age (Kraft, 1994). In return for this cut, employers would provide on-the-job training. The idea behind this move was to provide training for young, unskilled workers who have a very high unemployment rate. An estimated 30,000 protesters took to the streets to denounce this action and 73 police and 90 demonstrators were injured (Kraft, 1994). Britain, unlike other European countries, is creating many new jobs, but they are relatively poor paying ones (Milbank, 1994). Fifteen years of Conservative Party rule has weakened labor unions and average wages have dropped. Owners of companies are suggesting that Britain is again becoming competitive with the rest of the world but some workers are not sold on what is happening. A 44-year-old British loan officer currently working for $6.74 an hour says, "In days gone by, they never would have got away with this" and calls the pay "a nightmare" (quoted in Milbank, 1994:A1). Such anger and frustration is understandable—he used to make

$22.46 an hour in his old job, before he was laid off two years ago.

The Japanese Enterprise

When General Douglas MacArthur, leader of the allied military forces in Asia, became the head of the United States' occupation forces in Japan, he took steps to dismember the institutions held responsible for the war. The wealthiest families, who were industrial leaders, were taxed out of power (Hatcher, 1987). The wartime political leaders were forced out of office. Japan was disarmed and its military brass was left powerless. The Ministry of Home Affairs, which had been in charge of "thought control" during the war, was eliminated. But the economic bureaucracies were left largely intact because only they had the technical ability to bring Japan back from the economic graveyard. To a degree, too, they were misunderstood by the occupying American forces. One of these bureaucracies, the Ministry of Munitions, evolved into the Ministry of International Trade and Industry, known now by its acronym, MITI. Most postwar prime ministers have at some time been part of the industrial bureaucracy, often connected with MITI. "MITI sets strategic goals and directs companies in and out of selected industries and sectors. Together with other ministries, MITI has been the control tower of Japanese industry" (Hatcher, 1987:16).

The American scorn for Japanese accomplishments was deep and hard to dislodge. The U.S. auto industry continued to wallow in luxury, with high wages, a heavy burden of million-dollar executives, gross inefficiencies, and little attention to engineers with new ideas. The conviction of invulnerability was unshakable. Germany sent its little Volkswagens to the United States, but they were only a very minor problem. No one worried about Japan.

Then came the lean years for the U.S. auto industry, when Ford and General Motors both slipped in sales and Chrysler (before Lee Iacocca's herculean efforts) faced bankruptcy.

Japan had not only learned quickly from the United States and Western Europe, as was generally acknowledged, but was unexpectedly capable of production, managerial, technological, and labor innovations. Nothing illustrates the case better than the work of W. Edwards Deming, a technical expert who had served the United States admirably in pushing for high-quality war equipment during World War II. After the war, he was ignored by U.S. industry and sent by the government to Japan. The Japanese were impressed with him almost to the point of awe. Here was the man whose quality control in the production of military equipment had so much to do with their defeat, and now he was willing to discuss his ideas with them. He became the godfather of Japanese quality control and of improved production techniques. Famous throughout Japan, he was almost unknown in America. For a number of years, while innovation became synonomous with the Japanese auto industry, the overconfident U.S. auto industry stagnated. It was not until the late 1980s that the U.S. auto industry appeared to be definitely back on track, and by then much of the market had been lost. At the same time, the electronics industry and high technology in general were being challenged.

While European capitalist countries were suffering unemployment rates of 10 to 20 percent through late 1993 (Milbank, 1994:A1), Japan had almost no unemployment, although it rose to around 2.6 percent by 1993 (Butler, 1993). Japanese per capita income rivalled that of any other country, even the United States. Sales soared. While America suffered from tremendous debt of several trillion dollars, and monthly trade deficits of billions of dollars, Japan appeared to have nothing to do but count her gains. While the United States and many other countries, especially the Soviet Union, exhausted much of their national product on military spending, Japan, in agreement with treaties, spent virtually nothing.

Japanese Dilemmas

Nevertheless, wise Japanese leaders saw problems over the horizon. Naohiro Amaya, an official of MITI, even before the great oil crisis of 1973, could see problems resulting from too few industrial resources and too much dependence on heavy industry. Although Japan had no iron ore, coal, or petroleum, it had expanded strongly into steel, shipbuilding, automobiles, and trucks. Amaya worried about this as early as the 1960s. Oil was becoming the central force in all leading economies of the world, and the Arabic countries were moving into a formidable position of control. Japan would be a hostage to the Arabic nations because it imported all of its oil from them. Therefore, said Amaya, Japan must turn to high technologies that require little in the way of resources, but rely instead on the mentality and diligence of people (Halberstam, 1987:17–31).

Another problem Amaya saw was that much of Japan's advantage in the 1950s and 1960s had been in low wages, compared to those in Europe and the United States. But the Japanese labor force was becoming more skilled, more specialized, more indispensable, and better paid. Unless Japan could do better than other countries in quality and inventiveness, it might lose to industrializing countries whose labor forces were equally energetic but hungrier and willing to work for much less—Korea, Taiwan, Indonesia, or India, for example. In Japan, as in the West, the workers were becoming sufficiently well paid to be major consumers of the goods their country produced. Neither cheap labor nor cheap energy could save Japan any longer.

Amaya decided not only that industries requiring little fuel should be developed, but also that automobiles should use fuel efficiently. It was the fuel-efficient Japanese cars that struck the United States so forcefully during the oil crisis of the 1970s, and gained about 25 percent of the U.S. market for Japan. Another of his trade poli-

cies was that nothing should be done to antagonize Japan's greatest consumer, the United States. His theories about minimum fuel industries have been implemented by the rush into electronics, computers, stereos, VCRs, and microchips. Despite his warnings, though, antagonisms have developed; Japan has been accused of keeping unrealistically low prices on certain products in order to drive out the competition, and of using trade barriers against many agricultural goods. Increasingly, too, Japan—which once made cheap component parts for others—now hires cheaper labor abroad for such purposes, while training its own labor force for work at more technically sophisticated production. In this Japan is not alone; all industrial countries find some of their companies moving overseas for cheap labor. Japan is particularly successful in this attempt, as illustrated by her relations with Thailand, one of many labor-cheap countries.

Thailand and Japan

Japan has been investing huge sums of money in the economies of its Asian neighbors. Japan's investment in Thailand illustrates this trend. The rising value of the yen has given a trade disadvantage to Japanese goods produced at home, but an advantage to those produced by cheap Thai labor. Thai labor can be paid in the Thai currency (the *Baht*), which remains low in value. Japanese investments are bringing a boom to Thailand, but the Thais complain that none of their people is ever put into a managerial position, and no high technology is ever transferred to the Thais themselves. When the 100,000th Toyota pickup truck came off the line in Thailand, photographs were taken of the smiling plant manager and sales manager. Both were Japanese. In contrast, the last American executive of International Business Machines in Thailand was sent home in 1986, turning the executive jobs over to the Thais (Barber, 1987).

However, Japanese policy can change as the need changes. Fearing a loss of goodwill and investment opportunity in Thailand, Japan has supplied foreign aid to help Thai industry. Japan has also changed the nature of her operations in Thailand. Originally, Japanese foreign aid to Thailand was for the building of roads for trucks, which were imported from Japan as finished products. In the 1970s, truck parts were imported from Japan, but assembled in Thailand, giving employment to Thai workers. By the late 1980s, the trucks were being made in Thailand from parts produced in Thailand (Barber, 1987). It appears that Japan, when the need arises, can use diplomacy along with its foreign investments.

Trade Policies

In Thailand, trade policies seem to have changed in the direction of greater fairness. Years ago, Japan sometimes "dumped" goods in Thailand (sold them at less than production costs in order to undermine competition), but such policies in Thailand have been abandoned. One can still find examples of this practice, though. Australia negotiated to export beef to Japan. The agreement seemed to be very favorable to Australia, but there was a catch. The meat had to be inspected by Japanese inspectors, and there were only two such inspectors. Almost no meat could get through (Hatcher, 1987:15). Ted Holden (1992) explains how Japan's trade policies with Taiwan and Korea benefit Japanese corporations:

> Japan is putting the squeeze on Taiwan and Korea by gearing up production at low-cost manufacturing facilities in Southeast Asia. And though major Japanese companies have offered some technology to Korea and Taiwan, they have blunted the competitive challenge from these more powerful Tigers by holding back most state-of-the-art developments. At the same time, the Koreans and Taiwanese have become hooked on Japanese capital goods and industrial components, while Japan's market remains relatively closed. The result has been huge, growing trade surpluses in Japan's favor.

Americans, too, have complained about unreasonable requirements on goods that can be exported to Japan. The experience of Cochlear Corporation, a Denver-based firm that produces inner-ear implants, illustrates the problems foreign companies have in attempting to market their products in Japan. Cochlear is a very successful firm that has 70 percent of the world market (*National Journal,* 1993). Even though the company's product has been approved by the stringent standards of the U.S. Food and Drug Administration, the Japanese government's requirements and tests are keeping this product out of the country for a very long time. Clinical trials in Japan have been known to last more than seven years (*National Journal,* 1993).

Nearly all knowledgeable observers agree that a major key to Japan's success is governmental aid to exporting industries. In the United States, the government almost seems to create barriers to export. For example, when a U.S. industrial instruments corporation received an unsolicited order from England, its manager decided to enter foreign trade for the first time. He called the Department of Commerce office in San Francisco to ask about permits and how to proceed. The first office referred him to a second office. The second office referred him to a third. Then he was referred to a fourth, a fifth, and a sixth. The sixth office told him to call Washington, D.C., which he did. The Washington office referred him to yet another office. Finally, office number eight sent him the necessary papers, just as he was resolving, "Never again" (Eckhouse, 1988). Had he been in Japan, he would have been encouraged from his first phone call, supplied with an interpreter if he needed one, given special tax credits for helping with Japan's "Export or Die" campaign, and been regarded as a hero.

Problems for Japan

Not all goes smoothly for Japan. Its people complain of such high prices for land that they are no better off for housing than they were when the country was poor. For example, a 42-year-old graduate of Tokyo University earns $4,200 per month as a parts buyer for a manufacturer of construction machinery but can afford only a corrugated iron house no larger than a one-car garage (Jameson, 1992). The house has no indoor bath or shower and the kitchen is no bigger than a tiny walk-in closet.

Japan has been stagnating economically (Williams and Schlesinger, 1993), and has seen its stock market plummet (Hardy, 1994) and the value of its currency rise considerably (Williams, Forman, and Schlesinger, 1994; Sesit, 1994), which makes its products less competitive on the global market. Numerous factors explain Japan's current woes, including political scandals, the recent defeat of Prime Minister Hosokawa's political-reform package, and the new competitiveness of foreign companies, including American firms. Michael Williams and Jacob Schlesinger (1993) report that many Japanese are extremely pessimistic about their future. They report that Japanese books like *The Great Depressions Survival Guide* and *Gold Will Save Japan* have sold 120,000 and 30,000 copies, respectively.

Telecommunications has been the area in which Japanese companies have had the most trouble competing; in particular, interactive telecommunications (the consumer can interact and respond to the medium). Matt Miller's (1994) analysis of the latest technology in high-definition television (HDTV) illustrates the problems the Japanese are having in the area of telecommunications. Although Japanese HDTV is already on line—it debuted in late 1990—it relies on analog broadcasting while the HDTV being developed in the United States and Europe is based on digital technology. Although Japanese HDTVs are characterized by much clearer picture resolution than normal television sets, they are not selling very well in Japan. That is because they are very expensive ($6,000) and not very interactive. Furthermore, HDTV broadcasts only eight hours a day in Japan and the programs are, for the most part, the same as on regular TV.

That is not what HDTV from the United States and Europe will be like. European and United States HDTV will be extremely interactive and varied, relying on the "information highway" already being laid in the United States and Europe. According to Miller (1994), experts predict that as soon as the digital HDTV systems being developed in the United States and Europe come on line, the Japanese analog HDTV will become obsolete.

What accounts for Japan's problems in interactive communication? According to Miller (1994), three factors come into play: (1) Bureaucratic controls and turf battles. For example, cable television hardly exists in Japan, due to quibbling among overlapping bureaucracies; (2) Lack of software expertise. The Japanese have been much more successful with hardware than with software, and the latter is vital for interactive communication; and (3) Industrial policy. Traditionally, Japanese businesses and bureaucrats work together to devise ways to deal with critical technologies. However, once committed, they are very reluctant to shift technologies, even though better ones are shown to exist.

American writers Francis McInerney and Sean White (1993) agree with Miller about Japanese bureaucratic rigidity and inflexibility. They (McInerney and White, 1993:18) also suggest that "Japan's greatest successes and greatest failures are with its customers. Japanese companies that have best integrated customers into all aspects of design, production, and service have excelled. Those that have disregarded customers to pursue internal agendas have failed, often abysmally." McInerney and White (1993) continue by saying that foreign companies can beat the Japanese by recognizing four fatal flaws common to many Japanese firms and by taking advantage of this by treating the "customer" differently. The four "fatal flaws" (McInerney and White, 1993:18–19) are:

(1) Japanese are too vertically and horizontally integrated to respond quickly to changing customer needs; (2) They are too

centrally managed and bureaucratic to communicate effectively with overseas customers; (3) Their decision makers have little or no direct contact with overseas customers; and (4) The Japanese prefer to sell what they value most about themselves, usually their technology, rather than find solutions to their customer's problems.

Japan has worries about the future as Europe and the United States take its competition more seriously and try harder to meet it. There are also a number of newly industrialized Asian competitors, as compulsive about exports as Japan itself. Finally, Japan's neighbor, China, is growing at a rapid pace in the international market. But serious competition from China lies in the future. For the present, Japan's major concern is Korea.

FOUR TIGERS AND A DRAGON

Although the term *Newly Industrialized Country* (*NIC*) has been applied to several other countries, none has entered the age of industrialism (or possibly even postindustrialism) with such energy and drive as the semiperipheral countries referred to as "The Four Tigers": Korea, Taiwan, Singapore, and Hong Kong. Of the four countries, the largest and the one most feared by Japan is Korea.

Korea

Although a newly industrialized country, Korea is by no means a new country. Historical records of Korea go back to 1100 B.C., and legend goes back even further. At times in its history, Korea has made great achievements in art, literature, and science. It is not generally known, but movable type was used for printing in Korea before it was invented in Europe. Korea was also the first country to use armor-plated ships, which helped beat off an attempted Japanese invasion in 1592. Although maintaining its independence, Korea came to fear the outside world

and closed its ports to foreign trade for nearly 300 years, during which it became known as the *Hermit kingdom.* Like Japan, Korea was forced to open its doors to trade in the second half of the nineteenth century. Unlike Japan, it failed to move rapidly into modern industry and weaponry. In 1910 Japan succeeded in what it had failed to do three centuries earlier and conquered Korea.

Japan controlled Korea until 1945, when Japan was defeated in World War II. After the war, Korea was divided into two countries, with Soviet Communist troops occupying North Korea and U.S. troops occupying South Korea. Separate Korean governments were formed for the two countries. The United States, Russia, Britain, and the two Korean governments attempted for two years to develop a plan for reuniting Korea. The reunification did not occur, and the United States turned over the problem to the United Nations (UN) in 1947. The UN wanted supervised elections in Korea to choose one government for all of Korea. However, the Russians did not allow UN representatives into the North. In 1948 the UN supervised an election of representatives in the South. The representatives drew up a constitution and elected Syngman Phee president of South Korea. During the same year, the Communists announced the formation of the Democratic People's Republic of Korea in the North. Both the North and South Korean governments claimed to represent all of Korea.

At the end of 1948, Russia pulled all its troops out of North Korea and by mid 1949, the United States pulled its troops out of South Korea. North Korean troops invaded the South in June of 1950 and the Korean War was on. Soldiers from China assisted the North Korean troops and Russia provided much of the military equipment. The UN convinced 16 countries to send troops to help South Korea and 41 countries to send military equipment and other supplies. The United States supplied more than 90 percent of the troops and equipment. The war waged for three years but neither side prevailed. A truce was signed in July of 1953 but a permanent peace treaty has never been signed.

South Korea has had long periods of military rule, postponed elections, a bridled press, and considerable protest from students and labor throughout the latter half of this century. In 1993 Kim Young Sam was the first elected civilian president since 1961. Now, industry is heavily concentrated in a few giant companies.

Certain points in this brief history are important in understanding Korea. Korea is a literate country with high respect for learning and great pride in its national traditions, and lingering resentment against Japan. Divided from North Korea, South Korea has become a very populous and crowded country (43 million people squeezed into an area about the size of Indiana). Obviously, its only escape from dire poverty is to produce for the export market, which it does with zeal.

The giant corporations now driving the Korean economy are among "the most efficient economic machines the world has ever known" (Overholt, quoted in Powell et al, 1988). The drive of the Korean people is intense. At Hyundai Motors for example, management and workers enjoy referring to the Japanese as "the lazy Asians." One of the plant managers who works ten hours per day six days per week comes home exhausted, but he congratulates himself on having an easy way of life compared with his parents back on the farm (Halberstam, 1987:724).

Unlike the Japanese, who had to take several years to make their cars acceptable to the American and European markets, the Korean cars appeared suddenly, in acceptable form, and at prices neither America nor Japan could match. Korean cars immediately made a large dent in the market, especially in Canada. The Japanese, who had long looked upon Korea with contempt, could hardly believe they had a new challenger.

Like other peoples beginning to sample prosperity, the Koreans are agitating for better wages, and wages are going up. Like other countries in the competition, they are looking to innovation and quality to give them a competitive edge. Also, as in other countries facing rising wages, Korean companies are opening plants in peripheral countries where wages are lower than in their own country: India, Indonesia, Malaysia, the Philippines, and Mexico (Butler and Lawrence, 1993).

Taiwan

The second of the Four Tigers, Taiwan, is an island with an area only about the size of West Virginia, and a population of 20 million people. Like Korea, Taiwan was long ruled by Japan, having been wrested from China in 1895. In those days, Taiwan was known as Formosa. At the end of World War II, Taiwan received its independence, but events on the Chinese mainland disrupted what might otherwise have been a rather quiet island. The nationalists of China were defeated by Mao Zedong's Communist forces and retreated in large numbers to Taiwan. There the Chinese nationalists took control, under the command of Chiang Kai-shek, head of the Chinese Nationalist Party. After his death, his son, Chiang Ching-kuo, became ruler. Although the majority of Taiwanese (with the exception of about 2 percent of the original inhabitants) are Chinese by culture and language, those who were there long before Chiang Kai-shek's time regard the Chinese nationalists who took control as outsiders.

Despite the fairly dictatorial government of Taiwan, it was long regarded by the United States as the legitimate government of all of China. Favors in the form of military and economic aid were showered upon the little country and, for the Taiwanese, it paid off as foreign aid seldom does. Like Korea, Taiwan has seen a spectacular gain in production, trade, and prosperity. By 1992, it was showing trade surpluses of around $9 billion, and per capita income had risen to nearly $9,000—over 100 percent higher than it was in 1987 (*World Almanac,* 1994:814).

Chiang Ching-kuo was a practical ruler, more interested in the national bank account than in plotting war against the People's Republic of China, as his father had wished to do. Despite previous animosity, the People's Republic of

China sent condolences on his death in 1988, apparently seeking a rapprochement. Chiang was succeeded to power by Lee Teng-hui, a native Taiwanese. For the first time since World War II, no member of the old Nationalist Party of China heads the government. If Taiwan and China are linked as a semiautonomous state, China could have one of the Tigers to help its economic thrust into the world.

Singapore

Much smaller than Taiwan is Singapore, an island at the tip of the Malaysian Peninsula. Long part of the British Empire, Singapore was considered crucial as the guardian of the Strait of Malacca, between Malaya and Indonesia. Its location is still strategic for trade, because it sits astride the shortest sea route from China and Japan to India. Singapore is a major trade center with the world's largest container port, is the world's third largest oil refining center, and is a key exporter of disk drives (Naisbitt, 1994:252). In many ways, this tiny country is the most successful of the Four Tigers. The only Asian country with a higher standard of living than Singapore is Japan. The average annual per capita income of Singapore is $15,000 (Naisbitt, 1994:254). Although too small (224 square miles) to be a major competitor in the postindustrial world, Singapore is a good illustration of certain characteristics of that world: vast size and huge industrial resources seem to have been almost irrelevant in bringing prosperity to a well-educated people, with long experience in trade.

Hong Kong

Like Singapore, Hong Kong is mainly one city and its surrounding district. At present it is linked to Great Britain, but it is scheduled to be returned to China in July 1997. Hong Kong is a tremendous trade and financial center, despite its small size. Like the other three Tigers, Hong Kong maintains a trade balance greatly in its favor. Hong Kong's greatest importance is that it is becoming an increasingly major financial and trade center for China, especially since China appears to be moving away from rigid communism and drastically away from isolation (Naisbitt, 1994:218–219).

The government in Beijing promises to respect the present economic concerns of Hong Kong, apparently expecting Hong Kong to be a stimulus to the industrial and trade development of the Chinese mainland. Upon Hong Kong's separation from Great Britain, a new constitution will go into effect. In this document, China proposes that, for the next 50 years, Hong Kong "shall not practice the socialist system and policies, and will maintain the current capitalist system and life-style" (Gargan, 1988). If current trading patterns between Hong Kong and China are any indication of what the future holds, it appears these two entities will be very intertwined. As John Naisbitt (1994:218) asserts,

> When China opened its doors in 1978, Hong Kong was the first to walk through. Today, some 25,000 enterprises in Guangdong produce goods for Hong Kong companies. Combined, these businesses employ 4 million workers, which is four times the size of Hong Kong's manufacturing work force. Estimates are that as much as 20 percent of Hong Kong's currency circulation occurs in Guangdong. Success breeds success and Hong Kong businesses have begun to work in Shanghai, Bejiing, and many other Chinese cities. Mainland China also has surpassed the United States as the colony's largest trading partner. The reverse also is true. China's investments in the colony now surpass Japan's investments as well.

China: The Once and Future Dragon

The history of China goes back thousands of years, including a succession of dynasties that ruled the land until 1912, when China became a republic under the leadership of Dr. Sun Yat-sen. The struggling new republic faced numerous disasters. Japan invaded in a long and devastating war, which was followed by the eventual triumph of Mao Ze-dong's forces over what had changed from a republic to the rule of strong-man Chiang Kai-shek.

Mao Ze-dong was a genius at revolution, holding his forces together under impossible conditions and gaining strength and followers all the while. As ruler of China, however, he appeared to be a man so obsessed with revolution that the country was in constant turmoil. Policy shifts were frequent and extreme, and hundreds of thousands of people were executed. To his credit, he forced the unity of China, stopped its long period of civil wars, stopped its opium addiction, and developed a commune system that gave the peasants access to land. Above all, the people were fed, and intense and largely successful efforts were made to educate them and to promote good health.

The industries of Manchuria, built up during the long Japanese occupation of that province, were eventually revived (they had been devastated during World War II) and production began to rise slowly and hesitantly, encumbered by shifting policies in Beijing. After Mao's death in 1976, a struggle for leadership took place, but reforms in the early 1980s initiated a rapid increase in the rate of China's agricultural, industrial, and technical progress. The aged, but energetic and pragmatic, Zhao Ziyang became the General Secretary of the Communist Party. He and senior statesman Deng Xiaoping relaxed the economic grip of the government by allowing more local planning, and Zhao advocated more regulation of the economy by the market. Regulation by the market means allowing supply and demand to determine what will be produced and at what price. In this, he was obviously making a considerable compromise with capitalist principles. This compromise with capitalism has continued under the leadership of Premier Li Ping, who took over in April 1989.

At present, China is entering the world market on a vast scale. In 1992 China's exports exceeded its imports by $4.2 billion (*World Almanac,* 1993:752). As John Naisbitt (1994:179) has stated, one of the paradoxes of the 1990s is that the last great Communist country in the world is becoming the world's biggest market economy. He points out that if China maintains its current economic momentum, it will be the world's largest economy by the year 2000. It is already the world's third largest economy, behind the United States and Japan. Entrepreneurs have been given free rein in China and foreign companies are being encouraged to set up shop there. Incredible amounts of foreign currency are finding their way to China and the main business appears to be that—business (Naisbitt, 1994:180–225). Naisbitt (1994:183) states that "The entrepreneurs pretend they are doing it for the greater good; the Party pretends the country is still Communist." Naisbitt's (1994:179) comments regarding a trip he took to China put this country's development into perspective:

> I have never seen anything like it in my life. One hundred miles of uninterrupted construction. On an early morning in September of 1993 I arranged for a car and driver to take me from the Garden Hotel in Quangzhou (we used to call it Canton) to the railroad station in Shenzhen on the border of the New Territories of Hong Kong. Along this 160-kilometer corridor thousands of small and medium-sized factories, warehouses, and residential buildings are in various stages of construction, all being created by entrepreneurs. Because the traffic is so heavy (mostly trucks), the trip took more than four hours. Four hours of witnessing the largest construction project in the world.

We cannot forecast the future, but we do know that a determined nation, rising rapidly in educational level and in awareness of need, will likely become a major actor in the drama of international competition. It is our regard for China's history and our expectation of China's eventual success that has caused us to speak of the "once and future dragon."

THEORETICAL RAMIFICATIONS

It was argued previously in this chapter that world system theory provides one of the more useful perspectives on global competition. How can one use this perspective to understand the trends described here?

The work of sociologist Alan B. Simmons (1992) on the globalization of trade illustrates how world system theory explains global competition. According to Simmons, the globalization of trade that has mushroomed in the 1980s and early 1990s involves a number of key trends. First, production of goods is global, with parts manufactured in certain areas of the world and assembled in other places. Second, consumer markets have become globalized—goods are put together in one country and sold in many others. Third, globalization of trade involves the spread of "structural adjustment" programs which favor export-oriented development. That is, development may not result in products and services needed by the people in LDCs but in items needed by MDCs in their manufacturing enterprises. The fourth trend accompanying globalization of trade is the development of international trading blocs.

Simmons (1992) suggests that this globalization of trade is not accidental but deliberately planned by the developed, or core, countries. He also argues that one of the major effects of this globalization of trade is a pronounced differentiation between the "losers" and "winners" in economic development. The clear losers have been the peripheral countries, especially those on the African continent. The clear winners are the core countries such as the United States, Japan, and Germany. Other winners are some of the semiperipheral countries like South Korea, Hong Kong, Taiwan, Singapore, Malaysia, and Thailand. Simmons suggests that these semiperipheral countries have attracted investment and have been successful at exporting because they have reasonable political stability, progressive education polices, and relatively low wages. He also mentions that Mexico benefits from the globalization of trade due to its location next to the United States, its large labor force, and its industrial infrastructure.

The People's Republic of China is experiencing a building boom along the Pacific coast. In Shanghai, construction of several buildings overshadows young shoppers reviewing an old woman's produce for sale.

World system theory is also useful in explaining the rise and decline of core nations (such as the United States) on the world scene. World system incorporates two long-term factors: Periods of prosperity are followed by periods of economic stagnation; and there is a cycle of rise and decline in which core nations dominate the world system. According to Terry Boswell and Albert Bergeson (1987), America's economic problems can be explained by the fact that the above two cycles are intersecting—that is, the world economy is on a downswing and the United States is losing its dominant position to Japan and various other countries at the same time.

There is a weakness to the world system theory—its inability to see that the same kind of stratification, division of labor, and unequal distribution of wealth that exists among core, semiperipheral, and peripheral countries exists within all societies. We see in the next chapter that, just as the distribution of wealth among countries is widening instead of narrowing, so is the distribution of wealth within many countries. This is resulting in dire situations for a vast proportion of the planet's inhabitants.

SUMMARY

The world is experiencing a tremendous transformation. For thousands of years, humanity was organized in preindustrial configurations. The vast majority of peoples were hunters-gatherers and, later, farmers. With the Industrial Revolution, the majority of humans were employed in non-agricultural occupations—from mining coal to making automobiles.

The postindustrial age is based on knowledge and information, more than raw resources. The global economy is undergoing a tremendous transformation in which information and the handling of information constitute the key components of success. John Naisbitt (1994) argues that with the advent of microcomputers, the reduced cost of software, and relatively easy access to data files, the small, flexible, companies will be successful, and the large, multilayered bureaucratic companies will fail. He also foresees a proliferation of hundreds of new countries (like the recent addition of scores of new countries from the old Soviet Union and Eastern Europe) in the not too distant future. Countries with the greatest number of flexible, fast-changing corporations will be the most successful. National boundaries will be less and less important as information is increasingly set free from physical boundaries.

Though the nation-state may be becoming less important, it is still an important concept tied to material well-being and global competitiveness. World system theory suggests that the competitiveness of nations is related to their places in the pecking order of nations. The core countries, which tend to be developed and postindustrial, benefit from the underdeveloped nature of the semiperipheral and peripheral nations, and try to keep these countries from becoming developed. Multinational corporations, which tend to be based in core countries, are especially adept at taking advantage of low-wage labor in peripheral nations and dodging strict environmental laws.

Most African countries fall into the category of peripheral nation. Many Latin American countries are also peripheral but a significant number are moving into semiperipheral nation status. Also, many Asian countries such as South Korea, Taiwan, Singapore, Hong Kong, and China are semiperipheral nations but are rapidly developing into major competitive "players" on the world scene.

Though the core countries such as Japan, the United States, Canada, and European countries have huge competitive advantages over the semiperipheral and peripheral countries, they have witnessed incredible changes in their occupational and social class structures, which have produced serious problems for many individuals in these countries. In many of these countries, the transition to postindustrialism has resulted in the disappearance of well-paying unionized jobs requiring minimal education. The occupational structure in some developed countries, like the United States, is becoming bifurcated with a small, well-educated, highly paid class of professionals and a large growing class of less educated, poorly paid workers. The once heralded middle class is shrinking.

KEY TERMS

Free capitalism Economies characterized by limited government control or direction.

Ideal type A type that is definable and that is approached in the real world, but never completely realized.

Industrial societies Societies characterized by heavy industry powered by nonhuman labor.

Postindustrial societies Societies with declining percentages of activity in heavy industry and increasing percentages of activity in high technology, management, and services.

Preindustrial societies The term applied to the entire world before a series of inventions that replaced human and animal power with mechanical power and ushered in an age of factories and mass production. Applies to contemporary societies that still rely on human and animal power.

Primary industry Activity involving gathering or extracting raw materials.

Secondary industry Manufacturing.

Status panic The efforts of members of the middle class to maintain status in a world of rapidly changing requirements.

Tertiary industry Services.

Xenophobia An unreasonable fear or hatred of foreigners.

STUDY QUESTIONS

1. What are the differences between preindustrial, industrial, and postindustrial societies?

2. What is "status panic" and how is it related to the transition to postindustrialism?

3. Briefly summarize the perspective of world system theory on the competition among contemporary nations.

4. What barriers do the world's less developed countries face as they attempt to compete in the world marketplace?

5. Discuss the Communist route to industrialism. What problems were encountered under this system and what does the future hold for Communist nations, with regard to global competition?

6. Briefly discuss the problems faced by the United States in worldwide competition. How has the United States responded to these problems?

7. What kind of problems have been created in occupational and social class structures as a result of the transition to postindustrialism?

8. Discuss the "Japanese Enterprise" with regard to global competition. What problems are being faced by Japan today, with regard to global competition? How is Japan responding?

9. Discuss the recent advances of the "Four Tigers and a Dragon" on the world competition scene.

10. Imagine yourself as the ruler of the world. What policies would you institute to help the less developed countries of the world become more competitive?

ABUNDANCE
AND POVERTY

ittle José Gomez, a 6-year-old Mexican boy offers to clean the windshield of Diego Martinez's new Mercedes Benz as Diego waits in line to cross the border from Tijuana to San Diego. José lives with his family in a Tijuana shack built of used plywood. There is no indoor plumbing and insufficient room for José, his three brothers, two sisters, and parents. José would rather be playing baseball or soccer than cleaning windshields, but the $.20 he earns per windshield is needed to help put tortillas and beans on his family's table. José's father finds occasional work as a laborer, pulling weeds for wealthy San Diego homeowners. His mother sells trinkets to tourists in Tijuana.

Diego, who is 25 years old, lives with his extended family in an exclusive part of Tijuana. One would never guess the luxury that resides behind the walls of Diego's home. Like most expensive homes in Latin America, the exterior of Diego's home belies the wealth inside. Diego's house has everything that the most expensive house in San Diego has—an indoor swimming pool and spa, a sauna, a handball court, a tennis court, and the best furniture and art available. Diego is fortunate to belong to one of the elite families of Mexico who became extremely wealthy during the boom years of the 1970s. His family is worth $20 million and has invested in real estate in Tijuana and San Diego and in numerous retail stores in Tijuana. When Diego looks out his bedroom window, he see the shanties perched on the hillsides, awaiting the winter rains that are sure to wash many of them away.

The different fortunes of José and Diego reflect the tremendous disparity among people in the less developed countries. This enormous gap between abundance and poverty exists within nations, as in the case of José and Diego. The gap exists between nations as well, and represents one of the major problems of the world. Within nations, wide and widely recognized gaps between wealth and poverty foster bitterness, dependency, and alienation in the poorer population, and increase the crime rate. Research by Edward Muller (1988) shows a strong inverse relationship between income inequality and political stability—that is, as income inequality in a country becomes more extreme, the government is likely to break down. In fact, Muller found that the negative relationship between income inequality and political stability exists no matter how developed a country is—it applies to the most developed as well as the least developed countries. There is also evidence (Wilkinson, 1992) that the degree of income inequality within societies is strongly associated, in a positive direction, with national mortality rates.

On an international scale, the great and widening difference between wealthy nations and impoverished countries creates a host of problems. Workers in the poorer nations can only find work with foreign companies that have relocated there to take advantage of the cheap labor. They work for daily pay that is less than even the hourly pay in the United States and Western Europe. This breeds resentment on both sides: Workers in the poorer nations feel exploited by Western capitalism, and workers in the richer nations feel they have been robbed of valuable jobs. Conditions of poverty and animosity toward the wealthy play into the hands of revolutionary leaders, as in the case of the French Revolution. King Louis XVI, Queen Marie Antoinette, and thousands of French aristocrats lost their heads to the guillotine in this bloody revolution. Additionally, most poor nations accumulate debts that are virtually impossible to pay. They become dependent on richer nations that offer aid partly for humanitarian reasons, but also as insurance against revolution or against the possibility of the dependent nation's choosing the "wrong" side in international struggles.

The world, of course, is not neatly divided between countries (or regions) in which everyone is rich and others in which everyone is poor and miserable. One need only recall disclosures about the fabulous wealth and luxurious living of Ferdinand and Ismelda Marcos when they fled the impoverished Philippines—a country they had helped to impoverish. Poor countries usually have at least a few holders of great wealth who identify ideologically with, and work closely with, various multinational corporations. The leading industrialized nations have far more wealthy people, but they also have their poor. Nevertheless, there are parts of the world that by any historical standard can well be designated as highly affluent. Our first analysis will be of such countries. Next we turn to the problems of poverty and threatened poverty within those affluent countries. After that, attention will turn to LDCs of deep poverty and malnutrition and to questions as to how their populations are to be fed. A glance at Figure 9.1 will make clear the enormous contrast between rich nations and poor nations in per capita income. The average annual per capita income of more developed countries ($15,420) is more than 17 times greater than the per capita income of less developed countries ($870).

Although numerous perspectives explain the inequality both within and between nations, it is our opinion that the conflict perspective is best suited for this task. The world system perspective, which is a type of conflict view, is especially useful in explaining income inequality among nations.

It is important to note that inequality by itself is not a problem. As long as humans possess different levels of talent and different orientations and commitments toward work, humans will also have different incomes and degrees of

Tremendous disparity exists between wealthy and poor countries. The photograph above is of a Nobel Prize banquet at Stockholm's City Hall, where a multicourse meal is being served. The photograph below is of starving, emaciated men in Ayod, South Sudan.

wealth. A problem exists when inequality results in poverty or a perpetuation of vastly different chances of success among different groups of people. People are born into the world with vastly different life chances. The country one is born into is the first factor that affects one's opportunities in life. A child born in Nigeria or Bangladesh does not have the same opportunities as a child born in Japan or the United States. On average, people live in dire poverty in the first set of countries and relative abundance in the second set. However, being born in Japan or the United States does not assure freedom from poverty. Pockets of extreme poverty exist in these two countries, and the probability of being poor is associated with various factors, such as race. Inequality becomes problematic when one nation's fortune results in another nation's misfortune, or when one person's fortune results in another person's misfortune.

PEOPLE OF PLENTY IN THE MDCs

The Super Rich

History books tend to dwell on periods of war and upheaval, but occasionally they draw pictures of "golden ages" when everything seemed to go well. There was a Golden Age of Greece in the days of Pericles, and Gibbon started his monumental history of Rome with the Golden Age of the Antonines, characterized by constantly expanding trade, order within, and peace abroad. Such pictures leave out many conditions we would now regard as social problems—slavery, poverty, and draconian systems of justice (severe code of laws), for example. Nevertheless, those were periods when the average citizen might well have dreamed of ever increasing well-being, expecting his or her children and grandchildren to see more of the good things of life than he had known—a viewpoint similar to what United States citizens call "the American Dream."

"The American Dream" is a hypothetical condition of steady jobs, home ownership, education for the children, and an expectation that abundance will continue to increase. This idea originated in the United States but expresses the expectations of Canadians, Australians, and Europeans as well. Belief in the American dream has persisted in spite of such episodes as the Great Depression and occasional wars. In the post–World War II period, the dream of rising prosperity became more widespread than ever. France and Italy experienced a growth of industry such as they had never known. Germany rebuilt quickly, and production, sales, and income soared. Along with Sweden and France, it had to import workers from Turkey and North Africa to keep up with the strong demands for labor; similarly, the United States took a tolerant view of a stream of immigrant laborers from Mexico.

Japanese trade and industry grew even more rapidly than did trade and industry in the West. The Scandinavian countries, long accustomed to

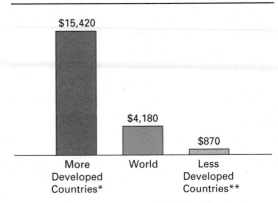

Figure 9.1
Per capita income in the more developed countries is more than 17 times greater than the per capita income in the less developed countries.

Income Contrasts, 1991 U.S. Dollars Per Capita

* All of Europe and North America, Australia, Japan, New Zealand, and the republics of the former USSR.

** All countries not included in More Developed category.

Source: Haub and Yanagishita, *1993 World Population Data Sheet* (Washington, DC: Population Reference Bureau, 1993).

comfortable living standards, continued to increase their production and their wealth. The former Soviet Union repaired the incredible devastation it had suffered in World War II. Although unable to match the prosperity of the West, the Soviet Union was able to clothe and feed its people in a minimal way and also provided basic education and health care. Bureaucratic inefficiency, so endemic to the former Soviet Union, continues to plague Russia and other republics of the former USSR, as do housing shortages and long waiting lines in front of stores. A recent analysis of the situation by a Russian scholar, Alexander Samorodov (1992), is unsettling because families are forced to allocate higher proportions of their incomes for food and because there are shortages of certain foodstuffs.

In Western Europe, Japan, and the United States, there are upper classes living far beyond the American dream. Their present standards of comfort and luxury would boggle the minds even of the titled aristocracies of earlier times. They jet from continent to continent both for business and recreation, often boasting homes and offices in several countries. They relax on the Riviera, yacht through the Caribbean, and buy up the diamonds of South Africa. Most such people are Americans or Europeans, but they are joined by increasing numbers of Japanese, Australians, South Africans, Asian Indians, and others. Among the more recent additions to the world of very great wealth and power are people from the Middle East whose fantastic fortunes were built originally from the ownership of oil, but in some cases augmented by intermediary roles—some legitimate but others not—in the sales of aircraft, guns, and missiles.

The extremely wealthy people of the world are now overwhelmingly of a business and industrial class. They are joined in some cases by traditional landowning classes, descendants of aristocrats, or by such recently enriched aristocracies as the House of Sa'ud in Arabia. More typical, though, are the rich families of the United States such as the Rockefellers, DuPonts, Mellons, and Tafts. These families never had titles but they have held great wealth for a long time and constitute an old upper class. The late C. Wright Mills (1958) researched the very rich of his time and concluded they were becoming a self-perpetuating class, as well as a class of people with growing influence in government and in all aspects of modern society. Moreover, the very rich wield this power over other classes without mixing with them. Their powerful companies and institutions (banking, insurance, etc.) back sympathetic politicians and lobby aggressively for legislation that is helpful to their interests. More recent sociological studies have generally born out Mills's point of view (Braun, 1991; Domhoff, 1970; Inhaber and Carroll, 1992; and Moore, 1979). Nevertheless, a very small number of people sometimes enter the level of the super rich. New industries (such as computers and software), resources, markets, and sometimes new craftiness lift new people to the highest levels of affluence.

However, the vast majority of people who make it to the highest levels of affluence began their ascent at already comfortable levels.

When we speak of the extremely rich, we are speaking of classes that have always existed to some degree. Their wealth is far greater than in the past, but perhaps relative to the rest of society it remains the same. The lord of a medieval castle, though his castle might have been uncomfortable by our standards, was undoubtedly looked up to with the same awe as people view the super rich of today. There were no television soap operas to picture their life-style but myths arose about them, troubadours sang about them, and everyone envied them.

The Upper-Middle Class

We will not go into detailed study of social classes here, but we must point out a few facts about social class that are important to our discussion of affluence and poverty. In the first place, in addition to the very rich, there are large numbers of people who, by the standards of earlier times, are also rich—people who own good homes, drive cars, go skiing in the winter and sailing in the summer, take trips overseas, deposit money to IRA accounts, watch their stocks grow, and live in "better" neighborhoods so that their children can enter the best schools. They live on a level of abundance that would be environmentally impossible for all the earth's 5.5 billion inhabitants. They are the **upper-middle class**. Their style of life and their incomes differ somewhat from country to country. In Scandinavia, they have to pay higher taxes than in the United States, for example, but they live very well and may have a greater feeling of security than their class equals elsewhere.

The upper-middle class people of whom we are speaking are business and professional people— scientists, technicians, managers, and the like, and are nearly always college educated. Their occupations and status relative to others tend to be similar in all industrial countries. In general, they have risen to their present positions through hard work, but often family background has had a lot to do with getting them started. Some studies have suggested that educational systems work in the direction of social-class stability, making sure that younger generations maintain the positions held by their parents. This has been an especially prevalent view among French sociologists. A study of France by Robinson and Garnier (1985) concludes that social-class perpetuation through education has been somewhat overstated. Although they acknowledge that educational opportunities are greatest for sons and daughters of people already holding upper-middle-class status, they found that some studies underestimated the great importance of business ownership. Robinson and Garnier argue that the passage of businesses down to family members is an even stronger source of social-class perpetuation than is educational advantage.

Other studies demonstrate great similarity among industrial countries in the pattern of social-class mobility and stability. Erikson, Goldthorpe, and Portocarero (1982) found great similarities in the countries they studied—England, the United States, France, and Sweden. In all countries, the greatest father-to-son continuity in job and in status was in farming, but there was also considerable continuity in well-paying, upper-middle-class positions. There was more fluidity in working class and lower-middle class, with at least a small upward movement for many of the latter.

Recent research in the city of Tianjin, in the People's Republic of China by Nan Lin and Yanjie Bian (1991), also shows the importance of family connections in predicting occupational success. For males, the employment status of their fathers was found to be a good predictor of how well the sons do occupationally. Family connections were found to be less useful for females; educational attainment was found to directly affect their status attainment.

In the former Soviet Union, fewer studies have been conducted on social class. Soviet insistence on a "classless" society was so great in the time of Joseph Stalin that sociology was ignored. Because sociology does more studies of social class than most other social or behavioral sciences, in the Stalinist view it was useless, except possibly for the capitalist societies. In more recent years, there have been sociological studies in the once Soviet-dominated world, especially in Poland (Vaughn, 1982). The Marxist viewpoint has been that social class is an unnecessary evil; but the arguments of some of the sociologists of the former Soviet world was that social class is an evil only if rooted in the ownership of the means of production—railroads, mines, factories, and so forth. It is possible now for sociologists from the former Communist bloc to acknowledge the existence of a reasonably affluent category of people, generally college educated and making important contributions in sciences, the arts, management and political leadership. In fact, with the former Communist bloc countries now experimenting with free enterprise, no one, including officials and scholars, has to pretend that social class distinctions do not exist.

It may seem strange that even intellectual people in the old Communist bloc failed to see the obvious fact that people who were well educated and in good positions would likely pass along their advantages to their children, even in the supposedly egalitarian Soviet Union. However, such thinking has its counterpart in the United States. To poor people, it seems obvious that the wealthy have more influence on government than do the poor. Yet, a study of attitudes by Joan Rytina and her colleagues (1970) found that well-to-do people think that opportunities are exactly even. The replies to one specific question are particularly interesting: "If one boy's father is president of the plant and another boy's father is a janitor there, will the two boys have an equal chance to become president of the plant some day?" The majority of wealthy, white people replied, "Yes, they'd have an exactly even chance." Poorer people, especially African Americans, did not agree. It is rather interesting that there should be this coincidence of perception among Communist theorists and wealthy, white U.S. citizens on the idea that the head start provided by an affluent home makes little or no difference. One's position obviously influences his or her thinking.

Viewpoints about social class notwithstanding, the fact is that in all industrial societies an upper-middle class comes into existence, needed for positions of management and technological and scientific advance. In all cases, there is a certain amount of upward mobility into the upper-middle class, but also a large amount of self-perpetuation. The upper-middle class lives with a fair degree of abundance in virtually all industrial societies.

It should be noted, however, that individuals in this privileged social class are encountering occupational problems and uncertainties that did not exist a few years ago. As noted in Chapter 8 (Global Competition), the economic and occupational structure of MDCs is undergoing a tremendous transformation, resulting in a much smaller number of full-time, secure positions in upper levels of management, finance, and business. David Hage and his associates (1993) discuss how this phenomenon has wreaked havoc on the lives of U.S. citizens who had impeccable degrees and credentials and spotless work records.

The Lower-Middle Class

A **lower-middle class** is also found in all industrial societies, made up of more poorly paid professionals, sales people, secretaries, and many types of service workers. Just where one draws the line between upper-middle and lower-middle class is difficult to know, partly because the two classes blend into each other gradually and partly because occupations differ in pay and status in different societies. In the United States, for example, elementary school teachers are poorly paid compared with other professionals and, on an income basis, might be called lower-middle class. In Japan, their pay and status are relatively higher, identifying them with the upper-middle class. In the old Soviet Union, more women than men were physicians. Their pay, however, was relatively low. On the basis of

Lower-middle class occupations, like check-out clerk, do not require significant amounts of education and do not pay so well as upper-middle class occupations do.

education and occupational authority, they would definitely be in the upper-middle class, but probably not on the basis of income.

When we reach the lower-middle class, we are speaking of a class that is not particularly affluent, but that is, nevertheless, a long way removed from hunger and deprivation, and that would look affluent to peoples of the less developed countries (LDCs). However, individuals in the lower-middle class generally do not have the savings and financial security that the upper-middle class has. Though they are likely to be buying their own modest homes, the equity in those homes constitutes the bulk of their net worth. And, while they are better educated than the working class, they do not have as much education as the members of the upper-middle class have.

The Working Class

The term **working class** describes people whose incomes may be about the same as lower-middle class (sometimes higher in unionized jobs), but whose jobs do not require as much training or hold as favorable status. Randall Collins (1975) has referred to the working class as "order takers" and the middle class as "order givers." Sociologists differ in the degree to which they would differentiate the two classes. Erik Wright and his colleagues (1982) speak of the proletarianization of the white-collar worker, implying that many people in sales and office jobs have no advantage either in pay or status relative to the working class. By their estimate, nearly half the people of the United States should be categorized as working class. Self-evaluations of social class place a majority of people in the middle classes. The reason for the high estimate by sociologists such as Wright is that they list people as working class if they have virtually no autonomy in their jobs and if their jobs require little enough skill that they can be replaced quickly and easily. Low level of skill means low level of bargaining power, except where unionization and collective bargaining exist. In most situations, working-class people have a better-than-average chance of losing their jobs and sinking into poverty. If the plant in which they work closes, they may find it extremely difficult to find work elsewhere. However, as noted, unemployment has recently become a serious problem for *all* social classes.

Working-class occupations, like ditch digging, used to be characterized by fairly good wages and job security. The restructuring of economies and occupations in the MDCs makes this less likely to be the case.

THE NEW POVERTY IN THE MDCs

Among the important subjects studied by economists are the ups and downs of business cycles, which to a certain extent are the products of the decisions made by various governmental agencies (such as the U.S. Federal Reserve Board, or the International Monetary Fund). These cycles are not always of short duration and typically work to protect the interest of securing capital. Stock markets rise and fall and corporate incomes vary. It is always hard to know in the middle of an upturn or downturn whether the trend is going to be of short or long duration. There is no certainty about long-term directions, but the 1970s, 1980s, and early 1990s have brought some disturbing indications for working people, with production shifts overseas and job

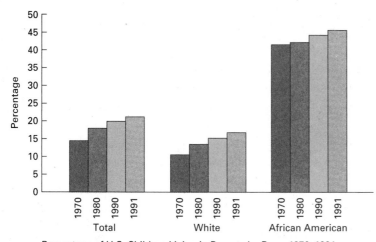

Percentage of U.S. Children Living in Poverty by Race; 1970–1991

Source: U.S. Bureau of the Census, *Statistical Abstract of the United States, 1993* (Washington, DC: U.S. Government Printing Office, 1993), p. 469, table 736.

Figure 9.2
The percentage of children in the United States below the poverty level has been increasing steadily since 1970, but especially so for African Americans.

losses at home. Countries with strong commitments to welfare legislation, such as Sweden, Denmark, and Germany, spend increasing amounts on retraining programs and unemployment insurance and there has been fairly strong public support for these programs, even among the well-to-do citizens (Gelber, 1983). As indicated in the previous sentence, "welfare" in the European sense of the word, is broader than what the term implies to most U.S. citizens—monetary relief to families with children and unemployed parents. The United States, especially during the first years of the Reagan administration, cut back on welfare expenditures, aid to cities, maternal care, and retraining programs. The poverty level increased to more than 15 percent of the total population and was more than twice that high for African Americans (see Figure 9.2). John Schwarz and Thomas Volgy (1993) argue that the U.S. Census Bureau's 1991 estimate of 36 million Americans being in poverty is a gross understatement. They assert that the Census Bureau's figure fails to account for the 26 million Americans who are technically above the poverty line but who, nevertheless, experience severe economic hardship. In another

article, Schwarz and Volgy (1992) point out that the use of the Consumer Price Index (CPI) to measure poverty is part of the problem. According to their calculations, the basic necessities of living, like rent, have been going up faster than the CPI but the "poverty line" has used the CPI since the late 1960s.

In England, small cuts were made in what had once been an all-free health-care program. Germany and France complained increasingly about foreign workers who had been welcomed a decade or so before when the humming industries of Western Europe required more laborers. Many workers from Turkey and North Africa went home. In the United States, Mexican workers continued to cross the border looking for jobs, but the welcome was no longer there. Legislation was passed making it illegal to hire them.

Relatively high proportions of unemployed citizens was not always viewed as normal. During the Truman administration (1945–1953), a Full Employment Act had been passed, acknowledging the intent of the government to maintain full employment. Although the act was a mere statement of philosophy with no enforcement provisions, it is interesting to recall that at that time

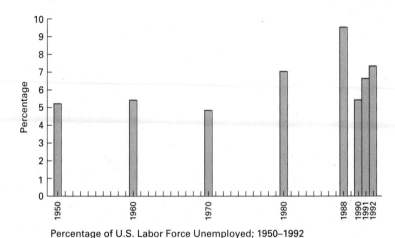

Figure 9.3
The post-war percentage of unemployed people in the United States reached an all-time high in 1988.

Percentage of U.S. Labor Force Unemployed; 1950–1992

Source: U.S. Bureau of the Census, *Statistical Abstract of the United States, 1993* (Washington, DC: U.S. Government Printing Office, 1993), p. 393, table 621.

full employment was defined as a situation in which 2 percent or less of the work force was unemployed. In the 1980s, unemployment in the United States climbed to more than 10 percent; when it fell back to 7 percent, the figures were celebrated as though full employment had been reached (Figure 9.3).

The United States was not the only country facing unemployment. The unemployment figure for England has hovered around 12 percent for several years. Germany, although considered more prosperous than England, had an unemployment rate of nearly 10 percent in 1986–1987. Even Japan, which for years had seemed immune to such problems, found its unemployment rate rising to about 3 percent in the late 1980s.

Besides those classified as unemployed in North America and Europe, there are many more people who are underemployed, meaning they have only part-time jobs or perhaps seasonal employment in agriculture. Unemployment is also a big problem in the less developed countries (LDCs), where far more people beg for jobs and get them only occasionally. Such problems as income gap and underemployment are much worse in poor countries than in the more developed countries (MDCs). Even so, one cannot ignore the bite of poverty and unemployment in the more affluent parts of the world.

The Income Gap

Unemployment obviously widens the gap between rich and poor, and so does a change from jobs in unionized industries to low-paying service jobs. In the United States, from the period just after World War II until the mid 1970s, there was a slight trend toward the equalization of income; significant gains were made for those with middle incomes and slight gains for those in the bottom fifth of income distribution. Since the late 1970s, the trend has been in the opposite direction. The rich become richer, the poor more numerous, and there is a decline in the number of people in the middle. Doug Henwood's (1992) analysis of both conservative and liberal scholarly work suggests that representatives from both ends of the political spectrum agree that the income gap between social classes in the United States will continue to widen, resulting in a sort of caste system.

Barbara Ehrenreich (1986) comments on the striking change for families with children in the United States. In 1968 the poorest families with children received 7.4 percent of total family income. By 1983 they were drawing only 4.8 percent of family income. Although the income distribution still makes a bell-shaped curve, with more people in the middle than at the extremes, Ehrenreich contends it is flattening out. Sales are up in such high-priced stores as Neiman Marcus and Bloomingdales and at such low-priced stores as K-Mart, but a number of stores in the middle range have not been doing well. By 1984 people living below the poverty level numbered 33.7 million, 10 million more than in 1978. Because poor families bear more children than do well-to-do families, the burden of poverty falls heavily on children. Denny Braun's (1991) comprehensive and seminal work, *The Rich Get Richer: The Rise of Inequality in the United States and the World,* validates the trends discussed by Ehrenreich, but also shows them to be true for other countries. At present, let us examine some of the causes, or alleged causes, of increased poverty. Some of the possibilities are demographic trends, government policies, industry policies, and agriculture.

Causes of Increasing Poverty in MDCs

Demographic Trends

At least a minor reason for unemployment is demographic (related to population changes). The very large numbers of people entering the labor force in the 1970s (a reflection of a high birthrate, or **baby boom,** from the mid 1940s to the mid 1960s) created an unemployment problem. Michael Moore (1987), speaking of his baby-boom generation complains that "our generation, unlike any other generation in the history of this country, is worse off than our parents." He is rather incensed that the baby-boom generation should be stereotyped as a generation of well-to-do, upwardly mobile professionals. Instead, he notes, taking figures from the Joint Congressional Economic Committee, that since 1973 young families have experienced a downturn in the percentage able to buy a home, and they spend 14 percent less on furniture and 30 percent less on clothes than did families of the same age a few years before that time. They are less able to save money, and they have less assurance that a college degree means success. Above all, they lack the traditional faith that things will soon be better. They have a sense of slipping backward.

It is partly coincidence, however, that the downturn in job opportunities has occurred during the baby boom or "crowded" generation. Ehrenreich (1986) presents figures indicating that the "crowded generation" accounts for only about one-third of the unemployment. As we have noted, unemployment is higher in England and Germany than in the United States, yet their post-war baby boom was not so pronounced as that of the United States. Insofar as a crowded generation is the source of an unemployment problem, it will eventually take care of itself. Nearly all industrial nations, including the United States and all of Western and even Eastern Europe are now experiencing a very low birthrate. The future demographic problem will be that of a rather small labor force at a time when the present baby-boom generation is moving into old age.

Government Policies

Government policies can obviously affect the degree to which poverty and unemployment persist and lead to suffering. Welfare measures, job-training programs, unemployment insurance, aid to families with dependent children, and the like alleviate the shock of unemployment, and job training programs give new hope. Such programs also have at least a minimal effect on equalizing incomes, because they are paid for by those able to pay and give to those in need.

Focus on the White Mountain Apache Nation

Poverty Can Be Reduced on Indian Reservations

The grinding poverty associated with Native American reservations in the United States includes extremely high rates of unemployment, low levels of education, and chronic alcoholism and drug abuse. Ever since the United States was formed in 1776, enormous damage has been inflicted on Native Americans by newcomers to this land. Their populations have been decimated by war and diseases brought from Europe, their land has been stolen, and their culture has been derided and ridiculed.

Though poverty conditions are still a reality on reservations, the fortunes of some reservations have improved. A 1988 federal law that gave tribes the right to set up gambling halls and casinos on their lands has resulted in sizeable infusions of money into some reservation economies. Native American tribes have been building health centers, schools, and homes from the proceeds from gambling operations. Not all economic success on the reservation is due to gambling, however. The La Jolla tribe in San Diego County has built a water park, which has greatly benefited the tribe. The Siletz tribe in Oregon is finding success in the timber industry, a business that sells plants to nurseries, and a smokehouse that sells salmon to tourists (Egan, 1991).

Though the White Mountain Apaches of Arizona have recently added a casino, other enterprises still provide the vast majority of the tribe's income (Eckholm, 1994). Their major industry is the Fort Apache Timber Company, which runs a sawmill in which more than 300 Apaches work for wages averaging $8.50 per hour. An additional 100 Apaches are employed by outside logging contractors. In 1993 the sawmill generated around $40 million and provided the tribe about $10 million in timber fees. Another industry on the White Mountain Apache

Reservation is the Sunrise Ski Resort, which employs 200 Apaches. When the snow is sufficient, this ski resort grosses $6 million and earns the tribe more than $1 million in profits. There are additional small enterprises on this reservation, such as "Apache Aerospace," a company with 15 employees that, in a joint venture with McDonnel-Douglas Aircraft, makes various components for the U.S. Army's Apache attack helicopter.

What explains the success of the White Mountain Apaches? One factor is the strong cultural identification these Native Americans have. All indications point to a continued increase in traditional ceremonies and activities. For example, the White Mountain Apaches celebrate the coming of age of 12-year-old girls by staging nine-day celebrations with copious amounts of food. Twenty-five years ago the White Mountain Apaches celebrated these ceremonies only a few times a year. Now there is at least one every weekend. The fact that the Apache language is still spoken on the reservation also indicates the strength of Apache culture.

A second factor in the economic success of the White Mountain Apaches is the way they have taken affairs into their own hands and the way they have been distancing themselves from the Bureau of Indian Affairs, the federal agency that has historically fostered dependency among Native Americans. Thirty years ago, this tribe was very dependent on the Bureau. Over the years however, strong tribal leaders and councils have dealt aggressively with government officials and other non-Indians to advance their tribal interests.

SOURCES: E. Eckholm. 1994. "The Apaches." *New York Times Magazine*, Feb. 27: 45–48; T. Egan. 1991. "Once Abolished by U.S., Tribe Forges Future." *New York Times*, Nov. 25: A1, D10.

In the early 1980s, the government of the United States sought to reduce its involvement in the economy, lessening welfare support, reducing regulatory functions, and following tax and investment policies more favorable to the rich than to the poor. Tax reforms passed in 1986

were expected to be more favorable to working-class people and to remove many "loopholes" (ways of avoiding higher taxes) in the law for the well-to-do; however, the tax burden of working-class people has not been altered much from what it was in the early 1980s. In 1980 the bottom 20 percent of U.S. taxpayers paid 8.4 percent in federal taxes; by 1990 they were paying 9.7 percent (Reich, 1991:199). The top 20 percent of taxpayers, however, saw their federal tax rate drop from 27.3 percent in 1980 to 25.8 percent in 1990. And, as Robert Reich (1991:199–200) points out, "The drop was even more precipitous for the very rich: By the end of the 1980s, the top 1 percent of American earners were paying a combined federal-state-local tax of only 26.8 percent, compared with 29 percent in 1975 and 39.6 percent in 1966."

Also there is no question that reductions in social programs in the 1980s and early 1990s has made the condition of the poor much worse in the United States than in most MDCs. In no other MDC has the rate of homelessness increased so rapidly as it has in the United States, nor even in the less affluent countries of Eastern Europe.

J. Larry Brown (1987) of the Harvard School of Public Health describes the effects of reduction in aid for the poor, effects felt especially by children. Brown defines *hunger* as "chronic insufficiency of the nutrients necessary for growth and good health." Thus defined, he says, there are 12 million hungry children and 8 million hungry adults in the United States, about 9 percent of the population. People, of course, can be malnourished because of ignorance of the right foods, but Brown cites studies indicating that the poor spend their food dollars quite wisely. He also argues that, since malnutrition had virtually disappeared in the 1970s and has reappeared now, the only way to explain it on grounds of ignorance would be to contend that the poor had suddenly become more ignorant than in the past.

Brown emphasizes a number of serious consequences of hunger among U.S. children: (1) the U.S. infant mortality rate (deaths of children between birth and age 1 per 1,000 live births) is higher than any of 18 other MDCs. Although other variables such as drug addiction among mothers with newborns may be partially responsible for the low ranking, poor nutrition is no doubt an important cause; (2) there has been an increase of babies born with lower-than-average birth weight because of poor maternal nutrition, which increases their chance of dying before the end of the first year; and (3) brain damage is possible for children who are inadequately fed during the first three years of life, a period of time when the brain should experience its most rapid growth.

Brown presents statistics to support his charge of neglect of the poor. For instance, there has been a drop in participation in food stamp programs from nearly 70 percent of the poor in 1980 to less than 60 percent in 1985. From 1975 to 1986, the percentage of jobless people receiving unemployment insurance dropped from 80 percent to 29 percent.

The better record on infant mortality rate for the countries of northwestern Europe than the United States (see Table 9.1) leads to the conclusion that they do better with nutrition for expectant mothers and infants. This does not mean, of course, that the United States is anywhere near the bottom of the list worldwide. The poorest countries, to be discussed later, have far higher infant mortality rates. The point is, though, that the United States could do much better; it is preeminent both in medical knowledge and in wealth.

Industrial Policies

The shortage of government aid makes the lot of the poor worse in a country like the United States

Infant Mortality Rate and Life Expectancy for Selected Countries, 1993							TABLE 9.1
Country	U.S.A.	Former USSR	Canada	Sweden	Norway	Netherlands	Switzerland
Infant mortality rate	8.6	28.0	6.8	6.2	7.8	6.5	6.9
Life expectancy	75	70	77	78	77	77	77

SOURCE: Haub and Yanagishita, *1993 World Population Data Sheet*, (Washington, DC: Population Reference Bureau, 1993).

than it is in many countries, but it does not account for the large number of poor people. Much more important are certain industrial changes that weaken the position of labor. New forms of world competition are posing problems for the wealthy industrialized countries. Complaints are heard about **deindustrialization**, meaning abandonment of industrial plants in countries with high labor costs, especially the United States, and the building of new plants in cheap-labor areas abroad (Bluestone and Harrison, 1982). One consequence of deindustrialization is a decrease in jobs with high pay, protected by unions, and an increase in low-paying jobs. A glance at Figure 9.4 will make this point clear. From 1980 through 1992, the annual percentage change in earnings and compensation has been negative. On the other hand, with the exception of 1980, the annual percentage change in output has been positive, reaching a 2.9 percent increase from 1991 to 1992. In short, U.S. workers are producing more and more for less and less compensation.

A Four-Nation Comparison Michael Buroway (1983), comparing England, United States, Sweden, and Japan, points out many differences in their industrial development. England industrialized much earlier than the others, with conditions of labor that were so bad as to make unionization inevitable and quite strong. In the United States, unionization was slower, partly because in earlier days workers had a frontier alternative to factory work. Although Sweden industrialized much later and without oppressive conditions of labor, it has the most highly organized labor force of all (87 percent unionized). Japan, the latest of the four to industrialize, has weak labor unions organized in each plant, not nationally. They are what U.S. labor leaders call company unions, the implication being that they are not very free from management.

Comparing the four countries on the basis of welfare legislation, Buroway finds that Sweden is by far the most benevolent, followed by England and the United States. In all three cases, welfare legislation has been sufficient to set something

Figure 9.4
Although the productivity of U.S. workers continued to increase from 1980 to 1992, their hourly earnings and compensation continued to decrease.

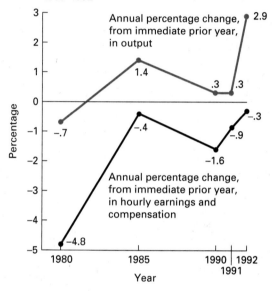

Productivity and Hourly Earnings and Compensation (In 1982 Constant Dollars): Annual Percentage Change, United States, 1980–1992

Source: Data for the production of this graph was taken from U.S. Bureau of the Census, *Statistical Abstract of the United States,* (Washington, DC: U.S. Government Printing Office, 1993), p.423, table 664, and p. 424, table 668.

of a floor under wages. In most cases, only people ineligible for welfare aid (often foreign nationals) will do sweatshop work for less than welfare would provide. In Japan, government welfare measures are minimal, but employers provide very considerable benefits. Life-long employment used to be one of those benefits, but recent changes in Japanese employment policy have made this an ideal. Increasingly, Japanese workers are having to contend with layoffs, just as workers in other industrialized countries must.

Buroway calls the Japanese system a type of "benevolent despotism" relative to labor. Workers

These auto workers in the Mitsubishi plant in Japan are able to provide meaningful ideas on the work process; auto plants in other parts of the world are emulating this model.

are given large benefits and, of great interest to workers in other countries, they are often consulted for ideas about work efficiency and product quality. However, there is no question that management is ultimately in charge. Unions are weak. The Japanese model, Buroway concludes, probably represents the face of the future. Labor loses its independence when the company can threaten to move to a country of much lower wages or to speed up the pace of automation. The only question is whether there will be anything benevolent about despotism over labor.

Bluestone and Harrison (1982:15,42–43) give some disturbing figures on the movement of American industry overseas. In the 1970s, runaway plants cost the United States between 450,000 and 650,000 jobs. During the period from 1950 to 1980, United States business investments abroad increased from $12 billion to $192 billion, and the trend continues. In their most recent work, Harrison and Bluestone (1988) have dealt with what has happened to U.S. workers who *do* have jobs. The truth of the matter is that there has been a U-turn in the U.S. standard of living. They work more hours and harder for less money, less security, and less power to impact their employment situation.

A recent example of plant closings concerns General Motors (Schwartz and Turque, 1987). In 1987 General Motors eliminated 29,000 jobs. Now, when attempting to negotiate wages, workers are never allowed to forget how lucky they are to have jobs at all. Workers complain of unkept promises made to them for their earlier wage concessions, but the fear lingers that no further concessions might mean lower company earnings and lower earnings could mean more plant closings. When workers have no bargaining power, the industrial situation fits well with Buroway's definition of "despotic." Besides the possibility of moving overseas, some companies have the alternative of farming out some of their work to smaller plants in low-wage parts of the country or getting around wage and hour laws by paying employees on a piece-work basis. Buroway gives the United States and Italy as prime examples of this means of keeping down wages.

While discussing the pressures toward less worker autonomy, we must not forget that Sweden, with high wages and a strong welfare commitment, manages to prosper. So does Japan, with a labor system that locks workers firmly to the concerns they work for, but that is nonetheless benevolent.

What advantage do those two countries have that keep their industries doing better than industry in the United States, England, France, or Germany? The answer does not lie in low wages. Sweden is a high-wage country, although its unions have practiced a *solidaristic wage policy*, meaning that they have tried to limit demands to keep prices of their products competitive in the world market. Like Japan, Sweden depends heavily on exports. In the case of Japan, wages are not so high as those in the United States, but considering the *nenko system*, which guarantees lifelong employment, the pay difference is not very great. Wages are certainly not the only reason for the success of Japan or Sweden.

Becoming Competitive   The term *competitiveness* has become a buzz word in the United States, but it is well worth serious consideration. What characteristics do two countries as different as Sweden and Japan share that keep their exports moving? They have maintained a competitive advantage through (1) high-quality products, (2) labor efficiency, and (3) governmental-industrial cooperation. In *The Next American Frontier*, Robert Reich (1983) argues that these three interrelated goals must be pursued by any country that wishes to remain competitive. Japan, Sweden, and Germany have long had close governmental-industrial cooperation in seeking markets, establishing quality control, and making sure labor is well treated and used with the maximum efficiency. Especially in Japan, labor loyalty to the firm is of great importance. Reich (1983:285) points out that during the decades from 1960 to 1980 many countries made rapid gains on the United States in gross domestic product (GDP) per capita; Sweden, Switzerland, Denmark, and Germany all showed greater efficiency than the United States by the latter date, although none of them had come even close to matching the United States in 1960. All the other countries have more elaborate and consistent programs for job training than does the United States, and their educational systems are more demanding, particularly in science and mathematics.

Reich (1983:265) contends that many countries are clever enough to work always toward improving the skills of their own people, even when investing abroad. Thus Japanese companies invest in the United States and hire U.S. workers, but their most highly skilled technicians and top managers are Japanese. Reich cites that France follows the same policy, accepting U.S. investment, but demands that the plant be built

Coca-Cola, a United States–based multinational corporation, can be found in virtually every corner of the world—in this case, Ho Chi Minh City, Vietnam.

in France so that French technicians will be trained. In many cases (automobiles are the best known), Japan has been restricted in its exports to the United States, but it has turned out a higher percentage of higher-priced products to make up for the loss in quantity. In this, as in many decisions, Japan is guided by MITI (Ministry of International Trade and Industry), which also helps to make sure that promising new industrial techniques are quickly disseminated throughout Japanese industry. This contrasts sharply with the exclusive patents in the United States. At present, Japan continues to invest heavily in the United States. About 250,000 Americans are now employed in Japanese firms in the United States, and the number is expected to rise to 1 million by the mid 1990s. American workers are well treated but, to succeed, they must learn to show much greater loyalty to the firm than is common here. They may eventually rise in position, but probably not all the way to the top. Jeff Copeland and his colleagues (1987), in making an assessment of Japanese concerns in the United States, appear to agree with Reich about how top levels of skill and management are kept in Japanese hands.

The fact that Japanese and other foreign investments remain strong in the United States is good evidence that the rest of the world does not expect the United States to undergo a financial collapse. With the right policies (discussed in the prior chapter), the United States can no doubt improve its competitive position, save jobs, and train a more technically skilled work force. There will still be poor people, of course, including many elderly and handicapped people and many dependent children. The United States must pay more attention to this problem, and must also deal with some serious problems in the agricultural sector of its economy.

The Agricultural Sector

In later pages, more will be said about agriculture in the poorer lands of the world. However, poverty among farmers is not limited to the poor and LDCs. It is found in the United States, Canada, Japan, and parts of Western Europe. The underlying problem is that economic forces are making large farms more profitable than middle-sized or small farms. Farm machinery has gone up in cost. In fact, prices of American-produced farm machinery are high enough that Japan is now entering the farm-equipment market on a large scale. Fertilizers and pesticides are high priced, and the costs of irrigation go up as ground-water levels decline. The small family farm of American tradition consisted of rather small acreage, worked by a team of horses, and it usually included cows, chickens, and other farm animals as part of the family living. That type of farm has disappeared and turned into a much larger-scale operation. Average farm size increased from 152 acres in 1930 to 467 acres in 1991 (Figure 9.5). Actually, though, such a figure understates the size of farms that are the sole means of support of their owners. Such farms usually run to over 1,000 acres. The average size is smaller due to the existence of many small acreages that are not the sole means of support of their owners.

Jeffrey L. Pasley (1987) discusses the three-way division of U.S. farms. There are large farms, large enough for their owners to afford and make full use of farm machinery and supplies and even to fight politically for subsidies and markets. At the other extreme are small farms that are sidelines for their owners, who live mainly on income from other jobs or pensions. The owners are not necessarily affluent, but they are generally not living in poverty or in fear that one more bad harvest will make paupers of them. It is in the intermediate sector that the real problem lies, in farms large enough to occupy the full time of their owners and be their only means of livelihood, but farms too small to be prosperous under present conditions. Their owners are usually not impoverished in the sense of not having shelter or enough to eat, but they are impoverished in the sense of having constant anxiety about whether they can hold on to their farms.

Besides rising prices of farm production, another problem for modern farmers is that

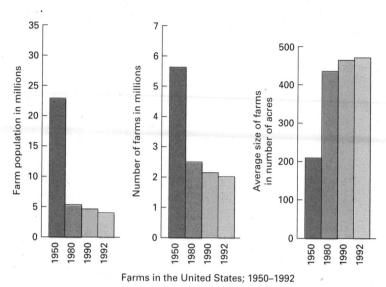

Figure 9.5
The number of farms and farmers in the United States continues to decrease while the average acreage of a U.S. farm continues to increase. Although these figures are for the United States, they represent a worldwide trend. In Latin America, India, and Southeast Asia, farms grow in size and small farms are forced out of production.

Farms in the United States; 1950–1992

Sources: Adapted from U.S. Bureau of the Census, *Statistical Abstract of the United States, 1987* and *1993* (Washington, DC: U.S. Government Printing Office).

foreign markets are shrinking. As we saw in a previous discussion of the Green Revolution, many countries that once depended on large imports of grain and other commodities are now self-supporting in farm products. In a typical year, even India buys far less grain than it once did.

Western countries have used different forms of government intervention to prevent a sudden collapse of too many farms. The United States resorts to farm subsidies and government help in the foreign marketing of grain. Sometimes farm surpluses are bought up by the government and later given to the poor, sent overseas for famine relief, or sold at bargain prices abroad. In the past, U.S. citizens have sometimes been angry to learn that Communist bloc countries were getting U.S. produce at bargain prices. All kinds of policies are considered necessary to prevent a farm collapse. Consequently, the number of farms drops off slowly rather than in one great catastrophe.

Other industrial countries have problems with their farms. In France and Germany, fewer farmers are needed. A number of special agreements about farm products had to be made in order to establish the Common Market, an economic union of nine European countries that

is also known as the European Economic Community (EEC). Even in the former Soviet Union, the number of people employed in agriculture has declined, although their farming is not nearly so efficient as that in North America.

A particularly interesting case of protection of farmers is found in Japan (Fallow, 1987). Japan, with a land area slightly smaller than California, has a population of more than 120 million. Much of its land is mountainous and much of the remainder is taken up by towns and cities, airports, roads, and railroads so that less than 15 percent is farmland. Much of that farmland is devoted to rice, grown on minute farms, often only 150th the size of an average American farm. The government subsidizes rice production, paying about $6 billion per year to farmers to produce rice. Because of the cost of subsidization, rice sells in Japan for much more than it would cost if it were purchased abroad and imported. And rice is a staple of the Japanese diet!

Why does Japan go to such lengths to preserve rice cultivation? Part of the reason is tradition. In Japan, rice is a ceremonial, as well as a nutritious, food. A consequence of the attitude about rice is that farmers have far more clout in parliament

Modern farms in the United States are becoming larger and require the use of expensive equipment like this combine.

than their numbers would warrant. Their votes are major factors in keeping up the Japanese mercantilist philosophy that Japan must always be a heavy seller and a light buyer, thus maintaining what it regards as a favorable trade balance.

The "rice plot" in Japan is in some ways unique, but in a more important way it is repeated in the United States, Canada, France, and many other places. For the small producer, it is a way of life that can be maintained only artificially. Small-scale farmers in much of the industrialized world, whether in poverty or relative comfort, feel themselves standing at the edge of an abyss, about to fall over unless they receive some government help. (Later in this chapter, we note that similar problems exist for small farmers in many of the LDCs, but their economic condition is infinitely worse.)

LANDS OF POVERTY

Sometimes it is argued that poverty in the United States and other industrialized countries is only **relative poverty**, which means that the poor are suffering only in comparison to other citizens, not because they lack food and shelter. We cannot accept this view even for the United States, partly because of the sheer number of homeless people, which may be as high as 3 million (Levitas, 1990), but even more important because of the food shortages for poor children. Earlier we mentioned, the work of J. Larry Brown (1987), which estimated the number of hungry children in the United States to be 12 million. This is a travesty, given that the United States exports $39.3 billion worth of agricultural goods annually (*World Almanac*, 1994:124). Even considering arguments for calling poverty in MDCs relative, there is no question that in most of the world's poor countries, poverty is absolute.

Nancy Birdsall (1981), in a study of poverty that includes all the world except the Communist and former Communist countries (about which it is hard to get reliable data), found that 780 million people live in absolute poverty. Someone living in **absolute poverty** has less income than is necessary to ensure a minimum daily diet of 2,150 calories per person per day. Converted to constant U.S. dollars, this amount averages an annual per capita income of $200. The proportions of population below this cut-off line range from about 50 percent in the poorest countries of the world—India, Bangladesh, Indonesia, and many sub-Saharan African countries—to 13 percent in better-off developing countries like Brazil, Mexico, and Iran (Birdsall, 1981).

Whereas the more industrially developed countries have individual average annual incomes ranging from $3,000 or $4,000 to $15,000, a majority of the world's inhabitants live on less than $1,000 per year, in many cases very much less. The average income in China is estimated at $370 per year, and in India, $330 (Haub and Yanagishita, 1993). These two countries together make up about one-third of the earth's population. Bangladesh is even poorer than India, with an average annual income of only $220.

It is in Africa, however, that the largest numbers of the poorest countries are found. In Ethiopia, the annual per capita income in 1991 was only $120, Burkina Faso and Mali were slightly better off. Guinea-Bissau, Malawi, and Zaire all have estimated per capita annual incomes of less than $230 (Haub and Yanagishita, 1993).

In some countries of Africa, starvation was rampant in the 1980s and early 1990s. Parts of Sudan and Somalia and much of Ethiopia have had a series of severe droughts, and hundreds of thousands of people were wiped out by starvation. Particularly in Ethiopia it was charged that, although supplies were brought in, there was no transportation to get them to the needy. Furthermore, the government was accused of indifference. People farther west in Africa suffered severe droughts and starvation in the 1970s, especially in the area bordering the Sahara Desert. It is feared that overgrazing along the desert borderlands is causing the Sahara to expand, a condition called **desertification** (discussed in the next chapter). Far to the south in Mozambique, civil war has resulted in multitudes of refugees, all malnourished, and many dying of hunger. In the case of Mozambique, however, the reason is probably not a failure of productivity, but the disruption of normal markets by war.

In the poorest of the poor countries, we need no definition of hunger in terms of calories; people simply waste away and die. Even in places that have not undergone starvation in recent years, there is hunger of the type previously

Overgrazing along the desert borderlands is causing the Sahara Desert to expand.

defined by Brown: a poor enough diet to cause retardation in height and weight and to cause a very large percentage of deaths among newborns. Chad, a country of more than 5 million people in an area nearly as large as Alaska, has a life expectancy for males of 45 years and for females of 48 years (Haub and Yanagishita, 1993). Although people in the United States might be ashamed of the infant mortality rate of 8.6 per 1,000 live births, the infant mortality rate for Chad is 127 (Haub and Yanagishita, 1993). The country has 94 physicians. In Ethiopia, life expectancy and infant mortality rates are similar to Chad's.

Despite their being poor countries, India and China both do somewhat better in child care and life expectancy than Ethiopia or Chad. India's infant mortality rate is 91 per 1,000 births and life expectancy is 58 years for males and 59 years for females (Haub and Yanagishita, 1993). This parity in life expectancy between the sexes is unlike most of the world, where women, on average, outlive men by about seven years. The probable reason for the parity in India is that boys are wanted by families more than girls, so if there is not quite enough food to go around, the boys get the larger share. Also, a proportionately higher percentage of women die in childbirth than in wealthier nations. China manages to provide much better health care with 2.7 million physicians, compared to India's 379,000. China's life expectancy is 68 years for men and 71 years for women (Table 9.2)

Latin America is a region of the world with far more than its share of poverty. We will pay particular attention to Mexico because of its proximity to the United States, then to Bolivia as a representative of the very poorest of Latin American countries. Brazil will be described as a country with very deep poverty despite considerable industrial development.

Mexico

Mexico, as of 1980, had a per capita income of $1800, a life expectancy of 64 and 68 years, respectively, for males and females, and an infant mortality rate of 53 per 1,000 live births. By 1993 per capita income had improved somewhat (U.S. $2,870), life expectancy had changed very little (66 years for men and 73 years for women), and the infant mortality rate decreased considerably (38 per 1,000 live births) (Haub and Yanagishita, 1993). Although Mexico struggles under a terribly heavy foreign debt and is plagued by unemployment and declining income from oil exportation (due to the worldwide drop in oil prices), living standards are not so bad as in the other countries just mentioned. This may be surprising to people who have seen the outlying slums of Tijuana or Mexico City, but poverty is much worse in Bangladesh and parts of Africa.

The Mexico–United States border has become busier than ever with the flight of United States businesses to places of low labor costs. Every day, border crossings are jammed with trucks from Nogales, Tijuana, and Ciudad Juarez bringing goods produced by United States companies in Mexican *maquiladoras* (Copeland and Harmes, 1987). In 1982 the hourly wage in Mexico equalled about $2.00 in U.S. currency. Because of the sharp decline in the value of the peso (Mexico's unit of currency), wages had fallen to the equivalent of $.75 by 1986. United States companies with *maquiladoras* across the border employed about 250,000 Mexican workers, but the number of Mexicans working for foreign firms increase to 275,000 the following year as Japanese firms like Sanyo, Sony, and Hitachi followed the 1,000 U.S. companies operating south-of-the-border plants. Although Mexicans may prefer higher wage jobs, many of them settle for jobs in *maquiladoras* because half of the

Infant Mortality Rate and Life Expectancy for Selected Countries, 1993							TABLE 9.2
Country	Chad	China	Ethiopa	India	Mali	Burkina Faso	Zaire
Infant mortality rate	127	53	127	91	111	119	98
Life expectancy	47	70	46	59	45	52	52

SOURCE: Haub and Yanagishita, *1993 World Population Data Sheet* (Washington, DC: Population Reference Bureau, 1993).

These workers in a *maquiladora* in Nogales, Mexico, are assembling Sears garage-door openers for a fraction of the pay U.S. employees would receive.

Mexican work force has no full-time employment. Foreign industry is happy with this situation, but U.S. workers are not happy with the job competition. Workers in the United States are losing their $15-per-hour jobs to nonunionized Mexicans who will do the same work for about $.40 per hour.

Bolivia

Bolivia is worth special consideration as one of the poorest countries in the Americas. A large country, about the size of Texas and California combined, Bolivia has a population of only about 8 million (Haub and Yanagishita, 1993). Most of the country is high and mountainous and not very productive, with neither fertile soil nor temperate climate. Life expectancy is well below that of Mexico—59 years for males and 64 years for females. Infant mortality is the same as that of the poorest countries of Africa, 89 per 1,000 live births. Although not suffering the starvation of Ethiopia and Somalia, Bolivia is a place of extreme poverty.

In 1986 the United States government, in an attempt to fight drugs, entered an agreement with Bolivia to eradicate much of its cocaine production (Guillermoprieto, 1986). The result illustrates

both the facts of poverty and the difficulty one government has in direct interference with another. American troops, 174 of them, were sent to Bolivia with the approval of the Bolivian government to stamp out cocaine-processing plants. At first the operation seemed successful, but later it had to be given up. Too many Bolivian peasants depend on the production of cocaine leaf as their only means of subsistence. The government feared a possible uprising, or *coup d'état*, that might be backed by powerful cocaine interest. The antidrug operation threatened to reduce further Bolivia's inadequate income without reducing cocaine production because there was an immediate rise in production in nearby countries.

Brazil

Brazil has the distinction of being the largest Latin American country (3,200,000 square miles), the most populous (152,000,000), the most industrialized, and the most indebted ($44,000,000,000). It demonstrates that rapid industrial development does not necessarily spell prosperity for the people if the distribution of wealth is extremely unequal. From the mid 1960s until 1985, Brazil was ruled by a succession of military leaders, amid constant charges

The great inequality in Brazil is illustrated in Rio de Janeiro where poor, homeless children sleep on the street, while wealthy people stroll in the background.

of dictatorial oppression and torture. During that period, hundreds of thousands of square miles of rain forest were cleared, Amazonian Indian lands were seized, and attempts were made to open up the interior regardless of possible environmental damage. Mining, agriculture, and manufacturing grew rapidly. With rising prices of goods on the world market, Brazil was able to borrow vast amounts of money, expecting repayment to be easy as profits continued to rise. However, the great energy squeeze starting in 1973 increased production costs so much that the anticipated profits did not materialize. Brazil found itself with a staggering debt. Although industrial development and mining have resulted in great wealth for many Brazilians, the standard of living among the poor is very bad. An analysis by Goldsmith and Wilson (1991) of the Northwest segment of Brazil shows that, despite industrialization, poverty is endemic and social inequality is extreme. Average per capita annual income in 1991 was $2,920 (Haub and Yanagishita, 1993). Life expectancy is 64 years for males and 71 years for females and infant mortality is 63 per 1,000 live births (Haub and Yanagishita, 1993).

Brazil is characterized by greater inequality than any other country in the world. The poorest 20 percent of the population receives only 2 percent of income while the richest 10 percent receives more than one-half of the income (Braun, 1991:77). Jane Kramer (1987), after spending considerable time in Brazil, calls Rio de Janeiro and its surroundings "a place where twelve thousand people go swimming at the beach while twelve million people go hungry." Although the statement is exaggerated, it points not only to extreme poverty for many, but also to much bitterness about it. She is describing a town not far from Rio called, ironically, *Campos Eliseos* (Elysian Fields). The description is anything but elysian (which means "paradise"):

> There are no paved roads once you get to *Campos Eliseos*, no sewers, no garbagemen collecting trash. If there is an epidemic, no one comes to *Campos Eliseos* to vaccinate the children. If there is dengue or meningitis, or encephalitis, no one sprays here the way they do in any of the fancy Rio neighborhoods. It is a standing joke in *Campos Eliseos* that the local mosquitos have a deal with the government. (Kramer, 1987:54)

According to Kramer, the last few years under civilian government have greatly reduced police cruelty, but made little change in poverty.

According to Kramer, there is a saying in Brazil that "miracles are a better bet than social justice or a living wage"(Kramer, 1987:72). The reason for such little change in poverty in Brazil is associated with the type of development in Brazil. When development is tied to foreign capital and when foreign investment dictates the terms of development, the typical poor Brazilian is not likely to see his or her lot much improved.

Causes of Poverty

In some cases, as noted in comments on parts of Africa, part of the reason for poverty is geographical. The region just south of the Sahara Desert, called the Sahel, sometimes has a series of good years during which human population and herds of animals increase. Then come droughts and famine. Foreign aid can help in the short run, but in the long run the environment will have to be much better managed or birthrates will have to decline.

Often the environment is quite favorable to life, but there is severe poverty nevertheless. Vital statistics on many of the poorest countries tell part of the reason. In many of the poorer lands, from 40 to 50 percent of the population is 14 years old or younger. By comparison, in the United States only 22 percent of the population is 14 years old or younger. Children put a strain on the economy. In some cases, like Bangladesh, the countries are already overpopulated. Even where more people can be supported, it is difficult to take care of too many dependent children. Not only is the population balance between children and adults unfavorable, but often health is poor. We have already noted how much lower life expectancy is in the LDCs than in the MDCs. The World Health Organization, the Peace Corps, and many governments attempt to improve health conditions in LDCs, but progress is slow. Malaria remains the world's biggest killer. (The topic of dependency is discussed further in the next chapter).

Another striking fact about statistics on the poorer countries is a generally high rate of illiteracy. In Haiti, only 53 percent of the adult popula-

tion can read. Literacy is also rather low in Central America but is better than 81 percent in Brazil and 90 percent in Mexico. Literacy rates are even higher in countries of intermediate wealth: Chile's literacy rate is 92 percent, Argentina's is 95 percent, and Uruguay's is 96 percent.

Economic factors also play a role in perpetuating poverty. In many poor countries, the few wealthy people depend on land for their income rather than investing money in trade and industry. Virtually no middle class develops, and trade is in the hands of foreigners. Sometimes a major crop is traditional such as coffee in Colombia, although a far more productive crop could be grown instead, possibly soybeans or yams. Often water supplies or transportation systems have not changed for centuries but could be improved with joint effort. Peace Corps members have helped provide wells or brought in running water or built bridges. Much as they are to be lauded, much larger changes are needed. Lengthy highways and new industries often depend on foreign loans or investment by multinational corporations. Foreign loans involve payment of interest, sometimes in amounts that can be crippling, as in the cases of Brazil and Mexico. Investments by multinational corporations can also be a mixed blessing, as we will discuss later. However, uneven distribution of land ownership remains a key problem.

In much of the impoverished world, large amounts of land are held by a relatively small number of owners. Plantations are opened to produce crops for export, such as bananas, coconuts, coffee, or sugar. Hence, land that once supported a peasant and his family, through the raising of chickens and farming of corn or other subsistence products, is now producing food for export.

For example, in El Salvador, plantations that produce food for export take up half the farmland of the country, including *all* the best land. Now 350,000 displaced peasants try to scratch out a living on barren hillsides, so steep that three-quarters of their farms suffer severe erosion (Goldsmith and Hildyard, 1984:183–184).

An even more appalling example occurred during the early 1970s, when 100,000 people died of starvation in the Sahel. While their landless people starved, Sahelian countries were exporting 60 percent of their agricultural produce to Europe (Goldsmith and Hildyard, 1984:177–178).

For reasons partly connected to the Green Revolution, the African production of cash crops for export has increased phenomenally. Since the early 1960s, "coffee production in Africa has quadrupled; the output of tea has increased sixfold; that of sugar threefold; cotton and cocoa production has doubled, and the output of tobacco has risen 60 percent" (Goldsmith and Hildyard, 1984:177–178). Those crops occupy the best agricultural land, but they are exported to Europe and the United States. Meanwhile, food production for the people declines. In some cases, drought has contributed to the decline, but much of the problem is that most of the food produced is exported. If there were industries in the cities to employ the displaced peasants, all would be well. But cities in LDCs are besieged by thousands of displaced country people, who find work only occasionally, and often resort to crime or prostitution. When new industries open up in the cities, they do not necessarily make things better.

Foreign Investments in Poor Lands

A few poor countries have been heavily subsidized from abroad in ways that have started them on the road to industrial development. Taiwan and South Korea, both subsidized by the United States, are such semiperipheral countries. The former Soviet Union subsidized Cuba, which helped Cuba to achieve good levels of health and education (96 percent of adult men and women can read and write), but not what we would call a high standard of living. The demise of the Soviet Union meant a cessation of aid to Cuba, and the island is suffering as a result.

The majority of the poorest lands have not received massive aid from governments and built their industry, but have received foreign investment of a more limited type. It might be assumed that investments by multinational corporations would be an unquestionable boon to underdeveloped lands, but considerable research by sociologists calls this assumption into question. Christopher Chase-Dunn (1975), in a cross-cultural study, came to the conclusion that foreign investments in underdeveloped countries often widen the gulf between rich and poor and distort the economies. By *distortion of the economies* of peripheral nations, Chase-Dunn refers to uneven development, promoting only one sector of the economy and ignoring the rest. For instance, investment may be only in mining. Roads and facilities are built for exploiting the mines; peasants are moved from the area; politicians are well paid for permitting the development, but the country as a whole sees little or no benefit. When penetration by multinational corporations is in agriculture or forest products, far more poor people are moved off their lands. In their study of 59 less developed countries, Dale Wimberley and Rosario Bello (1992) found that foreign investment has an exceptionally harmful effect on food consumption in peripheral countries.

Volker Bornschier and Ballmer Cao (1979) of the University of Zurich come to the same conclusion about the widening gap between rich and poor, but add a note about power distribution. Particularly in former colonies of one of the European powers, there is usually a well-organized elite, accustomed to the ways of foreigners and easy for foreign investors to deal with. By linking their interests with the new multinational corporations, they increase their wealth and their power.

Richard Rubinson (1976) is another sociologist who found that foreign investments do little or nothing for the poor people of less developed countries. He says that in many of the older industrialized nations the time came when wealthy capitalists were willing to see some of their wealth "trickle down" to the workers and the dispossessed. However, Rubinson's cross-national study found this does not necessarily happen in developing countries. In older industrialized countries, part of the reason for both an increase of wealth and a lowered resistance to sharing wealth lay in great economic diversification. There were many fields of enterprise to enter. Some required highly skilled labor, and occasionally there were worker shortages. The new situation is different, says Rubinson, in that separate countries, especially less developed countries, do not represent separate systems of economic development; increasingly they are all very minor parts of the world economy. Therefore, the world economy might need Country A solely for copper or chromium and Country B only for bananas or sisal. Small countries that have not developed independent, aggressive business interests become severely limited to only one, or perhaps a few, products on the world market. Prices and conditions of production and sale are set on the outside. This, concludes Rubinson, is a reason that there is little movement toward the equalizing of incomes in many of the poorest lands. It is also a reason for danger because lands of extreme inequality become politically unstable. Core countries with investments in them, such as the United States, meet the danger by trying to prop up the regimes that have handed out favors to the multinational corporations.

The encompassing work of Denny Braun supports the conclusion that foreign investment in LDCs generally has more negative than positive effects. Braun's chapter on multinational corporations (1991:95–135) delineates the process by which these huge corporations "buy" the goodwill of elites in LDCs, in exchange for all sorts of favors. In the end, concludes Braun, the LDCs find themselves in a buyer's market, and the MDCs are setting the terms—terms that benefit the MDCs at the expense of the LDCs.

Another cause of poverty in the peripheral countries is the action of the World Bank and the International Monetary Fund (IMF). Though these world financial institutions are thought by many people in the core countries to be instrumental in the development of peripheral countries, evidence suggests that the actions of the World Bank and the IMF impede the development of the peripheral countries. The work of G.

Hancock (1991) shows that rather than helping the poor in the peripheral countries, the "aid for development" put forth by the World Bank and IMF ends up benefiting global corporations situated in core countries and the small number of elites in the peripheral countries who have been coopted. The late British sociologist Tom Bottomore (1993:84) summarizes the negative impact of the World Bank and the IMF: "The relation of these agencies to the developing countries is shaped above all by the interests of capitalism, and the policies of the World Bank and the IMF in particular have contributed massively to the impoverishment of a large part of the third world (and to the destruction of the natural environment), while at the same time creating or strengthening in these countries small, wealthy, and frequently corrupt elites."

Inequality Without Boundaries

In this and previous chapters we have used the world system perspective to explain inequalities of various kinds. Some scholars argue, however, that inequality may be a phenomenon that will be removed from national and international boundaries and systems. Robert Reich (1991) asserts that, increasingly, the economic success of individual citizens of a particular country, is independent of their nationalities. He argues that modern corporations are characterized by their global webs and even though their home base may be in a particular country, the success of a particular corporation does not necessarily equate to success for citizens of that country. That is because the activities of corporations, whether they are building automobiles or computers, are decentralized all over the planet. Reich also makes the point that in the future, individuals around the world will fit in three occupational categories: routine production services; in-person services; and symbolic-analytic services. The first category includes the least skilled positions that require little ability or imagination, such as plugging a certain electronic component into computers on an assembly line. The second occupational category of in-person services is quite similar to the first but differs in that the services must be provided person-to-person. The last category of symbolic-analytic services includes occupations that involve considerable education and imagination. People skilled at problem solving and adept at manipulating various kinds of symbols—whether words, data, or oral and visual representations—find themselves in this category. Examples of symbolic-analysts are design engineers, software engineers, research scientists, investment bankers, biotechnology engineers, and public relations executives. Reich asserts that these individuals are becoming independent of their geographical communities and have a global network. Furthermore, their services are sought after more and more, on a worldwide scale. And, they are rewarded handsomely for their work. In fact, their incomes are escalating rapidly while the incomes of people in the first two occupational categories are decreasing. This growing disparity between symbolic-analysts and others is occurring in all nations. Reich makes the argument that though symbolic-analysts may operate on a global scale, they still reside in specific nations. They should be concerned with spreading their wealth to the other groups, if for no other reason than their own safety. Reich also asserts that it is the responsibility of nations to increase the skills of their citizens, to make them competitive with citizens of other countries.

We can conclude this section of the chapter by saying that the people of the world, especially the less developed segment of the planet, will continue to be treated with far greater inequality than seems fair. But it is a very productive world. Will we at least be able to end starvation?

CAN THE WORLD BE FED?

Whether the world can be fed depends on certain variables. If natural resources are ruined, water polluted beyond use, and other important aspects of ecology ignored, the answer is a fairly obvious "No." A negative answer would also have to be given if population in the LDCs continues to increase indefinitely. However, if the earth is even reasonably well managed and if population levels off in the decades to come, the answer to the question is a qualified "Yes."

Increasing Productivity

In 1970 Norman Borlaug was awarded the Nobel Peace Prize for his contribution to the world in the field of nutrition. Borlaug, a U.S. citizen of Norwegian descent, had spent a lifetime at work on strains of grain that would be high in yield, resist rust and various diseases, and be adaptable to soil and weather conditions in many countries and continents. Most of his research on wheat had been carried out in Mexico, which at the time his research started had to import about half of its wheat. Borlaug's research, funded by the Rockefeller Foundation, eventually resulted in a strain of wheat that doubled Mexico's yield, making it self-supporting in that important commodity.

What happened in Mexico also happened in the immeasurably more populous country of India. At the request of then Prime Minister Indira Gandhi, Borlaug went to study conditions in India, and concluded that his new wheat would prove adaptable to conditions there. By 1968, for the first time, Gandhi was able to announce to her people that India had reached a state of self-sufficiency in wheat, with a record harvest of 100 million tons (Doyle, 1985:259–261). The new wheat spread rapidly to Pakistan and has been used to some extent in much of the world. The case of India is particularly striking. A generation or so ago, India was stereotyped as a country always short of grain and often in a state of famine. Now it is only in times of unusual failures of the monsoonal rain pattern that India falls short of her newfound self-sufficiency in wheat.

Norman Borlaug is by no means the only person working on new varieties of grain and other foods. So many improvements of seed have come about that we now speak of a Green Revolution. All seed companies are busy producing many types of grain: wheat, corn, soybean, rye, and especially rice. In some parts of Southeast Asia, as a result of new strains, rice yields have doubled and doubled again. The seed companies have motivations other than humanitarianism in improving seed. New developments bolster profits.

A man trying to balance the self-interested pursuit of profit with socially responsible investment is Dwayne Andreas, sometimes called the "Soybean King." Like Larry Brown, quoted previously, Andreas is concerned about the damage malnutrition does to people. He is particularly interested in greater production of soybeans, not just because of his vested interest, but because they are higher in protein than any other vegetable. He has developed a number of nutritious drinks containing soybean oil—drinks that he gives away to poor countries. His contention is that it would be possible to provide a meal, enriched with soy protein, for $.50 per day. Such a meal for those who are chronically hungry "would increase IQs by one-third, and would make people four to five inches taller and 20 to 25 pounds heavier, and thus capable of more sustained work" (see Kahn, 1987). As fairly substantial proof of his contention, Andreas cites a case in Ghana where a Norwegian concern built a cement plant. Workers were provided the kind of meal Andreas describes, and they gained an average of 35 pounds in 18 months. "When people can gain that much, you know that previously they were starved," says Andreas.

Kahn (1987) gives another illustration of how great a change can sometimes be made for very small investments. Andreas had an interview with Mikhail Gorbachev not long before Gorbachev became General Secretary of the Soviet Union. Gorbachev complained to Andreas that cattle in the USSR produced 20 percent less meat than the same breed of cattle in the United States. He had already found that the reason was a shortage of protein in their feed. Andreas immediately found a customer for many tons of soybeans, convincing Gorbachev that they would make the difference and increase Soviet beef production by 20 percent, for absolutely no additional cost. The soybeans would cost no more than the grains they would replace.

Great though the increase in food production has been, much more must be done. On the optimistic side, it seems likely that much more *will* be done. Experimentation in the time-honored techniques of selective breeding and cross-breeding continue. Much more dramatic, however, is the dawning of an age of genetic engineering (changing gene codes on chromosomes). Already in the United States, seed companies are showing a great interest, backed by investments, in genetic engineering possibilities. Genes can be altered. Quite possibly many new strains of grain will outproduce anything yet developed. New possibilities include food that has far greater resistance to frost damage. Genetic engineering has produced a type of bacteria that, when sprayed on plant leaves, would keep them from freezing even in temperatures as low as 18° F. Regarding such bacteria, a word of caution is in order. Some people worry that if such bacteria were released they might cause unforeseen problems. Could they further heat the atmosphere? Developers are confident the answer is "No," but we are, of course, dealing with the unknown. Moreover, we really do not know the long-term human health consequences (over generations as well as individuals' lives) of genetic engineering. Although genetic engineering may help solve some food production problems, it should be kept in mind that "technological fixes" are not available to solve all our problems.

Lingering Doubts

Despite exciting progress, doubts linger about feeding the world. Another quotation from

Andreas is in order: "Look, it takes a new flour mill every week somewhere on earth just to feed that week's new mouths." From the comment on flour mills, he is led to thoughts about food animals—cattle and chickens, for example—that constantly increase in numbers and go on eating, eating, eating. Every day there are more cattle and chickens eating grain, while hungry people go looking for bread. Lester R. Brown, Hal Kane, and Ed Ayres (1993:36–37) report that the proportion of the world's grain being fed to animals has shown no sign of decreasing. It remains around 37 percent. The direct feeding of people with wheat, soybeans, yams, and the like would cut out the intermediary (in this case an animal) and bring about enormous food savings. Feeding animals as intermediaries is too costly. Also, evidence is increasing that there are health benefits from eating a plant-based diet. Most people who eat meat actually consume too much protein, which can impede absorption of other important nutrients. Aside from its super-dose of protein and hefty percentage of calories from saturated fat, meat has nothing else nutritionally to offer. It contains absolutely no fiber, which is now being investigated as a sort of "buffer" against certain kinds of intestinal cancer. So, in addition to providing more high-protein plants for people to consume, eliminating animals from our diet would have a positive health effect.

In addition to grain and meat as sources of food for the world's population, there is the fish harvested from the oceans. As in the production of grain, there has been a leveling off and an actual per capita decline since 1989. Figure 9.6A shows that 1989 was the record catch, and subsequent catches have fallen short of the 1989 harvest and show no signs of increasing. In fact, Figure 9.6B suggests that the projected seafood supply per person (taking future catches and world population projections into account) will decline as we enter the twenty-first century.

Figure 9.6
The world fish harvest has started to decrease, and is projected to continue to decline.

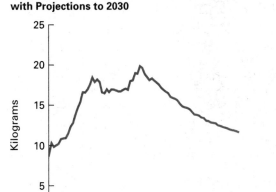

A. World Fish Harvest, 1950–1992

Source: Cited in L. R. Brown. 1994. *State of the World 1994,* p.179.

B. World Fish Harvest per Person, 1950–1992, with Projections to 2030

Source: Cited in L. R. Brown. 1994. *State of the World 1994,* p.182.

How Green Is the Green Revolution?

There is more to the story of India's Green Revolution. In 1972 there was a drought, and wheat again had to be imported. That is no reflection on the Green Revolution, but it is a reminder that nature often thwarts the best laid schemes. In thinking about whether the world will be fed, we must always allow for the possibility that things will not go as planned. Furthermore, there is evidence that declines in world grain production can have serious effects. As Table 9.3 shows, all regions of the planet, including North America, have witnessed decreases in per person production of grain, relative to the peak production year of that region. Lester Brown (1991:11–15) discusses four factors that explain this decline: (1) substantial acreage of marginal or highly erodible land is being abandoned, worldwide, for grain production purposes; (2) underground water tables are falling and aquifers are being depleted worldwide—water tables under parts of the North China Plain are dropping up to 1 meter per year, and the huge Ogallala aquifer under part of the U.S. breadbasket (Nebraska, Oklahoma, and Texas) is being slowly depleted due to irrigation; (3) air pollution is beginning to reduce crop production—in the U.S. it is estimated that air pollution has resulted in a 5 to 10 percent reduction in crop yield; and (4) the backlog of unused agricultural technology is declining.

There are other serious concerns regarding grain production (Doyle, 1985). One problem is that we market ever growing tonnage of only one or two strains of wheat or corn, increasing the vulnerability of the food supply. If a large percentage of a country's (or the world's) grain product is genetically identical, then it will all be subject to the same disease if a new disease appears. In some respects, there was more insurance in an old, traditional agriculture in which a hundred differences in seed strains could be found even in limited areas. One type might be vulnerable to a new disease, but another would be immune. Doyle's (1985:262) opinion is that

The Green Revolution was facilitated by hybrid plants, which require vast amounts of artificial fertilizer, herbicides, and water.

now there is a greater possibility of widespread disaster. History backs up Doyle's concern. From 1845 to 1847, Ireland experienced a terrible potato famine. The Irish had grown very dependent on the potato as a food supply. Thus, when a plant disease wiped out the crop, about three-quarters of a million people died of starvation and hundreds of thousands were forced to migrate to other lands. All of this occurred while the Irish government was exporting lamb and pork for profit.

Another concern about agriculture and food production was brought to the forefront of world attention in 1973 and for several years thereafter. The OPEC nations (Organization of Petroleum Exporting Countries, a cartel of 13

Regional and World Grain Production per Person, Peak Year and 1990	TABLE 9.3			
Region	Peak production		1990 Production	Change since peak year
	(year)	(kilograms)	(kilograms)	(percent)
Africa	1967	169	121	−28
E. Europe & Soviet Union	1978	826	763	−8
Latin America	1981	250	210	−16
North America	1981	1,509	1,324	−12
Western Europe	1984	538	496	−8
Asia	1984	227	217	−4
World	1984	343	329	−4

SOURCE: Based on U.S. Department of Agriculture, Economic Research Service, *World Grain Database* (unpublished printouts) (Washington, DC: 1990), with updates for 1990 harvest; cited in L. R. Brown, 1991. *State of the World*: p. 13.

nations that includes Mexico, Venezuela, and 11 Middle-East countries) managed to raise the price of oil drastically. Most fertilizers are petroleum products. The price of petrochemical fertilizers in India had been $50 per ton in 1971; in 1973 the price shot up to $225 per ton. By 1980 India was spending as much per year on fertilizer as it had paid 20 years before to import wheat! Not only was the price of fertilizer much higher, but the new crops of the Green Revolution demanded more of it. The new agriculture also demanded more irrigation and more use of farm machinery.

Rising Costs and Poverty

The new crops are best developed and most profitable on large acreages. In poor countries, the majority of agriculture had been family subsistence farms. All family members worked on the farm, growing traditional crops that were, perhaps, lower in yield than the new ones, but that could be depended on to grow in the same soil year after year. Farm animals were also the major source of fertilizer. With new crops, the possibility of making considerable money increased, but it depended on fertilizer, pesti-

cides, irrigation wells, and tractors. All these things cost money. Consequently, just as in the United States, there was a tendency to increase farm size, but there were fewer farms.

The family-type farm, although still common, is on the decline. Because of increased production costs, the cost of food has risen. The Green Revolution, then, widened the gap between rich and poor, even though far fewer agricultural imports are needed. In Communist countries such as China, most agriculture is collectivized. The result is that people lack a sense of ownership and are regimented by the government, but they are not driven out of farming by larger competitors. In India the peasants have more political freedom, but few options other than leaving their farms to seek jobs among the dispossessed of the city.

SUMMARY

The distribution of income and wealth is extremely uneven, both within and between nations. And this disparity is getting larger, not smaller. The "have" nations are becoming richer while the "have not" nations become poorer. One of the main causes of this growing disparity is the way multinational corporations invest in LDCs. Peripheral nations often experience a distortion of their economies because the type of development encouraged by multinational corporations usually does not benefit the general population, but only the small elite coopted by the multinationals. Other causes of this growing disparity are: huge debts that the less developed countries have incurred (with very high interest rates attached); an unwillingness, on the part of the more developed countries, to agree to more equitable terms of trade that would benefit the less developed countries; the increased importance of information and knowledge as keys to higher income, and the fact that the less developed countries are "out of the loop" on developments in these areas; extremely high rates of population growth in the less developed countries that make it very difficult for these countries to lower their unemployment rates and to become developed.

The disparity in the distribution of wealth within nations is greater in some nations than in others. Brazil has the greatest disparity of wealth in the world, with a tiny number of extremely rich people and huge numbers of extremely poor individuals. The United States is also characterized by an extremely skewed distribution of income and wealth. Such a skew is not so apparent as in Brazil, because poor people in the United States are not so destitute as those in Brazil. The middle class is decreasing in the United States, while the proportions in the lower classes are increasing. The very rich in the United States are becoming even more wealthy.

The nations of Europe, specifically the northern, Scandinavian countries, are characterized by more even distributions of wealth and income. These countries have traditions of comprehensive welfare systems, funded by fairly high tax rates. Thus, there is a forced reallocation of income, wealth, and resources through income and inheritance taxes.

There is also the question of whether the increasing number of people on the planet can be adequately fed. The Green Revolution gave us hope for a number of decades that we could, indeed, feed a growing world population. However, there is evidence that the Green Revolution may have run its course and that it may be difficult to feed the world's growing population. One way to address this problem is for the more developed countries to reduce, if not eventually eliminate, the consumption of meats and dairy products. These types of food require more resources to produce than grains, which can be consumed directly by humans, with fewer health risks.

KEY TERMS

Absolute poverty The condition of having less income than is necessary to ensure a minimum daily diet of 2,150 calories per person per day.

Baby boom: The large cohort of people born from the mid 1940s to the mid 1960s.

Deindustrialization The abandonment of industrial plants in countries with high labor costs, and the building of new plants in cheap-labor areas.

Desertification: The expansion of a desert area, caused by overgrazing along the desert borderlands.

Green Revolution: The massive increase in crop yields produced by new hybrids of grain that require artificial fertilizers, pesticides, and irrigation.

Lower-middle class The social class made up of more poorly paid professionals, sales people, secretaries, and many types of service workers.

Relative poverty The concept that poverty in the United States and other industrialized countries is not real, that people are poor in comparison to other citizens, not because they lack food and shelter.

Upper-middle class The social class directly beneath the "super rich" and characterized by high income, high education, and high-status occupations.

Working class The social class of people who have incomes similar to lower-middle class individuals, but whose jobs do not require as much training or hold as favorable status.

STUDY QUESTIONS

1. What is the American Dream? What factors are making this dream difficult to realize?

2. What distinguishes the super rich from the upper-middle class?

3. What are the differences between the lower-middle class and the working class?

4. Briefly discuss the new poverty in the more developed nations. What factors might explain this?

5. Discuss the causes of poverty in the less developed nations.

6. How does foreign investment in poor countries contribute to increased poverty?

7. What is meant by "distortion of the economies" of peripheral nations?

8. Discuss Robert Reich's future occupational categories (routine production services; in-person services; and symbolic-analytic services).

9. Briefly discuss the history of the Green Revolution.

10. What are some possible limitations to the Green Revolution?

ENVIRONMENTAL

POLLUTION

*I*n 1992, authorities in Mexico City closed schools, curtailed industrial production by shutting down hundreds of factories, and banned a million automobiles from roads and highways. This action was necessitated when the city's ozone level reached nearly 400 points. An ozone level of 100 points can irritate sensitive people and 300 points can make healthy people sick (Bales, 1992). Later that year, Santiago, Chile, experienced a similar circumstance—four of every ten motor vehicles were banned, factories were shut down, and people were forced to wear air-filter masks (Long, 1992). These tragedies helped focus public attention on the global nature of pollution.

Year by year, more pollutants are added to the world's air, water, and soil. Industrialized nations, in their search for cheap energy, depend heavily on petroleum and coal, which pollute the upper atmosphere with the products of combustion. At the same time, they try to rid themselves of urban sewage and industrial waste, which is spewed into coastal estuaries by the millions of tons. Increasingly, too, the less developed countries fall in line with the patterns of the leading industrial countries, looking for industrial products to be derived from the burning of coal and other fossil fuels for cheap energy. Both the more developed countries (MDCs) and the less developed countries (LDCs) have agricultural pests, which they try to eradicate with deadly pesticides. As pesticides poison the insects and rats, however, they can profoundly harm many other species, including our own.

ECOSYSTEMS AND THE BALANCE OF NATURE

An **ecosystem** is the combination of interrelationships among the total number of species in an area, as well as the relationships of those species to the physical components of the area such as soil, water, and climate. Paul and Anne Ehrlich (1970) illustrated the concept of an ecosystem with a description of a pond that is rich in life. Organic debris (deteriorating animal and vegetable matter at the bottom of the pond) supports water plants and plankton, upon which a great variety of microorganisms, insects, and fish depend. Some of the fish feed on mosquitoes or on smaller fish, and some of the birds above the pond nourish themselves with the fish. If something were to kill the plankton in the water, the whole complicated chain of life would be broken and species would die. Even eliminating the mosquitoes, which may seem like a good idea, would reduce the number of crickets, which

eat mosquitoes, and thus reduce the number of blackbirds, which depend on the crickets for much of their food. Shooting the blackbirds could result in a plague of crickets. The case of the blackbirds and crickets is a simple illustration of the **balance in nature.** Under natural conditions, a sustainable number of each species survives, meaning they are in balance with other species in their ecosystem.

In some respects, the ecosystem concept is similar to a sociologist's use of the word *society.* In a society, members are interdependent, and large numbers of members play different roles in the system. Just as the extermination of the plankton in the ecological system of the pond could bring death to the whole system, the elimination of farms and agriculture could exterminate a whole human society. Unlike natural ecosystems, a social system has cultural values, beliefs, and attitudes that culminate in laws. In ecosystems, nature alone makes the laws. At this point, though, we come to yet another similarity between social systems and ecosystems: Neither can completely ignore the laws of nature. When human societies interfere too drastically with ecosystems, destroying physical components or important species, and reducing the quality of life for all, a price must be paid.

Worldwide Ecosystems

Accounts of small areas of imbalance, such as the pond, bring an important question to mind: Are ecosystems generally small and self-contained, mere ponds, villages, hillsides, or islands, or can they be much more extensive? Is the entire earth one great ecosystem?

To answer the question about the extent of ecosystems, let us return to the comparison between ecosystems and social systems. Standard definitions of a social system include the phrase, "somewhat separate from other social systems." The implication is that social systems are entities. It is true that Chinese society is separate from the

Air pollution is so bad in Mexico City that residents, like this mail carrier, have to wear masks. The cement factory in the background has been called the worst polluter in the Valley of Mexico.

Even inside the classroom at Benito Juarez School, children have to wear face masks to protect them from polluted air. The school is located near a cement factory that adds particulate matter to the smoke-filled atmosphere.

societies of Europe and those of the Americas; French society is separate from the societies of Germany, Poland, and Great Britain, and so forth. Nevertheless, all those societies trade with one another; all of them have picked up cultural traits from one another; and in many cases they have even imported each other's flora and fauna, thus modifying ecosystems as well as social systems. Still, no society lives in total isolation. When the bubonic plague struck humankind

centuries ago, it recognized no national boundaries, just as AIDS knows no national boundaries. When a great nuclear disaster occurred at Chernobyl in the former Soviet Union, the fallout spread around the world, affecting Europe more than the Americas, but contaminating the environment almost everywhere to some degree. All contaminants in the atmosphere spread beyond their points of origin, and the whole world shares only one atmosphere.

EXTENT OF POLLUTION: WATER

Water is in many ways the essence of life, and water pollution is a subject of enormous importance and scope, affecting rivers, lakes, seas, oceans, and underground basins known as aquifers. The pollution of rivers, lakes, and seas is enormous and diverse, but there are certain common themes in the stories of their contamination. By looking first at a number of important rivers, we will see that they are being forced to serve too many functions, including disposal of human and industrial waste as well as irrigation needs and the quenching of human thirst.

The Ganges River

In recent years, the problems of three rivers have been prominent in the news: the Rhine in Western Europe and the Ganges which runs through India. To a degree their problems are not unique, but they do tell us something about their particular cultural and geographic areas. The Rhine, in German tradition, is the beautiful river of the Lorelei, romantic medieval castles and tourist cruises. The Ganges is a sacred river to India, in ancient belief flowing from heaven and purifying all things both physically and spiritually. For centuries people have bathed in the Ganges for spiritual purification, and believers have wished to have their ashes thrown into the Ganges after cremation. These customs continue, but vast increases in population and the growth of industry have created problems that almost defy imagination.

Every day, 234 million gallons of untreated sewage is discharged into the Ganges from the 27 cities and innumerable towns along its banks. Along with sewage goes industrial waste from 300 chemical plants and factories. The Indian government is undertaking an ambitious plan to clean the river, but programs receive far less support than is necessary. One reason is that industrialists and cities along the banks will not share the costs of the cleanup. More resistance comes from tradition. To the faithful, purification is a spiritual matter. The Ganges (*Ganga Ma*, or Mother Ganges, in Hindu), according to mythology, came into existence when Ganga, the Goddess of Water, flowed from heaven to earth to free the souls of human beings. To a great many Indians, therefore, the river is literally a god. *Ganga Ma* purifies regardless of her burden of wastes.

The government is concerned with a unique type of pollution not found in the Western world. Every year, 42,000 bodies are cremated on pyres of wood and thrown into the Ganges. Often the cremation is not complete, so thousands of partly burned bodies, along with 5,000 tons of ash, are ceremonially tossed into the river. In addition, an estimated 100 uncremated bodies are simply floated down the river by families too poverty-stricken to afford firewood. To deal with this situation, the government is importing thousands of carnivorous turtles, which it hopes will feast on the remains. But turtle meat is a delicacy, and India is a country of many hungry people (Tempest, 1987), so it is uncertain how effective this solution will be. Additionally, the government is beginning to insist that electric equipment be used to cremate more efficiently, preventing the gruesome sight of partly burned bodies and saving wood. Firewood is in increasingly short supply in many parts of the less developed world. Resistance to the government plan comes from cultural tradition, religion, and from the vested interests of industrialists and taxpayers. In virtually all cases, in wealthy and poor countries, one of the most important causes of pollution is the cost of preventing or cleaning it up (Yerkey, 1987).

The Rhine River

The Rhine is a river of international importance, rising in Switzerland, then forming part of the French-German border, flowing through Western Germany, then through the Netherlands, and into the North Sea near Rotterdam. A heavy concentration of industry along the Rhine has caused serious pollution. A disastrous chemical spill occurred in 1969, when a mere 200 pounds of an extremely toxic chemical, endosulphan, fell from a barge and poisoned the water for many miles. Thousands of dead fish floated down the Rhine. Even worse was the chemical spill that began at Basel, Switzerland, in November 1986. A fire broke out in a warehouse belonging to Sandoz, one of Switzerland's largest chemical companies. When firemen turned water hoses on the flames, the structure gave way, and 30 tons of chemicals, mainly pesticides and herbicides, were dumped into the Rhine. Later a second spill included the equivalent of two tons of mercury (Hull, 1986).

European officials were outraged when investigations revealed that another Swiss chemical manufacturer had deliberately dumped about 105 gallons of atrazine (a herbicide) into the Rhine the evening before the Sandoz fire. Such incidents as the poisoning of the Rhine and the fallout of radiation from Chernobyl have heightened awareness of the environmental problem. After the spill on the Rhine, protesters demonstrated with banners saying, TODAY THE FISH, TOMORROW US (Hull, 1986:37).

Although the deadly chemical spill occurred in a part of the world that one might expect to do better environmentally than India, the ecological disaster was greater than anything that has occurred on the Ganges. The food chain was broken at the plankton level because of the mercury poisoning, which meant death to the insects and larvae that had lived on the plankton, which in turn meant death to the eels (a delicacy of European diet) and fish that live in the Rhine. Finally, a large number of the ducks, gulls, and cormorants that winter along the Rhine was also exterminated. It will be many years before the Rhine is again rich in marine life; it never will be if such disasters recur (Watson, 1987). Figure 10.1 shows the countries that have been affected.

Narrow economic self-interest contributes to the problems of the Rhine. Laborers see jobs at

Figure 10.1
Tons of chemicals were dumped into the Rhine River at the point indicated. As the chemicals were washed downstream to the North Sea, they broke the food chain at the plankton level, killing insects, eels, fish, and water fowl.

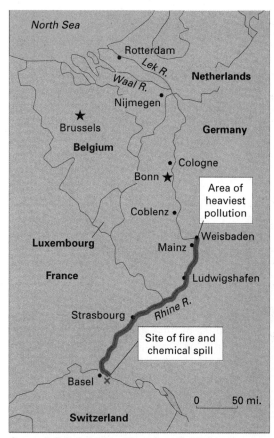

Source: J. B. Hull, "A Proud River Runs Red," *Time*, Nov. 24, 1986: 36–37.

stake if industries are heavily regulated, inspected, and forced to clean up. The results could be lower profits and possible plant closings. The German Green Party has taken environmental issues to heart, and European governments, pressured by various "green movements," seem to have become very progressive on environmental issues. But, as a prominent ecologist observes, "they are still not very good at enforcing their antipollution laws" (Elmer-DeWitt, 1992:54).

The Mississippi River

River pollution is by no means limited to Europe and Asia. The enormous Mississippi River is a U.S. region of heavy pollution that is an ongoing problem but attracts little attention. A disastrous flood, such as the one in the spring and summer of 1993, is more newsworthy. We debate whether to build levees higher and higher, how much the government should do for flood victims, and whether to stop people from settling in the most vulnerable areas. Little attention is given, though, to another problem of the Mississippi River: Large sections of it have been polluted for decades, and pollution spills over its banks along with flood waters. Michael H. Brown (1986) speaks of the Mississippi River as "The National Swill." The river begins its course, without pollution, in the tranquil countryside of Minnesota. Downstream contaminants are added, but the river is so vast that it can handle quite a lot of contaminating effluent—but how much? Increasing amounts of industrial waste, sewage, and particularly herbicides, pesticides, and fungicides are added. A chemical known as 2,3,7,8-tetrachlorodibenzofuran, "furan" for short, has been found in the Mississippi's waters. It has killed experimental guinea pigs at a concentration of only ten parts per billion, which amounts to a single drop in 1,280 barrels of water. Farther down the river at a tiny town a few miles below Hannibal, Missouri, one encounters a sign that reads:

CAUTION: HAZARDOUS WASTE SITE
DIOXIN CONTAMINATION
STAY IN CAR. MINIMIZE TRAVEL.
STAY ON PAVEMENT.
DRIVE SLOWLY.

Before its toxicity was realized, dioxin was mixed with oil and used for dust control or grading fill for roads. It has been used at more than 40 sites in Missouri alone. Much of it has entered streams, joining hundreds of other toxins that make the lower Mississippi into a flowing nightmare, "a chemical soup beyond scientific understanding" (Brown, 1986:57). Despite the final caution on the sign, it would seem tempting to drive fast to get out of there. The little town is now a ghost town; its 2,200 inhabitants have fled because it was unsafe for human (or animal) habitation. Dioxin is about 70,000 times more toxic than cyanide, the chemical that was mixed with Kool Aid in the mass suicide at Jonestown in Guyana, South America.

The Mississippi River, because of its size (2,348 miles) and the number of tributaries flowing into it, varies greatly in contamination from place to place. There are places in which one is warned not to eat the fish. Fishing is banned for 30 miles around Memphis where chlorinated hydrocarbons are manufactured for use in electrical insulation. People who eat the fish get skin rashes and sore throats. In Des Moines, Iowa, agricultural chemicals seep from the river into the wells of drinking water. Tap water is so contaminated that nitrate levels are featured nightly on local television stations ("Vital Signs", 1991). Downstream in Louisiana, the situation is worse. Louisiana produces about 25 percent of the nation's pesticides and also has many oil pits. In one year, says Michael Brown, Louisiana generated more than 16,000 pounds of wastes for every person in the state. Brown quotes a local fisherman as saying, "Everybody's scared. I wake up coughing and choking. We have to leave the house at times. I seen some black stuff in the heads of the crawfish, and you can taste it in the fish. The smell comes right out of the frying pan" (1986:63). It is probably no coincidence that the lower Mississippi finds itself a black dot on the cancer maps; many of its contaminants are carcinogenic.

Actually, much is spent on cleanup of the Mississippi, but the cost is overwhelming. One cultural factor involved in the "national swill" is not too different from that of the Ganges—the feeling that the great river can absorb any amount of pollution but still cleanse itself. That is true only to a point, and in the cases of the Ganges, the Rhine, and the Mississippi, that point has been exceeded. In all three cases, an important reason for continued pollution is economic. We have developed a way of life that calls for pesticides, herbicides, fungicides, and many other toxins that sometimes mingle together in river waters, transforming themselves into something even more deadly. Nevertheless, there is great economic need for such toxins. In the short run, the benefits are seen as outweighing the detriments, except in extreme and dramatic cases leading immediately to deaths and/or injuries on a large scale. To a marked degree in all countries, the tendency is to try deadly substances first, then investigate their lethal properties. In looking at other problems of water systems, we see the same lack of foresight. The problems are not beyond control, but they call for more knowledge and much more caution.

Dams and Environmental Problems

When great dams are built to impound thousands of acre-feet of water (an acre-foot = 43,560 cubic feet), the projects are matters of enormous pride to the countries building them. Hoover Dam on the Colorado River, completed in 1936, was called one of the wonders of the world. One of the proudest achievements of the early days of the Communist government in the former Soviet Union was the building of gigantic dams for flood control and hydroelectric development. By the 1930s they looked upon their dams as proof of their system's success. More recently, Kremlin leaders planned a vast diversionary system to bring water from the Ob River, which flows into the frozen Arctic Sea, down to the semiarid regions of Central Asia. However, former First Secretary Mikhail Gorbachev abandoned the project for two reasons: the costs were prohibitive and, more important, the ecological damage

outweighed the benefits. The Soviet Union already has enough polluted seas and lakes to attract the attention of such progressive leaders as Gorbachev and current President Boris Yeltsin.

In less developed countries, building gigantic dams is even more a matter of national pride than in the more developed countries; these dams are symbols of progressive development. However, they often cause environmental catastrophe. For example, by the late 1970s, India had invested more than $12 billion in the construction of 1,554 large dams to redirect rivers and generate power. But the affected areas are now three times more likely to flood during monsoons, the rain is less likely to percolate through the soil, and huge areas of earth have dried up and become unusable for agriculture (Postel, 1991). In spite of these effects, India is currently planning a $10 billion irrigation and hydroelectric project in its Narmada Valley that includes about 3,000 dams. If the project is completed, it will displace 100,000 people from villages, increase sediment and salinity in the river, and submerge farms and forests (Dorfman, 1992).

Damming the Nile

Since the beginning of recorded history, the Nile River has been the life blood of Egypt. In ancient times, the mysterious rise and fall of the river was attributed to the gods. Ancient Egyptians believed the river was sacred; its waters were poured from heaven. Through the long millennia of history, its seasonally rising waters were diverted through natural and manmade channels to produce crops. The water flooded the land for many days, soaking in thoroughly, and depositing silt to feed the later plantings of grain. In the autumn, the stumps of grain or corn left standing would return to the ground, helping the enrichment process. Cattle, goats, and other farm animals provided further fertilization for the soil so that it retained its fertility through time.

The Nile Valley was a rather simple ecosystem in which grain harvests depended on the labor of the *fellahin* (peasants), and they in turn depended on grain for life. Crops and farm animals all survived because of the Nile, as did the entire human population from the peasants to the Pharaoh. Pharaohs and dynasties came and went, but the Nile flowed forever; and just as eternal was the connection between water, silt, and grain. The Nile also built a rich delta at its mouth, extending the land area and preventing saltwater intrusion from the sea.

Each part of an ecosystem affects every other part. The water, the channels, the crude pumps, and the hard work of the *fellahin* were parts of the ecosystem that everyone could see. But with the coming of modern times, the silt the Nile deposited each season began to appear unnecessary. The world was producing artificial fertilizers from petrochemicals on a vast scale. Why use the laborious systems of antiquity? Why not join the world's great rush to agricultural modernity?

The old system had a long-time efficiency about it, but could not be pushed beyond its natural limits. With its rapidly growing population, Egypt needed more irrigated land. To increase output, the Egyptians built a dam on the Nile to store water and produce a constant flow, and to spring a second annual crop out of the soil. Crop production increased, especially production for export, with many acres of grain replaced by cotton. The cotton made money for landowners, but took up land that had once produced food for the people. Then came the dream of a much higher dam at Aswan so that, as the then ruler of Egypt, Gamal Abdel Nasser, said, "The largest lake ever shaped by humankind (would become) a source of everlasting prosperity" (Goldsmith and Hildyard, 1984:246). The dam was completed in 1970, cotton exports increased and hydroelectric power helped establish industries. Egyptians took great pride in their new dam, an accomplishment they believed to be unsurpassed anywhere. But the expected prosperity did not materialize due to such factors

as more mouths to feed, more land devoted to export crops that did little or nothing for the people, increased military spending, and the high costs of imported goods and services.

By the mid 1970s, worries developed concerning decreasing fertility of the land as well as the ever-rising cost of petrochemical fertilizers. "I say in all candor, as loudly as possible, I am worried, extremely worried, because of the threat to the fertility of our soils," said Sayyid Marei, who was the Egyptian Minister of Agriculture at that time (Goldsmith and Hildyard, 1984:61). He worried too, about the increasing salinity of the soil since there were no extended periods of fallowing of the land, and the land held enough moisture to bring up salt from deep below through capillary action.

Meanwhile, the delta of the Nile, which had grown for the past 6,000 years, began to shrink. In one decade it suffered a deficiency of 600 million tons of sediment which previously had reached the sea. The nutrient-rich sediment helped maintain fisheries in the nearby water— yet another part of the ecological system affected by the high dam. Now much of the sediment that once nourished farmlands and/or reached the delta settles under the water impounded by the Aswan High Dam.

Not only can an ecosystem be disturbed by the demise of some of its elements (floodwaters and silt in the case of Egypt), but sometimes new elements are introduced that disturb the balance. For example, bulinus snails flourish in aquatic weeds and spread schistosomiasis, a parasitic disease that attacks the bladder and the genitals or the spleen and liver. In some cases, cirrhosis of the liver develops; it is often fatal, always debilitating and painful. In the past, when the land surrounding the Nile lay fallow, it dried completely and killed the snails. Now, stagnant water supports aquatic weeds, which harbor the snails. In some communities of Egypt, the incidence of schistosomiasis approached 100 percent (Goldsmith and Hildyard, 1984:82).

A number of plant pests that attack corn, cotton, and other crops have also been introduced and have spread in the altered ecological conditions.

Can this distressing list of problems in the Nile Valley be cause for us to call the high dam "Nasser's Folly?" Actually, Nasser was praised for what seemed almost a messianic dream. Egypt needed to increase agricultural production and to develop hydroelectric energy that would attract industry. Economically, building the high dam seemed like a forward step. Ethnocentrically, such a project was very appealing to a proud people who had been under foreign rule for centuries. Furthermore, such dams have been built in many other countries, including LDCs like Nigeria, Ghana, India, and Sri Lanka, and MDCs such as the United States, Canada, and the former Soviet Union. As in Egypt, most of these dams were welcomed by the people and government, but have produced many unforeseen consequences. Goldsmith and Hildyard (1984) find more harm than good in virtually all of them. Their case may be exaggerated, but they correctly emphasize that nearly always money is appropriated and dams are built without prop-

erly considering the long-term effects. Lack of drainage and, especially in very warm climate, serious health problems usually accompany new dams and irrigation systems.

Irrigation and Diseases

Not only is schistosomiasis a plague in Egypt, but its worldwide incidence is on the rise. It now affects more than 100 million people, twice as many as suffered from the disease 30 years ago, causing suffering for all its victims and death for many. Malaria, a disease once considered under control and about to be eradicated, has made a dramatic comeback and now affects about 160 million people. Two other diseases spread by insects in areas of standing water are filariasis and onchoceriasis found in West Africa and also in southern Egypt and Sudan. The former can cause such severe swelling of body parts that the only treatment is amputation. The latter, often called "river blindness," is out of control in Ghana and Burkina Faso, where it has left whole villages of people blind (Goldsmith and Hildyard, 1984:72–84). Before large dams and canals were developed, the spread of such

A World Health Organization helicopter sprays biodegradable pesticide on blackfly larvae. The blackfly spreads river blindness.

disease was curbed during dry periods of the year; now there are no dry seasons to hold diseases in check. In the 1990s, it is possible to kill the germs causing river blindness, but its actual eradication awaits better health care.

Sociological Effects of Great Dams

There are a few cases, as in modern China, where the lands irrigated by new dams and canals are held collectively by the peasants to promote social equality. But the more common result of such water projects is the ultimate dispossession of the peasants of the land. Irrigation projects are financed by multinational corporations or governments, and usually result in large plantation agriculture. People who once worked small patches are removed from the land and must look for jobs in the rapidly growing cities (see Chapter 7). This process goes on in most of the world's agricultural areas as fewer people are needed on the land. Even in the United States, water costs make it impossible for small farmers to compete with huge agribusiness conglomerates. Although the law gives preference to small family farms in the use of water from government dams, there are ways to beat the system, and water is often sold at bargain rates to very large farm corporations (Myers, 1984).

The quality of drinking water can also be a problems in MDCs. Fifteen million people in the United States consume unsafe water. Although the Safe Drinking Water Act was signed into law in 1974, a study published in 1988 found 2,100 contaminants in U.S. water systems: 97 of them were known carcinogens (elements that cause cancer), 82 can cause mutations, 28 are toxic, and 23 promote tumors. Of 446 water systems tested by the Environmental Protection Agency, only 60 met federal standards (Sivard, 1992).

In LDCs, as more dams are constructed, less potable (drinkable) water is available to the people. About 40 percent of the world's population simply does not have enough water. Many

governments choose to channel water resources toward agricultural projects rather than to their people. Ironically, there are LDCs in which poverty and hunger grow as new irrigation projects are developed, because the irrigation helps produce crops for export, not for the indigenous population. Consequently, there are countries around the globe with hungry people selling food to affluent nations. Although some of that income helps with industrialization, often much more of the money goes to military expenditures (Sivard, 1992). Figure 10.2 shows that many more billions of dollars are spent annually on weapons than on grain.

The Oceans

In the early nineteenth century, the romantic poet, Lord Byron, wrote glowingly of the ocean:

Figure 10.2
Although more money was spent on grain than on military arms in the 1960s, the situation reversed in the 1980s. As the Cold War began to wind down in the 1990s, the gap (approaching $40 billion in the mid 1980s) should begin to close.

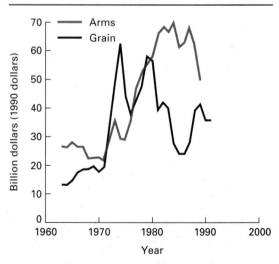

World Arms and Grain Trade, 1963–1991

Source: L. R. Brown, C. Flavin, and H. Kane, *Vital Signs 1992,* (New York: W. W. Norton, 1992), p. 104.

A thousand fleets sweep over thee in vain.
Man marks the earth with ruin; his control
Stops on the sea; upon that watery plain
Thou alone holdst sway; thou goest forth
Dread, fathomless, alone.

A century and a half later, we have to admit that the ocean, too, can be marked with ruin. The ocean no long "goest forth alone," nor is it uncontaminated by "a thousand fleets." It carries fleets of oil tankers, some holding as much as a half million tons of petroleum, which occasionally spills in the ocean and causes ecological disaster. It absorbs untold millions of tons of herbicides, pesticides, domestic and industrial sewage, heavy metals, radioactive fallout and radioactive waste, mercury and arsenic, and tanks of poisons originally intended for chemical warfare. In New York harbor and its surroundings, the ocean receives a daily dosage of 2,600 tons of carbon, 780 tons of oil and grease, 520 tons of nitrogen, 230 tons of copper, and sizeable amounts of lead, mercury, and polychlorinated biphenyls (PCBs), a family of very toxic and persistent chemicals used in plastics, electrical insulators, and hydraulic fluids (Myers, 1984).

It is not known how much pollution the oceans can handle. In earlier times, when human population was relatively small, the ocean seemed a great purifier that could receive and cleanse all the world's wastes. In modern times, however, this is clearly not true. We feed the oceans more nonbiodegradable substances, such as grease, oil, and plastics. Added to these are dangerous chemicals, ever increasing in number and toxicity. We also have problems of radioactivity, which did not exist in the past, brought on by the vaporizing of tiny Pacific atolls by atomic bomb testing and oceanic dumping of radioactive wastes. No one knows how much of these pollutants can be absorbed, but enough damage has been done already to make environmentalists apprehensive.

The worst ocean contamination occurs in harbors and estuaries and on the continental shelves, which are the relatively shallow parts of the ocean close to shore. Although continental shelves and estuaries make up only 10 percent of ocean area, they produce 90 percent of all known marine plant and animal life (Naar and Naar, 1993:844). In addition to a majority of fish, they produce practically all shrimp, scallops, oysters, crabs, abalones, and squid. Philip Elmer-DeWitt points out that the "real threats to the oceans, accounting for 70 percent to 80 percent of all maritime pollution, are the sediment and contaminants that flow into the seas from land-based sources—topsoil, fertilizers, pesticides, and all manner of industrial wastes" (1992:44). He points out also that every country contributes to the problem, generally in proportion to its size. However, countries that aggressively harvest their forests cause greater pollution because the clearing of forest land increases runoff into the oceans. Figure 10.3 shows various types of contamination afflicting the continental shelf of the 48 contiguous United States. And, just north of the U.S. border, Canadian beluga whales produce milk that contains PCBs at 3,400 times the safe levels for drinking water (Satchell, 1992).

When pollutants enter the food chain, they go through **bioamplification**. Bioamplification is the increasing concentration of pesticides as they pass upward from plankton and aquatic plants to higher forms of life. For example, mercury enters the tiny plankton, eaten by larger organisms, which are in turn eaten by fish, which are eaten by people. In Minimata, on Japan's southern Island of Kyushu, mercury poisoning resulting from the eating of mercury-contaminated fish killed 700 people and crippled 9,000 more. Chisso Corporation, a coastal factory that had for years been dumping its mercury-containing waters into Minimata Bay, was eventually discovered to be the source of the contamination, but only after many people suffered and died. Hospitals are still treating the crippled and brain-damaged victims. The sickness is characterized by blindness, tremors, seizures, paralysis, unconsciousness, and genetic deformities. People from

Figure 10.3
Even the oceans are contaminated by pollutants. Water along the northeast seaboard, the eastern coast of Texas, and several areas in California, Oregon, and Washington is home to fish that now show high levels of toxic chemicals. Large sections of the Gulf of Mexico and both coastal areas of the United States are closed to commercial fishing.

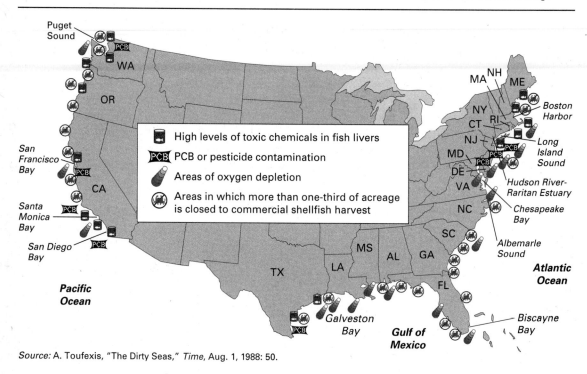

Source: A. Toufexis, "The Dirty Seas," *Time,* Aug. 1, 1988: 50.

Minimata have found it virtually impossible to marry because prospective mates fear the possibility of deformed children. Although courts found Chisso Corporation criminally negligent, there is no way to eradicate the mercury from Minimata Bay, so the whole bay has been filled with dirt (Weisskopf, 1987). Figure 10.4 shows how effluence from multiple sources eventually ends up in the world's oceans.

Oil spillage presents another assault on the planet's oceans. Worldwide attention was drawn to the coast of Alaska in 1989 when the *Exxon Valdez* grounded on Prince William Sound, an ecologically fragile area. As the ship split apart, the 10.8 million gallons of oil it carried gradually seeped into the ocean and onto the coastal land mass, killing virtually

every life form in the region (Parrish, 1992). It was a tragic accident, but an even greater catastrophe was caused quite deliberately two years later. With Iraqi troops in full retreat as Operation Desert Storm wound down in Kuwait, Saddam Hussein ordered his fleeing soldiers to blow up about 700 oil wells. The explosions produced a cloud of smoke so thick that sunlight was completely blocked out, and 390 million gallons (1,450,000 tons) of crude oil spilled into the Persian Gulf. Once the wellhead fires were extinguished, it took about a year for the air to clear. There are still about 30 large lakes of oil on the land, and the Gulf remains so polluted that many of the people living nearby suffer from respiratory disease. Ibrahim Hadi, president of Kuwait's Environ-

Figure 10.4
Oceans become the ultimate dumping ground for various types of pollutants. Acid rain, pesticides, fertilizer, heavy metals, raw sewage, oil spills, and other debris are cast into the world's oceans. Inevitably, contamination enters the food chain, eventually negatively affecting the human beings who produced the original pollutants.

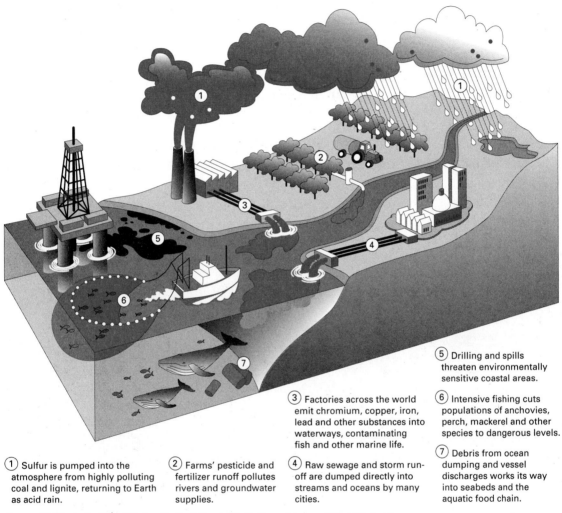

5. Drilling and spills threaten environmentally sensitive coastal areas.

3. Factories across the world emit chromium, copper, iron, lead and other substances into waterways, contaminating fish and other marine life.

6. Intensive fishing cuts populations of anchovies, perch, mackerel and other species to dangerous levels.

7. Debris from ocean dumping and vessel discharges works its way into seabeds and the aquatic food chain.

1. Sulfur is pumped into the atmosphere from highly polluting coal and lignite, returning to Earth as acid rain.

2. Farms' pesticide and fertilizer runoff pollutes rivers and groundwater supplies.

4. Raw sewage and storm run-off are dumped directly into streams and oceans by many cities.

Source: "A Day in the Life of Mother Earth: A Special Earth Summit Issue of World Report," *Los Angeles Times*, June 25, 1992: H7.

mental Protection Agency, says that it will take years to clean up the mess, and it will cost at least $20 billion. He claims he will send the bill to Saddam Hussein (Easterbrook, 1992).

Such disasters can help focus the public's attention on ongoing social problems. As a result

of the *Exxon Valdez* calamity, for example, the United States passed the Oil Pollution Act of 1990. Under the provisions of this law, the owners of large tankers have an increased liability (up to $200 million), must clean up their spills, and must contribute up to $1 billion worth

Figure 10.5
Oil and water don't mix, yet the world's oceans have been subjected to dozens of major oil spills from tanker ships. Spills of these magnitudes (10,000 gallons or more) cost millions of dollars to clean up and have a negative effect on all oceanic life.

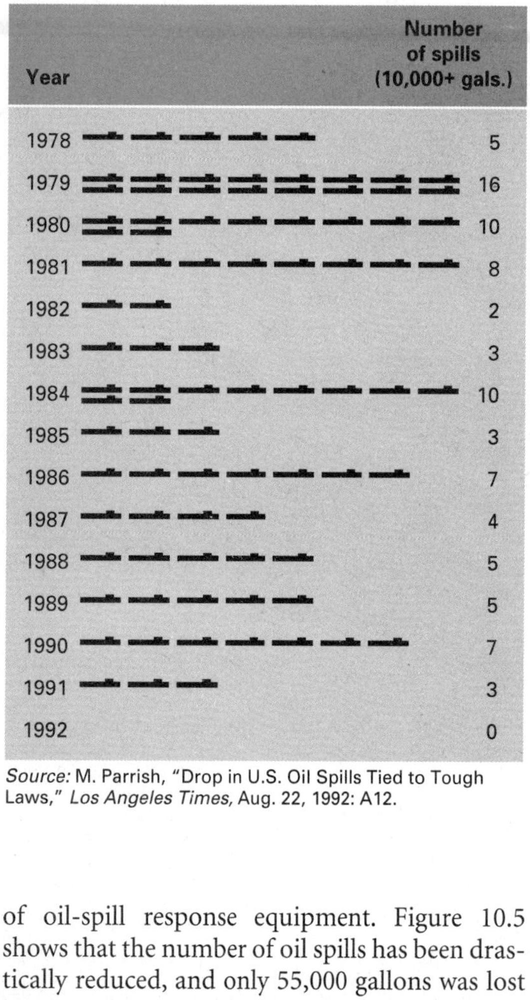

Year	Number of spills (10,000+ gals.)
1978	5
1979	16
1980	10
1981	8
1982	2
1983	3
1984	10
1985	3
1986	7
1987	4
1988	5
1989	5
1990	7
1991	3
1992	0

Source: M. Parrish, "Drop in U.S. Oil Spills Tied to Tough Laws," *Los Angeles Times,* Aug. 22, 1992: A12.

of oil-spill response equipment. Figure 10.5 shows that the number of oil spills has been drastically reduced, and only 55,000 gallons was lost in 1991. However, although events like the *Exxon Valdez* disaster and Hussein's environmental terrorism grab the media spotlight, most oil damage to the oceans comes from municipal and industrial drainage, the pumping of bilges and tanks on ships, and other routine events (Wright, 1991:538).

Seas and Lakes

Probably no seas on the surface of the earth have been devastated more thoroughly than those in regions that fell under the geopolitical influence of the former Soviet Union. The Aral Sea, located between Uzbekistan and Kazakhstan is a case in point. According to Lester Brown (1991), the sea has dropped 40 feet in the last 30 years and has lost the majority of its volume. One must now travel up to 30 miles from its former coastline to get to its polluted waters. Thirty years ago, fishermen hauled 160 tons of fish from it each day. Now, frozen fish are trucked in from the Baltic Sea.

James Rupert (1992) claims that the cause of the destruction was the Soviet government's lack of public accountability. Because it was dangerous for citizens to criticize the government, questionable plans could be implemented without protest. It must be admitted, though, that nearly all countries have instituted environmentally questionable policies. Competition has become so intense that any means of increasing production has been pursued with callous disregard for the future. In the case of the Aral Sea, the water of the Amu Darya and Syr Darya rivers (Figure 10.6), the two major sources of fresh water for the Aral Sea, were diverted from the sea in order to grow cotton in the desert region. As the river flow slowed, the sea gradually shrank. Figure 10.7 shows that in 1960 the sea covered 25,800 square miles. After three decades of assault due to governmental policies, only 13,000 square miles are left, and it continues to dry up.

On the northeastern edge of the former Soviet Union lies the Baltic sea, the tragic victim of both European and Soviet policies (Figure 10.8). Its major problems started at the end of World War II when Allied Forces seized hundreds of thousands of Nazi chemical weapons and casually tossed them into the sea. Today, the containers holding the chemicals are corroding, and the deadly gases are leaking into the already polluted waters. Peter Green observing from Lithuania and Estonia, and David Bartal looking from

Figure 10.6
Two rivers that used to supply fresh water to the Aral Sea (center), Syr Darya and Amu Darya, were diverted to an arid region of the former Soviet Union. Soviet decision makers thought that it was more important to produce cotton, using the river's waters, than to preserve the sea.

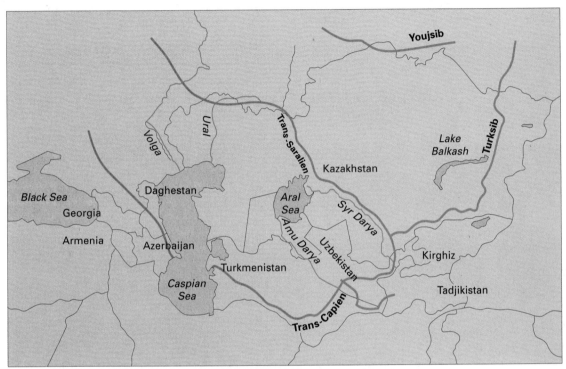

Source: G. Chaliand and J. P. Rageau, *Strategic Atlas: A Comparative Geopolitics of the World's Powers,* Third Edition (New York: HarperCollins, 1992): p. 100.

Sweden and Denmark (1992:47), create a poignant image: "Pink foam lines the beach. Greenish-brown sewage hugs the shore before it merges into the dull, slate-blue of the deeper sea."

With most financial resources tied up in the military arms race, Soviet planners neglected the need for sewage treatment plants in Kaunas, Lithuania's second largest city, so raw sewage is discharged directly into the Baltic. Other cities have only rudimentary systems. The sea has also been a dump for radioactive waste, toxic chemicals, and heavy metals discarded by the former Soviet Union and the recently formed Common-

wealth of Independent States. Yevgeny Usov of Russia's neophyte Green Party says, "The Baltic Sea is known as the chamber pot of Europe" (Simon, 1992:6). To make matters worse, two of Europe's filthiest rivers, the Oden and the Vistula, empty into the Baltic's basin. The Vistula River, which flows through Poland, is a relatively clean river until it reaches the industrialized areas where it picks up an incredible amount of pollution. Each day the Vistula dumps 12,000 pounds of zinc, 165 pounds of cadmium, 1,650 pounds of copper, 1,100 pound of lead, and 470 tons of organic matter, mostly fertilizers and untreated sewage, into the Baltic (Powers, 1992). Under such intense

Figure 10.7
Once one of the world's great seas, the Aral has been shrinking for more than three decades. In the 1960s (light area) it covered 25,800 square miles and was a major source of fish. By 1991 (dark area), it had shrunk to 13,000 square miles. Now, fish are trucked into the region because the water that is left in the Aral is too polluted for fishing.

Figure 10.8
When the Baltic republics of Estonia, Latvia, and Lithuania were under the control of the former Soviet Union, government leaders decided that it was more important to put its money into the arms race than to squander it on sewage treatment plants. Consequently, raw sewage drains from the Baltic republics directly into the Baltic Sea, which is already polluted from many other sources.

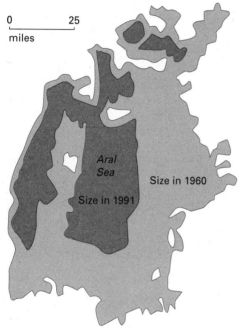

Source: J. Rupert, "Death of a Desert Sea," *Washington Post National Weekly Edition*, July 6–12, 1992: 10.

Source: G. Chaliand and J.-P. Rageau, *Strategic Atlas: A Comparative Geopolitics of the World's Powers,* Third Edition (New York: HarperCollins, 1992): p. 98.

siege, it is no wonder the deeper parts of the sea are already dead, and the upper levels are dying.

Whatever the environmental problems concerning the Soviet Union's rivers and lakes, the United States and Canada are in no position to gloat. The two countries share the only lakes comparable in size to the Aral and the Baltic Seas. The Great Lakes have suffered pollution levels hard to rival in any part of the world. William Ashworth's (1986) authoritative book, *The Late Great Lakes*, details implications of present-day or approaching environmental death. There are, he says, 60,000 major generators of toxic wastes in

the United States, producing about 90 billion pounds of hazardous material per year. Nearly one-fourth of the disposal of those toxic materials is within the Great Lakes Basin, draining into the Great Lakes. Canada produces much less toxic waste than the United States, but a larger percentage of it within the Great Lakes Basin. Ashworth gives examples of Canadian pollution, but singles out the United States's side of the border, near Niagara Falls, as the place of highest concentration of poisoned land and water. The Niagara area includes the notorious Love Canal and a place called the Model City Site, "where radioactive wastes left over from World War II's Manhattan Project are migrating toward Lake Ontario in open ditches" (Sheaffer and Stevens, 1983:215).

Water: Quantity and Quality

The building of large dams in much of the less-developed world has greatly increased the quantity of water available, but not the quality. As we have seen, water supplies are infested with deadly microorganisms as well as pesticides, herbicides, and fungicides. In many cases, industrial waste from factories drawing hydroelectric power from the new dams is added to the brew. Where there is no sewage system, canals and rivers serve as sewers, although generally not in China, where human wastes are returned to the soil to serve as fertilizer. More than half the people of the less developed counties lack access to water that is free from harmful bacteria or chemicals. Ponds and rivers are often the main source of drinking water for rural people. The consequences of drinking impure water from such sources are dysentery and other diarrheal diseases, including cholera, which kill more than 1,000 children per hour throughout the world (Myers, 1984:-120–121). Even in urban areas where running water is available, one is usually advised to drink only bottled water.

We cannot deny that there are places in the United States and Europe where people are also advised to drink bottled water, usually because of chemical pollution or radioactivity. Nevertheless, in wealthy, industrialized countries, water supplies are clean enough so that the majority of people need only turn on the tap to get potable water.

But even in the MDCs, the future quality of water supplies is a matter of some concern. Are water supplies remaining pure, or are they facing contamination? Equally important, are water supplies adequate now and for the future, especially in countries with extensive arid or semiarid regions, such as much of Australia, the western United States, and Central Asia?

In the Russian city of Novokuznezk, the air is fouled by a steel factory. Mismanagement of the environment by the leaders of the former Soviet Union has left the rivers polluted, one-quarter of the drinking water unsafe to drink, and 35 million people living in cities where the air is unsafe to breathe.

Regarding the first question, current trends are not very reassuring. The vastly increased use of chemicals and the spread of industrial plants to more parts of the world make the chemical-pollution problem nearly universal. Chemical wastes are often dumped in the very places where they will do the most possible harm to water supplies—in the lakes and rivers or in pits deep enough to draw in surface water after every rain. Although not specifying whether they are

Water-Scarce Countries, 1992, with Projections for 2010[1]			TABLE 10.1
		Per capita renewable water supplies	
Region/Country	1992	2010	Change
	(cubic meters per person)		(percent)
Africa			
Algeria	730	500	−32
Botswana	710	420	−41
Burundi	620	360	−42
Cape Verde	500	290	−42
Djibouti	750	430	−43
Egypt	30	20	−33
Kenya	560	330	−41
Libya	160	100	−38
Mauritania	190	110	−42
Rwanda	820	440	−46
Tunisia	450	330	−27
Middle East			
Bahrain	0	0	0
Israel	330	250	−24
Jordan	190	110	−42
Kuwait	0	0	0
Qatar	40	30	−25
Saudi Arabia	140	70	−50
Syria	550	300	−45
United Arab Emirates	120	60	−50
Yemen	240	130	−46
Other			
Barbados	170	170	0
Belgium	840	870	+4
Hungary	580	570	−2
Malta	80	80	0
Netherlands	660	600	−9
Singapore	210	190	−10
Additional countries by 2010			
Malawi	1,030	600	−42
Sudan	1,130	710	−37
Morocco	1,150	830	−28
South Africa	1,200	760	−37
Oman	1,250	670	−46
Somalia	1,390	830	−40
Lebanon	1,410	980	−30
Niger	1,690	930	−45

[1]Countries with per capita renewable water supplies of less than 1,000 cubic meters per year. Does not include water flowing in from neighboring countries.

SOURCE: S. Postel, "Facing Water Scarcity," in L. R. Brown, et al., *State of the World 1993* (New York: W. W. Norton, 1993), p. 25.

directly above usable water sources, the Environmental Protection Agency listed 20,766 sites of chemical dumps, of which 812 were placed on a national priority list to be cleaned (*World Almanac*, 1993:149). Clean Water Acts were passed in the United States in 1972 and amended in 1977 and 1990, but improvements have been slow. A 1986 measure, passed over President Reagan's veto, increased the funding for water cleanups. However, in the mid 1990s with a Democratic administration in conflict with a Republican Congress determined to cut the national budget, it is not likely that money will be appropriated to clean up chemical dumps. Meantime, the League of Women Voters of California reports that 2,449 wells in California's Central Valley are contaminated with pesticides, including some that have been outlawed since 1977 (Adler, 1991). California's problems are of particular interest because that state uses nearly half of the agricultural pesticides employed in the United States. The use of pesticides escalates in California as insect pests build up immunity to a toxin, or the natural enemies of those pests are killed off by pesticides. Stronger doses of toxins are used or new toxins are developed. The situation has become so overwhelming in California that the Environmental Protection Agency recorded about 100,000 violations of its water quality standards in 1990 alone (Brown, Flavin, and Postel, 1991:26)! Unfortunately, this promises to become the established pattern for many parts of the world. Table 10.1 shows the extent of water scarcity now and projected to the year 2010 in various countries.

Turning to the next question, which can be just as worrisome to the MDCs and to the LDCs: How are water supplies holding out? For many years the supplies have increased in countries either because of the building of dams or the drilling of more and deeper wells. In either case, however, possibilities are limited.

Wells at the southern border of the Sahara Desert, for example, encouraged larger stocks of cattle and goats, which led to overgrazing. There is a limit to how much water can be pumped out of the ground. In virtually all countries, the use of water constantly increases, due in part to such factors as increases in population and the amount of water used by individuals. Additionally, people who eat a lot of meat use much more water than those who live largely on grains. Each pound of beef, for example, is produced at a cost of about 2,464 gallons of water and nine pounds of feed (Nash, 1992).

Industry also requires increasing amounts of water. A moderate-sized paper mill uses as much water as the residents of a city of 1 million people. A ton of steel requires about 30,000 gallons of water in its manufacture (Sheaffer and Stevens, 1983:69–70).

The result of increased water use is a constant search for more water. In Israel, drip agriculture is used extensively to save precious water. Drip agriculture is a system by which each plant is given its supply of water through tubes that release only the amount needed, drop by drop. In the United States there are very few examples of such scrupulous water conservation. More typically, water is used with considerable abandon: If the well runs dry, we drill deeper. Consequently, the United States is using water faster than nature can replenish the supply. Figure 10.9 shows that rain seeps through soil into an aquifer, where some is stored for use as drinking water or for irrigation while some moves through the aquifer to the ocean. Although in most parts of the country our "bank account" of groundwater is very large, it is being overdrawn. In 1950 the United States pumped 21 billion gallons per day from underground; by 1990 it was pumping more than three times that amount, 75 billion gallons daily (Davis, 1992:457).

Building more dams cannot always compensate for underground water depletion. Yet in such dry areas as Kazakhstan (just south of western Siberia) in the former USSR (see Figure 10.6) or the western United States, construction of dams and aqueducts continues to increase. Demand for such projects in the United States has remained strong; in the late 1970s President Carter lost

Figure 10.9
In a balance of nature, water replaces itself through the hydrologic cycle. Water evaporates into the atmosphere, supplying moisture to clouds. Clouds concentrate water vapor into rain. Precipitation flows through the soil and is purified as it travels through aquifers. Ultimately, it returns to its original source.

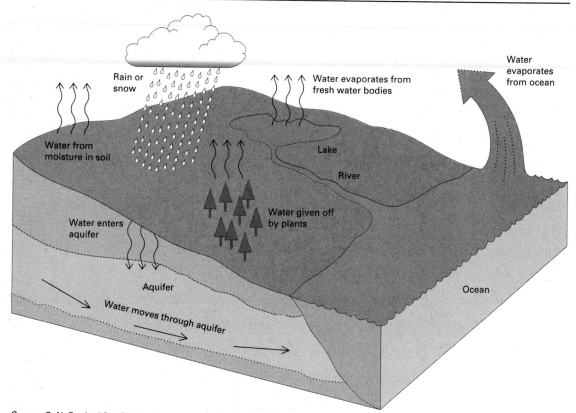

Source: S. N. Davis, "Our Precious Ground Water," *The World Book Year Book: 1992* (Chicago: World Book, 1992), p. 459.

substantial political support when he tried to slow dam building. Carter believed that careful studies of environmental impact and economic soundness should be made before further funding. Carter's unpopular opinion implied that perhaps we are reaching the end of dam sites that are profitable to develop. Building dams in the West with federal money causes the East to help pay for developments from which it will not benefit directly. The main problem, though, is a lack of adequate rivers to impound. Southern

California, always thirsty, already taps considerable amounts of water from the Colorado River (300 miles away), Owens Valley (300 miles away), and Northern California (from 300 to 500 miles away), and has set its sights on the Columbia River in the state of Washington (almost 1,500 miles away).

An expert on water problems, Sandra Postel (1990), argues that we have reached the limit of new water sources. As of 1987, the Bureau of Reclamation agreed, announcing no plans for future dams. The Clinton administration has actually considered the destruction of several dams, including the Edwards Dam on the Kennebec River in Maine and the Glines Canyon Dam and the Elwha Dam in the state of Washington (Gup, 1993).

Proposals to end water scarcity range from new but somewhat out-of-reach techniques, to old-fashioned but reliable ones. One suggestion has been to convert ocean water to fresh water through desalinization. However, the high cost of this process puts it completely out of range for agriculture or industry. Other ideas include towing icebergs from Alaska and pumping ice from the Arctic. But for the present, the real solution is conservation. Rather than dumping billions of gallons of chemically treated sewage into rivers to be carried down to the ocean, why not use it for farms? The idea is by no means new nor untried. The great nineteenth-century novelist and poet, Victor Hugo, was extremely interested in the problem and was instrumental in bringing about a cleanup of the hideous sewers of Paris and using the reclaimed water for many acres of beautiful gardens.

Reclaimed sewage has supported some of the most successful agriculture in France for many decades. Many of the cities of Germany and England follow the same plan. The treated sewage water irrigates crops, then seeps downward into underground aquifers, being further cleansed by vegetation, sand, and limestone, which, for many purposes, is the world's best filter. The idea is by no means exclusively European. In Michigan, 13 municipalities use their reclaimed sewage water on farms, and there are similar examples in Illinois, Colorado, California, and New Jersey. The city of Lubbock, Texas, profits from a large farm nearby that has been irrigated with the effluent from Lubbock's sewage treatment plant since the 1930s. The result is not only a large and highly profitable farm, but the water seeps down to the underground basin, further purifying itself as it goes. While many other municipalities in the vicinity

complain of lowered water tables, Lubbock has no water shortage and is able to maintain very large green parks and three small lakes.

Before closing the subject of water conservation through reuse, however, we must be reminded that if the water is contaminated by hazardous chemicals, held in solution, the purification process becomes virtually impossible. Such contaminants are not filtered out by sand or other earth materials through which they pass. Either they must be combined with other chemicals that change their toxic nature, or the water must evaporate and return to earth again as rain before it is pure. There are, though, cases in which even the rain is not pure.

EXTENT OF POLLUTION: AIR

Air pollution is to some degree a phenomenon of the entire world because there is constant circulation in the atmosphere. Pollution from one area blows into another. Sometimes the pollution is beyond human control, like the eruption of Mt. Pinatubo in the Philippines in 1992, which belched so much volcanic ash into the atmosphere that it had a slight cooling effect on climate throughout the world. More frequently, the pollution is manmade, like that from the explosion of the nuclear plant at Chernobyl in 1986.

The usual case of air pollution is much less dramatic, however. It is little noticed at first, and thought of as a problem for other people. "London fog" can be thought of as the prime example of early air pollution. It was a dense, choking pollution caused by coal smoke rising from hundreds of thousands of chimneys in the city. In 1952 pollution was blamed for 4,000 deaths and tens of thousands of illnesses in London (French, 1990:99). However, it was seen as solely the problem of London, and it was being cleaned up. Central heating replaced fireplaces, and coal was replaced by oil. Surely the same could have happened throughout the world. But oil prices rose dramatically in 1973, and coal came back into its own. Prices became an important factor in decisions of whether to pay attention to pollution. Many cities now resemble London of a century ago. In such cities, though, coal is not the only problem. Automobiles and trucks pour their emissions into the air. Some cities cope with these problems fairly well. Others fail utterly.

Factors Involved in Pollution

Level of Development

The level of industrial development correlates with pollution. As a broad generalization, it can be said that societies that live largely by small-scale agriculture are minimal polluters of the air; but if they catch up to the modern world and spread tons of pesticides, they can become heavy polluters.

At the opposite end of the developmental scale are societies learning to cope with air pollution. We have just mentioned that London no longer suffers from old-fashioned London fogs. Most of the cities of Western Europe, the United States, and Canada have worked to prevent degradation of air quality. The same cannot be said for much of Eastern Europe and certainly not for many of the LDCs.

Typically, the level of air pollution becomes worse in cities of the less developed world as they are rushing to catch up. In some cases, the air is not only bad, it is lethal. According to a study commissioned by the World Bank (*World Developmental Report*, 1992) air quality is growing worse, particularly in two measurements: suspended particulate matter (SPM) and sulfur dioxide (SO_2). As the name implies, **suspended particulate matter** consists of all the tiny particles in the air—coal dust, soot, smoke, bits of cattle dung, straw, and so on. Such air particles are a problem where household heat and the cooking of food both depend upon open fires, fueled by cattle dung, straw, wood, or coal. Dense populations greatly increase cooking fires

and dirt in the air, which accounts for 300,000 to 500,000 premature deaths each year. The World Health Organization has set standards for air safety, and finds that such cities as Bangkok, Beijing, Calcutta, New Delhi, and Tehran exceed the standard at least 200 days per year.

The other pollutant in the World Bank study, **sulfur dioxide** (SO_2), is a heavy, choking gas, easily liquefied for bleaches and cleaners. Sulfur dioxide enters the air through the burning of coal and oil, but the coal is much the worse of the two. It is widely used in developing countries to fuel plants that generate electricity. Electric development in China illustrates the importance placed on output regardless of pollution. In 1980 China started work on a plan to triple its electricity-generating capacity by the year 2000. The plan calls for the use of coal in all new plants, and for converting oil-burning plants to coal because coal is cheaper. Such heavy coal burning increases sulfur dioxide and other pollutants in the air. It is one reason deaths from cancer are five to seven times higher in Chinese cities than in the countryside (L.R. Brown, 1987:53).

Geography and Climate

In some cities, it is particularly difficult to have clean air. Los Angeles, the city that coined the word *smog*, was long singled out for having the dirtiest air in the United States. One reason was that the sprawled-out nature of the city, combined with very little public transportation, caused people to drive motor vehicles more miles than in any other city. However, part of the problem was geographical. Los Angeles rests on a coastal plain and enjoys warm weather but often has very little air circulation. Hence, air pollution accumulates, eyes burn with smog, and people with respiratory problems are advised to stay quietly at home. Los Angeles, however, has met its problem head on. By cleaning up industries, outlawing leaded gasoline, and requiring catalytic converters in cars, Angelinos have improved the air quality to a rate better than it was 20 years ago.

Other cities with poor air circulation are in worse shape.

The Mexico City metropolitan area has an estimated population of 16 million, whereas the Los Angeles area has about 12 million. But size is a minor factor in pollution. Mexico City is built on a high plain, with volcanic peaks rising much higher and cutting off air circulation for long periods of time. Mexico lacks the funds for a thorough cleanup, but has improved the quality of its gasoline in recent years. Mexico is industrializing, but like so many countries in the early stages of industrialization, postpones its environmental problems for another day. Meantime, one looks out from Mexico City toward the spectacular volcanic peaks to the east and sees nothing but smoke, haze, and smog.

Ankara, Turkey, is another city with geographical problems. Sitting in a high valley surrounded by even higher mountains, Ankara has long periods of little or no air circulation. The 2,500,000 inhabitants burn coal for heating, making the atmosphere even more unhealthful than that in Mexico City. It is said that breathing the air of Ankara brings the lung-damage equivalent of smoking three packs of cigarettes per day. Unlike Mexico City, Ankara is very cold in the winter, so that coal burning increases, and so does the choking feeling that comes from a high concentration of sulfur dioxide. A cold climate is a geographical factor affecting pollution, as it does in Ankara, unless there are heavy winds that prevent stagnation of air.

Size and Congestion

The size and congestion of cities would be expected to have a bearing on pollution, and this seems to be the case, but mainly with cities in LDCs. Tokyo, with its enormous population of 20 million (even more, if Yokohama is included in its metropolitan area) does not make the "worst air" list, nor do New York and London (see Figure 10.10). The "worst air" list is made up mainly of cities from less developed countries

that are striving to catch up. In their haste to become competitive, they fail to pass laws and regulations to minimize air pollution, as well as water pollution. Los Angeles is the only large city of the United States that appears on the "worst air" list, for reasons mentioned before: frequent air stagnation and a record amount of motor vehicle traffic.

Trade and Transport

At least 12 European countries are part of the European Union, whose economic ties are growing ever closer. Goods shipped from one member nation to another are no longer subject to tariff. The borders between member countries are hardly more significant than the lines separating the states of the United States. The new rules of commerce are leading to growth for Europe's internal market, which in most respects is good news. However, the internal market will produce a 30 to 50 percent increase in cross-border truck traffic by the year 2010. This increase in traffic will lead to an 8 or 9 percent increase in SO_2 emissions and a 12 to 14 percent increase in nitrogen oxide emissions (French, 1990). People in the French, Swiss, and Italian Alps are already disturbed by the increased traffic, noise, and pollution. Sometimes solutions to one problem exacerbate other problems.

Europe is not alone in increased traffic. The trade agreements among the United States, Canada, and Mexico will undoubtedly increase truck traffic and add to pollution, even though increased trade is as welcome here as in Europe. The only way to have the benefits of trade without paying the costs in pollution is to continue improving the efficiency of gasoline engines and to increase the use of railroads, which do less polluting per ton of cargo.

Acid Rain

Acid rain is rain containing high concentrations of acids, produced from sulfur dioxide, nitrogen

Figure 10.10
Dense populations produce large quantities of pollution. Consequently, the world's most densely populated regions are also those with the worst environmental problems.

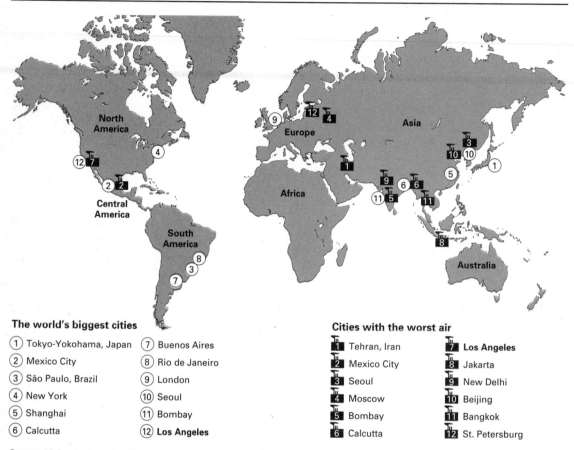

The world's biggest cities

① Tokyo-Yokohama, Japan   ⑦ Buenos Aires
② Mexico City   ⑧ Rio de Janeiro
③ São Paulo, Brazil   ⑨ London
④ New York   ⑩ Seoul
⑤ Shanghai   ⑪ Bombay
⑥ Calcutta   ⑫ **Los Angeles**

Cities with the worst air

1 Tehran, Iran   7 **Los Angeles**
2 Mexico City   8 Jakarta
3 Seoul   9 New Delhi
4 Moscow   10 Beijing
5 Bombay   11 Bangkok
6 Calcutta   12 St. Petersburg

Source: "A Day in the Life of Mother Earth: A Special Earth Summit Issue of World Report," *Los Angeles Times*, June 26, 1992: H7.

dioxide, selenium, arsenic, and other chemicals. The polluting chemicals come from the burning of coal, oil, and even wood, but especially from coal. Polluting chemicals in the atmosphere spread into forests, lakes, and fields. The United States spreads huge amounts of polluted, acid-containing air from the Midwest northward into the New England states, and from there farther north into Canada. The Canadian government has protested, and the United States government

has conducted one study after another trying to determine the cause of the bad air that results in acid rain. For many years, Canadian and American environmentalists have been sure of the answer. By 1986 the issue was no longer in doubt. Scientists tracked air pollution, and by 1986 were able to pinpoint its source. The selenium, arsenic, and other polluting substances in acid rain originated in the coal-burning industries of the Midwest (Wright, 1992). Twelve million tons of

Focus on the United States

A Revolutionary Car Can Be Efficient and Environmentally Friendly

In the 1970s, physicist Amory Lovins was the guru of "soft" energy. He argued that it makes a lot more sense to conserve energy and to produce energy from renewable sources such as solar, wind, and geothermal, than to use "hard" energy sources like coal, oil, and nuclear energy. At the time, he was considered a "fruitcake" by the "hard" energy proponents. Twenty-five years later, the United States has adopted many of Lovins's "soft" energy ideas.

The nation may also benefit from Lovins's current project—designing a revolutionary automobile that combines attributes of both gas-powered and electric cars. At his Rocky Mountain Institute, Lovins and his associates have designed and are promoting an automobile that is not plagued with the problems normally associated with electric vehicles.

Most electric vehicles have many batteries, often weighing more than 1,000 pounds, that are good for only 80 miles before needing a recharge. What distinguishes Lovins's design from standard electric vehicles is that his car is powered by a small, motor-scooter-sized engine and is also powered by electricity generated by the engine as well as the braking system. When the brakes are depressed, the forward momentum of the car's wheels turn a small electrical generator until the vehicle comes to a stop. Electrical energy produced from this new braking technology is stored until an extra burst of speed is needed to go up a hill or merge into freeway traffic. The fuel used by this automobile is clean-burning fuel, like alcohol or natural gas, and the range of this car exceeds current gasoline-powered cars.

Lovins's car is able to use a very small engine because the vehicle weighs only 25 percent as much as current small cars. This is because ultralight composite materials such as fiberglass, Kevlar, carbon fibers, and other plastics are used instead of steel. Although these materials are more expensive than steel, only a small amount is used because of the car's small size. Also, because color can be mixed with the composite materials, the cost of painting (an expensive component of producing steel cars) is saved. Using composite parts instead of steel also cuts down the number of body parts from 300 or 400 to six.

Because Lovins's car is so lightweight, it will get from 100 to several hundred miles per gallon. Due to this and its use of low-pollution fuels, Lovins's car will produce 100 to 1,000 times fewer emissions than current vehicles.

A serious impediment to current electric vehicles is their high cost, up to $20,000 more than gasoline-powered vehicles. Lovins thinks his car can be produced at a reasonable cost, probably cheaper than current models. He is of the opinion that the production cost trend line for his car will be similar to that of personal computers, with prices dropping as competition heats up.

The implications of this type of car for addressing the problems of resource depletion and environmental pollution are far-reaching, not just for the United States, but for the planet.

SOURCE: S. La Rue. "Electricity + Alternative Fuel = Supercar: Revolutionary Electric Vehicle May Conquer Drawbacks of Low Range and High Cost," *The San Diego Union-Tribune,* July 20, 1994, "Quest" column.

---

acid from United States coal furnaces blows into Canada each year, kills the fish in Canadian lakes, and heavily damages forests.

Acid rain changes the chemical balance in lakes, rivers, and rain-derived moisture in the soil. It destroys and kills many species, and prevents new growth. Acidified water leaches important plant nutrients out of the ground. It also damages building materials such as marble, limestone, sandstone, and bronze. Historic buildings, monuments, and works of art deteriorate when exposed to acid rain.

Solutions to the acid rain problem are not impossible, but they are expensive enough to create tremendous resistance from vested interests. Emission controls, consisting of the chemical treatment of coal to reduce the level of sulfates it contains, can be installed at coal-burning factories. Despite the initial costs of such procedures, the United States and Canada would benefit from the control of emissions.

The United States itself sustains more damage from acid rain than was previously believed. Besides damaging forests of the Northeast and Canada, acid rain now threatens forests of the Southeast, the Washington-Oregon Cascades, the Sierra Nevada of California, and the Rocky Mountain National Parks.

Like Canada, Sweden and Norway suffer from acid rain blown into their lakes and forests from the south. The chemical balance of lakes is upset, making the water lethal to many kinds of fish. Farther south, many trees in Germany's Black Forest are dying because of acid rain. Farther eastward, Poland depends heavily on burning coal in its northern factories in its struggle to develop industrially. Its factories cause a heavy fallout of acid rain on its southern forests (Ostman, 1982).

Less developed countries also have problems with acid rain. Xishuangbana National Nature Reserve in China suffers from some of the worst acid-rain damage in the world. In the rain forests of the Amazon, particularly in Brazil, seasonal burning of the forests to clear land for exploitation produces acid rain. In sub-Saharan Africa, this is a year-round process as acid rain, resulting from burning savannah, pours down on the tropical forests. No major region of the world is immune from this environmental hazard.

OLD VALUES AND NEW PRIORITIES

Knowledge is power, and it always has been. Having learned about our mistakes can we use that knowledge to undo damage and prevent further pollution and contamination? The answer is a qualified "yes." We already have technology that causes less pollution than that which we are presently using, but knowledge alone is not enough. We will have to change our values and restructure our priorities.

In the prosperity experienced by the MDCs after World War II, we began to perceive consumption as an end in itself. The 1950s were designed in the advertising firms of Madison Avenue in New York and their equivalents in London, Paris, and other key cities. The packaging of products was raised to an art form. The general equation that defined advanced societies was "more is better." Today, American children have an average of $230 per year in pocket money, more money than the poorest half-billion people live on annually per capita (Durning, 1991).

Figure 10.11 shows the acceleration of consumerism. Only 15 percent of U.S. households had air conditioning in 1960, by 1988 64 percent luxuriated in air cooled with environmentally harmful chlorofluorocarbons. In 1960, only 1 percent of households had a color television set; by 1990, 93 percent of families viewed their favorite shows in living color. And, ownership of microwave ovens and videocassette recorders is growing at an even faster rate. These patterns are mimicked in Western Europe and Japan, and it probably will not be long before the people of newly industrialized nations like South Korea and Singapore begin to emulate the fashions of the wealthy countries.

While consumerism keeps us happy with television and videos and computer games, it diverts us from former pastimes. We don't play basketball or softball very much; we watch it on television instead. That way we avoid exertion in our entertainment, to the dismay of health authorities. We also avoid such simple pleasures as playing with the dog or taking a walk through the woods. Such pleasures defeat the whole aim of consumerism.

Aldous Huxley, in *Brave New World* (1932), predicted the perfect consumer society. In his

Figure 10.11

Although the basic values of U.S. citizens were challenged during the 1960s and early 1970s, consumerism emerged virtualy unscathed. Today nearly everyone has at least one color television. Most households also have air conditioners, microwave ovens, and video cassette recorders. The production of so many consumer goods constantly increases industrial waste and environmental problems.

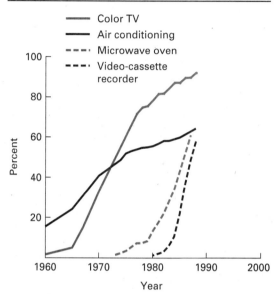

U.S. Household Ownership of Appliances, 1960–1988

Source: A. Durning, "Asking How Much is Enough," in L. R. Brown, Ed., *State of the World 1991,* (New York: W. W. Norton, 1991), p. 154.

vision of the future society, children were conditioned from infancy onward to hate nature. Otherwise they might enjoy such pleasures as exploring the forest or swimming in the river. Such activities do not consume products, so no one makes money from them. The *Brave New World*'s citizens spent most of their spare time in stores buying goods so as to keep up sales and prosperity.

It is plain that in many respects, prosperous MDCs have reached Huxley's *Brave New World*. Contrary to Huxley's expectation, many people

still enjoy nature, but largely because we have changed nature into a great consumer. Enjoyment of nature, for many people, requires off-road vehicles and/or motorbikes or a speedboat at the coast. In the winter, many people require snowmobiles; otherwise, it might be too strenuous getting over the snow. Such equipment increases the pollutants in the air, both by its manufacture and by its use.

Occasionally, we see cyclists on country roads and are annoyed at them for getting in the way and slowing down the traffic. Yet the future depends on people with "bicycle" values rather than "racy automobile" values. Of course, we will not suddenly abandon our autos, but it is hard to see how their expansion can go on forever. Imagine the world we would have if the two or three billion people of Asia were all enjoying automobiles, off-road vehicles, motorbikes, snowmobiles, and motorboats, all produced in smoky factories, spewing their poisons into the air. Surely a livable earth could not survive such an assault.

If we can change our values of consumerism to those of conservation, perhaps we can still have a pleasant life on earth. Nature must be regarded with reverence, not hated and conquered. (At the end of the next chapter, we will summarize the steps that must be taken to revitalize the earth, according to Japan's 100-year plan.)

SUMMARY

In some respects the whole earth is one great ecosystem in which pollution affects populations far from its source. In the way they are now treated, rivers have often become arteries for the spreading of pollution. The Ganges, Rhine, and Mississippi have all been described as conduits of industrial waste, including deadly chemicals; the former two are also carriers of sewage. The Nile is a river whose historic function of enriching

Egypt's soil has been terminated by a great dam. Dams on tropical rivers, although they may have some uses, often spread diseases, especially malaria and schistosomiasis.

Vast though the oceans are, they are also subject to pollution, especially along continental shelves, which are the source of 90 percent of edible marine life. Many lakes are also polluted. This is true of the Great Lakes, but the Aral Sea is the world's worst example. Just as rivers and lakes have been overused, so have underground aquifers, which bodes ill for future water supplies.

The air is also polluted, especially in countries rushing hard to industrialize. The more developed countries have taken measures, although insufficient, to clean up the air. Large cities with too little air circulation (e.g., Los Angeles, Mexico City) have particularly severe air pollution. Even worse are cities with cold winters where citizens burn coal in open fireplaces, which was once true of London and is still true of Ankara, Turkey. The burning of coal for the purpose of generating electricity is the largest source of the air pollution that causes acid rain. Chemicals picked up by the rain sicken forests and kill fish in lakes. Canada complains of such pollution blowing in from the United States. Scandinavia has the same complaint against countries to its south.

Finally, we conclude that changes in values from consumerism to conservation will be necessary to save the world from drowning in a sea of pollution.

KEY TERMS

Acid Rain Precipitation that has been polluted with toxic chemicals; some sources of acid rain are sulfur dioxide, nitrogen dioxide, selenium, and arsenic.

Aquifer Natural, underground storage chamber for water, usually permeable rock, sand, or gravel.

Balance of nature A condition that allows a sustainable number of each species to survive.

Bioamplification The increasing concentration of pesticides as they pass up the food chain.

Ecosystem A system of interrelationships among all of the plants and animal species in an area, including the relationships among the species and the physical environment, like soil, water, and climate.

Exxon Valdez Tanker ship that was responsible for a huge oil spill along the coast of Alaska in 1989.

Filariasis A disease, spread by insects from standing water, that causes body parts to swell to such an extent that amputation is the only treatment.

Fungicides Chemical compounds designed to kill fungus.

Herbicides Chemical compounds designed to kill vegetation.

London fog Dense, choking air pollution, caused by smoke from burning coal; especially prevalent in London.

Nonbiodegradable substances Substances, like oil or plastic, that do not chemically decompose in nature.

Onchoceriasis "River blindness," spread by insects from standing water; virtually out of control in West Africa.

PCBs Polychlorinated biphenyls, very toxic chemicals, used in plastics, electrical insulators, and hydraulic fluids.

Pesticides Chemical compounds designed to kill insects and other pests.

Potable water Water suitable for human consumption.

Schistosomiasis A parasitic disease that attacks the bladder and genitals or spleen and liver; the source is snails that live in standing water.

Sulfur dioxide A choking gas that enters the air when coal or oil is burned.

Suspended particulate matter Tiny particles of coal dust, smoke, fecal matter, or similar materials that "float" in the air.

STUDY QUESTIONS

1. What is an ecosystem? What is meant by the expression "balance in nature"? How is an ecosystem like a society?

2. What problems do the following rivers have in common: The Ganges, Rhine, and Mississippi?

3. What kind of environmental problems are caused when dams are built on rivers?

4. In what ways are oceans polluted?

5. What is bioamplification? How are food chains affected by pesticides?

6. How have government policies affected the Aral Sea?

7. How does the production of beef negatively affect the environment?

8. How is an area's degree of air pollution related to its level of economic development?

9. How does acid rain come into being? What is its effect on the environment?

10. How do the prophesies in Aldous Huxley's *Brave New World* relate to today's values in more developed countries?

GLOBAL
DESTRUCTION

If Charles Darwin were alive today, his work would most likely focus not on the origins of species but, rather, on the obituaries of species.

MOSTAFA K. TOLBA, EXECUTIVE DIRECTOR OF THE UNITED NATIONS ENVIRONMENTAL PROGRAM ("CITINGS," 1991A:8)

The destruction of the natural resources needed for future generations is an unpardonable crime.

OSCAR ARIAS, FORMER PRESIDENT OF COSTA RICA AND NOBEL PEACE PRIZE WINNER ("CITINGS," 1991A:8)

Seeing is believing and I'm no longer reluctant to say I'm scared of atomic power. Any rational person should be. Surely we can keep the lights on around the world without the dangers that have created a nuclear hell here on Earth.

S. DAVID FREEMEN, GENERAL MANAGER OF THE SACRAMENTO MUNICIPAL UTILITY DISTRICT, UPON RETURN FROM A TWO-WEEK VISIT TO THE (FORMER) SOVIET UNION TO MARK THE FIFTH ANNIVERSARY OF THE CHERNOBYL ACCIDENT. ("CITINGS," 1991B: 9)

We are the first species in the history of life to go out of control on a global scale.

HARVARD BIOLOGIST E. O. WILSON ("CITINGS," 1992:8)

These quotations show the wide range of concern over the environment. In the previous chapter, we discussed environmental pollution, but the people quoted above are speaking of more than just pollution. They are concerned with destruction. Most kinds of pollution can be stopped and their damage reversed. Destruction is in all cases difficult to reverse, and usually impossible. When vast acreages of the Brazilian rain forests are destroyed and the soil in which they grew is washed away, restoration is impossible. Similarly, when the South Pacific Bikini Atoll was blown up with nuclear bombs in 1946, its inhabitants had to be removed for all time, and all its wildlife died. Equally irreversible is the extinction of species, which goes on apace as human beings destroy the habitats of other species or poison them. In this chapter we will discuss elements of the environment whose survival is threatened.

First we turn to the development that at times has threatened all forms of life on earth: nuclear power.

THE NUCLEAR AGE

The development of the nuclear age is of great interest sociologically. It demonstrates that once science has reached a particular point in its development, new ideas will flourish rapidly. It also shows that no one country has a monopoly on scientific genius; people of many countries made discoveries leading to the atomic age. History of the nuclear age also illustrates a problem that worries many people: There is a tendency to charge ahead on new developments regardless of their social consequences. At least a few scientists feared that a nuclear bomb might start a chain reaction that would destroy the earth, but that didn't stop them. Finally, as the following pages demonstrate, a major new invention has unforeseen results.

The Road to Atomic Energy

For more than two thousand years, the idea of the Greek philosopher Democratus had been accepted: Matter is made of infinitely small particles called atoms, and atoms are indestructible. But scientists raised questions. Dmitry Mendeleyev of Russia found regularities about atomic numbers, and wondered if there were outer orbits to atoms. Maria Sklodowska (Curie) (1867–1934) of Poland wrote her doctoral thesis on elements that give off rays. She moved to France where she met and married Pierre Curie, and the two of them refined radium, an element that glows in the dark. They received the Nobel Prize for their work, and the scientific world lauded their achievement. What strange force

An atomic bomb explodes on Bikini Atoll in the South Pacific. The atoll has been so contaminated that it will not be inhabitable for generations into the future.

was at work? Were some kinds of atoms being changed to energy?

In 1905 Albert Einstein (then of Germany; later a U.S. citizen) developed an equation giving the relationship between matter and energy, $E = MC^2$, meaning energy equals mass times the square of the speed of light. The power of the atom would be tremendous. Atomic power, it was hoped, might supply all the energy needs of the earth.

The whole world was interested. In 1920 Robert Rutherford of New Zealand and Niels Bohr of Denmark explained atomic energy. Leo Szilard of Hungary moved closer to the atomic age by suggesting the possibility of a chain reaction in which one exploding atom in a mass would cause all the others to explode. In 1941 Enrico Fermi, an Italian-American scientist, went a long step farther and produced a controlled chain reaction.

Meantime, Germany was at work. Two German scientists, Otto Frisch and Lise Meitner, found that a chain reaction would change matter into energy with the shattering force Einstein had predicted. Meitner fled Germany and came to the United States.

Enrico Fermi, Leo Szilard, Edward Teller, and other atomic scientists became increasingly worried for fear Germany would develop an atomic bomb. They persuaded Albert Einstein to write to President Roosevelt, which he did. The result was an operation called the **Manhattan Project.** With the greatest possible secrecy, leading scientists worked out the details, and produced an atomic bomb. One was exploded at White Sands, New Mexico, exceeding all expectations in power and devastation. Some scientists had been certain about the result. Some, as stated before, feared that the chain reaction might destroy the earth.

Two other bombs had been made. On August 6, 1945, one of them was dropped on the Japanese city of Hiroshima, killing close to 100,000 people. Three days later, a second atomic bomb was exploded over Nagasaki, Japan. The nuclear fallout from these two bombs so conta-minated the environment that people continued to sicken and die for years afterward, and the effects of exposure to radiation caused birth defects to many thousands of people in the next generation.

At the time it was thought a great victory. The Japanese surrender came on September 2, 1945, a little sooner than it might have come otherwise. The United States alone held the bomb. It was also assumed that atomic power would give the world limitless and safe energy and that radiation would have many uses. The Western world ignored, at least temporarily, certain generalizations made earlier: no country holds a monopoly on scientific genius; when scientists make one great discovery, it leads to many more; in many cases the attitude toward new inventions will be "full speed ahead and damn the consequences." Above all else, the world had been changed, and its people would never again feel as sure of survival into the future as they had in the preatomic age.

THE NUCLEAR RACE

In the years after World War II, atomic weapons were exploded in the Nevada test sites and also in the South Pacific at Bikini Atoll. Although the United States had a brief monopoly of atomic bombs, the nation's leaders reasoned that the Soviet Union would eventually have its own atomic arsenal; consequently, frequent tests were considered necessary to keep ahead of the Soviets.

Soviet Bombs

Soviet developments were more rapid than had been expected. Even during World War II, Soviet intelligence had learned of U.S. work with nuclear power at Alamagordo, New Mexico. Early in the 1940s, Joseph Stalin, then dictator of the USSR, gave nuclear physicist Igor Kurchatov orders to produce an atomic bomb by the end of the decade.

Figure 11.1

Long before the nuclear meltdown at Chernobyl, there were atomic disasters in the former Soviet Union. In 1962 an explosion on the island of Novaya Zemlya (top, center) produced a two-mile fireball and spread fallout over all of the major cities of northern Europe.

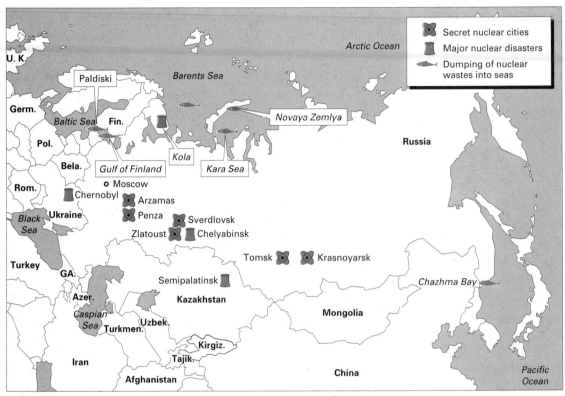

Source: M. Dobbs, "Sacrificed to the Superpowers," *Washington Post National Weekly Edition*, Sept. 20–26, 1992: 14.

Kurchatov set up plants in the city of Kasli in the Ural Mountains between Sverdlovsk and Chelyabinsk (Figure 11.1), and work proceeded. After the devastation of Hiroshima and Nagasaki, the research pace became frantic. Kurchatov was joined by two other scientists of great ability, Igor Tamm and Andrei Sakharov, who were also ordered to work on a hydrogen bomb. On schedule, in 1949, near Semipalitinsk in Central Asia, the first nuclear bomb of the Communist world was exploded.

The Soviet scientists continued work at their plant in the Urals where atomic reactors were built, and radioactive materials were stored. It is believed that carelessness with trenches for waste was what eventually caused the radioactive mass to reach a critical level in 1957 (Marbach, 1986). An enormous blast occurred. Hundreds were killed and hundreds more soon died from the effects of the fallout. Villages in the vicinity were vacated and burned so that their inhabitants would not return and be contaminated with radioactivity. A nearby forest gradually died. There were high incidences of cancer in the regions surrounding Kasli for years afterward. Although the disaster was kept as secret as possible, details were learned by American intelligence.

In the United States, testing continued at the Nevada test sites without spectacular disasters. However, the tests produced a kind of "creeping disaster." Years later, researchers found that a particularly deadly element in nuclear test fallout was Iodine–131 which concentrates in the thyroid gland. They found that thyroid disease in St. George, Utah, downwind from the test sites, was four times as common as in the population as a whole (Miller, 1986). This discovery stimulated a more thorough analysis of the downwind population, the results of which are shown in Table 11.1.

Despite growing fears about nuclear fallout, the level of testing in both the United States and the Soviet Union rose markedly in the 1960s as President Kennedy and Premier Khrushchev engaged in a bitter struggle. This struggle between the two world leaders reached its apex in 1962 when U.S. surveillance revealed that the Soviet Union was installing atomic weapons in Cuba, less than 100 miles from the coast of Florida. Kennedy confronted Khrushchev, who initially refused to remove the missiles. Eventually, after Khrushchev backed down in the Cuban Missile Crisis, the two men worked out an agreement to stop all atmospheric testing. This came also in 1962, soon after the most horrifying nuclear blast in history had occurred over Novaya Zemlya Island (Figure 11.1), producing a fireball two miles in diameter, and raining fallout on the Soviet cities of Archangel and Murmansk, all the cities of Scandinavia, and to some extent the entire world. Andrei Sakharov had vocally opposed the test; his protest landed him in prison. He had become convinced, as had many U.S. scientists, that every test explosion would eventually result in thousands of deaths (Miller, 1986).

Types of Cancer Among People Living Downwind from Nevada Test Sites	TABLE 11.1	
	Times expected rate	
	1958–1966	1972–1980
Leukemia	5.3	3.5
Lymphoma	—	1.9
Thyroid cancer	4.3	8.2
Breast cancer	—	1.9
Colon cancer	—	1.7
Stomach cancer	5.6	1.8
Melanoma	1.5	3.5
Brain cancer	3.1	1.7
Cancer of bone and joints	10.0	12.5

SOURCE: R. L. Miller. *Under the Cloud: The Decades of Nuclear Testing* (New York: The Free Press, 1986), p. 326.

The apparent goal of all this research and testing was to develop bombs of greater and greater destructive capacity. This evidently emanated from a theory called **deterrence**. The idea was that if country A could visit nearly total destruction on country B, then B would never dare attack A. Many countries seem to have accepted this theory; Great Britain exploded its first nuclear bomb in 1952, France in 1960, and China in 1964. It is also suspected that India, Israel, and Pakistan either have or could quickly assemble a nuclear arsenal. Another nine countries are known to have made inquiries, internationally, to obtain nuclear devices.

Particularly worrisome in regard to nuclear development is North Korea, one of the few remaining Communist countries. North Korea has resisted nuclear inspection by the United Nations. After negotiations, the North Koreans agreed to open some areas, but not others, making extremely suspicious their pronouncements of having no nuclear development.

The Carnegie Endowment for International Peace estimates that by 1990 the U.S. and the USSR had between 25,000 and 30,000 nuclear weapons in their arsenals. Additionally, Great Britain had 300, China had 350, and France had 600 (Spector, 1993:5b). The fact that so many weapons exist seems ridiculous when one considers that, during World War II, between 40 million and 50 million soldiers and civilians were killed, and all of the nations that participated used the equivalent of 6,000,000 tons of TNT. The bomb dropped on Hiroshima in 1945 was only 15,000 tons, and it leveled 4.5 miles of that city. By 1986 the world's nuclear stockpile had reached 16,000,000,000 tons. That's more than 6,000 pounds of TNT-equivalent nuclear explosives for each man, woman, and child in the world, and a single bomber can carry 8,000,000 TNT-equivalent tons of weaponry (Sivard, 1986).

According to Michael Renner (1993:128–129), the global nuclear arsenal reached its peak in 1988. By 1991 the United States, Russia, Belarus, Kazakhstan, and Ukraine had about 18,300 offensive warheads. Belarus, Kazakhstan, and Ukraine had committed themselves to eliminating their arsenals under the agreements of the Lisbon Protocol of 1992. However, their weapons will simply be moved to Russia. But according to the **Strategic Arms Reduction Treaties** (START I in 1992 and START II in 1993), the United States and Russia will reduce the number of warheads to about 6,500 by the year 2003. Still, that is enough firepower to annihilate all living things on the surface of the earth.

The "Benevolent" Atom

Despite worries about nuclear war, most of the world at first accepted the idea that atomic energy would have many benevolent, peace-time uses, the most important of which would be energy development. With nuclear power, air pollution caused by the burning of fossil fuels like petroleum and coal could be avoided. Eventually the "blessing" of atomic energy came under dispute for several reasons: (1) costs of development were much higher than expected, (2) the disposal of wastes was a problem to which

no acceptable solution could be found, and (3) a series of disasters or near-disasters has occurred in nuclear power plants (Figure 11.2). Atomic power problems are great enough that some countries have projected almost no further development after 1990, as is the case with Sweden, West Germany, the Netherlands, and Switzerland. France, however, depends heavily on atomic power and continues its nuclear-power programs. The United States leads the world with 111 nuclear power plants and 65 research reactors. Worldwide there are almost 500 power reactors and more than 300 research reactors (see Table 11.2).

Chernobyl

Although there have been many nuclear accidents throughout the world, the most devastating one to date took place in 1986 at Chernobyl in the USSR, close to the city of Kiev. In an experiment to see how long the steam-driven turbines would generate electricity in the case of a power cut-off, the officials in charge shut off the plant's cooling system. Early in the morning of April 26, 1986, two gigantic explosions occurred, the second one blowing the top off the reactor building. A blazing inferno inside thrust radioactive isotopes into the atmosphere, which was first reported by Sweden where radioactive fallout had increased alarmingly. Eventually, the Soviet Union admitted the accident and, several days later, took steps to protect its people. Chernobyl and surrounding areas were evacuated, and children from Kiev and the vicinity were sent off to summer camp early. There were, nevertheless, 31 deaths at the time of the accident and estimates range between 20,000 and 100,000 for the number of people who will die before their time because of the fallout (Marbach, 1986). Poland was badly contaminated with radioactivity; so was Scandinavia and more distant England.

The aftermath of the accident illustrates the tendency for governments to conceal facts from their people. The USSR took several days to let

Nuclear Accidents	
1957	Windscale, England, near Liverpool. Fire in a plutonium-production reactor spread radioactivity. Estimate 39 cancer deaths.
1957	Kasli, USSR. Enormous chemical explosion in tanks of nuclear waste, hundreds of deaths. Site and nearby villages evacuated ever since.
1961	Idaho Falls, Idaho. Accident in experimental reactor. Three killed.
1966	Detroit, Michigan. Enrico Fermi breeder-reactor malfunction, partial meltdown. Radioactivity released into cavern, which had to be sealed.
1969	Lucens Vad, Switzerland. Coolant malfunction in underground reactor. Radioactivity released into cavern, which had to be sealed.
1971	Monticello, Minnesota. Water system overflowed; 50,000 gallons radioactive water released into Mississippi River, some entering St. Paul water system.
1975	Brown's Ferry, near Decatur, Alabama. Accidental fire burned electrical controls. Supply of cooling water lowered to dangerous level.
1979	Three Mile Island reactor, Middletown, Pennsylvania. Loss of coolant, partial meltdown. Evacuation of area, widespread panic.
1979	Near Erwin, Texas. Uranium released from secret fuel plant. Approximately 1,000 people contaminated with five times as much radiation as would be received normally in one year.
1981	TVA's Sequoyah Plant, Tennessee. Leak of 100,000 gallons of radioactive coolant; eight workers contaminated.
1981	Tsuruga, Japan. During repair work, 100 workers exposed to radioactive material.
1986	Gore, Oklahoma. Nuclear-material cylinder burst. One worker killed, 100 hospitalized.
1986	Chernobyl, USSR. Radioactivity spread over much of Europe, caused 31 deaths at time or soon after. Many thousands of cancer-related deaths expected.

Figure 11.2
Major nuclear accidents have occurred since the mid 1950s. Nobody knows how many people have been exposed to radioactive elements. The greatest disaster occurred at Chernobyl in the former Soviet Union in 1986. Thousands of cancer-related deaths are expected because of the fallout, which may have affected the entire world to some degree.

Source: World Almanac and Book of Facts, 1994. (Mahwah, NJ: World Almanac), p. 551, except for Monticello and Erwin, which were cited in the 1987 edition.

people know what had happened at Chernobyl. In the Bavarian part of Germany, milk was badly contaminated with radioactive cesium (a source of leukemia). The milk was not sold to the German people but 252 railroad carloads of powdered milk were approved by local officials for sale to Nigeria and Egypt—a common way of treating the less developed countries. Fortunately, officials at the seaport of Bremen refused to grant export permits (Egger, 1987). A few months later, a Brazilian court disclosed that West Germany, Italy, and France had been sending food to Brazil that contained ten times as much radioactive cesium as Brazilian law would

| Nuclear Reactors as of December 31, 1992 | | | | | TABLE 11.2 |
Country	Power reactors	Research reactors	Country	Power reactors	Research reactors
Algeria	0	2	Korea, South	14	3
Argentina	3	6	Libya	0	1
Australia	0	3	Malaysia	0	1
Austria	0	4	Mexico	2	2
Bangladesh	0	1	Morocco	0	1
Belgium	7	6	Netherlands	2	3
Brazil	2	4	Norway	0	2
Bulgaria	6	1	Pakistan	1	1
Canada	22	14	Peru	0	2
Chile	0	2	Philippines	0	1
China	3	12	Poland	0	3
Colombia	0	1	Portugal	0	1
Czechoslovakia	14	4	Romania	4	2
Denmark	0	2	South Africa	2	1
Egypt	0	1	Spain	9	1
Finland	4	1	Sweden	12	2
France	61	19	Switzerland	5	5
Germany	21	28	Taiwan	6	6
Greece	0	2	Thailand	0	1
Hungary	4	3	Turkey	0	2
India	15	5	United Kingdom	38	10
Indonesia	0	4	United States	111	65
Iran	0	2	former USSR	52	24
Israel	0	1	Venezuela	0	1
Italy	0	5	Vietnam	0	1
Jamaica	0	1	Yugoslavia	1	3
Japan	55	19	Zaire	0	1
Korea, North	1	2			
			Total	477	301

SOURCE: R. L. Sivard, *World Military and Social Expenditures 1993* (Washington, D.C.: World Priorities, 1993), p. 13.

permit—another consequence of Chernobyl that advanced countries attempted to unload on developing countries.

In much of Western Europe (with Sweden a notable exception), governments have tried to downplay the Chernobyl disaster, not wanting their people to become too strongly opposed to their nuclear plans. French Electrical, the agency in charge of French nuclear development, has apparently been able to convince the French people that their industrial future and prosperity depend upon atomic energy (France is lacking in oil or any large amount of coal). Opposition is stronger in Germany where a 1986 opinion poll showed 69 percent opposition to the building of further nuclear plants (Egger, 295).

One year after the Chernobyl disaster, repercussions continued with antinuclear demonstrations in Western Europe. In Britain, Germany, the USSR, Italy, and Greece people began to question the credibility of government pronouncements regarding safety. Radioactivity levels throughout Europe remained higher than governments would admit. Fish from many

In shifts lasting only one minute, soldiers in protective clothing begin to clear the debris from Chernobyl. Incidentally, radiation levels were so high that the black and white film used in the photo was damaged. Color film would have been destroyed.

Finnish lakes were too contaminated to eat. Laplanders, pastoralists who herd reindeer in northern Scandinavia, found their ancient way of life threatened because reindeer meat and milk became too contaminated for human consumption. As far away as western England and Wales, farmers were afraid to eat mutton from their sheep because of the contaminated grass they ate. Immediate proximity to Chernobyl was not necessarily the key to how much radioactivity entered individual ecosystems. To no one's surprise, much of Scandinavia was badly affected, as were East Germany, Austria, Czechoslovakia, and Hungary. More surprising was heavy lingering radioactivity in parts of Italy and the British Isles (Begley, 1987). Seven years after the accident, cesium was found beneath 66 feet of snow near the top of Mont Blanc in the French Alps, 15,781 feet above sea level. Eventually, the snow will turn to water and drain down the mountain into streams and rivers. About half of the radiation will still be present on the mountain top in the year 2016—30 years after the Chernobyl disaster ("Earth Week," 1993).

Eight years after the disaster, Chernobyl-type reactors are still in use, inviting another explosion. A Russian writer tells us that people around Chernobyl take nuclear pollution as a way of life, "a process that humankind is doomed to live with for tens of thousands of years" (Martz, 1994).

Nuclear Waste

Another problem is finding a safe way to discard nuclear waste. In the United States, scientists have yet to discover a method for disposing of the nuclear waste from Fermi's 1940s experiment, currently buried under a foot of concrete and two feet of dirt on an Illinois hillside. Additionally, the United States has 80,000 tons of irradiated fuel and hundred of thousands of tons of other radioactive waste (Lenssen, 1991).

Conditions in the successor states of the Soviet Union are much worse. There are 15 Chernobyl-type nuclear reactors currently in operation in Russia, Ukraine, and Lithuania. There may be close to three dozen other nuclear plants that are so badly deteriorated that they pose a real threat to human life (Burt, 1993). Additionally, there have been accidents not involving nuclear power plants. For example, in 1989 the Soviet nuclear submarine, Komsomolets, sank off the coast of Norway. It is leaking cesium, but at levels too low to be of immediate concern. But the ship carried nuclear torpedoes, armed with 28 pounds of plutonium that is so powerful that just a tiny speck can kill a human being. The plutonium has a half-life of 24,000 years and, if scientific estimates are correct, that plutonium started seeping into the water in 1992 (Jackson, 1992). It will eventually contaminate huge expanses of the ocean. And this is not an isolated incident. Similar stories can be told about such accidents in the Chazma Bay near Vladivostok in 1985, the *Lenin* in the Barents Sea, and a string of abandoned nuclear vessels floating off the coast of Murmansk (Pasternak, 1992). The full and long-term effects of all this nuclear flotsam and jetsam may never be known.

Finally, there are the deliberate acts of Soviet leaders who seem to have had a total disregard for human life. Beginning in 1949, the Mayak plutonium plant began dumping nuclear waste into the Techa River, near Chelyabinsk. Many villages downriver use the river as a source of drinking water or for bathing. By the late 1950s, signs prohibiting bathing were posted along the river, but there was no explanation for the warning. Most villagers simply disregarded the signs.

The river water is also used for irrigation, and now radiation is present in the grass and soil. Cows feed off the grass, and radiation enters the food chain. In one village, four of every five persons are chronically sick. Babies are born with deformities. Three generations of village people have now been affected with high incidents of anemia and cancer. More nuclear waste from Mayak was spilled into Lake Karachi; eventually the lake dried up and high winds spread radioactive dust over a huge area. In 1992 Russian officials estimated that about 450,000 people had been affected by the combined events at the Mayak plant (Dobbs, 1992) and 300,000 people were being treated for radiation sickness (L. R. Brown, 1992:174–190).

Sometimes, MDCs minimize the risks to their own people while deliberately disregarding risks to others by locating factory operations that generate nuclear waste outside their national boundaries. One such case involves Japan, an industrial giant, and a tiny village, Bukit Merah, in Malaysia. Japan's Mitsubishi company created a subdivision called Asian Rare Earth Company to process an element called monazite into yttrium, which is used to coat the interior of television tubes. However, Asian Rare Earth Company's factory was not located in Japan, but

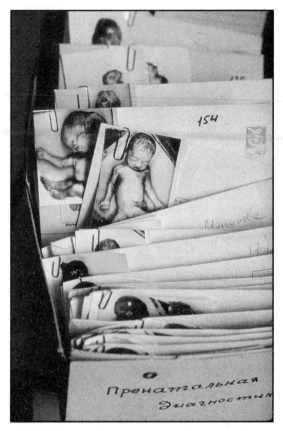

Deformed babies can be found in many small villages along Russian rivers that have been contaminated with radioactive waste.

in Bukit Merah. The by-products from the factory, radioactive thorium hydroxide and radon gas, were released into a stream behind the factory. Soon, area children were dying from rare forms of cancer. Doctors also noticed tremendous increases in lead poisoning, decreases in white blood cell counts, and increases in miscarriages and birth defects. Investigators traced the source of all the problems to Asian Rare Earth Company, which had started operating in 1982. The factory was finally closed in 1992, but the damage had been done (Wallace, 1992).

Nations that possess nuclear weapons and reactors must find safe ways to dispose of their radioactive wastes, ways that do not threaten the life of the planet. The social and economic costs may well run into the hundreds of billions of dollars, but we cannot maintain or expect poor nations to achieve a reasonable standard of living in an overly irradiated world. Because the material retains its radioactivity for thousands of years, extraordinary means must be taken to dispose of it. All possible means are dangerous and expensive. Some are violations of international law.

Technical Options for Dealing with Irradiated Fuel			TABLE 11.3
Method	**Process**	**Problems**	**Status**
Antarctica ice burial	Bury waste in ice cap	Prohibited by international law; low recovery potential, and concern over catastrophic failure	Abandoned
Geologic burial	Bury waste in mined repository	Uncertainty of long-term geology, groundwater flows, and human intrusion	Under active study by most nuclear countries as favored strategy
Seabed burial	Bury waste in deep ocean sediments	May violate international law; transport concerns; nonretrievable	Under active study by consortium of 10 countries
Space disposal	Send waste into solar orbit beyond earth's gravity	Potential launch failure could contaminate whole planet; very expensive	Abandoned
Long-term storage	Store waste indefinitely in specially constructed buildings	Dependent on human institutions to monitor and control access to waste for long time period	Not actively being studied by governments, though proposed by non-govt'l groups
Reprocessing	Chemically separate uranium and plutonium from irradiated fuel	Increases volume of waste by 160 fold; high cost; increases risk of nuclear weapons proliferation	Commercially underway in four countries; total of 16 countries plan to reprocess irradiated fuel
Trans-mutation	Convert waste to shorter-lived isotopes through neutron bombardment	Technically uncertain whether waste stream would be reduced; very expensive	Under active study by United States, Japan, former Soviet Union, and France.

SOURCE: N. Lenssen, *Nuclear Waste: The Problem That Won't Go Away* (Washington, D.C.: Worldwatch Institute, 1991), p. 22.

Table 11.3 shows the processes, problems, and status of some methods that might be used for disposing of nuclear waste.

Nuclear Secrets

In late 1993 and early 1994, both nuclear super-powers—the former USSR and the United States—admitted that their respective governments had covered up nuclear incidents. In the late 1950s, the Soviet Union was frantically trying to catch up with the United States's fleet of nuclear submarines. The accelerated pace caused workers to be sloppy and to take shortcuts. Two workers were killed in an explosion and six women died when they were overcome by fumes while the ship was being built. A welder's sloppiness caused solder to drip into a pipe that was to carry coolant to the ship's reactor. The ship was christened the *K-19* and was set off to sail in a simulated war game in 1961. During maneuvers, the pipe cracked, and the reactor overheated. The temperature in the reactor room soared higher than 140° Fahrenheit, the highest marking on the gauge. We'll never know how hot it really was.

The captain made a decision to try to save the ship. He asked three-man teams of volunteers to work on repairing the pipe in five- to ten-minute shifts, wearing only raincoats and gas masks. Within two hours, some of the volunteers were so red skinned, swollen, and bleeding through their pores that they were unrecognizable. Those who could whisper begged to be killed. Eight died within two days. Those who made it to the hospital were so radioactive that everything they came in contact with at the hospital had to be destroyed. In all, 22 volunteers died within two years.

The entire crew was sworn to secrecy, a pact they kept for 33 years. Survivors of the *K-19*, which they called the "Hiroshima," still suffer the effects of exposure to nuclear radiation. Unbelievably, after the ship had been gutted, it was put back into service. It was finally decommissioned in 1972 when 28 more sailors died in an onboard fire (Bivens, 1994).

In 1993 the Department of Energy revealed that the United States had conducted more than 200 secret nuclear tests, some of which had released radioactivity into the air. It was also disclosed that doctors and scientists had conducted more than 800 experiments on more than 600 Americans. As part of the experimentation, radioactive material was injected into pregnant women to find out what effect it might have on fetuses and on the children after they were born (Healy, 1993).

If anything was said to the victims of the research it was apt to be, "Would you take part in an experiment to help the war effort?" Doctors in the 1940s and 1950s were less inclined than now to explain procedures to patients. In addition, there was a pervasive atmosphere of secrecy. Whatever agreement was obtained would not meet modern standards for informed consent (Watson, 1993).

Nuclear Alternatives

We have discussed the dangers of nuclear accidents and radioactive fallout. In the previous chapter, we pointed out that air pollution from petroleum products and especially from coal is very dangerous. Limited world resources of petroleum, and the very serious acid rain caused by burning coal, make neither source of energy appear very promising for the future. That is why we rely more and more on nuclear energy. The problem is obviously one of finding alternatives. Sources of energy that had once seemed antiquated are being revived here and there, such as windmills and even a few commercial sailing ships. Minor new sources of energy have also been found, such as geothermal energy, long a major power source for Iceland, and now used in Japan, Hawaii, Indonesia, and other places of hot funnels and other volcanic activity. The use of such energy is helpful, and energy conservation is even more helpful. The demand for energy constantly increases and, so far, most conservation programs have been small-scale and not especially far-reaching. The demand for energy would be many times higher than it is now if the less developed counties ever reached anything even close to the living standards of the wealthier countries. Consequently, a new major source of energy is needed if nuclear energy is to be avoided.

For many years, environmentalists have argued that solar energy will become the nonpolluting driving force of the future. Barry Commoner (1979) has lectured widely and written books on the subject of solar energy and believes it is the hope of the future. The costs are too high at present, but Commoner contends that solar energy costs can be reduced by greater inventiveness and mass production. Yoshihiro Hamakawa (1987) agrees about a bright future for solar energy, which already helps considerably with heating houses and other buildings in Japan. Hamakawa writes enthusiastically about the increasing role of photovoltaic cells, whose cost is being reduced constantly by the use of new materials and new techniques. The cost of energy produced by photovoltaic cells is only one-tenth as much as it was ten years ago, and Hamakawa predicts it will be only one-tenth its present cost by the end of the century. Japan's Sunshine Project, started in 1974, aims at meeting a large part of Japan's energy needs through sun power by 1995. Japan has an even greater incentive than many other countries to find new sources of energy because it lacks both petroleum and coal, and its people have a great dread of nuclear plants. These very problems may push Japan into leadership in a solar age.

While we wait for the innovations of the future, however, some scientists have turned their attention to natural gas, which produces 30 to 60 percent less carbon dioxide than does oil or coal, while generating an equal amount of energy. It is among the simplest of hydrocarbons, being neither a liquid (like oil) nor a solid (like coal). Its greatest advantage is that, by the time it reaches the burning stage, it has lost its sulfur, so it adds no sulfur dioxide to the environment

(Figure 11.3). It is predicted that natural gas will soon power cars and buses and will be used to run electric power plants (Flavin, 1992). But, like oil or coal, it is a limited resource, and most experts see it as a stop-gap measure until clean sources of energy are developed.

POISON FOR EXPORT

Chemical pesticides widely used in the United States are also manufactured for export and sold to farmers who cannot read English and so have no warning of their hazards. In Haiti, for example, chemicals ruled too toxic to be used in

Figure 11.3
Nuclear power was initially seen as a clean way to produce electric energy. Unlike traditional methods it produces no nitrogen oxides or sulfur dioxides. However, disposing of nuclear waste is a problem. In the 1990s, natural gas, which is relatively nonpolluting, is a likely alternative.

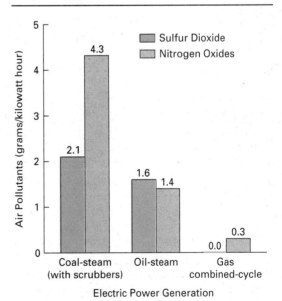

Source: C. Flavin, "The Bridge to Clean Energy," World Watch, July–Aug., 1992.

the United States and other industrialized countries are sold at general stores. Clerks scoop out the toxic powders with their bare hands and dump them into unlabeled plastic bags. The drums in which the toxins arrive are sold, unwashed, to peasants for water containers. There is an irony in the story: Some of those poisons may well come back to the very doorstep of their manufacturers. The United States imports food from the Caribbean that is contaminated with the very poisons that the government has ruled too poisonous for domestic use (Gelber, 1981).

Because the less developed countries are less rigid in their supervision of toxic materials than are the industrialized countries, it is not surprising that manufacturers of hazardous materials move their plants to such countries. By 1975 El Salvador was producing 20 percent of the world's supply of parathion, a very strong pesticide (Myers, 1984). Because of lack of regulations, accidental pesticide poisonings are much more common in the less developed countries than in the major industrial countries. The former use only 15 percent of the world's pesticides, but account for 75 percent of pesticide poisonings (Myers, 1984:128). In 1982, for example, the government of Egypt spent more money per capita on pesticide subsidies than it spent on health care in 1991 (Postel and Flavin, 1991:170–188). Such subsidies encourage farmers to use pesticides to excess.

Governments rely heavily on pesticides to satisfy immediate agricultural needs, often without considering the long-term effects. Furthermore, encouraging the use of chemical pesticides discourages farmers from developing nonchemical controls, such as integrated pest management, which makes use of natural predators of pests. Other nonchemical solutions include different planting patterns and developing pest-resistant crops (Brown, Flavin, and Postel, 1991).

Pesticides are not the only contaminants exported from wealthy countries to poor ones. Because of strict standards in the United States

for the disposal of lead car batteries, some companies export the batteries to a recycling plant near São Paulo, Brazil. The environmental controls there are so lax that more than 85 percent of the workers have lead concentrations in their blood that exceed the recommended limit in the United States (French, 1993:158–179). Hilary French says that the "export of waste is perhaps the most celebrated example of the world economy serving as purveyor of hazard" (French, 1993:165). For example, over the past several years, at least ten million tons of waste have been exported. About half of that has gone to Eastern Europe, where regulations are rather lax.

Just south of the U.S. border, there are about 2,000 U.S.-owned manufacturing plants. These plants notoriously discharge solvents and toxic chemicals, including heavy metals like mercury, into rivers and streams. The Rio Alamar in Tijuana, just south of San Diego, California, contains five times the amount of mercury allowable under California standards. Contact with this heavy metal is known to cause brain damage and birth defects. South of Arizona, Mexican groundwater supplies, which provide drinking water to residents, are contaminated by discharges from *maquiladoras*. Similar conditions exist south of Texas. But, such environmental degradation has effects on the United States, as well. In 1990 investigators found that the level of lead on the U.S. side of the Tijuana River was almost 100 times the U.S. maximum standard. Lead, when injested by human beings, attacks the brain and nervous system (McDonnell, 1993).

Some optimists believe that, as the North American Free Trade Agreement (NAFTA) develops, safeguards against pollution and destruction will be included in the various agreements negotiated among Canada, the United States, and Mexico. But, certain existing U.S. standards might actually be lowered. The NAFTA is similar to a localized version of a three-decade-old program, called GATT (General Agreement on Tariffs and Trade). These agreements are constantly being renegotiated and revised. According to rules proposed in 1993 (Figure 11.4), the amount of DDT and other pesticides allowed on food imported to this country may be hundreds to thousands of times the present U.S. standard (Bauerlein, 1993). However, in a three-way treaty by the United States, Canada, and Mexico, each country would have far more influence than in GATT.

Bhopal

Union Carbide, an American-founded multinational corporation, established one of its largest plants in India. In December 1984, a cloud of toxic gasses escaped from the Union Carbide plant in Bhopal, India, spreading through the town of Bhopal and the little shantytowns on its fringes. Initially, it was reported that at least 2,500 people were killed and about 200,000 were injured, making Bhopal the greatest industrial accident in history. A later and more thorough study of subsequent deaths placed the figures much higher. Dan Kurtzman (1988), who studied the Bhopal incident over a four-year period, is convinced that efforts were made to minimize the figures, which he concluded should be about 8,000 dead and 300,000 injured. The majority of the thousands of injured people were injured very badly, so badly that many of them will never be able to work again. The episode was terrifying, as people fled through the streets trying to get away from the suffocating fumes. Much of the response to the tragedy shows not only callous disregard on the part of the industrial world, but

Pesticide Residues Allowed on Your Food Under Proposed GATT Rules

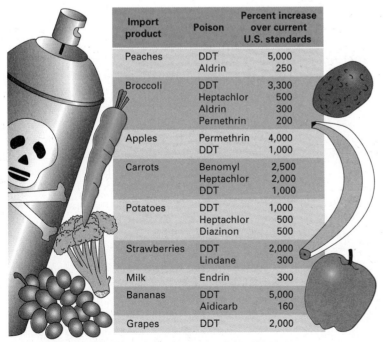

Import product	Poison	Percent increase over current U.S. standards
Peaches	DDT	5,000
	Aldrin	250
Broccoli	DDT	3,300
	Heptachlor	500
	Aldrin	300
	Pernethrin	200
Apples	Permethrin	4,000
	DDT	1,000
Carrots	Benomyl	2,500
	Heptachlor	2,000
	DDT	1,000
Potatoes	DDT	1,000
	Heptachlor	500
	Diazinon	500
Strawberries	DDT	2,000
	Lindane	300
Milk	Endrin	300
Bananas	DDT	5,000
	Aidicarb	160
Grapes	DDT	2,000

Source: M. Bauerlein, "GATTzilla," *Utne Reader,* Jan.–Feb., 1993: 19–21.

Figure 11.4
The U.S. Department of Agriculture's rules regarding the amount of pesticide residue allowed on agriculture produce is hundreds to thousands of times more strict than the proposed regulations for the General Agreement on Tariffs and Trade. These agreements are constantly being renegotiated, however, and regulations may become stricter at any time.

also insensitivity on the part of the Indian government toward its own people.

According to reports by many investigators of the tragedy, the Bhopal catastrophe combines extreme carelessness, indifference to regulations, indifference to warnings, and indifference to the lives of people. According to David Weir (1987), Union Carbide had been ordered by the Indian government to relocate its operation to the "obnoxious industries zone," 15 miles out of town. Union Carbide ignored the order and the government did not follow through. Weir also tells us that an Indian reporter had given warning in local newspapers only a month before the tragedy. The reporter had learned of an unpublished report by Union Carbide admitting many dangerous conditions. Other investigators found that even the warning alarm of the plant was not in operation (Morehouse and Subramanian, 1986). It had been turned off because a series of warnings of minor problems had been embarrassing to the corporation. In addition to the inoperative alarm, Weir lists six safety systems that were out of commission, including gauges measuring pressure and temperature (Weir, 1987:36).

Kurtzman's work concentrated on the stories of people killed and injured, but he also gives insight into official indifference to the suffering. According to Kurtzman (1988), a corporate executive from the United States, who went to investigate, was at first sympathetic. However as potential costs mounted and the corporation plotted its defense, sympathy and good intentions melted away.

Even in discussions of settlements, Union Carbide showed the contempt for people that often occurs as MDCs look at LDCs. Corporate executives reasoned that the life of an Indian worker was worth a little less than 2 percent of the average settlement paid for the life of an American worker who was killed on the job: an American life equals $500,000, and an Indian life equals $8,500 (Morehouse and Subramanian, 1986:58–64). Such reasoning has terrible significance for environmentalism, pointing to greater

profits in parts of the world where accidents cost relatively little. The original proposal for damages put forth by Union Carbide was for about $200 million to $300 million, an amount considered by the Indian government to be so grossly inadequate as to add insult to injury. Meanwhile, as negotiations between the corporation and the government were drawn out, thousands of people, including those who were horribly injured, received little or no help. Thousands of people suffered irreversible lung damage, and many people are still dying early deaths because of the accident. Union Carbide has sold many of its assets in an attempt to escape just payment. David Weir lists approximately $5 billion in sales (Weir, 1989:197–199).

Other Bhopals?

The possibility of other tragedies similar to the one at Bhopal cannot be dismissed. The relationships between the interests of governments trying to attract industry at any cost and corporations looking for a license to pollute in one of the less developed countries are mutually attractive and make more problems seem likely. The major theme of David Weir's book, *The Bhopal Syndrome* (1987), is that more "Bhopals" will occur, sometimes small, but adding up to thousands of lives. He is not optimistic even about the United States, pointing out that 75 percent of Americans live fairly close to a chemical plant, in most cases without realizing the fact.

The worst troubles can be expected in the LDCs, occasionally by explosions, but frequently by a creeping death coming from contaminated chemical plants. In their rush to industrialize, many countries have failed to develop necessary regulations and health facilities. Europe and North America in their early stages of industrialization treated their laborers badly, but they lacked the thousands of deadly and explosive chemicals now being used all over the world. A new chemical plant in Tanzania leaves its workers completely unprotected. In Cairo, dye and pesticide plants spew poisons into the Nile in the most crowded areas. Guatemala's pesticide plants are in the middle of cities. In Malaysia, pesticide plants are built next to schools. Everywhere, workers build shantytowns near the chemical plants, and governments let such hazardous living quarters mushroom (Weir, 1987:97–104).

ENVIRONMENTAL DESTRUCTION: WILDLIFE, FORESTS, LAND

Occasionally an event mentioned in the newspapers causes momentary concern about the extinction of one species or another. The last California condor existing in the wild was caught in the spring of 1987 to be kept with a handful of other members of her species, the final survivors. Attempts to breed the species in captivity have been successful, but such isolated triumphs do not guarantee the continuance of the species. In fact, tiny remnants of a species are often doomed, partly because they lack the genetic variability needed to make a breed vigorous. The inbreeding that must take place with only ten or twenty surviving members of a species raises doubts as to whether even the best intentions and the best care humans can provide will suffice for survival.

We can understand the importance of the statement above if we know about the significance of **biodiversity,** which means an environment has great diversity of species or diversity within a species. Life developed on earth about 600 million years ago. Over time, millions of species came into being. These species include microorganisms, fish, insects, birds, plants, and human beings. The integration of these species has made life on earth possible. Exactly how many species exist is not known. Only 1.4 million species have been identified, but scientists believe that the total number of species may be somewhere between 10 million and 80 million (Ryan, 1992a:2–26). Surveys of the rain forests of

Panama suggest that there may be 30 million insect species alone (*The Universal Almanac,* 1993).

Whether a species survives depends upon the survival of its habitat and of other species on which it depends. Equally important for survival is biodiversity *within* the species. If only one strain of the species exists (a condition called **monoculture**), its future is precarious. It may be unable to overcome new diseases or even slight environmental changes. As we approach the twenty-first century, we are witnessing the greatest threat to biodiversity since the extinction of the dinosaurs 65 million years ago, and we see a concomitant shift to monocultures. The danger of these changes can be illustrated by the mid-nineteenth century experience of Ireland. A single strain of potatoes had been introduced to Ireland from South America. The potatoes were so productive that they became Ireland's major food supply. Then, in 1848, the Irish potato was struck by a blight that destroyed the crop and brought the "Great Potato Famine," which killed or forced the migration of millions of Irish people to North America as well as to England and Australia. Crop failure continued until new strains of potatoes, resistant to the blight, were brought in.

Despite the lessons of history, we are witnessing a drift toward monocultures. Sri Lankan farmers once grew about 2,000 varieties of rice; now they rely on five. Over the past 50 years, India produced almost 30,000 strains of rice; by 2005, Indian farmers may be planting as few as ten types. And 3,500 varieties of rice disappeared in Indonesia during the past 15 years. In the United States, which lost 15 percent of its corn crop in 1970 because of a lack of biodiversity, "71 percent of U.S. corn fields are planted in just six varieties, while nine varieties of wheat occupy half of all U.S. wheatland" (Ryan, 1992a:14).

The Great Extinction

The California condor is joined in the path toward oblivion by so many other species that the present century can be thought of as the age of the great extinction. We do not know for sure why dinosaurs became extinct. We do know, however, that an extinction of species is taking place now on a similar scale. The reason for the great extinction is the dominance of a single species of phenomenally prolific predators known as human beings. Zoologist Les Kaufman (1986:89) explains:

> The bounds of human habitability include nearly the whole globe, whereas the entire livable universe of other species can vanish overnight as one river is dammed or one hillside is laid bare.

For this reason, says Kaufman, between the years 1600 and 1900, bird and mammal species disappeared at the rate of about one every four years; now the rate of disappearance is about one per year. David W. Orr (1993:89) of the Elmwood Institute, which offers resources and training in environmental education, says, "If today is a typical day on planet Earth, we will lose 116 square miles of rain forest, or about an acre a second. We will lose 72 square miles to encroaching deserts. We will lose 40 to 100 species. We will add 2,700 tons of chlorofluorocarbons and 15 million tons of carbon to the atmosphere."

The most dramatic present-day cases of species extinction are taking place in Africa, carried out largely by poachers. In 1970 there were more than 50,000 black rhinos in Zimbabwe, in southern Africa; as of 1993 there were only 408 that have been verified as alive. Rhinos are killed only for their horns, which are highly valued in Asia as an aphrodisiac. In addition to shooting poachers on sight, the government has been tranquilizing the rhinos and removing their horns with chainsaws, making the animals worthless to poachers. Unfortunately, it costs between $350 and $1,800 to dehorn a single rhino (depending on the amount of flight time in helicopters), and the horn grows back in about three years. So, the procedure must be performed many times on each animal during its lifetime (Satchell, 1993:76). Elsewhere throughout Asia and Africa, the worldwide rhino population has plummeted from about 100,000 in the early 1970s to fewer than 10,000 in 1993. The major reason for the slaughter is that a pound of rhino horn sells for about $28,000, and the value will undoubtedly increase as the size of rhino herds declines (Satchell, 1993:69).

In 1900 about 100,000 tigers roamed the mountains and jungles of Asia; in 1993, only

Because they are hunted only for their horns, rhinos are tranquilized, their horns are removed with chain saws, and the animals recover. This is one of the stategies to deter poachers from killing the last of the rhinos.

6,000 were left. Theresa Telecky of the Humane Society of the United States told a congressional hearing, "At this rate of decline, there will be no rhinos left in $2\frac{1}{2}$ years and no tigers in less than five" (Satchell, 1993:69). The World Wildlife Fund (WWF), which has developed a Defense Fund to protect various species, is a bit less pessimistic, but even WWF officials estimate that by the year 2025 both species will disappear (Begley, 1993).

In the Central African Republic, poachers hunt elephants for their ivory and by 1986 had killed 8,000 out of 11,000. Throughout Africa, 60,000 elephants were slaughtered in 1985 alone, feeding a $500-million ivory industry. In some countries, the wildlife services are not so alert as in Zimbabwe; corruption and bribery allow poaching to go on. In 1989 the United Nations **Convention on International Trade in Endangered Species (CITES)** established a ban on African ivory among its 120 member nations. By that time, nearly half of the continent's elephants had already been wiped out, particularly in East Africa. Southern African nations, still relatively "rich" in elephants, are pressuring CITES to lift the ban. South Africa, for example, interprets "sustainable use" to mean managing herds and

killing a certain percentage of animals for economic gain. Proponents say that the money received from the sale of horn, meat, ivory, and hide can be used to protect the remainder of the herd. Without such funds to pay armed guards, they claim, an entire herd would be killed off by poachers (Satchell, 1993:69).

The "culling of herds" policy is controversial, especially to people who believe more elephants can be saved. Clem Coetsee, a conservationist working in Zimbabwe, has devised a means of saving many more. The reason, he observes, for loss of elephants is that they are badly distributed, pressing against means of existence in one area and missing in others. With help from British and American conservation societies, he is moving elephants as much as 650 miles from Gona-re-zhou (Place of the Elephants) in Zimbabwe to other wildlife preserves in Africa. So far, 600 have been moved successfully in groups of six or eight, thoroughly tranquilized and loaded onto tractor-trailers (Contreras, 1993).

The other animals of Africa—wildebeest, antelope, cheetahs, lions, baboons, chimpanzees—are also under threat, not because they bear valuable ivory, but for other reasons. In the first place, many of the bovines are a source of food for the

This matriarch elephant was shot and gutted eight hours earlier by government rangers in South Africa's Kruger National Park. Within 30 minutes, she will be skinned, boned, and butchered; her remains (ivory, hide, feet, fat, bones, and meat) will fetch between $3,500 and $6,500.

hungry people near them. Much more important, however, is that they occupy land desired by human beings. The human population of Africa is growing rapidly, and it gradually denudes the semiarid lands and pours into any arable land remaining. What is happening to the wildlife in Africa is what happened to Europe long ago. The human tide drowns all else.

In Africa, the two closest relatives of Homo sapiens, chimpanzees and gorillas, are severely threatened, not because they are hunted, but because human population moves into more and more of their territory. The orangutans of Indonesia are under threat for precisely the same reason. At the present rate of extinction, they have very few remaining years on earth. Most people are not concerned about the thousands of species that will die out of existence this year because most of them are insects. Many animals, birds, fish, and plants are endangered species, as Table 11.4 shows. They are all parts of the food chain.

Deforestation

Forests exist because of **photosynthesis**, a process that uses solar energy to form carbohydrates from a combination of water and carbon dioxide. It also produces oxygen. Lester R. Brown, Christopher Flavin, and Sandra Postel (1991:73) write, "Indeed, this process for converting solar energy into biochemical energy supports all life on earth." Our forests are, in fact, the earth's lungs. To destroy them is to destroy everything.

The destruction of forests generally precedes the extinction of other species in a direct cause–effect relationship. In the poorest lands of the world, tree destruction proceeds rapidly because people need wood for their fires. They have no other fuel with which to cook and, especially in tropical regions, very little food is safe from contamination unless it is cooked because of a lack of refrigeration. Consequently, tens of millions of cooking fires eat away at the forests,

stick by stick and branch by branch. The people are not so ignorant as to fail to realize they are, in essence, eating away their future, but they are poor, the pangs of hunger are now, and the future must be forgotten. The animal inhabitants of the forests, of course, find their habitats shrinking. Stripped of their cover, they are run down and killed. In parts of India and parts of Africa, wood is so scarce that cattle dung is burned for fuel, which means the soil is being robbed of its only fertilizer in the poorest parts of the world.

A question naturally arises: Is this dim picture of forest destruction true of all countries? What about Europe? The United States? What about the heavily forested Amazon and Southeast Asia? The reply is a matter of a little good news, but more bad news. Europe and the United States used up much of their forest lands long ago, but in recent years they have made efforts to preserve what remains. For example, a recent poll showed that Germans were so concerned about preserving their forests that they supported a Scandinavian proposal to cut sulfur dioxide emissions by 30 percent in ten years (Brown, Flavin, and Postel, 1989). Switzerland plans to spend $10 billion to save the forests. Part of the plan is to build a railroad across the nation to replace the use of trucks whose emissions pollute the air and damage the trees. Trucks now pay a $10 toll to travel on Swiss roads. When the railroad is completed, it will cost truckers $200 to cross the Swiss border (Kandell, 1993). Table 11.5 shows that a total of 22 percent of Europe's forests have been damaged, the worst case being in the Netherlands.

In the United States and Canada, a method of harvesting trees, clear cutting, denudes huge areas that were previously forested. Environmentalists in both countries oppose clear cutting, but Canada has very few restrictions against logging. For example, when British Columbia was founded in 1871, it was declared "crown land," meaning that it was a possession of the British government. The government decided

Some Endangered Species

TABLE 11.4

Common name	Range
MAMMALS	
Asian wild ass	Southwestern & Central Asia
Point Arena mountain beaver	U.S. (Cal.)
Bobcat	Central Mexico
Ozark big-eared bat	U.S. (Mo., Okla., Ariz.)
Brown or grizzly bear	U.S. (48 conterminous states)
Cheetah	Africa to India
Eastern cougar	Eastern N.A.
Columbian white-tailed deer	U.S. (Wash., Ore.)
Chinese river dolphin	China
Asian elephant	Southcentral, Southeast Asia
San Joaquin kit fox	U.S. (Cal.)
Gorilla	Central & W. Africa
Leopard	Africa, Asia
Asiatic lion	Turkey to India
Howler monkey	Mexico to S. America
Southeastern beach mouse	U.S. (Fla.)
Ocelot	U.S. (Tex., Ariz.)
Southern sea otter	U.S. (Wash., Ore., Cal.)
Giant panda	China
Florida panther	U.S. (La., Ark. east to S.C., Fla.)
Utah prairie dog	U.S. (Ut.)
Morro Bay kangaroo rat	U.S. (Cal.)
Black rhinoceros	Sub-Saharan Africa
Carolina northern flying squirrel	U.S. (N.C., Tenn.)
Tiger	Asia
Hualapai Mexican vole	U.S. (Ariz.)
Gray whale	N. Pacific Ocean
Wild yak	China (Tibet), India
Mountain zebra	South Africa
Red wolf	U.S. (Southeast to central Tex.)
BIRDS	
Masked bobwhite (quail)	U.S. (Ariz.)
California condor	U.S. (Ore., Cal.)
Hooded crane	Japan, former Soviet Union
White-necked crow	U.S. (P.R.), Dominican Rep., Haiti
Eskimo curlew	Alaska and N. Canada
Bald eagle	U.S. (most states), Canada
American peregrine falcon	Canada to Mexico
Hawaiian hawk	U.S. (Hi.)
Indigo macaw	Brazil
West African ostrich	Spanish Sahara
Golden parakeet	Brazil
Australian parrot	Australia
Attwater's greater prairie-chicken	U.S. (Tex.)

(continued)

BIRDS (continued)	TABLE 11.4
Bachman's warbler (wood)	U.S. (Southeast), Cuba
Kirtland's warbler (wood)	U.S., Canada, Bahama Is.
Ivory-billed woodpecker	U.S. (Southcentral and Southeast), Cuba

REPTILES	
American alligator	U S. (Southeastern)
American crocodile	U.S. (Fla.)
Atlantic salt march snake	U.S. (Fla.)
Plymouth red-bellied turtle	U.S. (Mass.)

FISHES	
Bonytail chub	U.S. (Ariz., Cal. Col., Nev., Ut., Wyo.)
Cave crayfish	U.S. (Ariz.)
Gila trout	U.S. (Ariz., N.M.)

PLANTS	
Florida golden aster	U.S. (Fla.)
Autumn buttercup	U.S. (Ut.)
Bakersfield cactus	U.S. (Cal.)
Santa Cruz cypress	U.S. (Cal.)
Maguire daisy	U.S. (Ut.)
Short's goldenrod	U.S. (Ky.)
Tennessee yellow-eyed grass	U.S. (Ala., Ga., Tenn.)
Mountain golden heather	U.S. (N.C.)
Cooley's meadowrue	U.S. (N.C., Fla.)
Wheeler's peperomia	U.S. (P.R.)
Chapman rhododendron	U.S. (Fla.)
Texas wild-rice	U.S. (Tex.)

SOURCE: *The World Almanac and Book of Facts, 1994* (Mahwah, NJ: World Almanac, 1994), p. 174.

that the best use of the land was to provide timber. To draw investment to the area, the government issued long-term logging rights to private companies, and timber harvesting soared. In fact, so much of the forest on Vancouver Island was destroyed that the government established the Forest Resources Commission in 1991. Its job is to bring sweeping changes to Canada's previous policy. However, as Figure 11.5 shows, by that time nearly half of the forest had been cleared (Derringer, 1993).

Although the United States actually produces more lumber than does Canada, it has stricter policies. Canada now allows clear cutting up to a maximum of 100 acres; in the United States, the maximum is 40 acres. In 1993 U.S. President Clinton set a difficult task for a commission of scientists, sociologists, and economists: "Explore every conceivable option for preserving the Northwest's ancient forests and its wildlife, while saving whatever can be saved of the once proud and productive timber industry" (Gup, 1993:38). The plan allowed for annual timber harvests of 1.2 billion board feet, but that is only one-third of the peak production period of the 1980s. An outraged logging industry spokesperson said the plan

Estimated Forest Damage in Europe, 1986 TABLE 11.5			
Country	Total forest area	Estimated area damaged	Portion of total area damaged
	(thousand hectares)		(percent)
Netherlands	311	171	55
West Germany	7,360	3,952	54
Switzerland	1,186	593	50
United Kingdom	2,018	979	49
Czechoslovakia	4,578	1,886	41
Austria	3,754	1,397	37
Bulgaria	3,300	1,112	34
France	14,440	4,043	28
Spain	11,789	3,313	28
Luxembourg	88	23	26
Norway	6,660	1,712	26
Finland	20,059	5,083	25
Hungary	1,637	409	25
Belgium	680	111	16
Poland	8,654	1,264	15
Sweden	23,700	3,434	15
East Germany	2,955	350	12
Yugoslavia	9,125	470	5
Italy	8,328	416	5
Other	12,282	n.a.	n.a.
Total	142,904	30,718	22

SOURCE: L. R. Brown and C. Flavin, "The Earth's Vital Signs." In L. R. Brown, Ed., *State of the World 1988* (New York, W. W. Norton, 1988), p. 14.

the forest continues to disappear. Although many Americans may think that jobs for human beings should take precedence over the habitat of a bird, birds are an important part of the ecosystem. Large birds control the population of rodents. Without owls, hawks, and crows, there would be an explosion of rats, mice, and other rodents. Small birds help protect humans from a plague of insects. The stomach of a dead North American woodpecker contained about 5,000 ants. Imagine the number of insects the bird would have devoured in its lifetime. Other birds, like hummingbirds, are necessary for the continued existence of flowers. Other birds scatter seeds throughout the world. Yet 70 percent of the world's 9,600 species of birds are declining, and about 1,000 species are facing extinction (Youth, 1994). In some cases, their habitats are destroyed to satisfy human needs for land space, lumber, and other purposes. In other cases, they are hunted for food. Despite legal protection, about 50 million songbirds end up on dinner tables each year in Italy (Gup, 1993:18). Table 11.6 shows actions that make birds disappear.

In Southeast Asia, much forest remains, but valuable teak and tropical hardwood forests are under attack, being cut more rapidly than they can recover. Other forests are under attack for the same reason that orangutans face extinction: Their lands are needed for rice, other crops, and other reasons. For example, the Kankanaey, forest-dwelling natives of Dalicno, on the island of Luzon in the Philippines, have been "pocket miners" as well as farmers. When not working their farms, they use hand tools to dig into the mountainside, searching for gold. Now a large international corporation uses bulldozers to level the forest and the mountain. In another Philippine village, the Banwa'on tribe is losing its forest because the government literally sold it to a logging company. Traditionally, the Banwa'on hunted the jungle successfully on a daily basis. Now, according to the chief, they are lucky to make a single catch a month. On the Philippines' Mount Apo, the Lumad tribe is losing its forest to the Philippine National Oil Company, which is

would cause the Northwest's already high level of unemployment to increase by 85,000. Clinton offered $1.2 billion to diversify the industry, but loggers were not satisfied. Environmentalists were equally outraged because 22 percent of the old growth forest remains vulnerable to the chain saw. They also pointed out that continued logging denudes more land, causing additional soil runoff that pollutes rivers and threatens to kill off the salmon. If the salmon die, then 60,000 additional jobs will be lost in fishing and related industries (Gup, 1993:39).

In addition, the conflict between the government and the logging industry has drawn attention to the possible demise of the spotted owl if

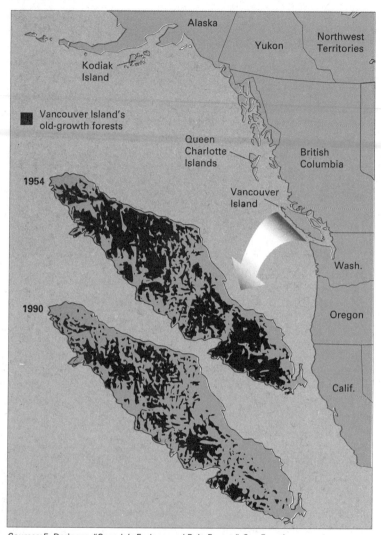

Figure 11.5
On Vancouver Island in British Columbia on Canada's west coast, government policies caused drastic reduction of the old-growth forests from 1954 to 1990. Although Canadian lumber is exported to all parts of the world, the United States is the largest customer.

Sources: E. Deringer, "Canada's Endangered Rain Forest," *San Francisco Chronicle,* July 19, 1993: A9. Sierra Club and Wilderness Society of Western Canada.

stripping the mountainside in search of geothermal power to help solve the country's energy crisis (Durning, 1992a).

In a publication for the Worldwatch Institute, Alan Thein Durning (1993) raises the question of who owns the forests. In many LDCs, the government claims rights to all forest land, regardless of the fact that the forests have been home to many hundreds of tribal people. In Borneo, the Galik people were among the dozens of tribes to have successfully managed their forests for hundreds of years. They carefully conserved their valuable ironwood trees, whose lumber is resistant to insects. Then, the government decided that it owned the forest and sold contracts to logging companies. Fearing they would lose everything, the Galik rushed to cut down the trees themselves. Durning comments,

Clear cutting forests in the Cascade Range, which stretches across the states of Oregon and Washington, denudes the land.

"In Borneo, as elsewhere, nationalizing the forests sabotaged traditional management, creating the free-for-all it purported to avert" (Durning, 1994:25).

Amazonia

By far the most gigantic of tropical rain forests is that of **Amazonia**. Larger than all of Western Europe, the Amazon is so vast it seems indestructible. But is it? Actually, prior to the last two or three decades, the life of the Brazilian rain forest seemed eternal. The Amazonian Indians burned off small patches of forest in order to plant corn, plantains, and other crops. The forest soil is thin and easily used up, so the Indians moved their gardens frequently, allowing the original forest cover to return. Amazonia was a vast, unified ecosystem, with more species of plants and animals than any other place on earth. Species of Amazonia show **ecological interdependence**, meaning one cannot thrive without the other. In return for debris from trees, insects work the soil and aid the decomposition of leaves into humus for roots. In some cases, interdependence is very specific. Only one type of bumblebee can spread pollen for Brazil-nut trees, and only the agouti, a large rodent, scatters the seed. Other species of trees depend upon particular wasps, birds, or ants. If any of these species is terminated, the trees eventually will die out (Prince, 1986).

Interference with the Amazonian ecosystem has proceeded on a large scale, however. In the 1970s, the Brazilian government attempted to aid the impoverished people of the northeast by moving them into the Amazon rain forest. The experiment was a dismal failure. The soil was too thin to sustain crops in any manner other than that of the Indians (Prince, 1986:87). Nevertheless, further attempts at cultivation have been made, often funded by the World Bank. Thousands of people have followed newly opened roads into the Amazon, deforesting hundreds of thousands of acres and exhausting the soil in a very short time.

The Brazilian government, with its ethos of expansion, continues to plunder the forest. The solid canopy of trees is now broken into sections, quite possibly breaking some of the links in an interdependent system. Dams have been built for hydroelectric power and thousands of acres have been inundated. Much land

Why Birds Are Disappearing	TABLE 11.6

Threats	Consequences
HABITAT LOSS	
Deforestation	At least half of the 250 bird species that breed in North America and winter to the south have declined in recent years.
Forest fragmentation	In North America, parasitic cowbirds infest more than half of other songbirds' nests in many areas where clearings have been cut into forests for roads or developments.
Overgrazing and plowing of grassland	Once-abundant species such as Eurasia's buzzards and North America's prairie chickens have all but disappeared.
Desertification	Whitethroat warblers that breed in Britain but winter in Africa have declined by 75 percent in 27 years.
Draining of wetlands	North America's most common ducks have declined by 30 percent in 27 years.
PESTICIDES	
	Widespread use of DDT in Africa has caused birds' eggshells to become too thin, leading to declines in populations of at least six birds-of-prey. Use of carbofuran on Virginia fields left tens of thousands of dead birds.
CHEMICAL CONTAMINATION	
Acidification of streams	Disappearance of fish has destroyed food supply for loons on northern lakes, and local extinction of the dipper in Wales.
Use of lead shot and sinkers	Consumption of lead scattered by hunters and fishers has caused widespread lead poisoning of swans, geese, ducks, and loons.
Oil spills	Persian Gulf War oil spills attracted and killed thousands of waterbirds. The *Exxon Valdez* spill killed 300,000 birds.
EXOTIC SPECIES	
	Introduction of the brown tree snake on Guam extinguished four of the island's five endemic bird species. Roaming house cats in Victoria, Australia, kill 13 million small animals per year, including members of 67 bird species.
OVERHUNTING	
	In Italy alone, 50 million songbirds end up on dinner plates each year.

SOURCE: H. Youth, "Flying into Trouble," *World Watch*, Jan.–Feb., 1994:19.

is ripped up in the frantic search for gold and other metals. As the forest diminishes, so does the number of species, along with genetic variety and potential products we will never know. Obviously, as the forest disappears, the land is no longer protected and much of it washes down to the sea. For example, less than 10 percent of the

Brazilian coastal forest that Charles Darwin observed in the 1830s survives today (Wolf, 1987). Durning (1992b) reminds us that cultural diversity, like biodiversity, depends on the maintenance of forests. In Brazil, 87 tribes simply disappeared during the first half of this century. Worldwide, he says, "the loss of cultural diversity

Figure 11.6
Damage from the edge effect can be reduced by changing the way trees are taken from forests. For example, two parcels of 10,000 acres of forest have been cleared of 2,500 acres of trees. The clearing pattern on the left leaves 5,156 acres undisturbed; the cutting pattern on the right leaves only 3,906 acres undamaged.

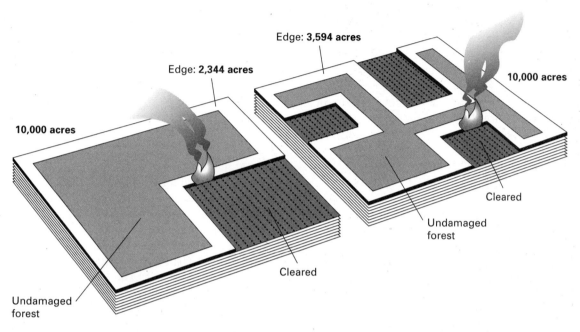

Source: From S. Budiansky, "The Doomsday Myths," *U.S. News & World Report,* Dec. 13, 1993: 87.

is keeping pace with the loss of biological diversity" (Durning, 1992:9).

Although scientists have known for many years of the terrible consequences, recent photographs of the Amazon, taken by the Landsat satellite, show that the habitat loss is worse than feared. The reasons become clear if we understand the edge effect. The **edge effect** is the tendency for trees and vines to be uprooted and otherwise damaged if they are at the edge of the forest, unprotected from winds, temperature changes, cattle, hunters, and other destructive elements (Budiansky, 1993). Figure 11.6 shows that deforesting one large section produces a smaller edge area than removing the same number of trees in smaller, but more numerous,

sections. Yet, the Brazilian government is allowing deforestation in a "fish-bone" pattern that maximizes the amount of forest subject to the edge effect. Taking this maximization into effect, Compton Tucker, a tropical forest expert, and David Skole, a physical scientist, determined that although there were 89,000 square miles of deforestation in 1988, there were actually 227,000 square miles of serious biological disturbance (Stevens, 1993).

In 1992 about 100 world leaders and 30,000 other participants descended on Brazil to attend the Earth Summit. On the eve of the meetings, the president of Brazil set aside an area, approximately the size of Hungary, for the exclusive use of the 10,000 remaining members of the Yanomami, an ancient Amazon tribe. Critics said the action was simply tokenism because he has not made similar provisions for other tribal peoples, like the Guarani, who live hundreds of miles south of the Yanomami, or the Sarare in Mato Grosso. But the president insisted that the Earth Summit would signal a turning point in how Brazil treats the environment (Serrill, 1992). Only time will tell how serious such politicians are.

Other areas that have suffered from significant levels of deforestation include Latin America, Asia, and Africa. Table 11.7 shows the annual rate of forest destruction for 87 countries during the 1980s.

Soil Destruction

Although one usually thinks of soil as something ubiquitous and eternal, the fact is that much of the land surface of the earth is covered with rock, ice, or unproductive sand or alkali, and the land that is covered with productive soil is subject to erosion and other problems. Soil cannot only be washed away; it can be filled with salt or toxins, waterlogged, or so filled with nuclear debris as to be "hot" and dangerous. Another way to do away with the soil is to simply pave it over with roads, airports, cities, and military installations. The soil is under attack in all these ways.

Deforestation leads directly to soil erosion. Obviously, the topsoil of Amazonia washes away as the forest is cleared. The same is true on a vast scale in tropical Africa and Indonesia. Elsewhere, high mountain areas are particularly subject to erosion if they are deforested. Annually, the Ganges River carries 250,000 tons of soil from deforested mountain slopes of Nepal, building a muddy island in the Bay of Bengal that now covers 15 million acres. Because of huge annual increases in population and, consequently, greater competition for land and natural resources, millions of Bangladeshis live on bars of silt and sand, called "chars," in the middle of the Bengal delta. A combination of a natural disaster (unusually heavy monsoonal rains) and

unnatural disaster (deforestation and building houses on chars) caused the area to flood in 1988, as it often does. The result was 1,200 deaths, hundreds of thousands of Bangladeshis suffering from diseases that spread as a result of contamination, and 25 million people left homeless (Jacobson, 1988).

In the United States, deforestation and misuse of land have led to heavy erosion. Winds swept through many western states in the 1930s, blowing away millions of tons of topsoil and creating the phenomenon known as the **dust bowl**. The loss of topsoil in the Great Plains, along with the deepening effects of the Great Depression, turned many farm owners into migrant workers in states like California. Jacobson (1988:8) calls such people "environmental refugees." Franklin D. Roosevelt's solution for future generations was to plant shelter belts of trees that cut the effect of the winds. His administration also took much sub-marginal land out of production, creating a kind of **soil bank**. But the soil bank plan of keeping land out of production has been largely abandoned. Consequently, the time might come when we face another dust bowl.

Whether because of deforestation, overgrazing, or poor farming methods, half of the world's arable land is suffering some degree of erosion. At present rates of erosion, all the land being expensively and painstakingly brought into production to feed the world's increasing population will be more than offset by land lost to erosion by the end of the century. Some effects of soil erosion are already evident. In the former Soviet Union, the production of grain was reduced by 20 percent between 1977 and 1991 because of the loss of soil (Brown, 1992b).

Soil erosion is not the only way soil can be lost. A second problem is **salinization**. When water stands for long periods, especially in hot regions, much of it evaporates. Water behind dammed reservoirs contains a little salt, which does not evaporate along with the water. So there is a cumulative effect: As the amount of water decreases due to evaporation, the concentration

Tropical Forest Area and Rate of Deforestation for 87 Countries, 1981–1990 (in thousand hectares)					TABLE 11.7
Region/subregion	Number of countries studied	Total land area	Forest area 1980	Forest area 1990	Area deforested annually 1981–1990
LATIN AMERICA					
Area Total	32	1,675,700	923,000	839,000	8,300
Central America and Mexico	7	245,300	77,000	63,500	1,400
Caribbean subregion	18	69,500	48,800	47,100	200
Tropical South America	7	1,360,800	797,100	729,300	6,800
ASIA					
Area Total	15	896,600	310,800	274,900	3,600
South Asia	6	445,600	70,600	66,200	400
Continental Southeast Asia	5	192,900	83,200	69,700	1,300
Insular Southeast Asia	4	258,100	157,000	138,900	1,800
AFRICA					
Area Total	40	2,243,400	650,300	600,100	5,000
West Sahelian Africa	8	528,000	41,900	38,000	400
East Sahelian Africa	6	489,600	92,300	85,300	700
West Africa	8	203,200	55,200	43,400	1,200
Central Africa	7	406,400	230,100	215,400	1,500
Tropical Southern Africa	10	557,900	217,700	206,300	1,100
Insular Africa	1	58,200	13,200	11,700	200
TOTAL					
	87	4,815,700	1,884,100	1,714,800	16,900

SOURCE: *The Universal Almanac 1993*, J. W. Wright, Ed. (New York: Andrews and McMeel, 1992), p. 574.

of salt in the remaining water increases. The salt content of the soil increases as well because when water evaporates from the soil, the salt remains. **Soil destruction** is a problem in Egypt, in India, and in the United States, especially in lands irrigated by the Colorado River. Lake Mead and secondary reservoirs on the Colorado are in hot desert lands of heavy evaporation, with a slight buildup of salt taking place. More pronounced is the buildup of salt in irrigation canals and fields, some of which is drained in runoff water that goes back to the Colorado River. One result is that the allotment of Colorado River water that goes to Mexico is so contaminated with salt that it is unusable. Consequently, the United States

has had to install expensive desalinization processes to provide Mexico with the amount of water guaranteed by treaty (Engle, 1993).

A third problem related to both soil erosion and deforestation is the production of cattle, sheep, and goats. All three species graze on rangeland. If there are too many for the land, **overgrazing** results—a loss of the stubble and chaparral that otherwise protect the soil. If there are too many of them in a small area, sheep will clip the grass much too short, and goats will even destroy small shrubs and trees. Cattle are not as destructive as goats, but they are a menace to the soil if there are too many of them for the acreage on which they graze. Although overgrazing occurs in

A strip-mining operation denudes a rain forest in the Amazon.

Throughout Central and South America, rain forests are cleared for cattle grazing. In many of these countries, beef is a valuable export. In Egypt, farmland that once produced food for people is now used to grow feed for cattle, whose meat only the rich can afford (Horowitz and Jackson, 1992:77). And, producing a pound of beef is an expensive proposition, regardless of the economic condition of the producer. According to Lester R. Brown (1993) of the Worldwatch Institute, cattle require about seven pounds of grain to produce one pound of beef. By contrast, pigs need about four pounds of feed and chickens require only two. Overgrazing and poor land management have contributed to a fourth means of soil degradation: **desertification**.

Much of the world's arable land is turning into desert. The worst cases of desertification are in Africa, where poverty-stricken populations, in need of food, sow steep slopes that will be washed away by rains in the next wet season, plow semiarid grasslands that will soon turn into dust bowls, or overgraze animals in ecologically fragile margins of deserts. Desertification is worse south of the Sahara, where grazing lands are being turned into desert at the rate of 250,000 acres per year. Evidence from satellite imagery shows that the desert spread 81 miles south in the period between 1980 and 1990. That's an increase of 16 percent in just ten years ("Satellite Finds Sahara Expanding," 1991). In Sudan, the desert advances about two miles per year. The picture is similar in Algeria, Tunisia, and Morocco (Figure 11.7).

Much of Central Asia, the western United States, western South America, western South Africa, and the larger part of Australia are arid or semiarid. All such lands are ecologically fragile. Their overuse can change them from somewhat productive grazing lands to total wastelands. Conversion into wasteland has taken place throughout history. Some authorities (Ehrlich and Ehrlich, 1982) contend that most of the Sahara Desert was once fertile land that has undergone desertification through the centuries.

the United States, Canada, Australia, and Russia, the greatest cattle problem occurs in India.

In a poor country like India, the effect of cattle can be devastating. India has more cows (196 million) than any other country and, except in the states of Kerala and West Bengal, it is against the law to slaughter them. The doctrine of Hinduism, the major religion of India, considers the cow sacred. But the activity of cattle can be destructive. Overgrazing causes a loss of grassland to weeds. The weeds are then consumed by goats, of which India also has the world's largest population. The soil is then left to the erosive effects of wind and rain (Brough, 1991).

Figure 11.7

Overgrazing and other misuses of semiarid lands are turning them into deserts. Between 1980 and 1990, the Sahara Desert in North Africa spread 81 miles south, causing the desert to grow by 16 percent. Desertification is also occurring in North America's southwest, parts of South America, across the subcontinent of Asia, and in Australia.

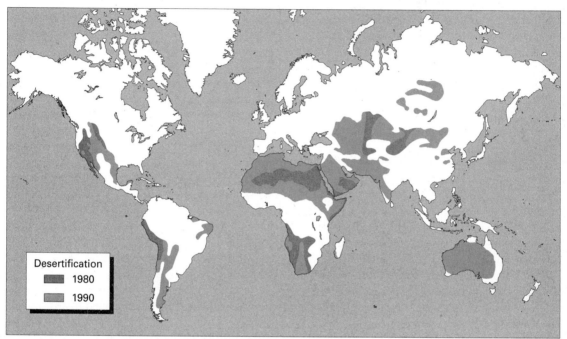

Desertification
1980
1990

Source: "Satellite Finds Sahara Expanding," *Los Angeles Times,* July 22, 1991: B3.

As soil continues to erode and desertification occurs, fertile farmland becomes scarce. Millions of people become environmental refugees, crossing national boundaries searching for sustenance. Lester R. Brown (1994:78) says that the "deteriorating balance between food and people in one way or another will increasingly preoccupy national political leaders, reorder national priorities, and dominate international affairs."

THE EARTH AS A GREENHOUSE

For many years, worries have increased about the possibility that certain substances thrown into the atmosphere are causing a **greenhouse effect**, gradually warming average temperature throughout the world. In fact, a 1990 report, written by 170 scientists from all over the world and prepared for the International Panel on Climate Change (IPCC), states that the earth's average surface temperature will rise by 5° Fahrenheit before the end of the next century unless we drastically change the way we live our lives and conduct our business. That is one-third of the temperature change since the last ice age, which occurred about 15,000 years ago (Stone, 1992). John C. Ryan (1992b:12) of the Worldwatch Institute writes, "A 5-degree warming would raise the Earth's temperature to its highest level in 100,000 years."

There is no better way of perceiving the earth as one vast ecosystem than visualizing it from above. What we would see is particulate matter, carbon dioxide, carbon monoxide, sulfur oxides, nitrogen oxides, hydrocarbons, and a class of substances called chlorofluorocarbons. The chlorofluorocarbons and all lighter gases make their way slowly into the upper reaches of the atmosphere known as the stratosphere. These substances do not hover merely above the industrial regions of the United States, Germany, or Japan, but they enter the circulatory system of winds and weather. They admit most of the short-wave radiation coming to the earth from the sun, but block much of the long-wave radiation reflected back from the earth. Because of an increase in the blocking agents that prevent escape of heat from the earth, the earth appears to be undergoing a gradual warming trend. The blockage of heat that would otherwise escape from the earth is the greenhouse effect.

More than two decades ago, Ward and DuBos (1972) presented evidence from volcanic eruptions to demonstrate that an increase in particulate matter in the upper atmosphere, rather than cooling the earth by blocking the sun's rays, has the effect of warming the earth by blocking reflected heat from the earth. In the great eruption of Mt. Agong, near Bali in Indonesia, a heating of two or three degrees took place and persisted for several years. Generalizing from that episode, "There is thus no doubt that gases and particles in the atmosphere do hang about, do have worldwide effects, and do raise the temperature" (Ward and DuBos, 1972:192). The eruption of Mt. Agong took place in 1963. The much earlier eruption of Mt. Krakatoa, also in Indonesia, must have had an even greater effect, because it was the most violent eruption in recorded history. There are eyewitness accounts of its blackening the atmosphere, but temperature was not carefully monitored then as it has been more recently.

We, of course, cannot do anything about volcanoes and their temporary effect on the atmosphere and temperature. Neither can we do anything about periodic changes that have brought ice ages and periods of warming over the course of geological time. Although there is no certainty about the matter, many geologists think we are moving into a warming period at present. If so, it would seem important for us to stop adding pollutants, which we are now doing at an accelerating rate, that will increase the warming trend. An intelligent policy under the circumstances would be to conserve our resources for bad times that might be coming. Instead, we continue to destroy much of the environment—air, water, and atmosphere.

The Carbon Dioxide Problem

Carbon dioxide, CO_2, is the gas formed by the burning of oxygen. In fires as well as in animal and human lungs, oxygen combines with carbon to form carbon dioxide. When the world's fires increased greatly, the amount of carbon dioxide in the atmosphere also increased. The increase has been mainly the result of burning fossil fuels, coal, and petroleum, which started with the Industrial Revolution and has increased ever since. Despite efforts in some countries to clean up these fuels, the amount of pollution continues to increase, and there is an accompanying rise in the amount of carbon dioxide being released into the atmosphere. Whether burning is clean or dirty, it always involves the formation of carbon dioxide. "In the past 150 years," writes Ryan (1992b:11), "humanity has burned enough fossil fuels and vegetation to increase atmospheric carbon dioxide by 25 percent."

Although the burning of fossil fuels is the primary problem in the carbon-dioxide increase, the burning of wood should also be mentioned. The world's forests are being burned faster than ever before, not only adding to carbon dioxide, but removing one of the air's purifiers. As previously mentioned, trees take the carbon from carbon dioxide and release free oxygen into the air. The world's supply of these oxygen producers is declining rapidly, while the carbon dioxide supply increases.

Methane

Another gas that scientists are concerned about relative to atmospheric heating is **methane,** a major component of the natural gas burnt for heating and cooking. Studies of air trapped in the ice of glaciers indicate that the amount of methane in the atmosphere had remained about the same until about 1600. Since then it has increased, although the cause is uncertain. It is estimated that methane will add another 20 to 40 percent to the global warmings expected from carbon dioxide by the year 2030 (Lester Brown, 1987:158–159). Methane is also called swamp gas because it rises from swamps where it is caused by decaying vegetation. Rice paddies are another source of methane, and so are cattle. We have complained of cattle relative to their cost in grain and in the results of overgrazing. At the risk of seeming unfair to cattle, we must add that a by-product of a cow's digestion is methane gas, which is released into the atmosphere. Although most people would not be concerned about cow belching or flatulence as major contributors to global warming, they actually produce more methane than the burning of vegetation, gas drilling, or coal mining (Horowitz and Jackson, 1992).

The warming of the earth of which we speak may seem infinitesimal. So far, it is hard to measure—a matter of perhaps half a degree in the last 50 years. There are two facts in the case, though, that should warn us against complacency; first, it takes extremely little change to have serious consequences. We can think of the earth at present as being in balance between too much glaciation and too much heat. If temperatures were to drop, which is not expected, the polar ice caps would advance. If temperatures were to rise, we could expect gradual melting of the polar ice caps, which would be accompanied by a rise in sea levels. According to IPCC calculations, the average sea level will rise between 12

and 43 inches by the end of the next century (Ryan, 1992b:12).

The second problem about the very slight rise in temperature is that it might not always be so slight. At present, the MDCs, Russia, and the new republics of Eastern Europe produce about 70 percent of the world's carbon dioxide. But Brazil, China, and India are industrializing, and a United Nations' scientific panel estimates that they may triple their carbon dioxide output by 2025 (Stetson, 1991). Table 11.8 shows the per capita carbon emissions from fossil fuels for selected countries. The anticipated increase might be accelerating because of another problem added to that of carbon dioxide—chlorofluorocarbons.

Chlorofluorocarbons

Chlorofluorocarbons, CFCs, may be even more of a hazard to the earth than the carbon dioxide and other pollutants previously mentioned. In 1974 Sherwood Rowland and Mario Molina, of the University of California at Irvine, came to the conclusion, based on computer-model calculations, that CFCs threaten the ozone layer in the upper atmosphere (cited in Linden, 1993). CFCs are the chemical propellants in most aerosol sprays. Although CFC spray propellants were

Per Capita Carbon Emissions from Fossil Fuels, 1989	TABLE 11.8
Country	**Carbon per capita 1989 (tons)**
United States	5.37
USSR	3.59
West Germany	2.86
Japan	2.31
China	.59
India	.21
Brazil	.38
Zaire	.03

SOURCE: M. Stetson, "People Who Live in Green Houses. . . . ," *World Watch*, Sept.–Oct., 1991:25.

banned in the United States in 1978, they are still widely used throughout the rest of the world. And in the United States, as well as elsewhere, they are a by-product of refrigerants, industrial solvents, and components of plastic foams. Seven hundred thousand tons of CFCs continue to rise into the stratosphere each year.

According to Peter H. Stone, a scientist at MIT's Center for Global Change Science, during the 1980s chlorofluorocarbons increased by 40 percent, methane by 10 percent, and CO_2 by 4 percent. "At these rates, CFCs would replace carbon dioxide as the major contributor to increases in global warming in 25 years" (1992:35–36). This problem is complicated by the discovery of a hole in the ozone layer above the South Pole in 1985. Ten years later, the hole was the size of Europe, 3.9 million square miles ("Science and Society," 1995). Scientists believe the damage was caused by a high concentration of chlorine monoxide (ClO), a chemical by-product of CFCs, in the atmosphere. In 1987, scientists at the National Aviation and Space Administration (NASA) found the same process beginning in the northern hemisphere. They calculated that in the late winter and early spring months there is a 40 percent depletion of ozone over the northern parts of the United States, Canada, Europe, and Russia (Lemonick, 1992).

When scientists theorized that CFCs threaten the **ozone layer,** they were mainly concerned with the problem of ultraviolet rays. Ozone, a molecule made of three atoms of oxygen, screens out almost all the ultraviolet rays coming from the sun to the earth. A decrease in ozone could result in the penetration of the atmosphere by more ultraviolet rays, causing mutations in DNA and producing more skin cancers. In fact, a 1992 United Nations Environment Program report predicted a 26 percent increase in the incidence of nonmelanoma skin cancers throughout the world if there is another 10 percent decrease in ozone.

Awareness of CFCs brings a new uncertainty into the heating problem, because it will take a very long time to know their effects. They rise so slowly that those released between 1955 and 1975

Figure 11.8
In 1985 scientists discovered a hole in the ozone layer above the South Pole. Chlorine monoxide, a by-product of chlorofluorocarbons (used in refrigerants, industrial solvents, and plastics), destroys the ozone. In 1992 NASA's Upper Atmosphere Research Satellitte photographed a huge cloud of chlorine monoxide. The striped area is the part of the world most affected.

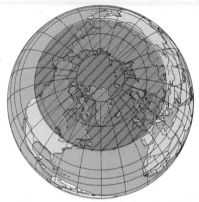

Source: M. D. Lemonick, "The Ozone Vanishes," *Time,* Feb. 17, 1992: 60.

are still rising toward the stratosphere. The atomic mathematics of CFCs is also disturbing: A single atom of chlorine can destroy up to 100,000 molecules of ozone. Brown, Flavin, and Postel (1991:17) point out that even "if CFC production were stopped immediately, ozone depletion would continue for two to three decades, and it would probably take decades for the upper atmosphere to recover."

If the expected loss of the ozone layer continues, ultraviolet light will do much more than increase the incidence of skin cancer. At a recent Environmental Protection Agency (EPA) conference, studies were presented showing the effects on marine life. It seems likely that blue-green algae that are somewhat resistant to ultraviolet light would increase, while there would be a decrease in the plankton that constitute the first link on the chain of aquatic life. The yield of the ocean might be sharply reduced.

Furthermore, increased ultraviolet light is believed to interfere with the process of photosynthesis, the process that converts solar energy to plant life and oxygen. There is some evidence from Australia that supports this theory. Scientists there attribute increases in ultraviolet light to damage in crops of wheat, sorghum, and peas, and also report a threefold increase in the incidence of skin cancer (Lemonick, 1992). These problems may worsen considerably in the future, because the ozone hole over the South Pole is widening. A study by the National Oceanic and Atmospheric Administration showed that, from late August to early October in 1993, the Antarctic atmosphere contained only 90 Dobson units (an internationally used measurement) of ozone, a record low. The previous record was 105 Dobson units, detected the previous year (Monastersky, 1993).

As the ozone problem accelerated, so did attempts to solve the problem. In 1986 the Montreal Protocol recommended that industrialized nations phase out the production of CFCs. In 1990 the Montreal Protocol was broadened to include industrial solvents not covered by the earlier agreement. Then, in November of 1992, representatives of more than half of the world's countries convened in Copenhagen, Denmark. They agreed to four provisions drawn up by Denmark's environment minister: (1) CFC production will be phased out by January 1996; (2) Halons, used in fire extinguishers, will no longer be used at all; (3) Methyl chloroform, used by dry-cleaning businesses, will not be produced after 1996; (4) hydrochlorofluorocarbons (HCFCs), a less damaging substitute for CFCs, will be gradually phased out by 2030 ("Ozone-Protection Treaty Strengthened," 1992). Figure 11.9 shows CFC offenders and their substitutes.

JAPAN'S 100-YEAR PLAN

A number of countries have signed various treaties to help preserve the earth's ecosystem. For example, representatives from 178 countries attended the Earth Summit in Rio de Janeiro in June 1992 and produced two important docu-

ments: a biodiversity treaty and a global warming treaty. The Biodiversity Treaty requires countries that signed the agreement to protect endangered species, invent their own plants and wildlife, and share research and technology with other nations. The United States, then under the Bush administration, was the only country that did not sign. However, President Clinton signed the treaty soon after he took office in 1993. The Global Warming Treaty recommends, but does not require, the signatories to cap their production of greenhouse gases like carbon dioxide and methane at 1990 levels. One hundred forty-three countries signed the agreement (Wright, 1993: 587), but the most comprehensive plan to save the planet was developed in Japan and is called **New Earth 21**.

New Earth 21

"New Earth 21" is a set of proposals developed by Japan's Ministry of International Trade and Industry (MITI) that is designed to renew the planet's ecosystem during the twenty-first century (see Figure 11.10). The proposals, analyzed by Yasuhiko Ishida (1993) of the Global Industrial and Social Progress Research Institute (GISPRI) in Tokyo, are divided into five ten-year tasks. Improving and implementing energy efficiency is the first priority. For example, GISPRI claims that governments should subsidize iron and steel industries while they invest in research to conserve energy. Once the new technology has repaid the investment capital, the subsidies would cease.

The goal of the second decade would be to develop clean energy production capabilities, which is of great concern to Japan, which lacks oil and coal. The search for energy includes photovoltaics, which utilize solar power, and wind energy, generated by miles of high-technology windmills. Geothermal energy will also be used, as it is now to some extent. Also GISPRI recommends safer nuclear reactors—a goal to which many object on the grounds that no nuclear reactors are entirely safe, and we still

Figure 11.9
The processes that produce foam packing material and cleansing agents account for nearly half the chlorofluorocarbons that destroy the ozone layer, which protects the earth from solar radiation. Another 20 percent comes from vehicle air conditioning. Most of the rest is from refrigeration and aerosol sprays. This illustration shows the pros and cons of some possible substitutes for chlorofluorocarbons.

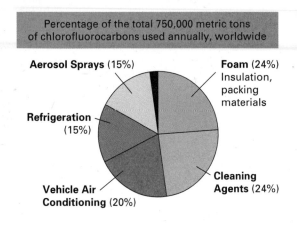

Percentage of the total 750,000 metric tons of chlorofluorocarbons used annually, worldwide

Aerosol Sprays (15%)
Foam (24%) Insulation, packing materials
Refrigeration (15%)
Cleaning Agents (24%)
Vehicle Air Conditioning (20%)

CFC Offenders and Substitutes

Key to Substitutes		
	Pros	**Cons**
HCFCs (hydro-chlorofluoro-carbons)	Break down more quickly in the atmosphere, posing less danger to the ozone layer.	If overused, could damage ozone. Retooled appliances may use more energy than original models.
HFCs (hydrofluoro-carbons)	Do not contain chlorine, thus are "ozone safe."	Safety questions such as flammability and toxicity still unsolved.
Hydrocarbons (such as butane, propane)	Cheap and readily available.	Can be flammable and poisonous. Some increase ground-level pollution.
Ammonia	A simple alternative for refrigerators.	Must be handled carefully.
Water and steam	Effective for some cleaning applications.	

Source: P. Elmer-Dewitt, "How Do You Patch a Hole in the Sky That Could Be as Big as Alaska?" *Time*, Feb. 17, 1992: 67.

don't know how to dispose of spent fuel. GISPRI recommends **breeder reactors,** which are nuclear reactors that generate atomic energy and create additional fuel by producing more fossil material than they consume. They are also thought to be safer than other reactors.

During the third decade, scientists will work on producing non–greenhouse-gas substitutes for chlorofluorocarbons, carbon-dioxide reutilization processes, and low-energy production technologies. The fourth decade will witness the benefits of **reforestation** and the **afforestation** (planting trees where they did not previously exist) of the deserts, projects that will have been started during the first decade. The major benefit, of course, will be carbon-dioxide absorption.

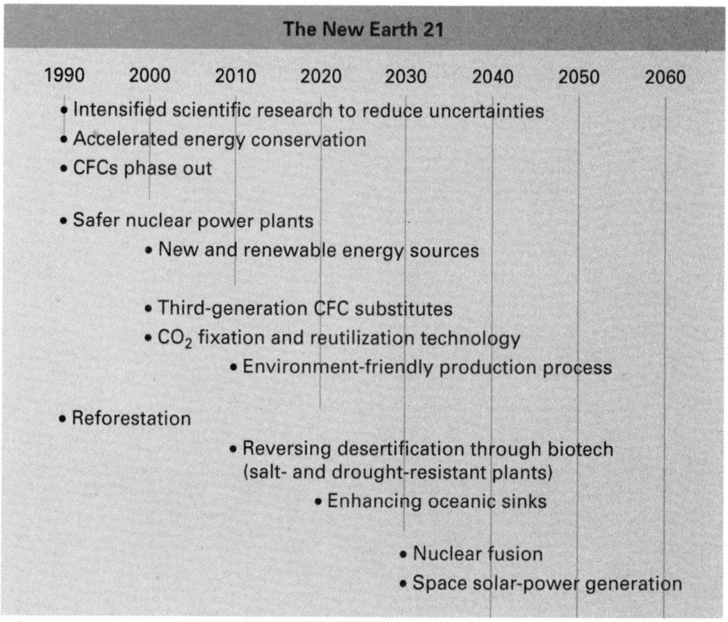

The New Earth 21

1990	2000	2010	2020	2030	2040	2050	2060

• Intensified scientific research to reduce uncertainties
• Accelerated energy conservation
• CFCs phase out

• Safer nuclear power plants
    • New and renewable energy sources

    • Third-generation CFC substitutes
    • CO$_2$ fixation and reutilization technology
        • Environment-friendly production process

• Reforestation
        • Reversing desertification through biotech
        (salt- and drought-resistant plants)
            • Enhancing oceanic sinks

                • Nuclear fusion
                • Space solar-power generation

Source: Y. Ishida, "Regreening the Earth: Japan's 100-Year Plan," *The Futurist*, July–Aug., 1993: 21.

Figure 11.10
Japan's Ministry of International Trade and Industry (MITI) has developed a 100-year plan to save the Earth. One key to this action program is to phase out use of chlorofluorocarbons within 20 years. All countries will have to adopt environment-friendly policies and develop new sources of energy.

The oceanic sinks will have been cleaned, and phytoplankton will be absorbing carbon dioxide.

During the fifth decade, scientists will work on a new generation of technologies, like utilizing fusion instead of fission in power plants, a system that is eminently safer and cheaper. More energy will be produced by orbiting solar-power plants, magma electricity that is generated from the earth's center, and superconductors that absorb virtually no energy. According to Ishida (1993:21), all of the programs during the first 50 years "will be implemented in a global partnership with all countries, including developed and developing countries alike." The last 50 years will be used to integrate the programs of the first 50 years and complete the work of regreening the world.

We will need to restructure our social systems also according to GISPRI. We will have to halt the overpopulation of urban centers, which will have to become more self-sustaining. Cities will have to be planned with more green areas to prevent the "heat-island" phenomenon that occurs when heat is trapped and reflected by environments that are mostly cement. Housing areas and work areas will need to be redesigned for the safety and comfort of energy savers, people who walk or bicycle to work. Buses and motorcycles must take priority over the automobile.

In the field of business, the "standard of . . . evaluation should be changed from sales, profit, and growth to new standards that indicate a beneficial role in society" (Ishida, 1993:24). Businesses will have to concentrate more on resource efficiency and less on time efficiency. Planned obsolescence will have to give way to products with long life spans that are easy to repair. Public education will have to play a leading role in pointing out that many causes for our current predicament is our adherence to "material affluence, impatience, and lack of consideration for future generations" (Ishida, 1993:24). It is

Focus on Germany

A Packaging Law to Save the Environment

You buy a 51-ounce box of raisin bran at the supermarket, and the clerk puts the box in a bag. When she asks, "Paper of plastic?" you are immediately presented with an environmental moral dilemma. Should you take the paper, knowing that it was made from a tree that has been cut down, or should you take the plastic and add to the world's nonbiodegradable garbage? In either case, when you get home, you throw away the bag and then open the box to find two smaller (25.5-ounce) boxes inside. Eventually, you'll throw away all three boxes and the two sealed wax paper bags inside the smaller boxes. That's a lot of garbage!

John E. Young (1991:40) points out that as "the dirty and expensive legacies of careless dumping have come to light, the most visible symptom of profligate materials consumption—the 'garbage crisis'—has generated political heat in communities around the world." Although not much heat has been generated in the United States, several West European nations, including Denmark, France, Sweden, and Switzerland have taken steps to cut back their consumption of raw material. Germany has taken the lead.

In 1991 Germany enacted the Ordinance for the Avoidance of Packaging Waste, which requires manufacturers to bear the responsibility for their packaging materials. According to Megan Ryan (1993:30), the "legislation divides packaging into three distinct categories—transport, secondary, and primary—and specifies reuse and recycling requirements for each." Immediately, manufacturers had to retrieve crates, pallets, and containers from retailers.

Secondary packaging—like the outer box for the raisin bran or cellophane wrapping—is discarded directly at the store. This section of the ordinance went into effect in April 1992. Retailers have to pay the recycling costs. So, retailers are putting pressure on manufacturers to discontinue secondary packaging.

Finally, since December 1993, primary packaging—milk cartons, plastic bottles, toothpaste tubes—is supposed to be returned to the stores, where retailers assume the responsibility for recycling. To encourage consumers to follow the law, there are substantial deposits mandated for bottles and cans. And, the law demands that more than 70 percent of beverage bottles, including beer, soft drinks, juice, wine, and milk be refilled (Ryan, 1993:31).

Germany is moving toward standardizing its plastic packaging by limiting manufacturers to just three types of plastic (Ryan, 1993:34). It is felt that by minimizing the types of plastics used, higher quality recycling can be accomplished. Recycling efforts are aided by a national garbage collection system. By contrast, in the United States, private and public garbage companies have concentrated on incinerating garbage. Young (1991:45) points out that state governments spend 39 times more money on incineration than on recycling. He also points out the "waste reduction, reuse, and recycling can reduce landfills by at least as much as incineration would" (Young, 1993:46).

Because Europe has literally run out of land in which to bury garbage, many other nations are looking for solutions for the problems of waste disposal. Like Germany, France has a national system for the collection of packaging materials. Denmark has a very effective bottle return system, and the Netherlands is developing a strategy to develop voluntary agreements among manufacturers to reduce waste (Ryan, 1993:34). Other industrial countries need to follow these examples because land is a finite commodity, even in geographically large countries like Canada and the United States.

Sources: M. Ryan. 1993. "Packaging a Revolution." *World Watch*, Sept.–Oct.: 28–34; J. E. Young. 1991. "Reducing Waste, Saving Materials." (In L. Stark, Ed.) *State of the World 1991* (New York: W. W. Norton), 39–55.

the opinion of GISPRI that the regreening of our planet will be impossible without everyone's help.

SUMMARY

By the end of World War II, the combined theories and work by an international community of scientists produced atomic power and the world entered the Nuclear Age. Testing of nuclear weapons by the United States and the Soviet Union caused many problems with nuclear fallout. After the nuclear arsenal reached its peak in 1988, some governments started to dismantle their weapons.

But, even the peaceful use of nuclear power has been problematic. The meltdown at Chernobyl spread nuclear fallout over much of the world. Disposing of nuclear waste has been hazardous to cities among the MDCs and villages among the LDCs. Both the former Soviet Union and the United States have kept atomic testing and nuclear accidents secret from the public. Because of the dangers associated with nuclear operations, scientists are looking for alternative sources of energy, like geothermal, solar, and photovoltaic power.

Pesticides, chemical wastes, and other poisons are exported from rich countries to poor ones, where they are often used or disposed of in harmful ways. Gases released from a Union Carbide plant in Bhopal, India, killed thousands and injured hundreds of thousands of people. Many potential "Bhopals" exist, especially in LDCs.

Today, the world is witnessing the greatest threat to biodiversity since the extinction of the dinosaurs. By moving toward monocultures, we risk losing many species. The most dramatic extinction of species is occurring in Africa. Elephants, rhinoceroses, and other animals are illegally killed by poachers. In Asia, tigers, too, are disappearing.

All over the world, forests are being cut down to provide lumber or to clear land for other uses. Poor countries often have to sell their forests to logging companies, which endangers birds and soil. Cultural diversity, like biodiversity, depends on the maintenance of forests. Deforestation leads directly to soil erosion. The soil also suffers from salinization, overgrazing, and desertification.

A greenhouse effect results from the release of various gases into the atmosphere. While oxygen-producing trees are declining, the production of carbon dioxide is increasing. Methane and chlorofluorocarbons (CFCs) contribute to the warming of the atmosphere. The CFCs have caused a hole in the ozone layer that protects the earth from excessive solar radiation.

Although several treaties have been signed by many countries to protect the earth, Japan's Ministry of International Trade and Industry believes that a single, comprehensive plan is needed. It will take a concerted effort over the next 100 years to prevent global destruction.

KEY TERMS

Afforestation The process of planting trees where they did not previously exist.

Amazonia The gigantic tropical forest of Brazil, in South America.

Benevolent atom Nuclear power used for nonmilitary purposes, like generating electric power.

Bhopal City in India where one of the worst industrial accidents occurred in 1984; gases escaping from the Union Carbide plant killed thousands and injured hundreds of thousands of people.

Biodiversity A variety of species, and a variety within a species.

Breeder reactor Nuclear reactors that generate atomic energy and produce more fossil material than they consume.

Carbon dioxide The gas that forms when oxygen is burned; it is increasing in the atmosphere.

Chernobyl Site of the most devastating nuclear accident located near the city of Kiev in the former Soviet Union

Chlorofluorocarbons Chemical propellants, used in aerosol sprays, that have caused a hole in the ozone layer.

CITES (Convention on International Trade in Endangered Species) United Nations agreement that seeks to protect species among the 120 member nations.

Clear cutting A pattern of cutting down forests that leaves the earth denuded.

Deforestation The destruction of forests.

Desertification The process by which arable land turns into deserts.

Deterrence The theory that having a large nuclear arsenal would protect a country from attack because other countries would fear nuclear devastation.

Ecological interdependence An environmental system in which one species cannot exist without one or more other species.

Edge effect Trees on the edge of a forest are more easily damaged than trees within the forest.

Greenhouse effect The result of releasing various gases into the atmosphere, that is warming of the world's temperature.

Manhattan Project The top-secret project, involving some of the greatest scientists in the world during World War II, to develop an atomic bomb.

Methane Gas produced from decaying vegetation; it is increasing in the atmosphere and adds to the greenhouse effect.

Monoculture Lack of biodiversity; dangerous because a single disease can destroy an entire species.

New Earth 21 Set of proposals, developed by Japan's Ministry of International Trade and Industry, that is intended to renew the earth's ecosystem.

Overgrazing A condition that results from too many animals and too many kinds of animals grazing on rangeland, destroying grasses and their root systems.

Ozone layer A band of molecules, made of three oxygen atoms, that surrounds the atmosphere and screens out ultraviolet rays from the sun.

Reforestation The process of replacing trees that have been destroyed.

Salinization The process by which salt is left in the soil after stored water evaporates.

Soil bank Land set aside and not used for agricultural production.

Soil destruction Soil that is ruined by salinization, overgrazing, and desertification.

Soil erosion Without the protection of plants, trees, and their root systems, top soil is washed by rain into the seas.

Strategic Arms Reduction Treaties (START) Two agreements, signed in 1992 and 1993 by the United States and Russia, to reduce the number of nuclear warheads in each country's possession.

STUDY QUESTIONS

1. What was the Manhattan Project? What was its product?

2. Explain how the "nuclear race" resulted in an oversupply of nuclear weapons.

3. Discuss the drawbacks to the "benevolent" atom. What were the consequences of the Chernobyl disaster?

4. List and discuss alternatives to nuclear power.

5. Why are toxic chemicals so much more dangerous in LDCs than in MDCs?

6. Describe the accident in Bhopal, India, and discuss its consequences.

7. What is biodiversity? Why are monocultures dangerous?

8. What is photosynthesis? Why are forests referred to as the "lungs of the earth?" How is *cultural* diversity threatened by deforestation?

9. What factors lead to soil destruction? In your answer, be sure to discuss salinization, overgrazing, and desertification.

10. What combination of forces is producing a greenhouse effect?

chapter 12

GLOBAL CORRUPTION, CRIME, AND THE DRUG TRADE

Ngima Dorji Sherpa is a member of a small ethnic group in Nepal that has great appeal to the outside world. The Sherpas have for many years been the providers of help for people lost in the Himalayas, and even more for mountaineers wanting to climb Mount Everest or other Himalayan peaks. Ngima, like most of his people, combines hardihood with good humor and is well liked.

In recent years, though, he has suffered bad times. There has been a great reduction in tourists and mountain climbers. Even worse, well-financed expeditions now go by helicopters to their high camps and have little use for Ngima's yaks. So when he was approached by some very nice friendly foreigners who offered him $16,000 for carrying a suitcase to Los Angeles, he couldn't resist. He is the sole support for his three younger brothers, one of whom is deaf and mute (Adam, 1994).

Ngima and four other Sherpas were flown to Bangkok, a drug-trafficking center, where each received a suitcase with a hidden compartment. Next they went on a great adventure, flying to Los Angeles. Because they had never committed a crime, they were not good at deception. Their nervous actions gave them away, and all were arrested by customs officials. But their plight has caused even the arresting officers to feel sorry for

them and to wish they could draw reduced sentences. That is impossible,
though, because the smuggling of drugs carries a ten-year minimum sentence.
Each of their suitcases contained about five pounds of heroin.

Ngima's story is a tiny incident in the world's enormous drug scene, but it illustrates several points about corruption. Just as the farthest reaches of the world are linked by travel and trade, so are they linked in the supplying of illegal drugs. No place is too remote for the underworld to reach if the profit is sufficient. We can also see from this story that honest people can be corrupted if in dire need, as was true of some of the refugees cited in Chapter 6. The account also shows that laws do not always accomplish their aim. The "nice, friendly people" who approached Ngima are the ones the laws are aimed at, but Ngima will serve ten years in prison under the terms of a minimum-sentence act. In the drug trade, as well as in financial schemes to be described next, those at the top of the pyramid are relatively immune from long prison sentences.

CRIME IN HIGH PLACES

Corruption is wide-spread and often crosses national lines. Although illegal drugs have much to do with global corruption, they are not the sole cause. We have just looked at a very minor case of corruption. Next we wish to look at a very large case of an extremely different kind, one involving what seemed to be respectable people. Respectable people run financial centers and governments, and yet they often rob the public. Later we will turn our attention to such underground organizations as the Mafia, to smugglers of people, weapons and drugs, and to the whole drug underworld. At present, let us look at stock market manipulation.

Financial Corruption: Wall Street

Bank robberies are dramatic and catch the news headlines, but many other crimes are less publicized and more profitable. Harper's Index estimates that $50,000,000 were stolen from federally insured U.S. banks in traditional bank robberies in 1989. In contrast, $1,000,000,000, or twenty times as much, was acquired through **fraud** and **embezzlement.** Financial manipulations in banks and on Wall Street are secret and hard to understand, but they involve enormous amounts of money. Through illegal use of secret information, "white-collar" criminals can tell which stocks will go up, buy those stocks, and make enormous profits. Such manipulation is illegal, but was widespread during the 1980s due to deregulation and a general "anything goes" attitude. The public was amazed to learn that Ivan Boesky and Dennis Levine had made $100 to $200 million dollars each through illegal stock manipulations. Then it was learned that Michael Milken had netted $550,000,000 in a single year (Stewart, 1991). All three were indicted, along with several others, and sentenced to terms in federal prison. Boesky had to pay more than $100,000,000 and Milken well over $1 billion in this, the biggest scandal ever to have rocked Wall Street. Milken was the biggest inside trader of all, and was involved in other financial scandals as well. He was tried and convicted on six felony counts. Nevertheless, he served only two years (Stewart, 1993). Contrast this with the ten years Ngima will serve.

Some people say this type of crime doesn't hurt anyone. Actually, though, it hurts all investors who have to compete with those who hold secret information. It hurts stock advisors

Insider trading on the stock exchange consists of gaining secret information about an approaching merger of corporations or other changes that might cause a particular stock to boom. Although illegal, insider trading became common before the practice was exposed in 1987–1988 in the biggest scandal ever to hit Wall Street.

whose reputations are damaged by an inability to keep up with the **inside traders.** Finally, it is the type of scandal that undermines confidence in the business system, which leads to cynicism.

At about the same time as the Wall Street scandal, the Department of Housing and Urban Development (HUD) was found guilty of favoring friends with loans and of serious mismanagement. By the 1990s it became clear that so much money had been misspent that the public would eventually have to pay for an $11.9 billion bailout of HUD (DeParle and Engleberg, 1993).

Not to be outdone in fraudulence, polluters with chemical wastes to dispose of were dumping such wastes, then escaping from the pools of poison left behind so that the government could not find them. They owed an estimated $270,000,000 for cleanup, but could not be found. Fears are that losses to the government, and subsequently to taxpayers, will run into the billions of dollars (Beamish, 1993).

All the above instances of stock market manipulation, favoritism with public funds, and escaping pollution cleanup are examples of white-collar crime. **White-collar crime** is crime committed by seemingly reputable people in the course of their business. It involves stockbrokers, oil companies, public officials, and any one else in a position to deal fraudulently with large sums of money. White-collar crime is not limited to one country, and often involves international corporations.

World Nature of Financial Scandals

Many cases of corruption have crossed national borders and become worldwide problems. Such is the case with the Bank of Credit and Commerce International (BCCI). The bank was laundering money from illegal sales of drugs and armaments on such a scale that it has been called the "Bank of Crooks and Criminals International." The BCCI, founded by Pakistanis as a third-world bank, has operated in 70 countries and bribed officials in at least 11, including the United States. When BCCI went through bankruptcy, 250,000 depositors lost their money and are now hoping for payment of a least a portion of it. Investigations are continuing and will probably take several years. Operators of the BCCI type are good at covering their tracks, just as they are good at laundering money. (**Laundering money** is the practice of hiding the source of illegally obtained money by depositing it in foreign banks or under false names, or both.)

Japanese Political Scandal

Scandal after scandal has rocked the leadership of the Liberal Democratic Party—actually a conservative party that has been dominant in Japan for more than 40 years. The greatest notoriety has gone to Shin Kanemaru, thought of as a "kingmaker" for the powerful Liberal Democratic Party. Although he does not hold office, he is what Americans would call a political boss. No member of his party has ascended to the premiership without his blessing. Yet Kanemaru is accused of accepting $4 million in questionable contributions from a mob-related businessman (Reid, 1992). But he is by no means alone in corruption. A Japanese correspondent, Yoichi Serakawa (1993) writes:

> Kanemaru has been roundly and fashionably maligned by party members disgruntled at his failure to help them line their own pockets while he creatively salted away a mini-Fort Knox for himself. (p. 18)

Serakawa goes on to explain that, although law forbids giving more than $12,000 to a politician, large sums are donated to parties, and appear to end up in politicians' pockets. Financial reports released in June 1993 indicate that many members of the Japanese Parliament have grown rich in office (Reid, 1993). Like American politicians, Japanese politicians speak loudly in favor of reform bills, but do not pass them. This has weakened Japanese trust in their government; 70 percent say the government no longer serves their interests (Associated Press, 1993). An important result has been a loss of power by the Liberal Democratic Party as of 1994.

European Corruption

Corruption also exists in much of Europe. In France, friends of former President Mitterrand are accused of having gained insider information from the president's office. Using their secret information, they made stock-market profits of $70 million in less than a week (Herrera and Duran, 1993). In Spain, officials are accused of accepting millions of pesetas from a German company that was bidding for work on building a high-speed train system. In Italy, large numbers of officials are facing arrest. In several countries, including all those formerly controlled by the Soviet Union, the sale of state-owned enterprises opens opportunities for profits by state officials.

CAUSES OF GLOBAL CORRUPTION

The cause of global corruption that comes to mind most readily is that business is increasingly conducted on a global scale. However, the scale of business activities would have no bearing on crime if a strong code of ethics were internalized by all people engaged in trade. We must turn to the question of why such codes of ethics are, in many cases, not honored.

Problems of Social Control

Emile Durkheim, a very insightful early sociologist (1858–1917), was interested in the problem of **social control,** that is, how a society gets its people to live up to its rules. He described two very different types of society—old, traditional society and modern society. In traditional society, he concluded, the problem of social control was relatively simple.

People in older societies were much more alike than they are now. They were held together by what Durkheim called **mechanical solidarity,** meaning they were almost as alike as mechanical products. Nearly all men farmed and nearly all women were mothers and housewives. Such a society obviously minimized freedom of choice. People were taught the rightness of things as they were and believed firmly in their traditional ways. Durkheim spoke of their laws as **retributive,** aimed at avenging society for any wrongs done. Such societies were severe, but not crime ridden.

According to Durkheim (1964), more modern societies are characterized as held together by **organic solidarity,** meaning all parts are interdependent. Thousands of different jobs are done, all necessary, and each contributes to the whole. However, people are no longer so alike as they were, nor do they believe so strongly in old customs and norms. Laws tend to be less severe. In fact, new laws are apt to be **restitutive** rather than retributive; that is, far more laws have to do with regulations of trade and industry or with compensation for injury—the types of laws enforced in civil court rather than criminal court. In Durkheim's view modern society would be preferable to traditional societies, but there would be a painful period of transition from one to the other, as people struggled to cope with much greater social complexity (Collins and Makowsky, 1972).

Societal Complexity and Crime

Although Durkheim's description of societal change is nearly 100 years old, it still rings true for a description of the change from rigid, traditional society to freer modern society. Societal complexity has grown since Durkheim's time, though, and new problems are involved in social control. As Durkheim expected, society has become increasingly vast and impersonal. The small villages in which people all knew one another and were bound to each other and to the norms are virtually gone. Crime, especially theft and fraud, are more common than in the past. Besides the problem of anonymity, there are far more goods to covet. In societies of much greater wealth than in the past, possessions seem to have

more social and psychological importance, making temptations greater.

Financial Crime: Larceny and Fraud

An analysis by Louise Shelley (1981) supports the conclusion that grand larceny and fraud are more common in urban-industrial societies than elsewhere. **Grand larceny** is theft on a large scale, with the amount differing from country to country. **Fraud** is deceit and trickery used to get someone else's property or money. Using statistics from **Interpol,** Shelley finds that for grand larceny, eight of the top ten nations fit the modern, urban image. The top ten nations for grand larceny were the following:

Country	Grand Larceny (per 100,000 people)
Italy	2,355
Bahamas	2,267
New Zealand	1,173
United States	1,744
Denmark	1,723
West Germany	1,611
Guyana	1,555
Scotland	1,486
Sweden	1,214
England and Wales	1,001

Shelley also gives rates for fraud, which show the same pattern of an increase in crimes against property in modern, urban countries.

Country	Frauds (per 100,000 people)
Sweden	705
France	625
Monaco	612
Denmark	454
West Germany	411
New Zealand	295
Finland	292
Australia	223
Bahamas	220
England and Wales	202

In this case, the only non–urban-industrialized countries (Monaco and Bahamas) are both playgrounds for the rich. More recent figures on crime tell the same story. With the exception of Bermuda and the wealthy United Arab Emirates, the top ten countries for theft are all modern, industrialized, and urbanized (Kurian, 1991: 209).

Interpol does not have statistics for all countries. The Soviet Union and its allies did not report at the time of Shelley's statistics. Nevertheless, many countries, both industrialized and less developed, did provide reports. The pattern is very suggestive of Shelley's conclusion: Crimes against property increase as countries modernize and urbanize. A report to the Secretary General of the United Nations in 1977 showed that crimes against property in less developed countries were rising at the rate of 2.5 percent per year, and the fastest increases were in places of rapid urbanization. A historical study of France and Germany shows the same tendency. Rates of theft increased as urbanization and industrialization increased in the early nineteenth century (Zehr, 1976). In the 1990s, reports from rapidly industrializing nations of Southeast Asia show the same trend toward both urbanization and corruption.

For violent crimes, the pattern is much more confusing. In murder rates, the United States has the dubious distinction of ranking much higher than any other urban-industrialized country, but ten of the less developed countries reported even higher rates to Interpol. Lesotho, the Bahamas, Guyana, Lebanon, the Netherlands Antilles, and Iraq head the list. The same holds true for Kurian's figures for 1991 (p. 207).

Opportunities and Crime

Along with a weakening of adherence to the norms goes greater opportunity to make money by devious means. We previously mentioned manipulations on Wall Street. In government, donations to campaign funds often amount to bribes. Companies that make large donations to political campaigns are often awarded lucrative government contracts. Smugglers find new routes by land, sea, and air for smuggling drugs,

weapons, people, or contaminated goods. The opportunities for such criminality increase as societies become more vast, complex, and involved in more problems than they seem able to manage.

THE COLD WAR, CRIME, AND POLICIES

Sociologists have studied the effects of war on rates of violent crime (they generally go up in the first few years after a war according to Archer and Gartner, 1982). But the Cold War was quite different. We do not know whether keeping a large military in a state of readiness for war has the same effect on crime as does actual war. We do know, though, that the Cold War had profound effects on governmental policies, which were very important in the drug problem.

Southeast Asia

For the United States and its allies, the Cold War caused a heavy preoccupation with preventing other countries from lining up with the Communist side. This accounts for the U.S. costly intervention in Vietnam, the U.S. support for the *Contras* in Nicaragua, various Afghan rebels against the Soviet-favored government, and many other interventions. Some of the interventions were on behalf of people who trafficked in drugs. The government had to decide whether its first concern was to stop the drug traffic or to stop communism.

In the 1950s, the United States helped the anti-Communist forces of southern China by sending military supplies, and it ignored their growing opium poppies to help raise money. The opium supply to the United States, which had been dwindling, began to increase (Kwitney, 1987). Later, the United States took over from France the task of trying to prevent a Communist victory in Vietnam. The United States again became involved with opium, both

Focus on Interpol

Attacking International Crime

The *International Criminal Police Organization,* (*Interpol*), the source of crime statistics from a large number of countries, is an organization that helps all member nations track down international criminals.

For many years, international crime has been a growing problem. It has become increasingly easy for criminals to flee the scene of their crimes, cross national boundaries, forge visas and other identity papers, change names, and pursue their criminal careers elsewhere. Interpol was founded at a small meeting in Vienna in 1923; since then it has grown from 20 members to more than 150, virtually all over the world.

The main work of Interpol is to act as a clearinghouse for information on criminals and crime. Contrary to common belief there is no "Man (or Woman) from Interpol" moving from country to country detecting criminals. Rather, Interpol collects criminal files the world over and passes information to countries seeking help to catch criminals who have fled their borders.

Interpol files list nearly three million names (counting aliases) and contain thousands of fingerprint cards and photos. Files are so well managed that experts can track down the right cards and descriptions in a few minutes. The descriptions are thorough, including race, height, weight, complexion, pigmentation, teeth, voice, gait, habits, vices, scars, moles, tattoos, deformities, nervous tics, aliases, and so on (Fooner, 1985).

A New York case illustrates how Interpol operates. Inspector Vitrano was keeping check on a hangout owned by Vince Rizzo, where many known mobsters met. One day, a dapper Englishman unknown to any New York authorities arrived. Seemingly very proper, the gentleman went by the name of Tony Grant. Vitrano called Interpol in St. Cloud, France. Soon the report came back: Tony Grant was an alias for Hyman Kiebanov, wanted in several European countries and in Argentina for jewel theft, fraud, and swindling. Interpol alerted authorities in Argentina, who told them that "Tony Grant" was suspected of cocaine operations in Chile. Chilean authorities in turn reported that "Tony Grant" was involved in a huge cocaine ring, smuggling cocaine into the United States. Just at that time, Rizzo disappeared, and was located in Germany. There, Interpol learned that both men were involved in a gigantic fraud, selling counterfeit American stocks and bonds in Switzerland, Italy, and Germany. Several confederates were also identified and arrested (Eds, Readers Digest Assn., 1982).

The crimes of greatest interest to Interpol include counterfeiting, drug trafficking, bank fraud, forgery, money laundering, and terrorism. The latter two crimes have presented special difficulties. Until the late 1980s, banks, especially banks in the Caribbean, had such strict rules of secrecy that they hid the identity of depositors, making it almost impossible to tell where drug money was hidden. In one case, $60 million from illegal drug sales was hidden in the account of a pizza parlor. It was common for small banks in the Caribbean to show assets in the billions of dollars.

Although the United States passed a Money Laundering Control Act in 1986, it applies only to banks within the United States. At about the same time, Interpol held a conference on the matter and was able to get most countries to cooperate better in running down money-laundering operations. Many criminal accounts were exposed (Fooner, 1989: 1–6).

International terrorism is another matter of great concern to Interpol, but Interpol is very cautious about cases of terrorism. Much terrorism is committed for political reasons, and Interpol tries to remain politically neutral. However, in the 1980s, at the urging of the United States and many less developed countries, Interpol took a more vigorous stand on terrorism, passing along information on terrorists to all members' police forces. Although it does not take a political stand against such organizations as the Irish Republican Army or the Moslem Hamas, it helps track down individuals in such organizations who commit acts of violence.

Interpol has expanded through the years, taking on more members and new duties, as in the case of antiterrorism. It has increased and internationalized

(continued)

(continued)

its staff at St. Cloud (just outside Paris). It has opened a separate office at the Hague, Netherlands, dealing entirely with forgeries and counterfeit money. Since Interpol is the best agency yet developed for fighting international crime, it is quite possible it will expand further.

SOURCES: Editors, Readers Digest Association, *Great Cases of Interpol* (Pleasantville, NY: Readers Digest, 1982; M. Fooner, *A Guide to Interpol* (Washington, D.C.: U.S. Dept. of Justice, 1985); M. Fooner, *Interpol: Issues in World Crime and International Justice* (New York: Plenum, 1989).

---

in an attempt to support allies and in inadvertently allowing heroin to reach its troops (Kwitney, 1987:45–50).

The U.S. Central Intelligence Agency (CIA) attempted to raise an army of Hmong, a dissident minority people, and received their military cooperation. Since many of the Hmong made their money by growing opium poppies, they would have been alienated if they could not sell their product. The CIA's Air America built landing strips in Laos. Those landing strips served for bringing in military supplies, but they also served for the export of opium (Freemantle, 1986:237–238).

Afghanistan

One of the biggest producers of opium poppies is the Golden Crescent, an area embracing territory in northern Pakistan and southern Afghanistan, and including the northeastern part of Iran. When Afghanistan was at war with the Soviet Union, the United States sent money, arms, and medical supplies to help. Afghans and Pakistanis now say that the United States turned a blind eye to the cultivation of opium poppies during the war. Poppies supplemented their meager incomes. Now they are economically dependent on opium, the most profitable crop they can grow, and so are some of the Pakistanis. It is estimated that 20 percent of the opium produced in the Golden Crescent ends up in the United States (Hussain, 1993).

Central America

In Central America, the picture during the Cold War was similar to that in Southeast Asia and Afghanistan. The United States was able to overlook transgressions of the Contras—who were trying to overthrow the left-wing government of Nicaragua. Jonathan Kwitney (1987), a reporter for the *Wall Street Journal,* wrote while the United States was strongly supporting the Contras,

> The Contra army the United States is now supporting to take over Nicaragua has in half a dozen documented cases made mutual benefit pacts with big-time smugglers bringing cocaine and narcotic pills into the United States. In every case, the Justice Department has turned a blind eye to this activity (p. 23).

Leslie Cockburn (1987) of CBS tells a more detailed story of trans-shipments of cocaine from the Medellín Cartel by Contras and their supporters, of shrimp boats engaged in the traffic, and of direct trades of drugs for weapons, apparently sanctioned by the CIA.

The U.S. drug policy at that time seemed self-contradictory. The United States fought drug suppliers on one front, but ignored, or even aided them, on another. With the collapse of the Soviet Union and intense fear of leftist regimes in any part of the world, the United States was free to pursue drugs more consistently, but had lost important battles before becoming fully engaged in the "war against drugs."

Profits from the opium-poppy fields of Afghanistan helped buy weapons for Afghan defense against Soviet troops and USSR-supported factions in the 1980s. Poppies remain a major crop for both Afghans and Pakistanis.

Even Manuel Noriega, the cruel and corrupt dictator of Panama, was praised by the Justice Department during the time he cooperated with the United States against Nicaragua, and his drug operations were ignored. It was only when he became too independent of U.S. policies that he was seized and brought to prison in the United States, probably for life (Chomsky, 1992:50–52).

Italy

For most of the period between World War II and the collapse of the Soviet Union, Italy had the biggest Communist Party in Western Europe. The result was a tendency for the majority of people to vote for the strongest of the non-Communist parties to avoid the possibility that the Communists and their allies could gain control. More than any other party, the Christian Democratic Party profited by the situation. For 47 years, the Christian Democrats were able to put together a coalition that prevented serious defeat at the polls. Their long-time leader, Giulio Andreotti, now under indictment for corruption, was elected Prime Minister seven times (Stille, 1993).

By the early 1990s, the Italian public became aware of massive corruption at the highest levels of government. Collusion with Mafia leaders has been rampant. Consequently, Italy is now on an anticrime crusade such as has seldom been seen anywhere. There is no longer any need to stick to the old political parties, so the Christian Democrats have lost control. High office holders have been thrown out, and many corrupt officials have been sent to jail. Mafia figures are finally being given long sentences; in the past, their sentences were just long enough to satisfy public demands to curb organized crime (Stille, 1993).

The Middle East

In the Middle East there was a long struggle between the United States and the former Soviet Union. The United States long supported anti-Communist regimes, including that of the Shah of Persia. The Shah was overthrown by Moslem fundamentalists, with both the United States and the Soviet Union losing out. Now support for Middle Eastern regimes has become a matter of trying to prevent further spread of Moslem fundamentalist regimes. To this end the United States heavily subsidizes Egypt, and sends moderate foreign aid to Pakistan. Both countries are accused of heavy corruption, partly because their governments are propped up by foreign aid, making it possible for them to put off needed changes (Murphy, 1993). Drugs from Pakistan continue to enter the international market.

Communist States

Communist philosophy had held that there would be no crime in a Communist state and that the Soviet Union was moving toward the Communist ideal. Nevertheless, there was considerable crime in the Soviet Union. In Shelley's analysis, the Soviet Union followed two separate patterns. The less urbanized parts resembled less developed countries in that violence (often accompanied by heavy alcohol abuse) was fairly common, but that crimes against property were uncommon. Property crimes occurred more commonly in the urbanized parts of the country. Little information about crime came out of the Soviet Union in most years, but in 1976 secret reports were made available. The rate for crimes against property was 1,064—about one-third the rate for the United States at the same time (Shelley, 1981:55). These figures seem plausible, since there was no financial freedom, not too much to steal, and heavy policing.

The crimes that have attracted most attention were political crimes, meaning any opposition to the Communist regime. The assumption prevailing among the Communist leadership was that all reasonable people could see the superiority of the Communist system. Those who could not see it must have something wrong with their minds. Thousands were sent to mental institutions, and many were not released until Gorbachev became prime minister and the Soviet system collapsed at the end of the 1980s. Heavy policing and horrible prisons were in the Russian tradition, but were intensified by a kind of paranoia about espionage and fear of the West.

Since the collapse of the Soviet Union, crimes against property have increased markedly. Some people blame the rise in such crime on Boris Yeltsin's economic reforms that have created a more open economic climate. General Ogorodnikov, head of the Ministry for Maintaining Social Order, sees other reasons (O'Brien, 1993). Free market conditions, he says, make crimes possible, but do not cause them. He points instead to a growing stratification in Russian society, resulting in great wealth for some and increasing poverty for others. The homicide rate has also increased, but remains well behind that of the United States (Russia, 6.1 per 100,000 people; United States, 9.8 per 100,000 people). Thefts rose far more than any other type of crime—about 50 percent between 1990 and 1992 (O'Brien, 1993).

Since 1992, however, new reports out of Russia make the crime situation appear much worse. The U.S. Department of Energy's Office of Threat Assessment studied the Russian Mafia in 1993. They found that crime organizations in Moscow and St. Petersburg force businessmen to pay 15 percent of their earnings in protection. Otherwise their businesses may be vandalized. The Russian Mafia may own as much as 50 percent of the nation's banks. Organized crime uses high-tech equipment that the government does not have. Many police, army officers, and government officials are corrupt (Hersh, 1994:67–68).

The Agency for International Development (AID) has insisted on the privatization of businesses and industries. To accomplish privatization, the government has issued vouchers to the citizens, which they can use to buy stock in corporations. However, it has been found that organized crime has counterfeited millions of such vouchers and used them to buy up the businesses and properties being offered.

Shelley, a specialist in the study of organized crime in Russia, says that organized crime threatens to dominate Russia. "Control will come," she says, "from the alliance of former Communist party officials with the emergent organized crime groups, groups that currently enjoy the preponderance of capital of the post-Soviet states" (quoted in Hersh, 1994:82).

It is feared, too, that organized crime in the former Soviet Union may get possession of plutonium or even of nuclear weapons (a subject discussed in the next chapter).

The People's Republic of China

China still exists as a Communist state in some respects, with many of the signs and slogans of the past. Nevertheless, in the more progressive parts of China, everyone is out to make money. Large numbers of independent enterprises have sprung up, especially in the big cities. The simple, frugal life of the past is replaced with more economic adventure in which some do well and others remain as poverty-stricken as ever. Corruption is on the rise. There are more and more cases of bribery and embezzlement on the part of party officials, according to the Chinese Academy of Social Science (Sun, 1993).

CRIMINAL ORGANIZATION

We have spoken of organized crime in the former Soviet Union and of its power. In many other places, organized crime corrupts governments and engages in such activities as shipping cocaine and heroin, illegal aliens, illegal military equipment, or charging businesses for "protection." Very prominent among criminal organizations is the Mafia. Today, the word **Mafia** is loosely applied to many crime rings, so we speak of a Colombian Mafia, a Russian Mafia, and so forth. However, the term originally applied to the crime rings of Sicily and southern Italy. At one time the Sicilian Mafia was regarded as a counterweight to oppressive government, especially before 1870, when Italy became united and independent.

Mafia Organizing Principles

Although the word *Mafia* is applied too broadly, the organization does, in fact, have its tentacles in many countries. It was originally organized on a familial basis, with many members being born into the organization. Others became members if they had godfathers in the Mafia, a title given to all important members. The Mafia was headed by a *capomafia* (Mafia head) and divided into cells. All members are treated as kinsmen unless they fail in their loyalty to the group, in which case they are likely to be murdered (Cressey, 1969).

The organizing principles of the Mafia sound old-fashioned, but newer strategies have kept the Mafia formidable. It corrupted officials and got some of its own members into political office. It collected protection money and became wealthy enough to bribe officials and to dominate crime organizations in other countries. There were internal fights, but no members dared turn against the organization until recently.

Italy Fights Back

In Sicily during the 1980s, internal fights and bloodletting became more severe than ever before. Salvatore Riina, whom even Mafia members referred to as *la belva* (the beast), had managed to put his own family, the Corleones, in charge of the 140 families in the organization. By 1981 his power was so great that he was able to have his rival bosses murdered.

Internal warfare resulted. As described by Alexander Stille (1993),

> This was no conventional Mafia war; it was a genuine extermination campaign. . . . Hundreds of friends and relatives, women and children (were) hunted down and murdered. And, once the war was won, Riina had many of his chosen assassins eliminated because they had become too powerful. All told, nearly a thousand people were killed (p. 69).

The result of Riina's excessive cruelty and tyranny has been that many former mafiosi have been willing to testify. Italy's laws have been greatly strengthened. Riina is in prison for life, and so are a score of his lieutenants. Italians who once feared to testify are strengthened by new laws giving them protection. Does this mean the Mafia is on its way out? Hardly. Alexander Stille (1993) points out that for years Sicily has been the poverty center of Italy, with the majority of jobs depending on patronage from the government, won by the political power of the Mafia. New sources of income may be necessary before Italy says a final farewell to the Mafia.

Mafia Tentacles

Another important worry about organized crime is that the Mafia has been able to cash in on many sources of wealth outside Italy and the United States. At the end of 1992, shortly before the arrest and conviction of Riina, the lead story in *World Press Revue* was, "Italy's Mafia Spreads Its Tentacles." The writer, Ed Vulliamy, notes that two of the most faithful fighters of the Mafia were killed by car bombs, and that more and more collusion between the legitimate world of government and business and the illegitimate world of the Mafia has been uncovered. At that time, Riina was believed to have subjugated the New York Mafia, the Corleones, to his clan. Meetings of Mafia families have included allies from Colombia and Venezuela. The Mafia families hold the drug markets of the French and Spanish Rivieras, as well as drug bases in Holland and Germany, and are believed to be organizing in Russia (Vulliamy, 1992).

The many steps toward the unification of Europe may have the unintended result of helping the drug trade. There is no longer careful inspection at boundary lines as in the past. The intended easier flow of legal goods has come about, but so has an easier flow of weapons and drugs. Whether a large increase in drug use in Western Europe will result remains to be seen, but at present the trend in drug use is upward. It is possible that the European police (**Europol**) will eventually gain the upper hand over the drug interests, but such an outcome would depend on further European negotiations to strengthen Europol (Flatscher, 1992).

Salvatore ("Toto") Riina, also called *La Belva* or "the beast," was head of the Mafia. His cruelty became so excessive (he had approximately 1,000 people murdered) that Italy rose against the Mafia as never before. People who had dared not speak out became willing to testify. Many Mafia leaders, including Riina, are in prison for life.

Another problem facing narcotics police in Europe is the attempt by refugees to cross borders into safe countries, and by others to make money for political causes.

Political Unrest and Crime

The people who have fled parts of former Yugoslavia or Albania number more than a million. Much larger numbers of refugees have come in from Russia and other East European nations, as well as Africa, the Caribbean, and the Middle East. The vast majority of refugees are honorable people who would not intentionally work for criminal elements; but if they are sufficiently desperate to escape their countries, they might agree to carry a small package with them in return for help in crossing borders and evading police.

Others smuggle drugs in order to get money for weapons to help fight for their causes. Albanians from Kosovo, fearing attack by the Serbs, are anxious for weapons. More than 1,000 Albanians are being held in Switzerland for trafficking arms and/or drugs. Iranians opposed to the present regime are deeply involved in the heroin trade to earn money to buy weapons. Kurdish rebels, trying to gain a homeland of their own, or at least to defend themselves against Iraq, also depend on the drug trade to get funds (Viviano, 1992).

The Russian police found 184 heroin-processing laboratories in Moscow, all run by Azeris (people from Azerbaijan) in order to get the money to buy weapons for their fight against the Armenians in Nagorno-Karabakh. Far to the south and west, people escaping oppressive regimes in Africa look for ways to get smuggled into Europe. Dealers will pay their way if they will swallow rubber sacks of heroin, to be retrieved somewhere on the other side of the Strait of Gibraltar. Many do so, and European police often find the bodies of people who died when sacks of heroin burst in their stomachs. In all such cases, innocent people are the cat's paws for drug dealers (Viviano, 1992).

Smuggling Rings: The "Snakeheads"

While people from Eastern Europe and Africa attempt to buy their way to a better life by importing drugs, thousands of Chinese seek their opportunity in America by paying all they have to gangs of smugglers whom they call **snakeheads**. Chinese trying to fulfill their dream of a new world will agree to pay from $20,000 to $50,000 for being transported overseas and smuggled into the United States. Both on the Pacific Coast and on the Atlantic Coast, ill-equipped, unseaworthy ships have had to be rescued by the United States Coast Guard, but in some cases not before many would-be immigrants died. Many of the smugglers' ships are hell holes, reminiscent of slave ships of long ago. The slave-ship comparison is apt in another way: The illegal immigrants lucky enough to get into the United States probably look forward to a life of debt slavery, working hard to pay off the criminal gang that brought them over. Failure to do so can mean death (Liu, 1993).

The Chinese illegals add to the American crime problem. Indebted as they are to criminal syndicates for having brought them to America, they may be forced into crime to pay their debts. They also create a serious problem for the immigration service. Those who are clever enough to do so file for political asylum status, usually given to those escaping from Communist countries. Those seeking asylum cannot be deported quickly, and are often released awaiting hearings, which can take a year or more. During their time of waiting for hearings, they can lose themselves in any of our large cities with sizeable Chinese populations (Liu, 1993).

Organized Street Gangs

From the beginnings of the crack trade in United States cities, illegal drugs have been peddled by youth gangs. There are advantages to having children as young as 10 years old engaged in the traffic. They look innocent. They are apt to be given shorter terms by courts. In all likelihood they will

Chinese refugees pay dearly to be smuggled into the United States. The smugglers are criminals, whom the Chinese call "snakeheads." Ships are wretched and unseaworthy, like this ship stopped by the U.S. Coast Guard at San Diego. Those who cannot pay for the voyage find themselves in debt or slavery and maybe forced into the drug trade.

become addicted themselves, hence another market for crack, amphetamines, or whatever. In time, young gang members show greater disregard for danger and more willingness to use extreme violence than would most mature adults. A few will make large sums of money and drive flashy cars. They will create the legend of what you can do "if you've got guts." The majority, though, will live miserable lives, addicted themselves, sometimes using up their own supply of drugs. Their death rate is very high (Prothrow-Stith, 1991:111–130).

The street gangs are particularly characteristic of American cities, but similar gangs, usually of adults, are becoming evident in European cities (Viviano, 1992). Such local gangs, of course, are at the bottom of the crime ladder, getting their supplies from more important dealers tied to the Mafia, the Medellín Cartel of Colombia, or other powerful crime organizations.

Bloods and Crips

The best known street gangs are the **Bloods** and the **Crips,** of Los Angeles origin. Each gang is a conglomerate of many smaller gangs, altogether

numbering into the thousands. There was an uneasy truce between them in the early 1990s. Their fights were once over turf, as with traditional city gangs, but eventually their "turfs" became markets for drugs. There have been large numbers of drive-by shootings over markets, for revenge, or for no particular reason. From Los Angeles, the Bloods and Crips have moved on to other cities—Phoenix, Denver, Las Vegas, San Francisco, San Diego, Portland. Eastern cities, especially Miami, New York, Chicago, and Washington, D.C., have similar gangs. In some cases, the gangs have been able to reach accommodations with the police. A Los Angeles police officer says, "It's no secret. There are a lot of cops on the gang payroll. We've fired lots of them for tipping dealers off before a raid" (Hackett and Lerner, 1987).

Smaller Cities and Gangs

Youthful drug gangs are found not only in big cities, but in smaller cities as well. A report on Wichita, Kansas, tells how the gangs operate to increase their markets. In December of 1989 Officer Brad Carey spotted a young man selling crack in one of the poor tenement districts. The young man identified himself as a member of the Crips and boasted that a flood of other Crips would follow him. The officer thought it was all bluster, but was greatly mistaken.

The Crips have made Wichita a crime center; drive-by shootings have become commonplace; in 1993 there were 14 gang-related homicides. Their first gang murder came on Easter of 1990 when one gang member gunned down a rival. A few months later, a young woman was kidnapped by four youths, raped, and stomped to death, in what turned out to be a revenge killing by members of a gang calling itself the "Insane Crips." Several hundred gang members were arrested in the period 1990–1993 but gang membership has grown to 1,250. Originally an exclusively male, African American gang, the Crips now include women, Caucasians, Hispanics, and Asians.

Such is the story of a small, Midwestern city once noted for being quiet and relatively free of crime. Killings have become inevitable because Wichita's gang members will not allow anyone to leave. Renaldo Cruz, age 15, tried to leave his gang. He was taken to a park, forced to his knees, and shot through the head (Gary Lee, 1993).

We have discussed the street gangs of American cities. Behind them, of course, are distributors with more power and wealth in the underworld. They receive their illegal drugs from sources that might be thousands of miles removed, but the means are always found to get supplies to the most lucrative markets.

DRUGS: INTERNATIONAL NETWORKS

The drug business is so profitable that powerful organizations form to control distributions, sometimes with the connivance of governments. The **Medellín Cartel** in Colombia is the best known organization, but there are other organizations in Latin America and East Asia, and, as we have seen, the Mafia is deeply involved.

Colombia

Much of the cocaine harvested in Bolivia and Peru is sent to Colombia for processing, and from there it is sent by ever changing routes to the United States and Europe. Medellín, Colombia's

Youth gangs involved in drugs and crimes are found in all major United States cities, even in smaller Midwestern cities like Wichita, Kansas.

second largest city, has been the drug center of Colombia and the murder capital of the world, although the **Cali Cartel** is moving Cali toward first position in drug trafficking. Colombians living in the United States are sometimes forced into working for the drug interests by threats against their relatives still living in Colombia (Montalbano, 1987).

Assassination is common in Colombia and has accounted for the deaths of 50 judges, 24 journalists, and hundreds of police officers. Killers for hire have been known to accept a murder assignment for as little as $10 dollars (Rosenberg, 1988). The United States, especially during the Bush administration, sent hundreds of millions of dollars in aid to Colombia, Bolivia, and Peru to help police the drug traffic and wipe out coca fields with pesticides.

Bolivia

Despite Colombia's enormous trade in cocaine, coca leaves are grown in larger amounts in Bolivia and Peru. Bolivia produces as much as 540,000 tons of coca leaf per year. For years, the production was controlled by Roberto Suarez and his son, whose income was estimated at about $600,000,000 per year (Freemantle, 1986). Such masses of money help explain why the drug traffic is hard to stop. The wealthy drug interests are seen as allies by the peasants, for whom the coca plant is the most profitable crop. The United States tried to persuade them to grow other crops, but those who did so are deeper in poverty than before and are angry at the United States (Farthing, 1992).

Peru

Like Bolivia, Peru is a country of great poverty and a long history of the use of cocaine in mild form. The ancient Incas paid workers partly in coca leaves, and the custom continued under Spanish rule. In more recent years, Peru has become a major exporter, sometimes with

government connivance, sometimes without. A radical revolutionary movement, known as the **Sendera Luminosa** (Shining Path) has arisen in Peru. In 1993 Alberto Fujimori became president of Peru, promising to make economic improvements. Instead, war intensified with the revolutionaries, each side accusing the other of being involved with drugs (Guillermoprieto, 1993).

Central America

We have mentioned Central America relative to Cold War policies. We need only add that Central America is reportedly growing as a place for transporting drugs northward. The drug interests are well armed with weapons left over from the civil war in Nicaragua between the United States–backed *Contras* and the Sandinistas, accused by the United States of being pro-Communist (Farah, 1993). For the most part, Central American governments lack the resources to stop the drug traffic, and some of them lack the will.

Mexico

It should surprise no one that the major drug cartels would look upon Mexico as a good place from which to transport their drugs into the United States. As a general rule, the president of Mexico cooperates with the United States; but a major drug cartel centered in Cali, Colombia, operates in Mexico. Most of the time the Mexican drug interests have been less violent than those in Colombia. However, with increasing organization and with directions from Colombia, Mexican drug traffickers have become increasingly ruthless, leading to the "Colombianization of Mexico" (Golden, 1993).

Spain

Because people from Colombia, Peru, and Bolivia speak Spanish and share cultural traits with Spain, they have not been looked upon with suspicion when they visit Spain. Often visas are not required. Consequently, an unobserved minority of Latin Americans now live in Madrid and Barcelona. Cocaine reaches these cities disguised as tourists' luggage. From there it is eventually trucked northward to France, Netherlands, Germany, and other parts of Western Europe. Because trade between the countries of the Economic Community is free and open, drug smuggling becomes easy (Viviano, 1992).

The New Opium War

The United States has sprayed Burmese opium fields with herbicides, sought an agreement with Pakistan to limit opium production to only enough for medical uses, and reached antidrug agreements with Thailand; but the drug problem is like the Hydra of Greek mythology—each time a head is cut off, two more take its place. When it looked as though Pakistan might cut down on opium production, the producers moved to Afghanistan. Now both countries produce more opium than ever before. Burma no longer cooperates with the outside world in attempting to control opium production, but even when it did, growers simply moved north into rebel-held territory (McConahay and Kirk, 1989). Burma is now the world's largest East Asian producer of opium, but the supply is swelled by Thailand, Laos, China's Yunan Province, and Sri Lanka. Considerable amounts of this illegal drug reach Europe through travelers and refugees from West Africa. Much of it is smuggled cross-country from Pakistan, Iran, and Afghanistan into Eastern Europe and from there to Western Europe. There it is rivaled by the cocaine trade from Latin America (Figure 12.1).

Huge profits keep the drug traffic flowing by land, by sea, and by air. Although the United States is by far the largest consumer of illegal drugs, the problem is growing in Europe.

Occasionally there are assurances that we are winning the "war on drugs," but Figure 12.2 is by no means reassuring. Although the United States has vastly increased spending on the drug war, up to $12 billion in 1992, we have not seen the results we would like. We can see from the second graph in Figure 12.2 that drug-related emergencies continue to be high, and that the number of drug users contracting HIV and AIDS continues to rise rapidly year by year.

It is time now to ask what these drugs are like, why they have such power over people, and whether some are more to be dreaded than others.

THE EFFECTS OF DRUGS

The drugs discussed here are the major ones defined as dangerous by government and law-enforcement agencies. To a certain degree, the naming of dangerous drugs is a political matter. Alcohol, which is enjoyed by large numbers of very important people, is not included in the list of dangerous drugs, even though it shortens the lives of many people and often leads to violence. Tobacco also escapes the list, even though it is losing some of the high status it once enjoyed. Tobacco kills far more people than any of the drugs listed, but it takes lives very slowly and is grown and used by respectable people. Cocaine, in contrast, belongs to the underworld; it takes lives rapidly, and often the lives of the young.

Cocaine

Cocaine is the type of drug called an **upper**, meaning a strong stimulant. It increases heart rate, blood pressure, and body temperature. Even in the mild form (chewing coca leaves) in which it was used centuries ago by the Andean Indians, it stimulated, helped overcome fatigue, and suppressed hunger and pain. In its more concentrated forms

Figure 12.1
The drug trade opens routes into Europe via several routes. *Route 1:* Drugs originating in Pakistan are smuggled to Eastern Europe, aided by dissidents trying to earn money for weapons. *Route 2:* Spain has been generous about admitting Latin Americans, but Latin American drug interests have exploited the Spanish connection and given Spain a serious problem with cocaine. *Route 3:* Drugs from the "Golden Triangle" of East Asia are sent to West Africa to be smuggled into Europe. *Route 4:* Sri Lanka smuggles drugs directly to Spain or Germany. *Route 5:* From Afghanistan, drugs are smuggled by Uzbec Tajik, and Azerbaijanis to Moscow, the Baltic States, and eventually to Germany and Holland.

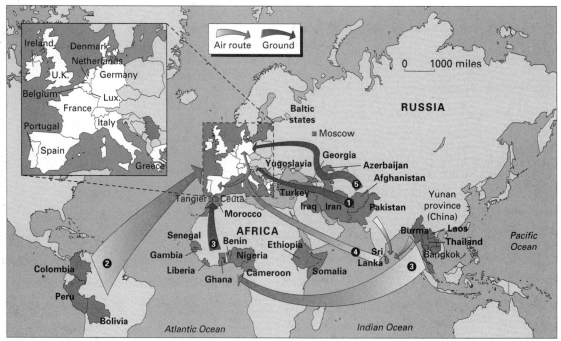

Source: San Francisco Chronicle, Dec. 17, 1992: A8.

(especially crack, which is smoked and therefore goes directly to the brain), it intensifies all these effects. It gives users an intense "high," and can lead to sleeplessness and irritability. It places a great strain on the heart, making it especially dangerous for people with heart trouble. Seizures and death have resulted from heavy use.

In some people, cocaine produces anger after the euphoria wears off. In one case, a newsboy, approaching the house of a subscriber to collect, was suddenly shot through the chest and killed. The killer had been on a cocaine binge and was

diagnosed as having cocaine-induced paranoia. Crimes directly caused by cocaine are few in number, however, compared with the crimes committed to get the money to buy drugs or committed in the course of peddling drugs (Giannini, 1993).

Crack

By the mid 1980s, despite reports of enormous seizures by the government, the supply of cocaine was increasing and the price was so low

Figure 12.2
Measured by drug-related health problems, it cannot be said that any real progress has resulted from the War on Drugs. Expenses continue to rise, but so do drug-related emergencies, which leads some people to look for new drug policies.

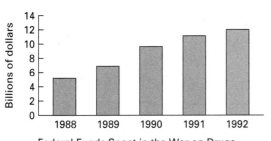

Federal Funds Spent in the War on Drugs

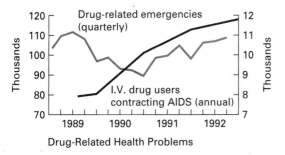

Drug-Related Health Problems

as to cut into its profitability. Then "crack" was invented. **Crack cocaine** is made by mixing powdered cocaine with baking soda and heating it until it's solid. Then it is broken into small pebbles known as rock or crack. It could be sold for as little as $5.00 a hit and still be profitable. Crack is smoked and goes directly to the brain, making its action fast and producing an intense high (Andre, 1987).

As Dr. Prothrow-Stith explains, experimenting with crack is much more dangerous than experimenting with alcohol or marijuana. Although, over time, alcohol and marijuana can be addicting, as well as detrimental to general health, their deleterious effects on the mind and body are not immediate. In contrast, it only takes

a few hits of crack to cause a powerful addiction. The high quickly passes, and users are left with "a destructive craving, gnawing in their bellies" (Prothrow-Stith, 1991:115). Soon all they can earn and all they can steal goes toward buying crack. Their physical decline is more rapid even than with heroin.

Heroin

Heroin and other derivatives of the opium poppy have been a problem for many years. Opium was once used very commonly in medicines, including soothing syrup for babies. It was the most common painkiller for wounded Civil War soldiers; eventually opium addiction became known as "the soldier's disease." Ironically, heroin, a very strong derivative of opium, was originally developed to cure opium addiction.

Heroin is a **downer,** inducing drowsiness and relieving pain. In England it is still used in hospitals to relieve pain, especially severe pain of terminal patients. American authorities have such a dread of heroin that it is never used, even when it might be the best pain reliever.

Despite its medical use, heroin is known primarily as a highly addictive drug, although in England and Holland, where it is medically administered to addicts, its users are able to live a nearly normal life. However, its continued use shortens lives. Heroin users often die, either from overdoses or from getting a bad batch of heroin. Hepatitis and AIDS are very common in heroin users because of shared needles. Addicts often resort to crime in order to support their habits. Prostitution is also a means of obtaining money for heroin. Unlike cocaine or alcohol, heroin does not rouse one to violence.

Speedballing

Injecting heroin and cocaine together, **speedballing,** gives greater euphoria than taking either drug alone (Freedman, 1988). Although the two drugs have opposite effects, one is not an anti-dote for the other. Both suppress the portion of the brain that controls breathing, and both are bad for the heart, making them very dangerous in combination. In 1982 the public was shocked to learn of the death of John Belushi after a fatal injection of the two drugs. Through the 1980s, deaths from speedballing increased fivefold. In 1994 the young actor River Phoenix died in the same manner as John Belushi.

A friend places flowers on the spot where River Phoenix died. Just as he was encountering success as an actor, Phoenix went to celebrate at the Viper Room. He used a combination of cocaine and heroin that, as is often the case, proved lethal.

Marijuana

Although two government commissions in the 1920s and 1930s pronounced marijuana no worse than alcohol, its use was punished severely, especially in the 1950s and 1960s. Many students spent years in jail for smoking "pot"; but it became clear they were not the dangerous crimi-nals described by the Bureau of Narcotics (Geller and Boas, 1971:46–47). Eventually, a number of states defined the use of marijuana as a misde-meanor rather than a crime, but many thousands of people are serving prison sentences for mari-juana offenses and in most states sentencing continues.

An argument continues over the effects of marijuana. It is something of a "downer"; in fact the word *stoned* is used in connection with mari-juana as well as with drunkenness from alcohol. The effects of marijuana are increased heart rate, impairment of short-term memory, lessened concentration and coordination, and an altering of the sense of time. The active ingredient in marijuana, THC, persists in the body and brain for several days, making it dangerous to use for fear of losing a job, if for no other reason. Some people contend that the heavy legal pursuit of marijuana users increased use of other drugs that were not so easy to detect in a urine test (Chomsky, 1992).

Students who are heavy users of marijuana usually find that their academic work suffers, just as with abuse of alcohol. As with alcohol, contin-ued heavy use tends to reduce fertility. All this adds up to strong arguments against heavy and/or long-term-use of marijuana. One hopeful observation regarding marijuana is that even at the height of its use in the 1970s, it tended to be a vice largely abandoned after the age of about 30 (U.S. Bureau of the Census, 1980). Later reports, however, indicate that if marijuana use ever declined, it made a strong comeback by the 1990s. Eric Schlosser (1994), after studying the growing of marijuana in the midwestern part of the United States, concluded that marijuana is among the biggest cash crops of the nation, if not the biggest. Despite all penalties, production and sales continue to rise.

Laws regarding marijuana use and sale are much more severe than most people think. The 1970s trend toward decriminalization came to an end during the Reagan administration. State laws are very severe in most states, but extremely inconsistent. Federal law makes it illegal to buy, sell, grow, or possess any amount of marijuana whatever. Penalties for a first offense range from probation to life imprisonment (for selling), and fines up to $4 million, depending on the quantity involved. Such laws, however, have not stopped marijuana use. In 1992 more than 340,000 people were arrested nationwide for marijuana offenses.

Hallucinogenic Drugs

Hallucinogens are drugs that affect perception, memory, and reason, and often cause the mind to produce illusions called hallucinations. The best known of them is LSD (lysergic acid diethylamide), which has also been described as psychotomimetic, meaning imitative of psychosis. The experiences of users differ widely, ranging from little effect to strange and vivid dreams, and even to terrifying psychological experiences and flashbacks as much as several years later.

During World War II, the U.S. office that eventually became the CIA was interested in some kind of "truth drug" that would cause captured spies to tell all they knew. Following the war, they learned of LSD, developed by a Swiss chemist. Some CIA officials were intrigued by its possibilities and gave it to large numbers of people, including hospital patients and enlisted men, often secretly and without their consent, an extremely unethical practice. The CIA even toyed

with the idea of slipping LSD into the drinks of leftist politicians in foreign counties to make them appear irrational (Lee and Shlain, 1986). Eventually LSD was abandoned by the CIA as dangerous and unpredictable. But by that time it had come to the attention of many people outside of government, and was fairly easy to make. It was used by artists and musicians and referred to in popular songs.

Use of LSD causes derangement of the thought processes. Sometimes the beautiful experiences sought for turn out to be terrifying, "a bad trip." Long-time use can lead to anxiety and depression, a certain amount of personality change, confusion, and impairment of memory. The United States government, whose CIA had become deeply involved with the drug, finally outlawed it. The annual University of Michigan survey of drug use among school students found that only 8.6 percent reported having tried the drug at least once, down from 17.3 percent when the survey was started in 1975. Use was up slightly from the previous year, however, causing some concern that it may be making a comeback (Isikoff, 1993).

Other Abused Drugs

Another dangerous illegal drug that should be mentioned is PCP, also called angel dust. In some people it causes a floating euphoria; however, it can produce violent behavior and a psychosis similar to schizophrenia, lasting for days or even weeks. Many people have died of erratic behavior produced by the drug and of its degenerative effects on the brain.

Although amphetamines are sometimes used under medical supervision to suppress appetite, use has declined because of the possible ill effects. Amphetamines are commonly referred to as "uppers" because they increase physical activity and restlessness. Prolonged heavy use can cause brain damage or produce a psychosis. Even low dosages over a period of time can produce drug dependency, the inability to live without it.

Other types of drugs are produced from time to time, to be sipped, smoked, sniffed, or shot into the veins. All have their dangers; many are deadly. Their use continues despite laws and punishments. Just how much has been accomplished in the struggle against drugs?

DRUG POLICIES AND THEIR RESULTS

Figure 12.3 shows one result of the drug policies: U.S. state and federal prisons have been filled to overflowing, and new ones are being built. State

prisons hold 840,000 prisoners; county jails hold 440,000; there are more than 2.7 million people on probation and 500,000 on parole, one third of whom are drug offenders (Nadelman and Wenner, 1994). Prisons sometimes become so crowded that courts find them in violation of our laws, and therefore order them to release some prisoners early. Ironically, the ones they release may be burglars, rapists, or even murderers, but usually not drug offenders. Federal law has demanded long minimum sentences for drug offenders, not to be shortened under any circumstances. About 50 senior federal judges are so frustrated with the system that they refuse to hear any more drug cases (Beck and Katel, 1993). The public demanded these rigid laws,

Figure 12.3
Although Americans in the 1990s express more dread about violent crime (murder, rape, robbery, aggravated assault), incarcerations for drug offenses have increased more rapidly. Many drug offenses carry mandated prison terms, meaning drug offenders cannot be released on bail. Consequently, criminals who have committed crimes of violence and crimes against the public order (gambling, prostitution, weapons charges, indecency) are sometimes released early to make room in the prisons.

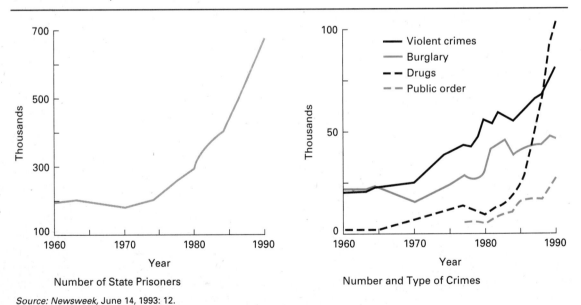

Number of State Prisoners

Number and Type of Crimes

Source: Newsweek, June 14, 1993: 12.

and no politician dared vote against a law designed to be tough on drugs. Despite long minimum sentences, arrest rates for drug offenders continue to rise. This questions the effectiveness of escalation of punishments as a deterrent to illegal drug use and sales.

Escalation of Punishments

When bad behavior is punished, but continues nevertheless, the first reaction is a demand for more severe punishment. This, of course, is part of the reason so many states have reinstituted the death penalty. A great majority of sociological studies of the subject have concluded that the death penalty has little or no effect on the murder rate (Archer and Gartner, 1984). Figures collected by Amnesty International (1992 Report) show that even giving the death penalty for peddling drugs will not necessarily work. Saudi Arabia executes drug peddlers and has virtually no drug problem. Iran executes drug peddlers, but has a big drug problem. Iran executed at least 775 people in 1991, many for drug offenses, and gave some of them 100 lashes before execution. The United States, of course, has done nothing of that kind, although it can execute people for repeated, large shipments of drugs. However, even as punishment has become more and more severe, there has been little positive result.

There are actually negative results from the escalation of punishments. One is that many people sympathize more with the drug user than with the law. Another is that present drug laws run contrary to concepts of justice. Very often, subordinates in drug organizations get very long sentences, while people at the top cut deals to get reduced sentences by betraying their associates (Beck and Katel, 1993). Often, as in the case of the Sherpas mentioned at the beginning of this chapter, the risky jobs go to relatively innocent people, while important members of crime organizations cannot be found.

One reason for imposing mandatory sentences was to make sentencing more just. According to the U.S. Sentencing Commission, this has not worked because one-third of the cases are plea-bargained through prosecuting attorneys. The Commission also found that blacks were given the mandatory sentence more often than whites. Sometimes the difference between a one-year sentence and a ten-year sentence depends on a single milligram of crack, which takes away the fairness of the law (Steinberg, 1994).

Besides the injustice of very uneven sentences and carelessness about accepting the testimony of informers, the justice system has instituted laws that call for seizures of property used in connection with drug sales or bought with drug money. Such cases are civil cases, which are easier to win than criminal cases. Under the authority of such a law, hundreds of millions of dollars worth of homes, cars, and businesses have been seized by the government. In June of 1993, however, the United States Supreme Court ruled unanimously that such seizures can go too far, violating the Eighth Amendment's provisions against excessive fines. The man on trial in the case was sent to prison for seven years for possession of cocaine with intent to distribute. His sentence stands, but he does not have to surrender his body shop and his home, his only possessions (Biskupic, 1993).

Alternative Policies

There is a growing consensus that policies have fallen far short of expectations. Attorney General Janet Reno agrees that jails have failed in the fight against drugs, but there is no agreement on alternative policies. The most extreme approach would be full legalization (Tacket, 1993).

Legalization

Those who argue that full legalization of drugs would be an improvement over present policies usually compare the drug trade with alcohol in the days of prohibition. Al Capone's gang was famous for supplying liquor illegally and for racketeering and murder. Once alcoholic drinks again became legal, the underground traffic was stopped and many criminals lost their profits. The legalization argument is that the same would happen with drugs. They would be available, but the price would fall and many criminals would be put out of business.

Opponents of such a policy argue that drug use would increase greatly, just as alcohol use increased at the end of prohibition. They also fear that full legalization would come too close to governmental approval of dangerous drugs. Nevertheless, many prominent citizens have spoken favorably of legalization, including the mayor of Baltimore, Maryland, Kurt Schmoke, and former Secretary of State George Shultz.

Selectivity

The idea of "selectivity," means treating use and abuse of different drugs in different ways. Much heavy spending of funds in the drug war goes for tracking down people who are growing marijuana plants in their basements. It might cut costs and criminal convictions to remove penalties on marijuana, or at least reduce such penalties to misdemeanors, as some U.S. states have done. Heavy penalties could remain only on drugs that are extremely dangerous, if they remain at all.

Education and Treatment

There are increasing suggestions to reverse present spending policy in fighting drugs. Instead of putting two-thirds of funds into inter-diction and punishment and one-third into education and treatment, the larger amount should apply to education and treatment. Attorney General Janet Reno suggests counseling as an alternative to jail. Only by accepting counseling and showing progress could a drug user avoid his or her sentence.

More approaches need to be tried. Switzerland, for example, another country with a serious heroin problem, is experimenting with giving addicts free heroin, morphine, or methadone in an effort to block sales by the underworld. England has long used the same policy for heroin addicts. The results have not been a total success, but England has far less heroin addiction than does the United States. In some cases, heroin addiction is treated with methadone, which may succeed, but actually only substitutes one drug for another, admittedly a less harmful, drug. More experimentation with pharmaceuticals might replace dangerous drugs.

As mentioned previously, more drugs seem to be flowing into both Eastern and Western Europe than ever before. We cannot look forward to a drug-free world, but we can restore many users and addicts to a sufficient degree of health so their lives might not be spent behind bars at public expense and they might contribute to society. Doing so might prevent the overcrowding of prisons, leading to early release of violent criminals to make room for drug abusers.

European Policies

Arnold Trebach of the Drug Policy Foundation calls for a "harm reduction" approach to drugs. He does not call for full legalization of drugs, but advocates a number of the policies of the European Frankfurt Resolution, signed by 15 European cities and provinces, including Zurich, Amsterdam, and Rome. The resolution calls for easing prohibitions on marijuana, the free availability of clean needles, and treatment for all who seek it (Horgan, 1993). Most of the major cities of Europe follow more of a harm reduction program than does the United States (Horgan, 1993). Methadone (to get off heroin) is more likely to be available in Europe than in the United States, although Baltimore and Boston have good programs. Drug treatment programs, under the Frankfurt Resolution, are to be user friendly, not administered under threat of jail as the alternative.

None of this means that illegal drugs will disappear, either from Europe or the United States. Treatment can be far more humane than at present, however, and may save the cost of keeping hundreds of thousands of people in prisons.

SUMMARY

Financial corruption is widespread in urban, industrial nations, which is consistent with sociological theory. Crime, but not necessarily violent crime, is believed to become more common in huge, anonymous populations than in rural societies.

The Cold War has also influenced crime rates, especially associated with illegal drugs. Drug interests were often ignored as long as they cooperated against the Communists. In Italy, fear of a large Communist party caused people to vote for corrupt parties as long as they were anti-Communist. Many government leaders had ties to the Mafia.

In the Middle East, government corruption feeds Islamic fundamentalist propaganda, which contends that only strict adherence to traditional Islamic laws can restore honesty.

Russia is plagued with heavy corruption as it moves into modern capitalism and away from a police state.

Criminal organizations grow more easily on an international scale now than in the past, partly because of the enormous profits in drugs, and partly because of ease in transporting drugs.

We briefly describe major drugs, and give some information about how the drug habit is spread. More effort must be made in treating drug addiction, as in most of Europe, rather than punishing it and flooding the prisons.

KEY TERMS

Bloods Violent street gang of Los Angeles origin, engaged in drug trade and often in street warfare. Now found in many large U.S. cities.

Cali cartel A drug cartel centered in Cali, Colombia, now operating in Mexico, transporting drugs to the United States.

Crack cocaine Cocaine processed into a solid that is broken into small pebbles that are smoked. Very powerful, fast acting, and extremely addictive.

Crips Violent street gang of Los Angeles origin, engaged in drug trade and often in street warfare. Now found in many large U.S. cities.

Downers Drugs that have a depressing effect on the body, inducing drowsiness and relieving pain, especially the case with opium and its derivatives.

Embezzlement Stealing money or stock entrusted to one's care; a crime committed by a trusted insider.

Europol A European police force serving members of the European Common Market. Similar to, but with fewer members than, Interpol.

Fraud Use of deception to gain other people's money or property.

Hallucinogens Drugs like LSD, that cause visual and/or auditory hallucinations.

Insider trading Gaining secret information as to which stocks are likely to go up, usually because of mergers of corporations, and using that **infor**mation to buy the stock.

Interpol An international police force to which most countries belong, that helps especially in finding escaped criminals and counterfeiters.

Grand larceny Theft of money or personal property. In many countries, grand larceny is theft of something worth more than a specified amount, and petty larceny is theft of smaller amounts.

Laundering money Placing money in foreign, secret bank accounts, to escape taxation or to hide money gained illegally, usually in the drug trade.

Mafia A term now applied to almost any well-organized crime group dominant in a particular country. Originally a Sicilian crime group, organized on a familial basis.

Mechanical solidarity Durkheim's concept of older societies held together by great similarity of their people and strong beliefs in old customs and norms.

Medellín cartel A drug organization centered in Medellín, Colombia; once the most powerful such organization in Latin America.

Moslem fundamentalism Moslems wishing to reinstate the laws of the Koran, do away with secular states, and have their countries dominated by the Islamic religion.

Organic solidarity In Durkheim's analysis, modern societies held together by interdependence of members, who engage in great varieties of work and are not so homogeneous as in older societies.

Restitutive law Laws calling for regulation of trade, definition of property rights, and such, as contrasted to harsh criminal law.

Retributive law Law of punishment or revenge. In Durkheim's analysis, typical of older societies held together by strong beliefs in norms and customs.

Sendera luminosa (Shining Path) A violent Communist revolutionary movement in Peru, accused of being in the drug trade.

"Snakeheads" A slang term used by the Chinese for people who smuggle illegal immigrants from East Asia into the United States.

Social control How a society gets its people to live up to its laws and mores.

"Speedballing" Using cocaine in conjunction with heroin to get a "super-high." Frequently lethal.

"Uppers" Drugs that are strong stimulants, increasing heart rate, temporarily overcoming fatigue, and often resulting in sleeplessness and irritability.

White-collar crime Crime committed by seemingly respectable people in the course of their business, including bribery, price-fixing, insider trading, false advertising, and so forth.

STUDY QUESTIONS

1. Explain mechanical solidarity and organic solidarity as described by Durkheim. What bearing do they have on crime?

2. What are the characteristics of countries that rank highest in larceny and fraud?

3. How does government corruption play into the hands of Islamic fundamentalists in the

Middle East? Is there any parallel in Christian fundamentalism in the United States?

4. How did the Cold War help drug interests in the drug-supplying nations?

5. What are the grounds for the contention that corruption in Italy was helped by the Cold War?

6. Changes in the former Soviet Union have generally been for the better. Why, then, have crime rates risen drastically?

7. What characteristics of the Mafia have made it a successful criminal organization?

8. Why has the United States had only very limited success with its policy of helping Latin American countries suppress the production of cocaine and other drugs?

9. What causes people to try illegal drugs and get "hooked"?

10. Argue the case for and against a highly punitive war on drugs, for full legalization, and for a policy somewhere between the two extremes.

chapter 13

DEADLY
COMBAT

elestine Mazimbaka clenched the side of his wooden chair while the interrogator hammered out his responses on a manual typewriter:

"How did you kill him?" the typist asked.

"With a machete."

"Where did you hit him?"

"I just beat him in the back of the neck. He didn't die right away. We put him in a hole in the ground and hit him again" (Zarembo, 1994).

Mazimbaka claims he was simply following his district administrator's orders when he plunged his machete into the neck of a drinking companion. Mazimbaka was a Hutu, and the man he killed was a Tutsi. The two tribes had lived together in peace at many times. They spoke the same language. Many of them had intermarried. But when the Hutu president was killed in an air crash in the spring of 1994, Hutus claimed it was the work of Tutsi saboteurs. Suddenly, large numbers of Hutus followed a government radio message, "Kill Tutsis or they will kill you." And they killed huge numbers, perhaps as many as one million. Now a new government, led by Tutsis, but including many moderate Hutus, is appealing to the United Nations to punish those guilty of attempted genocide (the killing of an entire people). Mazimbaka is charged with murder, but he claims he was only following orders.

The bloody conflict between the Hutu and Tutsi tribes of Rwanda was noted in the study of racial and ethnic problems in Chapter 6. The Tutsis, although a minority, had been the upper class. There had been conflicts between the two groups, but since the independence of the country in 1961 it had appeared that differences were declining and internal strife might be at an end. Old animosities can be reawakened by even minor incidents, however, especially if there are incendiaries in the population beating the drums of war, which was the case in Rwanda.

There have been many ethnic wars in recent years. We think first of the former Yugoslavia in this respect, where Serbs battle Moslems and Croatians in a land that was once held together by a powerful dictator, Josip Broz Tito, who died in 1980. The former Soviet Union also comes to mind. There have been ethnic fights in the former Soviet Republic of Georgia, and a war between Armenia and Azerbaijan, two former Soviet republics. The Soviet Union linked many ethnic groups under one central system that demanded their loyalty. The colonial empires of Britain, France, Netherlands, and Belgium, controlled interethnic strife in many places. Under Belgian administration, for example, Hutu-versus-Tutsi fights were never the horrible slaughter that they became in 1994. However, the old days of colonialism as well as of the Soviet Union are gone. There is more freedom in the world, but not necessarily peace.

So far, we have spoken of ethnic wars as though ethnic conflict is the only cause of war. Such is very far from the case. Causes of war are many and complex. Wars have been so constant in human history that some people, even scholarly people, have concluded that war is a part of human nature and that the world may never achieve peace.

THE DUBIOUS HUMAN NATURE ARGUMENT

The position that human nature leads to war dates back to English philosopher Thomas Hobbes (1588–1679), who argued that only a strong autocratic state could maintain peace; otherwise human life, as in primitive times, would be "solitary, poor, nasty, brutish, and short." In more recent times, the argument about the essential aggressiveness of human nature has been championed by Konrad Lorenz (1967), an animal ethologist. Lorenz compares human nature with animal nature, concluding that humans have an **aggressive instinct,** comparable to that of many animals. The tragic difference, according to Lorenz, is that animals usually have built-in behavior patterns that cope with aggression. He uses the wolf as an example. Wolves fight for dominance, but the fighting stops when one of them submits. Some kind of inborn behavior mechanism prevents the dominant wolf from killing the vanquished. Humans, on the other hand, will fight to the death, especially in the mass slaughter known as war.

The Lorenz theories have been accepted by many animal ethologists as well as by members of another academic discipline called sociobiology. **Sociobiology** is the study of the biological basis for human and animal social behavior; it assumes that much behavior is genetically determined. The most prominent sociobiologist, Edward O. Wilson (1978), says that if such traits as aggressiveness and male dominance occur universally, there is something instinctive about them.

A REFUTATION: MALLEABLE HUMAN NATURE

The majority of sociologists are less than enthusiastic about the views of animal ethologists and sociobiologists. In fact, they believe in a **malleable human nature,** that there are no human instincts whatever. The concept of an aggressive instinct appears overly fatalistic, and adds little to what we know about war. Although human history has been bloody, there are tribes of preliterate people who do not go to war (Denton, 1968), and many modern societies have shown no tendency to fight. Even male

"What's amazing to me is that this late in the game we still have to settle our differences with rocks."

dominance, which sociobiologists look upon as instinctive, differs greatly from society to society. Among the Hopi and Zuñi Indians, for example, women are so dominant in some respects (ownership of the house and corn supply) that one has to look hard for evidence of male dominance. Actually, males *do* dominate in the priestly realm, but in little else. If either war or male dominance is instinctive, we would expect more uniformity in degree.

One prominent anthropologist, Marvin Harris (1977), links male dominance and warfare and finds them related to level of cultural development. Regardless of what basic nature may be, he points out, there is a strong correlation between the level of warfare and the pressure on resources. This is especially true with the development of agriculture in settled populations and towns. Such a development gives marauding and ill-fed tribes an interest in attack and plunder, and more settled populations a reason to develop techniques of defense. In this way, war is explained in terms of economics and human interaction rather than instinct, and allows for an analysis of various causes of war.

THE CAUSES OF WAR

Harris has written mainly on the growth of warfare from raiding by small bands to the sacking of cities in early civilizations. Our present concern with warfare is predominantly about the kind of massive and devastating conflict seen in two world wars, and in Vietnam, Afghanistan, and the Persian Gulf. Another type of warfare with which we are concerned is typified at present by Yugoslavia, where conflicting ethnic groups fight over territory and independence. Revolutions pitting one social class against another and one ideology against another have also been common, as characterized by Nicaragua in the 1980s.

In all types of warfare, the reasons for fighting are complex. There is usually a distinction between real cause for fighting and idealistic justifications for fighting. There is often, too, a distinction between underlying causes for war and mere precipitating events. The killing of an archduke in Sarajevo was the incident that touched off World War I, but there were many basic causes that pitted two world alliances against each other. Sometimes the precipitating event seems trivial, as in the case of The War of Jenkins' Ear (1739). Jenkins, an English captain, was captured by the Spanish, who cut off his ear. Because England and Spain were on the verge of war, the incident was enough to precipitate a war and make one captain's ear very famous.

Wars of Conquest

Wars of conquest are as old as written history. Because all cultures develop norms they do not like to admit violating, excuses are nearly always found for wars of conquest. The conquistadors seized Mexico and Peru for gold, for land for settlements, and for impressed labor; but the glorified reason was to convert the heathens to Christianity and hence save their souls. When the United States expanded westward, a common rationalization for robbing Native Americans of their land was "Manifest Destiny," meaning that God obviously intended the land to belong to the United States. When Yermak Timofei and his Cossacks

conquered much of Siberia, they claimed it was to bring the native peoples under the civilizing influence of the Tsar, Ivan the Terrible. In Hitler's conquests, he claimed to be bringing a new world order, to be dominated by those he regarded as a superior strain of human beings, the Aryans. From ancient times to modern, conquest has been a major motive for warfare, sometimes involving vast territories, and sometimes small but desirable areas, as in Iraq's attempted conquest of Kuwait.

Territorial Disputes

In many cases, two or more countries have what they consider legitimate claims to the same territory. One of the most famous historical cases is that of the provinces of Alsace and Lorraine. Although France has held the territories for many years, they were taken by Germany in the Franco-Prussian war of 1870–1871. In World War I they were reclaimed by France. In 1942 Germany again seized them. At the end of World War II, the provinces again became French. With unification trends going on in Western Europe, it seems unlikely that such territorial disputes will arise again in the foreseeable future. In Eastern Europe, however, conflicting territorial claims for the various parts of what was once Yugoslavia have caused bloody fighting which may continue far into the future. Such problems could easily arise in parts of Africa, where territorial boundaries conflict with ancient tribal claims.

Irredentism

The word *irredentism* is from the Italian *irredenta*, meaning territories occupied by Italian people, but not incorporated into Italy. Irredentism, then, is the policy of trying to reincorporate lands that once belonged to a particular country or people. Irredentism was very important to Italy, much of whose historical lands had been taken by Spain, France, or

Territorial Changes in Europe

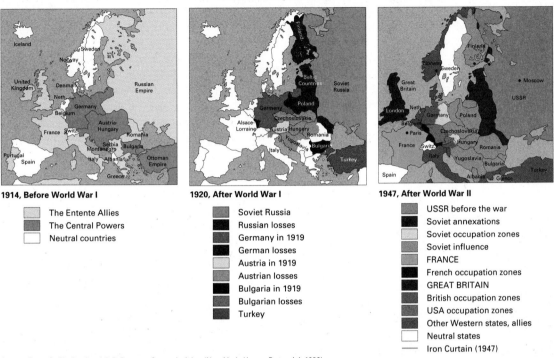

1914, Before World War I

- The Entente Allies
- The Central Powers
- Neutral countries

1920, After World War I

- Soviet Russia
- Russian losses
- Germany in 1919
- German losses
- Austria in 1919
- Austrian losses
- Bulgaria in 1919
- Bulgarian losses
- Turkey

1947, After World War II

- USSR before the war
- Soviet annexations
- Soviet occupation zones
- Soviet influence
- FRANCE
- French occupation zones
- GREAT BRITAIN
- British occupation zones
- USA occupation zones
- Other Western states, allies
- Neutral states
- — Iron Curtain (1947)

Source: From G. Chaliand and J. P. Rageau, *Strategic Atlas,* (New York: Harper Perennial, 1992).

Figure 13.1
When borders are changed, as they have been after major European wars, there are always pressures for restoring the old order, or "irredentism." Nationalistic Germans probably eye the territory to the east that was once theirs. Russian nationalists call for restoration of Russia's 1914 boundaries.

Austria. Irredentism led to the unification of Italy under such Italian patriots as Victor Immanuel II, Cavour, and Garibaldi. Note that a strong patriotic fervor for the cause of unity was necessary for irredentism to come about—a sentiment that usually accompanies war.

The word *irredentism* is now applied far beyond the borders of Italy. In East Asia, Japan is attempting to regain the Kurile Islands, which had been taken by the Soviet Union at the end of World War II. The expectation is that some kind of compromise will be made in the matter

without shots being fired. The war in former Yugoslavia involves an attempt to unite Serbia with territories inhabited largely by Serbs.

The boundaries of many Arabic states are somewhat arbitrary. Syria has designs on the Bekaa Valley of Lebanon, claiming it was historically Syrian. Iraq claims that Kuwait is an artificial state, carved from territory that was once part of Iraq and that is inhabited by displaced Iraqis.

As an extreme case of irredentism, we could cite Israel. In ancient times, the land that is now

Israel was the home of the Jewish people. The Palestinian Arabs, however, believe the land to be theirs by right of many centuries of occupation. Two cases of irredentism collide. The result has been outright war interspersed with years of riots and unrest.

Irredentism is similarly a factor in Ireland, which was occupied for centuries by the British. The Republic of Ireland achieved independence in 1949, but the six counties of northern Ireland remain a division of the United Kingdom. Although tensions continue in Northern Ireland between the Unionists, who wish to unite with Great Britain, and the Nationalists, who wish to be part of the Republic of Ireland, there is a declared end to the fighting and hope for peace through diplomatic efforts.

The Fight for Resources

Taking territories for the sake of resources cannot be distinguished in all cases from the wars of conquest. Historically, nations have fought for gold, iron, and coal. Today, the most coveted resource is oil. When Iraq seized Kuwait, the prize was not a small desert Emirate, but nearly one thousand producing oil wells and with them, a chance to raise the price of oil on the international market.

A problem for the industrial world is that nearly all the enormous reserves of oil are not located in France, Germany, Japan, or even the United States (once oil independent) (Yergin, 1990). The greatest oil supplies are in Arabia, Iran, Iraq, Libya, and Algeria, as well as in some of the Central Asian Moslem countries. By no means are all of them unfriendly to the United States, but they all have their interests to pursue, and the majority of them are politically volatile. Syria has ambitions in Lebanon. Iraq plans a

The natural resource most coveted by industrial nations is oil. Willingness to fight for it was demonstrated in the Persian Gulf War against Iraq. Vast reserves of oil give many Middle Eastern countries great power.

comeback in military power. Islamic fundamentalism and rejection of Western culture has made the United States an enemy of Iran. Saudi Arabia and the Persian Gulf Emirates are friendly to the United States and the West generally, but they are all kingdoms where Islamic fundamentalism might gain control, ending favorable relationships with the United States.

Conflicting forces are also at work in the former Soviet republics of Kazakstan, Uzbekistan, Turkmenistan, Tajikistan, and Kyrgystan, as Iran, Turkey, and Saudi Arabia all seek to woo them. As of the mid 1990s, they appear eager to reassert their Islamic beliefs, but not eager to become Islamic states having clerical rule.

Trade: From Competition to Conflict

Most of the world's nations have engaged in foreign trade, seeking products they desire, and trying to make money on goods they have for sale. When trade is carried on peacefully and within agreed norms of fair play, it is what economists call international competition, by which everyone gains. Competition, however, is not always within the norms. Conflicts, both violent and nonviolent, arise when one nation or group seeks to eliminate competing nations by any means. The conquest of the Americas resulted in English and Dutch privateers attacking Spanish ships in an attempt to get their share of the gold of the New World. English accounts describe such privateers as Drake and Hawkins as patriotic heroes; Spanish accounts depict them as pirates. The violation of norms of fair play are often rationalized as necessary, perhaps even noble. But such actions can lead to war, as they did frequently with England, Spain, Holland, and France.

In more recent times, trade rivalries continue to cause fighting. In World War I, the growing trade rivalry between Germany and Britain roused suspicions and fears which, in turn, figured in the arms race and countervailing alliances of the time. In the Persian Gulf War, much of the motive was to ensure that Iraq could not gain too much power over the oil trade. At present, no countries are fighting wars over trade, but charges and countercharges are made as to who is engaged in "fair" trade policies and who is not. The United States and Japan continually accuse each other of unfair trade practices. This type of trade quarrel will most likely stop short of shooting, but it could lead to high import duties and other barriers to trade that would probably prove harmful to both sides.

Economic Depressions

At the end of World War I, Germany suffered a disastrous inflation which, in effect, financially wiped out the middle class. It was followed by an equally disastrous depression which put millions out of work and destroyed all confidence in the future. Although the United States and Great Britain were also suffering from the Great Depression, their situations were less severe. Much more important, Germany was able to find scapegoats for its economic depression: the Treaty of Versailles that ended World War I and the Jews.

Hitler and his followers claimed that the Treaty of Versailles had caused the economic depression by cutting down on German territory and making Germany pay reparations. The Nazis further claimed that Germany had not really lost World War I. Conspirators, they claimed, mainly Jews, had gained control of the German government and signed the Treaty of Versailles. The Nazis confiscated all property of the Jews, then shipped them east to death camps where 6 million were killed in gas chambers. Although economic depressions can lead to political instability almost anywhere, the German response was in some ways unique. To explain it, one must add to it German humiliation over loss of a war, the terrorism used by the Nazis to hold the

German population in line, and a determination to seize more territory even if it meant war.

Obviously, not all countries go to war as a result of economic depression, but such conditions lead to discontentment and often irrational thinking. Ethnic minorities or foreign countries are convenient targets of blame.

Ethnic Wars

Ethnic minorities have been the victims of terrorism and oppression very often in history, as in the case of the Chinese in Southeast Asia, the Jews in various parts of Europe, the Gypsies in Eastern Europe, and the Armenians in Turkey. War, rather than submission to oppression, can result if oppressor and oppressed are nearly equal in numbers and power. For example, the Ibos of Nigeria fought a war for the independence of their land (Biafra) from 1967 to 1970. After heavy military losses and starvation, however, they were finally forced to yield. Since many other African countries have borders that ignore tribal identity, there are possibilities of further ethnic strife. In South Africa today, hostility between the Zulus and other South African blacks has slowed progress toward racial equality.

The breakup of the former Soviet Union made many former Soviet nations independent. Russia remains the world's largest country, but its population includes about 30 million non-Russians. At the same time, all parts of the former Soviet Union contain Russian minorities, a total of about 25 million people. A potential problem is with the Russian minorities. In at least one former Soviet Republic (Tajikistan), 25,000 Russian troops are fighting antigovernment guerrillas. The Russians are supporting a government that suppresses free speech (25 journalists have been killed), but that apparently works in line with Russian interests (Associated Press 1994).

Paul A. Gobel, of the Carnegie Endowment for International Peace, sees danger in Russian minorities (Gobel, 1992). He quotes several Russian generals as being of the opinion that

Russia should still have enough control over former parts of the Soviet Union to be able to interfere on behalf of Russian minorities. Russian President Boris Yeltsin does not fully agree with this position, which could lead to military action. Russian traditions, dating to pre-Communist times, argue that military leadership will eventually reassert itself. On the other hand, the popularity of Yeltsin's ethnically liberal policies indicates that democratic forces may prevail. Another helpful note, according to Gobel, is that most of the new countries have adopted liberal positions on citizenship and minority rights, which gives grounds for hope that there will be no reason for Russian intervention in ethnic matters.

While we speculate over whether ethnic conflicts will arise in and around Russia, such conflicts have already become bitter and bloody in the former Yugoslavia. Yugoslavia is extremely diverse culturally; Croatia and Slovenia are predominantly Roman Catholic, while the southern parts, including Serbia, are primarily Orthodox. Many Bosnians are Moslems, but there are also Orthodox Serbs and Catholic Croatians in Bosnia. The people are further divided by historical memories of wars, conflicting alliances, and uneven input into the struggle for independence from the Ottoman (Turkish) Empire. More recently, the Serbs have accused the Croats of collaboration with the Germans in World War II.

The animosity has grown so great that the Serbs are now calling for "ethnic purity," that is, allowing only Serbs in Serbia and other areas with large numbers of Serbs. In the confused three-way struggle, any group may be victimized. Serbs and Croats fight each other, but sometimes make truces. The Moslems are victimized most often, partly because of ancient animosities, partly because of religious differences, but primarily because they are in the way of a greater Serbia.

Religious Wars

Religion is one aspect of the interethnic strife in Yugoslavia. It is also part of what has divided

Kazakhstan and the other former Soviet republics of Central Asia from Russia. Since their independence, the new Central Asian republics have been building mosques and returning to Islamic worship which, like other religions, had been largely suppressed during the years of Communist rule. For the most part, the Moslem leaders of the vast region (larger than the United States) are Sunis and moderates, wanting Islamic influence but not a return to strict Koranic law, which might require public executions or stoning. There could, nevertheless, be ethnic and religious strife in the future as a conflict for their loyalty continues. Turkey, whose people are Moslems but whose government is separated from religious control, is attempting to win influence in the area, most of which was once ruled by the Turkish Ottoman Empire. Iran, a land of fanatical Shiite Islam, also tries to spread its influence. Wealthy Saudi Arabia pays for many of the new mosques, and undoubtedly expects to gain allies through such generosity (Lane, 1992). Turkey, Iran, and Saudi Arabia, potential rivals in Central Asia, already have a certain amount of animosity toward one another.

Religious wars have been prominent in the past. The Crusades of the Middle Ages, for example, were an attempt to win the Holy Land of Jerusalem for the Christians. The **Thirty Years' War** (1618–1648) began as a war between Protestants and Catholics. The Austrian Empire led the Catholic cause; Germany was divided; the Scandinavian countries were Protestant. Political rivalries became involved to such a degree that eventually Catholic France subsidized Protestant Sweden to enter the war and save the Protestants from disaster. The Thirty Years' war was one of the bloodiest in history, wiping out half the population of the German province of Brandenburg, according to some estimates.

The dividing of territory in imperialistic wars, as well as emigration and immigration, have left ethnic and religious minorities in nearly every country. Consequently, religious wars are very common; the struggles between Arabs and Israelis in the Middle East and between Catholics and Protestants in Northern Ireland are prime examples. India is another nation plagued with religious struggles. When Britain recognized its independence, India included its present boundaries as well as what is now Pakistan and Bangladesh, both Moslem countries. Britain attempted to divide the territory so that Pakistan would be primarily Moslem and India primarily Hindu. However, centuries of migration left minorities in both territories. As a result, there have been frequent outbursts of violence between Hindus and Moslems. Additionally, Sikhs (a religion founded in the sixteenth century) struggle for independence from the Hindus in India. The Sikhs believe in only one god (monotheism) and the Hindus have many

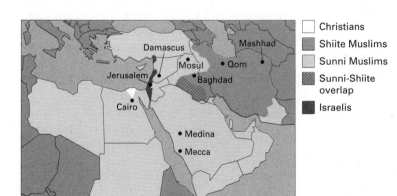

Christians
Shiite Muslims
Sunni Muslims
Sunni-Shiite overlap
Israelis

Damascus
Mashhad
Mosul
Qom
Jerusalem
Baghdad
Cairo
Medina
Mecca

Figure 13.2
Religion often plays a major part in war, as in the long struggle between Jews and Moslems over Israel. Moslems are also fighting Christians in the south of Sudan. Even in some parts of the Arabic world, tensions run high between Sunni and Shiite Moslems.

gods (polytheism), but their fights are more over territory and shrines than over beliefs.

Islamic Fundamentalism

The **Islamic fundamentalist** movement brought an end to the rule of the Shah of Iran and to United States influence in that country. Since then, there has been fear of the spread of such a movement—probably one of the reasons U.S. President Bush had sought to back Iran's enemy, Iraq, in the days before Iraq's invasion of Kuwait.

In the last election held in Algeria (1991), the Moslem fundamentalists won, but the election was voided by the government. Revolution may well be the final outcome.

Islamic fundamentalism has also taken hold in Sudan, the largest country in Africa, where fighting has continued for 36 of the last 50 years. By 1991 the National Islamic Front (NIF) had taken control of the northern part of the country and was gaining the upper hand in the south, much of which is populated by the Dinka and other non-Moslem tribes and by Christians. During days of famine, the government made it nearly impossible for food to get through to the South, apparently attempting to win the war through starvation (Hamburg, 1992).

According to Raymond Bonner (1992), an American journalist who spent considerable time in Sudan interviewing high ranking officials, the man in power is Hassan al-Turabi, an educated, articulate leader, but a determined fundamentalist fanatic. He is now receiving financial aid from Iran, with whose help he is buying weapons and aircraft from China. Turabi has brought several pronounced changes into Sudan:

1. The *Sharia* (strict Koranic law requiring cutting off the arms of thieves, the stoning of prostitutes, and the hanging of murderers) is being reinstated.
2. Women, who had been relatively liberated in Khartoum and other Sudanese cities, must

again wear a veil and not be seen on the streets after 5:30 P.M. Bonner learned of the severe flogging of three teenaged girls for allowing their hair to show.
3. Terrorist groups are being trained in Sudan, probably with Iranian help.
4. Political activities are banned. Political dissidents are sent to "ghost houses," secret places where they are interrogated and tortured. A few prisoners have had their genitals crushed.
5. Education is increasingly controlled by the NIF.
6. Foreign policy aims at spreading the NIF and similar organizations such as the Moslem brotherhood into positions of authority throughout North Africa, including Egypt, which is threatened by the turn of events in Sudan.

Raymond Bonner ends his discussion of Sudan with the comment, "Islamic fundamentalism is fast replacing communism as the ideology that most frightens the United States, yet the fear has not yet reached the state at which Washington might engage in actions against an Islamic government" (Bonner, 1992: 83).

Anti-Moslem Fanatics

Extremism on one side can easily become an excuse for extremism on the other side. Serbia is reported to have turned its full rage against the Moslems of Bosnia, calling them Islamic fundamentalists, and accusing them of plotting a *Jihad* (Holy War) against Christian Serbia. No United Nations observers or journalists place any credence whatever in such a story (Maas, 1993). It illustrates, however, how people can be stirred by the revival of religious hatreds.

Although we have said much about Islamic fundamentalism, the majority of the world's Moslems, such as the Egyptians, the Turks, the peoples of Central Asia or of Malaysia and Indonesia, are peaceful and progressive. Although highly critical of the fundamentalists, Bonner

Islamic guerrillas, returning from their victory in Afghanistan, are prepared to help other guerilla forces against such secular states as Egypt and Algeria. Their goal is religious domination.

capable of claiming the full devotion of their followers, of rousing strong emotions, and of trying to give meaning to life. Although religion has shown more survival power, strongly held ideologies, especially Nazism and communism, have had profound effects on history. Both have been characterized as "secular religions" because of the fervor with which they have been embraced.

The ideology of Nazi Germany made war inevitable, unless the rest of the world was willing to recognize Germany as its master. The ideology was so exclusively racist at first that Nazism, by definition, could have no allies. Eventually, though, Fascist Italy joined Germany, and so did Japan. Hitler recognized the Japanese as the master race of the Far East. As is usually the case, certain liberties were taken with the ideology to suit the government's needs.

More recently, the ideology that was looked upon as the greatest threat to world peace was communism. Because communism did not laud any one race or ethnic group as the "master," its appeal became more widespread. China followed the Marxist ideology into its own brand of communism, as did Cuba. The Soviet Union and China both supported Communist movements in many parts of the world, while the United States took the lead in supporting regimes that were under attack, sometimes regimes that had nothing to be said in their favor except that they opposed communism.

At present, no ideology similar to communism or Nazism threatens the world, although, as noted above, radical Islamic fundamentalism threatens parts of it. In other parts of the world, new types of fanatical ideologies could easily arise or old ideologies could reappear, especially in times of economic crisis.

reminds us that "Islam is. . . in fact a religion as committed to justice and concern for the poor as Christianity or Judaism is" (Bonner, 1992: 74). Fanaticism is as common to Christianity as it is to Islam. Such fanaticism was especially evident in the days of the burning of heretics and witches.

Ideology and War

Religion and **ideology** (beliefs about how to run society) have some of the same traits. They are

Revolutions and Surrogate Wars

Although the United States was born in revolution, it has often opposed revolutionary movements, especially revolutions believed to be Communist inspired. Some contend that it was the only alternative. Others feel the United States frequently ended up on the wrong side, supporting cruel repressive regimes against popular uprisings of the people and thus being seen as oppressors. The only "revolutions" the United States supported were those of rebels against left-wing regimes, as in Nicaragua and Angola. In the 1970s, the United States helped to reinstate the Shah of Iran, which later resulted in bitter hatred for the United States on the part of the Shiite Moslems who gained and still hold power. The United States became "the great Satan," and the target of terrorist actions. Although not involved militarily in Iran, the United States lost heavily in business assets, and 250 Americans were held hostage for nearly two years.

The Korean and Vietnam Wars are prime examples of what historian Paul Kennedy (1987) calls **surrogate wars.** His meaning is that the wars were really between the United States and the Soviet Union, but were fought largely by other people and in other countries. As of June 1988, just before it became clear that Gorbachev wanted to bring peace, there were 25 wars in progress around the world, killing an estimated 3,000,000 people per year (Bonner, 1992: 74). Some of the conflicts were religious or ethnic, but the majority were against existing regimes, led by revolutionists. In most cases, one side was receiving aid from the United States or the Soviet Union. Table 13.1 lists the serious surrogate wars of the 1980s.

OTHER CAUSES OF WAR: ARMS RACES AND FEAR

It would be difficult to exhaust all possibilities in looking for the causes of war. In earlier times in Europe, jealousies between ruling families were involved, as in England's War of the Roses

	Surrogate Wars of the 1980s	TABLE 13.1
Country	Number of Deaths, 1980–1988	Status, early 1990s
El Salvador	65,000	Uneasy truce
Nicaragua	30,000	Settled by election
Peru	10,000	Still in progress
Afghanistan	100,000	Soviet withdrawal, but factional fighting
Angola	213,000	Truce
Mozambique	2,000,000 (rough estimate)	Slight progress toward peace
Ethiopia	Widespread starvation	New government, continued starvation
Cambodia	500,000 in 1970s	Uneasy truce
Philippines	60,000	Downturn in fighting

NOTE: Vietnam is not included here because the Vietnam War ended in 1975.

(1455–1485) in which the houses of York and Lancaster fought for the crown of England, and the War of the Spanish Succession (1700–1715) fought to prevent the French royal family from inheriting the throne of Spain.

Sometimes war results from a serious miscalculation, as in the Persian Gulf War. The United States had supported Iraq financially and militarily almost until the day of the invasion of Kuwait (Farrell, 1992). For this reason, Saddam Hussein concluded wrongly that the United States would not enter the conflict.

Arms races are closely related to wars. Fear of other countries' intentions, whether justified or not, can lead to arms races, which further escalate fear. Thus, fear of war can be a self-fulfilling prophecy. Fear can lead to a search for allies, until two potential foes are constantly looking for help in order to maintain a **balance of power.** Balance of power is sometimes thought of as a means of maintaining peace, but it can actually be a major factor in war.

BALANCE OF POWER

In many cases, a motive in warfare is to prevent a deterioration in the power status of one's own country. In much of European history, Great Britain was engaged in diplomacy and frequent wars to keep any power from dominating Europe, whether Spain, France, or Germany. The balance of power was involved in World War I: France, Great Britain, and Russia aligned against Germany, Austria-Hungary, and Turkey. Each side feared the other was gaining the upper hand, so neither dared back down a single inch. Then a precipitating event occurred—the murder of an Austrian archduke in Sarajevo.

A similar balance of power in more recent years involved the United States and its allies (NATO) against the Soviet Union and its allies, the Warsaw Pact. Because of the nuclear threat, the balance of power became known as the balance of terror. The fear of each side for the other led to stockpiling enough nuclear weapons to have destroyed every city in the world many times. One study (Ehrlich et al., 1984) concluded that the stored weapons were enough to have brought a long winter to the earth in which the majority of life would perish. Some argued that the book exaggerated the case. In the early days of the Reagan administration, some of the president's advisers even thought a nuclear war would be winnable, but few agreed. The Reagan administration pursued a policy of trying to get far ahead of the Soviet Union in strength—a policy that would have upset the balance. Robert McNamara (1987), who had served in the Department of Defense during the Kennedy administration, argued for the more conventional view: The safest situation is to have the two sides approximately equal in power. Otherwise, the side that feels it is falling behind

in the race may strike before the situation gets worse. Fortunately, Mikhail Gorbachev brought the arms race to an end. The principle of balance of power remains and may arise in other situations in the future.

Military Balance and Surrogate Wars

Most of the "surrogate" wars discussed were fought to preserve the balance of power. The United States became rigidly determined to see no further expansion of Communist regimes anywhere in the world. The Soviet Union could turn down no opportunity to do what it thought would strengthen its position relative to the United States. These attitudes led to disastrous miscalculations in Vietnam and in Afghanistan.

Historian Barbara Tuchman (1984) singles out several wars that have all the qualities of madness. One is the war in Vietnam. Even as the expense of the war in money, equipment, and lives mounted intolerably, dedication to the war remained, with no one seeming able to find a way out. Even the North Vietnamese were puzzled as to why the United States was in the war. Did it expect to find oil? Gold? It would take hills and then abandon them. Was this because it failed to find what it was looking for?

Whatever the puzzlement of the North Vietnamese, in the thinking of many American leaders, especially Presidents Johnson and Nixon, the goal was to stop the spread of communism. The statement had been made by Eisenhower that if Vietnam fell to the Communists, the other Southeast Asian countries would fall "like a row of dominoes." No attempt was made to assess the staying power of such countries as Thailand, Malaysia, and Indonesia. The final success of the North Vietnamese proved the so-called domino theory to be seriously faulted.

Why were futile policies followed so long? The social psychologist Irving S. Janis (1983) attributes such errors in judgement to **groupthink,** or the tendency of people belonging to a close-knit group to think alike under many circumstances.

T o w a r d   A   S o l u t i o n

Focus on the United States and the USSR

Avoiding Armageddon

During the period referred to by Winston Churchill as the "balance of terror," there was a well-founded fear that weaponry had reached such a stage that humankind might indeed accomplish the destruction of life on earth. Nuclear bombs, including intercontinental ballistic missiles, were proliferating in the Soviet Union and the United States, and each country pointed its weapons at the other.

A book published in 1984 warned of the possibility of such massive destruction that human life might be exterminated. The title, *The Cold and the Dark* (Ehrlich and Sagan, 1984), set the theme: If a large part of the nuclear weapons in possession of the two superpowers of the time should be used in a great war, the atmosphere would be so contaminated as to cause a long period of nuclear winter over the earth. For two or three years the sun's rays would barely penetrate at all, so there would be a very long night and extreme cold.

An astronomer, Carl Sagan, and a biologist, Paul R. Ehrlich, were the main authors of *The Cold and the Dark*, but many prominent scientists were consulted, and the thesis of the book was widely accepted.

In connection with the study that produced *The Cold and the Dark*, Soviet scientists were invited to meet with American scientists. A Soviet radiobiologist, Alexander Kuzin, pointing out that humans are more easily damaged by radiation than most other species, predicted that "An ecological imbalance will arise, which will contribute to the dying out of the small population of humans that will have survived the immediate consequences of a nuclear catastrophe" (Ehrlich and Sagan, 1984: 150).

Despite the growing fear of nuclear war, production of nuclear weapons continued. As of 1987, when the stockpiling of bombs was at its height, the United States had 12,386 strategic nuclear weapons, and the USSR had 10,054 (Sivard, 1988). Strategic weapons are designed as ground-based or submarine-based weapons, to be delivered by long-range missiles. MX missiles carry warheads with 200 times the destructive force of the bomb that destroyed Hiroshima. In addition to strategic weapons were tactical weapons which, rather than being hurled across oceans and continents to strike the heartland of an enemy country, were designed for use in military operations at relatively short range. Eastern Europe feared they would be used in the territory of the Soviet satellites—Poland, Czechoslovakia, Hungary, and Romania. These tactical weapons made up the rest of the estimated 50,000 nuclear weapons in the hands of the United States and the USSR by 1990.

While scientists on both sides of the Iron Curtain repeated their warnings, both the Soviet Union and the United States continued arming, each fearing the other might strike the first blow. However, as pointed out in *The Cold and the Dark*, nuclear war might kill those who are using it as well as those who are the targets. Sagan was asked if either side could gain a real victory if it launched an attack without warning and utterly destroyed its enemy before the enemy could strike back. Sagan replied (Ehrlich and Sagan, 1984):

> We have an excellent chance that if Nation A attacks Nation B with an effective first strike, then Nation A has thereby committed suicide, even if Nation B has not lifted a finger to retaliate. (p. 16)

This was probably part of the truth perceived by Mikhail Gorbachev in 1987 when he began a series of reforms that amounted to a complete reversal of nuclear policy for the Soviet Union. Intelligence prevailed on both sides of the Iron Curtain: both sides chose survival.

We face a future in which nuclear weapons might yet be used, but not the great masses that were stockpiled by the United States and the Soviet Union. Those weapons are being stored or dismantled. Reason has prevailed and Armageddon, the war to end all wars, has been avoided.

SOURCES: P. R. Ehrlich, C. Sagan, D. Kennedy, and W. O. Roberts, *The Cold and the Dark* (New York: W. W. Norton, 1984); R. L. Sivard, *World Military and Social Expenditures* (Washington, D.C.: World Priorities Press, 1988).

Policy leaders surround themselves with like-minded advisors. They tend also to develop a feeling of invulnerability, and to underestimate the enemy. Each person backs up the other in these feelings until there is no doubt in anyone's mind that they are right. Although Janis used other examples, his conclusions seem to apply very well to Vietnam. We could also add some insights from John R. Raser (1969), who points out that even if subordinates have doubts about the leader's judgment, they are likely to remain silent. Furthermore, as anxieties grow, judgment becomes less clear, and often only one alternative can be seen.

Whatever the explanations, Vietnam cost more than 55,000 American lives, approximately 3,000,000 Vietnamese lives, and in the vicinity of $1 trillion.

Afghanistan

Had she written her book a few years later Barbara Tuchman could well have applied the term *March of Folly* to yet another war in which the United States and the Soviet Union lined up on opposite sides. The king of Afghanistan was overthrown in 1973 and a republic established;

but five years later, pro-Soviet forces overthrew the government and seized power in Kabul, the capital of Afghanistan. The new government was unable to establish its authority throughout the land, so the Soviet Union sent forces to its rescue. The result was a ten-year struggle in which 14,000 Soviet soldiers were killed, nearly all of Afghanistan was torn up with shelling, and 3,000,000 Afghans fled to Pakistan. At best, Afghanistan is a very poor country; war has reduced it to misery. Although Soviet forces withdrew in 1989, the government they had supported hung on to power in Kabul until early 1992, largely because of ethnic and religious divisions among the opposition.

There can be little doubt that the Soviet Union was also a victim of groupthink. In high councils there was little or no expressed opposition until the time of Mikhail Gorbachev. The Afghan War has had a number of after-effects that were not anticipated. Land mines strewn throughout the country and then abandoned, continue to kill people (the same is true in Vietnam). Although a moderate faction gained control in Kabul in 1992, fears persist that an Islamic fundamentalist group might eventually win. Other war-related problems extend far

Wars have long-lasting consequences. Afghanistan, Cambodia, and Vietnam are still littered with land mines, and thousands of people are being killed, blinded, or mutilated every year. Incredibly, people in northern France have been killed in recent years by land mines planted during World War I.

beyond the Afghan border. In order to finance the war, opium production and export increased, contributing to the drug epidemic in the United States and elsewhere. American-made weapons left over from the war are being smuggled out of the country, ending in the hands of various revolutionaries and in Iran. Large numbers of well-trained guerrilla soldiers are leaving Afghanistan for other troubled areas. They have joined antigovernment forces in Algeria and Tunisia, and some may have joined in the Jihad (holy war) against Israel (Fineman, 1991).

Military Balance and Economic Drain

At the end of World War II, the United States rode high as the wealthiest nation in the world, able to launch an assistance program (The Marshall Plan) to help rebuild Germany and Japan. It appeared that an American age had dawned.

The Soviet Union was also a winner in the war, able to occupy and force into its sphere of influence most of Eastern Europe. The USSR had problems the United States did not have, however. One was the enormous task of rebuilding after wartime devastation. The other was the lack of an atomic weapon, which the USSR needed to remain competitive with the United States. Every effort was exerted for atomic development, and by 1950 the Soviet Union entered the nuclear arms race, which escalated until the late 1980s. Although the Soviet Union fell far behind most industrialized nations in consumer goods, it kept fairly well abreast of the United States in weaponry. However, the arms race proved a severe economic strain for the USSR. Although it was well known that the Soviet people lived poorly compared with people in Western Europe or the United States, most Americans were surprised in the late 1980s when then Soviet Prime Minister Gorbachev called for "economic restructuring." He had, in fact, pronounced the Soviet economic system a failure.

The more efficient capitalist system of the United States was better able to withstand the mili-tary costs; but even here the financial drain is obvious. The national debt increased to nearly $3 trillion by the end of the Reagan administration. The national defense budget had risen from $134 billion in 1980 to a high of $303.6 billion in 1989, followed by a slight downturn as fear of the Soviet Union receded. With such military spending, there was obviously less funding for highways, bridges, inner-city rehabilitation, schools, work-fare programs, and other government services. Even though fear of the Soviet Union declined, there were other pressures to keep up military spending, pressures from the military-industrial complex.

THE MILITARY-INDUSTRIAL COMPLEX

The production of weaponry plays an important role in the U.S. economy, and the economies of other major arms producers, as it does in the national defense. The national budget always includes military spending, which increases with the potential for military involvement worldwide. In 1993, for instance, the U.S. Congress needed to cut $6 billion from a military budget of $280 billion. It was suggested that almost the entire cost could be cut by eliminating two stealth bombers (at $500 million each) and two Seawolf submarines (at just over $2 billion each). The cuts were opposed on grounds that eliminating those four weapons would result in heavy layoffs and possible bankruptcy of the companies that produced the weapons. A compromise had to be made because the district of a powerful congressman was involved (Roark, 1987).

When U.S. President Dwight Eisenhower gave his farewell address upon leaving office in 1960, he warned the people of the United States to beware of the development of a military-industrial complex. The speech was rather surprising in that Eisenhower had been a military man most of his life, and he related strongly to both military and industrial leaders. The **military-industrial complex** is an unofficial alliance of the military service and the industries that supply the military. They are mutually dependent and help each other in fulfilling their perceived needs. An industrial producer, such as a major aircraft or ship builder or a producer of any other of the incredibly expensive technologies of modern war, is almost sure to agree with the military services that new types of equipment are badly needed. Not only that, but if sophisticated new equipment has been developed, industry will find it easy to convince the Pentagon that it is badly needed. Until the late 1980s, the defense industry's first step in selling military equipment was to create a scare by finding that a far more advanced piece of equipment was possible, and that the Russians might be working on it. The Pentagon would agree. Thus, industry and the military would work hand-in-glove toward a military buildup. Even with little fear of Russia, members of U.S. Congress from districts that produce military hardware may well face defeat in the next election unless they can produce orders for their districts. Jobs are at stake, possibly even plant closings, unless the equipment continues to pour out. Even universities and research institutions that draw research funds from the Pentagon might suffer from a slow-down in defense spending. In fact, Department of Defense funding of university research doubled between 1977 and 1987 (Roark, 1987). These are the types of problems Eisenhower had in mind when he said:

> We must guard against the acquisition of unwarranted influence, whether sought or unsought, by the Military-Industrial Complex. The potential for the disastrous rise of the misplaced power exists and will persist. (Tempest, 1983:3)

The Military-Industrial Complex and Political Leadership

Not only is there a natural harmony between the producers of military equipment and the military establishment, but political leaders are frequently included. Fear of a potential enemy cannot be ignored by heads of state, as is illustrated by a famous conversation between U.S. President Eisenhower and Soviet Premier Khrushchev. Eisenhower commented to Khrushchev on how military leaders always tried to persuade him that more funds were needed.

> Eisenhower: "(If I turned them down), they would reply, 'We have reliable information that the Soviet Union has already allocated funds for their own such program. Therefore, if we don't get the funds we need, we'll fall behind the Soviet Union.' So I gave in. That's how they wring money out of me. They keep grabbing for more and I keep giving it to them. Now tell me, how is it with you?"

> "Yes, it's just the same," said Khrushchev. (Tempest, 1983: 4)

The military-industrial complex has not only influenced political leaders in their decisions, it has played a role in the election of leaders, even when it was doubtful that an increase in weapons' production was needed. Both John F. Kennedy and Ronald Reagan gained support by claiming the United States was falling behind the Soviet Union in the arms race, and vowing to increase military spending in order to catch up. In both cases, the validity of the claim that the United States was behind at all was questionable. In fact, after Reagan was elected, his own Commission on Strategic Forces concluded that the United States was not falling behind (Scheer, 1982: 67–68). Similarly, Kennedy's Secretary of Defense claims that Kennedy was unknowingly given exaggerated data by the Air Force, which desired more missiles (McNamara, 1987). It is generally believed that the position of the United States in military power was frequently made to look weak by military and/or industrial groups with a vested interest in escalating the arms race.

The military-industrial complex could easily become a factor in war, helping to create an arms

Figure 13.3

Despite loud calls for drastic cuts in military expenses, the military budgets of the 1990s will never fall below $250 billion. Is all the money needed and used carefully, or is the expense pushed along by the military-industrial complex of which Eisenhower warned?

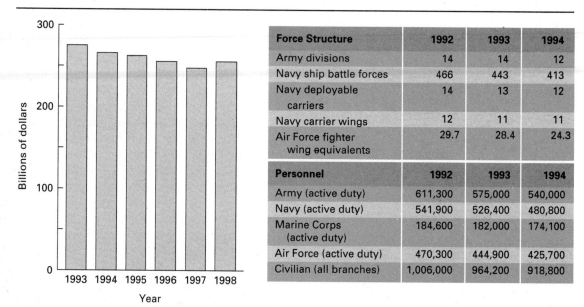

Force Structure	1992	1993	1994
Army divisions	14	14	12
Navy ship battle forces	466	443	413
Navy deployable carriers	14	13	12
Navy carrier wings	12	11	11
Air Force fighter wing equivalents	29.7	28.4	24.3

Personnel	1992	1993	1994
Army (active duty)	611,300	575,000	540,000
Navy (active duty)	541,900	526,400	480,800
Marine Corps (active duty)	184,600	182,000	174,100
Air Force (active duty)	470,300	444,900	425,700
Civilian (all branches)	1,006,000	964,200	918,800

Proposed Pentagon Spending

Source: Washington Post National Weekly Edition, April 4–11, 1993.

race to which a potential enemy would feel obligated to respond by increasing its own military budget. The arms race that eventually found the United States and the Soviet Union facing each other with a total of about 50,000 nuclear bombs could possibly be duplicated in the future.

CHALLENGES TO A SUPERPOWER

Since the collapse of the Soviet Union, the United States has remained the world's only superpower. With no powerful military rivals, one might expect a spectacular drop in defense spending, but the actual decline is only slight. Since modern history has no example of a unipolar world (a world in which the supremacy of one power has long gone unchallenged), it seems reasonable to maintain considerable military spending, although some would call present spending excessive. At present the United States appears to be arming against any possible challenges. Is it trying also to become the world's police force?

Policing the World

Although there had been much opposition to heavy American involvement in world affairs after World War I, most U.S. leaders since World War II have been activists in foreign policy. The United States helped establish the United Nations, and gained United Nations approval in the Korean War and the Gulf War. Just as important, the United States has assumed world leadership in large numbers of other commitments: to NATO, to Israel, to Afghanistan, to Egypt, to Kuwait, and to Saudi Arabia. As mentioned, the United States supported existing regimes in a large number of surrogate wars and used its diplomacy and economic power to promote human rights, and to strengthen the economies of Latin American nations. The United States maintains forces in Germany, Japan, Korea, Kuwait, and Cuba's Guantánamo Bay, to say nothing of farflung naval forces.

Some argue that these commitments have gone far beyond meeting emergencies that threaten U.S. national security. The long struggles in Vietnam and in Central America as well as the years of supplying weapons and funds to Afghanistan are cases in point. For a long time, the United States had appointed itself the world's police force, extending U.S. influence all around the world. Had the United States gone too far?

Paul Kennedy, in *The Rise and Fall of the Great Powers* (1987), does much more than discuss military power at various times in history. He looks into the forces that have undermined the preeminence of great powers even when they win victory after victory. One of the great problems he points out is overextension:

> The United States now runs the risk, so familiar to historians of the rise and fall of previous great powers, of what might roughly be called **imperial overstretch**: that is to say, decision makers in Washington must face the awkward and enduring fact that the sum total of the United States' global interests and obligations is nowadays far larger than the country's power to defend them all simultaneously. (Kennedy, 1987: 515)

Although it is true that the Soviet Union has collapsed as a military power since the above statement, U.S. forces remain vastly extended to all the countries and alliances previously mentioned. Additionally, there are a Mediterranean fleet, a North Atlantic fleet, an East Pacific fleet, a West Pacific fleet, and smaller, but formidable, forces in the Indian Ocean and the Persian Gulf. Is the United States as capable as ever of supporting so many fleets, to say nothing of armies, air commands, and nuclear facilities? Quoting again from Kennedy:

> The fundamental grand strategic dilemma remains: the United States today has roughly the same massive array of military obligations across the globe as it had a quarter-century ago, when its shares of world GNP, manufacturing production, military spending, and armed forces personnel were so much larger than they are now. (Kennedy, 1987: 521)

Such matters as relative financial power and industrial output are certainly as important to world leadership as military power. In these respects the United States has declined relatively from a high point after World War II, when such present-day rivals as Japan and Germany were in ruins. It is also significant that the U.S. national debt is the largest in the world.

A Pragmatic View

In view of the many commitments that could be financially devastating, the future might hold a foreign policy more narrowly pragmatic than that of the past. William G. Hyland (1992) argues that the United States can no longer afford foreign ventures without first considering the economic consequences and assessing whether its allies would support such an action. In the case of Russia, Hyland's pragmatism would call for a wait-and-see policy before becoming too strongly committed to any one leader, even Boris Yeltsin. It is more practical, Hyland says, to expect reverses in Russia than to take a leap of faith and assume all will be well. Judging from Russian history, it seems quite likely that the Russia of the future will be a fairly autocratic state, although it probably will not return to communism. We can expect quarrels between

Figure 13.4
The British and French foreign empires following World War I are examples of what Paul Kennedy calls "imperial overstretch," or commitment to defend and supply far too much territory. One-fifth of the land area of the world was part of the British Empire. Is the United States also in a state of "overstretch"?

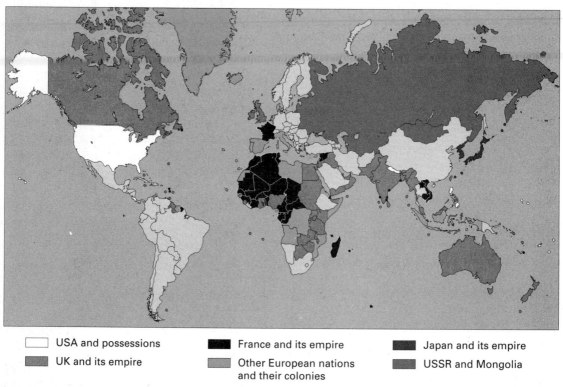

	USA and possessions		France and its empire		Japan and its empire
	UK and its empire		Other European nations and their colonies		USSR and Mongolia

The Colonial World Following World War I: Imperial Overreach?

Source: G. Chaliand and J. P. Rageau, *Strategic Atlas* (New York: Harper Perennial, 1992).

Russia and other parts of what used to be the Soviet Union, but settlement of such quarrels should be left up to Russia or to Europe. Even if Russia becomes a somewhat autocratic state, according to Hyland, it is likely to remain friendly to the United States. He bases this conclusion on the possible threat to Russia from both Europe and Asia.

Aid for a Superpower: Western Europe

Western Europe has been moving toward unity since the founding of the **European Economic Community** (EEC) in 1958. The present Common Market includes Belgium, Denmark, France, Germany, Greece, Ireland, Italy, Luxembourg, Netherlands, Portugal, Spain, and the United Kingdom. These countries have nearly eliminated barriers to trade, cross-border investment, and the right of workers to move from one country to another. There are occasional haggles over farm subsidies, but progress toward unity continues. Germany is becoming the driving force behind an economy that grows rapidly most of the time, despite the occasional recessions. Along with its European partners, Germany has access to a wide European market. It has an economic system similar to that of the

United States, but more supportive of workers' rights and health insurance. The German economy is also one in which industry and government are close partners, which many economists consider a competitive advantage over the United States (Burstein, 1991: 16–23). Germany has gained another advantage by being first to open markets in Eastern Europe, particularly Czechoslovakia, Hungary, and Poland. To all these advantages, Germany adds yet another: very little military expense. Ironically, the United States, although sometimes in a less favorable economic position, continues to maintain armed forces in Germany for the protection of NATO.

Germany's military forces are very limited and, by German law, are prohibited from foreign involvement. Germany since World War II has shown great pride in its economic accomplishments, but has opposed any military role outside Europe. Journalist William Pfaff (1992: 62) speculates that "there may have been a permanent mutation in German political conviction and ambition, toward North European or Scandinavian-style neutralism or noninterventionism, replacing the aggressive nationalism that has marked Germany's modern historical record."

Others still worry about whether Germany will again become ambitious for territories now held by Poland (part of East Prussia and Silesia) that were held by Germany before World War I. A 1990 questionnaire found that 50 percent of French and English respondents and nearly 70 percent of Poles feared a unified Germany (Burstein, 1992:213). The vast majority of Germans, however, including Chancellor Kohl, are content with present boundaries. It is disturbing to find a Neo-Nazi movement in Germany, but at present it is small and includes only what could be called a lunatic fringe. The movement aims to stop immigration and to expel foreigners, who have come from southern Europe and Turkey in search of jobs or more recently as refugees from Yugoslavia. In view of the strong drive for European unity it seems unlikely that the neo-Nazis will gain the upper hand. To a great degree the nations of Western Europe are burying their separate nationalisms in a commonwealth of nations.

Japan and East Asia

In the years after World War II, Japan realized that its economic survival depended on turning out superior products for the world market. Partly under the direction of the Ministry of International Trade and Industry (MITI), Japan turned to a system of quality control in production techniques that is unsurpassed anywhere in the world. Its success was earned through intelligence and hard work, and the United States helped by selling Japan advanced technology (Halberstein, 1989). It was also aided by an economic system in which government and industry worked together more closely than they do in the United States, probably even more so than in Germany. Japan has also concentrated on industries that call for great brain power (Japanese even use the expression Brain Power Index), and preferably little waste of materials.

Japanese trade policies have been criticized in the United States. Rules and regulations have severely limited the kinds of American goods that can enter the Japanese market, and trade negotiations on such matters are difficult.

The more important point is that Japan has become as much of an economic challenge to United States leadership as has Western Europe. It also appears that Japan aims to win strong economic allies in East Asia, especially in Thailand and Indonesia, possibly even China. The Japanese emperor has broken tradition by visiting both Thailand and China, suggesting possible development of a trading block similar to that of Western Europe. The emperor's visit may indicate Japanese concern with the rapid rise of China. Such developments are completely within international law and custom, but point further to the difficulty of maintaining a superpower position in the world. It suggests that the world will be dominated by not one but three power blocks: America, Western Europe, and East Asia. Although the situation should pose no threat to peace, it could endanger the preeminent power of the United States. Threats to peace at present seem to be coming from elsewhere.

THREATS TO WORLD PEACE

Earlier in this chapter, causes of war were discussed. Fortunately, not all of those are threats at present, although such situations could develop. However, some of the threats to world peace spring from the fragmentation of old political orders along ethnic lines. Other problems are that nuclear threats and arms races have not disappeared.

Fragmentation

In discussing the causes of wars, we have already spoken of the breakups of the Soviet Union and of Yugoslavia. Such **fragmentation** has a potential for disaster. The former Soviet republics have managed to separate without much bloodshed, except in the cases of a brief civil war in Georgia and a war between Azerbaijan and Armenia (1991–1993), as well as Chechnya's attempt to break away from Russia in 1994–1995.

The war that erupted in Yugoslavia, however, has been much more bloody and called for United Nations peacekeepers (see Chapter 14). The war was the result of ethnic fragmentation, when former Yugoslavia broke up and all the larger ethnic groups declared independence. As noted, the Serbs demanded ethnic purification of parts of Bosnia that had a sizeable number of Serbs in them. The bloodshed continues while the UN attempts to negotiate cease-fires and peace.

Will the fragmentation process continue through the 1990s and lead to more wars? Already there have been skirmishes in Moldova and in formerly Soviet Georgia. Benjamin Barber (1992) wrote an article on fragmentation entitled "Jihad Versus McWorld." He uses Jihad (an Islamic holy war) as a symbol of the fragmentation of existing countries (Palestine and Yugoslavia, for example);

and he uses the international growth of McDonald's fast-food restaurants as a symbol of how economic growth tends to unite countries. Barber's McWorld concept includes not only fast foods, but a world tied together by technology, communications, commerce, and a need for environmental policies.

Barber's conclusion is that although fragmentation will still exist, cooperation to achieve shared goals will be a stronger force. In countries already economically advanced, people are more interested in material prosperity than in long-ago wars. The trend toward unification in Europe certainly spells out the desire for economic progress, rather than for revenge or territorial expansion. One could hardly find a better example of the trend than the plans for a joint German-French army, to become effective in 1995 and to serve the 12 nations of the Western European Union.

Nuclear Threats

When the cold war came to an end and the former Soviet Union and the Western World were no longer threats to each other, there was a feeling of relief everywhere. The world still had many problems, but it did not face immediate destruction. This continues to be the case, but there are still worries about nuclear weapons and their proliferation.

The United States monopoly on nuclear weapons ended soon after World War II, when France and Great Britain developed such weapons. Such a development did not worry the United States, but the development of Soviet bombs five years later and of Chinese nuclear weapons in 1962 were much more worrisome. However, a **Nuclear NonProliferation Treaty** was signed in 1968, in which the atomic powers promised not to assist any other countries in developing atomic weapons. Some countries without atomic weapons claimed that the treaty was a device for keeping all power in the hands of the United States, France, Great Britain, the Soviet Union, and China. Consequently, several other countries have tried to produce atomic weaponry and thus crash the **nuclear club.**

Proliferation

Despite the NonProliferation Treaty, additional countries have developed atomic weapons. As early as 1983, India is believed to have had 12 to 20 atomic bombs at its disposal, South Africa 20, and Israel between 100 and 200 (Kidron, 1983: 36–37). Since its great governmental changes, South Africa has said that it is destroying its nuclear weapons, but no proof has been forthcoming.

Besides these countries believed to have atomic weapons are several more about which the world is suspicious. Iraq was working on nuclear weapons at the time of the Persian Gulf War. Since then, suspected sites of atomic weapons plants have been destroyed and UN inspections have gone on. There have also been worries for fear Libya or Iran may be working on an atomic bomb.

One of the countries high on the list of suspicions is North Korea, one of the few remaining Communist countries. The United Nations has sent inspectors, but North Korea has restricted the areas they can inspect, a very suspicious action. In October 1994, U.S. President Clinton went to North Korea and worked out an arrangement by which North Korea would agree to inspections, but in return other countries agreed to help build two reactors in North Korea purely for the development of power. Tensions have subsided for the moment, but we never know when another nuclear crisis might develop.

Nuclear proliferation has also occurred in Pakistan. In the spring of 1990, Pakistan and India were on the verge of war over the disputed state of Kashmir. India had massed two hundred thousand troops and threatened invasion. Pakistan, which had been defeated by much larger and more populous India, was determined it would never be defeated again. American intelligence sources concluded that Pakistan had at least six and maybe as many as ten nuclear weapons ready for use, and that the decision had been made to resort to nuclear war rather than

face another defeat (Hersh, 1993). U.S. President Bush sent an envoy, Robert Gates of the CIA, to negotiate a settlement. Gates said that the two countries seemed almost unable to back down from their confrontation. "I was convinced that if a war started it would be nuclear," he said (Hersh, 1993: 58).

Eventually war was avoided. The incident was kept very quiet, partly to avoid further inflaming India and Pakistan, but also, according to Hersh (Hersh:1993: 57), because the Reagan administration had aided Pakistan in getting the bomb. Pakistan had aided the United States against Soviet forces in Afghanistan, and the United States repaid with high-tech materials for the bomb. This obviously ran contrary to agreements in the Nuclear NonProliferation Treaty.

Where Are the Bombs?

The former Soviet Union has agreed with the United States to drastic reductions in numbers of nuclear weapons, and the two countries no longer have their nuclear arsenals aimed at one another. Indications are that intentions are good on both sides. Some of the weapons are not in Russia, but in Kazakhstan, which became nuclear without intent because Soviet bombs were made and stored in what is now its territory. Kazakhstan is cooperating with Russia on disposal of bombs, so there would seem to be no problem. Actually, though, two problems have arisen: (1) Russia is very careless about the storage of bombs and about the count of bombs, and (2) criminal organizations in Russia are so powerful that they may steal and sell fissionable materials or even bombs.

Neither Russia nor the United States checks up on the number of nuclear weapons the other has. Consequently, only guesses can be made. The CIA told Congress in 1992 that it estimated Russia's count of nuclear warheads as 30,000 with a margin of error of 5,000. Russian carelessness with nuclear materials is exemplified by this case: Enriched uranium was stored in a Quonset hut, protected only by a padlock and two Russian militiamen with hunting knives (Hersh, 1994: 78).

Regarding the possibility that nuclear weapons or other nuclear materials may be stolen, Hersh (1994: 68) states, "There is powerful evidence that organized crime in the former Soviet Union has been systematically seeking access to the nuclear stockpiles, with their potential for huge profit." Such reports may be based mainly on rumor, but they are serious enough so that the most important American nonproliferation intelligence unit—the Department of Energy's Z division—is now engaged in an intensive review of the potential nuclear threat from Russian organized crime (Hersh, 1994: 74).

Terrorism

Terrorism is the use of violence or threats of violence to impose one's will upon others. Terrorism can be used by governments against their own people through torture, executions, and other violations of human rights. The type of terrorism we are concerned with here, however, is that of secret groups attempting to force their will upon nations. The Irish Republican Army (IRA) has until recently used acts of terrorism, especially bombings, to force the British to unite Northern Ireland with the Irish Republic.

The Middle East is the region in which acts of terrorism are most common, and a place where terrorism and counterterrorism have long gone on between Arabic nationalists and Israelis. As of the present, the aims of the Middle Eastern terrorists are twofold. First of all, they want to destroy Israel, or at least force the Israelis back into very narrow boundaries. Second, many of them aim at bringing about fundamentalist Moslem states in the Middle East. They strongly oppose such countries as Egypt and Algeria, whose people are mainly Moslem, but whose governments separate church and state. The radical fundamentalists want a return to strict Koranic law.

With these dual aims, it is not surprising that terrorists strike not only at Israel but at moderate political leaders in Arabic states. The previous president of Egypt (Anwar Sadat) was assassinated for making peace with Israel and for opposing Islamic fundamentalism. President Mubarak, who succeeded Sadat, has received many threats on his life. Because the United States is an ally of Israel, it is also a subject of attack by Islamic fundamentalists. This appears to explain the bombing of the World Trade Center in New York in February, 1993. Six people were killed and nearly one thousand injured.

Terrorists bombed the New York World Trade Center in February 1993 in the most deadly attack of its kind in the United States until then. Four men were convicted and sent to prison for life. Later, a more widespread plot to blow up the United Nations building and other targets was discovered. The terrorists and their leader, Sheik Omar Abdel Rahman, stood trial in 1995; they are probably facing life sentences.

Various countries have been suspected of aiding fundamentalist terrorists: Libya, Sudan, Syria, Iraq, and Iran. Another important source of aid is charitable donations from wealthy Arabs (Coll and LeVine, 1993). Charity is often diverted to revolutionary purposes, although that sent to Croatia to help Moslems in Bosnia is definitely charitable.

Saudi Arabia, a conservative kingdom, tries to prevent charitable donations from going to revolutionaries. The largest governmental support of terrorists at present comes from Iran, a country anxious to export its Islamic revolution. In Tehran are the offices of two of the major radical Islamic groups—Hezbollah from Lebanon, and Hamas, in the Gaza strip (Coll and LeVine, 1993). Terrorism supported by Iran can strike at moderate Moslem states as well as at Israel (see Figure 18.5).

The Threat to Peace

Part of the danger of terrorism, of course, is a matter of deaths and injuries from terrorist attacks plus the fear that airplanes will blow up in the sky, as they have, or that buildings, trains, or buses will be bombed, as they have. Another serious problem is that terrorism can interfere with the peace process. At present, the terrorists appear to be frustrated. Yasser Arafat, leader of the Palestine Liberation Organization (PLO), and Prime Minister Yitzhak Rabin of Israel, have shaken hands and tried to make peace. Israel also succeeded in making peace with King Hussein of Jordan. It was probably their fear of peace that led members of Hamas to bomb a bus in Tel Aviv and kill 21 people. Israel wants peace, but it is well known as a country that will strike back hard if its future is threatened. Yasser Arafat, who also wants peace, will be in the difficult position of trying to enforce law in the Gaza Strip and keep down terrorism. If he is unable to do so, it is quite possible that President Rabin will use the provisions of a joint Israeli-PLO Declaration that allows the Israeli army to maintain order in the Gaza strip under emergency circumstances. In such a case, the peace

process in Israel might unwind. The Israelis are hopeful of continuing peace, but fearful of such a need for intervention. They are living between joy and terror. It is quite possible that terrorist attacks will increase for the immediate future in an attempt to keep the peace agreements between Israel and the PLO from holding. On the other hand, if peace continues, the terrorist groups may give up or turn to legitimate political opposition.

The Arms Trade

In 1989 the United States sold $8 billion worth of weapons to the less developed countries. In 1990 it sold $18.5 billion worth of weapons to the LDCs. In 1992 sales increased to $35 billion ("The Arms Bazaar," 1992). The United States accounted for the sale of 50 percent of the weapons supplied to other countries. Most of the sales were to countries of the Middle East, including Saudi Arabia, Egypt, Israel, Kuwait, Bahrain, and the United Arab Emirates. The sales were allegedly for *defensive* weapons, but they included F-15E fighter-bombers and other advanced equipment designed for attack. The official reason for U.S. sales is to maintain good relations with Saudi Arabia and other Arabic nations. At the same time, the United States sells arms to Israel to keep it from being attacked by any one or a combination of its Arabic neighbors. The United States is, in short, maintaining a balance of power in the Middle East, or attempting to, despite the problems associated with such a road to peace.

Other reasons for weapons sales can be found. There are high profits in arms sales. Even more important, most of the countries listed as major buyers of the United States' arms are oil-producing nations. As Daniel Yergin (1990) points out so well, at the present stage of the world's technological development, no major war could be won without access to a vast supply of oil. So even at the risk of offending Israel, an alliance with Saudi Arabia must be maintained.

In looking for reasons for arms sales, remember what was said previously about a military-industrial complex. Many U.S. industries depend heavily on military spending and on military

Figure 13.5

Charitable donations go from wealthy Arabs to help the poor or to help wartorn Bosnia. Much money is diverted to revolutionary and terrorist groups, however, especially in Iran and Sudan. Saudi Arabia fears the revolutionaries and tries to make sure donations go only to charity.

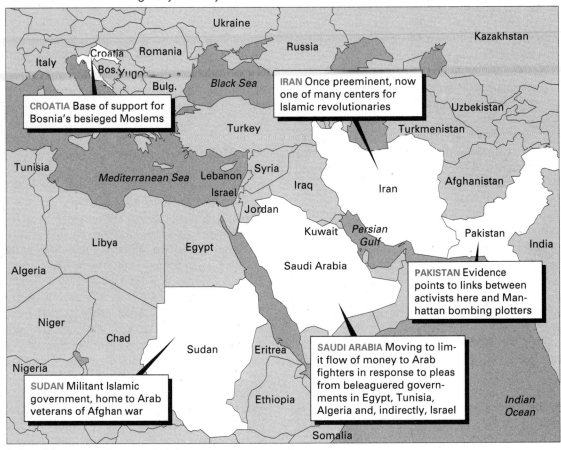

Bases of Support

Source: Washington Post National Weekly Edition, August 16–22, 1993.

sales. Jobs are in the balance, as are profits, military careers, and seats in Congress. What applies to the United States applies also to other countries that supply and sell weapons: Great Britain, France, Germany, Russia, and China. These countries produce most of their own weapons and profit from sales to developing nations, which are kept poor and in debt largely because of their military expenditures.

By no means do all of the weapons sold to LDCs go to those who can afford them, like Saudi Arabia and the Arab Emirates. Egypt makes heavy arms purchases even though its people are desperately poor. In less developed as well as in developed countries, military spending is much higher than spending on education and many times greater than spending on health.

Arms Sales and a Balance of Power

Although there are supposedly legal controls over the sale of weapons, especially high-tech weapons still regarded as secret, there are many violations

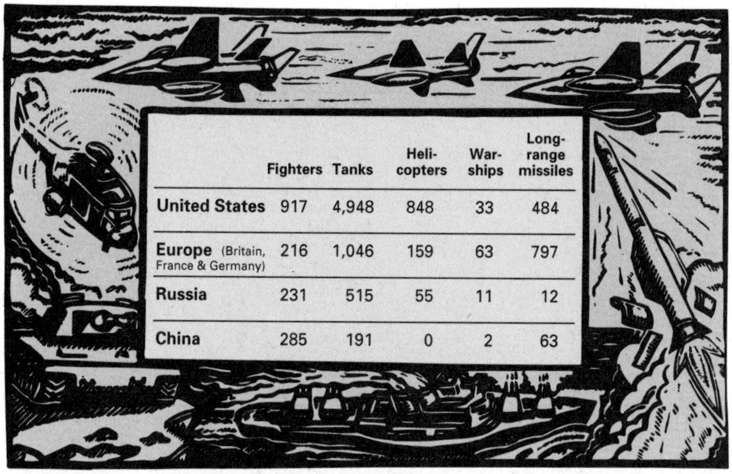

	Fighters	Tanks	Heli-copters	War-ships	Long-range missiles
United States	917	4,948	848	33	484
Europe (Britain, France & Germany)	216	1,046	159	63	797
Russia	231	515	55	11	12
China	285	191	0	2	63

Main Exporters of Military Equipment, 1989–1992

Source: *Wall Street Journal*, Jan. 28, 1994.

Figure 13.6
Arms producers are always eager to sell weapons at large profits, and countries suspicious of their neighbors are eager to buy. The United States is the biggest seller of weapons, and the Middle Eastern countries are the biggest buyers. Each year they buy more than the previous year.

of such regulations. Both Saddam Hussein and Muammar Quaddafi received help from European corporations in developing chemical plants to be used for poison gas. The United States supplied weapons to help Iraq against Iran in the years before its own war with Iraq. This was contrary to the frequently violated international regulations against neutral nations trading with belligerent nations.

At present, Israeli military sources complain that some of the arms technology of the United States delivered to Saudi Arabia "may continue along a circuitous course through Pakistan to Iran" (Kurzman, 1992). Such technology may be providing the Iranians the knowledge to produce nuclear weapons. Pakistan is building ties with Iran because it fears India, and its fear of India leads it to search for new allies. Such developments make India nervous, so it has arranged to buy rocket engines from Russia that would be capable of delivering nuclear explosives. The United States has protested, but to no avail (Reuters, 1992). India is also entering into trade and cultural agreements with Israel, apparently in an attempt to win an ally. Thus, suspicions have led to more sophisticated armaments and a possibility of two opposing alliances pointing their missiles toward each other. In a nightmare

of the future, the two sides could keep increasing their weaponry and their suspicion and fear of each other, increasing the risk of all-out war.

Alliances in the Middle East are unstable and shift rapidly. It may be that in a few years, other agreements between Middle Eastern countries will replace those mentioned above. For the present, however, the situation described illustrates how armaments and fears can feed on each other until, in the less dreadful case, countries impoverish themselves purchasing weapons or, in the worst case, they go to war.

Unpleasant though this discussion of arms races and nuclear weapons has been, remember that not all arms buildups lead to war; the United States and the Soviet Union stopped short of mutual destruction. It was our contention in the first pages of this chapter that war is not an inevitability of human nature. What can be done to improve prospects for peace and human rights? This is the theme of the next chapter.

SUMMARY

The idea that human nature makes wars inevitable is refuted. Many causes of wars are presented: conquest, territorial disputes, irre-

Heavy weapon sales between the United States and Saudi Arabia reflect an ulterior motive on the part of the United States—staying on good terms with the world's largest oil producer. Modern U.S. industry and military defense are impossible without the oil that Saudi Arabia possesses.

dentism, need for land and resources, trade competition, economic depressions, ethnic and religious conflicts, fear, and arms races. Wars between satellite countries of the former USSR and the United States in the period before the collapse of the Soviet Union are explained as surrogate wars.

The dubious role of balance of power in an attempt to preserve peace is presented, as well as the concept of a military-industrial complex.

The United States is characterized as the world's only remaining superpower. Does this mean the United States should police the world, or must the UN and NATO play prominent parts?

Among threats to world peace is the fragmentation of the former Yugoslavia and the former Soviet Union. Conversely, there are pressures that should be working toward closer linkage of the world's nations.

High among threats to world security is an irresponsible arms trade and an increasing number of countries that have nuclear weapons or are developing them.

KEY TERMS

Aggressive instinct An explanation for the frequency of violence and war, accepted by sociobiologists but rejected by sociologists.

Balance of power A situation in which two antagonistic countries or alliances attempt to keep approximately even military strength so each will be afraid to attack.

Ethnic wars Wars caused primarily by antagonisms between two or more ethnic groups, like the war in Yugoslavia in the early 1990s.

European Economic Community (EEC) A trade union of nearly all the countries of Western Europe joined in a common market to reduce or eliminate tariffs.

Fragmentation The breakup of larger countries into small ones, like the former Yugoslavia, Czechoslovakia, and Soviet Union.

"Groupthink" A term coined by Irving Janis for the tendency of people belonging to close-knit groups to think alike, especially in tense situations.

Ideology A strong belief or set of beliefs about how society should be run, such as communism and fascism.

Imperial overstretch Historian Paul Kennedy's term for the tendency of the strongest nations to expand too far, like the United States' commitment of its forces to saving the regime in South Vietnam.

Islamic fundamentalism The belief of many Moslems that their governments should be ruled by the laws of the Koran, not by secular states.

Jihad A holy war on behalf of Islam, such as that advocated by some extremist Palestinians to destroy Israel.

Malleable human nature The view that human nature is changed by socialization, not determined by instinct.

Military-industrial complex The cooperation of the military forces and the industries that supply them to pressure the government into larger and larger appropriations of funds for military spending.

Nuclear club A term for countries that had nuclear weapons before a treaty of 1968 (United States, USSR, France, Great Britain, and People's Republic of China).

Nuclear Nonproliferation Treaty, 1968 A treaty signed by the nuclear powers (United States, USSR, France, Great Britain, and People's Republic of China) promising not to help any other country obtain nuclear military power, and signed by many other countries promising not to develop nuclear weapons.

Sociobiology A study of the biological basis for human and animal social behavior, considered of doubtful value by most sociologists.

Surrogate wars Historian Paul Kennedy's term for wars between minor countries that became part of the fight between the United States and the USSR.

Terrorism The use of violence or the threat of violence to impose one's will on others.

Thirty Years' War A war in Central Europe mainly between Catholics and Protestants, 1618–1648; the most devastating war in European history.

STUDY QUESTIONS

1. Argue the case of whether human nature is naturally so aggressive that war is inevitable.

2. In view of what you studied in previous chapters about the environment, what deadly conflicts might you expect over resources?

3. Have ethnic wars become more likely now than they seemed to be as recently as ten years ago? Why?

4. Explain the term *surrogate wars*. What damage did they do to both sides?

5. What is the meaning of the term *balance of power?* Under what conditions does it seem to preserve peace? Under what conditions can it make war worse than it otherwise would have been?

6. What is Moslem fundamentalism? What seems to be its causes?

7. How do politicians become involved in the military-industrial complex?

8. What can be done to prevent the spread of nuclear weapons to increasing numbers of countries?

9. Argue the case for American intervention in Haiti or other countries in which dictators replace duly elected leaders.

10. There are reasons for thinking modern trade, communications, and exchange of information will link the world's peoples close together. There are also cases in which it looks as though the world is going to fragment into more and smaller countries. Which do you expect to see happen?

chapter 14

HUMAN RIGHTS
AND WORLD
COOPERATION

President Suharto
Presiden RI
Istana Negara
J1. Veteran
Jakarta Pusat
INDONESIA

Dear President Suharto,

I wish to bring to your attention a matter which greatly troubles me. On January 16, 1993, 9-year-old Junyonto was detained on suspicion of stealing a wallet. He was tortured by police in Indramayu, West Java, and then forced to watch and participate in the torture of his parents.

In the police station, Junyonto was beaten and burned with cigarettes until he told police that he had stolen the wallet and given it to his parents. The following day his mother, Dasmen, and his father, Sudarmono, were detained. Dasmen was tortured by the police but still denied knowledge of the wallet. Then the police brought in Junyonto and forced him to beat his mother. She lost consciousness and was rushed to the hospital where she remained in a coma for three days. Junyonto was made to watch while his father was kicked and punched until he collapsed. Sudarmono was taken to the hospital, but was dead on arrival.

A local outcry forced the police to promise that those responsible would be brought to justice. Five police personnel were reported to have been detained and transferred to the Military Police for questioning. However, nothing more was heard after these announcements.

I am aware that torture and ill treatment are prohibited under the Indonesian Criminal Code, the Code of Criminal Procedure, and by various ministerial regulations. It is unfortunate that these laws and regulations have not prevented ill treatment and torture.

I urge your government to conduct a thorough and impartial investigation into the torture of Junyonto and his parents and into the death of his father. I further urge your government to make clear its opposition to the use of torture by ensuring that the perpetrators of this crime are promptly brought to justice before a civilian court.

Sincerely,

This letter was sent by **Amnesty International,** an organization dedicated to promotion of human rights, in November 1994. It relates one of hundreds of cases of human-rights violations reported by human rights organizations. Often, as in this case, they occur under governments that have promised to respect human rights, but that leave such cruelties unpunished. To many governments, the concept of human rights is something to endorse for outward display, but not to act upon in treatment of the people. A true belief in human rights has evolved slowly.

THE EVOLUTION OF HUMAN RIGHTS

The term **human rights** means that all people have certain rights from which they cannot morally or legally be deprived. Many are established by precedent in British law or in the first ten amendments to the Constitution of the United States: freedom of speech and religion, guarantees of a fair trial and of freedom from torture, and many more. These and others are in the Declaration of Human Rights adopted by the United Nations. As the story of Junyonto and his parents makes clear, however, human rights are flagrantly violated.

Human Rights as a Concept

The modern concept of human rights has few roots in history. The ancient Greeks allowed male citizens to vote and granted them trial by jury, but such rights did not extend to women or to slaves. The idea of writing down the laws so that everyone could know them could be thought of as a guarantee against being punished by the mere whim of a policeman or magistrate. Written legal codes go back at least as far as Hammurabi, King of Babylon in the eighteenth century B.C. Rome is also famous for its legal codes, which were stern but consistent. In the days of the Roman Republic, male citizens were allowed to vote, but neither in Rome nor in Greece was such a right extended to women, slaves, or noncitizens.

The discussion of what we now regard as human rights began during the Enlightenment, a philosophical movement of the eighteenth century. Philosophers of the period rejected dogma and tradition and looked for enlightenment through reason. They also believed in humanitarian goals and social progress. John Locke (1632–1704) of England and Jean-Jacques Rousseau (1712–1788) of France both believed in the **social contract**—the idea that governments were started by an agreement in which the ruler was given authority to rule, and in return promised to recognize the rights of the people. Other people of great importance in the development of human rights were Voltaire (1694–1778), a strong advocate of freedom of religion, and Condorcet (1742–1794), who argued that women should have rights equal to those of men.

Human Rights as National Policy

Long before the Enlightenment, England had taken the first steps toward a guarantee of rights. King John was forced to sign the *Magna Carta* in 1215, the earliest European document guaranteeing rights for the people, in this case the right of trial by jury. The right applied to nobles and freemen, but not to serfs, and it was violated by later kings. Nevertheless, it was the beginning policy for human rights in England.

Toward the end of the Enlightenment, a much more revolutionary document was written—the Declaration of Independence. A few years later,

the **Bill of Rights** was ratified by the newly established United States, another landmark in the legislation of rights. In France, the ideas of such writers as Rousseau and Voltaire were incorporated into a document known as the **Declaration of the Rights of Man,** and the ideas of the French and American revolutions began to spread throughout Europe and Latin America.

Human Rights as Mores

Recall that long-established beliefs in rights and wrongs are *mores.* They are ingrained in a people's thinking. If it has been traditional to torture prisoners, the society will see that as the right and proper way to do things. If slavery has always been accepted, people will look upon it as the only way to make the economic system work. The American Bill of Rights did not promise freedom to the slaves; and when the Declaration of Independence said "All men are created equal," it meant only white men, not slaves, and not women.

However, as rights are accepted by the legal system, they gradually come to be looked upon as time-honored mores. It is now seen as morally wrong to torture prisoners, hold slaves, or deny equal opportunities to women, although the latter right is often violated.

HUMAN RIGHTS AS A WORLD ISSUE

As more cultures accept such rights as freedom of speech and religion, fair trial, and freedom from torture, we hope that the human rights agreed upon by the United Nations will become moral norms for all the peoples of the world. Many countries, usually under dictators or military rule, violate the rights of their peoples and try to hide their prisons and summary executions from the world. It is harder to hide tyranny now than in the past, however, with the all-seeing eyes of news cameras everywhere. There are also a number of human-rights organizations that are watching, reporting, and protesting.

The United Nations Declaration of Human Rights

The United Nations Charter makes frequent references to human rights. All members pledge to achieve "universal respect for and observance of human rights and fundamental freedom for all, without distinction to race, sex, language, or religion." However, an important disagreement arose immediately between the Soviet Union and the Western democracies. The Soviet Union maintained that the important rights of the people were economic rights such as the right to a job, to an education, and to free health care. (These rights were granted in the Soviet Union, but because of its low level of productivity, the health care was minimal.) The United States and its allies insisted that the important human rights were freedom of speech, press, religion, and to a fair trial.

A Declaration of Human Rights was drawn up in 1948, including both the Western and Soviet viewpoints. This served as a statement of principle to which all UN members agreed. However, it was not until 1966 that the UN was able to draw up a **covenant** of human rights. The difference between a declaration and a covenant is that the former is a mere statement of principles or goals, whereas a covenant is a promise on the part of members to carry out the provisions. The United States did not sign the Covenant on the grounds that it would interfere with its sovereignty.

Despite their agreement to the UN Covenant of Human Rights, many nations continued to violate its terms. The USSR, for instance, did not grant freedom of speech or press and had hundreds of thousands of political prisoners. Large numbers of dictators in Latin America, Africa, the Middle East, and East Asia completely

ignored the issue of human rights. There were no provisions for the enforcement of the Covenant of Human Rights, so it continued to be violated even by countries that had approved it. In addition to the Charter and the Human Rights Covenant, many nations have participated in declarations and conventions on such subjects as genocide, racial equality, economic and social rights, equality of women, and humane treatment of prisoners. Although the declarations are often violated, they have accomplished the important task of laying down definitions of right and wrong and the meaning of human rights on a global scale. Although frequently violated, documents such as those in Table 14.1 provide standards by which to judge all countries.

TABLE 14.1 U.N. Documents Pertaining to Human Rights	
1945	Charter of the United Nations
1948	Universal Declaration of Human Rights
1948	Convention on the Prevention and Punishment of Genocide.
1959	Declaration of the Rights of the Child
1965	International Convention on the Elimination of All Forms of Racial Discrimination
1966	International Covenant on Economic, Social, and Cultural Rights
1966	International Covenant on Civil and Political Rights
1967	United Nations Declaration on the Elimination of Discrimination Against Women
1975	The Helsinki Accords of Europe and North America (adds to political rights, right to travel, to reunite families, to interethnic marriages)
1975	Declaration on the Protection of All Persons from Torture and Other Cruel, Inhuman, or Degrading Treatment or Punishment
1993	World Conference on Human Rights. Special attention to Women's Rights; Proposed High Commissioner on Human Rights

Source: Adapted from Marvin E. Frankel and Ellen Saideman, 1989, *Out of the Shadows of Night*, New York. Delaconte Press, 1987.

Declarations Versus Realities

Levels of compliance with the UN human-rights documents has varied. Through the 1970s, conditions seemed to be taking a turn for the worse in at least three parts of the world (Meltzer, 1979). First, quite a number of Latin American nations were ruled by very repressive dictators, the worst being Argentina, Chile, Uruguay, Paraguay, and Bolivia. Dictators also held much of Southeast Asia: Indonesia, Malaya, the Philippines and, to some degree, Thailand. Finally, there was the enormous Soviet Union and its allies, who kept thousands of prisoners in Siberian labor camps. In Communist China, too, government was oppressive, prisoners were "reeducated" in harsh institutions, and in some cases used as forced labor for the state, virtual slavery.

Failures in Human Rights

Even dictators and other violators of rights found it advantageous to sign declarations and covenants promising human rights. It improved their images in the world, even though, in attempted secrecy, suppression of speech and press, execution, and torture continued. Such cases were of extreme concern through the mid 1980s. Violations persisted due to several factors including the conflict between the Communist and non-Communist world, as well as traditional mores that did not include human rights. Finally, there was the problem of enforcement—a problem that still exists.

Communism and Anticommunism

In Chapter 12, we noted that the struggle against Communist regimes in many cases took precedent over the war against illicit drugs. Similarly, the anti-Communist struggle was deemed so important that the United States was willing to support cruel and repressive regimes as long as they were anti-Communist. For example,

knowledge of government death squads and government-approved massacres in El Salvador were ignored, and support for the government continued (Danner, 1993). Even during the administration of President Carter, who was greatly concerned about human rights, the United States continued to give foreign aid to gross violators of human rights, including the Philippines, Indonesia and Iran (before the overthrow of the Shah). President Carter eventually cut off aid to Argentina, Uruguay, and Ethiopia in 1977. Aid continued to flow to Iran until the Shah was overthrown in 1979, despite Iran's having the highest execution rate in the world and one of the world's highest torture rates. The fear was that if the Shah were overthrown, Iran might align itself with the Soviet Union—a fear that proved groundless (Meltzer, 1979).

The Soviet Union was one of the greatest violators of human rights, and was nearly impossible to deal with. Long negotiations secured the release of a few famous scientists and writers, but hundreds of thousands of others were held prisoner in Siberia. Fear of further strain on East–West relations preempted attempts to interfere in the affairs of the Soviet Union.

Traditions of Cruelty

In much of the world, human-rights advocates just deal with entrenched custom. We use the word *mores* to refer to human rights but, as we have seen, much older mores have insisted on cruel punishments. Throughout history, witches were burned at the stake and other culprits were flogged, boiled in oil, or broken on the wheel. Such punishments were regarded as right and proper. Peter the Great of Russia (1682–1715) was not by nature a sadist, but when there was suspicion of mutiny in the palace guard, he had all members flogged to death (Massie, 1986). Torture was the traditional way to wring out confessions, even false ones. Much of the world still subscribes to this view.

The Problem of Enforcement

As noted, there were no provisions for enforcement of the Covenant of Human Rights, a weakness frequently found in the United Nations. A little reflection makes it clear why enforcement is difficult. In the first place, it would interfere with **national sovereignty.** Each country wishes to run its internal affairs in its own way and is hesitant to take away such a right from another country. Recall that the United States did not sign the Covenant on Human Rights for this reason. Another problem is that of what to do about violations by a particular country. If the UN should decide to punish the People's Republic of China for its political prisons, what form would the punishment take? An attempt to boycott Chinese goods, for example, would give a trade advantage to countries that break the boycott. Refusing to trade with a country can be effective only if virtually the whole world follows such a policy. In the case of South Africa, enough countries boycotted goods or withdrew investment to be effective, and such policies are credited with bringing apartheid to an end. Enforcement by economic means, then, is possible, but only in extremely rare circumstances.

In a case or two, World Bank policies and United States foreign aid policies have been used to influence nations in the direction of human rights, but this works only for countries in serious need of aid.

Other Barriers to Human Rights

Possibilities for human rights are lessened also by one-party systems, military regimes, and dictatorships, which are common in many of the countries that had colonial status before World War II. This applies to much of Africa. Such regimes, aware of their limited support, have

suppressed the opposition in order to ensure their political survival.

Religious fanaticism provides yet another cause for suppression. If a country comes under intolerant religious rule, as in Iran and Saudi Arabia, nonbelievers are silenced. A government fearing seizure by a fanatical religious movement may become extremely repressive to prevent a religious coup d'état, as in Egypt and Algeria. Fanaticism on one side leads to fanaticism on the other side.

Desire for trade and profit can also lead to the ignoring of human rights. At present, the United States and most other MDCs continue to trade with countries that flagrantly violate human rights.

The fall of the USSR has led to much progress in human rights. Soviet political prisoners were gradually released, Russian Jews were allowed to migrate, the former Communist satellite countries of eastern Europe ousted the Communist leaders, and the Berlin Wall came down. Not all the new regimes were models of democracy, but most of them were an improvement over what had gone before. Fear remained that ethnic strife might increase. By 1991 the human-rights group called Freedom House, produced a map showing more democratic than nondemocratic countries in the world (Mathews, 1991).

Limited Progress

The freeing of the Communist bloc seemed to be the beginning of a "new world order", a term used by former U.S. President Bush. The new world, however, was not entirely new. Although the Communist dictatorships in Europe fell, and so did some of the anti-Communist dictatorships formerly supported by the West, many dictatorships remained, and new ones were born. In fact, Freedom House released a discouraging report just two years after its optimistic report, finding an increase in the number of "not free" nations.

Many former Soviet countries remain nondemocratic: Serbia, Romania, and Bulgaria, for example. Several other countries were listed as more repressive of rights than they had been. Egypt's government felt greater need for strong measures to quiet the Islamic extremists. Some of the other countries listed are Ivory Coast, Tunisia, Bahrain, Oman, and the United Arab Emirates (*Los Angeles Times*, 1993). Elsewhere, the billion or more people of Communist China remain far from free, as do subjects of the brutal regimes of North Korea and Myanmar (Burma). In Angola, one of the longest wars in history continues, with no attention to human rights on either side. Warfare inevitably increases the abuse of human rights.

Additionally, Amnesty International accuses some United States' allies of long records of torture, especially Guatemala and El Salvador. Fear of terrorists has increased the severity of laws and made it increasingly difficult to prosecute police or other officials responsible for the torture of prisoners (*Amnesty International Report*, 1992). Saudi Arabia is a close ally of the United States whose laws violate UN standards of human rights. Its laws are severe, and traditional punishments for crime are cruel. Strict **Sunnite** Islamic law is enforced.

Poverty-stricken Philippine nationals work as servants in Saudi Arabia, but their Christian religion is outlawed. The ruling Sunnite Moslems also consider **Shiites** (the other major Moslem sect) heretics and subject to arrest on religious grounds. Public executions are held, and people have even been executed for "blasphemy," that is, making irreverent statements or cursing. In her book, *Princess* (a biography of an Arabian princess), Sasson speaks of a place in Riyadh that foreigners call "Chop-chop Square." "That is where our criminals lose their heads or their hands on Fridays, our day of religion" (Sasson, 1992:77–78).

We have given examples of countries that violate human rights. We now turn to an attempt to rate countries the world over on their observance of human rights and, in the process, to point out the rights that are violated—in all cases, rights that have been agreed to in UN declarations and/or covenants.

HUMAN RIGHTS RATINGS

Among the literature on human rights is a survey compiled by Charles Humana (1992). In it, he rates 104 countries on their compliance to human rights. He uses 40 criteria of human rights, weighting them so that, for example, routine practice of torture counts against a country much more than a failure to permit trade unions. On this basis, countries are given scores ranging from a theoretical 100 (best) down to 0 (worst). Ranking in the high 90s are Belgium, Czechoslovakia, Denmark, Finland, Hungary, Netherlands, New Zealand, Norway, Sweden, and Switzerland. Other Western industrial nations, such as the United States, Canada, France, and England are rated generally in the low or middle 90s. The lowest ratings go to Myanmar (Burma), China, Iran, Iraq, Sudan, and Vietnam—all with scores below 30.

Table 14.2 shows the best (Finland) and the worst (Iraq) countries for human-rights policies. Finland scores 99 out of a possible 100. Iraq, which ties with Myanmar for the world's worst, scores only 17; Iraq violates 31 of the 40 rights listed.

Among the less developed nations, scores average considerably lower than in Western Europe, the United States, and Canada; two exceptions are Costa Rica and Uruguay, which rank with the United States at 90. Scores of 40 to 60 are common in Africa. Although South Africa was given a score of only 50 in 1991, its standing is much higher now that apartheid has ended and blacks are given the right to vote and hold office.

Human Rights—the Best and Worst

TABLE 14.2

Human Rights Granted	Finland	Iraq
Political, legal equality for women	yes	yes
Social, economic equality for women	yes	yes
Equality for ethnic minorities	yes	no
Independent newspapers	yes	no
Independent book publishing	yes	no
Independent television networks	yes	no
All courts independent of government control	yes	no
Independent trade unions	yes	no
Free from deprivation of nationality	yes	no
Considered innocent until proven guilty	yes	no
Free legal aid when necessary	yes	yes
Free from secret trials	yes	no
Brought up for trial promptly (slight delays in rural courts)	yes	no
Free from search without warrant	yes	no
Free from arbitrary seizure of property	yes	no
Interracial, interreligious, and civil marriage permitted	yes	yes
Sexual equality in marriage, divorce	yes	yes
Free to practice any religion	yes	yes
May use contraceptive pills and devices	yes	yes
Noninterference by state in private affairs	yes	no
Free to travel in own country	yes	no
Free to travel abroad	yes	no
Freedom of assemblage	yes	no
Free to teach ideas	yes	no
May monitor human rights violations	yes	no
Right to publish in ethnic language	yes	yes
Free from forced labor, slavery, child labor	yes	no
Free from killings, "disappearances"	yes	no
Free from torture by state	yes	no
Free from labor conscription	yes	no
Capital punishment abolished	yes	no
Free from flogging, corporal punishment	yes	no
Free from long imprisonment without charges	yes	no
Free from compulsory membership in state political party	yes	no
Free from compulsory religion in school	yes	yes
Free to produce artistic works	yes	yes
Free press	yes	no
Untapped phones, uncensored mail	yes	no
Peaceful political opposition tolerated	yes	no
Multiparty elections, honest	yes	no

SOURCE: C. Humana (1992). *World Human Rights Guide.* (New York: Oxford University Press, 1992).

Human Rights and the Major Powers

Certain of the world's major countries are of special interest regarding human rights. The United States, though a freedom-loving country, ranks slightly below England and France largely because of racial conflict, executions, its support for tyrannical governments in Central America, and its failure to ratify the UN Covenant on Human Rights. Had Humana written after such abuses came to light, he would have probably taken the United States to task for its atomic experiments on human beings in the 1940s through the 1960s. Elderly patients, prisoners, and the mentally retarded were subjects of experiments, often without their knowledge. Subjects were given up to 100 times as much radiation as is considered safe (Watson, 1993). Although less was known then than now about dangers of radiation, the carelessness and lack of concern for subjects were beyond reason.

The United Kingdom is criticized for certain restrictions on information, and for miscarriages of justice in its policies regarding Northern Ireland. France scores 94, but is accused of discrimination against North African Moslems and less than full equality in pay for women.

Although Germany scores as high as any of the major European countries, it is criticized for unequal treatment of women and for not curbing violence against foreigners. Although there are worries about a resurgence of something similar to Nazism, the German government ranked in the high 90s in Humana's 1991 index.

Japan

Japan, scoring 82 on the human-rights index, is well above the world's average, but below Western European standards. The government has argued that "rights are developed within a particular culture and political system" (Peek, 1992), and contends that the United Nations has little to do with human rights. As Peek explained, the policy of limiting rights had the secret purpose of keeping the Liberal Democratic Party in control (ousted in 1993), as well as keeping patriarchal control in families. Duties and position, it was said, are more important than rights. Nevertheless, the United Nations has had an impact on Japan, encouraging women and other minority groups to protest their inequality. The Ainu (the non-Japanese indigenous people of Hokaido) complain of unequal treatment, as do the Burakumin (also called the Eta), a traditional lower caste whose jobs were leather work and burial of the dead (Smythe, 1952).

Russia

The Soviet Union was one of the most repressive countries in the world. Since its collapse, the Russian people have known a short period of freedom to speak their minds, to gain access to news, and even to travel if they have the money. Their human-rights problems may not be over, however. The government, fearing a resurgence of antidemocratic forces, has closed down magazines and newspapers in some cases and has arrested some of the most stubborn opponents of Russian President Yeltsin's regime. Boris Yeltsin may not wish to become a dictator, but it is difficult to protect human rights when governmental control is shaky. Furthermore, when corruption is rampant, police power may be increased in order to curb it, which could be a step toward dictatorship (Remnick, 1993).

A major problem with a new order in Russia was analyzed by a prominent sociologist, Talcott Parsons, many years ago (Parsons, 1951). In his analysis, based largely on Communist Russia, the old order tends to remain even when revolutionary changes are attempted. The problem is twofold: first, the new leaders were socialized in the old order and can't completely change their habits of thought; and second, the people most experienced at running affairs belonged to, and often remain loyal to, the old order. This has become a problem for Boris Yeltsin. In order to keep control, he must depend on military leaders who are interested in military power, not human rights. Two well-known news analysts, Evans and Novak (1993) contend that the army is interested in extending Russian control throughout most of what used to be the Soviet Union.

China

In Humana's analysis, the People's Republic of China ranks fifth among the world's most oppressive nations. There is no freedom of speech or expression, and beatings, electric shocks, and shackles for prisoners are common. Political activists are considered criminals; hundreds of thousands were executed after the 1989 demonstration for freedom at Tiananmin Square. Even home life is monitored by neighborhood watch groups. Amnesty International reports similarly that hundreds of thousands of people were held without charge in Tibet. Amnesty's informants have learned of 1,050 executions in 1991, and believe the number to be much higher (*Amnesty International*, 1992).

Despite reports of oppression in China, U.S. trade policy in both the Bush and Clinton administrations has extended **Most Favored Nation** (MFN)trade status to China. The United States profits greatly from trade with China, and many people think profit outweighs human rights.

A conference of major nations bordering the Pacific Ocean was held in Seattle, Washington, in November 1993. The United States was determined to increase trade with the growing economies of East Asia, including China, Thailand, Malaysia, Singapore, and Indonesia, none of which had good human-rights records. East Asian countries resented having the human-rights issue brought up and took the same position as Japan, that each country, not the United Nations, should be the judge of what rights it gives to its people. Ironically, most had signed the United Nations Covenant of Human Rights. The trade agreements were continued despite the utter lack of progress in human rights. One year later, the president of the United States visited Indonesia again to try to expand trade. Although human-rights criticisms

Chinese political prisoners in a Peking prison, drying cabbage. Despite protests from the UN and threats from the United States to suspend most-favored nation trade rights, China continues to hold thousands of political prisoners and to work them virtually as slaves.

were voiced, no solid commitments were obtained from Indonesia.

INTERNATIONAL ACTION ON HUMAN RIGHTS

The UN has never accepted the policy that human rights are purely internal affairs. Attempts have been made to gain compliance with UN declarations and conventions, especially against torture and genocide and in favor of the rights of women and children. In general, however, the UN has only the power to investigate, report, and recommend, not the power to enforce.

Governmental Organizations of the UN

The United Nations investigates reports of human-rights violations, although mainly in extreme cases. For many years, there were unfavorable reports and attempts to isolate South Africa. Such sanctions are probably part of the reason for a marked change in South Africa. The UN Human Rights Commission has condemned both Turkey and Egypt for torture of prisoners. The same commission has reported on torture and killings by government forces in El Salvador, even though the civil war there is officially over. These reports do not mean that anything drastic will happen, but they give support for reformist elements within El Salvador, or whatever country comes under UN censure. No country likes to have its dirty linen aired in public.

The United Nations also has a High Commissioner on Refugees, whose staff attempts to help people escape from oppression. In the last few years, the commission has helped refugees from Bosnia. A few United Nations members have died in an attempt to rescue people (Louyot, 1993).

Use of Financial Power

Just as human-rights violations are sometimes overlooked because of economic profitability, economic sanctions (punishments) can be used for violations of human rights or for other idealistic reasons. Linked to the UN is the World Bank, which makes loans to many countries. The loans usually depend on the government's effort to put financial matters into order. The World Bank has adopted new policies, however, that reflect a growing interest in human rights. In May 1992, the World Bank refused a loan to Malawi on the grounds that its dictator, Hastings Banda, flagrantly denies human rights to his people. The bank had also taken a similar action against Kenya, citing both human-rights violations and corruption.

Similarly, the United States, which has always been a major supplier of foreign aid, began cutting foreign aid to 35 countries in 1993. Seven of those countries were denied aid on the grounds that they are run by abusive dictatorial regimes. Prominent among those being dropped from foreign aid is Zaire, whose dictator, Mobutu Sese Seki, has cost the United States more than $1 billion over the last ten years, while his regime has grown more abusive and cruel and his people poorer (Associated Press, 1993). As previously discussed, the United States frequently supported anti-Communist dictatorships during the Cold War. With the demise of the Soviet Union, the United States has begun to break ties with some of the countries that do not comply with American democratic ideals.

It must be noted, though, that the United States has not turned to total idealism in foreign aid. Egypt continues to be one of the largest recipients of U.S. aid, despite UN charges of torture. The U.S. government has chosen to support the present regime in Egypt to prevent a takeover by radical Islamic Fundamentalists.

The United Nations and its members have taken other actions over human rights and other issues. The Gulf War against dictator Saddam

Hussein, intervention in Somalia, Cambodia, and other countries will all be discussed in the context of international cooperation. Specialized agencies of the UN also play direct or indirect roles in human rights. The International Labor Organization, the World Health Organization, and the Food and Agriculture Organization have helped promote the right to fair labor practices and freedom from disease and hunger.

Nongovernmental Organizations

Numerous independent organizations try to promote human rights throughout the world. The oldest active organization is the Anti-Slavery International, founded in Great Britain in the early 1800s. Another very old, but still active, human-rights organization is the French Federation for the Rights of Man, founded in 1902, following a long fight to obtain justice for an army officer sent to Devil's Island on a false charge of treason.

Years later, during World War II, an International League was formed to promote human rights; its members participated in drawing up the Charter of the United Nations. Human Rights Watch was founded in the 1940s and investigates and reports on conditions all over the world; it has many subgroups such as Asia Watch, Americas Watch, and Africa Watch. Another major human rights organization is Amnesty International.

In all cases, the watch groups are aided by heroic people in oppressed nations, who gather information, report atrocities, and keep organizations in North America and Europe informed. They risk imprisonment or even death for human rights (Weschler, 1994). Sometimes diplomatic intervention saves them, and often not, but the struggle goes on.

Amnesty International

The major work of Amnesty International is to gain information about people being held in prison (often writers, political leaders, and others whose lives are at risk for nonviolent opposition to the ruling regime) and/or under torture. It attempts to persuade free governments to intervene diplomatically. Another policy—and one in which anyone can participate—is to flood the offending government with letters of protest, letters by the thousands and tens of thousands (e.g., the letter to Suharto at beginning of this chapter). Countries in need of trade or loans do not want to offend the nations they are lobbying; they worry if their prisoners have a lot of support in those nations. Although a few releases are obtained, many prisoners die before the letters are acknowledged.

A Contrast: Governmental and Nongovernmental Organizations

The first international conference on human rights in 20 years was held in Vienna in 1993. Delegates representing the majority of the world's governments were there, as well as delegates representing Amnesty International, Human Rights Watch, Asia Watch, Helsinki Watch, and many other **nongovernmental organizations** (NGOs). The NGOs attempted unsuccessfully to pressure the UN to establish a High Commissioner for Human Rights. When the request was denied, the delegates finally called on the Assembly to at least consider it, a serious letdown. The UN delegates did, however, reject the arguments of a number of Asian nations that human-rights standards cannot be universal, but depend on the customs of each country. Such an argument implies that if torture is customary, it is perfectly all right.

Women's Rights delegates were among those at the Human Rights Conference. They were able to make progress on rights for women. For the first time, a United Nations organization explicitly recognized violence against women as a violation of human rights. Women delegates from many countries attended, including those from LDCs, in some cases able for the first time to report on the abuses they had suffered for being women (Kirshenbaum, 1993).

The governmental delegates were more restrained than those representing NGOs. They were unable to speak out forcefully on issues that might offend delegates. The Dalai Lama was not allowed to speak for fear of upsetting Chinese sensibilities. The NGO delegates provided a meeting hall and a forum for him, a man whose country had been seized and denied its human rights. Both groups showed deep concern over the treatment of children, many of whom fall victim to slavery.

Slavery and the Anti-Slavery International

Few people realize how common slavery is in the world. The London-based Anti-Slavery International (ASI) finds that more people are in slavery now than when the organization was founded in 1839. Its present estimate is that about 200,000,000 people are held in slavery, many of them women and children. Some are chattel slaves, some debt slaves, some sex slaves (Jacobson, 1992).

Chattel slaves are the personal property of their owners and can be bought and sold. **Debt slaves** are people forced to work for a person or company to pay debts, a condition also called *peonage* and declared unconstitutional in the United States. Sex slavery, as described here, is the holding of women against their will for the purpose of prostitution. A very similar practice is that of keeping a woman servant or housekeeper and insisting that she give her sexual favors to men of the household.

Even if chattel slavery exists, it is denied by most countries. But in Mauritania in northwest Africa, it is not. Here the buying and selling of slaves continues. One very elderly slave says freedom came only after "they used me up and

threw me out like trash" (Masland, 1992). That way his owner would not have to feed him in his old age. Chattel slavery also continues in Sudan which is located south of Egypt, where thousands of Dinka tribesmen have been sold by other ethnic groups. In recent years, slavery has been found in Mozambique on the southeast coast of Africa, where people fleeing the war have been abducted and sold into slavery (Jacobson, 1992).

Debt slavery is far more common than chattel slavery. Sometimes the plantations that people work for provide housing and also have a general store, owned by the company, at which workers can buy on credit. Prices are high, so workers fall into such deep debt that they must work for years in virtual slavery but never get out of debt. For example, hungry and impoverished Haitians go to work cutting sugar cane in the Dominican Republic. There they run into debt to the company store. The same system is used in the brick factories of Pakistan and in many carpet factories of India, Pakistan, and Bangladesh. The same system was once common in agriculture in the United States and, despite its being outlawed, is still occasionally found.

An alternative to debt slavery for some is to sell children into slavery. In Thailand, thousands of children are sold by their families to work in the sweatshops of Bangkok or in brothels (Jacobson, 1992). In India, similar conditions exist in carpet factories.

Sex slavery takes on many forms. In some cases, parents sell daughters into prostitution or enforced marriage, or for the sex tourism of Thailand and the Philippines. Boys are also sold as sex objects. The sale of women and girls into prostitution or forced marriage occurs throughout Asia, Africa, and the Middle East. The ASI has also documented cases of poor women sent to the United States or Europe as "mail-order brides," actually to be used as prostitutes (Jacobson, 1992).

INTERNATIONAL COOPERATION

We have learned of international conventions and covenants that set rules about human rights, but also of nations that break such agreements. We pointed out that a small degree of control can be exerted if the World Bank refuses loans to flagrant violators of human rights, or if the United States refuses foreign aid to such countries. Public opinion has a degree of force in many countries, but for dictators who owe their survival to terrorizing their own people (Iraq's Saddam Hussein or Zaire's Mobutu Sese Seki, for example), world opinion is meaningless. As everyone knows, force was used effectively against Hussein in Iraq, but that was quite unusual. Why is it so difficult for the world's leading powers to bring outlaw nations into line? What prevents law among nations from being forceful?

Children can inherit the debts of their parents and be forced to work alongside them in debt slavery. This Pakistani child will spend his life in fields of mud, making bricks.

National Sovereignty

One of the basic obstacles to gaining compliance with international agreements is the concept of national sovereignty. A sovereign nation is one that has the right to make all its own decisions without consulting a higher authority. This concept, along with nationalism (the feeling that nations are the ultimate object of loyalty and power), arose in the Western world only during modern history. In much earlier times, the Roman Empire had united much of Europe. After the fall of the Roman Empire, the prestige of the Vatican grew until the medieval popes were able to exert a modicum of authority and reduce the level of fighting that had erupted between city-states and bands of knights. Wars went on, but usually between small territories, or as crusades to gain the Holy Land. Papal authority, always fragile, was devastated by the Protestant Reformation and, a century later, by the Thirty Years' War (1618–1648) between Catholics and Protestants. Nation-states, of which France, England, and Spain were the first to emerge, became a law unto themselves. This was especially apparent in England where Henry VIII had defied the pope and made himself the head of the Church of England. The idea of the sovereignty of nation-states continues to this day, despite attempts at universal law.

International Law

If nations are sovereign, meaning laws unto themselves, how can there be international law? Usually the word *law* implies enforcement; but it is extremely difficult to force laws on and enforce laws in nations that define themselves as sovereign. Nevertheless, the term **international law** has been used at least since the end of the Thirty Years' War. At that time, Grotius, known as the father of international law, wrote *On the Law of War and Peace*, in an attempt to end some of the savagery of war (Hartman, 1967). International law, according to Grotius, called for such agreements among nations as treating diplomats with respect, maintaining trade relations, humane treatment of prisoners of war, and not killing civilians in times of war. These principles are all recognized as part of international law, but are often violated. There have also been various attempts to outlaw warfare, but they have been scorned by nations determined on aggression.

The Concert of Europe

Since international law falls far short of what would be necessary to end war in the world, other attempts have been made to establish order in international affairs. A Congress of Vienna was called in 1815 after the fall of Napoleon, with Austria, Russia, Prussia, and Great Britain attending. The former three formed the **Holy Alliance**, with the announced purpose of keeping peace in Europe and making sure there were no more revolutions. Every attempt was made to return Europe to the old order that existed before revolutions in the United States and France. The term **Concert of Europe** was used to describe the era of peace and monarchical rule.

In 1848 there was another revolution in France, as well as several other revolutions in Europe. The Holy Alliance was at an end; but a type of Concert of Europe continued in the form of meetings of the great powers to work out problems. Chancellor Bismarck (1805–1898) of Germany had made war on France in 1870, but nevertheless considered himself a peacemaker. He held conferences in Berlin to work out compromises between Austria and Russia, who were rivals for control of the Balkans, and between Britain and France, who were expanding their empires into Africa.

Bismarck was sure he had worked out a system whereby anything like a world war could be avoided; but a realignment came about as France and Britain both became suspicious of Germany. Rivalries and fears mounted. Each side felt threatened by the other and, as usual, there was no real authority outside the national states involved. The Concert of Europe had broken down. An Austrian archduke was assassinated in Sarajevo in 1914 and World War I was under way.

The League of Nations

Following World War I, a more ambitious attempt was made to ensure international cooperation and prevent further wars, The League of Nations. Although the League was proposed by U.S. President Wilson, the United States did not join, which cast a cloud over the League from the beginning. The League proved incapable of reigning in countries determined on aggression. It was powerless to stop Japan from invading Manchuria (1931) and Italy from seizing Ethiopia (1936). Hitler, seeing the successes of Japan and Italy, remilitarized the Rhineland contrary to the terms of the Treaty of Versailles, annexed Austria and Czechoslovakia, then invaded Poland, causing England to declare war. Although the League had provided a forum for hearing international disputes and did well at investigating the acts of aggressors, its failures were more conspicuous than its successes. The League was abandoned at the end of World War II, replaced by the United Nations.

THE UNITED NATIONS

Among the agreements made by the winning powers in World War II was a plan calling for a United Nations. It was hoped that the UN would be a stronger organization than the League of Nations had been. A charter for the United Nations was drawn up in 1945, stating its purpose of preserving peace and freedom, and outlining its structure and procedures. Like the League, the United Nations is built around six main parts (called organs). The most important of them are the Security Council, the General Assembly, and the Secretariat. A fourth organ is the Economic and Social Council (ECOSOC), which hears reports from member nations on economic and social problems. An organ of declining importance is the Trusteeship Council, whose duty it was to supervise territories (called trusteeships) that were placed under supervision of one of the major countries after World War II. It was understood that they would eventually become independent. Palau Island in the South Pacific, administered by the United States, was the last trusteeship; it became independent in 1994. Rwanda, so prominent in the news for massacres occurring there, was a Belgian trusteeship until 1962, when it was granted independence.

Courts and Tribunals

The remaining organ of the United Nations is the **World Court,** which was actually established in 1899 and later became part of the League of Nations, then of the United Nations. The World Court (officially The International Court of Justice) meets in The Hague (Netherlands), and hears disputes between and among nations that ask for its services. For example, the United States and Canada have submitted arguments about fishing rights in the Gulf of Maine (1984). Both countries agreed to abide by the decisions,

as is usually the case. The International Court has no enforcement power.

The United Nations also established a **War Crimes Tribunal** in Nuremburg following World War II that tried many of the German leaders for crimes against humanity, especially for genocide of the Jews and Gypsies. The cases of genocide, torture, and other crimes against humanity in the former Yugoslavia and in Rwanda are causing the UN to take another strong stand against violations of human rights. The Security Council has established an international tribunal to try people accused of genocide in Rwanda (Albright, 1994) and another court, at the Hague, to try cases of torture and genocide in the former Yugoslavia.

Besides the major organs mentioned above, there are a large number of specialized agencies, some of which we will examine next. After that, we will analyze the three most important organs: Security Council, General Assembly, and Secretariat.

Specialized Agencies

The specialized agencies show that a very large amount of international cooperation does, indeed, take place. The oldest of these agencies, the *United Postal Union,* is much older than the UN, and was created to facilitate delivery of mail to all countries, which is an important service usually taken for granted. The list of specialized agencies is very long and growing, but we mention eight to give some idea of the amount of international cooperation that takes place:

1. The *Food and Agriculture Organization (FAO)* tries to increase levels of nutrition in the world by improving farms, forests, and fisheries, dispersing information about pests, overuse of land, and other food problems.

2. The *World Health Organization (WHO)* fights widespread diseases such as malaria, tuberculosis, cholera, and AIDS. It aims at immunization of all children against childhood diseases and cholera. It

declared smallpox eradicated in 1979 and aims to eradicate polio by 2000 (U.S. Department of State, 1992). It also works to develop vaccines against such diseases as malaria and schistosomiasis.

3. The *International Labor Organization (ILO)* attempts to improve working conditions, occupational safety, and provide information regarding employment.

4. The *International Atomic Energy Agency (IAEA)* promotes peaceful applications of atomic energy and discourages its use for military purposes. It also promotes use of safety measures in atomic energy plants.

5. The *UN Environmental Program (UNEP)* assists developing countries to implement environmentally sound policies. It tries to prevent contamination of air and international waterways, and helps analyze climate change, especially the so-called greenhouse effect.

6. The *UN Children's Fund (UNICEF)* provides assistance to mothers and children in developing countries. It tries to establish community-based health facilities funded mainly through private contributions.

7. The *International Maritime Organization (IMO)* was established to promote international cooperation in shipping, especially to promote safety at sea. The IMO has also drawn up an international convention on oil pollution preparedness.

8. *The UN Educational, Scientific, and Cultural Organization (UNESCO)* promotes education and science and exchange of cultural ideas and viewpoints. The United States dropped out of UNESCO because of what it regarded as an anti-Western bias. Most major nations belong, and its bias may decline now that there is no Soviet Union to influence it.

These organizations give some idea of the causes the United Nations promotes. They aim to make the world more cooperative and agreeable, but the primary purpose of the UN is to preserve world peace and human rights. The Preamble to the United Nations Charter begins, "We the Peoples of the United Nations determined to save succeeding generations from the scourge of war, which twice in our lifetime has brought untold sorrow to mankind . . ." Next, the Charter lists human rights, justice, and social progress, then provides organizational rules of procedure.

As an organization to preserve peace, the United Nations at first appeared to have been stillborn. The only way to get the major powers to agree to such an organization was to give them special privileges, which are provided in the organ known as the Security Council.

The Security Council

The UN **Security Council** has primary responsibility for maintaining world peace, and permanent seats on the Council were given to the winners in World War II, the **Big Five**: the United States, the Soviet Union, Great Britain, France, and China. Each of these countries has the power to veto important measures passed by the Security Council. Hence, for 40 years or more the Security Council was deadlocked—the Soviet Union was able to veto any resolution contrary to its interests or the interests of its allies. The same veto power was given to the United States, Great Britain, France, and China (which in those days was the government of Taiwan, not the People's Republic of China). Because their interests were similar, they seldom had occasion to use the veto. Although there are ten impermanent members of the Security Council to represent the rest of the world, their power can be vitiated by the Big Five.

Consequently, the UN has been able to mediate between India and Pakistan, censure South Africa for racism, pacify Cyprus, and attempt to bring order in Cambodia. But when the United

The United Nations, just after a vote to oust Iraq. Although the UN has often found it difficult to take drastic action, it was able to agree to the Persian Gulf War against Iraq.

States and the Soviet Union were confrontational, it could not stop Soviet troops from crushing uprisings in Hungary and Czechoslovakia, or stop U.S. support for an oppressive regime in El Salvador, or stop the superpowers from atomic testing or atomic stockpiling.

The present situation is more encouraging, as illustrated by Security Council's action in Iraq. Not only did it approve the Gulf War, but it subsequently imposed an embargo on Iraq. No oil can be exported from Iraq until its government agrees to all terms laid down by the UN: no aggression against Kuwait; no atomic or chemical weapons; no attacks against Kurds or Shiites; and acceptance of UN inspectors to make sure all terms are honored. Because of severe need in Iraq, the UN may allow it to sell enough oil to earn income for food and medicine, but no more. In this case, the UN is resolute, and it appears that Iraq will eventually have to conform (Goshko, 1994).

The General Assembly

The most democratic of the major organs of the UN is the **General Assembly.** All members have a seat in the General Assembly, and each country has one vote. India, now approaching a population of one billion, has the same voice as San Marino, which has 23,000 people. Despite this disproportionate representation, the General Assembly provides a forum for the world, especially for the less developed countries that have no voice elsewhere.

Surprisingly, the General Assembly has assumed powers not written into the Charter. In 1950, when North Korea (a Communist state) invaded South Korea, the General Assembly, at the suggestion of U.S. President Truman's Secretary of State, Dean Acheson, adopted a **Uniting for Peace Resolution.** The resolution stated that insofar as the Security Council was unable to act to maintain peace, the General Assembly would call upon member nations to contribute forces for the purpose. Consequently, a defensive war was launched against North Korea in the name of the United Nations. The Russian delegates had walked out of the Security Council, making it possible for the Council to turn the matter over to the General Assembly. The Soviet Union never again walked out.

There were no other cases similar to the Korean War while the Soviet Union remained intact and in opposition to the United States and

Secretary-General Boutros-Ghali (center) is a man of strong opinions who would like to see more peace-enforcement power in the hands of the UN. However, he has at his disposal only the troops that member nations volunteer.

its allies. The Vietnam War did not become a United Nations operation, and the Gulf War against Iraq came after the fall of the Soviet Union. In other ways, however, the General Assembly continued to show inventiveness, promoting conferences on environmental problems, world hunger, refugees, human rights, and women's rights.

The Secretariat

The administrative staff of the United Nations is the **Secretariat,** the chief of which is the Secretary-General. Under the secretary-generalship of the Peruvian diplomat, Perez de Cuellar, and under the leadership of the Egyptian Boutros Boutros-Ghali, the duties of the office have increased. Many decisions have had to be made about intervention in one place or another, to prevent starvation in Somalia, to try to get goods and supplies to the besieged people of Bosnia, to try to end civil wars in Angola and Mozambique, and to prevent another "killing fields" in Cambodia. (Cambodia became known as the "killing fields" in 1975 when the Khmer Rouge, a fanatical Communist party, seized control and executed an estimated 1,000,000 people.)

Secretary-General Boutros-Ghali is a controversial figure of strong opinions and of proven ability. He helped bring about a peace treaty between Egypt and Israel—a treaty that has lasted. In the UN, he is an interventionist, who would like the UN to play a stronger role in Bosnia but, of course, he can only do what the Security Council approves and supports with military troops. He is highly regarded in Egypt, even though he belongs to a minority religion, Coptic Christian, in an overwhelmingly Moslem land (Preston, 1994). On the negative side, he is often seen as hard to reason with once he has made up his mind.

Peacekeeping

The Secretary-General has been overwhelmed with civil wars and other problems. Peacekeepers for the UN find themselves thrust into civil wars into which none of the great powers would dare venture alone. It is hard to get the great powers to bear the cost of such operations or to give clear guidance as to what should be done. Military troops can be raised only from countries willing to send them, and many countries are uneasy about turning their troops over to the United

Figure 14.1

Most people do not realize how much work the United Nations does in terms of peacekeeping around the world.

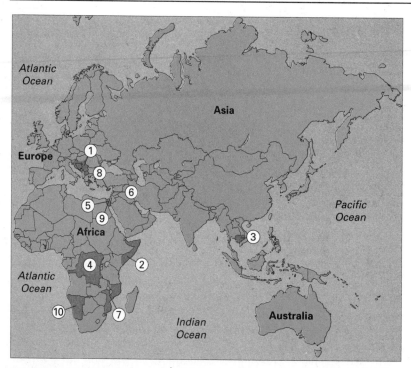

Largest U.N. Peacekeeping Operations

	Area	Force size	Fatalities	Dates	Result
①	Former Yugoslav Federation	30,500	77	March 1992 to present	Unresolved
②	Somalia	22,300	100	May 1993 to present	Unresolved
③	Cambodia	22,000	55	March 1992 to Sept. 1993	Elections
④	Belgian Congo (now Zaire)	19,800	234	July 1960 to June 1964	Secession put down
⑤	Sinai Desert (between Eqyptian and Israeli forces)	7,000	52	Oct. 1973 to July 1979	Peace treaty
⑥	Lebanon	6,900 max. strength (now 5,200)	195	March 1978 to present	Still keeping peace after 16 years
⑦	Mozambique	6,800	10	Dec. 1992 to present	Heading towards elections
⑧	Cyprus	6,400 max. strength (now 1,200)	163	March 1964 to present	Still keeping peace after 30 years
⑨	Sinai Desert (between Eqyptian and Israeli forces)	6,100	90	Nov. 1956 to June 1967	Six-day War followed their removal
⑩	Namibia	4,400	6	April 1989 to March 1990	Elections

Source: Los Angeles Times, May 3, 1994: H1.

Nations alone. Conversely, though, the major powers find it convenient to turn world problems over to the United Nations, sometimes making the UN a whipping boy for problems no one can solve. If one country alone intervenes, it is sure to be accused of aggression or trying to exert power over the rest of the world. Several countries have been particularly cooperative in sending troops for peacekeeping, Canada leading the list.

The Secretariat has other problems. It is accused of being a vast, expensive, and rigid bureaucracy (Branigan, 1993). Its inefficiency has slowed its refugee program so badly that many refugees go hungry unnecessarily. Also, inefficiency makes peacekeeping operations more costly than necessary. Annual reports, once started, are said to go on forever and to grow through the years, resulting in a paper avalanche. Even Boutros-Ghali is critical of much of the staff, saying about half the UN employees do no work whatever.

Expanding UN Powers

The decrease in tensions between the former Soviet Union and the Western world has made it possible for the UN to become much more active than in the past. However, if it is to be the world's guardian of peace, more powers are needed, as seen not only by the Secretary-General, but by many others as well. Michael Renner, speaking for World Watch (Renner, 1993), outlines important necessary changes: (1) the United Nations to date has been a **peacekeeper,** but it needs to also be a **peacemaker;** (2) the UN must be given much more responsibility regarding arms races and the proliferation of nuclear weapons; (3) the distribution of power within the UN must be changed to become equitable. Let us pursue each of these suggestions.

Peacemaking Versus Peacekeeping

In most cases in which the United Nations has intervened, it has sent peacekeeping forces. In Cambodia, for example, the conflicting forces made a peace agreement first, then UN troops came in to see that the terms were kept. Unless the situation in Cambodia takes a turn for the worse, it can be considered a success. As of 1995, the situation continued to look hopeful. In Bosnia, on the other hand, there has been no meaningful truce as of the time of this writing. Consequently, UN forces are limited to giving medical aid and trying to get food to the hungry, not to keeping a peace that does not exist. More than 70 "peacekeepers" have been killed.

In Somalia, however, the UN intervened in an attempt to make peace. It was decided by both the United States and the UN that at least one leading Somali warlord, Mohammed Aidid, should be disarmed. To do so meant making peace rather than just maintaining it. But when U.S. soldiers were killed in an ambush, demands for disengagement from Somalia became overwhelming, and U.S. troops were withdrawn. The UN was left in control of the situation, but was ill prepared and lacked sufficient troops (Richberg, 1993). The details are complicated, but the conclusion is obvious: The United Nations cannot go in forcibly to stop wars, even small wars, unless it has a dependable supply of troops at its command.

The suggestion by World Watch (Renner, 1993) is to adopt new rules that include a well-trained force. Such a force would have to be made up of participants from several countries, all trained together and used to working together. Otherwise, internal frictions can arise. With such a force, rules should be firm enough to make intervention mandatory in many situations. For example, if intervention had been immediate and forceful in Bosnia, war could have been stopped before it escalated to the point it has now reached. Even the bloody massacre in Rwanda might have been prevented by quick action by the United Nations if it had a force at its disposal for immediate action.

Such a change in rules might not meet overwhelming opposition. By 1994 the UN was

Toward A Solution

Focus on Canada

Canadian Peacekeepers

Certain countries have been very generous in providing troops, the so-called Blue Helmets, for the purpose of supervising truces between warring countries or factions. Foremost among such countries is Canada, whose troops have participated in all the peacekeeping missions of the UN. Other countries that have participated in a large number of such missions include Bangladesh, Malaysia, Poland, Sweden, Norway, Italy, Argentina, France and the United Kingdom (Meisler, 1994).

Canadian troops have served in Palestine, Korea, Cyprus, Egypt, India, Pakistan, New Guinea, Zaire, Yemen, Lebanon, Nigeria, West Irian (Indonesia), Cambodia, Iran, Iraq, and Kuwait. In Kuwait and Iraq, Canadian forces were engaged in a war, not just a peacekeeping operation.

Although very supportive of UN causes, Canada steered clear of engagements in "surrogate wars." In the case of the Vietnam War, which was not a UN operation, Canada was in strong disagreement with the United States and did not participate, although several thousand Canadians volunteered for the U.S. armed forces.

Although Canada has taken part in the largest number of peacekeeping operations, a few other countries sent more troops in total numbers. All of them are countries with much larger populations than Canada. As of 1994, France had the largest number of troops committed (6,600), followed by India (5,890), Pakistan (5,690), Bangladesh (4,412), and the United Kingdom (3,233). Canada's 2,312 troops represent as many in proportion to her population as France and the United Kingdom are supplying, and vastly more than the other three countries. In contrast, the United States has only 714 men engaged in peacekeeping operations. The United States was the biggest contributor to the Gulf War and, years ago, to the Korean War. Nevertheless, there is a certain amount of resentment over the very thin contribution of the United

States, although it bears the largest share of financial costs (Meisler, 1994:H5).

Peacekeeping has never been easy. In theory, troops are involved in cases in which both participants have asked for peace, but in Bosnia that is not the case. Eight Canadian soldiers have been killed and 80 wounded, mainly in attempts to get food and medical supplies to suffering civilian populations. (Thompson, 1994:114).

When we ask why Canada has been willing to make so many contributions to United Nations causes, one answer is that Canada sees clearly the need for collective security and for stopping small wars before they become big ones. As one of the founding members of the UN, Canada has generally regarded prevention as the best means of bringing a degree of order to the world (Thompson, 1994:113). The idea of United Nations peacekeeping as a key element of modern defense policy has many American supporters as well. Reports from the U.S. Naval Academy, Johns Hopkins School of Advanced International Studies, and Columbia University push the idea of international peacekeeping because they see no alternative (Meisler, 1994:H1). As Secretary General Boutros Boutros-Ghali has said, "Public opinion in the United States is not eager for that country to play the role of world policeman. The United Nations is there to do that job, and there is a consensus that despite all the difficulties. . . the only forum existing today to play this role is the United Nations" (Meisler, 1994).

It may well be that the future safety of the world will depend more on countries that play important roles in peacekeeping than on major powers or even superpowers.

Sources: S. Meisler, "Keeping the Peace," *Los Angeles Times*, May 3, 1994:A5–6; W. C. Thompson, *Canada 1994* (Harpers Ferry, W.V.: Stryker-Port Publications, 1994); J. Holmes, "Canada and the United Nations," *Canada Today/Canada D'Aujourd'hui*, 2 C1 1994:1–10.

Warlord Aidid haranguing a crowd in Mogadishu, Somalia. A UN attempt at peace-making failed, partly because the U.S. decided to withdraw its forces, but partly because Somalia was ruled by clans and warlords rather than a central government.

discussing the idea of a standing peacekeeping force. French General Gambiez leads a campaign for such a force. Action would be much faster if the troops could be trained together. According to Gambiez, as of April 1994, France and 17 other countries had agreed to provide peacekeeping forces on a permanent basis (Meisler, 1994).

Weapons Control

The world has spent $30 trillion on weapons since World War II. The arming continues, and the United States is the major supplier. In fact, the United States supplies more weapons than Russia, France, Britain, and Germany combined (Copeland, 1993). Recall that among the specialized agencies of the United Nations is the International Atomic Energy Agency, which attempts to limit nuclear technology to peaceful uses. The UN has attempted inspections in many places, the most recent being North Korea. As was true earlier in Iraq, the government long appeared to be playing nuclear hide-and-seek, limiting the areas in which inspection is permitted in return for trade benefits and technical assistance. Obviously, much stronger policies are

needed. After the death of its long-time dictator, Kim Il Sung, North Korea finally agreed, in the summer of 1994, to full inspection.

Other agreements on nuclear weapons have been made. The United States, Great Britain, and Russia have agreed to cease testing for the time being. President Kravchuck of Ukraine, has promised to destroy all nuclear weapons (the third largest stockpile in the world). Only the People's Republic of China and France have tested nuclear weapons as recently as 1995. China, however, has recently become more interested in trade and prosperity than ever before. It might be induced to stop testing if it would otherwise face trade restrictions. France antagonized much of the world with nuclear tests in the South Pacific in the late summer of 1995. There were protests from Greenpeace and also demonstrations in France against government policies. Because France has the veto power, it cannot be censured by the UN. It is quite possible, though, that there will be a political change in France.

We must not look only at China and France in connection with nuclear noncompliance. A number of countries have built or are attempting to build nuclear weapons (discussed in Chapter 13).

Although the UN has taken stands against nuclear and chemical weapons, it has not taken a strong stand regarding more conventional weapons, except land mines. At present the UN is involved in the costly attempt to eradicate millions of land mines in Cambodia. Copeland (1993) reports an estimated 85 million land mines in countries that have fought in recent years. Meantime, the accuracy and deadliness of missiles increase, and missile stockpiling becomes more widespread. John Galtung, Professor of Peace Studies in Stockholm, believes we have far more to fear from missiles than from nuclear weapons. Nuclear weapons have the same problem as poison gas: They are almost as dangerous to the sender as to the target, because they leave radioactivity in the air, in water currents, and in the food chain, and may possibly cause a nuclear winter (Galtung, 1992). The United States, he says, is willing to forego nuclear weapons, while ordering up more than 8,000 cruise missiles. Galtung (1992) continues:

> From the merchant's point of view, these are the weapons of the future. Rockets are now being sold in arms bazaars in Miami. . . . There will be more willing buyers for these weapons than sellers. There is no alternative to creative conflict resolution as long as disarmament only clears space for even worse arms, and arms embargoes only stimulate local production. (p.52)

In Galtung's opinion, creative conflict resolution should be a task for the United Nations. Renner (1993) argues that the UN should also have the power to inspect for such weapons, not just for nuclear weapons.

Organizational Changes

Although the United Nations has been able to function to some degree despite the veto power, the veto has often placed the Security Council in stalemate. Another problem is that less influential countries resent the Security Council as a device for keeping the real power in the hands of the Big Five: the United States, Russia, Britain, France, and China. At present, Russia does not use its veto power, and China has often abstained rather than cast a veto. Nevertheless, the possibility of deadlock remains. Renner suggests that the great powers may eventually compromise somehow on the veto power for the sake of saving the UN, which they need. "Even militarily powerful states," he contends, "seek the mantle of legitimacy that the UN confers" (Renner, 1993:58).

The other difficult organizational problem is that of recognizing change in the world's power structure. Why should the present Big Five exclude other highly productive and populous countries such as Germany, Japan, India, Italy, or Brazil? It would be rash to extend veto power to them, but they could be made permanent members of the Security Council.

Probably, changes will be made in the United Nations in the future, and its functions will increase. As we have seen, the UN is called upon more and more often when international problems arise. However, it has had a variable record in solving problems. Are there ways to extend international cooperation except through the UN?

ALTERNATIVES IN INTERNATIONAL COOPERATION

We have mentioned attempts to bring international order—the buildup of the concept of international law, the Concert of Europe, and defensive alliances. All these are part of traditional diplomacy, which does not depend on a United Nations. Such types of diplomacy are still at our disposal and are used. Direct diplomacy is in progress between the British and the Irish Republican Army. Much direct diplomacy brought together an international alliance against Iraq in the Persian Gulf War, even though United Nations backing was obtained; and Israel and the Palestine Liberation Organization negotiated a settlement after 40 years of fighting. Then why not rely on United States leadership, NATO, various alliances, and direct diplomacy?

The United States as Global Cop

Margaret Thatcher (1993), British prime minister from 1979 till 1990, said:

> The UN has its uses. People talk there, and they will help to keep the peace, but when you have an aggressor, it's the leadership of America and other like-minded nations who know that, unless the situation is dealt with, it will get much worse (p.12).

It is quite true that the real leadership in the Korean War and in the Persian Gulf War came from the United States. In the first case, the United States saw the conquest of South Korea by Communist North Korea as an intolerable boost to its enemies. In the Iraqi invasion of Kuwait, the United States saw a threat to its oil supply as equally intolerable. Freedom and democracy figured heavily in the speechmaking, but Kuwait was no more a democracy than was Iraq. Oil was what mattered, although it must be admitted that the dictator of Iraq was more vicious than the average dictator. The point is that self-interest figures heavily in the decision for a major country to go to war. In Korea and Iraq it seemed worthwhile. In Vietnam, it seemed worthwhile at the time, but eventually the war was a failure, the cost in lives and money and equipment was intolerable, and the United States drew back from military engagements that looked like possible quagmires.

For a long time, the war in former Yugoslavia appeared to be a potential quagmire, and the United States hesitated to take a leadership role.

The UN troops stationed there—British, French, Canadian, Dutch, and others—were not even adequate for peacekeeping purposes. Far more troops would be needed. Congress feared the American people would not tolerate deep involvement and considerable loss of life in such a conflict. Americans considered the war to be more a European than an American problem. They also felt that the United States could ill afford to take leadership in too many ethnic wars or they would bankrupt the country. Eventually, though, England and France began building an immediate strike force, and the United States thought the fighting could be done mainly from the air. The United Nations had nothing like the necessary forces to actually make war. It looked increasingly as though action would have to be taken by the organization whose duty had always been to guard Europe—NATO. Unlike the UN, NATO has a standing army of great power (see Table 14.3).

The North Atlantic Treaty Organization

Figure 14.2 highlights the members of the North Atlantic Treaty Organization (NATO) which was created after World War II to guarantee mutual protection of its members against the Soviet Union and its allies. The latter linked together in a treaty organization known as the Warsaw Pact. The Warsaw Pact has ceased to exist, but NATO continues. As the map shows, Greece and Turkey are also members of NATO, although some distance from the North Atlantic. Not shown in the map are the United States and Canada, which are also members. Each member country assigns troops to the organization to serve under a united command. Table 14.3 lists the number of troops committed to NATO by member countries as of October 1993.

The North Atlantic Treaty Organization is an example of international cooperation. Its military staff, centered in Brussels, has given the organization a unity of command rare in world

Figure 14.2
The North Atlantic Treaty Organization faces questions for the future. Will it include former Warsaw Pact nations? And what is its role now that the former Soviet Union has disbanded?

☐ NATO members
(Also U.S. & Canada)

■ Former Warsaw Pact members
(Excluding former East Germany)

Source: San Francisco Examiner, Jan. 9, 1994: A12.

history. The present Chairman of the Joint Chiefs of Staff of the United States, General Shalikashvili, was a member of the Supreme Command of NATO. The North Atlantic Treaty Organization did much to ensure safety from the Soviet Union for its member nations, but it now faces new questions: Can such an alliance stay together when it no longer feels immediate threat? If so, can it find new functions?

In answer to the first question, it can be said that alliances are seldom long lived. In the case of NATO, however, there is still enough threat from the East that it may continue. If such a bellicose leader as Zhirinovsky became presi-

dent of Russia, he would pose a threat to Eastern Europe. Eastern Europe is concerned with such a possibility, and Poland, the Czech Republic, Slovakia, Hungary, and Lithuania are pleading for NATO membership. Instead, it appears they will be offered membership in a "Partnership for Peace." This partnership calls for closer military cooperation with Eastern European countries, but not full membership in NATO. One reason for refusing full membership in NATO to the countries of Eastern Europe is that Russia might see such a policy as a threat against its sovereignty. Traditionally, defensive alliances have been alliances against a

Troops Assigned to NATO, October 1993	TABLE 14.3
Member country	Number of troops
Belgium	80,700
Canada	5,100
Denmark	29,200
France (does not participate in united NATO command)	402,000
Germany	447,000
Great Britain	281,900
Greece	159,300
Iceland	not available
Italy	354,000
Luxembourg	800
Netherlands	93,000
Norway	32,700
Portugal	58,300
Spain	217,000
Turkey	560,300
United States	154,700

SOURCE: *San Francisco Examiner,* Jan. 9, 1994:A12.

with Bosnian atrocities and struck forcefully against the Bosnian Serbs, restoring a certain amount of faith in the alliance. The motives were at least partly humanitarian, but there was also fear that the war might spread. At present, it is too early to know how successful NATO action will prove. The UN approved the action, but with no standing army could not have struck with such force. Such alliances as NATO will probably have to be depended upon in the future unless the UN becomes a much stronger organization than at present.

Direct Diplomacy

Direct diplomacy, or the meeting of diplomats of two or more quarreling nations, has always been one means of settling disputes. We mentioned that such diplomacy has been successful between Great Britain and the Irish Republican Army. Even more surprising was the announcement of negotiations between Israel and the Palestinians, which resulted in an agreement for Israel to cede to the Arabs the Gaza Strip and Jericho, if the Arabs would agree to give Israel diplomatic recognition and concede that Israel has a right to exist. The two sides continue their talks. Although there are many possibilities for a breakdown of the peace process, at present, it appears to be moving forward.

Direct diplomacy is used only occasionally. Often negotiations have to be pushed by an outside power or the United Nations. Even in the Israeli–Arab case, Norwegian diplomats had worked long and hard to bring the two sides together. Such diplomacy, of course, will and should continue. It is also possible to take disputes to the World Court, another organ of the UN, but very few international cases are referred to the Court. A frequently used type of diplomacy is for one nation to offer its "good offices" to get two disputants together. This strategy will undoubtedly continue, even though it is more common to take up such disagreements in the UN.

possible enemy. Extension of NATO might cause Russia to feel targeted as the enemy. Another objection to such a broad extension of NATO is that some present NATO members are not comfortable with an alliance with their former Warsaw Pact enemies (Elliott and Nagorski, 1994).

Critics of the Partners-for-Peace proposal fear it might be merely an easy letdown for countries that feel a real need for protection. Before World War II, Czechoslovakia had an alliance with Great Britain and with the Soviet Union, but no one came to its defense against Nazi Germany. Eastern Europe fears that unless full NATO membership is granted, history will repeat.

It has been feared, too, that NATO will not act forcefully. For three years, only the slightest support was given in Bosnia for UN peacekeepers. Then, finally, the NATO allies were fed up

Economic and Trade Alternatives

It was pointed out that both the United States and the World Bank have, in a few cases, cut off the money supply of countries applying for aid but failing to honor human rights commitments. At present, the United States is negotiating with the People's Republic of China to stop supplying missiles to Iran and to observe human rights. At stake is China's desire to continue to have most-favored-nation trade status. A firm commitment in this area could be quite effective, although there are strong doubts as to whether it will come about. Many people credit the end of apartheid to cutting off trade to South Africa. Cutting off trade with Serbia eventually caused Serbia to stop sending help to the Serbians in Bosnia. There appears to be a point in human emotions when hatred of the enemy is more important than one's own welfare. Many countries, though, strongly desire the trade status of most-favored nation. Nearly all countries see the need for trade.

Growing International Trade

While speaking of monetary policies and trade, we should return to a comment made at the beginning of this chapter: Throughout the world, trade restrictions have been falling away in recent years. In the fall of 1993, a trade agreement known as NAFTA (North American Free Trade Agreement) was approved by Mexico, Canada, and the United States. Over a 15-year period, it will gradually eliminate nearly all tariffs among the three countries. At the beginning of the same year, a new level of unity came to the EEC (European Economic Community). Added to existing free trade agreements was an agreement on a common currency approved by a majority of the members.

In the same year, an even more gigantic world trade agreement was reached, the **General Agreement on Trade and Tariffs** (GATT), approved by 117 nations, including the United States (Thomas, 1993). This means a drastic slashing of tariffs on manufactured goods and considerable cuts in tariffs on agricultural goods. One result will be a reduction in prices paid by consumers in member countries. It means, among other things, that all people will eat better, unless food production is reduced drastically by environmental problems. Besides more goods to buy, another possible result will be stronger bonds between countries, especially if the new agreements are accompanied by prosperity.

We stress trade agreements because they demonstrate the ability of many of the world's nations to cooperate for their own economic betterment. It can also be argued that a large increase in trade will make it more expensive and more difficult to break off friendly relations with other countries and return to deadly combat.

Much of the world appears to be drawing closer together, especially Western Europe and North America. It remains to be seen whether desire for trade, economic cooperation, and a will to survive will be stronger than the disintegrative forces of ethnic hatreds, nationalistic ambitions, and the suppression of human rights.

SUMMARY

The United Nations has attempted to define and promote human rights on a world scale. Many of the MDCs—Western Europe, the United States, Canada, Australia, and New Zealand—do quite well, and Eastern Europe and Russia have made great progress in the last few years. Many countries flagrantly violate human rights. Finland is singled out as the world's best country for observing human rights, and Iraq as the worst, but China, Iran, and many others are nearly as bad.

Action to pressure countries to meet human rights standards includes persuasion, exposure for violations, denial of foreign aid, and, rarely, cutting off trade. Nongovernmental organizations are also helpful in getting prisoners released and stopping torture and summary executions. Even slavery is still widespread in the world.

International cooperation has grown gradually, not only in trade, but in attention to world health and food supply and environmental problems. The Blue Helmets (UN forces) have been called out many times to keep peace. Suggestions are made for strengthening the UN in both peacekeeping and peacemaking. The UN must depend on military forces offered by member countries. Such regional alliances as NATO also represent increased international cooperation, as do increasingly generous trade treaties and policies.

KEY TERMS

Amnesty International An independent, privately funded organization that works for human rights throughout the world; especially concerned with people imprisoned and/or tortured for political or religious beliefs.

Big Five The permanent members of the Security Council of the United Nations, who possess the veto power: United States, Russia, China, Great Britain, and France.

Bill of Rights The first ten amendments to the Constitution of the United States, a major document in the development of human rights.

Chattel slavery A system of total slavery in which slaves are born into slavery, are the property of their masters, and can be bought and sold on the market.

Concert of Europe Originally an alliance between Austria, Russia, and Prussia, aimed at keeping peace in Europe and ensuring kingly rule in all countries; in the late nineteenth century, a term applied to occasional meetings of the European powers to resolve their differences and avoid war.

Covenant of the United Nations An agreement to a United Nations resolution and a promise to abide by its terms.

Declaration of the Rights of Man A document of the French Revolution (1789) that declares the rights of the people, especially freedom of speech and religion.

Debt slavery A system, often found in agricultural work, whereby people are forced to work for a person or company to pay off debts—debts that have been imposed upon them fraudulently.

Economic sanctions Attempts to force a country into line by bringing it financial injury, usually through boycotting its goods.

General Agreement on Tariffs and Trade (GATT) International agreement gradually reducing tariffs among member countries (most of the world).

General Assembly The United Nations organ that includes all member nations as equals; makes nonbinding recommendations.

Holy Alliance An alliance between Austria, Russia, and Prussia, formed after the fall of Napoleon in 1815, and promising peace. Replaced by, and often confused with, the Concert of Europe.

Human rights Rights that belong to all people, laid out in United Nations human rights documents, but not agreed to by all countries.

International law The idea of right and proper relations among nations, such as humane treatment of prisoners and diplomats, helping distressed ships at sea, and no deliberate killing of civilians in wartime. Unlike most law, this has no provisions for enforcement.

League of Nations An international organization formed after World War I to keep peace. Unsuccessful; replaced by the United Nations.

Magna Carta A document that King John of England was forced to sign in 1215, granting right of trial by jury to all nobles and freemen; a landmark in the development of human rights.

Most Favored Nation (MFN)   A country accorded this status receives all the best trade rights and privileges.

National sovereignty   The idea that a nation has a right to make all its decisions without consulting a higher authority.

North Atlantic Treaty Organization (NATO)   A defensive alliance of most Western European countries, Canada, the United States, Greece, and Turkey; to prevent aggression from the Soviet Union; NATO continues despite the demise of the USSR.

Nongovernmental organizations (NGOs)   Organizations not representing governments, but attending sessions of the General Assembly or Economic and Social Council; for example, women's rights groups, environmental groups.

Peacekeepers   Troops sent by UN members to try to keep peace between former belligerents; they serve under the UN banner and wear the blue helmets of the UN.

Secretariat   The administrative branch of the UN, headed by the Secretary-General, who serves a four-year term.

Security Council   The branch of the UN specifically charged with keeping peace; includes the Big Five, with veto power, which at times leaves the Council unable to act.

Shiites   One of the two major sects of Moslems, including nearly all Iranians, some Iraqis and Syrians.

Social contract   The theory of some early advocates of rights for the people (John Locke and Jean-Jacques Rousseau) that governments were started when people made an agreement with their rulers that they could rule, but in return must give rights to the people.

Sunnites   The largest of the Moslem sects, including most Saudi Arabians, Egyptians, and other North Africans.

United Nations Charter   A document drawn up in 1945 outlining the organization and purposes of the United Nations, including calls for peace and human rights.

Uniting for Peace Resolution   A resolution by the UN General Assembly that called for UN members to make war to save South Korea from invasion from the North; important because it was a way around the veto power of the USSR.

Veto power   *See* Big Five.

War Crimes Tribunal   A special international court, meeting in Nuremburg after World War II to prosecute leading Nazis for war crimes.

World Court (International Court of Justice)   A court meeting in The Hague, Netherlands, to hear disputes between and among nations, but lacking enforcement power.

STUDY QUESTIONS

1. What is the meaning of the phrase "human rights as mores?"

2. Now that communism is no longer a threat, what are the major barriers to human rights?

3. How would you answer the charge that the Western world is imposing its values on the East, especially on the People's Republic of China?

4. What are the most important rights missing from Iraq, Iran, China, and other countries very low on the human rights list?

5. What kinds of slavery are still fairly common in parts of the world?

6. What is the conflict between the idea of national sovereignty and such organizations as the UN and NATO?

7. What is the basic problem in the UN Security Council that has often immobilized the UN?

8. Would it be a good idea to expand UN powers by giving it standing military forces to serve if called for by the Security Council?

9. An alternative to depending on the United Nations would be to have the United States act as world policeman. What would be the problems with that course of action?

10. The chapter ends with the hope that increased foreign trade may make the world less likely to go to war. Does this seem overly optimistic? Why or why not?

Credits

Glossary

Absolute poverty The condition of having less income than is necessary to ensure a minimum daily diet of 2,150 calories per person per day.

Acid Rain Precipitation that has been polluted with toxic chemicals; some sources of acid rain are sulfur dioxide, nitrogen dioxide, selenium, and arsenic.

Acute hunger Hunger in poverty-stricken, resource-poor, and overpopulated countries, where very high proportions of the populations are on the verge of starvation.

Afforestation The process of planting trees where they did not previously exist.

Age structure The manner in which a population is distributed with regard to age.

Age-dependency ratio The ratio of people under the age of 15 and over the age of 65 relative to the rest of the population.

Ageism A systematic stereotyping of, and discrimination against, people because they are old.

Aggressive instinct An explanation for the frequency of violence and war, accepted by sociobiologists but rejected by sociologists.

Amazonia The gigantic tropical forest of Brazil, in South America.

Amnesty International An independent, privately funded organization that works for human rights throughout the world; especially concerned with people imprisoned and/or tortured for political or religious beliefs.

Anomie A sense of being without rules; confusion that occurs when norms are changing rapidly.

Apartheid A South African policy, ended in 1992, to divide blacks and whites into separate societies; extreme segregation.

Aquifer Natural, underground storage chamber for water, usually permeable rock, sand, or gravel.

Aryan invasion Invasion of India around 1500–1200 B.C. by an Aryan-speaking people, who are believed to have imposed, or at least strengthened, the caste system.

Baby boom: The large cohort of people born from the mid 1940s to the mid 1960s.

Balance of nature A condition that allows a sustainable number of each species to survive.

Balance of power A situation in which two antagonistic countries or alliances attempt to keep approximately even military strength so each will be afraid to attack.

Barrio A section of a U.S. city inhabited by poor Spanish-speaking people, usually of Latin American descent.

Benevolent atom Nuclear power used for nonmilitary purposes, like generating electric power.

Bhopal City in India where one of the worst industrial accidents occurred in 1984; gases escaping from the Union Carbide plant killed thousands and injured hundreds of thousands of people.

Big Five The permanent members of the Security Council of the United Nations, who possess the veto power: United States, Russia, China, Great Britain, and France.

Bill of Rights The first ten amendments to the Constitution of the United States, a major document in the development of human rights.

Bioamplification The increasing concentration of pesticides as they pass up the food chain.

Biodiversity A variety of species, and a variety within a species.

Bioethics An academic and research discipline that deals with the ethical implications of medical advancements.

Blended families Families formed when divorced individuals remarry and one or more children from previous marriages are involved.

Bloods Violent street gang of Los Angeles origin, engaged in drug trade and often in street warfare. Now found in many large U.S. cities.

Bourgeoisie Literally, the middle class in France, generally used to refer to people who own the means of production.

Breeder reactor Nuclear reactors that generate atomic energy and produce more fossil material than they consume.

Cali cartel A drug cartel centered in Cali, Colombia, now operating in Mexico, transporting drugs to the United States.

Carbon dioxide The gas that forms when oxygen is burned; it is increasing in the atmosphere.

Case study method The research approach in the social sciences that involves a small number of respondents who are studied in detail.

Caste A rigid system of social classification designated at birth, in which movement from one class to another is impossible and intermarriage between castes is forbidden.

Chattel slavery A system of total slavery in which slaves are born into slavery, are the property of their masters, and can be bought and sold on the market.

Chernobyl Site of the most devastating nuclear accident located near the city of Kiev in the former Soviet Union

Child molestation Adult sexual acts with children.

Chlorofluorocarbons Chemical propellants, used in aerosol sprays, that have caused a hole in the ozone layer.

Chronic hunger Hunger in very poor countries, where most people are not in immediate danger of dying, but where food is so scarce that it is inadequate for health, growth, and energy needs.

CITES (Convention on International Trade in Endangered Species) United Nations agreement that seeks to protect species among the 120 member nations.

Clear cutting A pattern of cutting down forests that leaves the earth denuded.

Cognitive dissonance Attempt to simultaneously hold two or more perceptions that are inconsistent.

Community A group of people who share a common territory and meet their basic physical and social needs through daily interaction with one another.

Concentric-zone model The model developed by R. Park and E. Burgess that sees cities comprised of circular zones, with business zones in the center and residential zones emanating toward the exterior.

Concert of Europe Originally an alliance between Austria, Russia, and Prussia, aimed at keeping peace in Europe and ensuring kingly rule in all countries; in the late nineteenth century, a term applied to occasional meetings of the European powers to resolve their differences and avoid war.

Conflict perspective Emphasis on the conflicts and clash of interests between and among various social classes and groups.

Conflict theory The type of sociological theory that perceives social strife at almost every level of society.

Constellation of values A set, or certain mix, of numerous values.

Control group The group in an experiment that is not given the stimulus.

Core societies The dominant, economically well-developed societies in world systems theory.

Covenant of the United Nations An agreement to a United Nations resolution and a promise to abide by its terms.

Crack cocaine Cocaine processed into a solid that is broken into small pebbles that are smoked. Very powerful, fast acting, and extremely addictive.

Crips Violent street gang of Los Angeles origin, engaged in drug trade and often in street warfare. Now found in many large U.S. cities.

Crude birthrate (CBR) The number of births, per 1,000 people, for a population during a year.

Crude death rate (CDR) The number of deaths, per 1,000 people, for a population during a year.

Cultural lag The inability of social structure and culture to keep up with rapid technological change.

Cultural universals The family functions that are found frequently around the world: reproduction, socialization of children, transferral of inheritance, and regulation of sexual behavior.

Cycle of abuse Abusive behavior that is experienced and learned and passed from one generation to the next.

Debt slavery A system, often found in agricultural work, whereby people are forced to work for a person or company to pay off debts—debts that have been imposed upon them fraudulently.

Declaration of the Rights of Man A document of the French Revolution (1789) that declares the rights of the people, especially freedom of speech and religion.

Deferred gratification Putting off immediate pleasures for later gratification.

Deforestation The destruction of forests.

Deindustrialization The abandonment of industrial plants in countries with high labor costs, and the building of new plants in cheap-labor areas.

Demographic transition theory The theory that describes how countries move from a stage with high fertility and high mortality (with little if any growth), to a stage with high fertility and low mortality (with considerable growth), to a stage with low fertility and low mortality (with little if any growth).

Demography The statistical description and analysis of human population.

Dependent variable The factor that the researcher is interested in explaining.

Desertification: The expansion of a desert area, caused by overgrazing along the desert borderlands.

Deterrence The theory that having a large nuclear arsenal would protect a country from attack because other countries would fear nuclear devastation.

Discrimination The practice of treating people of different ethnic groups unequally, usually because of prejudice against them.

Displaced Persons' Act of 1948 An immigration act making it possible for the United States to admit many people, largely Jewish, fleeing Europe after World War II.

Double standard of morality Different standards of sexual behavior for men and women; men are expected to be sexually experienced, while women are suppose to remain virgins until marriage.

Doubling time The number of years it will take a country to double its population.

Downers Drugs that have a depressing effect on the body, inducing drowsiness and relieving pain, especially the case with opium and its derivatives.

Ecological interdependence An environmental system in which one species cannot exist without one or more other species.

Economic sanctions Attempts to force a country into line by bringing it financial injury, usually through boycotting its goods.

Ecosystem A system of interrelationships among all of the plants and animal species in an area, including the relationships among the species and the physical environment, like soil, water, and climate.

Edge effect Trees on the edge of a forest are more easily damaged than trees within the forest.

Egalitarian authority Power is shared by all parties, in a marriage by husband and wife.

Embezzlement Stealing money or stock entrusted to one's care; a crime committed by a trusted insider.

Emigration The movement of people out of a country of which they are natives or long-term residents.

Eopolis The Greek term to describe tiny villages or "pre-cities" characterized by homogeneity and no differentiation of labor.

Ethnic cleansing A term used by the Serbs of former Yugoslavia, meaning to rid what they consider their territory of all non-Serbs by driving them out or killing them.

Ethnic group A group of people sharing a common culture or way of life.

Ethnic wars Wars caused primarily by antagonisms between two or more ethnic groups, like the war in Yugoslavia in the early 1990s.

Ethnocentrism A condition in which a group or society feels that its way is right and that its people are somehow superior to other groups or societies.

Eugenics The science of improving human beings through selective breeding.

European Economic Community (EEC) A trade union of nearly all the countries of Western Europe joined in a common market to reduce or eliminate tariffs.

Europol A European police force serving members of the European Common Market. Similar to, but with fewer members than, Interpol.

Euthanasia The act of killing an individual who is hopelessly sick, hence, often referred to as "mercy killing."

Experiment A test to see if a particular stimulus has an impact on another variable.

Experimental group The group, in an experiment, that is given the stimulus.

Exxon Valdez Tanker ship that was responsible for a huge oil spill along the coast of Alaska in 1989.

Family An intimate kin-based group consisting of at least a parent-nucleus, the minimal social unit that cooperates economically and assumes responsibility for the rearing of children.

Female infanticide The killing of female babies.

Fertility The actual number of births within a population in a given year.

Feudal society A society with the social, economic, and political structure of medieval Europe and other preindustrial societies.

Filariasis A disease, spread by insects from standing water, that causes body parts to swell to such an extent that amputation is the only treatment.

Fragmentation The breakup of larger countries into small ones, like the former Yugoslavia, Czechoslovakia, and Soviet Union.

Fraud Use of deception to gain other people's money or property.

Free capitalism Economies characterized by limited government control or direction.

Freedom of Access to Clinic Entrances Act Congressional act passed in 1994 that makes it a federal crime to block the entrance to an abortion clinic; established a "free zone" of 300 feet around clinics and hospitals.

Functionalist perspective The point of view that the agreements of society are the glue that holds the whole together.

Fungicides Chemical compounds designed to kill fungus.

Gay bashing Speaking ill of, and in the extreme, committing violence toward people simply because they are homosexuals.

Gemeinschaft The close, personal village where everyone knows everyone else and where order is maintained through tradition and custom, rather than reliance on law.

General Agreement on Tariffs and Trade (GATT) International agreement gradually reducing tariffs among member countries (most of the world).

General Assembly The United Nations organ that includes all member nations as equals; makes nonbinding recommendations.

Generalized other, taking the role of A person's ability to respond to the values and norms of people in general.

Genocide The killing of an entire racial or ethnic group, as in Hitler's attempt to exterminate the Jews.

Gesellschaft The large and associational type of social organization where the people are governed by the rules of business and legislature.

Ghetto Originally, the Jewish quarter of European cities. Now applied to sections of cities where minority ethnic groups live, usually due to social or economic pressures.

Grand larceny Theft of money or personal property. In many countries, grand larceny is theft of something worth more than a specified amount, and petty larceny is theft of smaller amounts.

Green Revolution: The massive increase in crop yields produced by new hybrids of grain that require artificial fertilizers, pesticides, and irrigation.

Greenhouse effect The result of releasing various gases into the atmosphere, that is warming of the world's temperature.

"Groupthink" A term coined by Irving Janis for the tendency of people belonging to close-knit groups to think alike, especially in tense situations.

Hallucinogens Drugs like LSD, that cause visual and/or auditory hallucinations.

Harijans The very lowest people in the caste system of India, the "untouchables."

Herbicides Chemical compounds designed to kill vegetation.

Hidden hunger Hunger where peoples' stomachs may be reasonably full, but their diets lack adequate protein, minerals, and vitamins.

Holy Alliance An alliance between Austria, Russia, and Prussia, formed after the fall of Napoleon in 1815, and promising peace. Replaced by, and often confused with, the Concert of Europe.

Human rights Rights that belong to all people, laid out in United Nations human rights documents, but not agreed to by all countries.

Hypercities Cities with 15 million or more inhabitants.

Ideal type A type that is definable and that is approached in the real world, but never completely realized.

Ideology A strong belief or set of beliefs about how society should be run, such as communism and fascism.

Immigration The movement of people into a country of which they are not natives.

Imperial overstretch Historian Paul Kennedy's term for the tendency of the strongest nations to expand too far, like the United States' commitment of its forces to saving the regime in South Vietnam.

Independent variable The factor that explains variation in another, dependent variable.

Industrial societies Societies characterized by heavy industry powered by nonhuman labor.

Infant mortality rate The number of deaths of infants between birth and 1 year old per 1,000 live births.

Infanticide The murder of infants.

Insider trading Gaining secret information as to which stocks are likely to go up, usually because of mergers of corporations, and using that information to buy the stock is illegal.

Institutional racism Racial discrimination that results from long-established, habitual ways of a society, such as housing discrimination that continues even when outlawed.

Interactionist perspective The perspective that is micro in nature, and that focuses mainly on the behavior of individuals and small groups of individuals.

Internal migration The movement of people from one region of a country to another.

International law The idea of right and proper relations among nations, such as humane treatment of prisoners and diplomats, helping distressed ships at sea, and no deliberate killing of civilians in wartime. Unlike most law, this has no provisions for enforcement.

Interpol An international police force to which most countries belong, that helps especially in finding escaped criminals and counterfeiters.

Islamic fundamentalism The belief of many Moslems that their governments should be ruled by the laws of the Koran, not by secular states.

Jihad A holy war on behalf of Islam, such as that advocated by some extremist Palestinians to destroy Israel.

Latent function The unintended and little noticed function for which an institution or policy is designed.

Latent problem A problem that is in the making and not yet readily apparent.

Laundering money Placing money in foreign, secret bank accounts, to escape taxation or to hide money gained illegally, usually in the drug trade.

League of Nations An international organization formed after World War I to keep peace. Unsuccessful; replaced by the United Nations.

Less developed countries (LDCs) Societies that are not yet developed economically and that have large proportions of extremely poor people.

London fog Dense, choking air pollution, caused by smoke from burning coal; especially prevalent in London.

Lower-middle class The social class made up of more poorly paid professionals, sales people, secretaries, and many types of service workers.

Machismo A sense of power and manliness.

Mafia A term now applied to almost any well-organized crime group dominant in a particular country. Originally a Sicilian crime group, organized on a familial basis.

Magna Carta A document that King John of England was forced to sign in 1215, granting right of trial by jury to all nobles and freemen; a landmark in the development of human rights.

Malleable human nature The view that human nature is changed by socialization, not determined by instinct.

Manhattan Project The top-secret project, involving some of the greatest scientists in the world during World War II, to develop an atomic bomb.

Manifest function The intended function for which an institution or policy is designed.

Maquiladoras Factories located in Mexico, near the United States–Mexico border, that use low-wage Mexican labor and specialize in the assembly of components sent from developed countries.

Matrilineal descent Family heritage traced through the woman's family; generally children take the mother's family name.

Mechanical solidarity Durkheim's concept of older societies held together by great similarity of their people and strong beliefs in old customs and norms.

Medellín cartel A drug organization centered in Medellín, Colombia; once the most powerful such organization in Latin America.

Megalopolis A very large urban area formed by the merging of metropolises and their suburbs.

Methane Gas produced from decaying vegetation; it is increasing in the atmosphere and adds to the greenhouse effect.

Metropolis A large, busy city that often serves as the capital of a country, state, or region.

Migration The physical movement of people into or out of a geographic region.

Military-industrial complex The cooperation of the military forces and the industries that supply them to pressure the government into larger and larger appropriations of funds for military spending.

Misogynist attitudes Antifemale attitudes.

Monoculture Lack of biodiversity; dangerous because a single disease can destroy an entire species.

Monogamy A marriage of one husband and one wife.

More developed countries (MDCs) Postindustrial societies like the United States, Japan, and European countries where people live with some level of abundance.

Mores Moral beliefs and practices of a society.

Mortality The actual number of deaths within a population during a year.

Mos Singular of *mores.*

Moslem fundamentalism Moslems wishing to reinstate the laws of the Koran, do away with secular states, and have their countries dominated by the Islamic religion.

Most Favored Nation (MFN) A country accorded this status receives all the best trade rights and privileges.

Multiple-nuclei model The urban model stating that cities tend to be made up of numerous centers of nuclei, which are surrounded by different kinds of activities.

National Origins Act of 1921 A federal act to limit immigration from each country on the basis of how many that country had contributed already to the United States population.

National sovereignty The idea that a nation has a right to make all its decisions without consulting a higher authority.

Negative euthansia Allowing a person to die, but not aiding the process.

New Earth 21 Set of proposals, developed by Japan's Ministry of International Trade and Industry, that is intended to renew the earth's ecosystem.

Nonbiodegradable substances Substances, like oil or plastic, that do not chemically decompose in nature.

Nongovernmental organizations (NGOs) Organizations not representing governments, but attending sessions of the General Assembly or Economic and Social Council; for example, women's rights groups, environmental groups.

Norms The behaviors accepted and expected within a society.

North Atlantic Treaty Organization (NATO) A defensive alliance of most Western European countries, Canada, the United States, Greece, and Turkey; to prevent aggression from the Soviet Union; NATO continues despite the demise of the USSR.

Nuclear club A term for countries that had nuclear weapons before a treaty of 1968 (United States, USSR, France, Great Britain, and People's Republic of China).

Nuclear family A family consisting of two parents and their natural or adopted children.

Nuclear Nonproliferation Treaty, 1968 A treaty signed by the nuclear powers (United States, USSR, France, Great Britain, and People's Republic of China) promising not to help any other country obtain nuclear military power, and signed by many other countries promising not to develop nuclear weapons.

Onchoceriasis "River blindness," spread by insects from standing water; virtually out of control in West Africa.

Organic solidarity In Durkheim's analysis, diverse modern societies held together by interdependence of members, who engage in great varieties of work and are not so homogeneous as in older societies.

Overgrazing A condition that results from too many animals and too many kinds of animals grazing on rangeland, destroying grasses and their root systems.

Ozone layer A band of molecules, made of three oxygen atoms, that surrounds the atmosphere and screens out ultraviolet rays from the sun.

Participant observation The research technique that involves the researcher joining the group under investigation.

Patriarchal authority Power is held by males; females are subordinate.

Patrilineal descent Family heritage traced through the man's family; generally children take the father's family name.

PCBs Polychlorinated biphenyls, very toxic chemicals, used in plastics, electrical insulators, and hydraulic fluids.

Peacekeepers Troops sent by UN members to try to keep peace between former belligerents; they serve under the UN banner and wear the blue helmets of the UN.

Peripheral societies The dependent, less economically developed societies in world systems theory.

Permanent settlers Immigrants who are not facing the severe and dire forces faced by refugees, but who desire to move to another country to improve their lives.

Personal interview In-depth, lengthy interviews of respondents in a case study.

Pesticides Chemical compounds designed to kill insects and other pests.

Pogroms Organized attacks on the Jews in Russia in the nineteenth and very early twentieth centuries, often encouraged by the government.

Polis The Greek term to describe the early cities which were independent political entities and the source of the only government that existed.

Polyandry The status of one woman being married to several men.

Polygamy The status of one women being married to several men or one man being married to several women.

Polygyny The status of one man being married to several women.

Population The total group in which the researcher is interested.

Population momentum The population dynamic that sees the current age of a population as an important force in the future size of that population. A young population is assured of growing, even if couples have replacement-level fertility.

Pornography Pictures, videos, printed material, or other matter that exceeds the community standards of decency and stirs sexual interest.

Positive checks Those factors (famine, pestilence, war, and disease) discussed by Thomas Malthus, that increase mortality and bring population back into balance with the food supply.

Positive euthanasia The actual termination of the life of a hopeless and suffering patient.

Postindustrial societies Societies with declining percentages of activity in heavy industry and increasing percentages of activity in high technology, management, and services.

Potable water Water suitable for human consumption.

Preindustrial societies The term applied to the entire world before a series of inventions that replaced human and animal power with mechanical power and ushered in an age of factories and mass production. Applies to contemporary societies that still rely on human and animal power.

Prejudice An unfounded negative attitude about a subgroup of people based on preconceived notions.

Preventive checks Those factors (celibacy, deferment of marriage, and "moral restraint" within marriage), discussed by Thomas Malthus, that decrease fertility.

Primary industry Activity involving gathering or extracting raw materials.

Priorities What we are willing to do, either passively or actively, about our feelings of right and wrong.

Pro-choice The attitude that a woman has a right to a legal abortion.

Pro-life The attitude that abortion is wrong; abortion is the taking of a life.

Proletariat Those who must sell their labor for whatever price the bourgeois class is willing to pay.

Pronatalist policies Policies designed to increase fertility.

Prostitution The exchange of sexual activities for money or other considerations.

Public records Social and economic data gathered by public agencies and used by researchers.

Race A term applied to divisions of the human species based on inherited differences in appearance such as skin color, eye shape, hair type, and bone structure.

Racism The discredited belief that race is a very important determinant of behavior and that some races are superior to others.

Rate of growth The rate of natural increase plus the rate of net migration.

Rate of natural increase (NI) The crude birthrate minus the crude death rate.

Reference groups Groups with which a particular person wishes to identify.

Reforestation The process of replacing trees that have been destroyed.

Refugees People who have been uprooted, left homeless, or forced to flee one geographic region to settle in another.

Relative poverty The concept that poverty in the United States and other industrialized countries is not real, that people are poor in comparison to other citizens, not because they lack food and shelter.

Research methods The techniques, ranging from qualitative to quantitative, that social scientists use in their research.

Restitutive law Laws calling for regulation of trade, definition of property rights, and such, as contrasted to harsh criminal law.

Retributive law Law of punishment or revenge. In Durkheim's analysis, typical of older societies held together by strong beliefs in norms and customs.

Salinization The process by which salt is left in the soil after stored water evaporates.

Sample A subset of a population that a researcher selects for investigation.

Scapegoat A person or group who is blamed for problems of which he, she, or they are not guilty.

Scapegoating The practice of blaming the ills of society on an unpopular person or group

Schistosomiasis A parasitic disease that attacks the bladder and genitals or spleen and liver; the source is snails that live in standing water.

Scientific method An approach to investigating a topic that relies on both logic and observation.

Secondary industry Manufacturing.

Secretariat The administrative branch of the UN, headed by the Secretary-General, who serves a four-year term.

Sector theory The urban model developed by Hoyt that sees cities made up of wedges going from the center to the extremities, following major transportation arteries.

Security Council The branch of the UN specifically charged with keeping peace; includes the Big Five, with veto power, which at times leaves the Council unable to act.

Self-concept The mental image one has of herself or himself.

Sendera luminosa (Shining Path) A violent Communist revolutionary movement in Peru, accused of being in the drug trade.

Serial Monogamy Situations in which, at any one time, one man is married to one woman but, at different periods of their lifetimes, husbands and wives are married to two or more spouses.

Sexual harassment Unwanted sexual advances; usually made repeatedly by someone in a position of power over the victim.

Sexually transmitted disease (STD) Diseases, like syphilis, gonorrhea, and AIDS, that are passed from person to person through sexual acts.

Shiites One of the two major sects of Moslems, including nearly all Iranians, some Iraqis and Syrians.

"Snakeheads" A slang term used by the Chinese for people who smuggle illegal immigrants from East Asia into the United States.

Social contract The theory of some early advocates of rights for the people (John Locke and Jean-Jacques Rousseau) that governments were started when people made an agreement with their rulers that they could rule, but in return must give rights to the people.

Social control How a society gets its people to live up to its laws and mores.

Social isolation The situation in which the family is not integrated socially into the community.

Social problems Situations, policies, or trends that are (a) distressing or threatening to large numbers of people, (b) contrary to the moral beliefs of the society, and (c) partly or wholly correctable through the actions of social groups.

Social survey A survey of a population or sample that relies on a questionnaire to elicit information on a particular topic.

Socialization The process by which an individual learns to think and act in a particular culture.

Sociobiology A study of the biological basis for human and animal social behavior, considered of doubtful value by most sociologists.

Soil bank Land set aside and not used for agricultural production.

Soil destruction Soil that is ruined by salinization, overgrazing, and desertification.

Soil erosion Without the protection of plants, trees, and their root systems, top soil is washed by rain into the seas.

"Speedballing" Using cocaine in conjunction with heroin to get a "super-high." Frequently lethal.

Statistics Analytical techniques that allow us to compare what was expected from a theory to what was actually observed.

Status panic The efforts of members of the middle class to maintain status in a world of rapidly changing requirements.

Stimulus That which is administrated to the experimental group but not the control group, in an effort to test cause and effect.

Strategic Arms Reduction Treaties (START) Two agreements, signed in 1992 and 1993 by the United States and Russia, to reduce the number of nuclear warheads in each country's possession.

Strict monogamy The "till death does us part" version of monogamy in which a spouse will only remarry in the event of the other spouse's death.

Subculture theory A perspective that sees urban residents involved in numerous groups and communities where meaningful relationships and ties are forged.

Sulfur dioxide A choking gas that enters the air when coal or oil is burned.

Sunnites The largest of the Moslem sects, including most Saudi Arabians, Egyptians, and other North Africans.

Surrogate wars Historian Paul Kennedy's term for wars between minor countries that became part of the fight between the United States and the USSR.

Suspended particulate matter Tiny particles of coal dust, smoke, fecal matter, or similar materials that "float" in the air.

Terrorism The use of violence or the threat of violence to impose one's will on others.

Tertiary industry Services.

Theoretical perspective A particular way of explaining or making sense out of the social world.

Theory The logical aspect of science that explains how and why a certain phenomenon exists.

Thirty Years' War A war in Central Europe mainly between Catholics and Protestants, 1618–1648; the most devastating war in European history.

Total fertility rate (TFR) The total number of children that each woman (on average) would have during her reproductive years, if she patterned her fertility after the age-specific birthrates (rates for age categories of women) in existence at that time.

Transfrontier metropolis An urban area situated on an international border.

United Nations Charter A document drawn up in 1945 outlining the organization and purposes of the United Nations, including calls for peace and human rights.

Uniting for Peace Resolution A resolution by the UN General Assembly that called for UN members to make war to save South Korea from invasion from the North; important because it was a way around the veto power of the USSR.

Upper-middle class The social class directly beneath the "super rich" and characterized by high income, high education, and high-status occupations.

"Uppers" Drugs that are strong stimulants, increasing heart rate, temporarily overcoming fatigue, and often resulting in sleeplessness and irritability.

Urbanization The process by which a society sees increasing proportions of its population residing in urban areas and declining proportions living in rural areas.

Values The feelings and beliefs that define notions of right or wrong.

Vested interest A special economic or political interest that one has in a social practice, policy, or institution.

Veto power *See* Big Five.

War Crimes Tribunal A special international court, meeting in Nuremburg after World War II to prosecute leading Nazis for war crimes.

White-collar crime Crime committed by seemingly respectable people in the course of their business, including bribery, price-fixing, insider trading, false advertising, and so forth.

Working class The social class of people who have incomes similar to lower-middle class individuals, but whose jobs do not require as much training or hold as favorable status.

World Court (International Court of Justice) A court meeting in The Hague, Netherlands, to hear disputes between and among nations, but lacking enforcement power.

World systems theory A conflict perspective developed by Immanuel Wallerstein that explains the status and well-being of a society based on where that society is located in the global economic stratification system

Xenophobia An unreasonable fear or hatred of foreigners.

Youth wave The large number of currently young children who will be entering their reproductive years in the future.

Zero opinion analysis Theory that resources are finite so that one person's gain requires another person's loss.

Zero-sum game The situation played out with the belief that someone's gain equals another person's loss.

References

Chapter 1

Babbie, E. 1992. *The Practice of Social Research*, 6th ed., Belmont, CA: Wadsworth.

Boulding, K. E. 1985. *The World as a Total System*. Beverly Hills, CA: Sage.

Condon, G. E. 1994. "Ukraine OKs Deal to Scrap Nuclear Arms." *San Diego Union-Tribune*, Jan. 11, Part A: 1.

Dickens, C. 1948. *A Tale of Two Cities*. New York: Grosset and Dunlap.

Gale, R. P. 1987. "More Chernobyls Unavoidable." *Los Angeles Times,* June 27, Part I: 3.

Ganguly, D. 1987. "India's Carpet Kids: Court Fights Age-Old System of Slavery." *San Francisco Examiner,* Apr. 12, Part A: 19.

Gans, H. J. 1971. "The Uses of Poverty." *Social Policy,* July–Aug.

Hochschild, A. 1989. *The Second Shift*. New York: Viking.

Marwick, C. 1992. "Dermatology Academy Drafts Skin Cancer Warning." *Journal of the American Medical Association,* 268(21): 3041.

Marx, K. 1867. *Capital: A Critique of Political Economy.* Republished in 1975 by International Publishers, New York.

Mead, G. H. 1934. *Mind, Self, and Society.* Chicago: The University of Chicago Press.

Merton, R. K. 1957. *Social Theory and Social Structure*. New York: The Free Press.

Mills, C. W. 1951. *White Collar*. New York: Oxford University Press.

———1956. *The Power Elite*. New York: Oxford University Press.

———1959. The Sociological Imagination. New York: Oxford University Press.

Perlman, D. 1987. "Research Schools up in Arms over Defense Cuts." *San Francisco Chronicle*, Nov. 17, Part A, 5.

Rokeach, M. 1960. *The Open and Closed Mind*. New York: Basic Books.

Santiago, A. M. 1993. "Comments from the Special Collection Editor: Global Perspectives on Social Problems—Current Issues and Debates." *Social Problems*, 40 (2,): 207–212.

Simpson, G. 1963. *Emile Durkheim*. New York: Thomas Y. Crowell.

Sivard, R. L. 1993. *World Military and Social Expenditures. 1993.* Washington, DC: World Priorities.

Thurber, J. 1956. "Oliver and the Other Ostriches." *Further Fables for our Times*. New York: Simon and Schuster.

Tierney, K. 1982. "The Battered Women's Movement and the Creation of the Wife-Beating Problem." *Social Forces*, 29: 207–220.

U.S. Bureau of the Census. 1993. *United States Statistical Abstract, 1993*. Washington, DC: The U.S. Government Printing Office.

Wallerstein, I. 1979. *The Capitalist World Economy*. Cambridge, England: Cambridge University Press.

Weir, D. 1987. *The Bhopal Syndrome*. San Francisco: Sierra Club Books.

Chapter 2

Aguirre, B. E. 1985. "Why Do They Return? Abused Wives in Shelters." *Social Work*, 30: 350–354.

Ahlburg, D. A., and C. J. De Vita. 1992. "New Realities of the American Family." *Population Bulletin*, 47: 1–44.

Anderson, J. W., and M. Moore. 1993. "The Burden of Womanhood: Too Often in the Third World, a Female's Life Is Hardly Worth Living." *Washington Post National Weekly Edition*, Mar. 22–28: 6–7.

Arendell, T. 1986. *Mothers and Divorce: Legal, Economic and Social Dilemmas*. Berkeley: The University of California Press.

Boo, K. 1992. "Grow Up, Twenty-Somethings. You Can Go Home Again." *Washington Monthly*, 24, (4): 31–37.

Cherlin, A. 1978. "Remarriage as an Incomplete Institution." *American Sociological Review*, 84, (3): 634–650.

Clausen, J. 1993. *American Lives: Looking Back at the Children of the Great Depression*. New York: Free Press.

Coontz, S. 1992. *The Way We Never Were: American Families and the Nostalgia Trap*. New York: Basic Books.

Dancer, L. S., and L. A. Gilbert. 1993. "Spouses' Family Work Participation and Its Relation to Wives' Occupational Level." *Sex Roles*, 28, (3/4): 127–145.

Davidson, J. K., Sr., and N. B. Moore. 1992. *Marriage and Family*. Dubuque: W. C. Brown.

Dawson, D. A. 1991. "Family Structure and Children's Health: United States, 1988." *Vital Statistics*, Series 10, No. 178 (June).

Duncan, G. J., and S. D. Hoffman. 1985. "A Reconsideration of the Economic Consequences of Marital Dissolution." *Demography*, 24 (4): 485–497.

Easterlin, R. 1989. *Birth and Fortune: The Impact of Numbers on Personal Welfare*. Chicago: The University of Chicago Press.

Eggebeen, D. L., and D. T. Lichter. 1991. "Race, Family Structure, and Changing Poverty Among American Children." *American Sociological Review*, 56 (Dec.): 801–817.

Friedl, J., and M. B. Whiteford. 1988. *The Human Portrait: Introduction to Cultural Anthropology*, 2d ed. Englewood Cliffs, NJ: Prentice-Hall.

Furstenberg, Jr., Frank F. 1990. "Divorce in the American Family." *Annual Review of Sociology*, 16: 379–403.

———and A. J. Cherlin. 1991. *Divided Families*. Cambridge: Harvard University Press.

Gelles, R. J. and M. A. Straus. 1987. "Is Violence Toward Children Increasing? A Comparison of 1975 and 1985 National Survey Rates." In R. J. Gelles, *Family Violence*, 2d ed. Newbury Park, CA: Sage.

Glass, J., and V. Camarigg. 1992. "Gender, Parenthood, and Job-Family Compatibility." *American Journal of Sociology*, 98, (1): 131–152.

Glenn, N. D. 1992. "What Does Family Mean?" *American Demographics*, 14, (6): 30–35.

Goldscheider, F. K., and L. J. Waite. 1991. *New Families, No Families?* Berkeley and Los Angeles: University of California Press.

Goldstein, D., and A. Rosenbaum. 1985. "An Evaluation of the Self-Esteem of Maritally Violent Men." *Family Relations*, 34: 425–428.

Gordon, L. 1988. *Heroes of Their Own Lives: The Politics and History of Family Violence.* New York: Viking.

Harry, J. 1983. "Gay Male and Lesbian Relationships." In Eleanor D. Macklin and R. H. Rubin, Eds., *Contemporary Families and Lifestyles.* Beverly Hills, CA: Sage.

Haub, C. and M. Yanagishita. 1994. *1994 World Population Data Sheet.* Washington, DC: The Population Reference Bureau.

Howard, M. C., and J. Dunaif-Hattis. 1992. *Anthropology: Understanding Human Adaptation.* New York: HarperCollins.

Iwao, S. 1993. *The Japanese Woman: Traditional Image and Changing Reality.* New York: Free Press.

Jamieson, K. M., and T. J. Flanagan (Eds.). 1989. *Sourcebook of Criminal Justice Statistics*, 1988. Washington, DC: U.S. Department of Justice, Bureau of Justice Statistics.

Kellam, S., et al. 1977. "Family Structure and the Mental Health of Children." *Archives of General Psychiatry*, 34: 1012–1022.

———1982. "The Long-Term Evolution of the Family Structure of Teenage and Older Mothers." *Journal of Marriage and the Family*, 44: 539–554.

Kephart, W. M., and D. Jedlicka. 1991. *The Family, Society, and the Individual*, 7th ed. New York: HarperCollins.

Laslett, P. 1992. "Europe and 1992: Europe's Happy Families?" *History Today*, 42 (Mar.): 8–11.

Lenski, G., and J. Lenski. 1987. *Human Societies: An Introduction to Macrosociology.* New York: McGraw-Hill.

Morgan, S. P., A. McDaniel, A. T. Miller, and Samuel H. Preston. 1993. "Racial Differences in Household and Family Structure at the Turn of the Century." *American Journal of Sociology,* 98 (4): 798–828.

Murphy, C. 1993. "Pulling Aside the Veil: Women in the Arab World Struggle Against Male Dominance and Religious Taboos." *Washington Post National Weekly Edition*, Apr. 12–18: 10–11.

Pillemer, K., and D. Finkelhor. 1988. "The Prevalence of Elder Abuse: A Random Sample Survey." *Gerontologist*, 28 (1): 51–57.

Pleck, J. H. 1992. "Work-Family Policies in the United States." In H. Kahne and J. Giele, Eds., *Women's Lives and Women's Work: Parallels and Contrasts in Modernizing and Industrial Countries.* Boulder, CO: Westview Press.

Popenoe, D. 1993. "Renewing Families" *Current*, 350 Feb.: 36–41.

Riche, M. 1991. "The Future of the Family." *American Demographics*, 13, (3): 44–47.

Robertson, N. 1987. "Ethiopia: Amazon Fighters." *Third World Week*, 2 (12): 1–2.

Roscoe, B., and N. Benaske. 1985. "Courtship Violence Experienced by Abused Wives: Similarities in Patterns of Abuse." *Family Relations*, 34: 419–424.

Rosenthal, J. A. 1988. "Patterns of Reported Child Abuse and Neglect." *Child Abuse and Neglect*, 12: 263–271.

Russell, D. 1986. *The Secret Trauma: Incest in the Lives of Girls and Women.* New York: Basic Books.

Steinmetz, S. K., S. Clavan, and K. F. Stein. 1990. *Marriage and Family Realities: Historical and Contemporary Perspectives.* New York: Harper and Row.

Straus, M. A. 1990. "Family Violence." In D. Olson and M. K. Hanson, Eds., *2001: Preparing Families for the Future.* Minneapolis: National Council on Family Relations.

Sun, L. H. 1993. "The Feminization of Poverty: In China, Mao's Promises of Equality Are Giving Way to the Bad Old Days." *Washington Post Weekly Edition*, Apr. 5–11: 9–10.

Szinovacz, M. E. 1983. "Using Couple Data as a Methodological Tool: The Case of Marital Violence." *Journal of Marriage and the Family*, (45): 633–644.

U.S. Bureau of the Census. 1989. "Child Support and Alimony: 1985." *Current Population Report* P–23, no. 154. Washington, DC: U.S. Government Printing Office.

U.S. Bureau of the Census. 1991. "Money Income of Households, Families, and Persons in the United States: 1990." *Current Population Report* P–60, No. 174 Aug.: Table 13. Washington, DC: U.S. Government Printing Office.

U.S. Bureau of the Census. 1991b. *Statistical Abstract of the United States*, p 459. Washington, DC: U.S. Government Printing Office.

Wadsworth, M. E. J. 1979. *Roots of Delinquency.* New York: Barnes and Noble Books.

Weitzman, L. J. 1985. *The Divorce Revolution: The Unexpected Social and Economic Consequences for Women and Children in America.* New York: The Free Press.

Zinn, M. B. and D. S. Eitzen. 1990. *Diversity in Families*, 2d ed. New York: HarperCollins.

Chapter 3

"Abortion as a Contraceptive." *Newsweek*. 1988. June 13, 71.

Adler, J. 1993. "Sex in the Snoring 90s." *Newsweek*, April 26:. 55–56.

Anderson, J. W. and M. Moore. 1993. "The Burden of Womanhood." *Washington Post National Weekly Edition*, Mar. 22–28: 6–7.

Associated Press. 1987. "Extremist Pressure: Textbook Censorship Still Alive, Group Says." *San Francisco Chronical*, Sept. 1: A3.

Beck, M., K. Springen, and D. Foote. 1992. "Sex and Psychotherapy." *Newsweek*, April 13: 55–57.

Bem, S. L. 1993. *The Lenses of Gender: Transforming the Debate on Sexual Inequality*. New Haven: Yale University Press.

Billy, J. O.G., N. S. Lansdale, W. R. Grady, and D. M. Zimmerle. 1988. "Effects of Sexual Activity on Adolescent Social and Psychological Development." *Social Psychology Quarterly*, 51: 190–212.

Bullough, V. 1976. *Sexual Variation in Society and History*. New York: John Wiley.

Caldwell, J., and A. Ilves. 1989. "Dignity and Realism Sought for Gays." *San Francisco Chronicle*, Apr. 20: A33.

Carlson, C. S. 1992. "Sex Scandal Rocks Georgia Prison." *Santa Rosa Press Democrat*, Sept. 8:. A12.

Coser, L. A., S. L. Nock, Patricia A. Steffan, and D. Spain. 1991. *Introduction to Sociology*. San Diego: Harcourt Brace Jovanovich.

Davenport, W. H. 1962. "Sex in Cross-Cultural Perspective." In F. A. Beach, Ed., *Human Sexuality in Four Perspectives*. Baltimore: Johns Hopkins University Press.

Durkheim, É. 1951. *Suicide*. Transl. by J. A. Spaulding and George Simpson. Glencoe: The Free Press.

Engels, F. 1884; 1972. *The Origin of the Family, Private Property and the State*. New York: International Publishers.

Enloe, C. 1988. *Does Khaki Become You? The Militarization of Women's Lives*. Boston: Unwin Hyman.

Eskenazi, M. and D. Gallen (Eds.). 1992. *Sexual Harassment: Know Your Rights*. New York: Carrol and Graff.

Ford, C. S., and F. A. Beach. 1951. *Patterns of Sexual Behavior*. New York: Ace Books.

Freedman, E., and B. Thorne. 1984. "Introduction to Feminist Sexuality Debates." *Signs*, Autumn: 102–105.

Galtney, L. 1992. "Mothers on the Run." *U.S. News & World Report*, June 13: 22–24.

Gies, F., and J. Gies. 1987. *Marriage and the Family in the Middle Ages*. New York: Harper and Row.

Gregerson, E. 1986. "Human Sexuality in Cross-Cultural Perspective." In D. E. Byrne and K. Kelly, Eds., *Alternative Approaches to the Study of Sexual Behavior*. Hillsdale, NJ: Lawrence Erlsbaum Associates.

Grube, J., R. Kleinhesselink, and K. Kearney. 1982. "Male Self-Acceptance and Attraction Toward Women." *Personality and Social Psychology Bulletin*, 8: 107–112.

Henslin, J. M. 1995. *Sociology: A Down-to-Earth Approach*. Boston: Allyn and Bacon.

Hoebel, E. A. 1960, *The Cheyennes: Indians of the Great Plains*. New York: Holt, Rinehart and Winston.

Hunt, M. 1974. *Sexual Behavior in the 1970s*. New York: Dell.

Ingrassia, M. 1994. "Virgin Cool." *Newsweek*, Oct. 17: 59–69.

Jacobson, J. L. 1992. "The Other Epidemic." *World Watch*. May–June: 10–17.

Johnson, A. G. 1992. *Human Arrangements: An Introduction to Sociology*. Fort Worth: Harcourt Brace Jovanovich.

King, P. and B. Cohn. 1993. "Why Won't Packwood Quit?" *Newsweek*, Mar. 15, 36.

Kinsey, A. C. W. Pomeroy, and C. E. Martin. 1948. *Sexual Behavior in the Human Male*. Philadelphia: W. B. Saunders.

Kinsey, A. C., W. Pomeroy, C. E. Martin and P. Gebhard. 1953. *Sexual Behavior in the Human Female*. Philadelphia: W. B. Saunders.

Kusha, H. R. 1992. "Iran's White Revolution and Its Outcome for Iranian Women." In J. Ferrante, Ed., *Sociology: A Global Perspective*, Belmont, CA: Wadsworth.

Lancaster, J. 1992. "Does Anyone Allow Gays to Serve in the Military?" *Washington Post National Weekly Edition*, Dec. 7–13, 14.

Larkin, J. 1988. "The Spirit of '76 Was Pretty Sexy." *San Francisco Chronicle*, Aug. 30: A6.

Laumann, E., R. Michael, S. Michaels, and J. Gagnon. 1994. *The Social Organization of Sexuality*. Chicago: University of Chicago Press.

Lemonick, M. D. 1995. "An Armed Fanatic Raises the Stakes." *Time*, Jan. 9: 34–35.

Lenski, G., J. Lenski, and P. Nolan. 1991. *Human Societies: An Introduction to Macrosociology*. New York: McGraw-Hill.

MacFarquhar, E. 1994. "The War Against Women." *U.S. News & World Report*, Mar. 28: 42–48.

Males, M. 1993. "In Defense of Teenage Mothers." *The Progressive*, Aug.: 22–23.

Marx, K., F. Engels, 1848. Trans. S. H. Beer. 1955. *The Communist Manifesto*. New York: Appleton-Century-Crofts.

Mead, M. 1949. *Male and Female*. New York: New American Library.

———1966. *Coming of Age in Samoa*. New York: New American Library.

Miller, J. 1992. "Women Find Freedom in Islamic Restriction." *The Fresno Bee*, Dec. 17: A–21.

Moreau, R. 1992. "Sex and Death in Thailand." *Newsweek*, July, 20: 50–51.

Nathan, P. E. and S. L. Harris. 1975. *Psychopathology and Society*. New York: McGraw-Hill.

National Advisory Commission on Obscenity and Pornography Report. 1970. Washington, DC: U.S. Government Printing Office.

Nobile, P., and E. Nadler. 1986. *United States of America Versus Sex*. New York: Minotaur Press.

O'Kelley, C. 1980. *Women and Men in Society*. New York: Van Nostrand.

Plant, R. 1987. *The Pink Triangle: The Nazi War Against Homosexuals*. New York: Henry Holt.

Pope, V. 1994. "To Be Young and Pretty in Moscow." *U.S. News & World Report*, Mar. 28: 56.

Reinisch, J. M., and R. Beasley. 1990. *The Kinsey Institute New Report on Sex*. New York: St. Martin's Press.

Robertson, I. 1989. *Society: A Brief Introduction.* New York: Worth.

Sachs, A. 1994. "The Last Commodity: Child Prostitution in the Developing World." *World Watch*, July-Aug.: 24–30.

Schaefer, R. T. 1993. *Racial and Ethnic Groups.* New York: HarperCollins.

Shearer, L. 1985. "Why Teenage Pregnancy Rates Are Rising in the United States." *Parade*, Sept. 15: 10.

Smith, P. 1989. "Sex in American History." *The Nation*, Jan. 31: 221–223.

Stewart, E. W., and J. A. Glynn. 1984. *Introduction to Sociology.* New-York: McGraw-Hill.

Tuller, D. 1993. "Advocates Fighting for Russia's Imprisoned Gays." *San Francisco Chronicle*, Oct. 18: A1, A8,

United Press. 1989. "Sex Education in the United States Is Taught Too Late, Teachers Say." *San Francisco Chronicle*, May 3: A17.

Waller, D., P. King, and E. Salholz. 1992. "Deepening Shame: The Scandal That Is Rocking the Navy." *Newsweek*, Aug. 10: 30–36.

Whitman, F. L., and M. J. Dixon. 1980. "Occupational Choice and Sexual Orientation in Cross-Cultural Perspective." *Homosexuality in International Perspective.* In J. Harry and M. S. Das, Eds., New Delhi: Vikas Publishing House.

Wilkes, P. 1993. "Unholy Acts." *New Yorker*, June 7: 62–79.

World Almanac and Book of Facts. 1995. Mahwah, NJ: World Almanac.

World Bank. 1993. *World Development Report 1993: Investing in Health.* New York: Oxford University Press.

Wright, J. W. 1993. *The Universal Almanac.* Kansas City: Andrews and McMeel.

Yang, C.-K. 1959. *The Chinese Family in the Communist World.* Cambridge: MIT Press.

Chapter 4

Anderson, O. W. 1989. *The Health Service Continuum in Democratic States: An Inquiry into Solvable Problems.* Ann Arbor: Health Administration Press.

Black, R. F., S. Collins, and D. L. Boroughs. 1992. "The Hidden Cost of AIDS." *U.S. News & World Report*, July 27: 49–59.

Brownlee, S., K. Schmidt, and E. Ransdell. 1992. "Origins of a Plague." *U.S. News & World Report*, Mar. 30: 50–52.

Califano, J. A., Jr. 1986. *America's Health Care: Who Lives, Who Dies, and Who Pays.* New York: Random House.

Castro, J. 1991. "Condition: Critical." *Time*, Nov. 25: 34–42.

Chandler, W. U. 1986. "Banishing Tobacco." *State of the World 1986.* In L. R. Brown, Ed. New York: W. W. Norton.

———Choices in Dying. 1993. *State Statutes Governing Living Wills and Appointment of Health Care Agents.* New York: Author.

"Cholera Spreads through Somalia." 1994. *Bakersfield Californian*, Mar. 30: A10.

Clark, M., M. Gosnell, and D. Shapiro. 1991. "When Doctors Play God." *Newsweek*, Aug. 31: 48–54.

Clinton, J. J. 1985. *Health, Population, and Nutritional Systems in LDCs: A Handbook of Family Care.* Washington, DC: U.S. Government Printing Office.

Collins, S. 1993. "Saving Lives Isn't Cheap." *U.S. News & World Report*, June 7: 56–58.

Cowley, G. 1993a. "The Endless Plague." *Newsweek*, Jan. 11: 56–59.

———1993b. "The Future of AIDS." *Newsweek*, Mar. 22: 47–52.

Cowley, G., E. A. Leonard, and M. Hager. 1992. "Tuberculosis: A Deadly Return." *Newsweek*, Mar. 16: 53–57.

David, H. P. 1992. *Eastern Europe: Pronatalist Policies and Private Behavior.* Washington, DC: Population Reference Bureau.

Doka, K. J. 1992. "When Gray Is Golden: Business in an Aging America." *The Futurist*, July–Aug.: 16–20.

Easterbrook, G. 1993. "The National Health Care Phobia." *Newsweek*, Sept. 6: 22–25.

Efron, S. 1993. "As Russian Quality of Life Slips, Preventable Diseases Soar." *Los Angeles Times*, Aug. 17: A8.

———1994. "Russia's Epidemic of Shame." *Los Angeles Times*, Apr. 5: A1, A10.

Ferreri, G. 1987 "Death by Choice." *World Press Review*, Dec.: 51.

Foley, J. D. 1993. *Sources of Health Insurance and Characteristics of the Uninsured: Analysis of the March 1992 Current Population Survey.* SR–16, Issue Brief No. 133. Washington, DC: Employee Benefit Research Institute.

Fuchs, V. R. 1983. *Who Shall Live? Health, Economics, and Social Choice.* New York: Basic Books.

Ginzberg, E. 1994. *Medical Gridlock and Health Reform.* Boulder: Westview Press.

"Globe and Mail." 1992. Cited in "The World Battles a Deadly Plague." *World Press Review*, Jan.: 12.

Goldberg, C. 1992 "Every Day a Sick Day for Russia." *Los Angeles Times*, Aug. 23: A1, A12–A13.

Goliber, T. J. 1989. *Africa's Expanding Population: Old Problems, New Policies.* Washington, DC: Population Reference Bureau.

Gonzales, P., and V. Kotowitz. 1993. "Speaking of International Relief." *Los Angeles Times*, Apr. 20: H6.

Gorman, C. 1992. "Is Health Care Too Specialized?" *Time*, Sept. 14: 56.

Haney, D. Q. 1993. "Class Differences in Death Rates Appear To Be Widening." *San Diego Union-Tribune.* July 8: A10.

Havemann, J. 1992. "Diagnosis: Healthier in Europe." *Los Angeles Times*, Dec. 30: A1, A9.

Hiltzik, M. A. 1989. "Guinea Worm: How and Where This Crippling Disease Strikes." *Los Angeles Times*, Nov. 6: B3.

———1991. "AIDS Spells Disaster for Africa." *Los Angeles Times*, Dec. 28: A14.

Himmelstein, D. U., and S. Woolhandler. 1992. *The National Health Program Chartbook.* Cambridge: The Center for National Health Program Studies.

The Hunger Project. 1985. *Ending World Hunger: An Idea Whose Time Has Come.* New York: Praeger.

Kane, H. 1993. "Cigarette Smoking Drops Again." In L. R. Brown, H. Kane, and E. D. Ayres, Eds., *Vital Signs,* New York: W. W. Norton.

Kaser, M. 1976. *Health Care in the Soviet Union and Eastern Europe.* London: Croom Helm.

Kennedy, P. 1993. *Preparing for the Twenty-first Century.* New York: Random House.

Klima, G. J. 1970. *The Barabaig: East African Cattle Herders.* New York: Holt, Rinehart and Winston.

Kraft, S. 1987. "Toll Threatens Hard-Earned Gains in Nation with Meager Sources." *Los Angeles Times,* Aug. 9: 2, 4–5.

————1992. "Africa's Death Sentence." *Los Angeles Times Magazine,* Mar. 1: 12–16.

Long, W. R. 1992. "Cholera: One Year Later." *Los Angeles Times,* Jan. 15: A3.

Mann, J. 1988. "60 Minutes," Feb. 14.

McGirk, T. 1993. "New Strain of Cholera Is Sweeping South Asia." *San Francisco Examiner and Chronicle,* May 30: A3.

Monmaney, T., and P. McKillop. 1988. "The Return of Tuberculosis." *Newsweek,* Feb. 22: 68–71.

Moody, M. 1993. "Speaking of River Blindness." *Los Angeles Times,* Nov. 23: H6.

Moreau, R. 1992. "Sex and Death in Thailand." *Newsweek,* July 20: 50–51.

Mosley, W. H., and P. Cowley, 1991. *The Challenge of World Health.* Washington, DC: Population Reference Bureau.

Nelson, H. 1988a. "Soviet Goal: Resuscitate Health Care." *Los Angeles Times,* May 15, Part I: 1, 16.

————1988b. "Soviet Goal: Resuscitate Health Care." *Los Angeles Times,* May 15: I1, I16.

————1988c. "Soviet Health Care Reaches the Isolated." *Los Angeles Times,* May 15: A19–A20.

————1988d. "Sweden Considering Private Care for Some Health Needs." *Los Angeles Times,* Mar 7: 10.

"Officials Fear Cholera Outbreak in Somalia May Turn Epidemic." *Los Angeles Times,* 1994. Feb. 28: A17.

Perlman, D. 1994. "Top Scientists Gather for Ninth AIDS Conference." *San Francisco Chronicle,* June 5: A10.

Pol, L. G., M. G. May, and F. R. Hartranft. 1992. "Eight Stages of Aging." *American Demographics,* Aug.: 54–57.

"A Question of Color." *Time,* 1992. Oct. 12: 33.

Reedly, M. 1994. "One Lives, One Dies." *Los Angeles Times,* Feb. 2: A16-A17.

Roark, A. C. 1992. "U.N. Calls Many Child Deaths Preventable." *Los Angeles Times,* Dec. 17: A1, A34.

Roemer, M. I. 1991. *National Health Systems of the World, Vol. 1: The Countries.* New York: Oxford University Press.

Rosenblatt, R., E. Chen, Chris Erskine, and Ken Oelerich. 1993. "Health Care and You." *Los Angeles Times,* Sept. 23: A6.

Rosenthal, M. M. 1987. *Health Care in the People's Republic of China.* Boulder, CO: Westview.

Samuelson, R. J. 1993. "Health Care: How We Got into This Mess." *Newsweek,* Oct. 4: 30–35.

Schieber, G. J., J. P. Poullier, and L. M. Greenwald. 1993. "Health Spending, Delivery, and Outcomes in OECD Countries." *Health Affairs,* 12 (2): 120–129.

Shapiro, J. P., and D. Bowermaster. 1994. "Death on Trial." *U.S. News & World Report,* Apr. 25: 31–39.

Shearer, L. 1990. "Intelligence Report." *Parade Magazine,* May 13: 14.

Shilts, R. 1987. "In Cold Blood: Why the Reagan Administration Ignored Its Own Advisor on AIDS." *Mother Jones,* Nov.: 26–44.

Stolberg, S. 1993a. "Fears Cloud Search for Genetic Roots of Violence." *Los Angeles Times,* Dec. 30: A1, A14.

————1993b. "Nipping Violence in the Bud." *Los Angeles Times,* Dec. 31: A1, A26.

Terris, M. 1990. "Lessons from Canada's Health Program." *Technology Review,* Feb.–Mar.: 27–33.

Thomassie, J. 1991. "The Cholera Epidemic." *Los Angeles Times,* Apr. 9: H6.

"UNICEF Says Seven Million Lives Could Be Saved." *San Francisco Chronicle,* 1987. Dec. 10: A33.

"U.S. Announces Plan to Fight Drug-Resistant Tuberculosis." *San Francisco Chronicle,* 1992. May 1: A10.

Wahl, G. 1987. "Analyzing China." *World Press Review.* Nov.: 50.

Weissman, J. S., and A. M. Epstein. 1994. *Falling Through the Safety Net: Insurance Status and Access to Health Care.* Baltimore: The Johns Hopkins University Press.

Wilkinson, T. 1993. "Prostitution, Prejudice Fuel AIDS Epidemic in Honduras." *Los Angeles Times,* July 27: H1, H4.

World Almanac and Book of Facts. 1994. Mahwah, NJ: World Almanac.

World Bank. 1993. *World Development Report 1993: Investing in Health.* New York: Oxford University Press.

World Health Organization. 1994. "More Women Infected by AIDS Virus." *The Futurist,* Mar.–Apr.: 62–63.

Wright, J. T. Ed. 1993. *The Universal Almanac.* Kansas City: Andrews and McMeel.

Wright, R. 1992. "Three Faces of Hunger." *Los Angeles Times,* Dec. 15.

Chapter 5

Associated Press. 1984. "French Population Aging Causes Worry." *Bakersfield Californian,* p. 22.

Binstock, R. H. 1988. "Aging, Politics, and Public Policy." *The World and I,* 3 (12): 533–547.

Bongaarts, J. 1991. "The KAP-Gap and the Unmet Need for Contraception." *Population and Development Review,* 17 (2): 293–313.

Bouvier, L. F. 1984. "Planet Earth 1984–2034: A Demographic Vision." *Population Bulletin,* 39 (1): 1–39. Washington, DC: Population Reference Bureau.

Bouvier, L. F., and R. W. Gardiner. 1986. "Immigration to the U.S.: The Unfinished Story." *Population Bulletin*, 41 (4): 1–50. Washington, DC: Population Reference Bureau.

Brown, L. R. 1987. "Analyzing the Demographic Trap." In L. R. Brown, *State of the World 1987*. New York: W. W. Norton.

———1991. "The New World Order." In L. R. Brown. *State of the World 1991*. New York: W. W. Norton.

Brown, L. R. and E. C. Wolf. 1986. "Reversing Africa's Decline." In L. R. Brown, *State of the World 1986*. New York: W. W. Norton.

Butler, R. W. 1969. "Ageism: Another Form of Bigotry." *Gerontologist*, 9: 243–246.

———1989. "Dispelling Ageism: The Cross Cutting Intervention." *Annals of the American Academy of Political and Social Science*, 503 (May): 138–147.

Buttner, T., and W. Lutz. 1990. "Estimating Fertility Responses to Policy Measures in the German Democratic Republic." *Population and Development Review*, 16 (3): 539–555.

Chomitz, K. M. 1987. "Demographic Influences on Local Public Education Expenditure: A Review of Econometric Evidence." In Committee on Population, Commission on Behavioral and Social Sciences and Education, National Research Council. Ed., *Demographic Change and the Well-Being of Children and the Elderly* (45–53). Washington, DC: National Academy Press.

Davis, K. 1949. *Human Society*. New York: MacMillian.

Day, A. T. 1985. *Who Cares? Demographic Trends Challenge Family Care for the Elderly*. Washington, DC: Population Reference Bureau.

Diaz-Briquets, S., and L. Perez. 1981. "Cuba: The Demography of Revolution." *Population Bulletin*, 36 (1): 1–41. Washington, DC: Population Reference Bureau.

Ehrlich, P. R. 1968. *The Population Bomb*. New York: Ballantine.

Friedlander, D., and C. Goldschieder. 1984. "Israel's Population: The Challenge of Pluralism." *Population Bulletin*, 39 (2): 1–39. Washington, DC: Population Reference Bureau.

Goldsmith, E., and N. Hildyard. 1984. *The Social and Environmental Effects of Large Dams*. San Francisco: Sierra Club Books.

Goliber, T. J. 1985. "Sub-Saharan Africa: Population Pressures on Development." *Population Bulletin*, 40 (1): 1–46. Washington, DC: Population Reference Bureau.

———1989. "Africa's Expanding Population: Old Problems, New Policies." *Population Bulletin*, 44 (3), Washington, DC: Population Reference Bureau.

Haub, C., M. Mederios., and M. Yanagishita. 1987. *World Population Data Sheet 1987*. Washington, DC: Population Reference Bureau.

Haub, C. and M. Yanagishita. 1992. *World Population Data Sheet 1992*. Washington, DC: Population Reference Bureau.

———1993. *World Population Data Sheet 1993*. Washington, DC: Population Reference Bureau.

———1994. *World Population Data Sheet 1994*. Washington, DC: Population Reference Bureau.

Haupt, A. 1987a. "China's Birth Rate Reported on Rise." *Population Today*, May.

———1987b. "How Romania Tries to Govern Fertility." *Population Today*, Feb.: passim.

Heymann, D., J. Chin, and J. Mann. 1990. "A Global Overview of AIDS." In N. Alexander, H. Gabelnick, and J. Spieler, Eds., *Sexual Transmission of AIDS*. New York: Wiley-Liss.

Hohm, C. F. 1975. "Social Security and Fertility: An International Perspective." *Demography*, 12 (4): 629–644.

Hohm, C. F., F. Galloway, C. Hanson, and D. Biner. 1985. "A Reappraisal of the Social Security-Fertility Hypothesis: A Bidirectional Approach." *Social Science Journal*, 23 (2): 149–160.

Johansson, S., and O. Nygren. 1991. "The Missing Girls of China: A New Demographic Account." *Population and Development Review* 17 (1): 39–42.

Kammeyer, K. C. W., and H. L. Ginn. 1986. *An Introduction to Population*. Chicago: The Dorsey Press.

Keyfitz, N., and W. Flieger. 1990. *World Populaiton and Aging: Demographic Trends in the 20th Century*. Chicago: The University of Chicago Press.

Klingholz, R. 1987. "The March of AIDS." *World Press Review*, Feb.: 57.

Kraft, S. 1992. "Africa's Death Sentence." *Los Angeles Times Magazine*, Mar. 1: 1, 4, 14.

Luther, N. Y., G. Feeney, and W. Zhang. 1990. "One-Child Families or a Baby Boom? Evidence from China's 1987 One-Per-Hundred Survey." *Population Studies*, 44 (2): 341–357.

Lutz, W. 1994. "The Future of World Population." *Population Bulletin*, 49 (1). Washington, DC: The Population Reference Bureau.

Malthus, T. R. 1798. *An Essay on Population*. New York: Augustus Kelly, Bookseller; reprinted in 1965.

Martin, L. G. 1989. "The Graying of Japan." *Population Bulletin*, 44 (2). Washington, DC: Population Reference Bureau.

McMahon, M. K., and C. F. Hohm. 1994. "The Age-Dependency Ratio: Is It an Accurate Measure of Dependency?" Presented at the 1994 Annual Meeting of the Pacific Sociological Association. San Francisco, CA.

Merrick, T. W. 1986. "Population Pressures in Latin America." *Population Bulletin*, 41 (3): 1–50. Washington, DC Population Reference Bureau.

Newland, K. 1979. "International Migration: The Search for Work." *Worldwatch Paper 33*. Washington, DC: Worldwatch Institute.

———1994. "Refugees: The Rising Flood." *Worldwatch Paper*. Washington, DC: Worldwatch Institute.

Omran, A. 1971. "The Epidemiologic Transition: A Theory of the Epidemiology of Population Change." *Milbank Memorial Fund Quarterly*, 49 (2) Part 1:509–530.

Preston, S. H. 1984. "Children and the Elderly in the U.S." *Scientific American*, 251 (6): 44–49.

Robinson, L. H. and S. E. McLees. 1982. "Africa Officials Express Attitudes about Population Growth." *Intercom*, 10 (3), Mar.

Rosenbaum, W. A., and J. W. Button. 1989. "Is There a Gray Peril? Retirement Politics in Florida." *Gerontologist*, 29: 300–306.

Serril, M. S. 1987. "In the Grip of the Scourge." *Time*, Feb. 16.

Simmons, A. B. 1992. "Sixty Million on the Move." *UNESCO Courier* (Jan.): 30–33.

Sokolovsky, J. 1982. "Introduction: Perspectives on Aging in the Third World." In J. Sokolovsky, Guest Ed., *Aging and the Aged in the Third World: Part I, Studies in Third World Societies*, No. 22. Williamsburg, VA: College of William and Mary, Department of Anthropology.

Stanton-Russell, S., and M. Teitelbaum. 1992. *International Migration and Internaitonal Trade*. New York: World Bank.

Stone, M. 1987. "Q. and A. on AIDS." *New York*, Mar.: 36.

Streib, G. F., and R. H. Binstock. 1990. "Aging and the Social Sciences: Changes in the Field." In R. H. Binstock and L. K. George, Eds., *Handbook of Aging and the Social Sciences*, 3d ed. San Diego: Academic Press.

Tien, H. Y. 1983. "China: Demographic Billionaire." *Population Bulletin*, 30 (2): 1–42. Washington, DC: Population Reference Bureau.

Tien, H. Y., Z. Tianlu, P. Yu, L. Jingneng, and L. Zhongtang. 1992. "China's Demographic Dilemmas." *Population Bulletin*, 47 (1): 1–44. Washington, DC: Population Reference Bureau.

United Nations. 1992. *Human Development Report*. New York: United Nations.

United Nations. 1994. *Programme of Action of the United Nations International Conference on Population and Development*. New York: United Nations.

UNFPA/United Nations Population Fund. 1993. *The State of World Population 1993*. New York: United Nations Population Fund.

van de Kaa, D. J. 1987. "Europe's Second Demographic Transition." *Population Bulletin*, 42 (1): 1–57. Washington, DC: Population Reference Bureau.

Visaria, P., and L. Visaria. 1981. "India's Population: Second and Growing." *Population Bulletin*, 36 (4): 1–55. Washington, DC: Population Reference Bureau.

Wallis, C. 1987. "You Haven't Heard Anything Yet." *Time*, Feb. 16: 54.

Weller, R. H., and L. F. Bouvier. 1981. *Population: Demography and Policy*. New York: St. Martin's Press.

World Bank. 1984. *World Development Report 1984*. New York: Oxford University Press.

Wrigley, E. A. 1969. *Population and History*. New York: McGraw-Hill.

Yi, Z., T. Ping, G. Liu, and X. Ying. 1991. "A Demographic Decomposition of the Recent Increase in Crude Birth Rates in China." *Population and Development Review*, 17 (3): 435–450

Zopf, Jr., P. E. 1984. *Population: An Introduction to Social Demography*. Palo Alto, CA: Mayfield.

Chapter 6

Amnesty International. 1992. *A Comprehensive Report on Human Rights Violence Around the World*. New York: Amnesty International.

Associated Press. 1993. "Cocaine Sentences Discriminate Against Blacks, Activists Claim." in *San Francisco Chronicle*, Aug. 26: 18–19.

Bonner, R. 1988. "Indonesia." *New Yorker*, June 6: 45–54.

Caughlin, W. J. 1969. "Caste System Still Operates in India." *Los Angeles Times*, Jul. 13: 1–2.

Cohen, R. 1967. "Slavery in Africa: Introduction." *Transaction*, Jan.–Feb.: 44–46.

Duke, L. 1993. "For Black America: The Search for Unity." *Washington Post National Weekly Edition*, Sept. 6–12: 13.

Epstein, E. 1993. "Moslems Get Even Angrier." *San Francisco Chronicle*, May 19.

Espinoza, S., and B. Pimentel. 1993. "U.S. Steps up Investigation of White Racist Terrorists." *San Francisco Chronicle*, Aug. 13: 1, 15.

———1993. "Immigration Backlash Explodes." *San Francisco Chronicle*, Aug. 27: 1, 6.

Garraty, J. A., and P. Gay. 1981. *The Columbia History of the World*. New York: Dorset Press.

Hill, H. 1973. "Anti-Oriental Agitation and the Rise of Working-Class Racism." *Society*, Jan.–Feb.: 44–53.

Ingrassa, M. 1993. "Endangered Family." *Newsweek*, Aug. 30: 17–29.

Kageyama, Y. 1993. "Xenophobia Thrives at Japanese Park Known as 'Little Tehran.'" *San Francisco Chronicle*, Apr. 29: A14.

Kramer, J. 1993. "Neo-Nazis: A Chaos in the Head." *New Yorker*, June.

Liebow, E. 1967. *Tally's Corner*. Boston: Little Brown.

Lifton, R. J. 1986. *The Nazi Doctors: Medical Killing and the Psychology of Genocide*. New York: Basic Books.

Long, W. 1988. "Brazil: No Equality for Blacks Yet." *Los Angeles Times*, Apr. 9: 1, 16.

Monroe, S. 1988. "Blacks in Britain: Grim Lives, Grimmer Prospects." *Newsweek*, Jan. 4: 32–33.

Morganthau, T. 1992. "Beyond Black and White." *Newsweek*, May 18: 28–30.

Mydans, S. 1993. "Immigration Opposition Grows." *San Francisco Chronicle*, June 28: A3.

Myrdal, G. 1964. *An American Dilemma*. New York: McGraw-Hill.

Neier, A. 1987. "Refugee Gulags." *The Nation*, Dec. 12: 363–364.

North, J. 1985. *Freedom Rising*. New York: Macmillan.

Oberg, K. 1940. "The Kingdom of Ankole in Uganda." In E. E. Evans-Prichard and M. Fortes, Eds. *African Political System*. Oxford University Press.

Olcott, M. 1944. "The Caste System of India." *American Sociological Review*, 9, Dec. 6: 648–657.

Ottaway, D. 1993. "Ethnic Cleansing's New Diaspora." *Washington Post National Weekly Edition*, Aug. 23–29: 10–12.

Otterbein, K. F. 1967 "The Evolution of Zulu Warfare." In P. Bohannon, *Law and Warfare: Studies in the Anthropology of Conflict*. Garden City, N.Y.: Natural History Press.

Pearce, D. M. 1979. "Gatekeepers and Housekeepers: Institutional Patterns of Racial Steering." *Social Problems*, Feb.: 323–342.

Pomfret, J. 1993. "Exodus in Europe." *Washington Post National Weekly Edition*, Aug. 2–8: 6–7.

Reuters. 1993. "Germans Say Racism Is National Problem." *San Francisco Chronicle*, Sept. 28: A12.

Richberg, K. 1994. "Is Africa Falling Apart?" *Washington Post National Weekly Edition* Sept. 12–18: 6–7.

Robinson, E. 1993. "Sweden's Ambivalent Embrace." *Washington Post National Weekly Edition*, Aug. 9–15: 8–9.

Sandalov, M. 1994. "California Blamed for Immigration Lies." *San Francisco Chronicle*, July 6: A3.

Sartre, J.-P. 1963. In F. Fannon, *The Wretched of the Earth*. New York: Grove Press, p. 8.

Shaefer, R. T. 1988. *Racial and Ethnic Groups*. Glenview, Ill.: Scott Foresman.

Sowell, T. *The Economics and Politics of Race*. New York: Quill.

Swardson, A. 1994. "Canadian Leaders Play Down Separatists' Win in Quebec." *San Francisco Chronicle*, Sept. 14: A12–13.

Taylor, P. 1993. "The War the World Forgot." *Washington Post National Weekly Edition*, Oct. 4–10: 16.

Thomas, R., and A. Murr. 1993. "The Economic Cost of Immigration." *Newsweek*, Aug. 9: 18–19.

Thornton, R. 1988. *American Indian Holocaust and Survival*. Norman, OK: University of Oklahoma Press.

Trachenberg, J. 1966. *The Devil and the Jews*. New York: Harper and Row.

Turque, B., S. Reiss, M. Liu, and A. Wolfberg. 1993. "Why Our Borders Are Out of Control." *Newsweek*, Aug. 9:25.

United Nations, *The State of World Population 1993*. New York: United Nations Population Fund.

U. S. Department of Health and Human Services. 1986. *Health—United States*. Washington, D.C.: U.S. Government Printing Office.

Vobejda, B. 1993. "No Exit: Isolated Urban Ghetto." *Washington Post National Weekly Edition*, Mar. 15–21: 6–7.

Williams, C. J. 1993. "A Tragic Portrait of Civilization Gone Wrong." *Los Angeles Times*, June 8: H–3, H–5.

Winter, R. 1994. "Rwanda Up Close and Horrible: Genocide." *Washington Post National Weekly Edition*, June 13–19: 23–24.

Chapter 7

Bose, A. 1990. "Urbanization in China and India." *Beijing Review* (Apr. 30–June 6): 22.

Chan, K. W. 1992. "Economic Growth Strategy and Urbanization Policies in China, 1949–1982." *International Journal of Urban and Regional Research* 17, (2): 275–305.

Cornish, E. 1991. "Building Utopia: Lessons from Brasilia." *The Futurist*, July–Aug.: 29–32.

Costa, F. J., A. K. Dutt, L. J. C. Ma, and A. G. Noble. 1989. "Trends and Prospects." In F. J. Costa, A. Dutt, L. J. C. Ma, and A. G. Noble. *Urbanization in Asia: Spatial Dimensions and Policy Issues*. Honolulu: The University of Hawaii Press.

Ficker, V. B., and H. S. Graves. 1978. *Social Science Urban Crisis*. New York: Macmillian.

Fischer, C. S. 1987. *The Urban Experience*. Orlando: Harcourt Brace Jovanovich.

Glasser, I. 1994. *Homelessness in Global Perspective*. New York: G. K. Hall.

Guldin, G. 1992. "Urbanizing China: Some Startling Conclusions." In G. Guldin, *Urbanizing China*. New York: Greenwood Press.

Hardoy, J. E. 1992. "Introduction." In R. M. Morse and J. E. Hardoy, Eds., *Rethinking the Latin American City*. Washington, DC: The Woodrow Wilson Center.

Harris, C., and E. L. Ullman. 1945. "The Nature of Cities." *Annals of the American Academy of Political and Social Science*, 242: 7–11.

Haub, C., and M. Yanagishita. 1993. *1993 World Population Data Sheet*. Washington, DC: The Population Reference Bureau.

Herzog, L. 1991. "Cross-national Urban Structure in the Era of Global Cities: The US-Mexico Transfrontier Metropolis." *Urban Studies*, 28, (4): 519–533.

Holston, J. 1989. *The Modernist City: An Anthropological Critique of Brasilia*. Chicago: The University of Chicago Press.

Hoyt, H. 1939. *The Structure and Growth of Residential Neighborhoods in American Cities*. Washington, DC: Federal Housing Administration.

Jacobs, J. 1961. *The Death and Life of Great American Cities*. New York: Random House.

Kasarda, J. D., and E. M. Crenshaw. 1991. "Third World Urbanization: Dimensions, Theories, and Determinants." *Annual Review of Sociology* 17: 467–501.

Kornblum, W. 1991. *Sociology in a Changing World* (2d ed.). Fort Worth: Holt, Rinehart, and Winston.

Langer, W. L. 1978. "The Black Death." In V. B. Ficker and H. S. Graves, *Social Science and Urban Crisis*. New York: Macmillian.

Lenski, G., and J. Lenski. 1987. *Human Societies: An Introduction to Macrosociology*. New York: McGraw-Hill.

Levitas, M. 1990. "Homeless in America." *New York Times Magazine*, June 10: 44–45, 82–91.

Linden, E. 1993. "Megacities." *Time*, Jan. 1: 30–38.

Margolis, M. 1992. "A Third-World City That Works." *World Monitor*, Mar.: 43–50.

Meinert, D. 1993. "Judge Blocks NAFTA, Cites Environment." *San Diego Union-Tribune*, July 1 Section A,: 1, 19.

Mohanti, P. 1983. "A Village Called Nanpur." *UNESCO Courier*, June: 11–14.

Mumford, L. 1961. *The City in History: Its Origins, Its Transformations, and Its Prospects.* New York: Harcourt, Brace, and World.

Pannell, C. 1992. "The Role of Great Cities in China." In G. Guldin, *Urbanizing China.* New York: Greenwood Press.

Park, R. E., and E. W. Burgess. 1925. *The City.* Chicago: The University of Chicago Press.

Perdue, W. D. 1986. *Sociological Theory.* Palo Alto: Mayfield.

Population Crisis Committee. 1990. *Cities: Life in the World's 100 Largest Metropolitan Areas.* Washington, DC: Population Crisis Committee.

Powers, C. T. 1981. "Ethiopia—Village Life Is Still Hard." *Los Angeles Times,* Oct. 30, Part I: 1, 10–12.

Reissman, L. 1964. *The Urban Process: Cities in Industrial Societies.* New York: The Free Press.

Rossi, P. I. 1989. *Down and Out in America: The Origins of Homelessness.* Chicago: The University of Chicago Press.

Sanchez, R. A. 1989. "Health and Environmental Risks of the Maquiladora in Mexicali." *Transboundary Resource Report,* 3: 1–3.

Sirjamaki, J. 1964. *The Sociology of Cities.* New York: Random House.

Sjoberg, G. 1973. "The Origin and Evolution of Cities." In *Scientific American, Cities: Their Origin, Growth, and Human Impact.* San Francisco: W. H. Freeman: 19–27.

Snow, D., and L. Anderson. 1993. *Down on Their Luck: A Study of Homeless Street People.* Berkley: University of California Press.

Snow, D., S. Baker, L. Anderson, and M. Martin. 1986. "The Myth of Mental Illness Among the Homeless." *Social Problems,* 33 (June): 407–423.

Street, D., and Associates. 1978. *Handbook of Contemporary Urban Life.* San Francisco: Jossey-Bass.

Suttles, G. 1967. *The Social Order of the Slum.* Chicago: The University of Chicago Press.

Thomlinson, R. 1978. "The Nature and Rise of Cities." In V. B. Ficker and H. S. Graves, *Social Science and Urban Crisis.* New York: Macmillian.

United Nations Centre for Human Settlement. 1990. *Shelter: From Projects to National Strategies.* New York: United Nations (International Year of Shelter for the Homeless).

United Nations. 1991. *World Urbanization Prospects 1990.* ST/ESA/SER.A/121. Department of International and Social Affairs. New York: United Nations.

Wilson, W. J. 1973. *The Declining Significance of Race.* Chicago: The University of Chicago Press.

———1987. *The Truly Disadvantaged.* Chicago: The University of Chicago Press.

Wirth, L. 1938. "Urbanism as a Way of Life." *American Journal of Sociology* 44: 1–24.

World Bank. 1990. *World Development Report 1990: Special Issue on Poverty.* New York: Oxford University Press for the World Bank.

Chapter 8

Balk, A. 1990. *The Myth of American Eclipse: The New Global Age.* New Brunswick: Transaction.

Barber, B. 1987. "Yen in Thailand: Investment or Imperialism?" *San Francisco Examiner,* Oct. 11: D1, D5.

Bell, D. 1973. *The Coming of the Postindustrial Society.* New York: Basic Books.

Bluestone, B. and B. Harrison. 1982. *The Deindustrialization of America.* New York: Basic Books.

Boswell, T. and A. Bergeson. 1987. "American Prospects in a Period of Hegemonic Decline and Economic Crisis." In T. Boswell and A. Bergeson, *America's Changing Role in the World System.* New York: Praeger.

Brooks, W. T. 1987. "No Proof That World Bank Lending Helps Poor Nations." *San Francisco Chronicle,* Dec. 16, Briefing Section: 9.

Butler, S. 1993. "Japan is No Tower of Strength." *U.S. News & World Report,* Nov. 22: 38.

Butler, S. and S. V. Lawrence. 1993. "The Lure of the Orient." *U.S. News & World Report,* Nov. 22: 34–38.

Church, G. J. 1993. "Jobs in an Age of Insecurity." *Time,* Nov. 22: 34–39.

Cooperman, A. 1994. "For Russians, Drop in Longevity Mirrors Decline in Quality of Life." *The San Diego Union-Tribune,* Feb. 4, Sec. A: 25.

Eckhouse, J. 1988. "U.S. Exporting Snafu." *San Francisco Chronicle,* March 14: C3, C11.

Forero, 1993. "Maquiladora Paradox: Companies Thrive, Workers Don't." *San Diego Union-Tribune,* Nov., 7, Part A 1, 17.

Gargan, E. A. 1988. "China Drafts Constitution for Hong Kong." *The Santa Rosa Press Democrat,* Apr. 28: A9 (reprinted from the *New York Times*).

Geiger, E. 1994. "Many Germans Now Homeless, as Economic Miracle Fades." *San Francisco Chronicle,* Feb. 10: 14: 18.

Gittleson, J. 1988. "Korean Workers Fight Low Wages." *San Francisco Examiner,* Oct. 18: D1, D4.

Goldberg, C. 1994. "Russia's Factory Failures Raise Fears for the Future." *The Los Angeles Times,* March 7, Sec. A: 4.

Hage, D., L. Grant, and J. Impoco. 1993. "White-Collar Wasteland." *U.S. News & World Report,* June 28: 42–52.

Halberstam, D. 1987. *The Reckoning.* New York: Avon Books.

Hardy, Q. 1994. "Japanese Stocks Plummet: Political Setback Is Cited." *The Wall Street Journal.* Feb. 25: C1, C17.

Hatcher, P. 1987. "Confronting the Problem." *World Press Review,* Aug.: 13–15.

Headden, S. 1993. "Made in the U.S.A." *U.S. News & World Report,* Nov., 22: 48–55.

Holden, T. 1992. "How Japan Keeps the Tigers in a Cage." *Business Week,* Aug. 17: 98D (3).

Ignatius, A. 1994. "Money to Be Made: For All Russia's Woes, It Offers Quick Riches to Deft Entrepreneurs." *Wall Street Journal,* Mar. 1, Sec. A.

Jameson, S. 1992. "Does Japan Ever Really Change?" *Los Angeles Times*, December 9: A1, A14.

Kennedy, P. 1988. *The Rise and Fall of the Great Powers*. New York: Random House.

Knight, R., J. Marks, and F. Coleman. 1993. "Push Comes to Shove: Western Europe Is Ailing, Angry, and Afraid of the Future." *U.S. News & World Report*, June 14: 53–64.

Kraft, S. 1994. "Tens of Thousands in France Protest Pay Cuts for the Young." *The Los Angeles Times*, Mar. 26: A10, A12.

Luttwak, E. N. 1993. *The Endangered American Dream*. New York: Simon and Schuster.

McGeary, J., and C. Booth. 1993. "Cuba Alone." *Time*, Dec. 9: 44–54.

McInerney, F., and S. White. 1993. *Beating Japan*. New York: Truman Talley Books/Dalton.

Milbank, D. 1994. "Unlike Rest of Europe, Britain Is Creating Jobs, But They Pay Poorly." *Wall Street Journal*. Mar. 28: A1, A5.

Miller, M. 1994. "Lost on the Info Highway: Japan's HDTV Not the Definition of Success." *The San Diego Union-Tribune*, Mar. 6: A1, A17.

Mills, C. W. 1951. *White Collar*. New York: Oxford University Press.

Morrow, L. 1993. "The Temping of America." *Time*, Mar. 29: 40–47.

Naisbitt, J. 1994. *Global Paradox*. New York: William Morrow.

National Journal. 1993. "How One Company Didn't Make It Big In Japan." *National Journal*, Apr. 10: 870–871.

Powell, B., et al. 1988. "The Pacific Century." *Newsweek*, Feb. 22: 42–48.

Reich, R. 1983. *The Next American Frontier*. New York: Times Book.

Rose, R. L. 1994. "Humming Mills: Once the 'Rust Belt,' Midwest Now Boasts Revitalized Factories." *Wall Street Journal*, Jan. 3, Part A: 1, 38.

Rosecrance, R. 1990. *America's Economic Resurgence*. New York: Harper and Row.

Sesit, M. R. "Dollar Falls 4% Against Yen in Trade Dispute." *Wall Street Journal*. Feb. 15: C1, C17.

Soto, E. C. 1988. "China's Private Initiative Fuels Development." *World Press Review*, Jan.: 22–23.

Simmons, A. B. 1992. "Sixty Million on the Move." *UNESCO Courier*. Jan.: 30–33.

Simons, C. 1987. "They Get by with a Lot of Help from Their Kyoiku Mamas." *Smithsonian*, Mar.: 44–52.

Talbott, S. 1992. "A Miracle Wrapped in Danger." *Time*, Dec. 7: 34–35.

Tyson, L. D. 1992. Who's Bashing Whom? Trade Conflict in High-Technology Industries. Washington, DC: Institute for International Economics.

Wall Street Journal. 1993. "U.S. Auto Production Expected to Outpace Japan's for a Change." *Wall Street Journal*, Dec. 21, Sec. C: 18.

Wallerstein, I. 1974. *The Modern World System*. New York: Academic Press.

———1979. *The Capitalist World Economy*. Cambridge, England: Cambridge University Press.

———1980. *The Modern World System II: Mercantilism and the Consolidation of the European World Economy*, 1600–1750. New York: Academic Press.

———1991. *Geopolitics and Geoculture*. Cambridge, England: Cambridge University Press.

Wessel, D. 1994. "The U.S. Economy May Dominate for Years." *Wall Street Journal*, Jan. 10, Part A: 1.

Williams, M., C. Forman, and J. M. Schlesinger. 1994. "Yen's Rise Poses Broad Threat to Japan Firms." *Wall Street Journal*. Feb. 16: A3, A12.

Williams, M. and J. M. Schlesinger. 1994. "Japan, Economically and Politically Ailing, Is Sinking into Gloom." *Wall Street Journal*. Dec. 29: A1, A10.

World Almanac. 1993. *The World Almanac and Book of Facts: 1994*. Mahwah, NJ: Funk and Wagnalls.

Chapter 9

Birdsall, N. 1981. *Population Growth and Poverty in the Developing World*. Washington, DC: Population Reference Bureau.

Bluestone, B., and B. Harrison. 1982. *The Deindustrialization of America: Plant Closings, Community. Abandonment, and the Dismantling of Basic Industry*. New York: Basic Books.

Bornschier, V., and T. B. Cao. 1979. "Income Inequality: A Cross-National Study of the Relationships Between MNC Penetration, Dimensions of the Power Structure, and Income Distribution." *American Sociological Review*, 44, June: 487–506.

Bottomore, T. 1993. *Elites and Society* (2d. ed.). London: Routledge.

Braun, D. 1991. *The Rich Get Richer: The Rise of Income Inequality in the United States and the World*. Chicago: Nelson-Hall.

Brown, J. L. 1987. "Hunger in the United States." *Scientific American*, 256, Feb.: 37–41.

Brown, L. R. 1991. *State of the World, 1991*. New York: W. W. Norton.

———1994. *State of the World, 1994*. New York: W. W. Norton.

Brown, L. R., H. Kane, and E. Ayres. 1993. *Vital Signs 1993: The Trends That Are Shaping Our Future. State of the World*. New York: W. W. Norton.

Buraway, M. 1983. "Between the Labor Process and the State: The Changing Face of Factory Regimes under Advanced Capitalism." *American Sociological Review*, 48, Oct.: 587–605.

Chase-Dunn, C. 1975. "The Effects of International Dependence on Development and Inequality." *American Sociological Review*, 40, Dec.: 720–738.

Collins, R. 1975. *Conflict Sociology*. New York: Academic Press.

Copeland, J. B., and J. Harmes. 1987. "The Rise of Gringo Capitalism." *Newsweek*, Jan. 5: 40–41.

Copeland, J. B., D. Shapiro, E. Williams, and N. Matsumoto. 1987. "How to Win Over a Japanese Boss." *Newsweek*, Feb. 2:46–48.

Domhoff, G. W. 1970. *The Higher Circles: The Governing Class in America.* New York: Random House.

Doyle, J. 1985. *Altered Harvest: Agriculture, Genetics, and the Fate of the World's Food Supply.* New York: Viking Press.

Ehrenreich, B. 1986. "Two Americas: Are We Becoming a Nation of Haves and Have Nots?" *This World.* Nov.: 9–12.

Erikson, R., J. H. Goldthorpe, and L. Portocarero. 1982. "Social Fluidity in Industrial Nations: England, France, and Sweden." *British Journal of Sociology*, 33:1–34.

Fallow, J. 1987. "The Rice Plot." *This World.* Feb. 15: 8–9.

Gelber, A. 1983. "The Welfare Crisis." *Newsweek*, July 25: 48- 51.

Goldsmith, E., and N. Hildyard. 1984. *The Social and. Environmental Effects of Large Dams.* San Francisco: Sierra Club Books.

Goldsmith, W. W., and R. Wilson. 1991. "Poverty and Distorted Industrialization in the Brazilian Northeast." *World Development*, 19: (5): 435–456.

Guillermoprieto, A. 1986. "Sharing in the Failure: Anti-Drug Operation Folds Its Tents." *Newsweek*, Nov. 24: 63.

Hage, D., L. Grant, and J. Impoco. 1993. "White Collar Wasteland." *U.S. News & World Report*, June 28: 42–51.

Hancock, G. 1991. *Lords of Poverty.* London: Mandarin Paperbacks.

Harrison, B., and B. Bluestone. 1988. *The Great U-turn: Corporate Restructuring and the Polarizing of America.* New York: Basic Books.

Haub, C., and M. Yanagishita. 1993. *1993 World Population Data Sheet.* Washington, DC: Population Reference Bureau.

Henwood, D. 1992. "A Caste of Millions." *UTNE Reader*, Jan.–Feb.: (49): 115–17.

Inhaber, H., and S. Carroll. 1992. *How Rich Is Too Rich? Income and Wealth in America.* New York: Praeger.

Kahn, E.F. Jr., 1987. "Profiles: Dwayne Oliver Andreas." *The New Yorker*, Feb. 16: 41–67.

Kramer, J. 1987. "Letter from the Elysian Fields." *New Yorker*, Mar. 2: 40–75.

Levitas, M. 1990. "Homeless in America." *New York Times Magazine*, June 10: 44–45, 82–91.

Lin, N., and Y. Bian. 1991. "Getting Ahead in Urban China." *American Journal of Sociology*, 97: 3, Nov.: 657–689.

Mills, C. W. 1958. *The Power Elite.* New York: Oxford University Press.

Moore, G. 1979. "The Structure of a National Elite Network." *American Sociological Review*, 44, Oct.: 692–712.

Moore, M. 1987. "We Are the Baby Bust." *This World*, Mar. 1: 12–13.

Muller, E. A. 1988. "Democracy, Economic Development, and Income Inequality." *American Sociological Review*, 53. Feb.: 50–68.

Pasley, J. L. 1987. "No More Little House on the Prairie." *This World*, Jan. 4: 13–14.

Reich, R. B. 1983. *The Next American Frontier.* New York: New York Times Books.

———1991. *The Work of Nations: Preparing Ourselves for 21st Century Capitalism.* New York: Alfred A. Knopf.

Robinson, R. V., and M. A. Garnier. 1985. "Class Reproduction Among Men and Women in France." *American Sociological Review*, 91, Sept.: 250–280.

Rubinson, R. 1976. "The World Economy and the Distribution of Income Within State: A Cross-National Study." *American Sociological Review*, 11, Aug.: 638–659.

Rytina, J. H., W. H. Form, and J. Pease. 1970. "Income Stratification Ideology." *American Journal of Sociology*, 35, Apr.: 703–716.

Samorodov, A. 1992. "Transition, Poverty, and Inequality in Russia." *International Labour Review*, 131 (3): 335–354.

Schwarz, J. E., and T. J. Volgy. 1992. "Out of Line: Why Poverty's Worse Than You Think." *New Republic*, 207 (22): 16–18.

———1993. "Above the Poverty Line—But Poor: One-Fourth of a Nation." *The Nation*, 256 (6): 191–193.

Schwarz, J., and B. Turque. 1987. "Collision Course? A Restless Auto Union Takes on Its Leaders." *Newsweek*, Feb. 23: 52.

U.S. Bureau of the Census. 1987. *Statistical Abstract of the United States, 1987.* Washington, DC: U.S. Government Printing Office.

U.S. Bureau of the Census. 1991. *Statistical Abstract of the United States, 1991.* Washington, DC: U.S. Government Printing Office.

U.S. Bureau of the Census. 1993. *Statistical Abstract of the United States, 1993.* Washington, DC: U.S. Government Printing Office.

Vaughn, M. 1982. "Socialist Stratification and Social Survival." *British Journal of Sociology*, 37, June: 157–178.

Wilkinson, R. G. 1992. "National Mortality Rates: The Impact of Inequality." *American Journal of Public Health*, 82: 8, Aug.: 1082–1085.

Wimberley, D. W., and R. Bello. 1992. "Effects of Foreign Investment, Exports, and Economic Growth on Third-World Food Consumption." *Social Forces*, 70 (4): 895–921.

World Almanac. 1993. *The World Almanac and Book of Facts, 1994.* New Jersey: Funk and Wagnalls.

Wright, E. O., D. Hachen, C. Costello, and J. Sprague. 1982. "The American Class Structure." *American Sociological Review*, 47, Dec.: 709–726.

Chapter 10

Adler, J. 1981. "The Browning of America." *Newsweek*, Feb. 23: 26–37.

Ashworth, W. 1986. *The Late Great Lakes: An Environmental History.* New York: Knopf.

Bales, R. 1992. "Mexico's Smog Sets a Record." *Los Angeles Times*, Mar. 16: A–1.

Brown, L. R. 1987. *State of the World.* New York: W. W. Norton.

———1991. "The Aral Sea: Going, Going. . . ." *World Watch*, Jan.–Feb.: 20–27.

Brown, L. R., C. Flavin, and S. Postel. 1991. *Saving the Planet.* New York: W. W. Norton.

Brown, M. H. 1986. "The National Swill: Poisoning Old Man River." *Science Digest*, June: 55–65.

Davis, S. N. 1992. "Our Precious Ground Water." *The World Book Year Book.* Chicago: World Book.

Dorfman, A. 1992. "Summit to Save the Earth: The World's Next Trouble Spots." *Time*, June 1: 64–65.

Durning, A. 1991. "Asking How Much Is Enough." In L. R. Brown, Ed., *State of the World 1991.* New York: W. W. Norton.

Easterbrook, G. 1992. "A House of Cards." *Newsweek*, June 1: 24, 29–33.

Ehrlich, P. R., and A. H. Ehrlich. 1970. *Population, Resources, and Environment.* San Francisco: Freeman.

Elmer-DeWitt, P. 1992. "Rich vs. Poor." *Time*, June 1: 42–46, 51–54, 58.

French, H. 1990. "Cleaning the Air." In L. R. Brown, Ed., *State of the World 1990.* New York: W. W. Norton.

Goldsmith, E., and N. Hildyard. 1984. *The Social and Environmental Effects of Large Dams.* San Francisco: Sierra Club Books.

Green, P., and D. Bartal. 1992. "Turning a Sea into Toxic Soup." *U.S. News & World Report*, Apr. 13: 47.

Gup, T. 1993. "It's Nature, Stupid!" *Time*, July 12: 38–40.

Hull, J. B., et al. 1986. "A Proud River Runs Red." *Time*, Nov. 24: 36–37.

Huxley, A. 1932. *Brave New World.* New York: New American Library.

Long, William R. 1992. "Anti-Smog Effort Not Working, Say Choking Chileans." *Los Angeles Times*, July 24: A5.

Myers, N. 1984. *GAIA: An Atlas of Planet Management.* Garden City, NY: Anchor Books.

Naar, J., and A. J. Naar. 1993. *This Land Is Your Land.* New York: HarperCollins.

Nash, M. 1992. "The Beef Against Beef." *Time*, Apr. 20: 76–77.

Ostman, R. 1982. *Acid Rain: A Plague upon the Waters.* Minneapolis: Dillon.

Parrish, M. 1992. "Drop in U.S. Oil Spills Tied to Tough Laws." *Los Angeles Times*, Aug. 22: A12.

Postel, S. 1990. "Saving Water for Agriculture." In L. R. Brown, Ed., *State of the World 1990.* New York: W. W. Norton.

———1991. "Emerging Water Scarcities." *The World-Watch Reader*, L. R. Brown, Ed. New York: W. W. Norton.

Powers, C. T. 1992. "Poland's Vistula River." *Los Angeles Times*, May 26: H4–H5.

Rupert, J. 1992. "Death of a Desert Sea." *Washington Post National Weekly Edition*, July 6–12: 10.

Satchell, M. 1992. "The Rape of the Oceans." *U.S. News & World Report*, June 22: 64–75.

Sheaffer, J. R., and L. A. Stevens. 1983. *Future Water.* New York: William Morrow.

Simon, S. 1992. "Europe's Chamber Pot." *San Francisco Examiner*, July 26: 6.

Sivard, R. L. 1992. *World Military and Social Expenditures.* Washington, DC: World Priorities.

Tempest, R. 1987. "India Bogged Down in Ganges River Cleanup." *Los Angeles Times*, Aug. 9, Part I: 1, 18, 20.

"Vital Signs" 1991. *World Watch*, Nov.–Dec.: 6.

Watson, R., et al. 1987. "The Blotch on the Rhine." *Newsweek*, Nov. 24: 58–60.

Weisskopf, M. 1987. "In Minimata, the City of Death, It's Hard to Tell if Life Goes On." *Washington Post National Weekly Edition*, May 11: 18.

World Almanac. 1987. New York: Newspaper Enterprise Association.

World Development Report 1992: Development and the Environment. 1992. Oxford: Oxford University Press.

Wright, J., Ed. 1991. *The Universal Almanac 1992.* Kansas City: Andrews and McMeel.

Yerkey, G., 1987. "Ganges Choked by Waste." *San Francisco Examiner*, Mar. 29: A25–A26.

Chapter 11

Bauerlein, M. 1993. "GATTzilla." *Utne Reader*, Jan.–Feb.: 19–21

Begley, S. 1987. "The Lessons of Chernobyl." *Newsweek*, Apr. 12: 50–56.

———1993. "Killed by Kindness." *Newsweek*, Apr. 12: 50–56.

Bivens, M. 1994. "Horror of Soviet Nuclear Sub's '61 Tragedy Told." *Los Angeles Times*, Jan. 3: A1, A6.

Brough, H. 1991. "Holy Cows, Unholy Trouble." *World Watch*, Sep.–Oct.: 19–21.

Brown, L. R. 1987. *State of the World.* New York: W. W. Norton.

———1992:a. "Launching the Environmental Revolution." *State of the World 1992.* L. R. Brown, Project Director. New York: W. W. Norton.

———1992:b. "Grainland Shrinks." *Vital Signs 1992.* New York: W. W. Norton.

———1993. "Meat Production Up Slightly." *Vital Signs 1993.* New York: W. W. Norton.

———1994. "Facing Food Insecurity." *State of the World 1994.* New York: W. W. Norton.

Brown, L. R., C. Flavin, and S. Postel. 1989. "A World at Risk." *State of the World 1989*, L. R. Brown, Project Director. New York: W. W. Norton.

———1991. *Saving the Planet.* New York: W. W. Norton.

Budiansky, S. 1993. "The Doomsday Myths." *U.S. News & World Report.* Dec. 13: 81–91.

Burt, R. 1993. "Potential for Nuclear Nightmare Still Exists." *Los Angeles Times*, Jan. 4: B7.

"Citings." 1991a. *World Watch*, May–June: 8.

"Citings." 1991b. *World Watch*, Nov.–Dec.: 9.

"Citings." 1992. *World Watch*, Jan.–Feb.: 8.

Commoner, B. 1979. *The Politics of Energy.* New York: Alfred A. Knopf.

Contreras, J. 1993. "Pack your Trunk and Off You Go." *Newsweek*, Dec. 6: 6.

Derringer, E. 1993. "Canada's Endangered Rain Forest." *San Francisco Chronicle*, July 19: A9.

Dobbs, M. 1992. "Sacrificed to the Superpowers." *Washington Post National Weekly Edition*, Sept. 20–26: 13–14.

Durning, A. T. 1992:a. "Last Sanctuary." *World Watch*, Nov.–Dec.: 18–25.

————1992:b. *Guardians of the Land: Indigenous People and the Health of the Earth*. Washington, D.C.: Worldwatch Institute.

————1993:. *Saving the Forests: What Will It Take?* Washington, D.C.: Worldwatch Institute.

————1994. "Redesigning the Forest Economy." *State of the World 1994*, New York: W. W. Norton.

"Earth Week." 1993. *San Francisco Chronicle*, June 18: A14.

Egger, D. 1987. "West Germany Pours Hot Milk." *The Nation*, Mar. 28: 293–295.

Ehrlich, P. R., and A. H. Ehrlich. 1982. *Extinction*. London: Victor Gollancs.

Engle, J. 1993. "Speaking of Water." *Los Angeles Times*, Dec. 14: H6.

Flavin, C. 1992. "The Bridge to Clean Energy." *World Watch*. July–Aug.: 10–18.

French, H. 1993. "Reconciling Trade and the Environment." *State of the World 1993*, L. R. Brown, Project Director. New York: W. W. Norton.

Gelber, A. 1981. "Pesticides' Global Fallout." *Newsweek*, Aug. 17: 53–55.

Gup, T. 1993. "It's Nature, Stupid!" *Time*. July 12: 38–40.

Hamakawa, Y. 1987. "Photovoltaic Power." *Scientific American*, Apr.: 87–92.

Healy, M. 1993. "U.S. Reveals 204 Nuclear Tests, Plutonium Exposure." *Los Angeles Times*, Dec. 8: A1, A20.

Horowitz, J. M., and D. S. Jackson. 1992. "The Beef Against Beef." *Time*, Apr. 20: 76–77.

Ishida, Y. 1993. "Regreening the Earth: Japan's 100-Year Plan." *The Futurist*, July–Aug.: 20–34.

Jackson, J. O. 1992. "Nuclear Time Bombs." *Time*, Dec. 7: 44–45.

Jacobson, J. L. 1988. *Environmental Refugees: A Yardstick of Habitability*. Washington, D.C.: Worldwatch Institute.

Kandell, J. 1993. "The Hole in the Swiss Trees Reclamation Plan." *Los Angeles Times Magazine*, Aug. 22: 22–23, 42–44.

Kaufman, L. 1986. "Why the Ark Is Sinking." L. Kaufman and K. Malloy, eds. *The Last Extinction*, Cambridge: Massachusetts Institute of Technology.

Kurtzman, D. 1988. *A Killing Wind: Inside Union Carbide and the Bhopal Disaster*. New York: McGraw-Hill.

Lemonick, M. D. 1992. "The Ozone Vanishes." *Time*, Feb. 17: 60–63.

Lenssen, N. 1991. *Nuclear Waster: The Problem That Won't Go Away*. Washington, D.C.: Worldwatch Institute.

Linden, E. 1993. "Who Lost the Ozone?" *Time*, May 10: 56–58.

Marbach, W., et al. 1986. "Anatomy of a Catastrophe." *Newsweek*, Sept. 3: 26–28.

McDonnell, P. J. 1993. "Foreign-Owned Companies Add to Mexico's Pollution." *Los Angeles Times*, Nov. 18: A1, A14–A15.

Martz, L. 1994. "Chernobyl." *World Press Review*, Aug. 3: 3.

Miller, R. L. 1986. *Under the Cloud: Decades of Nuclear Testing*. New York: The Free Press.

Monastersky, R. 1993. "Antarctic Ozone Level Reaches New Low." *Science News*, Oct. 16: 247.

Morehouse, W., and M. A. Subramanian. 1986. *The Bhopal Tragedy*. New York: Council on International and Public Affairs.

Myers, N. 1984. *GAIA: An Atlas of Planet Management*. New York: Anchor Books.

Orr, D. W. 1993. "Teach Kids Wisdom About the Earth." *Utne Reader*, Jan.–Feb. 87–90.

Pasternak, D. 1992. "Moscow's Dirty Nuclear Secrets." *U.S. News & World Report*, Feb. 11: 46–47.

Postel, S. and C. Flavin. 1991. "Reshaping the Global Economy." *State of the World 1991*, L. R. Brown, Project Director. New York: W. W. Norton.

Prince, G. 1986. "The Amazon: Paradise Lost." In L. Kaufman and K. Malloy, Eds. *The Last Extinction*. Cambridge: Massachusetts Institute of Technology.

Renner, M. 1993. "Nuclear Arsenal Decline on Hold." In L. R. Brown, H. Kane, and E. Ayres, Eds. *Vital Signs 1993*. New York: W. W. Norton

Rupert, James. 1992. "Death of a Desert Sea." *Washington Post National Weekly Edition*, July 6–12: 10.

Ryan, John C. 1992a. "Conserving Biological Diversity." *State of the World 1992*, L. R. Brown, Project Director. New York: W. W. Norton.

————1992b. "When Nature Loses Its Cool." *World Watch*. Sept.–Oct.: 10–16.

Satchell, M. 1993. "Wildlife's Last Chance." *U.S. News & World Report*, Nov. 5: 68–76.

"Satellite Finds Sahara Expanding." *Los Angeles Times*. 1991. July 22: B3.

Serrill, M. S. 1992. "Brazil's Two Faces." *Time*, June 8: 74–77.

Sivard, R. L. 1986. *World Military and Social Expenditures*. Washington, D.C.: World Priorities.

Spector, L. S. 1993. "The Nuclear Threat in the New World Order." *The 1993 World Book Year Book*. Chicago: World Book.

Stetson, M. 1991. "People Who Live in Green Houses." *World Watch*, Sept.–Oct.: 22–29.

Stevens, W. K. 1993. "Amazon Habitat Loss Worse Than Feared." *San Diego Union-Tribune*, June 30: E1, E3.

Stone, P. H. 1992. "Forecast Cloudy: The Limits of Global Warming Models." *Technology Review*, Feb.–Mar.: 32–40.

Tsipis, K. 1983. *Arsenal: Understanding Weapons in the Nuclear Age*. New York: Simon and Schuster.

The Universal Almanac 1993. 1992. J. W. Wright, Ed. New York: Andrews and McMeel.

Wallace, C. P. 1992. "A Question of Pollution and Power." *Los Angeles Times*. Dec. 8: H2.

Ward, B. and R. DuBos. 1972. *Only One Earth*. New York: W. W. Norton.

Watson, R. 1993. "America's Nuclear Secrets." *Newsweek*, Dec. 27: 14–17.

Weir, D. 1987. *The Bhopal Syndrome*. San Francisco: Sierra Club.

Wolf, E. C. 1987. *On the Brink of Extinction: Conserving the Diversity of Life*. Washington, D.C.: Worldwatch Institute.

Wright, J. W., Ed. 1993. *The Universal Almanac 1993*. Kansas City: Andrews and McMeel.

Youth, H. 1994. "Flying into Trouble." *World Watch*, Jan.–Feb.: 10–19.

Chapter 12

Adams, G. 1994. "Temptation Comes to Shangri-la." *San Francisco Chronicle*, Oct. 12: A1, A6.

Amnesty International Report, 1992. New York: Amnesty International Publications.

Andre, P. 1987. *Drug Addiction*. Pompano Beach, FL: Health Communications.

Archer, D., and R. Gartner. 1982. *Violence and Crime in Cross-National Perspective*. Hartford, CT: Yale University Press.

Associated Press. 1993. "Japanese Losing Trust in Government." *San Francisco Chronicle*, Apr. 6: A12.

Beamish, R. 1993. "Feds Often Stuck with Cleanup Bill." Santa Rosa *Press Democrat*, June 21: A3.

Beck, M., and P. Katel. 1993. "Kicking the Prison Habit." *Newsweek*, June 14: 32–33.

Biskupic, J. 1993. "High Court Limits Seizure of Property." *San Francisco Chronicle*, June 19: A2.

Chomsky, N. 1992. *What Uncle Sam Really Wants*. Berkeley, CA: Odonian Press.

Cockburn, L. 1987. *Out of Control: The Story of the Reagan Administration's War in Nicaragua*. New York: Atlantic Monthly.

Collins, R., and M. Makowsky. 1972. *The Discovery of Society*. New York: Random House.

Cressey, D. R,. 1969. *The Theft of a Nation*. New York: Harper and Row.

DeParle, J., and S. Englebery. 1993. "Huge Bailout Predicted in HUD Mess." *San Francisco Chronicle*, June 21: A2.

Díaz, J., and I. Durán. 1993. "Dirty Dealings in Europe." *World Press Review*, May: 10–11.

Durkheim, E. 1964. *The Division of Labor in Society*. New York: The Free Press.

Farah, D., and T. Robberson. 1993. "A New War Replaces the Old Ones." *Washington Post National Weekly Edition*, Apr. 5: 18–19.

Farthing, L. 1992. "Bolivian Coca Farmers Hurt by U.S. Anti-Drug Program." *San Francisco Chronicle*, Aug. 11: A10.

Flatscher, A. 1992. "Europe Begins to Fight Back." *World Press Review*, Dec.: 16–17.

Fooner, M. 1985. *A Guide to Interpol*. Washington, D.C.: U.S. Department of Justice.

Freedman, D. 1988. "U.S. Heroin Use Rapidly Increasing." *San Francisco Examiner*, June 19: A3.

Freemantle, B. 1986. *The Fix: Inside the World of Drugs*. New York: Tor Books.

Giannini, J. A. 1993. "How Cocaine Use Affects Violence." *USA Today*, Aug.: 11.

Golden, T. 1993. "Drug Gangs Colombianizing Mexico." *San Francisco Chronicle*, June 21: A8, A10.

Guillermoprieto, A. 1993. "Down the Shining Path." *New Yorker*, Feb. 8: 64–75.

Hackett, G., and M. A. Lerner. 1987. "L.A. Law: Gangs and Crack." *Newsweek*, Apr. 27: 35–36.

Herrera, J. D., and I. Durán. 1993. "Dirty Dealings in Europe." *World Press Review*, May: 9–10.

Hersh, S. M. 1994. "The Wild East." *Atlantic Monthly*, June: 61–86.

Horgan, J. 1993. "A Kinder War." *Scientific American*, July: 24–25.

Hussain, Z. 1993. "Pakistani Farmers Still Hooked on Poppies." *San Francisco Chronicle*, May 19: A6.

Isikoff, M. 1993. "Is Drug Use Heating Up Again?" *Washington Post National Weekly Edition*, May 10–16: 37.

Kurian, G., 1991. *New Book of World Rankings*. New York: Facts on File.

Kwitney, J. 1987. *The Crime of Patriots*. New York: W. W. Norton.

Lee, G. 1993. "A New Frontier of Violence." *Washington Post National Weekly Edition*, June 28–July 4.

Lee, M. E., and B. Shlain. 1986. *Acid Dreams: The CIA, LSD, and the Sixties Rebellion*. New York: Grove Press.

Liu, M., F. Gabney, S. Miller, and T. Morganthau. 1993. "The New Slave Trade." *Newsweek*, June 21: 34–41.

Martin, D. M. 1993. "Just Say 'No' to Informer Testimony." *San Francisco Chronicle*, Apr. 20: 19.

McConahay, M. J., and R. Kirk. 1989. "Over There." *Mother Jones*, Feb.–Mar.: 36–39.

Montalbano, W. D. 1987. "Debts, Drugs, and Democracy." *Los Angeles Times*, Aug. 30, Part IV: 1, 6.

Murphy, C. 1993. "How Corruption Fuels a Revolution." *Washington Post National Weekly Edition*, Apr. 5–11: 19.

Nadelman, E., and J. Wenner. 1994. "Toward a Sane National Drug Policy." *Rolling Stone*, May 5: 24–25.

O'Brien, C. 1993. "Economic Hardships Blamed for Crime Rise in Russia." *San Francisco Chronicle*, July 29: A14.

Prothrow-Stith, D., and M. Weissman. 1991. *Deadly Consequence*. New York: HarperCollins.

Reid, T. R. 1992. "Japanese Ruling Party's Kingmaker Admits to Graft." *San Francisco Chronicle*, Aug. 28: A15.

———1993. "Miyazawa Bails Out on Reform Bill." *San Francisco Chronicle*, June 6: A12.

Rosenberg, T. 1988. "Murder City." *Atlantic Monthly*, Nov.: 20–30.

Ross, Y. 1993. "Central America's Latest Wars." *World Press Review*, May 13: 20–21.

Schlosser, E. 1994. "Reefer Madness." *Atlantic Monthly*, Aug.: 45–63.

Serakawa, Y. 1993. "Dodging the Law in Japan." *World Press Review*, May 13: 18.

Shelley, L. 1981. *Crime and Modernization*. Carbondale, IL: Southern Illinois University Press.

Steinberg, N. 1994. "The Law of Unintended Consequences." *Rolling Stone*, May 5: 33–34.

Stewart, J. B. 1991. *Den of Thieves*. New York: Simon and Schuster.

———1993. "Michael Milken's Biggest Deal." *New Yorker*, Mar. 8: 58–64.

Stille, A. 1993. "The Mafia's Biggest Mistake." *New Yorker*, Mar.: 60–73.

Sun, L. H. 1993. "High Anxiety: China Is Stressed by Challenges of Change." *Washington Post National Weekly Edition*, July 5–11: 17.

Tacket, M. 1993. "Reno Says Jail Failing in Fight Against Drugs." *San Francisco Examiner*, May 5: A4.

Viviano, F. 1992. "Drug Trade Feeds World's Rebellions." *San Francisco Chronicle*, Dec. 12: 1, 8.

Vulliamy, E. 1992. "Italy's Mafia Spreads Its Tentacles." *World Press Review*, Dec.: 6–7.

Zehr, H. 1976. *Crime and the Development of Modern Society*, London: Rowan and Littlefield.

Chapter 13

"The Arms Bazaar." (1992). *San Francisco Examiner*, May 12, Sunday Punch Section: 36–37.

Associated Press. 1994. "Bloody Wave of Repression in Tajikistan." *San Francisco Chronicle*, Oct. 27: A16.

Barber, B. R. 1992. "Jihad Versus McWorld: How the Planet is Both Falling Apart and Coming Together." *The Atlantic*, Mar.: 53–63.

Bonner, R. 1992. "Letter to Sudan." *New Yorker*, July 13: 70–83.

Burstein, D. 1991. *Euroquake*. New York: Simon and Schuster: 16–23.

Coll, S. and S. LeVine. 1993. "A Global Militant Network." *Washington Post National Weekly Edition*, Aug. 16–22: 6–7.

Denton, R. K. 1968. *The Semai: A Non-Violent People of Malaya*. New York: Holt, Rinehart, and Winston.

Ehrlich, P. R, C. Sagan, D. Kennedy, and W. O. Roberts 1984. *The Cold and the Dark: The World After Nuclear War*. New York: Norton.

Farrell, J. A. 1992. "Scandal That Reveals How the United States Helped Arm Hussain." *Boston Globe*, reprinted in the *San Francisco Examiner*, May 17: A6.

Fineman, M. 1991. "Have Guns, Will Travel." *Los Angeles Times*, Apr. 7: H1, H8.

Gobel, P. A. 1992. "The Russian Military Under the Guise of a Commonwealth." *Washington Post National Weekly Edition*, July 27–Aug. 2: 24.

Halberstein, D. 1989. *The Reckoning*. New York: Avon.

Hamburg, J. 1992. "Iranian Aid Bolsters Khartoum's Regime." *San Francisco Chronicle*, May 18: A9–A10.

Harris, M. 1977. *Cannibals and Kings: The Origin of Culture*. New York: Random House.

———1987. *Our Kind*. New York: Harper and Row.

Hersh, S. M. 1993. "On the Nuclear Edge." The New Yorker, Mar. 29: 56–73.

———1994. "The Wild East." *Atlantic Monthly*, June: 61–84.

Hyland, W. G. 1992. "Re-Examining United States Foreign Policy." *Current*, May 1: 18–23.

Janis, I. S. 1983. *Group Think: Psychological Studies of Policy Decisions and Fiascos*. Boston: Houghton-Mifflin.

Kennedy, P. 1987. *The Rise and Fall of the Great Powers*. New York: Random House.

Kidron, M. and D. Smith. 1983. *The War Atlas: Armed Conflict–Armed Peace*. New York: Simon and Schuster.

Kurzman, D. 1992. "U.S. Arms Technology May Be Going to Iran." *San Francisco Chronicle*, May 19: A7–A8.

Lane, C. 1992. "Vukovar: Now It's Serb City." *Newsweek*, Aug. 3: 36–37.

Lorenz, K. 1967. *On Aggression*. New York: Bantam Books.

Maas, P. 1993. "Serbs as Defenders of the Faith?" *Washington Post National Weekly Edition*, Aug. 17–23: 18.

McNamara, R. S. 1987. *Blundering Into Disaster*. New York: Pantheon Books.

Pfaff, W. 1992. "Reflections: The Absence of Empire (Ethnic Europe)." *New Yorker*, Aug. 10: 62.

Raser, J. R. 1969. "The Failure of Fail-Safe." *Transaction*, Jan.: 11–19.

Reuters News Service. 1992. "Russia–India Rocket Deal Prompts U.S. Sanctions." *San Francisco Chronicle*, May 12: A11.

Roark, A. C. 1987. "Research: Emphasis is Military." *Los Angeles Times*, Apr. 12, Part I: 32, 34–35.

Ryle, J. 1993. "The Invisible Enemy." *New Yorker*, Nov. 29: 120–135.

Scheer, R. 1982. *With Enough Shovels: Reagan, Bush, and Nuclear War*. New York: Random House.

Sivard, R. L. 1988. *World Military and Social Expenditures, 1987–1988*. Washington, DC: World Priorities Press.

Tempest, R. 1983. "Servants or Masters: Revisiting the Military-Industrial Complex." *Los Angeles Times*, July 10, Part IV: 1–4.

Tuchman, B. 1984. *The March of Folly*. New York: Ballantine Books.

Webster, D. 1994. "Out There Is a Bomb With Your Name." *Smithsonian*, Feb.: 26–39.

Wilson, E. O. 1978. *On Human Nature*. Cambridge, MA: Harvard University Press.

Wright, R. 1992. "Report from Turkestan." *New Yorker*, Apr.: 53–75.

Yergin, D. 1990. *The Prize: The Epic Quest for Oil, Money, and Power*. New York: Simon and Schuster.

Zarembo, A. 1994. "Genocide Suspects Await Their Judges." *San Francisco Chronicle*, Oct. 18: A1, A15.

Chapter 14

Albright, M. 1994. "UN Security Council Establishes International Tribunal for Rwanda." U.S. Dept. of State Dispatch, Nov. 21.

Amesty International 1992 Report. 1992. New York: Amnesty International.

Associated Press. 1993. "U.S. to Cut Foreign Aid to 35 Nations." *San Francisco Chronicle*, Nov. 20: A6.

Briscoe, D. 1994. "Peace Dividend Wanted, UN Says." *San Francisco Chronicle*, June 2: A9.

Branigan, W. 1993. "UN Beset by Bureaucracy." *San Franciso Chronicle*, Sept. 22: A7-A8.

Bureau of Public Affairs. 1992. *United Nations Background Notes.* Washington, D.C.: U.S. Department of State. Oct.

Copeland, P. 1993. "Business Booms for U.S. Arms Merchants." *San Francisco Chronicle*, Dec. 5: 3.

Danner, M. 1993. "The Truth of *El Mozote*." *New Yorker*, Dec. 6: 50–133.

Elliott, M., and A. Nagorski. 1994. "The Learning Curve." *Newsweek*, Jan. 17: 24–25.

Epstein, W. 1991. "And Now the UN Century." *Bulletin of the Atomic Scientists*, 48: 22–23.

Evans, R., and R. Novak. 1993. "Russian Army is Pulling Yeltsin's Strings." *San Francisco Chronicle*, Nov. 8: A23.

Frankel, Marvin E., and Saidemann, Ellen. 1989. *Out of the Shadows of Night.* New York: Delaconte Press, 1987.

Galtung, J. 1992. "Worse Than the Bomb." *World Press Review*, July: 52–53.

Goshko, J. M. 1994. "Saddam Hussein May Have to Say 'Uncle' to UN." *Washington Post National Weekly Edition*, June 24–30: 19.

Hartman, F. H. 1967. *The Relations of Nations.* New York: Macmillan.

Humana, C. 1992. *World Human Rights Guide.* New York: Oxford University Press.

Jacobson, J. L. 1992. "Slavery, Yes Slavery Returns." *World Watch*, Jan.–Feb.: 9, 34.

Kirshenbaum, G. 1993. "After Victory, Women's Human Rights Movement Takes Stock." *MS*, Sept.–Oct.: 20

Los Angeles Times. 1993. "'93 Was a Bad Year for Democracies." Reprinted in *San Francisco Chronicle*, Dec. 18: A2.

Louyot, A. 1993. "A World In Exodus." From *L'Express* of Paris, reprinted in *World Press Review*, Nov.: 47.

MasJand, T. et al. 1992. "Slavery." *Newsweek*, May 4: 30–39.

Massie, R. K. 1986. *Peter the Great.* New York: Ballantine.

Mathews, T. 1991. "Decade of Democracy." *Newsweek*, Dec. 30: 35–41.

Meisler, S. 1994. "Keeping the Peace." *Los Angeles Times*, May 3: A1, A5.

Meltzer, M. 1979. *The Human Rights Book.* New York: Farrar, Strauss, Giroux.

Parsons, T. 1951. *The Social System.* New York: The Free Press.

Peek, J. M. May 1992. "Japan, the United Nations, and Human Rights." *Asian Survey*, 32: 217–229.

Preston, J. 1993. "When All the Pots Boil Over at Once." *Washington Post National Weekly Edition*, June 21–27.

————1994. "Boutros-Ghali Rushes In. . . " *Washington Post National Weekly Edition*, Jan. 10–16.

Remnick, D. 1993. "Letter from Moscow." *New Yorker*. Nov. 22: 51–65.

Renner, M. 1993. *Critical Juncture: The Future of Peacekeeping.* Worldwatch Paper No. 114: Washington, D.C.: Worldwatch Institute.

Richberg, K. B. 1993. "U.S. Left UN in Lurch in Somalia." *San Francisco Chronicle*, Dec. 9: A27.

Sasson, J. F. 1992. *Princess.* New York: Avon Books.

Smythe, H. H. 1952. "The Eta: A Marginal Japanese Caste." *American Journal of Sociology*, 58: 194–196.

Thatcher, M. 1993. Interview in "Intelligence Report." *Parade Magazine*, Dec. 12: 12.

Thomas, R. 1993. "The ABCs of the GATT Pact." *Newsweek*, Dec. 27: 23.

Thompson, W. C. 1994. *Canada 1994.* Harpers Ferry, WV: Stryker-Port Publications.

U.S. Department of State 1992. *Background Notes: United Nations*, III (5) Washington, D.C.: Bureau of Public Affairs: Office of Public Communication.

Watson, R., et al. 1993. "America's Nuclear Secrets." *Newsweek*, Dec. 27: 14–18.

Weschler, L. 1994. "The Sentries." *New Yorker*, Jan. 10: 70–73.

Name Index

Subject Index

Sex roles, 29–39. *See also* Family(ies)
in less developed countries, 29–32
in more developed countries, 32–39
Sex slavery, 441
Sexual abuse, 47, 78–79
Sexual harassment, 80–82
Sexuality, human, 18, 54–85
child molestation, 78–79
early sexual relations, 61–68
abortion and, 62, 66–68
academic achievement and, 61–62
sex education and, 62–65
sexual activity in U.S., 65–66
unwanted pregnancies and, 62
highly permissive societies, 58
homosexuality, 34, 61, 68–71, 122
pornography, 76–77
prostitution, 59–61, 71–76, 107
from conflict perspective, 72–73
in former Soviet Union and modern Russia, 73–74
in nineteenth and early twentieth century, 59–61
in Third World countries, 74–76
rape, 67, 77–78, 79
restrictive societies, 57–58
sex as source of normative problems, 56–58
sexual harassment, 80–82
sexual revolution, 58–61
silence regarding sex, 56–57
surveys of, 60–61
Sexually transmitted diseases (STDs), 64, 158–59. *See also* AIDS (acquired immune deficiency syndrome)
in Russia, 106–8
Sexual revolution, 58–61
Shah of Iran, 17, 379, 408, 410, 433
Shamans, 110
Sharia (strict Koranic law), 408
Shiite Islam, 407, 434, 435
Siberia, Cossack conquest of, 402
Sicilian Mafia, 381–82
Sikhs, violence between Hindus and, 407–8
Siletz tribe (Native American), 276
Singapore, 259
Single-parent households, 33–34, 45, 46, 182
Siriono people in Bolivia, 58
Skin cancer, 362, 363
Skinheads
in Germany, 191
violence of, 183–84
Slavery, 179–80, 441
absolute, 179
aftermath of, 179–80
Slovenia, 406
Smog, 320
Smoking, medical costs and, 93–95
Smuggling rings, 383, 384

Social class. *See also* Inequality
African American success and, 182, 225–26
lower-middle class, 271–72
postindustrialism and, 236
super rich, 268–69
upper-middle class, 236, 269–71
working class, 272
Social contract, 431
Social control, problems of, 374–75
Social isolation, 47
Socialization, 10
Social Organization of Sexuality, The (Laumann, Michael, Michaels, and Gagnon), 60–61
Social priorities, 4–6
Social problems
defined, 3–4
explaining, 2–13
in global perspective, 17–22
latent problems, 6–7
social priorities and, 4–6
sociological analysis of, 11–12
theoretical perspectives on, 7–11
Social Security, 100, 152
Social survey, 12
Societal complexity, crime and, 375–76
Society(ies)
core, 8, 237, 241, 261, 262
ecosystem compared to, 300
feudal, 203
gesellschaft, 202
highly permissive, 58
industrial, 234
peripheral, 8, 236–37, 241, 261
postindustrial, 234–36, 245–57
preindustrial, 234, 237–38
restrictive, 57–58
semiperipheral, 237, 239, 240, 241, 257–59, 261, 289
Sociobiology, 400
Socioeconomic status, medical inequality and, 100–102
"Soft" energy, 323
Soil bank, 356
Soil destruction, 356–59
Solar energy, 341
Solidaristic wage policy, 280
Solidarity
mechanical, 9, 374–75
organic, 9, 375
Somalia, UN intervention in, 449
Sotho tribe, 184
South Africa, 132
apartheid and, 184–86, 456
boycott of, 434
ethnic wars in, 406
European conquest of, 176
human rights rating for, 435